Turkish Foreign Policy s

This revised and updated version of William Hale's *Turkish Foreign Policy 1774–2000* offers a comprehensive and analytical survey of Turkish foreign policy since the last quarter of the eighteenth century, when the Turks' relations with the rest of the world entered their most critical phase.

In recent years Turkey's international role has changed and expanded dramatically, and the new edition revisits the chapters and topics covered in light of these changes. Drawing on newly available information and ideas, the author carefully alters the earlier historical narrative while preserving the clarity and accessibility of the original. Combining the long historical perspective with a detailed survey and analysis of the most recent developments, this book fills a clear gap in the literature on Turkey's modern history. For readers with a broader interest in international history, it also offers a crucial example of how a medium sized power has acted in the international environment.

William Hale is a former Professor of Turkish Politics in the School of Oriental and African Studies of the University of London.

Praise for previous editions

'an illuminating insight into the continuities as well as the changes in Turkey's relations with the outside world since the middle of the eighteen century ... a masterly study that includes useful historical maps and an exhaustively impressive bibliography.'

International Affairs

'an up-to-the-minute account that should satisfy all those who need to understand the motives of Turkish diplomacy today, and to evaluate its results ... One of the many merits of Hale's study is that it relates foreign policy to the Turkish domestic scene, in particular to government instability in the last decade and the mismanagement of the economy which started even earlier.'

Choice

'provides greater insight into Turkish foreign policy development and should be read by scholars seeking a thorough understanding of the impetus behind Turkey's changing role in international relations.'

Journal of Peace Research

'a meticulously researched and lucidly written book with an impressive biography and useful maps. Students and scholars of Turkish foreign policy will be well served by this book for years to come.'

International Journal of Middle East Studies

'a masterful, detailed study of Turkey's foreign policy after the end of the cold war and the disintegration of the Soviet Union and Yugoslavia ... a superb work, a gold mine of reliable and detached information on Turkey's domestic and foreign affairs. It is both a political history of Turkey and an excellent study of Turkish foreign policy based on official documents and publications as well as on most of the books and articles on the topic.'

The International History Review

Turkish Foreign Policy since 1774

3rd edition

William Hale

LONDON AND NEW YORK

First published 2000 by Frank Cass Publishers
Second edition published 2003 by Frank Cass Publishers
This edition published 2013 by Routledge
2 Park Square, Milton Park, Abingdon, Oxon OX14 4RN

Simultaneously published in the USA and Canada by Routledge
711 Third Avenue, New York, NY 10017

Routledge is an imprint of the Taylor & Francis Group, an informa business

British Library Cataloguing in Publication Data
A catalogue record for this book is available from the British Library

Library of Congress Cataloging in Publication Data
Hale, William M.
Turkish foreign policy since 1774 / William Hale
    p.cm.
        Includes bibliographical references and index.
        1. Turkey—Foreign relations—1918–1960. 2. Turkey—Foreign
relations—1960–1980. 3. Turkey—Foreign relations—1980– I. Title.
    DR477.H36 2012
    327.56009'034—dc23
                        2012006764

ISBN 978-0-415-59986-3 (hbk)
ISBN 978-0-415-59987-0 (pbk)
ISBN 978-0-203-10202-2 (ebk)

Typeset in Times
by Taylor & Francis Books

MIX
Paper from
responsible sources
FSC
www.fsc.org   FSC® C004839

Printed and bound in Great Britain by the MPG Books Group

Contents

A note on spellings

Since 1928, Turkish has been written in a version of the Latin script, and this has been used for spelling all Turkish personal and place names when writing of the period after the first world war. When writing of the Ottoman period, when Turkish was written in Arabic characters, the transliterations normally used by writers at the time have been adhered to, although this has resulted in some inconsistencies. Similarly, non-Turkish names originally written in the Arabic, Cyrillic or Greek alphabets have been rendered in the way normally used by English language writers, and the author must beg the forgiveness of specialists for any mistakes.

In the modern Turkish alphabet, the letters are pronounced roughly as in English, with the following exceptions:

a – short 'a', as in French, or the English 'u' in 'hut'.
c – 'j', as in English 'jam'.
ç – 'ch', as in English 'church'.
ğ – normally silent: lengthens preceding vowel.
ı – as in the first and last 'a's in 'banana'.
i – as in English 'bit': notice the upper case form İ.
ö – as in German, or the French 'eu' in 'leur'.
ş – 'sh', as in 'shut'.
ü – as in German, or the French 'u' in 'tu'.

Abbreviations

AKP	Justice and Development Party
AP	Justice Party
BDP	Peace and Democracy Party
BOTAŞ	Turkısh state pipelıne company
BP	British Petroleum company
BRIC	Brazil, Russia, India, China
BSEC	Black Sea Economic Cooperation project
BTC	Baku-Tiflis-Ceyhan oil pipeline
CENTO	Central Treaty Organization
CHP	Republican People's Party
CIS	Commonwealth of Independent States
CSCE	Conference on Security and Cooperation in Europe (later OSCE)
DECA	Defence and Economic Cooperation Agreement
DEP	Democracy Party
DİSK	Reformist Trades Unions Confederation
DP	Democrat Party
DSP	Democratic Left Party
DTP	Democratic Turkey Party, also Democratic Society Party
DYP	True Path Party
EC	European Community
ECO	Economic Cooperation Organization
EEC	European Economic Community
EU	European Union
GDP	Gross Domestic Product
GNP	Gross National Product
HADEP	People's Democracy Party
Hak-İş	Just Labour Unions Confederation
HEP	People's Labour Party
IFOR	Implementation Force (in Bosnia-Herzegovina)
İHH	Foundation for Human Rights and Freedoms and Humanitarian Relief
IMF	International Monetary Fund

ISAF	International Security Assistance Force (in Afghanistan)
KDP	Kurdistan Democratic Party
KFOR	Kosovo international peace-keeping force
KRG	Kurdistan Regional Government (in Iraq)
MHP	Nationalist Action Party
MSP	National Salvation Party
MÜSİAD	Independent Industrialists and Businessmen's Association
NATO	North Atlantic Treaty Organization
NGO	Non-governmental organization
NSC	National Security Council
OECD	Organisation for Economic Co-operation and Development
OEEC	Organisation for European Economic Cooperation (predecessor to OECD)
OIC	Organization of the Islamic Conference
OSCE	Organization for Security and Cooperation in Europe
PJAK	Party for a Free Life in Kurdistan
PKK	Kurdistan Workers' Party
PLO	Palestine Liberation Organization
PUK	Patriotic Union of Kurdistan
RCD	Regional Cooperation and Development
SACEUR	Supreme Allied Commander, Europe
SFOR	Stabilisation Force (in Bosnia-Herzegovina)
SHP	Social Democrat People's Party
SOCAR	Azerbaijan state petroleum company
SP	Felicity Party
TICA	Turkish International Cooperation Agency
TPAO	Turkish Petroleum Company
TRNC	Turkish Republic of Northern Cyprus
TRT	Turkish Radio and Television Corporation
TTOBB	Turkish Union of Chambers
Türk-İş	Turkish Trades Unions Confederation
TÜSİAD	Turkish Industrialists and Businessmen's Association
UNPROFOR	UN protection force in Bosnia
YAŞ	High Military Council
YTP	New Turkey Party

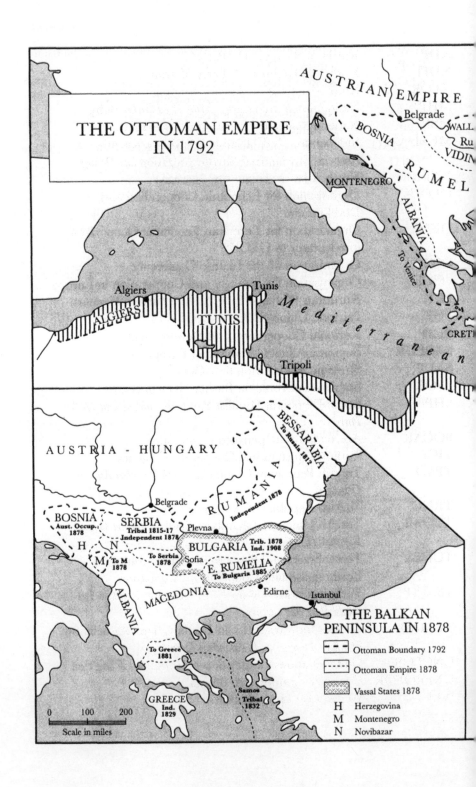

THE OTTOMAN EMPIRE
IN 1792

AUSTRIAN EMPIRE

Belgrade

BOSNIA

WALL

Ru

VIDIN

R U M E L

MONTENEGRO

ALBANIA

To Venice

Algiers

Tunis

A L G I E R S

T U N I S

M e d i t e r r a n e a n

CRET

Tripoli

AUSTRIA - HUNGARY

BESSARABIA
To Russia 1812

Belgrade

R U M A N I A
Independent 1878

BOSNIA
Aust. Occup.
1878

SERBIA
Tribal 1815-17
Independent 1878

Plevna

H

N

BULGARIA
Trib. 1878
Ind. 1908

M

To M
1878

To Serbia
1878

Sofia

E. RUMELIA
To Bulgaria 1885

ALBANIA

MACEDONIA

Edirne

Istanbul

THE BALKAN
PENINSULA IN 1878

‑ ‑ ‑ ‑ Ottoman Boundary 1792

- - - - - Ottoman Empire 1878

▨▨▨ Vassal States 1878

H Herzegovina

M Montenegro

N Novibazar

To Greece
1881

Samos
Tribal
1832

GREECE
Ind.
1829

0   100   200

Scale in miles

LDAVIA
Jassy

RUSSIA

1792

1774

1774

CRIMEA

Black   Sea

rne
Istanbul

rsa

Trabzon

GEORGIA

Caspian

Sea

irne

Ankara

DEREBEYS

Erzurum

zmir

NOMAD
TRIBES

Kayseri

DEREBEYS

Konya

Adana

Mosul

PERSIA

Aleppo

BAGHDAD

CYPRUS

Beyrut

SYRIA

Damascus

Baghdad

Sea

Akka

xandria

Jerusalem

Cairo

EGYPT

HIJAZ

WAHHABIS

Medina

Red

Aswan

Mecca

Sea

Jiddà

Suakin

HIJAZ

Massawa

Approximate limits
of the Empire

North African States
under Ottoman suzerainty

Areas under autonomous
and tribal rulers

Lands lost 1774 — 1792

200   400

Scale in miles

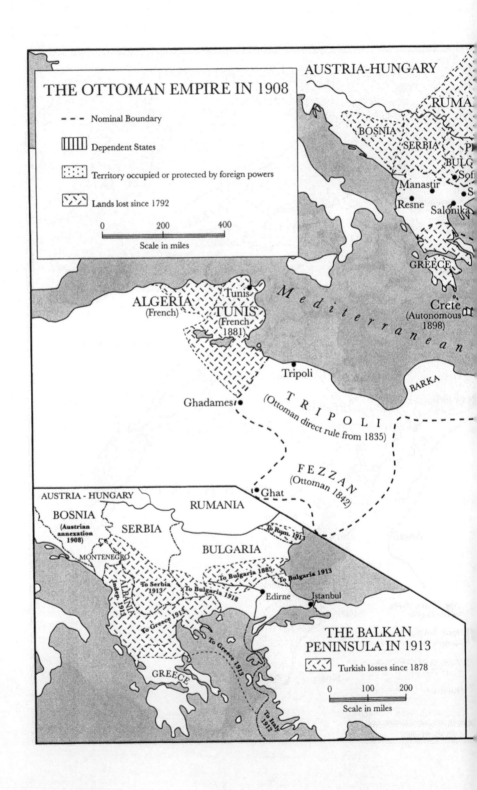

THE OTTOMAN EMPIRE IN 1908

- - - Nominal Boundary

|||||| Dependent States

[:::::] Territory occupied or protected by foreign powers

[\\\] Lands lost since 1792

0   200   400

Scale in miles

AUSTRIA-HUNGARY

RUMA

BOSNIA

SERBIA

BULG

Sof

Manastir

S

Resne

Salonika

GREECE

Crete
(Autonomous
1898)

Mediterranean

Tunis

ALGERIA
(French)

TUNIS
(French
1881)

Tripoli

BARKA

Ghadames

T R I P O L I
(Ottoman direct rule from 1835)

F E Z Z A N
(Ottoman 1842)

Ghat

AUSTRIA - HUNGARY

BOSNIA
(Austrian
annexation
1908)

SERBIA

RUMANIA

MONTENEGRO

ALBANIA
Indep. 1913

To Serbia
1913

BULGARIA

To Bulgaria 1885

To Rum. 1913

To Bulgaria 1913

To Bulgaria 1918

Edirne

Istanbul

To Greece 1913

To Greece 1913

GREECE

To Italy 1912

THE BALKAN
PENINSULA IN 1913

[\\\] Turkish losses since 1878

0   100   200

Scale in miles

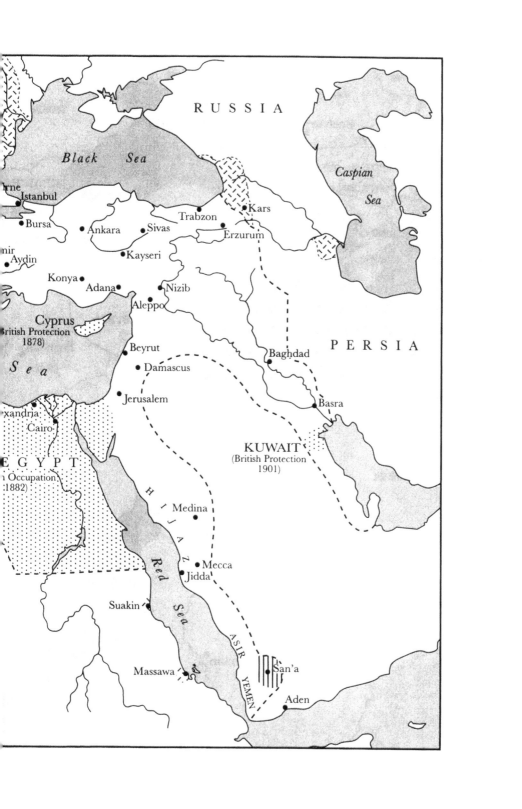

RUSSIA

Black Sea

Caspian Sea

PERSIA

Irne
Istanbul
Bursa
Ankara
Sivas
Trabzon
Kars
Erzurum
nir
Aydin
Kayseri
Konya
Adana
Nizib
Aleppo
Cyprus
British Protection
1878)
Beyrut
Baghdad
Sea
Damascus
Jerusalem
xandria
Cairo
Basra
KUWAIT
(British Protection
1901)
EGYPT
Occupation
1882)
H I J A Z
Medina
Red Sea
Mecca
Jidda
Suakin
A S I R
Massawa
San'a
YEMEN
Aden

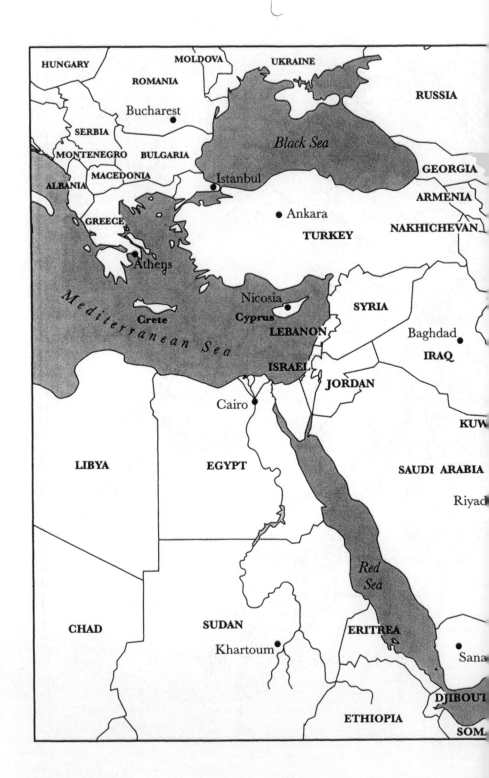

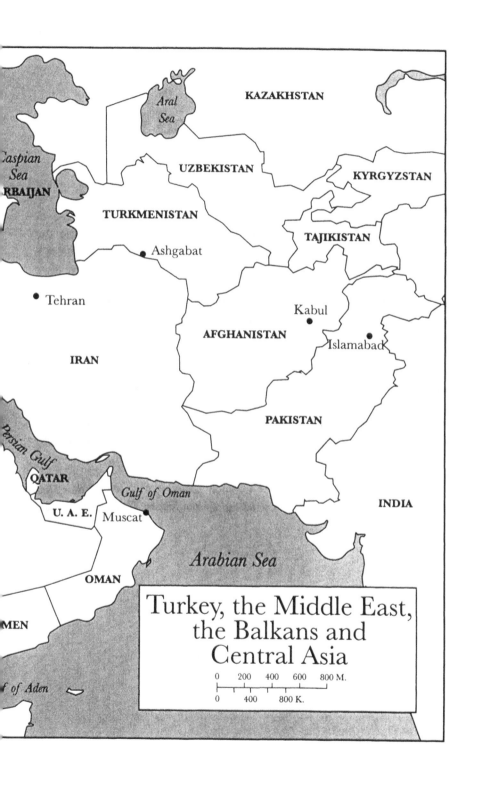

KAZAKHSTAN

Aral
Sea

*Caspian
Sea*

RBAIJAN

UZBEKISTAN

KYRGYZSTAN

TURKMENISTAN

TAJIKISTAN

• Ashgabat

• Tehran

Kabul
•

AFGHANISTAN

Islamabad
•

IRAN

PAKISTAN

Persian Gulf

QATAR

Gulf of Oman

INDIA

U. A. E.

Muscat •

Arabian Sea

OMAN

MEN

f of Aden

Turkey, the Middle East,
the Balkans and
Central Asia

0   200   400   600   800 M.

0   400   800 K.

Preface

The predecessor to this book, *Turkish Foreign Policy, 1774–2000*, was published by Frank Cass 12 years ago, with a second edition appearing in 2002. The huge changes in the intervening period, both in global politics and Turkey's position in the international system, have meant that it has had to be substantially rewritten, and a change of title thus seemed appropriate. In the case of the first five chapters, covering the period up to the end of the Cold War, the alterations of the text have been relatively minor, reflecting newly available information and ideas on the history of Turkey's international relations. The remaining seven chapters, covering the period since 1990, are mainly new, although some of the original text has been kept. To make way for the new material, the previous narrative has been shortened, with parts eliminated. Honest qualms are felt about this, but there seemed to be no alternative, if the book was not to become impractically long. Where it seemed appropriate, readers are pointed by the endnotes towards the more specialist literature to fill in the gaps. In the last seven chapters I have also abandoned the chronological approach in favour of a thematic one, since it was realized that not all readers will be reading the whole book straight through. Inevitably, this creates problems where the themes overlap. Thus, for instance, the story of Turkish policy towards the Middle East, especially Iraq and Iran, has been intimately bound up with that of relations between Turkey and the USA. Likewise, the Cyprus dispute plays a crucial role in the Turkey–EU relationship. To cope with this and similar cases, there are frequent cross-references to other parts of the text, so that readers will know where else to look.

I must again thank the many friends and colleagues, both in Turkey and abroad, who have helped me with the preparation of this book and its predecessor. My thanks are also due to both my publishers for their patience, and their scrupulous and scholarly editorial work.

William Hale
Istanbul
December 2011

Introduction

The first edition of this book was completed at the beginning of 2000 as an initial attempt to describe and analyse the evolution of Turkey's external relations since the late eighteenth century, while concentrating on the period since the Second World War. Since it appeared, Turkey's international role has been hugely enhanced and re-defined by the complex evolution of what looks like an unstable international system. This new edition aims to keep pace with these changes, while maintaining the historical perspective that was judged an essential feature of its predecessor.

For the statesmen of the nineteenth century, the Ottoman Empire was 'the eastern question'. For their twentieth-century successors, Turkey is alternatively seen as an emerging regional power or a vexing problem in the construction of a new Europe. On their side, many Turks have felt that their growing economy as well as the continued strategic importance of their country entitled it to carry greater international weight. Taking the story back to the late eighteenth century illuminates the continuities, as well as the changes in external policies. More broadly, the Turkish example can also offer some interesting pointers as to how medium-sized states have acted in the changing international environments of the last 200 years.

The main purpose of this book is descriptive, not theoretical. Hence, what follows does not seek to offer any new general theories in the field of international politics: the writer has to leave this to other and more expert pens. Nevertheless, the story it tells needs to be set in some sort of general framework. It tries to look outwards from Turkey, describing and analysing Turkish policies, rather than the policies of other actors towards Turkey. Using a realist perspective, the Turkish republic and the late Ottoman Empire can be fitted into the international system as a middle power. This is far from the only way of conceptualizing its international role, but for most of the period covered in this book it still seems the most realistic way of explaining Turkish policies.[1] Power is here defined as the ability to oblige other states to take actions that they would not otherwise have taken and to resist pressure to do so from other states. This power depends on a mixture of the country's military strength (which in the nineteenth century depended quite largely on its population) and its economic resources and level of development. Small powers have little ability to act independently in the international system, especially when compared to what were referred to as the 'Great Powers' in the nineteenth century or the superpowers during the Cold War era. Middle powers stand somewhere in between the two extremes of the scale – that is to say, they have some ability to resist pressure from more powerful states, and may sometimes be able to influence the policies of weaker ones, especially if they are geographically contiguous. Most crucially, they cannot normally fight a successful war against a major power. Hence, if they are threatened by a major power, the solution to their security problem must come from outside, either through an alliance or through the exploitation of a balance of forces between the great powers. Essentially, they are forced to adopt defensive strategies. In the Turkish case, the question of whether this could best be achieved by alliance or neutrality was a frequently recurring one, depending on the nature of the international system at the time and the country's position in it.[2]

Within a defensive strategy however, the decision as to whether to opt for an alliance is not an easy one. The advantage of an alliance is that it will help to deter an enemy, and that a small power may be able to use the alliance to influence its ally in a direction favourable to itself. However, dangers are also apparent. In Chapter 21 of *The Prince*, Machiavelli warns the ruler of a small state not to forge an alliance with a more powerful state unless he is forced to do so, since he will end up being 'under the will and pleasure' of his ally. The choice of ally is also a critical one, since the interests of the allies should at least be complementary if not identical, although one some occasions each ally may be protecting a different set of interests. Alternatively, to avoid the dangers of an alliance with a more powerful state, a middle power may prefer to gamble on one with a weaker partner, or a number of small powers.

Historical processes

While these general proposals may be said to have affected the positions and policies of small or medium states through modern international history, it is also clear that both are influenced deeply by the nature of the international system at the time. These changes have been fundamentally important for the Ottoman and Turkish states during the period covered in this book – that is, from the last quarter of the eighteenth century until today. Essentially, the international order can be seen as having undergone four systemic changes, through five successive phases, during this time.

During the nineteenth century, international politics were dominated by the five indisputably 'great powers' of Europe – France, Prussia/Germany, Austria, Russia and Britain – with no power in a hegemonic position. The preservation of peace, and the survival of small states, rested essentially on the preservation of a balance of power between the main European states. If one of them attempted to conquer a weaker power then it ran the risk that another great power, or alliance of powers, might see this as an attempt to alter the balance of power to its disadvantage and might launch a successful war against the aggressor. In this situation, alliances were normally short-run *ad hoc* accords, involving relatively little agreement on common political principles (as opposed to interests) between the participants. They could be overtaken by a new pattern of alliances as circumstances changed. In general, states also preferred to negotiate rather than fight and were prepared to stop fighting rather than eliminate an essential national actor. No one state was strong enough to conquer all the others, and the mutual jealousies of the major powers preserved even small or relatively weak states, which could not have done this by themselves.[3]

Between the early 1890s and 1914, the relationship between the European great powers began to move into a pattern of intense rivalry, with the emergence of two major alliances, between Germany and Austria-Hungary on the one side, and Russia and France, joined later by Britain, on the other. The cataclysm of the great war brought about the destruction of the nineteenth century balance of power system and of the assumptions on which it was perceived to have rested. With the establishment of the League of Nations, the hope was that commitments to collective security could achieve the task of keeping the peace, in which the balance of power system had catastrophically failed. The resultant international system has been described as unique and hard to categorize – it was not a balance of power system nor a bipolar one, but perhaps in transition to bipolarity. After 1933, with the rise of Nazi Germany, it developed into a quasi-bipolar system, similar to that of 1890–1914.

The period of the Second World War was clearly one of intense conflict and bipolarity, though the makeup of the two poles obviously altered at critical junctures – notably through the entry of the Soviet Union into the war, with the Nazi invasion of Russia in June 1941, and that of the United States and Japan, following the attack on Pearl Harbor in the following December. On the face of it, the position of the small or medium power in such a conflict seemed hopeless. If it tried to remain neutral, it could nevertheless still be invaded by one side or the other, depending on its geographical situation. If it joined an alliance, this might still be no effective defence against invasion by the opposing side. However, in certain fortunate circumstances, it could manage to stay out of the conflict, and might even gain from it if it was able to convince the belligerents that the cost of trying to coerce it would outweigh the benefits.[4]

Normally, the period of the Cold War, between 1945 and the late 1980s, is taken as the archetype of a bipolar global system. Reduced to its essentials, it was a struggle between the USA and the USSR, in which the role of other states was, at best, subsidiary. Two other features of the Cold War provided important contrasts with the pre-1914 situation. First, after 1949, both sides possessed nuclear weapons, whose number and effectiveness they steadily developed over the next four decades. Hence, peace depended not just on a balance of power, but a balance of terror. This deterred each side from starting a conventional war, at least in Europe, for fear that it might develop into a nuclear one. However, it also placed a very high premium on crisis management, since a false move would be hard to correct and liable to result in rapid escalation and mutual destruction. Second, the Cold War was seen as an ideological contest, in which political ideas and principles, not just material interests, were declared to be at stake. Even if small states might rank security or economic interests above ideological commitments, the broad political preferences of their leaders were almost bound to have some effect on how they positioned themselves in the global contest.

Although, in retrospect, the Cold War era marks a distinct phase in international politics, there were important changes in the international system between 1945 and the late 1980s. Following the Cuban missile crisis of 1962, the superpowers set up a process of *détente* designed to lower the risk of another potentially disastrous collision between them. This effectively opened a new chapter in the history of the Cold War. In this environment, small or medium powers outside Europe found it easier to opt out of Cold War alignment, and even saw moral advantage in doing so. Some of these conditions altered again during the phase of what has been called the 'Second Cold War' between 1979 and the mid-1980s. The most striking manifestation of this was the build-up in military expenditure, especially by the United States, after 1978, in response to a steady increase on the Soviet side during the 1970s. The Soviet invasion of Afghanistan at the end of 1979 was also an important turning point, since it showed that the USSR could be prepared to use force against a neighbouring but non-aligned state. This phase was effectively ended by changes within the Soviet Union, following the death of Konstantin Chernenko and his succession by Mikhail Gorbachev as Secretary-General of the Soviet Communist Party, in 1985.[5]

The end of the Cold War in 1989–90 and the formal dissolution of the Soviet Union at the end of 1991 left the United States as the world's sole superpower, as previously defined. Nonetheless, it was hard to define the new order as simply unipolar and it did not seem to have any clear historical precedent. There were some similarities with the situation that immediately followed the First World War, but the parallel was far from complete. Economically, the USA was still the world's most powerful state, but by the end of the first decade of the twenty-first century, its economy, like that of the European Union, was facing severe problems as the main locus of global economic power was shifting to Asia and a scatter of other fast-growing economies. Politically, also, American self-confidence was badly undermined by the disastrous invasion and occupation of Iraq. Nor did the end of the Cold War bring an end to Western alliances, which (most notably, in the case of NATO) continued to exist, since they still had important utility for both the United States and their small or medium power members even after the Warsaw Pact ceased to exist.

For the middle powers, especially those that, like Turkey, had previously been threatened by the USSR, the end of the Cold War had obvious benefits, since it removed the most immediate threat to their security. However, it did not by itself end regional conflicts. In fact, new ones were created by the collapse of communist hegemony in eastern Europe and the former Soviet Union. Globally a new emphasis on the international application of democratic norms, heightened in Turkey's case by the start of accession negotiations with the European Union, began to erode previous assumptions about unrestricted state sovereignty within national frontiers. Middle powers such as Turkey were thus faced with as many problems as in previous eras, even if their character had been changed.

The Ottoman and Turkish states and the international system

On the empirical evidence, most of the generalizations made about the position of small and medium powers in the international system fit the Turkish case quite aptly. On the one hand, in the world as it was before 1945, it was clearly weaker than the great powers of Europe. After 1945, it was still well behind the secondary powers, to say nothing of the two superpowers. On the other hand, it was not entirely powerless internationally, since it was often able to bargain with the great powers to its own advantage, and it had some regional power, both in south-eastern Europe and the Middle East, especially if its neighbours were not satellites or colonies of a great power or superpower.

The main factors affecting Turkey's international position have been its geographical situation, its natural and human resources, and its economic development, especially since the 1950s. On the first score, Turkey is the only state, apart from Russia, with territory in both Europe and Asia, and is affected by and affects international politics in both south-eastern Europe and the eastern Mediterranean, in Transcaucasia and the southern regions of the former USSR, and in the northern parts of the Middle East. Historically, Turkey's most strategically significant asset has been its control of the straits of the Dardanelles and Bosporus, on which Russia has depended for direct maritime access to the Mediterranean, and the only route through which Britain, France and later the United States could challenge Russia in the Black Sea (or try to assist it, during the First World War). Since the start of the Second World War, the development of air power, nuclear weapons and later of intercontinental missiles has reduced the role of conventional naval forces. However, it has not eliminated Turkey's strategic importance, since the possession of air bases on Turkish soil, and access for ground forces in time of war, gives any of the major powers a crucial advantage for actual or potential action in the northern part of the Middle East, the Balkans and Transcaucasia. In short, its geographical situation increases Turkey's international weight, but historically it also increased the chances of an attack by any of the great powers with ambitions in these regions, making it quite unrealistic for it to adopt a passive policy of opting out of international politics.

Turkey's natural and human resources also appear to put it in the middle power category. At 780,000 square kilometres, its land area is slightly less than that of France and Britain added together. During the nineteenth and early twentieth centuries, the population of the Ottoman Empire fluctuated erratically, due to frontier changes, wars and migrations (see pp9–10) but it was still large enough to raise a respectably large army, by the standards of the day. At the time of the foundation of the Turkish republic in 1923, the population was probably somewhere around 12 million, but better health conditions and reduced infant mortality raised this to an estimated 73.7 million by 2010. Given what is now a declining birth rate, the population is expected to stabilize at around 95 million by the middle of the twenty-first century. Meanwhile, Turkey's international strength is not limited by a shortage of manpower – in fact, there is a surplus rather than shortage of labour. As of 2010, 67 per cent of the population was aged between 15 (the minimum school leaving age) and 65, with only 7.2 per cent over that age, so the demographic time-bomb of an increasing dependency ratio that was hanging over the economies of Europe, China and Japan was still some way off. Over the last 70 years, Turkey has also made better use of its human resources. In 1927 (the earliest date for which statistics are available), the literacy rate stood at around 10 per cent and only a tiny proportion of the population had received higher education. By 2010, the reported literacy rate had risen to risen to around 93 per cent, while the proportion of the student age group in higher education was about 30 per cent. In educational terms, this leaves Turkey behind western Europe, but still ahead of most of the rest of the world's population.[6]

The country's natural resources also put it in a fairly favourable position internationally. Normally, it can produce more than enough food to feed its population and does not usually need to import more than a small quantity of agricultural products. It has sufficient deposits of most of the main industrial minerals, with the significant exceptions of oil, natural gas and hard coal. Nor is it dependent on the export of a single or limited range of products. Today, industrial exports – notably motor vehicles, textiles, clothing, steel and light machinery – have come to account for around 90 per cent of total exports. Politically, its main resource liability, apart from its lack of significant deposits of oil and gas, is its dependence on the advanced industrial states for modern military hardware. A domestic arms industry has recently been established, including the manufacture of jet fighters, but this is still heavily dependent on imported know-how and components. As in the cases of other middle powers, complete self-sufficiency is an unrealistic dream.

The Ottoman Empire was a poor and backward country, with virtually no modern industry and poor internal communications. Its dependence on foreign capital, both for economic development and staving off government bankruptcy, left it vulnerable to pressure from the leading industrial states. With the establishment of the republic, there was better financial management and a sharp reduction in the external debt, followed by a state-sponsored industrialization programme in the 1930s. Nonetheless, until the 1960s, Turkey remained a predominantly agricultural country, with low per capita incomes – in effect, a Third World country ruled over by a First World elite. Since then, there has been a rapid increase in the size and sophistication of Turkish industry, and of the economy as a whole, so that agriculture now accounts for only about 9 per cent of Gross Domestic Product (GDP), compared with around 30 per cent for manufacturing and construction, and 60 per cent for services – proportions close to those of the advanced industrial economies. Measured at current exchange rates, GDP has risen from $18 billion in 1968 to around $735 billion in 2010.[7] Using the more realistic conversion by purchasing power parities, GDP now stands at around $1,104 billion. This appears to give Turkey the world's 17th biggest economy, with a per capita average of $15,180 – just under half of that for the European Union as a whole, but higher than that of EU member states Bulgaria and Romania.[8] As the economy has grown, so has its dependence on foreign trade, which has risen from around 8 per cent of GDP in 1970 to 41 per cent in 2010.[9] In this way, economic growth has increased rather than reduced external dependencies. Meanwhile, what puts Turkey in a special class is that, since the world financial crisis of 2008–9, its economic recovery, measured by the annual GDP growth rate, has been far higher than those of the advanced industrial economies. In the global economy, the main emerging powers are commonly identified as the BRIC nations (Brazil, Russia, India and China) all of which are much larger than Turkey. However, the BRICs are followed by four others – Turkey, Indonesia, South Korea and Mexico – that each account for more than 1 per cent of world GNP, and can thus be expected to be part of a crucial shift in global economic and political power during the twenty-first century.[10]

1 Foreign relations of the late Ottoman Empire, 1774–1918

The Turkish republic was established in 1922–4, when the monarchy and the Islamic Caliphate were abolished, and Ataturk and his colleagues set out to create a new nation-state on the ruins of the Ottoman Empire. Constitutionally and territorially, the transformation marked a clean break with the Ottoman past. Nonetheless, the attitudes of the new state's rulers, as well as its citizens, were inevitably shaped by the experiences of the Ottoman period or what they learnt of them either formally or informally. Rather than attempt a full history of the Ottoman Empire's foreign relations during the last 150 years of its existence, this chapter attempts to summarize those aspects of the story that played an important role in shaping later attitudes. It starts by giving a brief sketch of the structure of the Ottoman state, as it affected its foreign policies, as well as the international system and the options available to late Ottoman policy-makers – some of which still affect confront their successors. A narrative section then attempts to illustrate these points by sketching in the main events in the foreign relations of the Ottoman Empire during the period. The concluding discussion assesses the implications of these events in forming later attitudes and policies.

The Ottoman state: Dilemmas and change

The central problem faced by the Ottoman Empire in the nineteenth century was both an internal and an external one. At the zenith of its power in the sixteenth and seventeenth centuries, the Sultan's government had ruled over a vast territory stretching from Hungary to the Crimea and from Tunis to the Persian Gulf, and had been the hegemonic power in the eastern Mediterranean. By the 1770s, in the west, Hungary and Transylvania had been lost to the Hapsburg Empire, while north Africa was ruled by local dynasties over whom Ottoman control was normally not much more than nominal. Nonetheless, the Ottomans still had formal sovereignty over a huge territory. Unfortunately they lacked the power to control it effectively internally or to protect it against external enemies. During the sixteenth century, the Empire had been equal if not superior to any of the European states in military, technological and economic advances, and administrative efficiency. By the last quarter of the eighteenth century it had fallen well behind the major European powers in all these respects. In effect, it was neither a great power nor a minor one, but a former great power in gradual eclipse, whose future became a continuing problem both for its own rulers and the leading European states.

In 1912, Count Johann von Pallavicini, the Austrian ambassador in Istanbul, suggested to his government that 'Turkey was not, and is not now, a state in the European sense of the word'.[1] Setting aside the counter-claim that the Hapsburg monarchy was itself something of an anachronism, Pallavicini's judgement would certainly have been true a century earlier. The Empire had been what is described as a 'tributary state', in the sense that the ruling class of army officers and state bureaucrats had no specific socio-economic foundation but extracted surplus from all sectors of the economy – agriculture, trade and industry.[2] It was 'tributary' also in the sense that those who exercised power in most of the Empire were tributaries, rather than the obedient servants, of the central government. While officially invested with power by the Sultan as governors or military commanders, they could often exercise it independently and by process of bargaining and manoeuvre with other local power-holders. In effect, the Empire could be seen as a series of local satrapies. In 1864, following a series of partial earlier reforms, and as part of a wide-ranging programme of reform known as the *Tanzimat* ('reorganization') a new law on provincial administration introduced a centralized system on the Napoleonic model. This provided in theory for a hierarchy of trained officials taking their orders from the centre and remitting regular revenues to it.[3] Nevertheless, in practice, and until the end of the Empire, state power remained dispersed and unreliable in outlying regions. In Istanbul and the other main port cities it was also limited by the capitulations – the special arrangements under which foreigners resident in the Ottoman Empire enjoyed fiscal and legal privileges. Since the European consuls frequently gave out citizenship of their states to members of the Christian communities who were natives of the Empire and were originally Ottoman citizens, these concessions came to have considerable importance: by the 1880s, resident 'foreigners' had come to account for as much as 15 per cent of the population of Istanbul.[4]

This administrative weakness was compounded by ethnic and religious heterogeneity. Westerners often referred to the Ottoman Empire as 'Turkey', and its people as 'Turks', but the Turks themselves preferred to speak of their Empire as the 'exalted Ottoman state' and its rulers as 'Ottomans' (even if they were not of the imperial dynasty) reflecting its lack of ethnic identity. Population figures for the Empire in the nineteenth century are often guesswork, since the government failed to carry out a population census in the accepted sense. However, from the 1830s, local officials were supposed to keep registers of the population in their districts, and calculations of the entire population were issued, based on these admittedly incomplete statistics. On this basis, it would appear that in 1844 (the first year for which we have remotely complete figures) the population of the territories actually, rather than nominally, controlled by the Sultan, was somewhere around 26 million. Of this about two thirds was Muslim (Turks, followed by Arabs, Kurds, Muslim Slavs and Albanians) and the remainder Christian (Slavs, followed by Armenians, Greeks, Christian Arabs and Albanians) with a small Jewish community.[5] By 1885, following territorial losses to the empire in the Balkans, which reduced the total while increasing the percentage of Muslims, the population had fallen to around 17–18 million, of which about 72 per cent was Muslim, but it then rose to around 21 million by 1906. In 1914, after the loss of virtually all the Empire's territories in Europe during the Balkan wars, the population had dropped back to 18.5 million, of which about 81 per cent was Muslim. Since the Ottoman government classified its citizens by religion (that is, as Muslims or Jews, or adherents of the different Christian denominations) we have no breakdown of the population by ethnic groups, but it would appear that in the last quarter of the nineteenth century, ethnic Turks only accounted for about 45–50 per cent of the population, and a lower proportion before that.[6]

The Ottoman state was largely non-assimilative and lacked the technical, economic and institutional resources to integrate its diverse populations into a single political community, even if it had wanted to. Hence, its society remained highly diverse. Its subject peoples retained their own languages and religions, with some degree of formal political autonomy. Non-Muslims could be seen as second-class citizens, in that they could not serve in the army and were subjected to special taxes, but were not subjected to forcible conversion. Each religiously defined community, or *millet,* had its own hierarchy, led in theory by its religious head, or *milletbaşı* (thus, the Patriarch of Constantinople for Orthodox Christians, the Chief Rabbi for Jews, and so on) and administered its own courts for personal status cases, as well as educational institutions.[7] Until the nineteenth century, this diversity did not pose too serious a challenge to the Empire's territorial integrity, since the vast majority of Ottoman citizens accepted traditional authority and identified primarily with local communities based on residence or kinship. If they saw themselves as part of a wider 'imagined community' then it was that of the religiously-based *millet,* not the ethnic or territorially-based nation.[8] However, modern ideas of ethnic nationalism began to affect the Greeks and Serbs in the early nineteenth century, and later spread to the Romanians, Bulgarian and Macedonian Slavs, and Armenians. Since Christianity and Islam were still the primary markers, most Muslims remained loyal to the Ottoman state until its end, although a successful nationalist revolt broke out among the mainly Muslim Albanians in 1910, and an embryonic nationalist movement had begun among the Ottoman Arabs just before the First World War. Left to itself, the Ottoman army could normally defeat a national rebellion by a single ethnic group, since the proto-nations were mostly geographically dispersed and often mutually hostile, but it could not do so if the rebellion were supported by one or more of the major European powers, or if a number of ethnic groups or emergent nations combined against it. Hence, the Empire was subjected to a process of gradual territorial dismemberment and ethnic cleansing.

During the nineteenth and early twentieth centuries, rebellions by the Christian minorities sporadically triggered off ruthless and brutal reactions by the Ottoman authorities which naturally aroused righteous indignation on the part of European statesmen and writers – as on the occasion of the massacres on Chios in 1822, the 'Bulgarian horrors' denounced by Gladstone in 1876, and the massacres and deportation of virtually the entire Armenian population of Anatolia in 1915. What western opinion almost entirely ignored was the fact that the Muslim populations of the Balkans, Crimea and Caucasia suffered equally appalling atrocities at the hands of the emerging Balkan nations and advancing Russian armies, and in far greater numbers. Well-documented calculations by Justin McCarthy and others show that between 1827 and 1922 around 5 million Muslims in Greece, the Crimea, the Caucasus, and the Balkans were killed, while about another 5.4 million were expelled and took refuge in the Ottoman Empire. A large proportion of these victims of Greek and Balkan chauvinism and Russian imperialism were ethnic Turks, but their numbers also included millions of Slavic Muslims and Crimean Tatars, plus the Muslim minorities of the Caucasus (Muslim Circassians, Abkhazians, Chechens, Azeris and Muslim Georgians) many of whom had not been under Ottoman rule, but fled to the Ottoman Empire since they recognized it as a 'kin state'.[9]

Of course, two wrongs do not make a right, and atrocities by one side cannot justify counter-atrocities by the other. At the same time, it is clear that the massacres and expulsions of these Muslim communities had profound effects on the Empire. First, the influx of refugees tended to enhance the effect of territorial contraction, by increasing the Muslim share in the total Ottoman population. Second, it created a profound sense of injustice and deep hostility towards those nations that had been responsible for it. By the 1920s, around one third of the population of what became the Republic of Turkey was probably composed of refugees or their descendants, creating a strong sense of shared suffering and solidarity. Third, it had important effects on the attitudes of the Ottoman rulers. What looked to Europeans like an effort to prop up a crumbling, corrupt and sometimes brutal empire, was seen by Ottoman governments and their Muslim subjects as a perfectly legitimate attempt to protect their own people against slaughter and exile, in the face of indifference or outright hostility on the part of the European powers.

The primary aim of Ottoman Sultans and statesman was to preserve their state and to protect its Muslim populations in these unpromising conditions, and this was almost the sole goal of the *Tanzimat* reforms. Apart from the attempted administrative modernization referred to earlier, reform and strengthening of their armed forces was naturally a major focus of attention. After a false start between 1789 and 1807, the construction of an effective modern army began with the destruction of the Janissary corps by Sultan Mahmud II in 1826, and had begun to yield results by the 1840s. Hence, as Feroze Yasamee suggests, after a period of pronounced decline between 1768 and 1839, Ottoman power began to revive after that date. After a system for conscription of Muslim males was introduced in 1869, the strength of the standing army was raised to around 200,000 by the 1870s, and 470,000 by 1897. During the First World War, some 2.7 million men were mobilized, although the maximum strength of the army probably failed to exceed 650,000 at any one time. Modern weapons and tactics, and an officer corps trained in both, also increased the Empire's military strength. As a result, the Ottoman army could still win battles (especially defensive ones) and even wars. Its main deficiencies were its almost total reliance on imported weaponry, its lack of logistical backup and modern transport, the financial weakness of the state and, above all, the sheer number and strength of its potential enemies compared with the relatively small size of the Muslim population and the immense length of frontiers it had to defend. Hence the government had to resort to diplomatic manoeuvring, rather than risk unaided military resistance to any major European power.[10]

Ottoman diplomacy: Aims, methods and policies

Careful diplomacy was thus the key to Ottoman survival. As has been suggested in the Introduction (pp2–3), it rested on exploiting the balance of power between the main European states – Russia, Britain, France and Austria, with Germany emerging as a major power in the last part of the nineteenth century – and their mutual fear that if either one or a coalition of powers destroyed the Ottoman Empire, this would provoke a major war with their rivals. In this way, the Empire lasted much longer than most European observers had expected. In effect, the Empire served as a classic example of how a relatively weak state – the supposed 'sick man of Europe' – could survive even in the heyday of European imperialism.

Since 'the eastern question' was a major focus of concern in nineteenth century diplomacy, the history of the policies of the major powers towards it has received a good deal of scholarly attention. Unfortunately, this has not been the case on the Ottoman side. Hence, while we have relatively abundant information on the diplomacy of the main European states, and the effects of Ottoman decline on their relations with one another, we have little direct information about what Ottoman governments thought or planned in the foreign policy field – and then only for the last quarter of the nineteenth century.[11] Most of what we know about the policies of Ottoman governments thus has to be inferred from their actions, or from what European diplomats believed and reported at the time.

Ottoman foreign policy was also affected by the institutional resources available to it. Until the last years of the eighteenth century, the Empire had no permanent diplomatic representatives abroad, although temporary diplomatic missions were frequently sent abroad for specific purposes. This defect was remedied during 1793–6 as permanent embassies were established in London, Vienna, Berlin and Paris, to be followed in due course by other capitals. Besides representing their government, the staff of these embassies were also supposed to find out about western technical and administrative advances, and thus came to play a major role in pushing forward the *Tanzimat* reforms. Originally, there was no separate foreign ministry: foreign policy was decided at the centre by the Grand Vizier (*Sadr-i Azam*) and its administration by the office of the 'Chief of the Scribes' (*Reisülküttab*) an assistant to the Grand Vizier, who also had responsibility for a variety of other functions. In 1835, however, his foreign policy and diplomatic responsibilities were transferred to a new Ministry of Foreign Affairs (*Umur-i Hariciye Nezareti*). The ministry continued to handle relations with the non-Muslim *millets* within the Empire until the 1880s. In the meantime, the post of foreign minister came to be one of the most important in the state, as leading statesmen of the *Tanzimat* interchanged this appointment with that of Grand Vizier. The Grand Vizier thus joined the foreign minister as an important determinant of foreign policy. At other times, a forceful and determined Sultan could take over the reins, reducing the foreign minister to relatively minor status: this was certainly the case during the reign of Abdul Hamid II (1876–1909).[12] Overall, however, the Ottoman Empire seems to have built up a reasonably effective foreign policy structure, not so different from those of other autocratic monarchies at the time, and probably more effective than other parts of the Ottoman state bureaucracy.

As an active foreign policy maker, Abdul Hamid II evidently had a low opinion of the way it had been conducted. Having suggested that every state needed a 'fundamental goal' and a 'policy which accords with its circumstances and position',[13] he regretted that:

> The Ottoman empire has no definite and decided goal and policy: in every question the person in power acts in accordance with his own opinion, and in the event of failure successor blames predecessor and predecessor successor, and in the process the sacred interests of the state suffer.

In fact, the Sultan probably did his predecessors as well as himself something of an injustice, since late Ottoman foreign policy was arguably more consistent and effective than he suggested. From around the beginning of the nineteenth century, Ottoman statesman had evidently recognized that the Empire could not win a war for territory with the major European powers unless it was supported by one or more of the others. They hoped that in the long run they could restore the Empire to its former strength by modernizing state structures and the economy, and by rebuilding its army and finances, but to do this they needed a fairly long breathing space, with sufficient external stability and security. They thus had to consider how to exploit the international situation to their advantage. Territorially, the principal threats arose in three main zones of conflict: first, in the Balkans, where emerging local nationalist movements, aided by Russia and sometimes by other powers, threatened to end Ottoman rule; second, in the straits of the Bosporus and Dardanelles, which it was assumed Russia aimed to dominate as a means of securing access to the Mediterranean and thus the world's oceans; third, in Egypt and to a lesser extent the rest of the Arab Middle East, where France and Britain had ambitions. Against this, it could be expected that, at least to some degree, Russia and Austria (aided later by Germany) could cancel one another out in the Balkans, Russia and Britain at the straits, and Britain and France in Egypt.

In this situation, Ottoman statesmen had two broad options in policies towards the major powers. One would be to avoid both conflicts and firm alliances with any of them, meeting each crisis as it arose, and relying on the workings of the balance of power to preserve the status quo. This policy would also avoid the danger that too close relations with any one power or group of powers might mean the subordination of Ottoman interests to those of the partner or partners. As an alternative, the Ottoman government could try to negotiate a reasonably stable alliance with one or more of the European powers. This assumed that one power could definitely be identified as the enemy, intent on destroying the Empire or reducing it to impotence, while another power or combination of powers could be potential allies, who were not capable of reaching an accommodation with the enemy, and were themselves genuinely committed to maintaining the Ottoman Empire. Which of these two broad options were adopted depended on the circumstances at the time, the relative strength of the main powers, and their perceived intentions, besides the situation on the ground in the zone or zones of conflict. At the same time, the Ottoman Empire had a clear interest in staying out of a war between the European powers, unless their conflict centred on its own territory: at most, it could hope to sell its friendly neutrality to whichever side offered it the most favourable terms.

If the second option were chosen, then Ottoman policy-makers obviously had to decide which power was the enemy and which others were actual or potential or actual allies. During the middle part of the century – that is, roughly between 1840 and 1878 – the answers to both these questions seemed fairly obvious. Russia was identified as the most serious foe, since it was best placed to launch a land invasion of Ottoman territory, it had an assumed interest in gaining control of or at least free passage through the straits, and presented itself as the patron and protector of the Sultan's Orthodox Christian subjects. On the other hand, Britain, supported on occasion by France and Austria, appeared as the obvious ally, since the British had a (probably exaggerated) fear that if Russia achieved its assumed ambitions at the straits, or managed to conquer or subordinate the Empire as a whole, then it could challenge British naval dominance in the Mediterranean and the sea route to India. However, this calculation could not be applied at all times or in all circumstances. In the first place, Russian power or ambitions might not be so far-reaching as the calculation assumed: faced with obstacles to the achievement of a maximalist and expansionist programme, Russia might be prepared to accept the status quo, or even to offer protection to the empire against other enemies. Equally, alliance with Britain was far from risk-free, or necessarily effective. In the first place, Britain had its own ambitions in Egypt and the Middle East, and might use an alliance with the Empire to further its own interests at Ottoman expense. Second, Britain was a naval rather than a land power, and was poorly positioned to prevent Russian territorial advances in south-east Europe or along the Empire's north-eastern border.[14] In effect, the British navy could not, by itself, reliably protect the Empire against the Russian army, or vice versa. Hence in certain circumstances the Ottomans might do best to avoid any alliances – the first broad option – or to seek an alliance with another power, maybe even with Russia. By the end of the century, Germany was emerging as the most likely candidate for alliance, although this connection eventually led to the Ottoman Empire's destruction in the First World War.[15]

Diplomacy in action: 1774–1918

These general observations about Ottoman foreign policy in the nineteenth century need some illustration and expansion, by reference to the main relevant events during the period and the way in which Ottoman statesmen coped with them. Needless to say, this exploration can only be introductory and cannot do more than give a summary sketch of the full story, which is well covered by a substantial quantity of scholarly literature.[16]

For most of the eighteenth century, the Ottoman Empire's main adversary had been Austria and its main ally France. This pattern was radically altered in the 1770s by Russian expansion to the Black Sea, as a result of which Russia replaced Austria as the most immediate threat. After defeat by Russia in the war of 1768–74, the Ottomans were forced to sign the treaty of Küçük Kaynarca of 1774. This gave Russia a foothold on the northern shores of the Black Sea, recognized the independence of the Crimea (previously a vassal-state of the Ottoman Empire) and allowed Russia navigation rights in the Black Sea as well as what was dubiously interpreted as a right of protection over Ottoman subjects of the Orthodox faith. Meanwhile, Austria helped itself to the formerly Ottoman territory of Bukovina in 1775. Russia annexed the Crimea in 1783 and, after another war of 1787–92, captured further territory between the rivers Dniestr and Bug. For the first time, Ottoman territory mainly inhabited by Muslims had been occupied by a Christian state. It had also become clear that the Empire was no match for Russia unless the Ottomans were supported by one of the other European powers.[17]

France's internal turmoil after the revolution of 1789 temporarily removed it as a counterweight to Russia, and the Napoleonic wars brought constant shifts in the kaleidoscope of the Ottoman Empire's alliances and enmities. Between 1799 and 1812, the Ottoman government was periodically either allied with or at war with all the main European protagonists. The traditional Ottoman *entente* with France was ended by Napoleon's invasion of Egypt in 1798. In response, the Ottomans signed a treaty with Russia in December 1798 which Britain adhered to in the following month. The British, aided by the Ottoman army, ousted the French from Egypt in 1801, but Russia did not

[margin handwritten note: Russian/ Austrian expansion into Ottoman land]

want to carry on the war with France and signed peace with it in October 1801, to be followed by the British and Ottomans in May and June 1802. However, the re-opening of the war between Britain and France in 1803 led to an Anglo-Russian alliance in April 1805: this was followed by an Ottoman–Russian agreement in September in which the two sides agreed to cooperate in the case of an attack by a third party.

This resurrection of the alliance between the Ottomans, British and Russians was nonetheless to be very short-lived. The overwhelming victories by Napoleon at Ulm and Austerlitz persuaded the Ottoman leaders that they had joined the wrong side: they never ratified the agreement of September 1805, and entered into negotiations with France in the summer of 1806. In response, Russian forces occupied the nominally Ottoman principalities of Moldavia and Wallachia (modern Moldova and part of Romania) in November 1806, causing the Ottomans to declare war the following month. In effect, the Empire had now joined France against Britain and Russia. In February–March 1807, the British and Russian fleets made an abortive attempt to capture the straits, but in July the tables were once again turned by Napoleon's peace agreement with Tsar Alexander I at Tilsit. The Ottoman Empire was now faced with the real danger that the French and Russians might partition its territory between them.

Fortunately for the Ottomans, Napoleon never decided what he wanted to achieve in the Balkans, since there was the danger that Austria and Britain would be the main gainers from an Ottoman collapse, and he was determined to prevent Russia from seizing the straits. Accordingly, the Russo-French partition plan was abandoned in 1808 – a good example of the balance of power system in operation. The position was strengthened by an Ottoman–British peace treaty of January 1809, under which the two sides confirmed the traditional rule that the straits would be closed in peacetime to all non-Ottoman warships. Meanwhile, the Russo-Ottoman war over the principalities dragged on, with periodic armistices, until early 1812, when the imminent attack by France forced Russia to come to terms. Under the treaty of Bucharest of May 1812, Russia held on to the formerly Ottoman territory of Bessarabia, but the Ottoman state regained sovereignty over Wallachia and Moldavia. Thereafter, it effectively dropped out of the Napoleonic wars. In spite of internal turbulence, and the fact that its military power was almost at rock bottom, it had managed to come through the conflict with relatively little loss of territory, by forming flexible alliances and exploiting the mutual rivalries of the European powers.[18]

During the complex crises of 1798–1812, the Empire's survival had mainly been threatened by direct territorial expansion by the major European powers: after this date, the main challenge came indirectly, from European support for rebellions by the Balkan Christian communities and its own vassals. A rebellion had begun in Serbia in 1804–5 under the Serb leader Karageorge, but this was crushed by the Ottomans in 1813 after the treaty of Bucharest allowed them to re-direct their forces against Serbia. However, in 1815 the revolt was re-started by Milos Obrenovich, who had Karageorge murdered in 1817. Meanwhile, Obrenovich had reached an agreement with the Ottomans under which Serbia remained within the Empire, but power was shared between him and the Turkish governor in Belgrade.

During the 1820s, two new players appeared on the Ottoman and Balkan scene, in the shape of Mehmet Ali Pasha, the Sultan's governor of Egypt, and a rising Greek resistance movement. A native of Kavala (now in Greek Macedonia) Mehmet Ali had arrived in Egypt after the expulsion of the French as a member of the Albanian contingent of the Ottoman army, and became governor of Egypt in 1805. Over the next 40 years, with the help of European (mainly French) professionals, he launched an impressive programme of modernization and strengthening of his armed forces and Egypt's economy and administrative structures. This achievement acted as a model for the Ottoman *Tanzimat* and converted him from a servant into a rival of the Ottoman Sultan. When a Greek uprising began in earnest in 1821, the Ottoman army was so weak that it was unable to defeat even the divided rebels. The task was left to Mehmet Ali, who landed his forces in southern Greece in February 1825, and had defeated the Greeks by the spring of 1826. This brought about naval intervention by the European powers. The combined fleets of Britain, France and Russia destroyed the Egyptian-cum-Ottoman fleet in the port of Navarino in September 1827, and Mehmet Ali's army withdrew. Eventually, Greece was established as an independent state in the southern part of its modern territory, and was recognized as such by the Ottoman government in 1832.[19]

For Sultan Mahmud II, the success of the Greek revolt had pointed up the urgent need to modernize his army and to dissolve the Janissary corps, which was the main obstacle to military reform. To achieve this, however, he needed a breathing space and a settlement with Russia, which in 1825 had threatened unilateral action on behalf of the Greeks. Accordingly, in October of that year, his government accepted the Convention of Akerman with Russia. This established the autonomy of Moldavia and Wallachia as well as Serbia within the Ottoman Empire, recognized Russian conquests in the Caucasus and allowed Russian merchant ships freedom of navigation throughout the Empire. Later, however, the defeat at Navarino hardened Mahmud's policy, and he refused to implement these provisions. In response, Russia declared war on the Empire in April 1828. By the summer of 1829 the Ottoman forces had collapsed: the Russians had captured Edirne (Adrianople) which is only some 170 miles north-west of Istanbul, and had advanced along the Black Sea coast as far as Trabzon. Nonetheless, the Russian army was also ravaged by disease. Correctly fearful that a total destruction of the Ottoman Empire might provoke a major war with France and Britain, Tsar Nicholas I decided to sue for peace. In the last analysis, Russia preferred to preserve a weak Ottoman Empire along its southern border, rather than risk its total dissolution. Under the treaty of Edirne of September 1829, the Russian hold over Armenia and Georgia (much of which had not been Ottoman territory anyway) was confirmed, and Russia only made small territorial gains at the mouth of the Danube. Once again, the balance of power, and cautious Russian policy, had prevented the general disintegration of the Empire.

This pattern repeated itself in the case of the next challenge to the Ottoman state, which came from Mehmet Ali. Frustrated by his failure to hold on to his conquests in the Greek peninsula, the Egyptian governor sent his armies into Palestine and Syria in October 1831. By February 1833 they had reached Kütahya, in western Anatolia, and Mehmet Ali seemed poised to succeed the Ottomans on the throne of Istanbul. Bereft of other support, Mahmud II turned to Russia, and in April 1833, 14,000 Russian troops arrived in the Bosporus with naval support. Under the treaty of Hünkâr İskelesi, signed in July, Russia and the Ottoman Empire agreed to help one another in case of outside attack. In a secret clause, Russia conceded that it would not call for Ottoman military and naval support if it were attacked by a third party, and in return the Ottoman government agreed to close the straits to foreign war-ships. Meanwhile, the Ottomans also agreed to recognize Mehmet Ali as governor of Syria, to which the Egyptian army withdrew. Britain had hitherto stood aside in the crisis, but the Hünkâr İskelesi treaty eventually stung the Foreign Secretary Lord Palmerston into action, since he mistakenly believed that its secret clause had given Russian warships free passage through the straits. He also appreciated the risk that the Ottoman Empire might be turned into a Russian protectorate. During the 1830s, France emerged as Mehmet Ali's main supporter, further complicating the situation for Britain. This danger was put to the test in 1839 when Mahmud decided to try to eject Mehmet Ali from Syria, but was decisively defeated at the battle of Nezib (Nizip in Turkish) in June. Before news of the defeat had reached Istanbul, Mahmud had died, to be succeeded by his 16-year-old son, Abdul Mejid, and the Empire was again dependant for its survival on European support. Fortunately for the Ottomans, the apparent indirect challenge from France, through Mehmet Ali, produced a Russo-British rapprochement. Under a convention signed with the Ottoman government in July 1840, Britain, Austria, Prussia and Russia agreed to protect the Sultan's government against Mehmet Ali, in return for an Ottoman declaration that the straits would be closed to all non-Ottoman warships in peacetime. The following September, the British fleet bombarded Beirut, and by February 1841, the Egyptian army had returned to its country, defeated by British and Ottoman forces and with no effective help from France. Under an agreement of June 1841, Mehmet Ali accepted the limitation of his army, in return for the hereditary governorship of Egypt, vested in his family.[20]

The defeat of Mehmet Ali marked the emergence of Britain as a more active player in the near eastern power game, and the Ottoman Empire's main ally for the next 37 years. Under the treaty of Balta Limanı of 1838, Britain also acquired a dominant position in the Empire's foreign trade. This was strengthened by British support for the principles of the *Tanzimat*, and those Ottoman statesmen who promoted it, such as Mustafa Reshid Pasha,

Ali Pasha and Fuad Pasha. In September 1841, the new British Ambassador, Stratford Canning, was instructed by the Foreign Secretary, Lord Aberdeen, that: 'The policy of Great Britain in the Levant has long been distinguished by a sincere desire to support the Turkish Power; and to avert the dissolution [of the Empire], either from the effects of internal convulsion or of Foreign aggression.' Britain hoped 'by promoting judicious and well considered reform, to impart some degree of consistency and stability to the government which is threatened by so many causes of dissolution'.[21] There is some room for doubt as to how influential British policy was in furthering the cause of reform. Ottoman internal policies were almost certainly more autonomous than foreign commentators supposed and, as Frank Edgar Bailey remarks, the *Tanzimat* reforms were 'essentially Turkish in origin'.[22] Admittedly, the imperial rescript (*Hatt-i Şerif*) of Gülhane of 1839, which promised an end to tax farming and pledged that all Ottoman subjects regardless of their religion would be treated equally and justly by the courts, was an important turning point, and was introduced more than partly as a means of winning foreign (particularly British) support against Mehmet Ali. However, the programme of modernization of the administration, the army and education had begun well before then, and continued for many years after Britain and the Ottoman Empire had drifted apart diplomatically. At the same time, the fact that British policy-makers believed that they were playing an important role in the *Tanzimat* almost certainly helped to stiffen British policy. For their part, Ottoman statesmen realized that they needed western support against Russia, although they did not necessarily favour Britain as their sole ally.

The policy of allying with the other European powers against Russia reached its apogee at the time of the Crimean War of 1854–5. The conflict began with a dispute between France and Russia in 1851–2 over the respective rights of the Orthodox and Latin churches in the Christian shrines of Jerusalem, but escalated in 1853 when the Russian General Prince Menshikov was sent to Istanbul as a personal representative of the Tsar. Menshikov demanded the restoration of all Orthodox privileges in Jerusalem and that Russia be given the right to protect all Orthodox Christians in the Ottoman Empire. This demand was quite unacceptable to both the Ottoman government and the western powers. In June 1854, Russia threatened to occupy the principalities of Moldavia and Wallachia, British and French warships were sent in response to the Dardanelles and Russia carried out its threat at the end of the month. In the ensuing war with Russia, the Ottoman fleet was destroyed in the Black Sea port of Sinop in November 1853, but in March 1854, Britain and France signed a treaty with the Ottomans committing themselves to defend Ottoman territory against Russia, and formally declared war. Meanwhile, Austria refused to support the Russian advance into Moldavia and Wallachia, and in June 1854, concluded a treaty with the Ottoman government in which the latter transferred its sovereign rights in the principalities to Austria until the conclusion of peace. With great reluctance, the Russians backed down: the Russian troops in Moldavia and Wallachia were replaced by Austrians in July–August 1854.

Having lost their original *casus belli,* the allies decided to replace it with an attack on the Crimea, with the aim of destroying Russian naval power in the Black Sea. The Crimean war began in September 1854, when British, French and Ottoman troops were landed in the peninsula, and was ended after the allies captured Sebastopol in September 1855. Under the Treaty of Paris, signed in March 1856, the Black Sea was closed to warships of all nations, but for small vessels for coastal protection: effectively, it had now ceased to be an Ottoman lake and had become a neutral one. The principalities were restored to Turkish suzerainty, but were to enjoy autonomous rights guaranteed by the powers. Similarly, the signatories agreed to respect the independence and integrity of the Ottoman Empire, and any state in conflict with it was to seek the mediation of a third power before resorting to force. In return, the Sultan's government agreed to give guarantees of good treatment of its Christian subjects: this was enacted by the issue of a new imperial decree, the *Hatt-i Hümayun,* in February 1856. Under the treaty, the Ottoman government was also invited to 'participate in the public law and concert of Europe'. To the uninitiated, this might seem a vague and pointless provision. To the Ottoman government, however, it had considerable significance, since it was treated as recognition of the Empire's status as a European power. The continuation of this recognition has since remained one of the Turkish state's main foreign policy goals.[23]

The Treaty of Paris ushered in a period of relative calm in the Empire's relations with the European powers that lasted until 1875: the Ottomans were affected by further upsets in the Balkans and the Lebanon,[24] but there were no international crises affecting their territories on the scale of those of 1831–3, 1839–41, or 1854–5. In 1871, an international agreement allowed Russia to resume its sovereign rights in the Black Sea, and thus reversed the neutralization provisions of the Treaty of Paris. This concession had no immediate practical effect since for many years afterwards poverty and the lack of a consistent near eastern policy prevented Russia from building a Black Sea fleet of any consequence. However, in 1874 a revolt began in Bosnia-Herzegovina that spread to Bulgaria in 1876 and set off shock waves that nearly proved fatal for the Empire. In 1875, as Anatolia was gripped by drought and famine, the Ottoman government announced that it was suspending payment on the huge foreign debt of £191 million that Sultan Abdul Aziz had accumulated, inviting intervention by the western governments to protect their bondholders. The financial problem was eventually settled in 1881 with the establishment of the international Council of the Ottoman Debt, but the political crisis was far more difficult to solve. The brutality with which the Ottoman forces suppressed the Bulgarian uprising alienated western liberal opinion, especially in Britain, and Russia threatened to intervene on behalf of its Orthodox Slavic brethren. Istanbul was further affected by internal turmoil, as Abdul Aziz was deposed by a virtual *coup d'état* in May 1876, to be succeeded by his nephew Murad. The hope of Midhat Pasha and other reformist Ottoman statesmen was that the new Sultan would agree to a constitution, with a representative parliament in which all the communities of the Empire would assent to Ottoman rule. However, Murad proved to be mentally unstable and it was not until December 1876, after he had been replaced by his brother Abdul Hamid, that the Empire's first and only constitution was proclaimed.[25]

Meanwhile, the European powers, who were generally unimpressed by the constitution, proposed governmental reforms and some territorial changes in the Balkans. In April 1877, Abdul Hamid rejected their reform proposals and declared war on Russia. Opinions on the Russian side were divided between pan-Slavists, led by the tsar's ambassador in Istanbul General Ignatiev, who wished to end Ottoman rule in the Balkans by setting up a chain of Russian-protected states, and the more cautious policies pursued by the foreign minister, Prince Gorchakov. Due to stout resistance by the Ottomans, who held out in the fortress of Plevna (Pleven) in northern Bulgaria until December 1877, the Ottoman–Russian war of 1877–8 was far from a one-sided match, but the Ottoman forces were eventually defeated. In the east, the Russians captured the vital fortress of Kars in November 1877. In the west, they took Edirne in January 1878, and advanced to the Ottomans' final defence lines at Çatalca the following month. These victories allowed the pan-Slavist school of thought to gain the upper hand in Russia. Under a treaty signed at San Stefano (now Yeşilköy, a suburb of Istanbul) in March 1878, Abdul Hamid's government agreed to the creation of a 'Greater Bulgaria', with a southern coastline on the Aegean, which was to be nominally tributary to the Sultan, but in fact under Russian military occupation for the next two years. Russia would gain territorial advances in Bessarabia (or southern Romania) and on the Ottoman Empire's north-eastern frontier. Serbia and Montenegro would gain further territory at Ottoman expense. In brief, had the treaty of San Stefano been implemented, Russia would have become the dominant power in the Balkans.

The main weakness of Russia – and an advantage for the Ottomans – was that the tsar's government was diplomatically isolated. None of the western powers wished to preserve the Ottoman Empire unaltered, but Britain opposed any settlement which would leave Russia in a strong position to take over the straits. With Germany now emerging as an important power-broker, Bismarck also wished to prevent a war between Russia and Austria over the Balkans. There was thus a good deal of coincidence between British, German and Austrian aims. At the height of the crisis in February 1878, the British fleet passed through the Dardanelles to Istanbul, and a war between Russia and Britain seemed a possibility. The outcome was settled at the congress of Berlin of June–July 1878, which ended with a treaty signed on 13 July. Under its terms the 'Greater Bulgaria' foreseen at San Stefano was dismantled. Bulgaria north and west of the Balkan mountains was established as an autonomous state under nominal Ottoman suzerainty and a Christian prince. The region to the south and east of this, known as 'eastern Rumelia', was to remain under Ottoman rule, but with a Christian governor and a Christian militia as well as some Ottoman garrisons (in fact, the Sultan never exercised this last right). The remainder of 'Greater Bulgaria' was returned to Ottoman government.

However, Serbia, Romania and Montenegro were recognized as independent states and Russia gained some territory from Romania as well as the formerly Ottoman districts of Kars, Ardahan and Batum in the east. Austria was allowed to occupy Bosnia-Herzegovina (though it remained nominally under Ottoman suzerainty until 1908) while Britain also took a share of the spoils by occupying Cyprus.[26] In effect, the treaty had bought the Ottoman Empire another uncertain lease of life, but at a very heavy price. Apart from its territorial losses in the east, it had lost all direct control of south-east Europe, except for a long and strategically indefensible arm of territory stretching from the present Greek–Turkish frontier into northern Greece, Macedonia and Albania. In terms of population, from a previous total of somewhere around 25 million, the Sultan had lost about 5.5 million subjects, almost half of whom were Muslims.[27]

With the Berlin settlement, the 'eastern question' moved off the top of the agenda for the main European powers for the next 40 years. However, this did not solve the central problems faced by Ottoman statesmen. Abdul Hamid had prorogued the Ottoman parliament indefinitely in February 1878, and virtually monopolized decision-making until 1908, both domestically and in foreign policy. The main problems he encountered were that his territory, especially that remaining in Europe, was very hard to defend, that the *entente* with Britain was fading, and that France's power in the near east had also waned. By occupying Egypt in 1882, Britain secured a vital stepping stone on the route to India that did not depend on Ottoman goodwill and it thus had less need to prop up the Empire in south-east Europe. At the same time, Abdul Hamid became very suspicious that Britain meant to break off the Arab provinces of his Empire, and establish a British sponsored Armenian state in eastern Anatolia. In fact, the Sultan had no way of preventing the British occupation of Egypt, nor could he prevent the union of the two halves of Bulgaria in 1885–6, and its emergence as a virtually independent state. His only consolation was that, thanks to internal upheavals and diplomatic pressure from Britain and Austria, the new Bulgaria was, for a time at least, anti- rather than pro-Russian.

Abdul Hamid was a pious Muslim and, unlike his predecessors, emphasized his position as Caliph, or nominal head of all the world's Muslims. Politically, this may have been of some value, by promoting Islamic unity against incipient Arab or Albanian nationalism. Although it depended on bluff, it may also have provided some leverage against those European powers, such as Britain, France and Russia, with large subject Muslim populations. However, the Sultan was pro-European in culture, and there is no evidence that he ever regarded a pan-Islamic state as a practical project. As an alternative, he continued the policy of modernizing the Empire's administrative and military machine, though with the objective of strengthening the Empire against the European powers, rather than improving the position of the Christian minorities, which was what the Europeans normally meant by 'reforms'.[28]

Initially, Abdul Hamid attempted to tackle his security problem by seeking a defensive alliance with Germany, as the one power that was too far away to threaten his Empire directly, but could offer him some protection against Britain and Russia. However, Bismarck turned down the Ottoman approaches in 1881–2: he had only recently constructed the 'League of the Three Emperors' between Germany, Russia and Austria in June 1881 and did not want to arouse Russian suspicions, although he did agree to the despatch of a German military mission to modernize the Ottoman army in March 1882. In 1886, at the prompting of the Grand Vizier Kâmil Pasha, there was some discussion of a renewed Anglo-Ottoman alliance. However, the British government backed off since it feared that an alliance with the Sultan might allow Bismarck to embroil Britain with Russia, and thus free Germany to attack France – a good example of the complexities of the balance of power system. The failure provoked some consideration of a Russian–Ottoman alliance, for which the Ottoman officials even drew up a draft treaty, but this project also came to nothing. Hence, after 1886, the Sultan moved back to the alternative option of trying to preserve friendly neutrality towards all the main powers, without forming an alliance with any of them.[29]

During the 1890s, European economic penetration into the Empire became a major focus of international attention – most notably, the proposal to construct a railway from Istanbul to Baghdad. After much trumpeted visits to the Ottoman Empire by Kaiser Wilhelm II in 1889 and 1898, a largely German-backed company received a concession for the project in 1903. This, combined with growing German trade with the Empire and the German role in modernizing the Ottoman army, convinced some later observers that the Empire was being converted into a satellite of Germany. In fact, in the years before 1914, Germany's share of the Ottoman Empire's foreign trade was still well behind those of Britain, Austria and France, and Germany only accounted for about 21 per cent of the total foreign capital invested in the Empire, compared with France's share of 49 per cent. In the event, the Baghdad line was not completed in its entirety until 1940, and Britain settled its differences with Germany over the railway in 1913–14.[30] Hence, it seems that there was nothing inevitable or economic about the Ottoman–German alliance in the First World War.

Meanwhile, the main problem faced by the Empire was still the rising tide of Balkan nationalism and the European powers' entanglement with it. A rebellion in Crete led to a brief war with Greece in 1897 in which the Ottoman armies won an easy victory, but pressure from the powers forced the Sultan's government to withdraw from the island and recognize it as an autonomous province under Ottoman suzerainty. By the early years of the twentieth century, attention had switched to turmoil in Macedonia, in which the Ottomans tried to play off Greek against Bulgarian nationalists. The European powers sponsored reform schemes but these had little effect. Eventually, the struggle in Macedonia provided the background for a revolution in the Ottoman army itself. In July 1908, a group of officers in the Third Ottoman Army, based in Salonika, rose in rebellion and demanded that the Sultan reactivate the 1876 constitution by reconvening the parliament which had been closed since 1878. Unable to resist his own army, Abdul Hamid rapidly capitulated. Free debate and a free press began again after the long years of royal autocracy, elections were held and the new parliament was duly inaugurated in December 1908. For the optimists, a new era seemed to have dawned in which all the diverse communities of the Empire would unite behind the principle of constitutional and representative government, under the banner of 'Union and Progress'.[31]

Unfortunately for the Empire, the brave hopes of 1908 proved stillborn. Before long the 'Young Turk' regime fell apart through internal struggles between liberals and 'unionists', resulting by 1914 in the establishment of an autocratic triumvirate of Enver, Mehmet Talat and Ahmed Jemal, three of the leaders of the original revolution. Austria seized the opportunity to annex Bosnia-Herzegovina in October 1908, while Bulgaria proclaimed its independence and Greece annexed Crete.[32] Without the shadow of an excuse, Italy invaded the Ottoman provinces of Tripoli and Cyrenaica (modern Libya) in September 1911, forcing the Ottoman government to cede the territory in October 1912.[33] The Albanians, a majority of whom were Muslims, rose in revolt in 1910, seeking a measure of self-government within the Empire, and achieved this in September 1912. Elsewhere in the Balkans, the Christians of the Empire pushed forward for independent statehood rather than a civic or supra-ethnic identity within the Ottoman state, strengthening the tendency towards a defensive Turkish nationalism on the other side. Hence, it is only at this point that one can begin to speak of 'the Turks' as a political rather than just an ethnic category.[34]

In foreign policy, it has frequently been assumed that the Young Turks initially favoured an alliance with Britain, as the supposed progenitor of democratic government. In fact, researches by Hasan Ünal suggest that, at best, their ideas were very vague, ill-formed and inconsistent. Turkish diplomacy was also constrained by the fact that, by the late nineteenth and earlier twentieth centuries, it was becoming more difficult to play off one European power against another, since the main European states were becoming divided into two camps, with France, Russia and later Britain on the one side, and Germany and Austria on the other. Before coming to power, the Young Turks' debates had shown a general hostility towards all the European powers, while after the revolution they switched to the opposite policy of trying to establish friendship with all of them. Initially, the picture was further confused by a division of power in Istanbul where the Grand Vizier Kâmil Pasha adhered to careful diplomacy, while some of the Young Turk leaders tried to follow an independent and more adventurous line. During October 1908 they made approaches to the British, French, Germans and Austrians, although this blunderbuss approach lacked logic, given the mutual hostilities of the European states.[35] Hence, their hopes were disappointed, and not just because relations with the Empire were badly handled, notably by Britain. Admittedly, the British government was extraordinarily badly served at the time by Sir Gerard Lowther, its ambassador in Istanbul between 1908 and 1913, and his staff, who had a deep hostility to the Young Turks and all their works, intrigued constantly against their government, and harboured outrageous and absurd prejudices against Jews, Freemasons, Turks, and Muslims in general.[36] However, this was not the sole or the most important reason for the failure of the projected alliance with Britain. In London, the Foreign Secretary, Sir Edward Grey, was working for an *entente* with France and Russia in an effort to preserve the continental balance of power against Germany, and did not want to provoke Russia by entering an alliance with the Ottoman Empire. Hence, when an Ottoman delegation arrived in London in November 1908 to propose an alliance, it was told by Grey that Britain wished to keep its hands free. After the outbreak of war with Italy, the Ottoman government again proposed a formal alliance, either bilateral or with the triple *entente* as a whole, but again learnt that Britain favoured neutrality.[37]

The Ottoman state was thus left without an alliance with any of the European powers when it faced its final trial of strength in the Balkans in 1912–13. In October 1912, the four states of the 'Balkan League' – Bulgaria, Serbia, Greece and Montenegro – launched an all-out attack on the remaining Ottoman territories in Europe. By itself, the Ottoman army could probably have defeated any of the Balkan nations individually, but it could not overcome an alliance of all of them. The Bulgarians, who bore the brunt of the fighting on the alliance side, had reached the Çatalca lines by November 1912, and captured Edirne in the following March. Under the treaty of London of April 1913, the Ottoman Empire ceded all of its territory west of the Enez-Midye line, including Edirne. In June 1913, the Istanbul government again approached the British for a defensive alliance but this was rejected on the grounds that it would unite 'all Europe' against Britain. However, the Ottomans were able to save some face, as well as territory, when Bulgaria fell out with its erstwhile allies Greece and Serbia over the division of their territorial spoils in Macedonia. Since the Bulgarians were forced to transfer most of their forces to their western front to fight the Serbs, Edirne was left virtually undefended. Turkish troops entered the city on 21 July, with Enver hogging the limelight – an advantage which he then used to project himself into a position of almost total power by his appointment as Minister of War on 1 January 1914. Meanwhile, the treaty of Bucharest of August 1913 brought the war to a close and the Turks' western frontier was fixed along its present line.[38]

The Balkan wars set the stage for the final drama in the Ottoman Empire's long history, when it entered the First World War on the German side. This fatal decision was preceded by negotiations with both sides, and apparently not regarded as inevitable by either of them. During the pre-war years, ultra-nationalist ideologues urged an alliance with Germany against the Slavs, who were seen as the Turks' natural enemies. In this literature, anti-imperialism was mixed with social Darwinism, so that struggle and war were seen as the only avenues to liberation.[39] The effects of these ideas should not be over-estimated, however, since it appears that the majority of the public and the government initially favoured neutrality, with Enver the only consistent advocate of an alliance with Germany. In May 1914, Mehmet Talat approached the Russians with an offer of alliance, but was turned down: the furthest

Russia was willing to go was to ensure Ottoman neutrality. Ahmed Jemal was similarly rebuffed by France when he visited Paris in July.[40] Important authorities on the German side, including Baron Hans von Wangenheim, Germany's ambassador in Istanbul, and General Liman von Sanders, head of the German military mission, opposed the idea of an alliance with the Ottoman Empire, on the grounds that it was too weak to be an effective ally. Against this Kaiser Wilhelm II favoured the alliance, for fear that the Turks would otherwise join the *entente*, and this view eventually won out on the German side.[41] On 2 August, the day after the war had begun in Europe, Enver negotiated a secret treaty with Germany, promising Ottoman support for the central powers if Germany's assistance to Austria led to war with Russia – a condition which was fulfilled four days later. However, Jemal and the other cabinet members were not informed of the agreement until after it was signed and for some time it was not certain that the Ottoman government would act on it.

A turning point was passed on 3 August when the British government – apparently unaware of the secret Ottoman–German agreement – commandeered two dreadnoughts that had just been built in England for the Ottoman navy and had been paid for by public subscription. This arbitrary decision turned public opinion against the British as few other steps could have done. Even at this late stage, however, Enver was still negotiating with the Russian ambassador N.K. Giers for an alliance with Russia in return for the restoration of western Thrace and the Aegean islands which had been lost to Bulgaria and Greece in the Balkan wars. The most Giers offered was a joint guarantee by Britain, France and Russia of Turkish neutrality and territorial integrity. Enver continued to insist on the return of the Aegean islands, as well as the abolition of the capitulations and the return of the commandeered warships, but France and Britain refused the last two conditions, and the negotiations broke down.

On the British side, Grey believed: 'Turkey's decision will not be influenced by the value of the offers made to her, but by her opinion which side will probably win and which is in a position to make the offers good.'[42] On this score, the Germans won a clear advantage on 10 August when the German battle cruisers *Goeben* and *Breslau* arrived in Istanbul, and were transferred to the Ottoman navy by a bogus sale. Germany had thus demonstrated a clear material commitment to aid the Empire and exploited the advantage created by Britain's mistake in impounding the two dreadnoughts. On 11 October, the German ambassador secretly promised delivery of 2 million Turkish pounds (£1.8 million) in gold if war was declared, and the arrival of the gold on 16 and 21 October sealed the deal. Without consulting the rest of the cabinet, Enver ordered the German admiral Souchon, now commanding the Ottoman fleet in the Black Sea, to attack the Russians. Souchon carried out his orders on 29 October. Russia declared war on the Ottoman Empire on 2 November and Britain and France followed suit three days later.

Enver's decision appears to have been formed by the expectation that the central powers would win a rapid victory in the war, that Russia would attempt to exploit Armenian resistance in eastern Anatolia to take territory from the Empire, and that alliance with Germany was the best way of preventing this. He went on believing this even after the battle of the Marne, on 5–12 September, had made it clear that Germany would not win a quick victory and might well lose the war. In effect, he had broken one of the ground rules of earlier Ottoman diplomacy, that the Empire should not join a war between the European powers unless its own territories were directly involved (which they were not). Previously, the Ottoman government had compensated for its internal weakness by playing off one European power against another, but Enver now threw away this advantage. Some later writers, such as Feroz Ahmad, admit that the Young Turks backed the wrong horse in 1914, but claim that 'events had shown that they had no other horse to back'.[43] Against this, it can be argued that they would have done much better to stay away from the race track.[44]

During the war, the future disposition of the Ottoman Empire's territories was the subject of intense and complicated negotiations between the *entente* powers. These were inconsistent with one another, and many of them later became dead letters after Russia's withdrawal from the war: moreover, the Ottoman government obviously had nothing to do with them. Three events during the war did however have a powerful effect on the post-war Turkish state's foreign policy and relations. Of these, the first was certainly tragic and is still bitterly contested. In January 1915 the Turkish forces fighting the Russians on the eastern front were devastatingly defeated at Sarıkamış, and the way opened for a large-scale Russian advance. In response, the Ottoman government ordered the deportation of the Armenian population of the region, which it rightly suspected of siding with the enemy. What happened then is sharply disputed. According to Armenian accounts, more than a million of their people were massacred in a planned genocide. Turkish or pro-Turkish accounts argue that the number who died during the transportation, or of conditions of famine or disease which also killed around 2 million Muslims, was about 200,000, and that a genocide was not ordered or carried out. What is indisputable is that by the end of the war, the Armenian population of Anatolia, which had formerly numbered about 1.3 million, had been virtually wiped out – either through flight, massacre or disease. Whatever the historical truth may be, the events of 1915 undoubtedly created a source of deep mistrust between Turks and Armenians that survives to this day.[45]

The second event had an equally important long-run effect on the Turks' relations with their Arab neighbours. The British-sponsored Arab revolt – led by the Hashemite family who had been the hereditary rulers of Mecca under the Ottomans – that began in the Hijaz in 1916, was a turning point in the history of Arab nationalism. For the Turks, it represented a treacherous stab in the back, after the official Ottoman declaration in 1914 that the war was a *jihad,* in which all good Muslims should join the fight against the infidel. The third event was further away, and the Ottomans played no part in it. Nevertheless, the Bolshevik revolution had profound effects on the Empire, as on all

Russia's neighbours. In the short run, it relieved the Ottoman army on a vital front, allowing the Empire to regain the territories lost to Russia in 1878, under the treaty of Brest-Litovsk of December 1917. As a result, in 1918 Turkish forces advanced into Transcaucasia in a pointless campaign. This was the only practical expression of the idea of pan-Turkish nationalism, or the union of the Turkic peoples of central Asia with those of Turkey, which was fashionable in Young Turk intellectual circles, but it soon came adrift. In the longer run, the revolution and the consequent turmoil in Russia severely reduced Russian power until the late 1930s, and even converted what had been regarded as the hereditary enemy into an ally, at least for a few years.

During 1915–16, two of the Young Turk leaders – Ahmed Jemal, now Commander of the Ottoman Fourth Army in Syria, and Rahmi Evranos, the governor of the Aegean province of Aydın – were not above trying to make side deals with the Russians and the British, in the hope of establishing themselves in power by taking the Ottoman Empire out of the war, but nothing came of these approaches.[46] As a result, the Ottoman government stayed in the war much longer than it could have done. During 1917 it could probably have arranged a separate peace with the British that would have left much of the Empire intact, if it had made a serious effort to do so. However, Enver did not lose confidence in a final victory for the central powers until June 1918. By September 1918, total defeat was staring him in the face. With the withdrawal of Bulgaria from the list of Germany's allies, the Empire was cut off from Germany, and faced with the serious danger of an advance on Istanbul from the west by *entente* troops. In Palestine and Syria, the Ottoman army expected almost certain destruction by vastly stronger British forces. Even then, Enver kept the truth from the cabinet, and it was not until he was removed from power through the installation of a new government under Izzet Pasha on 14 October that peace feelers were put out to the British.[47] These resulted in the signature of an armistice on the British battleship HMS *Agamemnon*, anchored off Mudros, on the island of Lemnos, on 30 October. Under its terms, all Ottoman troops were to lay down their arms and the straits were opened to the navies of the *entente*. The critical seventh clause of the armistice agreement also gave the *entente* powers 'the right to occupy any strategic points in the event of a situation arising which threatens the security of the allies'.[48] The war was finally ended, but the Ottoman state faced a very uncertain future.

Implications and legacies

For subsequent Turkish policy-makers, as well as the Turkish people, the most obvious and important lesson of the Ottoman state's long period of struggle and decline since the late eighteenth century was that, territorially and structurally, the Empire was not sustainable and could not be recreated. In effect, the late Ottoman rulers had been engaged in a long project of damage limitation, which had ultimately failed. Through careful diplomacy, they had been able to slow down the decline but they had never been able to create a long enough breathing space to reconstruct and modernize the Empire effectively, and might well have been unable to do so even if they had managed to secure external stability. The European powers had paid lip service to the principle of Ottoman sovereignty, and had frequently repeated the claim that they respected the Empire's territorial integrity, but in reality this respect was usually a fiction. The process of dismemberment of the Empire had been a long and gradual one, rather than a single and cataclysmic collapse, as many had predicted. Most commonly, a subject community would rise in revolt, would be defeated by the Ottomans, but would then win autonomy within the Empire thanks to support by one or more of the European powers. Autonomy would eventually be converted into full independence, after the next Ottoman defeat and a respectable length of time. This story had been repeated in the case of Serbia, Greece, Romania, Bulgaria, and finally Albania. Even when the Ottoman armies won a clear victory against an enemy state – as in the case of Greece in 1897 – political pressure by the European powers had reversed the verdict of the battlefield. In effect, the late Ottoman Empire had apparently been locked into a no-win situation.

This experience did not mean that the tactic of exploiting the balance of power had been wrong. The greatest mistake made by Ottoman foreign policy had been in 1914, when Enver had abandoned it (though how long the Ottoman Empire might have survived if it had remained neutral in 1914 is still an unanswerable question). At the same time, there were certain inescapable conclusions to be drawn from the late Ottoman experience. First, the future Turkish state would have to draw a firm line round those territories that it could reasonably expect to defend, either by itself or, if absolutely necessary, with the support of allies whose long-run interests were very close to its own. For the most part, this meant the territory inhabited by ethnic Turks, or other Muslims who were willing to integrate into or cooperate with the Turkish state. Ethnic Turks outside these boundaries could not be protected, except in rare circumstances where Turkish military force could be brought to bear.[49] Second, the nineteenth century experience encouraged a highly suspicious attitude towards any expressions of religious or ethnic separatism by non-Muslim or non-Turkish minorities remaining in Turkish territory. This derived not from innate prejudice but from the perception that, in the past, such movements had been used by rapacious foreign powers as a mask to hide their own imperialist ambitions. This reaction ignored the genuine humanitarian sympathies that might exist abroad for such minorities, but was none the less real for all that. The huge influx of refugees resulting from the Empire's contraction reinforced this feeling of betrayal by the west and led to a high degree of integration of the newcomers into the existing Turkish population of Anatolia. The modern Turkish nation was born in this melting pot.[50]

In other circumstances, this might have produced a nation of xenophobes, determined to cut themselves off from the outside world. That this was not so in the Turkish case was primarily due to the fact that, for the political elite, the western nation-state and its values still retained a powerful attraction as the sole practical model for national reconstruction – political, economic and cultural. Those outside the elite might still prefer traditional or Islamic values – as they were perfectly entitled to do – but only the most eccentrically conservative could deny the importance of western economic and technical achievements, or refuse to emulate them. The result was something of a love–hate relationship with the west. There was a natural desire to emulate the west in technical, economic and military terms, and to be recognized as a respected member of the western community of nations. This was balanced by a suspicion of western motives, and a fierce resentment of any sign of patronizing or dictatorial behaviour by western governments, which was not unjustified by past experiences.

Perhaps the most complicated and problematic element in the resulting political culture was its attitude to Islam. On the one hand, there can be little doubt that, even at the end of the Empire, most Turkish and Kurdish inhabitants of Anatolia still identified themselves in primarily religious terms, and continued to do so for many years. The Ottoman state had been defeated, but the idea that political authority should have a religious basis still remained common. On the other hand, most of the original Islamic political project lay in ruins. Muslims were not united in a single state, and had not been for centuries. Abdul Hamid had appealed for Islamic unity as a general principle, but even he had never treated it as a real political blueprint. Above all, Ottoman rule over the Arab Middle East and its holy places had been decisively ended, both by superior British military strength and what the Turks saw as Arab betrayal during the First World War. Hence, the idea of rooting the legitimacy of the state in Islam was greatly weakened and that of continuing the empire as a geographical entity almost entirely destroyed. On the other hand, Islam as a cultural and social system as well as a religious faith still commanded mass respect. How to integrate it into the structures and values of a modern state, with its concomitant foreign policy assumptions, still remains a problem for many Muslim Turks.

2 Resistance, reconstruction and diplomacy, 1918–39

Between 1919 and 1923, the Turks passed through the most critical turning point in their modern history. With the defeat of the Ottoman Empire in 1918, the victorious *entente* powers seemed poised to divide up almost all its remaining territory, thus practically extinguishing the Turkish state as an independent international actor. After the Russian revolution, the Bolshevik government withdrew the tsarist regime's claims to Turkish territory, making Britain the dominant power in the near east. Once the war was over, the Prime Minister David Lloyd George tried to give effect to this, by establishing British rule in Iraq and Palestine, and by using Greece as Britain's surrogate in Asia minor. Since Greece had been coerced into the war by Britain and France in July 1917, the Greek premier Eleutherios Venizelos was accorded a place at the Versailles peace conference in February 1919. On the basis of bogus population statistics claiming that the majority of the population was Greek, he put forward a grandiose claim to the whole of western Asia minor, eastern Thrace and all the Aegean islands. These claims were broadly supported by Britain and France, but opposed by Italy. What the *entente* powers failed to anticipate was the emergence of a powerful movement of national resistance that decisively defeated the partition project. Eventually, in 1923, this forced its former enemies to recognize an independent Turkey within what are virtually its present frontiers. The leader of the resistance movement, Mustafa Kemal Atatürk[1] then used his traditionally-derived authority as a 'Ghazi', the victor in a war against the infidel, to reconstruct the Turkish state on quite untraditional lines – as a secular republic, committed to modernism and a Turkish-ethnic rather than Muslim identity, with himself as President. This outcome was basically determined on the battlefield, not at the conference table. Nonetheless, the military victory would probably have been impossible without adroit diplomacy by Atatürk and his colleagues – in effect, the exploitation of the balance of power, and rivalries between the main European states, on which their Ottoman predecessors had relied.

Diplomacy, war and peace: 1918–23

While the First World War had still been raging, the *entente* powers had, in effect, written themselves vague and sometimes contradictory promissory notes for the territories of the Ottoman Empire. In 1915, reversing a century of policy, the British promised to hand over Istanbul and the whole straits region to Russia if the *entente* won the war, and secured French acquiescence to this. After the Russian revolution, the Bolshevik government renounced all claims to Turkish territory, but this still left open the fate of the straits as well as territories in eastern Anatolia which the tsarist government had occupied or claimed. After much negotiation, the *entente* powers' plans were eventually formulated as the Treaty of Sèvres, which was reluctantly accepted by the government of the last Sultan Vahdettin (Mehmet VI) in August 1920. Under this stillborn treaty, Ottoman rule in Istanbul would be maintained, but control over the straits placed under an international commission, on which the Ottoman government would have only minor representation. İzmir and the surrounding territory would be administered by Greece for the following five years, after which it could be attached to Greece, subject to a plebiscite. Eastern Thrace was separately allotted to the Greeks. In eastern Anatolia, Armenia would be established as an independent state in the provinces of Erzurum, Trabzon, Van and Bitlis (of which only a minority of the population had been Armenian). A scheme for 'local autonomy' for the Kurds, possibly leading to full independence, would be worked out by a commission composed of British, French and Italian delegates. The treaty provided for the severance of the Arab provinces of the Empire, which the Turkish nationalists broadly accepted, but a separate agreement between Britain, France and Italy recognized the 'special interests' of Italy in southern Anatolia, and of France in Cilicia (that is, Adana and the area to its north-east). In effect, the treaty envisaged that the future Turkish state would be reduced to a rump including only Istanbul and central and northern Anatolia, with very few resources and practically no freedom of action in the economic sphere.[2] Legally, the Treaty of Sèvres was quite invalid, since it was never ratified by the Ottoman or any other Turkish parliament. Nonetheless, it was important as a statement of the *entente*'s plans and its failure was a striking defeat for allied, especially British, policy.

Although these plans were not formalized until the Sèvres treaty was prepared in 1920, several of the states involved had moved to create *faits accomplis* for some time before. On 15 May 1919, Greek troops were landed in İzmir, primarily to pre-empt the Italians, who had been promised the region in separate inter-allied agreements of 1915 and 1917.[3] Meanwhile, in the spring of 1919, Italy landed troops in Antalya, while the French occupied Cilicia, and British, French and Italian forces were stationed in the straits. In response, huge protest meetings were held in Istanbul and local resistance movements organized in Anatolia. They were coordinated by Mustafa Kemal, the Turks' most distinguished general in the First World War, who had been sent by the Istanbul government to the Black Sea port of Samsun in May 1919, nominally to suppress attacks by the local Turks on Greek settlements in the area. Exploiting the underground organization known as Karakol ('The Guard') set up by Enver towards the end of the war, local resistance leaders in the 'Eastern Provinces Society for the Defence of National Rights', whose core was drawn from army officers and the middle ranking echelons of the old Union and Progress organization, met in Erzurum during July–August 1919. Here they elected Mustafa Kemal as chairman of their Representative Committee. The Erzurum congress also issued a proclamation declaring that 'the entire country within its [undefined] national frontiers is an undivided whole',[4] and that any foreign occupation of it would be resisted by force. These commitments were repeated at a second congress held in Sivas on 4–11 September, which established a national organization known as the Society for the Defence of Rights of Anatolia and Rumelia ('Rumelia' referred to Turkey's remaining European territory in Thrace). In effect, Mustafa Kemal, who moved his headquarters to Ankara on 27 December 1919, had now been made head of an embryo government over most of Anatolia, which was effectively outside the Sultan's control.

The ensuing struggle for Anatolia – or, as the Turks call it, the 'National Struggle' (*Milli Mücadele*) – was effectively divided into two phases. During the first of these, between June 1919 and March 1920, the nationalist resistance movement, which was still building up its military and political structure, evidently hoped that it might achieve its aims without facing a military showdown with the *entente* powers, and in collaboration with sympathetic members of the Sultan's government. It is suggested that at this stage Kemal planned to capture control of the imperial government rather than overthrow it.[5] A possible opportunity to do this occurred at the end of September, when the Sultan dismissed his subservient Grand Vizier and brother-in-law, Ferid Pasha, replacing him with Ali Rıza Pasha. The new Grand Vizier then sent his Navy Minister, Salih Pasha to meet Mustafa Kemal in the town of Amasya, near the Black Sea. Under the resulting 'Amasya protocol' of 23 October 1919, the two sides agreed that a new Chamber of Deputies, under the Ottoman constitution, would be elected and convened outside Istanbul, and that the declarations of the Sivas congress would be accepted by the Sultan's government, assuming they were passed by the Chamber. The elections, in which nationalist sympathizers won a handsome majority, were held during October–November, and the Chamber convened in Istanbul (in spite of the Amasya agreement) on 12 January 1920. On 28 January it voted through the 'National Pact' (*Misak-i Milli*), which effectively became the official statement of the nationalist aims. This accepted the loss of the 'portions of the Ottoman State which are populated exclusively by an Arab majority', and which were under occupation by the *entente* powers at the time of the Mudros armistice of October 1918, with which most Turks were apparently happy to cut their links. In effect, the nationalist resistance had decided not to try to re-build Turkish power in the middle east. However, the Pact declared that:

the whole of those parts [of the Ottoman Empire] whether within or outside the said armistice lines which are inhabited by an Ottoman Muslim [in effect, Turkish and Kurdish] majority, united in religion, in race and in aim ... form a whole which does not admit of division for any reason in truth or in ordinance.[6]

In reaction to the Chamber's defiance, and because they apparently feared some sort of link between the Turkish resistance and the Bolshevik regime in Russia,[7] the *entente* forces subjected Istanbul to a full military occupation beginning on 16 March 1920, allowing the Sultan to restore Ferid Pasha to power and arresting all the nationalist deputies whom they could lay their hands on. However, 92 deputies managed to escape arrest and assembled in Ankara, where they were joined by 232 new members elected by local branches of the Defence of Rights movement. On 23 April they opened their first session as the Grand National Assembly of Turkey, proclaiming their sovereignty in the name of the nation, although leaving open the question as to whether the Sultanate could be continued.

The publication of the Sèvres terms in April 1920, and their acceptance by the Sultan's government in August, effectively dashed hopes that the Turkish nationalists might be able to negotiate their way out of the partition plan, or could do so in collaboration with the Istanbul government. This opened the second phase in the struggle. For the nationalists, the prospects must at first have seemed daunting. After centuries of decline, the Ottoman Empire had just been defeated by the most powerful armies of the day. On the ground, the Turks had been unable to stem the advance of the Greek forces, which had captured Bursa and most of the Aegean region by the summer of 1920. Moreover, the nationalist movement could not make an undisputed claim to sovereignty, since the Sultan's government continued its existence until November 1922. Most foreign states continued to recognize it, maintaining their diplomatic missions in Istanbul rather than Ankara. The nationalists had difficulty in finding the personnel for their embryonic foreign ministry, which originally consisted of just three officials and a lady secretary. According to one story, passengers alighting from the train from Istanbul who were wearing neckties (an assumed sign of western culture) were asked whether they spoke any French. Those who did were immediately invited to join the foreign ministry, where they were given jobs regardless of their qualifications or profession. As time went on, officials from the old Istanbul government transferred themselves to the new ministry. It was not until after the proclamation of the republic in October 1923 that a regular ministerial and diplomatic structure was established, and it was only in the late 1920s that most foreign diplomatic missions in Turkey transferred their embassies to Ankara. By this stage, Turkey had started to build up an impressive cadre of trained diplomats who helped to maintain a fairly high degree of consistency and independence in the execution of policy.[8]

However, events were to show that the odds were less stacked against the Turks than they might have appeared. The *entente* governments could not enforce their partition scheme without a massive military commitment, but neither they nor their peoples were prepared for this. In April 1920, Marshal Foch reported that an army of 27 divisions would be needed to force the Turks to accept the proposed peace terms, but such forces were simply not available.[9] The only *entente* state with a clear national and territorial interest in Anatolia was Greece, but in the long run Greece was too weak to defeat the Turks without effective military support from Britain, which was not forthcoming. The French and Italians soon made it clear that they had no stomach for another bitter war with the Turks, and sought separate peace deals with them. The Sèvres scheme also excluded Russia, where the Bolshevik government had established effective control by the end of 1920, and aligned with the Turkish nationalists against the *entente*. Finally, the *entente* states were not only at odds with one another, they were also internally divided. Italy, always the weakest of the major European powers, was further weakened by internal convulsions, culminating in the Fascist takeover of October 1922. In Britain, Lloyd George's policy of full support for the Greeks, and the reduction of Turkey to impotence, was not supported by his Foreign Secretary, Lord Curzon who, while far from pro-Turkish, believed that peace would be impossible if the Greeks were allowed to take over large parts of Anatolia. Winston Churchill, the Secretary of State for War, took a more explicitly pro-Turkish line, since he wished to preserve a friendly and relatively strong Turkey as a barrier against the Bolsheviks.[10]

For their part, Mustafa Kemal and his colleagues were evidently aware of these weaknesses and divisions on the *entente* side, and fully prepared to exploit them. During 1920–1, the first occasion to put these policies to the test occurred on Turkey's disputed north-eastern border, where the collapse of tsardom and the consequent struggle between the Bolsheviks, their pro-tsarist opponents and local nationalist forces, created a constantly changing and unpredictable situation, but one that turned out to be to the Turks' advantage. In September 1918, just before the end of the First World War and as part of Enver Pasha's eleventh-hour Caucasian campaign, Ottoman troops had briefly tried to fill the power vacuum in Transcaucasia, and occupied Baku, the oil centre and chief city of Azerbaijan, but had then withdrawn under the Mudros armistice. Baku and Batum were occupied by the British in November 1918. The three Transcaucasian republics – Georgia, Armenia and Azerbaijan – had all declared their independence the previous May, and now moved to assert it, but were locked in mutual struggles over disputed territory. Meanwhile, General Denikin, the local leader of the anti-Bolshevik Russian forces, who was supported by Britain, refused to countenance any independence for the Transcaucasian republics, insisting on the aim of 'Great Russia, One and Indivisible'. By March 1919, realizing that they could not maintain substantial military forces in both Transcaucasia and the Turkish straits, the British decided to withdraw virtually all their troops from Transcaucasia by the end of the year. Denikin's forces had collapsed by December 1919.[11]

Mustafa Kemal had first struck up contact with the Soviets in May 1919, and broadly favoured their cause in Trancaucasia, primarily because he looked to Moscow for arms supplies to aid him against the *entente*, whereas the independent republics, especially Armenia, blocked the land bridge between Turkey and Soviet-controlled territory. He strictly abjured Enver's pan-Turkist ideas, declaring that 'neither Islamic union, nor Turanism may constitute a doctrine, or logical policy, for us'.[12] In effect, vague ideology was far less important than practical strategic considerations. In April 1920, Bolshevik forces made their first major step into Trancaucasia by taking over power in Azerbaijan, with Turkish support. Mustafa Kemal simultaneously wrote to the Soviet government promising support for the Bolshevik campaign. Turkey's biggest obstacle in Transcaucasia was Armenia, since the Armenians, unlike the other Transcaucasian nations, had substantial territorial claims against Turkey and had occupied the disputed provinces of Kars and Ardahan, which the Turkish nationalists regarded as legitimately theirs.[13] In September 1920, the Ankara government decided to take matters into its own hands by launching an invasion of Armenia. Left to themselves, the Armenians collapsed. By 30 October, Turkish forces led by General Kâzim Karabekir had swept through Kars to the frontier town of Alexandropol (later Leninakan – in Turkish, Gümrü). Under the treaty of Alexandropol signed on 2 December, the Armenians agreed to the present Turkish–Armenian frontier and denounced the Treaty of Sèvres. However, the Bolsheviks simultaneously took over Armenia and rejected the Alexandropol treaty.

Until early in 1921, the Soviet leaders seem to have believed that pro-communist forces could take over in Turkey and that there was therefore no need to reach an agreement with Kemal. They were rapidly disillusioned. On 28 January 1921, Mustafa Suphi and the leaders of the tiny Turkish communist party were drowned – almost certainly murdered – in the Black Sea off Trabzon. In the same month, the so-called 'Green Army' led by the guerrilla warlord Çerkes Ethem in western Anatolia, which was attached to a bizarre mixture of Islamism and socialism, was decisively defeated by the Kemalist forces. Kemal meanwhile outflanked the Bolsheviks by setting up his own 'official' communist party, which included leading members of his government, and even suggested that it would seek affiliation with the Third International. On the western front, on 10 January 1921, nationalist forces commanded by İsmet Pasha defeated a Greek attempt to break out from Bursa at İnönü, from which İsmet later took his surname. These events persuaded the Soviet government that they would do best to seek an accommodation with the Turkish nationalists and aid them against the entente. A communist takeover in Turkey could be postponed to an indefinite future. In the meantime, it was far more realistic to reach an agreement with Ankara. After a brief clash over the Georgian port of Batum, which had been occupied by the Turks on 5 March 1921, the two sides signed a Treaty of Friendship in Moscow on 16 March that fixed the north-eastern frontier of Turkey along its present line. Significantly, under Article 8 of the treaty, they agreed 'to forbid the formation or presence on their territory of organizations or groups claiming to be the government of the other country or part of the territory and also the presence of groups that have hostile intentions to the other country'.[14] Although this was not specifically provided for in the treaty, the Soviets also gave substantial financial aid to the nationalists, probably amounting to around 10 million gold roubles (the exact amount is disputed) plus large amounts of arms and ammunition.[15]

As Bülent Gökay suggests, the Turkish–Soviet accord resembled 'a business partnership rather than a unity of principles'.[16] Nonetheless, it was of undoubted value to the Kemalists, since it strengthened their material resources, freed them to concentrate their military efforts on their western front against the Greeks, and helped to convince the entente powers that they would be a permanent force to be reckoned with.

While these agreements with the Bolsheviks were being worked out, the Ankara government was also negotiating with the entente. At a conference convened in London in February–March 1921, concessions were offered on the Sèvres terms, but the Greeks refused any modification of their own claims and thus saved the Ankara government from the need to accept anything short of the conditions of the National Pact. As its Foreign Minister and the head of the nationalist delegation, Bekir Sami also secured the secret agreement of France and Italy to withdraw their forces from Anatolia in return for economic concessions. This solution was rejected by the Grand National Assembly, evidently with Kemal's assent, and Bekir Sami was forced to resign as Foreign Minister. However, the possibility of separate agreements with France and Italy, which would detach them from Britain and Greece, was clearly on the table. A further sign of this came in June, when the Italians began to evacuate their forces from Antalya. After some false starts, the French Senator Henri Franklin-Bouillon signed an agreement with the Ankara government on 20 October 1921 under which the French withdrew their forces from Cilicia, leaving substantial military supplies to the Turkish nationalists.[17] In effect, Kemal had neutralized France and Italy, leaving the war in Anatolia as a straight fight between the Greeks and Turks, with the British in an uncertain position at the straits.

These diplomatic moves were both accompanied and affected by the changing military fortunes of the two sides in Anatolia. On 1 April 1921, İsmet Pasha inflicted another defeat on the Greeks at a second battle of İnönü, but the Greeks then regrouped and on 10 July began a general advance in which they captured Eskişehir, Kütahya and Afyon, obliging the Turks to withdraw to the line of the Sakarya river, only 50 miles west of Ankara. The biggest battle of the war then ensued along the Sakarya between 23 August and 13 September, stopping the Greeks in their tracks and forcing them to retire to Eskişehir. This was the turning point in the war, since the Greeks had needed to gain a decisive victory over the Turks at the Sakarya if they were to win the struggle in the long run. With a lull in the fighting during the winter of 1921–2, Yusuf Kemal [Tengirşenk], Bekir Sami's successor as Foreign Minister, spent fruitless weeks in March 1922 in London and Paris trying to persuade the entente governments to accept peace on the basis of the National Pact. The furthest the British, French and Italian governments were now prepared to go was outlined in a statement of 27 March, accepting the restoration of Turkish sovereignty throughout Anatolia, an armistice and a Greek withdrawal once a peace treaty were signed. This was accepted by Greece, but rejected by the Kemalists who feared that the Greeks would use the armistice to recover and instead demanded an immediate evacuation. In July 1922, Kemal sent his trusted friend Fethi [Okyar] to London for renewed talks with the British, but this was just a device to gain time, pending the launch of a military offensive. This was opened on 26 August, and resulted in a decisive Turkish victory at Dumlupinar, near Afyon, and the capture of İzmir on 11 September.[18]

Flushed by victory, the Turks then turned north to deal with remaining Greek forces in eastern Thrace, but found their way blocked by a small allied garrison at Çanakkale, guarding the Dardanelles. The French and Italians withdrew their contingents, leaving the British to face the Turks unaided. In the last resort, the Lloyd George government was prepared to re-start a war against the Turks, but it was also ready to make important concessions to prevent this. This realism was reciprocated on the Turkish side. On 3 October, British, Turkish, Greek, French and Italian military representatives gathered in the town of Mudanya, on the southern shores of the Sea of Marmara, where they signed an armistice agreement on 10 October 1922. Under its terms, the Greeks were to evacuate eastern Thrace up to the river Maritsa (Meriç) within 30 days, and Turkish sovereignty over the region, as well as the straits and Istanbul, was recognized. In return the Turks promised to respect a neutral zone around the straits, pending the signature of a definitive peace treaty. To this end, invitations to a peace conference to be held in the Swiss city of Lausanne had been issued on 20 September to the governments of Britain, France, Italy, Romania, Yugoslavia, Japan, Greece, Turkey and the United States.[19]

The Lausanne conference opened on 21 November 1922, but only after encountering serious problems as to who was to attend. When the original invitations had been issued, the Soviet government had pointedly been left off the list, but this caused predictable protests from Moscow as well as from Ankara, where the Kemalists were anxious to avoid being isolated against the western powers. As a result, on 27 October, an invitation was issued to the Soviets, but on condition that they could only participate in those discussions that had to do with the future of the straits. Equally crucially, separate invitations were issued to the Ankara government and to that of the Sultan in Istanbul, although by this stage Vahdettin only exercised vestigial power. Kemal and his colleagues were naturally anxious to prevent a divided Turkish representation at Lausanne. Almost certainly, Kemal had had it in mind to end the rule of the Ottoman dynasty for some time, but this diplomatic acci- dent forced his hand. The Assembly dealt with the problem by the abrupt step of abolishing the Sultanate on 1 November. Sultan Vahdettin, the last of his line, went into exile on a British warship on 17 November 1922, leaving his cousin Abdul Mejid to carry on as Caliph, or nominal head of the world's Muslims, for another 16 months.

In the event, it was not until 24 July 1923 that a peace treaty between Turkey and the wartime entente was eventually signed at Lausanne. In the negotia- tions, the British, Turks and Soviets were the main players, with France and Italy principally concerned with the economic aspects of the eventual treaty and Greece too weak to have any effect on the outcome. In Britain, the Lloyd George government had fallen on 19 October 1922 – partly, but not entirely, as the result of the collapse of his policy in the near east – and Lord Curzon, as Foreign Secretary, was free to set the course of British diplomatic strategy. This essentially consisted of aiding the establishment of an independent Turkey as an anti-Soviet barrier, while protecting British interests. Such a policy had long been Curzon's preference, and it had in any case been made virtually inevitable by the startling revival of Turkish power between 1920 and 1922. As a memorandum by the British General Staff of October 1922 put it, 'we can no longer treat the Turks as a conquered nation to whom it is possible to dictate any terms we wish'.[20] From the British viewpoint, there was no further point in assisting the Greeks, who lost their claims to eastern Thrace and any territory in Anatolia. The river Maritsa was thus fixed as the land frontier between Greece and Turkey, where it remains to this day, though the treaty also established demilitarized zones along the Turco-Greek and Turco-Bulgarian frontiers. Under the treaty, the Aegean islands were granted to Greece, but for the Dodecanese (principally Rhodes) which were confirmed as Italian territory, and the islands of Tenedos (Bozcaada) and Imbros (Gökçeada), close to the entrance to the Dardanelles, which remained under Turkish sovereignty. The islands attached to Greece were also to be demilitarized.[21]

Britain's main interests, as Curzon saw them, were to secure freedom of passage for British warships through the straits, and the attachment of the disputed province of Mosul to British-ruled Iraq, rather than to Turkey. On the first score, Britain's interests were fairly consistent with those of the Turks, though inconsistent with those of the Soviets. In contrast to the positions taken by the British and Tsarist governments in the nineteenth century, the British now sought to have the straits opened to warships, while the Soviets aimed to keep them closed, since the Russian Black Sea fleet had been destroyed in the civil war. Meanwhile, the British wished to prevent the Turks from closing the straits to western navies, as Enver Pasha had done in 1914. The Turks, for their part, were prepared to allow limited access to the Black Sea for the navies of non-Black Sea states, so as to maintain a balance of power against Russia. The result was a compromise under which non-Black Sea powers gained limited access to that sea and both sides of the straits were demilitarized. These arrangements were to be supervised by an international commission.[22]

The second issue proved more difficult to settle, since British and Turkish interests directly clashed. The Turks based their claim to the province of Mosul on the grounds that it was part of the 'non-Arab' territories which were included within the putative Turkish state under the National Pact and had not been under British occupation at the time of the Mudros armistice. The fact that most of the population was ethnically Kurdish rather than Turkish did not persuade them to drop their claim, since İsmet [İnönü], the chief Turkish delegate at Lausanne, maintained that there were no differences between Turks and Kurds, and that 'the Government of the Grand National

Assembly of Turkey is the Government of the Kurds just as much as the Government of the Turks'.[23] This claim had some justification at the time, in that the Turkish Kurds had in general supported the nationalist cause against the Greeks. However, it was hotly disputed by the British, who were anxious to attach the Mosul province to Iraq as a defensive barrier against Turkey. Moreover, although they both denied it, both sides were keen to gain control of the rich oil resources of the province, which were suspected, but not proven, at this stage.[24] Although Atatürk had privately suggested to Turkish journalists in April 1922 that Turkey would not be prepared to go to war with Britain for the sake of Mosul,[25] İsmet refused to abandon the Turkish claim and the question was left unsettled when the treaty was signed, with an undertaking that both sides would come to an agreement within nine months.[26]

What were referred to as the 'economic' clauses of the treaty also proved to be extremely difficult to settle, and led to a long intermission in the negotiations during February–April 1922. For the Turkish side, the major objective was to secure international recognition of the abolition of the capitulations, which were regarded as a quite unacceptable limitation of the powers of a modern sovereign state.[27] The entente powers fought hard to maintain some special legal rights for foreign citizens living in Turkey, but were eventually forced to concede the 'complete abolition' of the capitulations under Article 28 of the treaty. In return, the Turkish government undertook to respect all concessionary contracts given to foreign firms before October 1914, and to maintain its import tariff at the relatively low levels established by the Ottoman customs tariff of September 1916, until 1929.[28] The Ottoman Empire's huge war debt to the central powers, put at £170 million sterling, was written off. Turkey's share of the Ottoman debt was fixed at TL gold 84.8 million (or £78 million sterling) with the remainder distributed to those parts of the Ottoman Empire, as of 1914, which had now become independent states. The foreign-controlled Public Debt administration, established in 1881 (see p20), was also wound up.[29]

Finally, in human and political terms, one of the most significant provisions of the Lausanne settlement was a Greek–Turkish convention on the exchange of populations, under which the Greek (or at least, Greek Orthodox) population of Anatolia, which apparently numbered around 900,000, was exchanged for the Muslim community of Greece, of around 400,000. While these massive movements of population helped to homogenize the population of both countries, the gain was bought at appalling human cost and ended centuries of generally peaceful coexistence between the two communities. An exception was also made in the case of the Greeks of Istanbul (then numbering about 120,000) and the Turks and other Muslims of western Thrace. As recognized 'non-Muslim minorities', the Christian and Jews remaining in Turkey were given the right to maintain their own educational and religious institutions, using their own languages, and the Orthodox Ecumenical Patriarchate was maintained in Istanbul. No such rights were accorded to the Turkish Kurds, who probably accounted for about 10–15 per cent of the population at the time, since they represented an ethnic rather than religious minority. At the same time, the draconian exchange of populations, combined with the massacres and deportation of virtually all the former Armenian community of Anatolia during the First World War (see p27) had a transformatory effect on the cultural and political landscape of the country. The population of Anatolia, of which about 20 per cent had been non-Muslim before the war, was now about 98 per cent Muslim, completing a long process which had begun in the nineteenth century.[30]

Settlements and challenges: 1923–39

With the signature of the Treaty of Lausanne of 1923, the new Turkish state passed its most critical test. It had at last achieved a degree of security and international recognition that its Ottoman predecessor had lacked ever since the last quarter of the eighteenth century. As a result, foreign policy could take second place to internal reconstruction. Hereafter, the constantly repeated mantra 'peace at home, peace abroad' (a phrase attributed to Atatürk, although there is no documentary evidence that he actually said it)[31] became the stated bedrock of Turkish policy. During the 1920s, Atatürk and his colleagues used this breathing space to transform the political institutions of their country and to try to reorient its society and culture on the basis of their secular-nationalist and modernist beliefs. On 29 October 1923, a republic was formally declared, with Atatürk as its President and İsmet İnönü its Prime Minister. The Caliphate – separated from the Sultanate since November 1922 – was abolished on 3 March 1924, and Abdul Mejid, the last Caliph, sent into exile. These changes were embodied in a new constitution, enacted on 20 April 1924, which confirmed the Grand National Assembly as 'sole rightful representative of the nation' and, among other things, fixed Ankara as the capital of the new state. The institutional reforms were continued into the social, legal and cultural spheres during the rest of the 1920s, notably by the abandonment of the old Islamic-based civil and penal codes in 1926, in favour of secular codes based on those of Switzerland and Italy respectively, and the compulsory change from the Arabic to the Latin script for written Turkish, in 1928. In the same year, the clause in the 1924 constitution declaring Islam to be the official religion of the state was withdrawn, although it was not until 1937 that 'secularism' was officially written into the constitution as one of the six guiding principles of the republic.

In domestic politics, Atatürk faced some serious challenges to his authority during the first half of the 1920s. Once the war against the Greeks had been won, many of the leaders of the nationalist movement, both civilian and military, assumed that Turkey could now be established as a parliamentary democracy on western lines, and were anxious to prevent Atatürk from making himself a dictator. In November 1924, they formed a Progressive Republican Party, in opposition to the ruling People's Party (later re-named the Republican People's Party). Atatürk's government was also opposed by those who refused to accept the abolition of the Caliphate and the establishment of a secular state, as well as sections of the Kurdish minority. In February 1925, the opposition took a violent turn, when a major rebellion was raised in the eastern provinces by a Kurdish tribal and religious leader, Sheikh Saiyid of Palu. The insurrection was rapidly suppressed in draconian fashion, and Atatürk and İsmet seized the opportunity to close down the Progressive Party and muzzle all potential opposition. An attempt on Atatürk's life in İzmir in 1926 produced another round of arrests and executions. Henceforth, and with only a brief interlude of limited pluralism in 1930, Turkey was run as a single-party state until 1945.[32]

Having won a reasonably favourable peace in 1923, Atatürk had no incentive to disrupt it. His primary objective was to raise Turkey to the 'level of modern civilization' and to reinforce the power of the state. Although not explicitly, 'modern' was in practice equated with 'European' or 'western', as the Kemalist government turned its back to the Muslim world. As Tevfik Rüstü Aras, then Foreign Minister, told the US ambassador Joseph Grew in 1928: 'Turkey is now a western power; the death of a peasant in the Balkans is of more importance to Turkey than the death of a king in Afghanistan.'[33] This ambition of being classed as a member of the European family continues to this day, as it is the main incentive for Turkey's project to obtain full membership of the European Union.

More immediately and materially, the Treaty of Lausanne had left Atatürk's government in a position of greater relative strength than its Ottoman predecessors, since it did not try to rule over territories that it could not defend and because Turkey now had virtually no non-Muslim minorities that foreign powers could exploit to undermine its territorial integrity. It was also aided by the external environment, since Russia, the traditional enemy, was too isolated and too convulsed by internal upheavals to represent a serious threat to Turkish security until the end of the 1930s. Instead, it had actually been converted into a friend. Unlike the other defeated states of the First World War, Turkey had reversed the defeat of 1918 by 1923, and thus acted as a generally conservative and anti-revisionist, rather than revisionist, force in European politics.

Between 1923 and 1926, the main item on Turkey's foreign policy agenda was the Mosul dispute with Britain, the principal piece of unfinished business left over from the Lausanne conference. For the Turks, giving the province to Iraq could be seen as a failure to achieve part of the objectives of the National Pact. On the other side, the British believed that the state of Iraq would not be viable, either militarily or economically, without Mosul, thanks to its important strategic position and expected oil resources. The Kurds were the biggest single ethnic group in the province, accounting for an estimated three quarters of the population, but the city of Mosul itself was Arab and there was also a substantial Turkish-speaking (or 'Turcoman') minority. Hence, neither Britain or Turkey had a strong moral case in ethnic terms. Nor was the idea of an independent Kurdish state a realistic option, given the political and economic circumstances of the time.

In accordance with their undertakings at Lausanne, Britain and Turkey engaged in bilateral negotiations during May–June 1924, but these failed to make any progress, and in August 1924, Britain referred the question to the League of Nations, of which Turkey was not a member. In the following month, the Council of the League decided to establish a commission of enquiry, to investigate the position on the ground. Not surprisingly, the commission failed to find a clear-cut case for an award to either Turkey or Iraq, but it rejected the idea that most of the local population preferred Turkey. Hence, its report, issued in July 1925, awarded the province to Iraq. The British government accepted this decision but it was predictably opposed by Turkey, which questioned its assumptions and opposed the Council's right of jurisdiction. This led to a referral to the Permanent Court of International Justice, which decided on 21 November 1925 that a decision by the Council would be binding on both parties. On 16 December, the Council then made a unanimous decision in favour of Iraq. For a time there was speculation that Turkey might defy the League and all the main western powers on this issue, fuelled by the fact that it signed a new Treaty of Neutrality and Friendship with Soviet Russia in December 1925. The British prepared plans to blockade the Dardanelles, although they were reluctant to resort to force. On the other side, the battle-weary Turks were ultimately not prepared to go to war over Mosul after their years of struggle, as Atatürk had predicted in 1922. Hence, after bilateral negotiations were re-opened in Ankara in April 1926, they accepted the League's decision, subject to a face-saving formula under which Turkey was to receive 10 per cent of the oil royalties payable in the Mosul province for the next 25 years.[34] The agreement was formalized in a treaty signed in Ankara on 5 June 1926.[35]

Relations with Greece were Turkey's other main foreign policy concern during the late 1920s. The population exchanges created complicated disputes over the disposition of properties left in each country by the emigrants and these were only partially settled by an agreement reached between the two governments in 1926. The expulsion of the Ecumenical Patriarch Constantine by the Turkish authorities at the end of 1924 provoked further ill-will on both sides, which was only defused when Constantine was succeeded by Patriarch Basil Georgiadis in May 1925. This allowed normal diplomatic relations, and the exchange of ambassadors, to begin in the summer of that year. The dispute over properties continued until 1929, by which stage it even appeared that the two countries might resort to force to settle the issue. However, in February 1930, Eleutherios Venizelos, who had now returned to the premiership in Greece, launched an unexpected initiative, telling the Greek parliament that he believed that Turkey was a peace-loving country that would not attack Greece. The Turkish government rapidly reciprocated, paving the way for another agreement, signed in June 1930, in which the dispute over properties was finally settled. At İsmet İnönü's invitation, the Greek premier, Turkey's former arch-enemy, visited Ankara and Istanbul in October 1930, to an enthusiastic public reception. On 30 October, the two countries signed a Treaty of

Friendship, Neutrality, Mediation and Arbitration, together with commercial and other agreements. The reconciliation was completed by a return visit by İnönü to Athens in October 1931, and effectively continued up to the time of the outbreak of the Cyprus dispute in the mid-1950s.[36]

The rapprochement with Greece was part of a general shift in Turkish foreign policy, in which Turkey sought to steer itself back into a position of equality and cooperation with the main western powers, without breaking its links with Moscow. Following energetic lobbying, in January 1931 it was invited to join the Commission of Enquiry established as a first step towards the establishment of a European Union launched by the French premier and Foreign Minister Aristide Briand. This project fizzled out after Briand's death in 1932, but for Turkey its main purpose was to confirm its identity as a member of the European family of nations, as well as promoting European peace.[37] More substantially, the main sign of this reorientation was Ankara's decision to join the League of Nations in 1932. As one of the defeated powers, Turkey had been left out of the League when it had been founded in 1919. During the Mosul dispute it had continued to view the organization with grave suspicion, as a body controlled by the imperialist powers, primarily Britain and France. This view was reinforced by Turkey's links with Soviet Russia, which took a similar view until the 1930s. Under a protocol of 1929 that renewed the Turco-Soviet treaty of 1925, both sides had pledged not to accept any undertakings to third parties without obtaining approval from the other. By 1931, the Turks had changed their position, seeing membership of the League as a necessary step to restoring their relations with the western powers. Hence, when they accepted an invitation to join the organization in 1932, they were careful to obtain Soviet approval and informed the Soviet government that they would not allow their obligations to the League to damage their relations with the USSR, assuming the latter did not attack a third state.[38] The position was naturally eased in 1934 when the Soviet Union itself joined the League. Henceforth, Turkey was a strong supporter of its principles. As the Foreign Minister Tevfik Rüştü Aras told the British Ambassador Sir Percy Loraine in 1935, 'the integral maintenance of the covenant of the League' was the foundation of Turkey's foreign policy.[39] Unfortunately, the Turks turned out to have joined the League at just the point when it lost what little power it had ever had, marked by the withdrawal from the League of Germany and Japan in 1933 and Italy in 1935. In attempting to preserve peace, Turkey, like other nations, had to look for other forms of security.[40]

As Europe moved towards war during the 1930s, the main focus of Turkey's security concerns lay in the Balkans – the traditional zone of danger for the Ottoman Empire – and the Mediterranean. With the removal of the threat from Russia, Italy initially emerged as the most powerful potential enemy, followed later by Germany. As in the past, the danger from the Balkans was complicated by internecine disputes between the Balkan states themselves and their individual weakness. Turkey's relationship with Italy was also an unstable one, as Mussolini's policies followed a highly erratic course. Initially, he had fanciful plans for settling Italian colonists in Anatolia, and in 1924 offered to help the British against the Turks in the event of a war over Mosul. Two years later he even considered launching an expeditionary force from Naples to grasp territory in Asia Minor, but backed off after the Turks responded with a partial military mobilization.[41] In 1928 he reversed this, in favour of a friendship offensive towards Turkey and Greece designed to counter French influence in the Mediterranean. Hence, in 1928, Turkey signed a Treaty of Neutrality, Mediation and Judicial Settlement with Mussolini's government. This acted as a model for the similar treaty signed with Greece in 1930, which was encouraged by Rome, as part of an eastern Mediterranean alliance that would protect Italy's flank in its contest with Yugoslavia over Albania. The treaty with Italy was renewed in 1932.[42] Apparently, it was not until 1933–4 that the tables clearly turned again, and Italy began to be seen as a potential threat to Turkey as well as most of the Balkan states. Mussolini's invasion of Ethiopia in 1935 was a crucial turning-point, since Turkey was an outspoken advocate of sanctions against Italy. Since it lacked sufficient naval forces to confront the Italians in the Mediterranean, Turkey joined Greece in asking the British for aid to build up their respective navies. The request was turned down by the British government on the grounds that it opposed 'any combination that might even have the appearance of being directed against Italy'.[43]

Turkish policy was also affected by divisions within the Balkans at this time. On the one hand, Greece, Yugoslavia and Romania, which had been on the winning side in the First World War and gained territory from it, took a pro-status quo or anti-revisionist position, while on the other Bulgaria and Hungary, which had lost it, were in the revisionist camp. Italy had also been on the winning side but was at odds with Yugoslavia and was hence a leading revisionist. In the military sphere, thanks to the demilitarization of the straits and the Thracian border under the Treaty of Lausanne, Turkey was at a serious disadvantage in seeking to defend its western frontier against an attack by Greece or Bulgaria, especially if the two states combined or were supported by Italy. Hence, a major objective of Turkish policy was to form an entente with at least one, or preferably both, of its two Balkan neighbours. More broadly, Turkey wished to keep war out of the Balkans, to prevent the Balkan states from squabbling among themselves and, as Loraine put it, to 'deprive [the] Balkans of their former character of a kind of Tom Tiddle's ground for the ambitions of great powers'.[44]

Although it does not seem to have been originally envisaged as an anti-Italian alliance, the rapprochement with Greece was a first step towards the realization of this strategy. It was extended in September 1933 by what was called an *Entente Cordiale* under which Greece and Turkey mutually guaranteed their common frontier in Thrace and agreed to consult with one another on all questions of common interest. In its wake, Turkey signed separate non-aggression pacts with Romania and Yugoslavia. Meanwhile, a series of four conferences was held of all the Balkan states between October

1930 and November 1933. This resulted in the conclusion of the Balkan Pact between Greece, Romania, Turkey and Yugoslavia in February–March 1934. Under the pact, the four states agreed that in the event of aggression against any of them, they would each guarantee the frontiers of the signatory state against the aggressor and would consult with one another in the event of any threat to peace in the region. The pact was a notable achievement, but it still fell far short of the original objectives of Turkish policy which, according to Aras, included the idea of a much broader pact under which Britain, France, Italy, the Balkan states and the USSR would all bind themselves together for mutual assistance. More specifically, the exclusion of Bulgaria was a serious disadvantage from the Turkish viewpoint. Until the last moment, Turkish diplomacy had put considerable effort into trying to bring in the Bulgarians, but Bulgaria was unwilling to drop its territorial claims in Macedonia (against Yugoslavia) or western Thrace (against Greece). Hence, the pact still left Turkey vulnerable to a potential attack by Bulgaria, possibly supported by Mussolini. Greece also insisted that its commitments under the Pact should not involve it in a war against Italy. This reservation was accepted, together with the general provision that none of the signatories were under an obligation to assist if one of them were attacked by Italy alone. Ironically, this was just the situation that eventually arose when Italy attacked Greece in 1940.[45] During the late 1930s, the Balkan pact became even weaker, as Yugoslavia and Romania drifted into the German orbit. Nor did it suffice to deflate Italian ambitions – indeed, Mussolini's most overt threats against Turkey came just afterwards, in March 1934, when he told the Fascist Congress that Italy's 'historical ambitions' lay in Asia and Africa, and later in 1934–6, when he refortified the Dodecanese.[46] Needless to say, both these moves were seen by Turkey as a threat and provoked a sharp reaction, but still left it with the task of finding a credible way of deterring Italy.

In July 1937, the Turks extended the principle of regional security pacts eastward, when Iraq, Iran, Turkey and Afghanistan concluded the Saadabad Pact, named after the Shah's palace near Tehran where the document was signed. This was not an entirely new idea, since the British had suggested a similar pact, with themselves included, in 1932, but the plan had been turned down by the Turks.[47] On this occasion, the British were invited to join the agreement but turned down the offer. The pact obliged the four states to preserve their common frontiers, not to interfere in one another's internal affairs, to commit no aggression against one another's territory and to consult together on all matters of common interest. The pact followed a separate frontier agreement between Iran and Turkey, signed in 1932. The Saadabad agreement was primarily a means of preventing frontier disputes between the four states and, for instance, a way of ensuring that neither Iran or Iraq would give any sustenance to Kurdish rebels on Turkish territory or vice versa.[48] There is no evidence that it was directed against the USSR – in fact, the original intention was that the Soviet government should join the pact. However, as Aras pointed out to the Grand National Assembly, it contained no provisions for mutual assistance or military commitments and had mainly psychological value.[49]

This brought the Turkish policy-makers back to the problem of increasing their country's security in a worsening international situation. According to one frequently repeated account, Atatürk had a conversation with the American General Douglas MacArthur in 1932 in which Kemal predicted that Germany would start another war between 1940 and 1946, that the United States would be drawn in and Germany would be destroyed, leaving the Soviet Union as the dominant power in Europe, and the USA and USSR the only real great powers. Unfortunately, there are no contemporary accounts of this conversation, putting the authenticity of the story in grave doubt.[50] However, it is quite clear that by the mid-1930s, Atatürk and his colleagues had real anxieties about the ambitions of Italy, and later Germany, as well as the lack of effective collective security arrangements between the other European powers. Until the autumn of 1939, the Turkish government seems to have assumed that its good relations with the USSR would give it security to the north, but this still left it vulnerable to an attack from the Balkans, or in the Mediterranean by Italy. To achieve greater security, Turkey had to achieve three objectives: first, to strengthen its military position in Thrace and the Dardanelles by removing the demilitarization restrictions contained in the Lausanne Treaty; second, to build up and modernize its armed forces; and third, to reach an accommodation and, if possible, a defensive alliance with Britain and France while preserving the entente with Moscow. Good relations with France and Britain were also essential to achieve the first two objectives. If Germany were to start another war, then Turkey must above all avoid falling into the trap of 1914.[51] As Aras explained to the British Foreign Secretary Anthony Eden in 1937: 'England was not merely a power, but a world power: she was ubiquitous: her interests lay everywhere.' If Britain entered the war, then Aras thought that it would defeat Germany – if not by itself, then with the help of the United States.[52] This time, Turkey had to make sure that if it could not stay out of the war, then it was at least on the winning side.

Of the three objectives, the first one turned out to be the easiest to realize. By late 1935, the British, as the principal architects of the straits regime of 1923, had come round to the realization that the benefits of allowing the Turks to remilitarize the straits outweighed the losses. Demilitarization reduced Turkey's capacity to defend itself against Italy, and was resented in Turkey as a restriction on the state's territorial sovereignty. On the latter score, the Turks had begun to raise the question of remilitarization in 1932, before the threat from Italy became clear. The British also realized that, in the last resort, the Turks might decide to remilitarize by unilateral action rather than international agreement, as Germany was to do in the case of the Rhineland in March 1936. Given a choice, the Turks preferred international agreement to an illegal remilitarization. Accordingly, an international conference of all the Lausanne signatories – with the exception of Italy, which refused the invitation – was convened at Montreux in Switzerland on 22 June

1936. On 20 July a new 'Convention Regarding the Regime of the Straits' was signed. The main objections to the new arrangements came from the USSR, which was prepared to accept remilitarization by Turkey, but wanted to secure free passage through the straits for Black Sea powers while closing them to other navies. In the event, it accepted a compromise under which Black Sea states were allowed to send warships into the Mediterranean in peacetime, subject to some tonnage restrictions affecting 'capital ships' which were defined as excluding aircraft carriers. Ships defined as 'light surface vessels, minor war vessels and auxiliary vessels' (in effect, warships of under 10,000 tons) whether of Black Sea or non-Black Sea powers, were granted free passage in peacetime.[53] Non-Black Sea states could send warships into the Black Sea to a maximum aggregate tonnage of 30,000 tons, or 45,000 tons if the fleet of the strongest Black Sea navy grew by 10,000 tons. In time of war, if Turkey were neutral, then warships of belligerents would not be allowed to pass in either direction. If Turkey were at war, or under threat of war, then it could close the straits to warships at its own discretion. A clause that was not contested in principle at the time but turned out to be of critical importance by the 1990s was the provision in Article 2 of the Convention that all merchant ships, whatever their flag or cargo, would enjoy complete freedom of navigation through the straits in war and peace. Most importantly from the Turkish viewpoint, Turkey regained the right to remilitarize the straits and the previous international control commission was wound up.[54]

Between 1933 and 1937, it appears that Turkey saw its main potential enemy as Italy, but by 1938 its principal concern had become the threat from Germany, the watershed being Hitler's takeover of Austria in March of that year. So long as Italy was seen as the only real threat, then the Turkish defence forces expected to deal with it on their own and with existing resources, by concentrating on coastal defences that could prevent a landing on the western coast of Turkey or the Aegean islands.[55] With the emergence of the danger of a German attack from the Balkans, the priority switched to the north-western land frontier with Bulgaria, but Turkey's existing armed forces were inadequate to deal with this threat, especially if offensive operations were considered. For most of the inter-war period, the government had deliberately sacrificed guns for butter, by concentrating its resources of developing the civilian economy, most notably through the first five-year industrialization plan launched in 1934. In 1938, the government increased the proportion of budget expenditure devoted to defence to around 44 per cent, from a low point of 23 per cent in 1932–3, but this still left the armed forces woefully short of modern equipment. In the same year, the total strength of the army was around 195,000 officers and men, but they were mainly armed with the weapons of the First World War. The army had very few tanks or armoured cars, and was still reliant on horses or mules for transport. As of 1937, the air force had just 131 front-line aircraft, of which only half were relatively modern, and the biggest ship in the fleet was still the cruiser *Yavuz,* formerly *Goeben* – Germany's fatal gift of 1914.[56]

By 1938, the Turks was seeking to increase their naval forces to float two new squadrons, to acquire 200–300 new front-line aircraft and enough modern ordinance to arm ten new divisions. It was clear that it would be impossible to achieve this without foreign assistance. Accordingly, Turkey obtained an armaments credit from the British worth £6 million in May 1938, followed by a further credit worth £25 million in October 1939.[57] In the economic sphere, Britain and Germany engaged in competitive aid giving during 1938, as Britain extended a trade credit of £10 million, matched by a loan of 150 million Reichsmarks from Germany. However, the Turks turned down a tentative offer of a neutrality treaty from Berlin and decided not to purchase any more arms from Germany, hitherto an important supplier, as from 1939. Unfortunately, little of the promised assistance from Britain and France arrived, thanks to British inability to part with it, and French reluctance to do so. In all this it appears that, far from Britain and France trying to push Turkey into war, the initiative came primarily from the Turkish side. In fact, Turkey acted as the suitor, with the British and French the reluctant *fiancées*.[58]

Amid all these concerns, the death of Atatürk in November 1938 produced no perceptible change in Turkish foreign policies, as İsmet İnönü succeeded smoothly to the presidency, with Şükrü Saracoğlu succeeding Aras as his Foreign Minister. Like Atatürk, İnönü took a keen interest in foreign affairs, although he was more cautious.[59] He was well-informed on the subject and was in close control of foreign policy throughout his period as President that lasted until 1950. His most important objective was to secure a defensive alliance with Britain and France without breaking Turkey's entente with the USSR. Essentially, he believed that defence of the Balkans rested on cooperation with the Soviet Union, and that of the Mediterranean with the British and French. However, attempts at forging a mutual security pact with the USSR, which had begun during the Montreux negotiations in June 1936, had produced no tangible result.[60] The British were also wary of the idea of an alliance. Sir Percy Loraine, as ambassador between 1934 and 1939, won credit for Britain's rapprochement with Turkey thanks to a personal friendship with Atatürk, but he supported the policy of negotiating with Hitler and Mussolini rather than fighting them.[61] When the Spanish civil war broke out in July 1936, Atatürk strongly opposed Mussolini's intervention on the rebel side and supported international efforts to prevent Italian submarines sinking ships bringing supplies from the Soviet Union to the republic.[62] Nonetheless, in facing up to Italy and Germany, British and French policy remained essentially passive: when Turkey offered Britain a full-scale alliance in the latter part of 1936, it was politely turned down.[63] At the end of March 1939, Aras, now the Turkish ambassador in London, proposed a non-aggression treaty between Poland, Romania, the USSR and Turkey, in which all the parties would combine against any party contravening it, backed up by a British guarantee. Turkey, Yugoslavia and Greece could also accede to the Anglo-Italian agreement of 1938 providing for a common policy in the Mediterranean. However, Poland and Romania were unwilling to cooperate against Germany and the

British turned Aras's proposal down. Hitler's occupation of Czechoslovakia on 15 March and the Italian invasion of Albania on 7 April then caused a delayed reaction in London, as the Prime Minister Neville Chamberlain belatedly realized that Germany and Italy would have to be resisted, by war if necessary. On 12 April, the British hastily offered Turkey the treaty of mutual assistance they had turned down less than two weeks earlier and gave guarantees of their security to Greece and Romania on the following day. After negotiations, a joint Anglo-Turkish declaration was issued on 12 May. This announced that 'pending a definite long-term agreement of a reciprocal character' and 'in the event of an act of aggression leading to war in the Mediterranean area' the two sides would give each other 'all aid and assistance in their power'.[64]

The Anglo-Turkish declaration left the Turkish government with two urgent diplomatic tasks: first, to develop it into a definite alliance including France; and second, to integrate it with their commitments to and expectations from the USSR. The main obstacle to building France into the prospective alliance was a continuing dispute between the Turks and French over the province of Alexandretta (Hatay), which was attached to French-ruled Syria up to 1939. As in the case of Mosul, there was no available solution to this that would have been fair to all sides on ethnic grounds. In the mid-1930s, the province's population of 220,000 included no less than five different linguistic groups practising 16 religious variations, of which Muslim Turks accounted for about 38–9 per cent, followed by Alawi and Ismaili Arabs (28 per cent) Sunni Arabs (10 per cent) and other groups, mainly Arab and Armenian Christians accounting for the remaining 23–4 per cent.[65] As part of the Franklin–Bouillon pact, Turkey had accepted the attachment of the province to Syria in 1921, subject to its administrative autonomy and the protection of the cultural rights of the Turkish community. This arrangement was confirmed by the Lausanne Treaty. Both the Ankara government and the local inhabitants seem to have been quite satisfied with this until 1936: during the 1920s, there were disagreements between Turkey and France over the exact course of the Turco-Syrian frontier, but these affected the central and eastern sections of the border, not Alexandretta.[66] However, in September 1936, the French government and Syrian nationalists initialled a treaty which would, if implemented, have given Syria independence by 1939,[67] causing the Turks to launch a vociferous campaign for incorporation of the province into Turkey. In 1938, local assembly elections produced a narrow majority in favour of retaining the status quo, but these results were ignored by the French authorities, who allowed Turkish troops to enter the province in July for joint patrols with the French. New elections were then held producing a pro-Turkish majority, and in September the local assembly declared a sovereign 'Republic of Hatay'. This paved the way for its incorporation into Turkey, although last-minute disagreements between Turkey and France prevented an accord on this just before the Anglo-Turkish declaration was signed. The problems were then overcome. On 23 June 1939, France and Turkey agreed to the legal cession of

Alexandretta and issued a joint declaration identical to that between Britain and Turkey of 12 May, removing the obstacle to French participation in the prospective Anglo-Turkish alliance. The transfer was contrary to France's undertakings to the League of Nations, since Article 4 of the mandate under which it ruled Syria stipulated that it could not cede Syrian territory to any 'foreign power', and the League never gave its formal consent to the cession. While the result was important to France in the context of its broader international objectives, it also created a lasting source of bitterness between Turkey and the independent Syrian state after the Second World War.[68]

During the following months, the British, French and Turkish governments engaged in intense negotiations over the political, military and economic terms of a proposed tripartite treaty. The Turks initially tried to develop the pact into an offensive engagement against Italy, rather than a purely defensive one, and proposed that Britain and France should declare war on Italy first and invade Italian territory with Turkish military help. On paper, however, the eventual treaty had a purely defensive character.[69] Meanwhile the German–Turkish relationship was naturally tense. The Anglo-Turkish declaration of May 1939 had come as a surprise to the Germans, and Franz von Papen, the German ambassador in Ankara since April 1939, unsuccessfully tried to prevent its development into a formal alliance. Von Papen came to Ankara with a considerable, although far from creditable reputation, since he had served in Turkey as an army officer during the First World War, had helped Hitler come to power during his period as Chancellor in 1932 and, as German ambassador in Vienna, had then paved the way for the Nazi take-over of Austria in 1938. His appointment had been strongly opposed by both Atatürk and İnönü when it had first been proposed in April 1938, and was only reluctantly accepted one year later.[70] His British opposite number was Sir Hughe Knatchbull-Hugessen, who had succeeded Loraine as British ambassador in February 1939. Von Papen's long-term goal was to convert the German–Italian axis into a triangular one, with Turkey as its third point, but to do this he first had to detach Turkey from the prospective Anglo-French alliance. His project failed at the first hurdle, since he could not overcome Turkish suspicions of Italy, which had naturally been sharpened by Mussolini's invasion of Albania. Although von Papen had apparently persuaded Berlin to soften its reaction to the Anglo-Turkish declaration, he protested strongly to Saracoğlu after the eventual signature of the tripartite treaty, on Ribbentrop's instructions. Similarly, in Berlin, Ribbentrop warned the Turkish ambassador Hüsrev Gerede that Turkey might suffer the same fate as Poland if it challenged Germany.[71]

In spite of the Turks' differences with the British and French, and objections from Germany, agreement in principal was reached on a draft treaty between Turkey, Britain and France on 1 September 1939. This assured Turkey of Anglo-French assistance if it were attacked by any European power, in return for Turkish assistance to the other two parties if they were involved in a war in the Mediterranean resulting from an act of aggression by any European power (read Italy) or if Britain and France found themselves at war as a result of their guarantees to Greece and Romania. Signature of the final treaty was then delayed until the Turks could reach a comparable agreement with the USSR. Discussions on this between Ankara and Moscow had in fact been proceeding for some time. During April–May 1939 the two sides had talks on a possible Black Sea security pact, but these failed due to the reluctance of Bulgaria and Romania to enter such an arrangement and the lack of enthusiasm shown by the British. The dialogue was re-launched by the Soviet government at the beginning of August, but the situation was then transformed by the signature of the Nazi–Soviet non-aggression pact on 23 August, which caused a sharp and hostile reaction in Turkey. The pact had a profound effect on the Turkish position, since the Turks had previously expected that the USSR could be brought into a defensive alliance against Germany. Hitler also expected that his pact with Stalin would frighten the Turks into cancelling the Anglo-Turkish and Franco-Turkish declarations and now put pressure on Moscow to reject a Turco-Soviet pact or at least to ensure that if such a pact were signed, then Turkey be detached from the western powers.[72]

On 25 September 1939 – just over three weeks after Germany invaded Poland and thus started the Second World War – Foreign Minister Saracoğlu arrived in Moscow but found it impossible to bridge the gap between Turkey's new friendship with the west and its previous one with the Soviets. Under German pressure, Stalin and Molotov insisted on a series of modifications to the proposed Turco-British–French treaty, culminating in a demand for the exclusion of Turkish aid to the Balkans in the case of German aggression, and the closure of the straits, both of which Saracoğlu rejected. On 17 October, İnönü telephoned the British and French ambassadors in Ankara to tell them that the talks in Moscow had broken down, and that the tripartite treaty should be concluded immediately.[73] The final document, which was signed on 19 October, was on the lines agreed to before the failure in Moscow. Under Article 1 of the treaty, Britain and France pledged to give 'all aid and assistance' to Turkey if it were attacked by another European power. A reciprocal obligation was assumed by Turkey 'in the event of an act of aggression by a European Power leading to a war in the Mediterranean area in which France and the United Kingdom are involved', or if France and Britain were involved in war as a result of their guarantees to Greece and Romania (Articles 2 and 3). Although the Turks had failed to reach a security agreement with the USSR, they were still anxious to avoid war with the Soviets. Accordingly, they secured a protocol to the effect that none of their obligations under the treaty would compel them to enter into a war against the Soviet Union. An additional secret agreement provided for a credit of £25 million to Turkey to buy war materials and an additional loan of £15 million in gold, repayable in Turkish commodities. Turkey was not obliged to fulfil its obligations under the treaty until all the war materials currently on order, as well as new orders to be covered by the gold loan, had been delivered. The attached Military Convention also provided that if Italy joined the war there would be a joint attack on the Italians in the Dodecanese, as soon as local command of the air and sea could be achieved, for which air bases would be constructed in Turkey. The Turks would also hold Bulgaria in check if it entered the war. Allied troops would be allowed to travel through Turkish territory, and Turkey would cooperate in the construction of whatever infrastructure was required. On all these points, the Turks had driven a hard bargain, but at this stage they seem to have been quite prepared to carry out their obligations under the treaty should the circumstances it envisaged arise. The Turkish press, which normally reflected official thinking, blamed Germany (and, indirectly, the Nazi–Soviet pact) for the outbreak of the war but still speculated that Italy and the USSR might stay out of it. Turkish diplomacy had failed to realize its optimum programme, but at the time Turkey still seemed to be strongly placed, at least on paper and with existing military assumptions.[74]

Turkish diplomacy, 1919–39: Some summary assessments

Turkey's foreign policy between the two world wars can clearly be divided into two phases, with the Treaty of Lausanne of 1923 marking the dividing line. During the first phase, the process of gradual territorial attrition of the late Ottoman Empire reached its ultimate stage, as the victorious powers prepared to partition even the Turkish and Kurdish inhabited heartland of the old Empire. In the last resort, the survival of the Turkish state depended on effective military resistance and political leadership, of which the Turkish people provided the first, and Atatürk and his colleagues the second. Without this, diplomacy would have been pointless. With it, diplomacy still helped to win the eventual victory. Essentially, Turkish foreign policy-makers, like their Ottoman predecessors, exploited the balance of power and the divisions among their opponents, besides a measure of good luck. The main difference from Ottoman days was that the new Turkish state was far more internally homogeneous than the Empire had been, and that its rulers set themselves limited and achievable goals. France and Italy were reluctant to back up their territorial claims with concerted or sustained military action and were effectively detached from the hostile coalition by 1921. The United States, which might have provided protection to an independent Armenia or Kurdistan on Turkish soil, virtually dropped out of international politics after the end of 1920. For their part, the Greeks over-reached themselves, deluded by misperceptions of their own strength and the durability and effectiveness of British support. Hence, they refused to negotiate effectively until it was too late. Both domestically and internationally, Lloyd George had gone out onto a limb in giving full support to the Greeks, especially after the turning point in the Greek–Turkish war marked by the battle of Sakarya in August 1921. His successors in government, most of whom had never fully supported his pro-Greek policy anyway, were prepared to accept the *fait accompli*, given that Britain and France were still left as the dominant powers in the Middle East, with its rich resources and strategic value. The last outcome also had the fortunate effect for Turkey of virtually removing the Middle East from its list of foreign policy concerns until 1941.

The Russian position was also crucial in this new balance of power, even though German power had been temporarily destroyed, and the Habsburg Empire removed. By the beginning of 1921, Russia was ravaged by years of war and internationally isolated. Nonetheless, contrary to western hopes and expectations, the Soviet government had established control over most of the old tsarist empire. Russia was still there as a force to be reckoned with, even if the western powers were reluctant to recognize it. The result was that the Turks could reverse the position of most of the nineteenth century, in which Russia had been the main potential enemy. The 1920s and 1930s were the first prolonged period in which they had an entente rather than confrontation with Russia since the Treaty of Hünkâr İskelesi of 1833. It also depended on a change of policy by the Soviets, when they decided to jettison the idea of sponsoring a communist revolution in Turkey early in 1921. Equally, the fact that they were anti-communist did not prevent the Turkish leaders from building up a useful business relationship with the USSR. The Kemalist regime was also pro-western, in the sense that it was committed to re-establishing Turkey as a western-style, secular state, but this was no reason for constructing an international alliance with the western powers, unless national security required it. Ideology was much less important than power politics in the formation of foreign policy.

After 1923, and until the mid-1930s, foreign relations took a back seat, as internal reconstruction and reform became the Turkish government's main priority, and the international situation did not seem threatening. For Turkish diplomacy, the main items on the agenda were problems left over from the Lausanne conference. Territorially, the Mosul settlement of 1926 was seen as a loss for the Turks, but the attachment of Mosul to Turkey would probably have brought Ankara more problems than advantages. If Turkey had won sovereignty over Mosul, then it would have had to co-exist with a far bigger Kurdish population, inhabiting a remote and mountainous country. Maintaining Turkish rule over Mosul would have been quite inconsistent with Turkish ethnic nationalism. Moreover, since the Iraqis regarded Mosul as a legitimate part of their territory, it would have created constant frictions with the independent state of Iraq. These problems would almost certainly have outweighed the value of controlling the Kirkuk oilfields. The most important benefit of the agreement at the time was that it paved the way towards a better relationship with Britain. The Turkish decision not to go to war over Mosul also demonstrated Turkey's realistic recognition of its own limitations.

The rapprochement with Greece was slower in coming, but when it came it was quite dramatic and effective. So far as one can judge, the Greek–Turkish treaty of 1930 derived mainly from an independent decision to bury the hatchet by both countries, rather than as a direct result of their relations with the rest of the world. Nonetheless, it aided a better relationship between Turkey and the western powers, symbolized by Turkey's accession to the

League of Nations in 1932. The shift was rendered more important with the emergence of the apparent Italian threat in 1933. This faced Turkey with essentially the same range of options as those confronting Ottoman policy-makers in the nineteenth century. Turkey could either stay out of alliances, relying on the balance of power to maintain security, or it could actively seek an alliance with one the main European powers, or a coalition of them. For a time, the Turks sought to delay the decision, by constructing a security pact with the Balkan states that, they unrealistically hoped, might be joined by Britain, France and the USSR. In principle, the resulting Balkan pact of 1934 was a worthy project, but it eventually failed, partly because of its technical weaknesses and partly because none of the Balkan states except Greece were ultimately prepared to stand up to the Axis.

Meanwhile, the restoration of Germany's international strength and ambitions had produced a far more serious threat, which was clearly recognized by the Turks by 1938, if not before. Atatürk scorned Mussolini, and according to one account he heartily disliked Hitler: he was disgusted by the Nazis' anti-Semitism, which was strongly attacked by İnönü in the Grand National Assembly.[75] However, the Turks had a healthy appreciation of Germany's military and economic power and realized that they needed security arrangements with the other European powers to meet it.[76] At no time during the 1930s did Turkey seriously consider a security pact with rather than against Germany, its former ally of the First World War: in fact both Atatürk and İnönü strongly criticized the alliance of 1914–18 that, they argued, had subordinated Turkish to German interests.[77] The alternative was an alliance with Britain and France that, the Turks hoped, could be combined with an effective security pact with the USSR. The forging of such an alliance was delayed until the last months before the Second World War, partly because of the dispute with France over Alexandretta, but more importantly because Britain rejected the idea until after the German invasion of Czechoslovakia in March 1939. The resultant alliance between Britain, France and Turkey appeared to be favourable to Turkey, although it was severely weakened by the Nazi–Soviet pact and hence the non-adherence of the USSR. In this respect, Turkish diplomacy had failed, defeated by the cynical tactics of the dictators. The need to expand and modernize Turkey's armed forces had also been unmet by 1939. With these exceptions, Turkish diplomacy seemed to have played a successful game, from what must have seemed a hopeless start.

3 Turkey and the Second World War, 1939–45

Because it had some importance in the history of the Second World War as a whole, Turkish diplomacy between 1939 and 1945 has received a good deal of scholarly attention – more so, for instance, than in the case of either the immediately preceding or succeeding periods. At first glance, it seems fairly straightforward and consistent. Although its government had signed a tripartite alliance with Britain and France in October 1939, Turkey remained a *de facto* neutral throughout the war, resisting strong pressure from both the Allies and Germany to join the war on their side. The careful balancing act is held up as an example of how a relatively small and militarily backward country could follow an independent path at a time of global struggle, and 'a striking example of a small state which was no helpless pawn in international politics'.[1] This policy could be seen as a natural outcome of Turkey's experiences since 1914, and the country's relative power and international position. All Turkey's leaders during the Second World War had first-hand experiences of the previous one and were naturally anxious to avoid repeating them. Saving the country from a return to the death and destruction of war was their overriding objective. Turkey's armed forces were too ill-equipped to hold off a counter-attack by either Germany or the Soviet Union effectively. Its political leaders were above all anxious to protect the security they had won in 1923. Assuming it was not invaded by one of the belligerents, Turkey had practically nothing to gain and everything to lose by joining the war.

This view has a good deal to recommend it, but it does not seem plausible as an explanation of Turkish policy throughout the war years.[2] If, for instance, İnönü and his colleagues had been determined to stay out of the war from the moment they signed the alliance with Britain and France in 1939, then one would have to conclude that they blatantly intended not to carry out their commitments under it, or that they thought that the circumstances under which they were supposed to do so would never arise. However, this would assume a degree of duplicity or naïveté on their part that is inconsistent with their overall policy performance. It is not supported by their policies during the first six months of the war, in which they accepted the principle of entering the war against Italy and Germany. Like other political leaders in most situations, they usually decided policy on the basis of the existing situation, their previous experiences and their expectations at the time. Hence, Turkey's wartime diplomacy can be seen as subject to significant shifts, adapted to the circumstances of a series of fairly distinct phases and to changes within these phases.

On the policy-making side, İnönü kept a tight control over decision-making throughout the period. The watchword of his approach was caution. He put great emphasis on gaining time, at which he was an expert, and avoided bold initiatives, adapting his policies to the circumstances of the moment. He was assisted by a trusted team of advisers, but the final decision rested with the President. Within the policy-making establishment, there were some individuals who apparently took a pro-Axis or distinctly pro-Allied position, but İnönü held them in check. Nor was the military command able to take an independent line. The Chief of the General Staff, Marshal Fevzi Çakmak, had been in the post since 1922, and had been appointed mainly because he was seen as a loyal supporter of Atatürk who could secure the political attachment of the army to the regime. During the war, he was much criticized for his conservative outlook on professional military matters. He had an uneasy relationship with İnönü, since he had been a rival candidate for the presidency when Atatürk died. However, he does not seem to have played an effective role in policy-making, and was eventually dismissed by İnönü in January 1944. Even before then, it appears that İnönü was usually able to bypass Çakmak by settling questions with his Assistant Chief of Staff, General Asım Gündüz, so that Çakmak's influence over İnönü was minimal.[3] Throughout the war, İnönü continued his close personal interest in foreign affairs. His principal foreign policy advisers were all experienced colleagues, notably Şükrü Saraçoğlu, who served as foreign minister from 1939 until he took over as Prime Minister in 1942, and Numan Menemencioğlu, the Secretary-General at the foreign ministry since 1929, who became foreign minister in 1942 and is regarded as the main source of ideas in Turkish foreign policy until his enforced resignation in June 1944.[4]

Shifting fortunes and policies, October 1939–June 1941

At the time it signed the tripartite alliance with Britain and France in October 1939, it appears that the Turkish government fully expected to carry out its commitments, and that it would join the war on the Allied side if the Axis powers invaded the Balkans, or Italy started a war in the Mediterranean, as the treaty provided. It was also expected that Turkey would be able to defend its own territory against likely invaders. Since 1934, the Turkish army had redeployed more than half its forces, with the bulk of its equipment and all its modern weapons, to eastern Thrace. A system of fixed fortifications was constructed, known as the 'Çakmak line', with which visiting British officers were impressed. Hence the initial assumption seems to have been that the Turks could hold off an invasion from the Balkans, although it was recognized that they had little ability to advance beyond their own frontier without extensive help. During October–November 1939 operational plans were discussed between Fevzi Çakmak, and Generals Maxime Weygand and Archibald Wavell, respectively French and British commanders in the Middle East. Çakmak agreed to allow the Allies the use of forward bases in Turkish territory for a campaign against Germany in the Balkans – an idea on which the British were markedly less enthusiastic than the French. He also stressed the need for 'effective and timely assistance' from France and Britain as an essential condition. As late as the spring of 1940, the three partners were still considering an attack on the Italian-held Dodecanese islands, which Çakmak considered would be of 'primary importance'. More broadly, it appears that İnönü shared the Anglo-French belief that the war on the western front would be a long one, that it would be fought on the Maginot line, and believed that the Allies would ultimately win, as in 1914–18. Apart from this, it was far from certain that Italy would join the war, or that Greece or Romania would be invaded by the Axis, so the circumstances for activating the alliance might not arise.[5]

Before long, however, both the Turks and the British had begun to revise some of their assumptions. On 29 May 1940, Çakmak reported to the ministry of defence the difficulties that the army would face in defending Thrace, especially due to the lack of motor transport. The failure of the Allies to deliver the promised armaments, together with Turkish appreciation of Hitler's lightning victory over Poland in September 1939, contributed to a more pessimistic assessment of their military position by the Turks. Meanwhile, it appears that the British had started to become worried that Turkey might not activate the alliance. In March 1940 the French proposed a plan for bombing the Soviet oil fields at Baku, so as to weaken Russia and prevent the large exports of oil that the USSR was supplying to Germany. To do this, the attacking aircraft would need to overfly Turkey. According to one account (that was later disputed), René Massigli, the French ambassador in Ankara, was given to understand from Saracoğlu that Turkey would turn a blind eye to this infringement of its airspace. However, the British were lukewarm towards the idea, since they correctly believed that the Turks might not be cooperative, or at least that it would be best not to test them on this. Aggression by the Allies against the USSR might give the Turks an excuse to stay out of the war, and Turkey's role as the bastion of the British position in the Middle East made it essential to retain Turkish support. The plan was thus dropped, mainly because of fears of the Turkish reaction. Later, Saracoğlu even denied the existence of an Anglo-French–Turkish plan to attack Baku.[6]

More crucially, the collapse of France in June 1940 dramatically reversed İnönü's expectations about the likely course of the war and Turkey's own role in it. Turkey's possible participation in the war had depended on the assumption that the French fleet would be available to oppose Italy in the Mediterranean if need be. İnönü and his government were incensed with the French for having pressed Turkey to join the fight against the Axis after they had known that their own defeat by Germany was inevitable, and there were calls in Turkey for an agreement with Germany in the face of a mutual danger from the

USSR. As Massigli later admitted, 'to remind Turkey of a promise given was one thing, but to invite her to rally to our cause on the very day of the evacuation of Paris was another'.[7] Turkish reactions to the dramatic alteration of the balance of power in the Mediterranean were also critical in the British decision to try to destroy the French Mediterranean fleet in July 1940, to prevent it falling into German hands.[8]

The results of this new situation became quite clear after Italy entered the war on 10 June 1940, and thus created the situation foreseen in Article 2 of the tripartite treaty, which would oblige Turkey to join the war on the Allied side. The problem was made still more acute on 7 October, when German troops began to enter Romania, and then on 28 October, when Italy invaded Greece from Albania, both of which events should have required Turkish belligerence under Article 3. The Turkish response to the Italian declaration of war was to back out of these requirements. A declaration of non-belligerence issued by the government on 26 June cited the protocol to the treaty that absolved Turkey from joining the war if this would involve it in armed conflict with the Soviet Union (see p52). The Turks also argued that, since their alliance had been with both Britain and France, the fact that France was now dropping out of the war relieved them of their obligations. For the British, the first excuse was not convincing, since there was no proof that if Turkey joined the war against Italy then it would be attacked by the USSR, and they pressed Turkey to fulfil its treaty commitments.[9] Clearly, the real reason for Turkey's failure to act was the expectation that, with France knocked out of the ring, Britain would be unable to give any effective support and that Turkey would be left to fight Italy and Germany virtually on its own. The fear that Stalin would then take advantage of the situation, at Turkey's expense, was a further reason for caution.

Meanwhile the success of Germany's *Blitzkrieg* tactics caused a radical revision of defence plans on the Turkish side. By March 1941, the expected line of defence, in the event of an invasion from the Balkans, had been moved back to western Anatolia, prospectively abandoning Istanbul to the enemy.[10] Obviously, İnönü's government had to avoid this if it could. Henceforward, estimates of Turkey's powers of resistance varied, but it was generally recognized that the primitive state of its internal communications, which were an obstacle to a successful invasion, also restricted the Turkish army's ability to defend its country. The Turks might be brave soldiers but their outdated equipment and lack of modern training, plus the extreme weakness of the air force, would have put them at a severe disadvantage in a war with either Germany or Russia. Above all, Istanbul and İzmir were virtually defenceless against a determined air attack.[11] After the summer of 1940, these considerations naturally informed all Turkish reactions to potential threats, or attempts to bring Turkey into the war on either side.

Although the events of 1940 forced the Turks to reconsider their position, this did not lead to a rapid rapprochement with Germany. Initially, Germany's aim was to secure the neutrality of Turkey – to ensure, at least, that it did not play an active role on the British side – and to try to prevent Italy from provoking the Turks into activating the alliance with Britain. After the dramatic German victories in the summer of 1940, von Papen (see p51) urged Berlin that Germany should go further, by trying to convert Turkey into a pro-German neutral so as to facilitate a German attack on the British in the Middle East. This could be achieved with the participation of Russia, which could be offered concessions at the straits. Hints were meanwhile dropped to the Turks that Germany would oppose such concessions if Turkey made some concrete demonstrations of sympathy for Germany, including the dismissal of Saracoğlu, who was seen as strongly anti-German. Predictably, this demand was categorically dismissed by İnönü.[12] Meanwhile, trade relations formed the main business of Turco-German diplomacy. During the 1930s, Germany had manipulated a system of clearing agreements and its non-convertible currency to gain a dominating position in Turkey's foreign trade, accounting for 51 per cent of its imports and 31 per cent of its exports, but this had no effect on Turkish policy. After the signature of the alliance with Britain and France, the Turks cut back their trade with Germany sharply, so that in 1940 these percentages were reduced to 12 per cent and 9 per cent respectively.[13] In June 1940, disagreements over trade arrangements with Britain led Turkey to secure a new commercial agreement with Germany. However, its duration was limited to only one year, the volume of trade was still limited and it did not include chromite, which was Turkey's most strategically vital potential export (see p66). As a result, Turkish–German trade in 1941 remained at almost exactly the same level as in 1940.[14]

The reaction of the British to the Turkish decision not to join the war was also ambiguous. Officially, Knatchbull-Hugessen protested against Turkish reluctance until after the Italian attack on Greece. Nonetheless, the Foreign Secretary Lord Halifax told the House of Lords on 11 July 1941 that the British government 'fully appreciated the circumstances which led to this decision of the Turkish Government' not to join the war.[15] Privately, a British military report estimated that if Turkey joined the war, and was attacked by Germany, then Hitler's armies could conquer the country in 16 weeks.[16] In effect, a belligerent Turkey would be more of a liability than an asset for Britain. The British came to realize that even if they could not officially accept the Turkish decision, there was little they could do about it, since they feared that further pressure on the Turks might push them towards Germany. By the end of January 1941, according to his own later account, Churchill had decided that it 'was obviously impossible to consider the treaty we had made with her [Turkey] as binding upon her in the altered circumstances'.[17] By February–March 1941, the Italian invaders had been pushed back by the Greeks, and the British were attempting to counter the impending German invasion of the Balkans by sending troops to Greece and reviving the Balkan pact. By this stage, however, they had realized that it would be pointless to try to get Turkey to join the war unless their overall military position improved dramatically, and hence they desisted from doing so.[18]

Throughout this period – indeed, throughout the war – a crucial concern for Turkey was the policy of the USSR. The Nazi–Soviet pact, and Russian demands to Saracoğlu during his visit to Moscow in 1939, had completely reversed the Turks' previous expectations of cooperation with the Soviets. The USSR was not only geographically close to Turkey, but the Moscow discussions of 1939 had also made it clear that it was, at the very least, likely to make demands at the straits that the Turks could not accept. In July 1940, Stalin accepted British mediation for an improvement in relations with Turkey, but insisted that this should be based on the participation of the Black Sea powers (presumably dominated by Russia) in the defence of the straits. This was unacceptable to the Turks, so the proposal came to nothing.[19] Moreover, Turkey's relations with the USSR were inevitably overshadowed by those of Stalin with Hitler. So long as the Nazi–Soviet pact lasted, there was the danger that Germany might offer the straits to Stalin as part of the price for his neutrality or even active intervention in the war on the German side. Negotiations between the Germans and Soviets in November 1940 showed that these fears were well-founded. Following the conclusion of the Three Power Pact for mutual aid between Germany, Italy and Japan on 27 September 1940, Molotov began to explore the possibility of Soviet collaboration with the Pact in conversations with Hitler and Ribbentrop in Berlin on 12–13 November. He emphasized that the USSR regarded control of the straits as essential to its security and claimed that he could reach an agreement with Turkey on this. The Germans responded by presenting him with a draft agreement on 26 November that, among other things, proposed a joint commitment to detach Turkey from its alliance with Britain, 'to recognise the extent of Turkey's possessions', and to secure a revision of the Montreux convention giving the USSR free naval access through the straits. However, Molotov regarded this as insufficient and demanded the establishment of Soviet military and naval bases at the straits. If Turkey agreed to join a projected four power pact (that is, Germany, Italy, Japan and the USSR) then the three other powers would guarantee its independence and territory. If not, then the 'the required military and diplomatic measures' would be taken. Bulgaria would also have to be induced to sign a mutual assistance pact with the USSR since, Molotov claimed, it was 'situated inside the security zone of the Black Sea boundaries of the Soviet Union'.[20]

These demands were too much for Hitler. Evidently, he did not want to hand over control over the straits and Bulgaria to Stalin, which would have ruled out a possible German attack on the British in the Middle East and encircled Germany from the south. Accordingly, the negotiations broke off with no positive result. Twenty-two days later, on 18 December, Hitler issued the fatal orders to begin preparations for his invasion of the Soviet Union ('Barbarossa'). Whether or not they knew of the German–Soviet negotiations at the time, the Turks certainly learned of them on 18 March 1941, when Hitler, anxious to show the Turks that he was on their side, told the Turkish ambassador in Berlin that he had flatly refused the Soviet demand for bases at the straits. On 25 March, the Soviet government declared that it would remain neutral in the event of a war between Turkey and the Axis, and this declaration was reciprocated by the Turks. Nonetheless, İnönü and his colleagues had been left in little doubt about Stalin's long-run ambitions.[21]

During 1940–1, events in the Middle East further embroiled Britain and Germany with Turkey. Following the fall of France, a pro-Vichy administration had installed itself in Syria. During the summer of 1940, the British considered schemes for intervening in the country to prevent it coming under direct German or Italian control. Turkey, it was suggested, could be offered territory in Syria, including Aleppo, as an inducement for cooperating in this. However, the idea was dropped, as the Turks showed no interest in it and the British feared the likely reactions in other Arab states to any Turkish intervention in Syria. On the Turkish side, there was probably a natural reluctance to provoke Germany. In March 1941, the Turkish government also went to some lengths to emphasize publicly that it did not have any territorial ambitions in Syria. When Saracoğlu met Anthony Eden in Cyprus on 18 March, he was reported by the British to have told the Foreign Secretary that Turkey did not covet territory in Syria as 'the Syrians were awkward customers and modern Turkey did not wish to include non-homogeneous peoples within her frontiers'.[22]

In April 1941, attention switched to Iraq as the government was overthrown by a pro-Axis junta, which installed Rashid Ali al-Gaylani, a prominent Iraqi nationalist politician, as Prime Minister. Rashid Ali then restricted British reinforcements of their troops and Iraqi forces besieged the British base at Habbaniya, some 25 miles west of Baghdad.[23] Although Rashid Ali had received hints of Axis aid, the Germans had not planned his takeover and were ill-prepared to assist him. Hitler had no clear plans to try to eject the British from the Middle East at this stage, and was anyway heavily engaged in the Balkans and in his preparations for Barbarossa. As a result, the Iraqi rebels acted too soon and Hitler too late. On 3 May, Hitler agreed to send German warplanes to Iraq and these played some role in the fighting against the British. The quickest way for the Germans to send arms to Iraq was to draw on the Vichy stocks in Syria, and on 5 May they obtained the approval of the Vichy government in France to this plan. An obstacle to it was the fact that the only railway from Syria to Iraq passed through Turkish territory, and the operation thus depended on Turkish permission. According to one source, the Turks had serious designs in Iraq, where the province of Mosul had only been reluctantly conceded in 1926, which they hoped to achieve in collaboration with either Britain or Germany.[24] However, if they did have such ambitions, they evidently decided not to push them home. It appears that four trains loaded with small arms completed the trip from Syria to Iraq in the second half of May, but the remainder of the planned consignment failed to get through (in fact, the arms that were sent made no difference to the military outcome in Iraq).[25] At the same time, the Turkish government was also engaged in fruitless attempts at mediation between Rashid Ali and the British. In negotiations with the Germans during June, Turkey refused

German demands for an agreement allowing the despatch of an unlimited quantity of German arms to Iraq and a defined number of troops across German territory. From the German viewpoint, the proposal was too late anyway, since the British had meanwhile moved forces into Iraq and overthrown Rashid Ali by 30 May. Meanwhile, the British were preparing to invade Syria, and on 2 June they again suggested to the Turks that they should occupy Aleppo as part of this. The proposal was turned down again by the Turks, though Turkey did concentrate forces on the Syrian border. With the idea of collaboration with Turkey now dropped, a mixed force of British, Indian, Australian, Arab and Free French forces invaded Syria on 8 June, as the last German units were withdrawn. The Allied forces completed the overthrow of the local Vichy administration in Syria on 14 July. Turkey had thus been able to get out of the crisis without any serious involvement on either side.[26]

In the spring of 1941, German advances in the Balkans were Turkey's main focus of concern. When Eden visited Ankara at the end of February, with a German attack on Greece looming, the Turks told him they were convinced that their turn would come next and that they were worried that the USSR might also attack them if they were involved in war with Germany. Soon afterwards, during April and May, the British position in the Balkans collapsed as Hitler conquered Yugoslavia and Greece. Additionally, German forces were now in full occupation of Romania and Bulgaria. Given that German troops were now only about 40 miles beyond its north-western frontier, Turkey was bound to try to reach some understanding with Berlin. Hitler was similarly inclined, since he wished to stabilize his southern flank in preparation for Barbarossa. The expulsion of Britain from the Middle East, involving an invasion of Turkey or at least its political subordination, could wait until after Russia had been defeated. Accordingly, on 4 March 1941, Hitler wrote a personal letter to İnönü assuring him that the German occupation of Bulgaria was in no way directed against Turkey but purely against the British in Greece, and that he had ordered his forces in Bulgaria not to go within 60 kilometres of the frontier with Turkey.[27] At a meeting with Mussolini in Salzburg on 29 April, Hitler claimed that 'Turkey was moving slowly but surely over to the Axis', that it would never be an enemy of the Axis and would at worst remain neutral: the Turks would also like to have Russia 'as far removed as possible from their territories'.[28]

How Turkish–German relations developed immediately after this is unclear, since there are two quite contradictory accounts. According to the first account, based on German records, Saracoğlu and von Papen discussed a full-scale alliance between Turkey and Germany during May 1941. Von Papen reported that, on 17 May, Saracoğlu told him that Turkey would be willing to abandon the alliance with Britain in return for large arms deliveries from Germany and recognition that Iraq was within Turkey's sphere of influence. This account relates that von Papen then prepared a draft treaty, which Saracoğlu had helped to prepare, that was cabled to Berlin on 23 May. This offered Turkey the cession of some Bulgarian territory near Edirne, two or three of the Greek

Aegean islands and 'the advancement of Turkish interests in the southern and eastern neighbouring zones' (presumably, in Syria and Iraq) as part of a Turkish–German alliance that would give Germany transit rights across Turkey.[29] The second account, also based on German records, suggests that the initiative for a treaty to allow Germany transit rights came from not from von Papen but from Ribbentrop, who suggested on 18 May that Turkey could be offered frontier rectification's near Edirne and possibly 'one or other island in the Aegean Sea'. If Turkey resisted this offer then Ribbentrop suggested that the Turks should be told that Germany was in a position to 'blot out the Turkish state within a few weeks'. The second account goes on to relate that von Papen opposed this plan, by arguing that the idea of getting Turkey to grant transit rights to Germany was just a vain dream, and that territorial offers would not have any effect on Turkish policy. It does not suggest that Saracoğlu ever agreed to a draft treaty. The only thing that can be said for certain is that the Turks rapidly abandoned the alliance project, if they had ever adopted it in the first place.[30]

Accordingly, the Germans had to be content with a simple mutual non-aggression pact with Turkey. In the Turkish–German Treaty of Friendship and Non-Aggression, signed on 18 June 1941, which was to be valid for ten years, the two governments agreed to respect each other's territorial integrity and to 'abstain from all action aimed directly or indirectly against one another'. However, the preamble to the treaty stated that these commitments were 'subject to the already existing arrangements of each party' – an obvious reference to the treaty with the British of 1939, as Saracoğlu pointed out to the Turkish parliament.[31] In his memoirs, Knatchbull-Hugessen relates that the Turks kept the British informed of their negotiations with the Germans, and that he decided that it would be counterproductive to oppose the non-aggression pact. However, it appears that at the time he criticized it strongly, as did the US government.[32] The signature of the treaty marked Turkey's furthest move towards a full, rather than merely *de facto* neutrality. Of course, the Turks could be criticized for cutting a deal with the Germans when they were supposed to be allied to the British but they probably had no safe alternative, given their strategic situation at the time. The most serious criticism of the treaty was that, in the long run, it might be of no value. After all, Hitler had broken virtually every important international agreement he had ever made, and he would have been perfectly capable of ignoring this one if and when he had been able and willing to do so. The point was made only four days later, on 22 June, when German forces finally invaded the USSR.

Walking the tightrope: June 1941–December 1942

The beginning of Barbarossa naturally caused a heartfelt sigh of relief in Ankara, since it was now unlikely that Hitler would have the forces to spare for an invasion of Turkey and the Middle East in the near future. Unsurprisingly, Turkey immediately proclaimed its neutrality in the conflict. However, the longer-term outlook was still dangerous. If the USSR won this new war outright, then it would probably be left as the dominant power in eastern Europe and able to dictate its own terms at the straits. On the other hand, if Russia collapsed and then capitulated, as it had in 1917, then Hitler might well fall on Turkey as his next victim. Obviously the best outcome for Turkey would be that Germany and the Allies would reach a negotiated settlement that would leave neither Germany nor the USSR in a dominating position in eastern Europe, or that they would fight one another to a standstill. As the Italian ambassador in Ankara Ottavio de Peppo put it: 'The Turkish ideal is that the last German soldier should fall upon the last Russian corpse.'[33] However, the Turks had no way of ensuring this ideal result. The best İnönü could do was to follow his own cautious instincts by playing for time, avoiding commitments and exploiting whatever opportunities arose to strengthen Turkey's position.

The fear that Germany would attack Turkey if the USSR were defeated was not baseless. The German archives show that in June 1941, before Barbarossa had begun, German military planners confidently expected to defeat Russia in three months. Following this, during the late autumn and winter of 1941–2, Germany would attack Egypt from the west and mass large forces in Bulgaria. Turkey would be forced to submit, preparatory to the launch of a German attack on the Suez canal through Turkey, Syria and Palestine, combined with an invasion of Iran from the Caucasus. In conversations with his dinner guests in September 1941, Hitler maintained that Turkey would join the Axis after the defeat of Russia and that the Turkish ambassador in Berlin, Hüsrev Gerede, whom he claimed was in favour of cooperation with Germany, might be made Turkish foreign minister. However, the planned operation did not depend on these predictions. German planners assumed that the Middle Eastern campaign could be finished in 85 days if Turkey cooperated, or in 145 days if it did not. Either way, the plan could be completed by the spring of 1942.[34] Even if they did not have the details of these plans, the Turks reasonably expected that Hitler had something of the kind in store. As early as July 1941, Fevzi Çakmak (who, paradoxically, was thought by both the Germans and the British to favour the German side) told the British Air Attaché that Turkey hoped that the Germans would exhaust themselves in Russia, since: 'We realise that if Germany has a quick success in Russia we will be the next sheep for slaughter.'[35] In January 1942, after the Germans had been halted before Moscow, İnönü told Knatchbull-Hugessen that he still expected an imminent invasion by Germany from Thrace, and had reinforced the Turkish positions there. Thereafter, the Turks continued to fear a sudden and probably catastrophic Luftwaffe assault on Istanbul, like that on Belgrade or Warsaw, against which they had virtually no effective protection.[36]

An important question in Turkey's relations with Germany during 1941–2 is whether Turkey hoped to gain territory in Transcaucasia and possibly other Turkic areas of the USSR, in collaboration with Germany, assuming Russia were defeated. Certainly, von Papen promoted the proposal, as a means of bringing Turkey over to the Axis side, and it had some support in Berlin.

Although Atatürk had strictly abjured pan-Turkism, it had continued as a fringe movement in Turkey during the 1930s. A so-called committee of experts on the 'Turanian' question was established in July 1941, consisting of convinced pan-Turkists, including Nuri Pasha, a brother of the Young Turk leader Enver Pasha and now a businessman in Turkey, and Professor Zeki Velidi Toğan, a well-known pan-Turkish historian. In August 1941, Nuri visited Berlin as what von Papen described as a fully accredited representative of the Turkish government, although Turkish sources deny this. At this stage, the Turkish government had evidently decided to test the temperature on this issue, through semi-official channels. In Berlin, Nuri urged the establishment of a pan-Turanian state stretching as far as the Chinese province of Xinjiang. However, both the Germans and Turks then abandoned this fantasy. Those Germans who favoured the idea also claimed Fevzi Çakmak as one of its supporters, but the furthest Çakmak was apparently prepared to go was to tell the Germans in May 1942 that he was willing to allow Turkish civilians to go to Germany to prepare for the establishment of separate states in the Turkic areas captured from the USSR. On the other hand, Hüsrev Gerede, who had supported the idea at first, bluntly turned down the proposal that Turkey should take over Turkic areas of the Soviet Union when Hitler suggested it to him in August 1941. It was obviously dropped completely, once it was clear that Germany was not going to crush the USSR anyway.[37]

Trade was also a significant thermometer of Turkish–German relations. Here, a vital issue for both the Germans and British was the supply of chromite, which is an essential ingredient in steel-making. Germany had no domestic supplies, but Turkey had accounted for about 16 per cent of world production in 1939. The problem for the Turks was that they were allied to a country that had little economic use for their products, given that Britain had alternative sources of supply of both chromite and the agricultural crops exported by Turkey. On the other hand, the Allies could have done severe damage to Germany's war effort if they could have denied the Germans access to Turkish chromite. In October 1939, the Turks had proposed to the British that they should sell them 200,000 tons of chromite per year for the next two years. This offer was later increased to 20 years. Since this was greater than Turkey's total pre-war production, it would have pre-empted Germany from the market for the duration of the war. However, in negotiations with the British, Numan Menemencioğlu insisted that Britain should also buy agreed quantities of Turkey's other exports, on the grounds that Germany, Turkey's previous customer, would refuse to take these products if chromite were not also on offer. The British turned this deal down and only promised to buy 50,000 tons of chromite per year in 1941 and 1942, with an option on that mined in 1943. In their 1940 trade agreement with Germany, the Turks had withheld chromite and Menemencioğlu assured the US and British governments that Turkey would not sell chromite to Germany. Nonetheless, in October 1941 a new arrangement was reached with Germany, known as the 'Clodius agreement', after its chief German negotiator, Karl Clodius. Under this, Germany was to receive a maximum of 90,000 tons of chromite in 1943 (that is, after the contract with the British expired) and 45,000 tons in 1944. The Clodius agreement also provided for the sale by Germany of substantial amounts of military and other essential equipment to Turkey. In the summer of 1942 Turkey received a loan of 100 million Reichsmarks for the purchase of arms from Germany – supplies that Britain could not match at the time. As a result, Turkey's trade with Germany recovered, to account for 28 per cent of Turkey's total imports and 25 per cent of its total exports in 1942. The signature of the Clodius agreement partly derived from the British failure to accept the proposed exclusive deal with Turkey, but it is likely that it also reflected İnönü's desire not to provoke Germany by withholding supplies of chromite, given his country's perilous situation. The arms loan from Germany was also a further means of building up Turkey's defences – possibly against Germany itself.[38]

One other action by the Turkish government did some harm to Turkey's relations with the Allies in the longer term, as well as the international reputation of İnönü's government, though the British did not publicly raise it at the time.[39] In November 1942, the government introduced a Property Tax (*Varlık Vergisi*), which was supposed to be applied on a one-off basis to wealthy farmers, businessmen and corporations. In theory, it was expected to have the perfectly reasonable aim of mopping up part of the windfall profits accumulated by speculators in wartime conditions. In practice, it was used by the local committees who fixed the tax assessments as a means of killing off commercial competition from members of the non-Muslim minorities who had remained in Istanbul after the Lausanne settlement (see p40). As a result, non-Muslims were assessed far more severely than Muslims. Of the total collected, 53 per cent was paid by non-Muslims, compared with 36.5 per cent paid by Muslims and 10.5 per cent by foreign citizens resident in Turkey. Those who failed to pay were shipped off to a labour camp in Aşkale, in eastern Anatolia that, for a middle-class Istanbuli, was the Turkish equivalent of Siberia. Collection of the tax was slowed down in 1943 and terminated in 1944, but by this time many innocent citizens had been ruined. Meanwhile, and quite paradoxically, Turkish intervention saved many thousands of eastern European Jews from the Holocaust, by aiding their clandestine immigration into Palestine. There thus seems to have been a complete disconnect between internal and external policies.[40] In the long run, the infamous Property Tax seriously damaged Turkey's international moral standing.[41]

Obviously, the beginning of Barbarossa also affected Turkey's relations with both Moscow and London, since Britain and the USSR were now fighting on the same side. Their first concern was to try to allay Turkish suspicions about Russian ambitions at the straits. Accordingly, on 28 July 1941, Stalin had told İnönü that he had no interest in revising the Montreux Convention. On 10 August, the British and Soviet governments issued a joint declaration, stating their fidelity to the Montreux rules, that they had 'no aggressive intentions or claims whatever regarding the straits' and that they were 'prepared scrupulously' to observe Turkey's territorial integrity. If Turkey were attacked by a 'European Power' (read Germany) then they would both come to its aid.[42] However, it does not appear that the Turks were reassured by these statements. Their suspicions were naturally strengthened by the Anglo-Soviet invasion and occupation of neighbouring Iran in August 1941. As the Turkish press pointed out, if the British and Russians had been prepared to invade a neutral country merely because it stood in their way, then they might be prepared to do the same to Turkey.[43] Following the death of Prime Minister Refik Saydam on 8 July 1942, Saracoğlu succeeded him, with Menemencioğlu becoming foreign minister shortly afterwards. After his appointment, Saracoğlu promptly announced that Turkey was 'equally loyal and friendly towards all opposing States'.[44] Nonetheless, in reality it had serious suspicions of all of them. On 8 August, von Papen reported a conversation with Saracoğlu in which Saracoğlu stated that he hoped for the collapse of the USSR, allowing Germany and Turkey to sign a separate peace agreement, and to sponsor the non-Slavic minorities in Soviet territory as enemies of Slavism. Saracoğlu had a further interview with von Papen on 29 August, in which he repeated his hope for the destruction of Russia, but added that Turkey would have to preserve its neutrality.[45]

On the British side, the Turks' misgivings were recognized, and it appears that both the British and Soviet governments realized that the best they could do would be to try to keep Turkey as a neutral buffer at this stage. At a meeting with Eden in December 1941, Stalin suggested that after the war, Turkey should be given the Dodecanese, certain territory in Bulgaria and possibly in northern Syria, but Eden replied that Britain could not commit itself to any post-war re-drawing of frontiers.[46] As Knatchbull-Hugessen states it in his memoirs, the British government adhered to this policy of accepting Turkey's *de facto* neutrality until the end of 1942. However, behind the scenes, and by August 1942, Churchill was trying to persuade his two allies (which now included the United States) that their next priority must be to try to knock Italy out of the war and bring Turkey in.[47] The second proposal, combined with the overall change in the tide of the war during the winter of 1942–3, was to prove the greatest problem for Turkish diplomacy from then until 1945.

Allied ascendancy: November 1942–May 1945

To fix the exact date when the tide turned in the Second World War is not easy. Clearly, the full entry of the United States into the war following the Japanese attack on Pearl Harbor in December 1941 was probably the decisive event which determined that, in the long run, the Axis would lose the war. However, this had little immediate effect on the war in Russia and north Africa, Turkey's immediate environment. Turkey's position was not effectively changed until the winter of 1942–3 – first, by the German defeat at el-Alamein in October–November 1942 and the consequent Allied landings in Algeria and Morocco, which ended the Axis threat to the Middle East, and second, the

German surrender at Stalingrad in February 1943, which made it virtually certain that Hitler's campaign in Russia would ultimately fail. In an ideal world, Turkish statesmen would have preferred a situation in which Germany accepted a peace deal with the western Allies before Stalin completed his conquest of eastern Europe, which would have left some German power in the region to balance that of Russia. However, this hope ran counter to realities. On the one side, Hitler insisted on fighting the war to the bitter end and attempts to overthrow or murder him were unsuccessful. On the other side, for the Allies the war was one of good against evil, and not just a conflict of national interests. Victory could only be won if the Third Reich was completely destroyed. The policy of demanding the unconditional surrender of Germany, announced at the Casablanca conference in January 1943, combined with Hitler's fanaticism, precluded the possibility of a negotiated peace between Germany and the western Allies. The Turks had to deal with the world as it was – in particular, with the Allies' campaign to bring Turkey into the war.

On this score, Turkish policy was determined, first by the fear that if Turkey joined the war on the Allied side with inadequate preparation or support it would still be very vulnerable to a retaliatory attack by Germany. Equally, Stalin might use Turkish entry into the war as an excuse for Soviet entry into Turkey. On the other hand, if Turkey bluntly rejected the Allies' proposals then it would be left dangerously isolated and in a very weak position to resist Soviet ambitions at the straits and elsewhere in the post-war world. The fear that Britain and America might offer control of the straits to Russia, as the price for keeping it in the war – as the British had done in 1915 – was constantly at the back of Turkish minds. Hence, İnönü and his colleagues had to play for time, to try to keep the Allies reasonably satisfied with Turkish intentions, but to avoid committing their country to war unless this was part of a concerted and coordinated military offensive by the western Allies in south-eastern Europe. Since the latter never materialized, Turkey stayed on the sidelines, running the risk of the second of the two dangers it faced.

The initiative for bringing Turkey into the war came principally from Winston Churchill, and was first outlined to the US ambassador in London, John G. Winant and to Anthony Eden on 9 November 1942. It depended on bringing military supplies into Turkey via Syria and elsewhere, and originally assumed that Turkey would invade the Balkans in the spring of 1943, so as to strike at Germany's southern flank. The main obstacles to pressing this project home were the reluctance of the Turks to get dragged into the war, objections from both the British Foreign Office, including Eden, who doubted its political practicality, and from military commanders, especially on the American side, who questioned its strategic viability.[48] Nonetheless, at the Casablanca meeting of Roosevelt and Churchill it was agreed that Britain should take the lead in trying to bring Turkey into the war on the Allied side. Apart from their opposition to the policy of demanding the unconditional surrender of Germany, the Turks were also perturbed by the idea that the Casablanca decisions meant that they were being put into some sort of British zone of influence.[49]

However, İnönü agreed to talk directly to Churchill at a hastily arranged meeting held in a train parked near Adana on 30–31 January 1943.

At the Adana meeting, İnönü's main objective was to avoid committing Turkey to war against the Axis, but to obtain the maximum of military supplies to Turkey and to warn Churchill about Stalin's likely post-war intentions. On the latter score, the Turkish leaders were worried that pushing Turkey into a war with Germany was intended to soften Turkey up for an invasion by Russia, and they were not persuaded by Churchill's reassurances on this issue. When Churchill suggested that air bases should be prepared in Turkey for the RAF, the Turks responded that even if German power was now not what it had been, Germany was still capable of reacting by overrunning the straits and reducing Istanbul and Turkey's few industrial installations to rubble. Hence, it was eventually agreed that Britain would not ask for any immediate commitments from Turkey, although consideration should be given to allowing the RAF to use Turkish airfields to attack the Romanian oilfields, the Dodecanese and Crete, and to the possibility of Turkish intervention in the Balkans if there were anarchy in the region. If it became belligerent, Turkey's territory would be fully guaranteed by Britain after the war (by implication, against Russia). The only clear and immediate commitment on both sides was that Turkey should receive an increased flow of arms and infrastructural support.[50]

Following the Adana meeting, military staff meetings between the British and Turkish sides began in February 1943. The British produced plans for building up Turkish facilities to receive British air and later ground detachments. The Turks dragged their feet at every turn, so as to delay the open deployment of British forces on their soil, citing endless problems of transportation and logistics. Turkish policy, evidently, was to postpone the date at which they might be required to enter the war indefinitely. However, Churchill did not abandon his strategy. Instead, the overthrow of Mussolini's government on 25 July 1943, and the subsequent surrender of Italy on 8 September encouraged him to induce the Turks to come down off the fence. The collapse of Italy immediately raised a question mark over the future of the Dodecanese. The British proposed to answer it by sending an amphibious force to occupy the islands, but when they launched an attempt to capture the Dodecanese in September–October 1943, the Turkish role was limited to transporting food and equipment to the British in small ships, and subsequently evacuating those British troops who escaped capture to the mainland. As it was, the Dodecanese operation was a disaster for the British, as the Germans had swiftly reconquered the islands by mid-November. It was also a serious setback for Churchill's diplomacy, since it showed that Germany still had the upper hand militarily in the eastern Mediterranean, and was still in a strong position to retaliate against Turkey if it joined the Allies in the war.[51]

While the struggle for the Dodecanese was still going on, the British continued with their diplomatic offensive in Turkey. At this stage, the idea of bringing Turkey into the war was still supported by the USSR. At meetings between Eden, Molotov and the US Secretary of State Cordell Hull in Moscow between 19 October and 1 November 1943, the Soviet foreign minister proposed that Turkey should be told peremptorily to join the Allies. At this stage, the Russians still wanted Turkish participation in the war, which they estimated would draw off 15 German divisions from the Russian front. Roosevelt later agreed that the Turks should be asked to allow the establishment of Allied air bases on its soil, and to enter the war by the end of 1943, provided that no Allied forces were committed to the area which were needed for the planned Allied invasion of France ('Overlord'). Eden put these proposals to Menemencioğlu at a meeting in Cairo on 5–8 November, although he assured the Turkish foreign minister that 'there was no intention to press the Turks to go into the war on an all-out basis'.[52] Menemencioğlu, however, was not persuaded, making it clear that nothing short of a definite Anglo-American commitment to invade the Balkans would make it feasible for Turkey to join the war. The mere establishment of Allied air bases in Turkey would be tantamount to a declaration of war against Germany, without providing Turkey with a sufficient role, and at a time when it was unprepared. When Menemencioğlu queried post-war Soviet intentions, Eden threatened that the Allies might not support Turkey against Russia if it failed to meet British wishes. The talks thus ended on a bitter and unproductive note. The furthest the Turks were willing to go was contained in a message of 22 November stating that Turkey was prepared to enter the war 'in principle', but only if it received adequate protection against a German attack.[53]

In spite of these evident problems, the Allied campaign to bring in Turkey as an active partner continued until early 1944. When the question was discussed at the Tehran conference between Churchill, Roosevelt and Stalin of 28 November–1 December 1943, Stalin began to shift his ground, opposing any diversion of forces to Turkey if this would mean the postponement of Overlord, and evidently regarded the question of Turkish entry as unimportant. Nevertheless, the conference concluded that it was 'most desirable' for Turkey to enter the war by the end of the year, and fixed 14 February 1944 as the date by which it should become an active participant.[54] These proposals were put to İnönü at a second conference in Cairo with Roosevelt and Churchill on 4–6 December 1943. Before leaving for Cairo, İnönü had received the authority from his government and the party group to enter the war if need be, and had agreed to attend only on condition that there was a free discussion on Turkey's position, and not just on the basis of decisions already reached at Tehran.[55] He and his colleagues were still perturbed by possible Soviet intentions, and mistakenly believed that it was the Russians, rather than the British, who were trying to push them into the war, with the British and Americans as their unwitting tools. They noticed that Soviet representatives were conspicuous by their absence at the discussions in Cairo and were again warned by Churchill that if they failed to join the Allies they might not be supported against Russia after the war. However, they decided not to harp on their suspicions of the USSR. Instead, İnönü continued to stress Turkey's military inadequacy and the shortfall in supplies from the

British (which the British in turn denied). Turkey's participation in the war, İnönü argued, would depend on the organization of a joint Allied offensive in the Balkans. As he put it: 'What would suit Turkey best would be that she should fight side by side with British and American contingents in her own part of the world.' However, this idea ran up against the rock of opposition by the American military chiefs to any substantial diversion of resources from Overlord. They considered that if Turkey came into the war, this would 'burn up our logistics right down the line', as General Marshall maintained. Even if he did not know the details of American military misgivings on this score, İnönü realized that Roosevelt was sceptical about the idea of bringing Turkey in, and exploited this difference between the British and Americans to delay action. As he later claimed, Roosevelt 'completely understood my reluctance to bring Turkey into the war'.[56] As a result, the conference closed on an inconclusive note, with the Turks only committing themselves to accepting a military mission to discuss the preparation of the proposed air bases and reserving the right to decide by 15 February 1944 whether they would allow the Allies to use them.[57]

Not unexpectedly, the new military staff talks provided for by the Cairo decisions soon ran into the sand. Von Papen, who was well-informed about the conference proceedings through the activities of the German agent 'Cicero', Knatchbull-Hugessen's valet, made it clear to the Turks that accepting Allied aircraft on Turkish soil would mean immediate war with Germany, and was assured by Menemencioğlu on 18 December that Turkey would remain neutral. Meanwhile, on 12 December, the Turkish government duly informed the Allies that Turkey would exercise its option not to receive Allied air detachments by the target date of 15 February.[58] A military mission arrived in Ankara, but left on 4 February 1944 after making no progress, and the British decided to stop their programme of re-equipping Turkey. By the middle of the year, the Soviet government had indicated that it had lost interest in bringing Turkey into the war, and opposed the use of British or American forces in the area, which would have blocked Stalin's post-war plans for a general Soviet take-over in south-eastern Europe.[59] The British also appear to have come round to the view that there was no point in pressing for immediate Turkish entry into the war by July 1944. By October 1944, when Churchill and Stalin held their famous Moscow meeting delineating spheres of influence in eastern Europe and giving the USSR dominant shares in Bulgaria and Romania, the idea of an Allied intervention involving Turkey in south-eastern Europe that would block the Soviet Union had evidently been pushed off the agenda. Churchill decided not to pressure Turkey to join the Allies, as this would merely have provoked the USSR without any military benefit: by this stage Soviet troops were in occupation of Bulgaria anyway.[60]

While these developments certainly weakened Allied pressure on the Turks, they did not mean that they could now cut themselves out of Allied diplomacy on the war. Their recognition that the Allied victory was now just a matter of time was manifested by several internal adjustments. The first of these was the enforced retirement of Fevzi Çakmak in January 1944. At 68, the Marshal was by now well over the normal age of retirement, and he would have needed a special dispensation from the President to continue in his command. His conservative views on professional military matters were an additional reason for retiring him. Almost certainly however, his pro-German reputation played a part in the decision, which was seen as an attempt by İnönü to improve his relations with the Allies. Other decisions that evidently had the same intention were the withdrawal of the scandalous Property Tax in March 1944 and the trials of those involved in pan-Turkist activities that began two months later.[61] In May 1944, Menemencioğlu also attempted to move matters forward with the Soviet government by proposing a Turco-Soviet treaty guaranteeing the independence of the Balkan states after the war. The Soviet response was that this could only be considered if Turkey entered the war without delay – a condition that they must have known was unacceptable to the Turks. Menemencioğlu concluded that the USSR wanted Turkey to participate in the war but only if it were 'assisted' by Soviet troops who would then stay on in Turkey after the war was ended.[62] Subsequently, İnönü's attempt to placate the western Allies, and especially the British, went further when Menemencioğlu himself was forced to resign on 15 June 1944, to be succeeded as foreign minister by Hasan Saka in the following September. The immediate cause of Menemencioğlu's departure was a complaint by the British that he had allowed the passage of six armed German ships to pass through the Bosporus, in defiance of the Montreux Convention (the Turkish counterclaim was that they were 'auxiliaries', whose passage in wartime was allowed under the convention). However, the underlying reason was the conviction of the British Foreign Office, and especially Eden, that Menemencioğlu was pro-German. Whether he really was is hotly disputed. It would probably be fairer to say that the policies he had followed had throughout been endorsed by İnönü, but that the president now wanted to be seen to be making a change of course, to placate the Allies.[63]

The most contentious issues in relations between Turkey and the Allies during the spring and summer of 1944 was caused by Allied pressure on Turkey to break commercial and diplomatic relations with Germany. During the first two months of 1944, the Turks had actually increased chromite shipments to Germany, causing sharp protests from the Americans and British, and even the consideration of putting an economic blockade on Turkey. This idea was abandoned since, among other things, it would make Turkey even more dependent on the Axis. In the event, diplomatic pressure proved enough. On 20 April, Menemencioğlu announced that chromite exports to Germany would cease immediately. He took this further on 26 May, by agreeing that Turkey would reduce its shipments to Germany of other strategic materials by 50 per cent and would give preferential orders from Allied sources. The process was rounded off on 2 August when Turkey formally broke off diplomatic relations with Germany, forcing von Papen to return to Berlin to face an uncertain future.[64]

While straightforward on the surface, the process of breaking Turkish links with Germany was accompanied by serious discussion that, even at this late stage, Turkey might join the war and play an active part in the future of the Balkans. This partly derived from wishful thinking by Menemencioğlu, to the effect that it might be possible to arrange a negotiated peace between Germany and the Allies that would prevent the USSR from taking over eastern Europe. In a dinner speech on 28 February 1944, he proposed the formation of a Balkan federation, under Turkish leadership, which would mediate between Germany and 'Pan-Slavic Europe'. The idea evidently had no support in either camp and fell by the wayside. However, an alternative plan for Turkish intervention in the Balkans was aired in July 1944, as Soviet forces were poised to occupy Romania and Bulgaria. The USSR had offered to declare war on Bulgaria if Turkey did, and the US ambassador in Ankara Laurence Steinhardt was convinced that Turkey would enter the war in the near future if it received additional war materiel as well as Soviet assurances regarding Bulgaria. Nothing came of the project, however – presumably because the Allies could not meet Turkish conditions. In the event, Soviet forces occupied Bulgaria in September 1944, causing a brief panic in Turkey that it might face a combined threat from Soviet and Bulgarian expansionism, which the western Allies might not oppose. Later, however, the Turks were reassured by British attempts to establish a stable government in Greece, and recognized their common interests with Greece and Britain. Hence, they withdrew their claims to the Dodecanese in November 1944.[65]

During the final phase of the war, between February and May 1945, the focus of Turkish attention switched away from the question of participation in the war towards Turkey's position in the post-war political order and the long-feared ambitions of Stalin at the straits. In the course of the Moscow conference of October 1944, Stalin claimed that the Montreux Convention was 'unsuitable' and a 'spearhead' aimed at Russia: he could not accept a situation in which Turkey might 'grip Russian trade by the throat', he maintained.[66] Against the advice of Eden and the Foreign Office, Churchill responded that Britain would have no objection to allowing free passage for Soviet warships through the straits and that the convention was now 'inadmissible' and 'obsolete'. Stalin did not make it clear exactly what he was demanding at the straits and, in Roosevelt's absence, no decision was taken.[67] The question came back onto the agenda at the last wartime meeting of the 'Big Three' held at Yalta on 4–11 February 1945, as Stalin again raised his complaints about the Montreux Convention. Churchill again accepted the principle of revision, although he and Eden added that Turkey should be given assurances that its independence and integrity would be guaranteed (an idea that was then dropped). The conference thus ended with the conclusion that the Allies would discuss the issue further, although with no specific Soviet proposals at this stage. The Soviet side did, however, agree that it would not make any approaches to Turkey without consulting its allies, and that it would take no action likely to damage Turkey's independence and integrity.

The Soviet Union's next step came on 19 March, when Molotov told the Turkish ambassador in Moscow, Selim Sarper, that unspecified changes were needed to the Turco-Soviet treaty of 1925, which was due for renewal in November 1945. Sarper replied that Turkey wished to continue a friendly relationship with the USSR, and would consider proposals made by the Soviet side. In fact, the Turks were naturally perturbed by what might be in store. Their anxieties were reinforced by a Soviet proposal made at the end of March that the future of the straits should be discussed purely at the bilateral level between Turkey and the USSR, suggesting clearly that Stalin wished to detach the Turks from possible western support. Meanwhile, on 19 March, the Soviet government formally denounced the 1925 treaty.[68] İnönü's government was thus faced with the likelihood that Stalin would make serious demands at the straits, without knowing exactly what these would be. Meanwhile another decision taken at Yalta, to the effect that membership of the proposed United Nations would be restricted to those states that had joined the war on the Allied side before the end of February 1945 induced Turkey to take the formal step of declaring war on Germany and Japan on 23 February. Even though they were probably quite uncertain of their future in the post-war world, the Turks were clearly anxious to play a part in its international institutions.

Turkey's neutrality, 1939–45: Tactics, strategies and implications

After the war, İnönü and his supporters were naturally anxious to stress the success of their wartime policies, both to their fellow-countrymen and to the western Allies. Turkey had come through the test without having fired a shot in anger and with no loss of territory or lives. By careful diplomacy, İnönü's government had saved the country from the horrors of war that had engulfed most of the rest of Europe, and had protected Turkey's independence and territorial integrity. Turkish and western observers stressed that, whatever the policies the Allies had adopted during the war, Turkish neutrality had been in the best interests of both sides. At the time, Knatchbull-Hugessen was apparently horrified by Turkey's failure to abide by its alliance with Britain the summer of 1940, but, as Brock Milman concludes, Turkey's entry into the war after the fall of France 'would have been the height of recklessness'.[69] It would probably have meant invasion and occupation by Germany – as in the cases of Greece and Yugoslavia – which would merely have been an additional burden for the Allies and might well have resulted in eventual Soviet occupation.[70] In spite of the non-aggression pact with Germany of 1941, Turkey's basic sympathies had been with the Allies all along, it was argued.[71] This claim may not be accepted, but it is hard to deny that İnönü and his government had effectively protected Turkey's own national interests. Without doubt, Turkey's most important interest was to avoid the destruction of war, without sacrificing its independence or any of the territory it had won in 1923. In this respect, İnönü and his colleagues were entirely successful. They showed skill in bargaining with both sides and were relatively immune to propaganda or internal political penetration from either. On the principle that countries do not have permanent friends but only permanent interests, Turkish diplomacy had done a remarkably effective job.[72] Like those of other neutral states, the Turkish economy suffered from wartime shortages. These were exacerbated by poor economic and financial management by the government,[73] quite apart from the scandal of the Property Tax. However, these economic problems were as nothing compared with those that would have been produced by invasion, the probable result of joining the war on either side.

To achieve these aims, İnönü and his colleagues successfully exploited Turkey's strategic position, adopting the classic method of playing one power off against another. Turkey's military weakness was a severe handicap in facing up to prospective invasions by either Germany or Russia, since it made it very hard to protect the straits against an enemy with a modern air force and mechanized ground forces. However, İnönü turned this weakness into a diplomatic asset by stressing Turkey's military unpreparedness to the Allies, and thus heading off pressure for joining the war as well as gaining military supplies. He was also able to benefit from differences between the British and Americans on the desirability of bringing Turkey into the war. The main cause of friction between Turkey and the Allies derived from the fact that whereas they had only one identifiable enemy, Turkey faced threats from both the Axis and the USSR. For the Turks, Stalin was as menacing as Hitler. However, the Turkish government was able to turn this to its advantage by, for instance, using the German threat as a reason for not joining the war on the Allied side, and that from the USSR for not carrying out its commitments under the 1939 tripartite treaty in 1940. Similarly, the danger of an attack from Russia was used as a means of deflecting German calls for assistance in 1941. This diplomacy was aided by a substantial helping of good luck. In 1940, Hitler's failure to reach an agreement with Stalin on a carve-up of the near east between them was obviously a life-saver for Turkey. The fact that Hitler also attached more importance to invading Russia than attacking the Middle East saved Turkey from a German invasion in 1941. Since Hitler's armies became bogged down and were eventually defeated in Russia, he was unable to carry through his second plan for knocking the British out of the Middle East, which would have required both the defeat of Russia and the invasion or political subordination of Turkey. At the end of the war, the fact that it was the British and not the Soviets who occupied Greece when the Germans withdrew in 1944 saved Turkey from being surrounded by a hostile power on three sides. None of these outcomes could have been determined by Turkey, but they undoubtedly helped it to survive as an independent state.

To say that Turkey was neutral during the war also disguises important shifts in its policies between 1939 and 1945, which were largely caused by changing Turkish perceptions of which side would win the war. 'Neutrality' is a loose term and can cover the position of strict and *de jure* neutrality adopted by, say, Switzerland, and the *de facto* neutrality espoused by Turkey. Between October

1939 and June 1940, Turkey was not only an ally of Britain and France by treaty, but apparently fully expected to be able to carry out its alliance commitments. By the spring of 1941, with the signature of the non-aggression pact with Germany, it had moved to a more fully neutral position, virtually equidistant between the two camps, referred to by Menemencioğlu as 'active neutrality'. In 1943, it shifted back towards the Allies, while remaining non-belligerent. During 1943–4, Turkish leaders repeatedly told the Allies that they would be willing to join the war, but only as part of a major Allied offensive in the Balkans. Turkish anxiety to prevent Stalin taking over south-eastern Europe was undoubtedly genuine, and if the British and Americans had been willing to commit substantial forces for an invasion of the Balkans in 1943–4, it seems possible that Turkey would have done so too.[74]

While Turkish diplomacy may have been successful in keeping Turkey out of the war, it can also be argued that it ended with one significant failure, since it left the Soviet Union in a dominant position in south-eastern Europe. Throughout the war, Turkish policy-makers, Menemencioğlu in particular, had attached cardinal importance to the idea of maintaining the balance of power between Russia and its western neighbours, especially Germany, by avoiding the total destruction of German power. This had been one of the main aims of Turkish diplomacy since the nineteenth century. However, during 1939–45 it proved to be quite unattainable, thanks to the Allies commitment to secure the unconditional surrender of the enemy and Hitler's determination to fight on to the bitter end. In an age of total war, both sides, Axis and Allied, fought for total victory. Abstract principles such as the balance of power could not be used for the mobilization of total populations or in the defence of either democratic or totalitarian ideologies. Hitler was being fought because his regime was totally evil, and not just because Germany had upset the balance of power. Hence the principle of not eliminating essential national actors, which was part of the balance of power system, went out of the window. In staying out of the war, the Turks had to take the risk that the classic mechanisms of power politics would re-assert themselves afterwards and that the western powers would forget wartime alliances so as to prevent Stalin from taking over the straits, or from turning Turkey into a Soviet satellite. Apparently, in 1944, Menemencioğlu believed that this risk was worth taking, that even if Turkey stayed out of the war the western powers would still support it against Russia in a post-war confrontation.[75] His prediction turned out to be right, but at the time the war ended there was no proof that it would, and Turkey still faced a severe challenge to its hard-won security.

4 Turkey and the Cold War, 1945–63
The engagement phase

On 18 July 1945, just as the Second World War was ending and the Cold War beginning, the veteran Turkish journalist Ahmet Emin Yalman suggested in his newspaper *Vatan* that, for Turkey 'the old eastern question has risen from its grave'.[1] His verdict was quite justified to the extent that, as in the period up to 1917, Turkey's territorial integrity and its future as an independent state were gravely threatened by a resurgent Russia, and Turkey urgently needed to find allies to fend it off. On the other hand, there were significant differences between Turkey's situation during the Cold War, and that of the Ottoman Empire before 1914. In the first place, the 'old eastern question' had largely been about the future of the Balkans, but these had been lost to the Turkish state in 1912–13, and later Turkish governments never tried to re-establish their old role in the region. Internal ethnic conflict, as a leading issue in the Turks' foreign relations, did not re-emerge until the late 1980s, when the Kurdish problem became a critical factor in Turkey's relationship with the western powers and its Middle Eastern neighbours. Meanwhile, Christian–Muslim conflict in the Balkans was stilled until the disintegration of Yugoslavia in 1991.

For the Turks, the most important feature of the post-war world was its bipolarity, and the fact that the USA and USSR were the only two players who really mattered. Hence, Turkey was unable to play one European power off against another, in a fluid and usually temporary pattern of alliances and rivalries, as the Ottoman government had been able to before 1914. In effect, the range of Turkey's options was far more limited than it had been during the early period. It could not opt out of the Cold War, relying on a balance of power between the two Cold War blocs to maintain its security, like most of its Arab neighbours and other Asian and African states, without running the serious risk of Soviet aggression or political domination. Nor did it have sufficient economic, technical and military resources to protect itself if it chose neutrality. On this account, it was virtually bound to seek a place in the western alliance. The nuclearization of the potential contest, and its consequent risks, were also crucial for an exposed ally such as Turkey. The Turks were to receive a sharp lesson in the realities of this danger in 1962, although catastrophe was fortunately avoided. The effects of the perception that the Cold War was also an ideological struggle are harder to assess. In spite of the

Turkish government's repeated claims of adherence to democratic values, it is likely that this factor was less important in motivating Turkey's attachment to the western alliance than traditional territorial and security interests. Essentially, Turkey was forced into the western camp in the Cold War because it was directly threatened by the USSR, rather than through an *a priori* commitment to liberal democracy (indeed, the causal chain may well have been the other way round). On the other hand, the nature of the ideological divide did have an important effect on Turkey's foreign policy options, in that the western alliance paid reasonable respect to the independence of small or medium-sized states, whereas Soviet communism did not. This factor reinforced the effect of immediate security considerations and the historical suspicion of Russia.

The effect of its Cold War alignment on Turkey's domestic political evolution between the mid-1940s and the early 1960s is more difficult to assess, since this was very far from being an externally dependant variable. At the end of 1945, İsmet İnönü took the bold step of dismantling the single-party structure and allowing the formation of an effective opposition party. This materialized as the Democrat Party, founded by two dissidents from the Republican People's Party, Adnan Menderes and Celal Bayar. In Turkey's first free and fair elections since the foundation of the republic, held in 1950, the Democrats were swept to power, with Menderes as Prime Minister and Bayar as President. At first glance, İnönü's decision might be seen as a result of clear foreign policy interests: if Turkey was gain admission to the western alliance, then it had to make itself respectably democratic. On the other hand, it is virtually impossible to prove that it was this simple logic which determined İnönü's choice, since there were powerful domestic factors pushing him in the same direction. Nor is there any there is no clear proof that the western powers demanded democratization in Turkey as a condition of their support.[2] İnönü was willing to admit in private that foreign policy considerations had affected his decision, but this seems to have been based on the general perception that the defeat of the Axis heralded the end of dictatorship world-wide, and the victory of democracy, rather than as part of a straightforward bid to win western support in the Cold War.[3]

In the event, the Democrats' victory produced few important changes in foreign policy. If anything, Menderes and his colleagues were even more committed to the west than İnönü had been, since they shared his strategic perceptions, and reinforced this by an attachment (at least in theory) to American-style economic liberalization. In foreign policy, they were, however, weakened by sharply declining domestic popularity and economic failures in the late 1950s. This briefly inclined them to look for some new alternatives but without any significant effect. The Democrats were overthrown by a military coup on 27 May 1960, which pushed foreign policy into the background but confirmed Turkey's commitment to the west. It was not until the mid-1960s that domestic political turbulence began to have serious effects on external orientations.[4]

The construction of the western alliance, 1945–52

At the end of the Second World War, the Turks had been left with the knowledge that Stalin was likely to push for a revision of the Montreux Convention in Russia's favour, and possibly other concessions, without knowing the exact nature of his demands. Nor could they be confident that the western powers would oppose him on this issue. It soon became clear that Stalin's project was remarkably similar to the one he had unsuccessfully proposed to Hitler in November 1940 (see p61). In March 1945, the Soviet government officially denounced the Treaty of Friendship with Turkey, which it had signed in 1925. Three months later, on 7 June 1945, Molotov told Selim Sarper, the Turkish ambassador in Moscow, that in return for renewing the treaty the USSR would demand a new straits convention, negotiated solely between Turkey and the Soviet Union. This would provide for the free passage of Soviet warships through the straits and their closure to non-Black Sea states, the establishment of Soviet bases at the straits, and the retrocession to Russia of the eastern provinces of Kars and Ardahan that had been returned to Turkey in 1921 (see p36).[5] Of these proposals, the Soviet plan for the establishment of Soviet bases seemed easily the most dangerous, since it threatened the establishment of a Soviet military presence, which could have been used to secure Russian political control over the country as a whole. This expectation was reinforced when Molotov hinted that the kind of treaty relationship the USSR wanted with Turkey would be similar to those it was establishing with Poland and the other satellite states. Sarper's reply was that Turkey could not consider allowing Russia bases at the straits, or re-negotiation of the 1921 Turco-Soviet treaty (in other words, the retrocession of Kars and Ardahan). Any revision of the Montreux Convention would have to be a matter for international negotiation and agreement. At a meeting in the presidential mansion in Ankara in the spring of 1945, İnönü expressed the view that there was no immediate danger of a Soviet invasion of Turkey as the Soviet Union's losses in the war were too severe, and it also had other commitments in eastern Europe. However, in October, the Turks had second thoughts about this assumption, due to a build-up of Soviet troops in Bulgaria, and temporarily halted demobilization of their own forces.[6] Throughout, there was a real fear on the Turkish side that the USSR wanted not only to gain control of the straits but also to convert Turkey into a satellite, as it was currently doing in the eastern European countries. Contemporary Soviet attempts to take over Iranian Azerbaijan, and maybe the whole of Iran, reinforced this perception, and combined with the Soviet reinforcements in Bulgaria to create a serious war of nerves between Turkey and Russia.[7]

After the delivery of these Soviet demands, the British, who saw them as a threat to their position in the Middle East, assured the Turks of their support and encouraged them to stand firm against them. However, at this stage the United States was very reluctant to take on distant commitments such as ensuring the security of the Turkish straits.[8] Hence, western opposition to

Stalin on this issue did not become explicit at the first post-war meeting of the 'Big Three', held at Potsdam on 17 July–2 August 1945. When Stalin repeated the proposals Molotov had earlier put to Sarper, Churchill pointed out that they went well beyond what he had suggested at Yalta. President Truman then made an unexpected intervention, proposing that the straits and all other international waterways should be put under international control – a project that, if carried out, would have returned Turkey to the position it had had between 1923 and 1936 under the Lausanne Convention (see p39). Although Stalin had failed to get British or American support for the establishment of Soviet bases at the straits, the conference ended on an inconclusive note, with the proposal that the three governments, plus Turkey, would conduct separate discussions.[9] In fact, nothing came of this.

We cannot know for certain whether Stalin was actually intending to invade Turkey in 1945–6: quite probably, his preference was to isolate Turkey diplomatically and then force its rulers to accept a treaty that would give the USSR control of the straits and then of the government as a whole. As Necmeddin Sadak, later the Turkish foreign minister, claimed in an article published in 1949, 'after the occupation of the Dardanelles, the Soviet Union would demand a Communist Government at Ankara and would impose one on Turkey'.[10] Essentially, the Turks had to assure themselves of a counter-vailing force if they were to oppose Stalin successfully. Diplomatic opposition would have been pointless if it had lacked the threat of a military response. Legally, the treaty with the British of 1939 was still valid and was Turkey's only existing alliance. However, it was doubtful whether post-war Britain had the power or resources to support Turkey against Russia effectively, and the British did not wish to draw attention to it, although the Turks were happy to drop the provision that it should not involve them in war with the Soviet Union (see p52).[11] Hence, Turkey had to try to secure American assistance. Essentially, what İnönü's government had to do was: first, to make sure that the USA and the other western powers would not support the Soviet demands; second, to obtain western financial support that would make it possible to maintain the mobilization of the armed forces (which was undertaken in response to the Russian offensive); and third, if possible to construct an effective alliance with security guarantees with the west, as a long-term means of ensuring security against Soviet power.

On 2 November 1945, the United States presented a note to the Turkish government proposing an international conference to discuss the revision of the Montreux Convention, at which the US would support the principle of free passage for the warships of Black Sea powers and limited access for the fleets of non-Black Sea states (which was what, in effect, the existing convention provided for). The fact that this response excluded the proposal for the establishment of Soviet bases was the most important point from the Turkish viewpoint.[12] This secured İnönü's first objective, but left him uncertain as to whether the west would be ready to give Turkey sufficient material support to make its diplomatic stand effective. On this point, a crucial change was that, by the beginning of 1946, President Truman had been converted by Soviet actions in Iran and elsewhere to adopt a much tougher approach than he had demonstrated at Potsdam. As he wrote in a letter (that he never actually mailed) to Secretary of State James F. Byrnes on 3 January 1946:

> There isn't a doubt in my mind that Russia intends an invasion of Turkey and the seizure of the Black Sea straits to the Mediterranean. Unless Russia is faced with an iron fist and strong language another war is in the making. Only one language do they understand – 'how many divisions have you?' ... I'm tired of babying the Soviets.[13]

Truman's forecast of likely Soviet actions appeared to be born out in March 1946, as the USSR reinforced its substantial military presence in Iranian Azerbaijan, thus threatening both Iran and eastern Turkey, as well as strengthening its forces in Bulgaria that could have been used against either Turkey or Greece. An important boost to Turkish morale came on 6 April 1946, when the battleship USS *Missouri* paid a visit to Istanbul, to wide public acclaim. Originally, the *Missouri* visit had been arranged to bring home the body of the former Turkish ambassador in Washington, Mehmet Ertegün, who had died in November 1944, but it was generally accepted as an important symbol of American support for Greece and Turkey against Russia.[14] However, it was still unclear what concrete form this support would take. Meanwhile, the diplomatic tussle over the straits continued. On 7 August 1946, the USSR delivered its long-delayed response to the American note of the previous November. This merely repeated the previous Soviet demands, although without reference to Kars and Ardahan. It proposed that the regime of the straits should come under the competence of Turkey and the Black Sea powers alone, and that Turkey and the USSR should organize 'joint means of defence of the straits'. In response, the Americans reiterated their position of November 1945, adding that an attack on the straits would be 'a threat to international security', and a matter for action by the UN Security Council.[15] On 24 September 1946, the Soviets suggested to the Turks that they should hold bilateral talks, preparatory to the revision of the Montreux Convention, but were again turned down. Subsequently, on 26 October, the Soviet government informed the British that it considered that a conference to consider a new straits regime would be 'premature', suggesting that it realized that attempts to persuade either Turkey or the western powers to accept Stalin's demands would be fruitless.[16]

In the event, this turned out to be the end of official diplomatic exchanges on the issue, but neither the Turks or the western powers could have known this at the time, and the propaganda war between Turkey and Russia continued for many years to come. Since the Soviet claims had not been officially withdrawn, Stalin could have re-opened his campaign whenever he wanted to. Hence, Turkey still had to find effective means of securing its defence. Meanwhile, Britain was in dire economic straits. On 21 February 1947,

Clement Attlee's government announced that it would no longer be able to carry the burden of economic support to Greece and Turkey. Elsewhere, President Truman's resolve was strengthened by the fact that the western powers had successfully faced Stalin down over Iran in 1946, allowing the Shah's government to resume rule over Iranian Azerbaijan at the end of the year. However, Greece was still ravaged by the destruction of war, with its government facing the prospect of defeat by communist insurgents backed by Albania, Yugoslavia and Bulgaria. By this stage the British and American leaders had been convinced for more than a year that the defence of Greece and Turkey was essential for the protection of western interests in the eastern Mediterranean and the Middle East. However, this point was not widely appreciated in America, where the newly elected and Republican-dominated Congress was determined to reduce government spending. Truman decided to face the challenge by presenting the Congress and public with the grim facts, and applying for their assistance. The 'Truman Doctrine' took the form of a speech to both houses of Congress delivered on 12 March 1947, in which the President asked for approval of a $400 million aid programme to Greece and Turkey, to last until the end of June 1948. The programme was passed by large majorities in both houses during the next two months.

The launch of the 'Truman Doctrine' marked a turning point in the history of the Cold War, as well as Turkey's search for post-war security. The internal political and economic situation was far more precarious in Greece than in Turkey, and Truman laid the main emphasis on this in his address to Congress (accordingly, $300 million was to be allocated to Greece, and $100 million to Turkey).[17] However, İnönü's government was also in serious need of foreign support to continue the military expenditure needed to deter Stalin, so economic assistance was an important advantage. More importantly, Turkey's inclusion in Truman's programme was a clear signal to the USSR that the USA was prepared to make a material rather than purely symbolic contribution to the defence of Turkey. As Necmeddin Sadak explains: 'The Truman Doctrine was a great comfort to the Turkish people, for it made them feel that they were no longer isolated.'[18] Since it bolstered the Greek government against the communist insurgents, it also helped to prevent Turkey's encirclement by satellite states on three sides.

During 1948, as an additional support, Turkey began to receive Marshall Aid, and thus became a member of the OEEC (Organisation for European Economic Co-operation, later OECD or Organisation for Economic Co-operation and Development). Between then and 1950 it received around $183 million in economic aid under the European Recovery Programme, and around $200 million in military aid. Although the Turks predictably complained that this aid was insufficient and that they had been admitted to the Marshall Aid scheme only after some delay, its availability was another advantage of their developing relationship with the USA.[19] Meanwhile, with the Berlin blockade, the Cold War assumed definite shape in Europe and its institutional structures began to emerge. In March 1948, Britain, France and the Benelux countries signed the Brussels Treaty, providing for economic collaboration and mutual self-defence, with strong support from President Truman. Subsequently, in November 1948, Turkey formally submitted an unsuccessful application for inclusion in any future Atlantic Pact. The Turks welcomed the fact that the western powers were now taking joint action against the Soviet threat, but were disturbed by its prospective confinement to western Europe, since their exclusion might send a signal to Stalin that the western powers were not prepared to protect Turkey. Among various alternatives, they promoted the idea that Turkey might take the lead in forming a pro-western alliance in the Middle East, as a means of restoring British faith in Turkey as an ally. Alternatively, a Mediterranean Pact could be established, similar to the Atlantic Pact, to include Britain, France, Greece and Turkey, and with US support. However, increasing expectations that Italy would be included in the Atlantic security system severely weakened the utility of a second structure. As the Turks argued, one could not cut the Mediterranean in two. There was also some discussion of a bilateral defence agreement with the United States, but this was blocked by the fact that Congress limited US defence spending to $15 billion in 1948–9, and then to the same amount in 1949–50. Although the Joint Chiefs of Staff emphasized America's strategic interests in Greece and Turkey, Secretary of State George Marshall opposed spreading limited resources over too wide an area.[20]

Hence, the only viable alternative for Turkey, as the Turks saw it, was to seek full membership of the Atlantic alliance. Apart from the far greater degree of security that this would bring, it would also signal Turkey's acceptance as a member of the western comity of nations – an aim going right back to the Treaty of Paris of 1856. For İsmet İnönü, an important aim was that, in his words, Turkey should be accepted as a 'respected member of the civilized world'.[21] A symbol of this commitment was Turkey's application for admission to the Council of Europe, which was accepted in August 1949. This attachment later turned out to have important implications for Turkey's adherence (or, rather, non-adherence) to human rights and other democratic norms, but at the time it was welcomed by Turkey as a sign of its acceptance as a European nation.[22]

The North Atlantic Treaty, signed on 4 April 1949, formalized the new alliance, but gravely disappointed the Turks, mainly because Italy had been included but Turkey and Greece rather pointedly left out. As Necmeddin Sadak, now the Turkish foreign minister, put it to Assistant Secretary of State Dean Acheson, the Turks were still preoccupied with the unanswered question 'Will the United States fight if the Russians attack Turkey?'[23] Membership of NATO was seen by the Turks as the only means of getting a positive answer to this question, but it was held up for three years by some complex obstacles. The most important of these was that the Truman administration initially tended to see Turkey as part of the Middle East rather than Europe, and assumed that US interests in the region were minimal compared with those of Britain. Given budgetary constraints between 1948 and 1950, the US army still preferred to concentrate its resources on western Europe. The British, meanwhile, were primarily concerned with trying to prop up their own crumbling power in the Middle East, and advanced the idea that, rather than join NATO, Turkey should take part in a British-led Middle Eastern defence system. The Turks were willing to consider such arrangements, but only on condition that admission to NATO was part of the deal. Accordingly, Turkey submitted its first unsuccessful application for membership of the alliance in May 1950.

The global situation was then radically changed by the outbreak of the Korean War in the following month, as a result of which the US defence budget for 1950–1 was sharply increased to $50 billion. This relieved the administration of the need to define Turkey's strategic location. Either way, the funds were now there to incorporate the Turks and Greeks into NATO. The events in Korea also demonstrated that the threat to western security was a global one, and not confined to western Europe, bringing in the two countries as actors in a potential world war that might include the Middle East. In July 1950, a month after the start of the Korean War, the new Democrat Party government led by Adnan Menderes announced the despatch of a Turkish brigade of 5,090 men to join the UN forces, as a clear sign of its commitment to the western camp. The new Prime Minister justified this commitment by arguing: 'If, today, we remain indifferent to the aggression against South Korea who, tomorrow, will come to our rescue when our mighty neighbour attacks us?'[24] Undoubtedly, Menderes and his colleagues were mainly concerned to exploit this apt opportunity to prove Turkey's value and loyalty to the west and thus gain admission to the Atlantic alliance. Only one week after the decision to send Turkish troops to Korea, they put forward a formal request to join the alliance. Over the next two years, the Turkish brigade in Korea was rotated twice, so that by the time the war ended in July 1953, more than 25,000 Turkish soldiers had served in Korea, with more than 10 per cent falling as casualties. Although US commanders initially doubted that they were battle-worthy, they fought with great distinction and were widely admired as fierce and courageous fighters.[25]

Initially, the reaction of the US military chiefs to Turkey's application to NATO was cautious. In September 1950, they were still only willing to offer Greece and Turkey associate membership of the alliance, with full membership as an eventual goal. Not surprisingly, the Turks turned down this prospect of second-class citizenship in the alliance. At the same time, the NATO Council of Ministers rejected a second application by Turkey for membership, saying that Turkey and Greece should merely be asked to participate in planning for the defence of the Mediterranean.[26] Shortly afterwards, however, a crucial change in US strategic thinking was effected by Dwight Eisenhower, as Supreme Allied Commander in Europe (SACEUR). As Eisenhower explained it in a message to Truman in January 1951, he saw Europe as shaped like a bottleneck, with Russia the wide part, central Europe the neck, and Spain the end. If Russia tried to move forward in the central bottleneck, then the western powers should attempt to hold it there, but also hit the wide part of the bottle hard from both flanks, using air and sea power. Turkey and Yugoslavia were essential to this strategy, as the main anti-Soviet countries on the southern flank. In the regional security context, Turkey would be vital to help repel a Bulgarian attack on Greece, but could not be expected to do so unless it were given a firm security commitment by the western powers.[27] Elsewhere, the engagement of Chinese troops in Korea in November 1950 suggested that the Soviet Union might strike anywhere – for instance, by launching an attack through one of its satellites on either Greece or Yugoslavia, following Tito's break with Stalin. At the end of a conference of US Chiefs of Mission in Istanbul and discussions with President Bayar in February 1951, George McGhee, then Assistant Secretary of State for the Near East, South Asia and Africa, urged the State Department that the US should give renewed attention to the admission of Greece and Turkey to NATO. Secretary of State Dean Acheson was converted to this view in late March 1951. Various alternatives, such as a series of bilateral pacts between the United States and the two countries, or some other multilateral arrangements between the US, Turkey, Britain and Greece, were considered less straightforward or effective.[28]

Fortunately for the Turks, Truman was convinced by these arguments, and in May 1951 decided to press for the admission of Greece and Turkey as full members of NATO. This left the Americans with the task of winning over the other NATO allies. Of these, British objections were the most troublesome, since Britain attempted to make Turkish admission to NATO dependent on Turkish agreement to put Turkish troops under British command in the event of war, as part of the plan for a Middle East Command that it was unsuccessfully trying to negotiate with Egypt.[29] The Scandinavian member countries, Norway and Denmark, also resisted the plan to admit Greece and Turkey since they were worried that this might drag them into a war in the Middle East, in which they had no interests. However, on 18 July 1951, the new British Foreign Secretary, Herbert Morrison, publicly announced a change of policy by Britain and supported the admission of Greece and Turkey to NATO. In response, Menderes' Foreign Minister Fuat Köprülü told the Turkish parliament on 20 July that if Turkey were admitted to NATO, then it would take on an unspecified defence role in the Middle East. At the meeting of the NATO Council of Ministers held in Ottawa in September 1951, the Americans were able to overcome objections from the other allies, and the Council eventually approved the plan unanimously. In particular, the British proposal that Turkey should be admitted to NATO only if it agreed to be part of the proposed Middle East Command as a prior condition was overruled by the Americans, although the Turks did agree to discuss the proposal after their admission. Arguments then followed as to how the new members could be fitted into the NATO structure, as a result of which it was decided that their ground forces would come under NATO's Southern Command. The Turks clung resolutely and successfully to this arrangement since, as Ekavi Athanassopoulou puts it, 'Ankara's wish for Turkey to be considered European and not Middle

Eastern was all-pervasive in the minds of the Turkish cabinet members'.[30] The Americans supported the Turks on this issue and again carried the day over the British. On this basis the extension of the alliance was officially approved at a meeting of the North Atlantic Council in Lisbon in February 1952. After six years, Turkish post-war policy had finally realized its paramount objective.[31]

In retrospect, the process of transition to full membership of the western alliance could be seen as Turkey's most important foreign policy change since the 1920s. On the Turkish side, the reasons for it are not hard to identify: the problem for the Turkish government was not to convince itself or its own people that they needed an alliance with the west but to convince the western powers that they needed Turkey. The end of the war had brought about a dramatic change in Turkey's strategic environment, which made the continuation of neutrality, or uninvolved dependence on the balance of power to maintain Turkey's security, a defunct option. Russian power was now resurgent, extending to the Bulgarian frontier in the west and Transcaucasia in the east. The possibility of a communist takeover in Greece also continued until the end of the Greek civil war in 1949. In eastern and central Europe, Germany and Austria had been eliminated as balancing powers. The Soviet threat was a clear and blunt one, which obliged Turkey to seek a western alliance. As Nikita Khrushchev later put it, Beria and Stalin 'succeeded in frightening the Turks right into the open arms of the Americans'.[32] Under previous conditions, Turkey would have been wary of accepting an alliance – including, as it did, the establishment of NATO air and naval bases on Turkish soil – for fear that this would convert it into a satellite of its allies. Such criticisms were later to surface during the 1960s, but were virtually absent at the time. Had the western alliance been led by Britain and France, the old imperialist powers, Turkey would probably have been chary of joining it, but the leadership of the United States, which was seen as being genuinely committed to protecting the independence of small states, convincingly overcame such objections.

On the western side, the reality of the Soviet threat, and Turkey's vital strategic situation, plus the solidity of the Turkish response, defeated suspicions about Turkey's commitment or reliability. For the western powers, Turkey was an 'unsinkable aircraft carrier'.[33] As an internal Foreign Office memorandum concluded in April 1948, 'there will be no neutrality for Turkey in any next war, and … the Turks recognise that they cannot play their old game'.[34] Like his tsarist predecessors, Stalin was not only threatening Turkey, but also western security in the Mediterranean and Middle East, so there was a strong confluence of western and Turkish interests. It may be argued that Stalin did not have inherently aggressive intentions against Turkey, but was merely seeking to strengthen the security of his own country. However, as the Turks and their allies saw it, absolute security for the USSR meant absolute insecurity for its neighbours.[35] At the same time, Turkish views about the shape of the alliance were much closer to those of the USA than those of Britain. Hence, Turkey was able to exploit America's dominant role among the western powers to its advantage. Domestically, Kemalist nationalism still had an almost exclusive hold over public opinion and pro-Soviet sympathies were virtually non-existent. A fellow-travelling Turkish Socialist Worker's and Peasant's Party was re-established in 1946, but, like the Turkish Communist Party originally set up in 1920, it was banned within a few months and had no internal underground support structure.[36] Hence, Turkey's attachment to the western alliance was far more straightforward than in the cases of, say, Greece or Iran, where Soviet power was trying to expand through internal penetration rather than threats of external aggression. In spite of the transition to multi-party politics in 1945–6, and the victory of the Democrats in the 1950 elections, there was virtually no disagreement about the main lines of foreign policy, which survived the transformation in domestic politics virtually unscathed. The only point of conflict was Turkey's participation in the Korean War – the first occasion on which Turkish troops had been sent abroad since the foundation of the republic. The decision was criticized by the Republican People's Party, now in opposition, on the grounds that parliament had not been consulted. It appears, however, that this derived from Menderes' tactics of presenting the move as a *fait accompli,* rather than opposition to the decision as such by İnönü. Participation in the Korean War was widely supported by the Turkish press, and apparently by public opinion generally.[37] In the existing climate, foreign policy was almost lifted out of Turkish internal political debates for more than a decade.

Alliance engagement and regional conflicts, 1952–60

During the 1950s and early 1960s, Turkey's commitment to and engagement with the western alliance was at its height. Admittedly, Soviet policies softened after the death of Stalin in 1953, but this had little effect on Turkish attitudes, since the Democrat Party government simply refused to believe that the supposed change of heart was genuine.[38] Nikita Khrushchev and his successors sought to replace confrontation with the west in the European theatre to Soviet support for what was now known as the Third World, where it was hoped that a pro-Soviet 'correlation of forces' would steadily undermine western power and influence. This merely changed the nature of the Turkish perception of the Soviet threat rather than removing it, since politically the Turks saw themselves as part of the First World rather than the Third. They were now perturbed not just by the Soviet military presence on their north-western and north-eastern borders (which was still there) but also by growing Soviet political penetration to their south, in the Middle East. Shifting patterns in the Balkans, especially Yugoslavia, were also a source of concern. Although relations with the western governments were not always entirely harmonious, Turkey had no other foreign policy interests that clearly conflicted with those of the main western powers, so the alliance seems to have been perceived as firm on both sides.

In May 1953, shortly after Stalin's death, the Soviet government publicly declared that it had withdrawn its claims to Kars and Ardahan, and that it did not have 'any kind of territorial claims on Turkey' (although it was not clear that it was dropping all its demands for a reform of the straits regime). Menderes' government accepted this 'with satisfaction', but made no further move to pick up the olive branch.[39] When the original term of the Montreux convention expired in November 1956, it was considered to have been automatically renewed, since none of the signatories had officially applied for its abrogation or amendment. Early in 1958, when Turkey was in serious economic difficulties, a delegation was sent to Moscow to sound out the Soviets on obtaining economic aid, but nothing came of this, and Turkey was later bailed out by an IMF rescue package.[40] There was another sign of a thaw in the Turkish attitude early in 1960, when it was announced that Menderes and Khrushchev would exchange official visits, but Menderes' government was overthrown by a *coup d'état* on 27 May 1960, before this could be accomplished. On 28 June 1960, Khrushchev wrote to General Cemal Gürsel, the head of the then military junta, proposing that Turkey should opt for neutrality, and suggesting that the two sides should hold talks on points which they had in common. This marked a change in Soviet policy, which was now demanding the neutralization (sometimes referred to as the 'Finlandization') of Turkey rather than its effective conversion into a satellite. However, Gürsel failed to respond, apparently because he wished to convince the western powers that the change of regime in Turkey did not herald any weakening of its commitment to the west.[41] Both the military government, and the civilian administration under İsmet İnönü that took over in November 1961, later turned down a $500 million aid programme from the USSR, since they feared that Moscow would demand political concessions in return. İnönü was also quick to allay suspicions that he might have a more neutralist policy than his military predecessors.[42]

Meanwhile, Turkish integration with western defence structures, and the western military presence in Turkey, developed apace during the 1950s. Three-quarters of Turkey's land forces were reserved for NATO purposes, under the Commander-in-Chief of Allied Forces, Southern Europe (CINCSOUTH) who was based in Naples, while the air force and navy were assigned to SACEUR. Under a series of bilateral and secret agreements, important US-cum-NATO facilities were constructed in Turkey including, most notably, an air base at İncirlik, near Adana, with other bases at Karamürsel, Çiğli and Diyarbakır, and radar stations at Karamürsel, Sinop, Samsun, Trabzon, Belbaşı and Diyarbakır. Naval facilities and storage centres were established at İskenderun (Alexandretta) and Yumurtalık. The US Air Force stationed strike aircraft armed with tactical nuclear weapons on Turkish soil, under an agreement reached in 1957, and by the late 1960s there were about 24,000 US military personnel on Turkish territory. US aid, equipment and training were also instrumental in modernizing the armed forces and in propping up the Turkish economy. Total delivered military assistance to Turkey between 1948 and 1964 came to $2,271 million, plus $328 million in deliveries of surplus equipment. Meanwhile, economic aid to Turkey between 1950 and 1962 totalled around $1,380 million, of which the vast majority came from the USA. To put these figures into context, Turkey's annual average exports during the 1950s came to around $320 million, and its annual imports to around $400 million. Almost certainly, Turkey would have found it virtually impossible to maintain a fairly high rate of economic growth during the 1950s (which it did) and greatly strengthen its defences at the same time, without this assistance.[43]

For the Turks, and especially for those who opposed Menderes, a worrying question was whether the US engagement with Turkey might include an American commitment to protect its government if it were threatened by internal opposition, in accordance with the 'Eisenhower Doctrine' proclaimed in 1957. The signature of a wide-ranging security agreement with the US in the spring of 1959 that, among other things, stated that the US would come to the aid of the Turkish government in the case of 'direct or indirect aggression' heightened these anxieties. Immediately after the coup that overthrew Menderes in May 1960, those responsible were worried that the deposed premier might have had some sort of secret agreement with the US to restore him to power in such an eventuality, and were heartily relieved when the western powers, as well as the USSR, rapidly recognized their new regime.[44] However, it was only at the end of the 1950s that such fears began to re-emerge: for the most part, later commentators were able to look back on the decade as a 'golden era' in relations between Turkey and the NATO powers.[45]

During the 1950s, Turkey was also engaged in two unsuccessful projects to extend western defence structures to the Balkans and the Middle East. The first of these invited comparison with the Balkan pact of 1934, but it was more limited in scope – being restricted from the start to Turkey, Greece and Yugoslavia – and was constructed in a situation in which the potential enemy, the USSR, was already in control of most of the region. However, as in the previous case, Italian participation was effectively excluded thanks to Italy's dispute with Yugoslavia over Trieste. On the other hand, the Turkish–Greek entente established in 1930 continued during the post-war years, thanks to both countries' alignment against the perceived Soviet threat, and their joint campaign to gain admission to NATO. In 1947, as part of the peace treaty with Italy, Turkey agreed to the transfer of the Dodecanese to Greece (a move it had accepted in principle in 1944) and it was agreed that the demilitarization applied in the other Greek Aegean islands under the Lausanne treaty would equally be applied in the case of the Dodecanese. Given that a large majority of the population of the islands was Greek, Turkey was in no position to oppose the transfer, even if it had wanted to.[46] Yugoslavia, however, occupied a more problematic position since, following Tito's break with Stalin in 1948, the United States became perturbed by the possibility of a Soviet invasion of the country. With US encouragement, Turkey and Greece began discussions with the Yugoslav government, which resulted in the signature of an Agreement on Friendship and Cooperation signed on 28 February 1953. This was, however, limited in scope and merely obliged the signatories to consult with one another on matters of common interest and to engage in military discussions.

The Balkan alignment did not become an alliance until 9 August 1954, when a Balkan Defence Pact was signed in Bled between the three countries. The pact declared that an attack on any of the signatories would be counted as an attack on all of them and that they would immediately take all measures, including the use of armed force, for their common defence. If it had been carried through, the pact would have had the effect of bringing Yugoslavia under the NATO umbrella, without making it a full member of the alliance. However, it became a dead letter almost as soon as it was signed. In 1955, Khrushchev made his peace with Tito, and thus removed the pact's main *raison d'être*. Tito later became one of the leaders of the non-aligned movement, whose earliest origins were supposedly marked by the Bandung conference of April 1955. At the same time, the Cyprus problem began to occupy a dominant position on the Greek foreign policy agenda, making it more difficult to follow a cooperative policy with Turkey. Hence, the second Balkan pact fell by the wayside even more quickly than the first.[47]

Turkey's other main foreign policy concern at the time was the Middle East, and was originally derived from British and American policies. During the early 1950s, the British wished to reduce their direct military presence in the region, signalled by the agreement with Egypt of October 1954 under which British troops were withdrawn from the Suez Canal zone. As a replacement, Britain wished to build up a Middle Eastern alliance system that would buttress the western and especially the British position. On the American side, John Foster Dulles, as Secretary of State in the Eisenhower administration from the beginning of 1953, aimed to construct a defensive chain to contain the USSR along its southern borders. British and American plans did not entirely coincide, since the British favoured incorporation of the core Arab countries, among whom British influence had traditionally been stronger, while the Americans put the main emphasis on the 'northern tier' of states that bordered the Soviet Union – that is, primarily Turkey and Iran. Either way, Turkey was seen as an essential participant in the project, since it was judged to be the strongest regional state militarily and was clearly committed to the west through NATO. For their part, the Turks had publicly announced in 1951 that they would take on a defence role in the Middle East if they were admitted to NATO. Apart from this commitment, they were also unlikely to oppose a project that enhanced Turkey's apparent value to the west and thus increased the chances of overall western support for Turkey. It appears, in fact, that at the outset Menderes had no clear-cut policy towards the Middle East, but wished to participate in western defence structures as fully as possible and to achieve economic and military aid additional to Turkey's entitlement as a member of NATO.[48]

During 1952–3, discussions took place regarding the possible formation of a 'Middle East Defence Organization' (MEDO), but these came to nothing since, among other things, the Arab states regarded the idea of cooperation with Turkey with grave suspicion. Apart from individual points of conflict, such as Syrian hostility over the annexation of Alexandretta by Turkey in 1939, Arab opinion tended to have a suspicious attitude towards the Turks, as the former masters of the Arab lands, and resented Turkish support for western policies on Palestine. Although Turkey had voted with the Arab states against the UN resolution partitioning Palestine in November 1947, it had recognized the state of Israel in 1949 and the two countries exchanged ambassadors at the end of that year. After the establishment of the state of Israel, around 62,000 Turkish Jews emigrated to Israel, leaving around 20,000–25,000 in Turkey today. In spite of the persecution that some of them had recently suffered, notably the infamous Capital Tax of 1942–4 (see p67), most of the emigrants retained links with Turkey and supported good relations between the two countries.[49] Meanwhile, the Israelis were anxious to develop the relationship as a way of breaking out of their diplomatic isolation in the Middle East, and because they thought it would give them a window to the Arab-Muslim world. Economic relations between Turkey and Israel also grew apace during the early 1950s.[50] However, once the Egyptians had signed an agreement with the British in 1954, the Menderes government became far more hopeful of negotiating an alliance with the main Arab states, especially Egypt.[51] The construction of a western-backed pact structure began in April–May 1954, with the signature of a Mutual Defence Assistance Agreement between Pakistan and the United States, and a 'Treaty of Friendly Co-operation' between Turkey and Pakistan. Meanwhile, Iraq signed a military assistance agreement with the US, and on 24 February 1955 it concluded the Baghdad pact with Turkey 'for their mutual security and their defence'. How this was to be achieved was left for later detailed arrangements. Turkey played a major role in bringing Iraq into the pact, which Menderes evidently saw as an important way of increasing Turkey's security along its southern borders and of enhancing Turkey's value to the west as an ally. He also managed to overcome Iraqi suspicions that the pact might be a cover for Turkish territorial ambitions in Mosul.[52] Britain joined the pact on 4 April, since the British knew that their existing security agreement with Iraq, which provided for two British air bases on Iraqi soil, was due to expire in 1957: hence, they needed this new agreement to help maintain their influence in the country. Pakistan acceded to the pact in September 1955, and Iran the following month. The five pact members met in Baghdad in November 1955, and set up a Council of Ministers and special committees for military planning, economic planning and counter-subversion. The United States never officially became a signatory, since the State Department still wished to preserve whatever chance there was of working with non-member Arab countries, such as Egypt and Saudi Arabia, and did not want to provoke Israel. Nonetheless, it was clear from the start that Washington was the principle paymaster and promoter of the project.[53]

The launch of the Baghdad pact provoked a storm of protest in the rest of the Arab world, especially Egypt, where the Iraqi government of Nuri al-Said was berated for having joined the western camp and having betrayed the Arabs in their common campaign against Zionism. Turkish attempts to persuade or pressure Syria and the Lebanon were quite unavailing and in Jordan

King Hussein nearly lost his throne in an upsurge of protest against possible Jordanian adherence to the pact. More broadly, the Suez crisis of 1956 caused fatal damage to British power in the Middle East, and hence to the Baghdad Pact concept, leaving the pro-western Middle Eastern states in a severely exposed position. Initially, the Menderes government strongly condemned President Nasser's nationalization of the Suez Canal. Later, however, it reluctantly fell in line with the United States, as its more powerful ally, in calling for an Anglo-French withdrawal from the canal zone. Meanwhile, the four regional members of the pact, pointedly excluding Britain, held a meeting in Tehran in November 1956, at which they strongly criticized the Anglo-French invasion of the canal zone and called for the withdrawal of Israeli forces from all Egyptian territory. According to contemporary reports, Menderes was instrumental in persuading the other pact members not to eject Britain from the organization.[54] The final blow to the Baghdad pact, in its original shape, came in July 1958, when a revolutionary *coup d'état* in Iraq overthrew Nuri and the pro-western Hashemite regime. Although a meeting of the other Baghdad pact states, meeting in London shortly afterwards, declared that 'the need which called the Pact into being is greater than ever',[55] it was clear that it could not survive in its original form. The headquarters and secretariat of the alliance were moved from Baghdad to Ankara in October 1958, and Iraq formally withdrew from it in March 1959.[56]

In August 1959, the remains of the Baghdad Pact were reconstructed as a purely northern tier alliance of Britain, Turkey, Iran and Pakistan, with the United States continuing its observer status, known as the Central Treaty Organization (CENTO). Like the Baghdad pact, CENTO suffered from serious structural weaknesses, since it had no centralized military command structure comparable to that of NATO, and amounted to little more than a pledge of mutual assistance in the event of aggression against one of the members (implicitly, by the USSR). Probably, the main value of CENTO in the eyes of its Middle Eastern members was that it gave them institutional mechanisms for obtaining arms and financial aid from the United States. As in the case of the Saadabad pact of 1937, the geographical dispersion and disparity of its members robbed it of much effective force as a defence organization. Since three quarters of Turkey's ground forces were allocated to NATO, it would have had little to spare to counter a Soviet attack on Iran, whose own forces were weak. Pakistan's adherence made little difference, since its main concern was to win American military aid and diplomatic support against India, and it had little interest in or capacity for military involvement in the Middle East. However, none of the members had any serious disputes with one another, so the organization officially survived until the Iranian revolution gave it the final death blow in 1979. Meanwhile, in 1964, the three member states had also attempted to give their relationship a stronger economic dimension by setting up an organization for 'Regional Cooperation and Development' (RCD). Here again, however, the effects were limited as the three countries had few economic synergies: essentially the linkage was a purely political one, with not much military or economic depth.[57]

While the story of the Baghdad pact is well known in outline, there is some doubt about what Turkey's attitude towards it was, or how seriously the Turks took the idea of regional collaboration. At the outset, it seems that the government was quite cynical about the idea of cooperation with the Middle Eastern nations. In March 1953, Dulles visited Ankara for discussions on the proposed Middle East Defence Organization. According to George McGhee, now the US ambassador in Ankara, Dulles was told by President Celal Bayar that he 'pledged to go forward with the efforts to build MEDO, if that were the policy of Turkey's allies, despite the belief that it would be a wasted effort'. Other evidence suggests that, at this stage, the Turks did not rate the value or practicality of a Middle East defence pact highly.[58] On the other hand, it appears that Turkey later took the lead in forming the pact with Iraq in 1955, and that the Turks were energetic, if quite unsuccessful, in trying to sell the project to Syria, Lebanon and Jordan. Menderes had apparently genuinely hoped for a more positive response from the Arab countries, and underestimated their antipathy to the west. In fact, the American and British governments were quite perturbed by Turkey's tough and threatening approach to the Syrians and Jordanians – which included, for instance, warning Syria that if it went ahead with the evolving security pact with Egypt then Turkey might break diplomatic relations with Damascus, and telling the Jordanian government that if it failed to join the Baghdad pact, and Jordan were then at war with Israel, then it might find the Turks fighting on the opposite side.[59] After the Suez fiasco, the US tried to fill the apparent power vacuum in the Middle East when Eisenhower launched his version of numerous presidential 'doctrines' in January 1957, pledging US support and the readiness to use US forces to protect any Middle Eastern state 'requesting such aid against overt armed aggression from any nation controlled by international communism'. The 'Eisenhower doctrine' was used to justify US support to King Hussein in his clash with internal pan-Arabist opponents in April 1957 and the landing of US marines in Beirut in Lebanon's incipient civil war in July 1958.[60]

By this stage, it appears that Adnan Menderes had a more Dullesian-than-Dulles phobia regarding the dangers of communist penetration in the Middle East, and that his western allies had to restrain him from taking a more aggressive stance in the region. During August and September 1957, there was a widespread belief in Washington and Ankara that Syria was in grave danger of takeover by local communists, met by Soviet complaints that the west was plotting to encourage its local allies to attack the country. Soviet arms deliveries to Egypt and Syria after the Suez war also alarmed both the Americans and the Turks. At the height of the crisis, Turkey massed troops on its southern border and, according to a contemporary Foreign Office report, it 'seems to have considered "going it alone" over Syria', although this would obviously have justified and strengthened the Soviet position.[61] In response, Khrushchev had threatened that if the crisis resulted in war, Turkey would not last 'even a single day'. Although the State Department emphasized that if Turkey were attacked, the US would carry out its defence commitments to the Turks 'with all its power', it appears that the British and Americans were gravely perturbed by Turkey's apparently aggressive attitude to Syria and feared that it might provoke a Soviet attack on Turkey that could lead to a full scale conflict between the two superpowers. Unexpectedly, the crisis ended with a change of course by the unpredictable Khrushchev.[62] On 29 October 1958, the Soviet leader attended a reception at the Turkish embassy in Moscow to celebrate the anniversary of the foundation of the Turkish republic, where he declared that 'there was no threat to the Middle East at all and that the whole affair had been misunderstood'.[63] Khrushchev's apparent decision to switch to something like a peace offensive with Turkey failed to pay any immediate dividends in his relations with the Menderes government, but it did at least defuse the crisis, and Turkey withdrew its troops.

In 1958, Turkey supported the American intervention in Lebanon, allowing the use of the İncirlik air base in support, although the operation was quite clearly outside its NATO remit. Immediately after the Iraqi revolution of July 1958, it also appears that Menderes strongly urged military intervention by Turkey to restore the previous pro-western regime, although whether he was overruled by his own generals on grounds of military impracticality, or by American pressure, is unclear.[64] In the aftermath of the revolution, the Israeli Prime Minister, David Ben Gurion, paid an unannounced visit to Turkey in August 1958, and Turkey and Israel agreed to a secret 'Periphery Pact' designed to link Israel, Turkey, Iran and Ethiopia. Apparently, this would have provided for Israeli technical and military assistance to Turkey, although whether it would also have involved Turkish military support for Israel in the event of another Arab–Israeli war is unclear. Apparently the alliance – if such it was – came to nothing and was certainly dropped after Menderes was overthrown in 1960.[65] What seems certain is that Menderes had been an enthusiastic supporter of the Baghdad pact project and was gravely upset by its failure. In fact, it is even suggested that he feared he might meet the same fate as the Iraqi King Faisal II and Prime Minister Nuri al-Said, who were murdered by the revolutionaries.[66] Overall, the idea that Turkey engaged in the Middle East purely as the servant of western interests, rather than on its own initiative, appears hard to sustain unreservedly.

During the second half of the 1950s, Turkey also became involved in another regional conflict that was to become one of its main foreign policy preoccupations in subsequent decades. Following the recognition of British rule in Cyprus in 1878 (see p22), Britain had formally annexed the island in 1914, and this annexation was recognized by Turkey under the Treaty of Lausanne in 1923. During the Lausanne negotiations, İsmet İnönü neglected to bring up the Cyprus question, for fear that this would make the British more intransigent over the abolition of the capitulations. While it would not be true to say that Turkey was entirely unconcerned about events in Cyprus between then and the 1950s, it does appear that both the Turkish government and the Turkish Cypriots, numbering about 20 per cent of the population, were broadly prepared to accept British rule, since this was seen as the best available alternative to *enosis*, or union with Greece, and an assurance of reasonably fair treatment of the Turkish community. Similarly, successive Greek governments refused to support the movement for *enosis,* out of a desire not to alienate the British.[67] Concern for the future of Cyprus only began after the pro-*enosis* movement began to gain momentum among the Greeks, both in Greece and in Cyprus, in the mid-1950s.

The dispute came into the international arena in September 1954, when Greece submitted its case unsuccessfully to the United Nations. In 1955, as the underground Greek terrorist organization EOKA began its campaign of violence on the island, the British called a conference in London with representatives of the Greek and Turkish governments. A plan providing for a measure of self-government under continued British sovereignty, with separate representation for the Greek and Turkish Cypriots was discussed, without agreement. In negotiations with the Iraqi Prime Minister Nuri al-Said over the proposed Baghdad pact in January 1955, Menderes expressed a clear preference for the continuation of British rule in Cyprus.[68] However, at the London conference, the Turkish foreign minister Fatin Rüştü Zorlu took the line that if British sovereignty were to end, then the whole island should revert to Turkey. Later, in 1956, the Turkish government shifted its position to pushing for partition, under which separate Greek and Turkish halves of the island would be transferred to Greek and Turkish sovereignty respectively. Apparently, this idea had originally been suggested by the British.[69] In general, the British encouraged Turkish resistance to *enosis*. As the Prime Minister Sir Anthony Eden later wrote: 'I regarded our alliance with Turkey as the first consideration in our policy in that part of the world.'[70] It also appears that Menderes built up Turkish protests as a means of distracting attention from his domestic failures. A shameful example of this occurred during the London conference of 1955, when demonstrations in Istanbul, which were apparently originally orchestrated by the government, got out of hand. A riotous mob looted or destroyed Greek (and some non-Greek) property in the city, persuading most Istanbuli Greeks to leave for Greece.[71] However, it would be quite wrong to argue that Turkish resistance to *enosis* was just artificial, or purely concocted by either the British or Menderes. Within Turkey, there was a good deal of real concern for the future of the Turkish Cypriots – probably more than on other foreign policy issues – and genuine resentment that the pro-*enosis* case virtually ignored their existence.[72] Apart from considerations of national honour and prestige, it was also argued that *enosis* would fundamentally change the strategic balance between Greece and Turkey in the Mediterranean, allowing Greece to surround Turkey on two sides. On these grounds, some Turks suggested that Turkey would have opposed *enosis* even if there had been no ethnic Turks on the island.[73]

Between 1956 and 1958, a series of plans for local self-government in Cyprus were put forward by the British government, but all foundered on the rock of Greek opposition, since the British would not yet concede the principle of sovereignty. Meanwhile, a full-scale revolt was mounted by EOKA. Archbishop Makarios, the political as well as religious leader of the Greek Cypriots, was first interned by the British in the Seychelles in March 1956, and then released in April 1957. By 1958, the struggle was assuming the shape of a Greek–Turkish civil war, rather than just a fight between the Greeks and the British. The turning point came at the beginning of 1959, when the British had recognized that they did not need to retain sovereignty over the whole of Cyprus to meet their aim of maintaining a strategic military base in the eastern Mediterranean. Initially, the Menderes government favoured the establishment of a federal state on the island, but then realized that the Greeks would reject this as a disguised form of partition. Equally, the Greek government conceded that *enosis* would be firmly opposed by both the British and the Turks. Hence, the Greek and Turkish governments came round to accepting the principle of an independent Cyprus, with a power-sharing constitution, as an alternative to either *enosis* or partition. An agreement along these lines was hammered out at a meeting between Menderes and Constantine Karamanlis, the Greek Prime Minister, in Zürich on 5–10 February 1959. It was accepted by the British government, the political leader of the Turkish Cypriots Dr Fazıl Küçük and, much more reluctantly, by the Archbishop, at a conference in London later that month.[74] At the time, Menderes described the London and Zürich agreements as neither a victory nor a defeat for Turkey, but as 'a compromise which was not against Turkey's national interests and which respected the other party's rights and interests'.[75]

The Cypriot constitution, based on the Zürich and London agreements, was issued in April 1960, and paved the way for the proclamation of the independent Republic of Cyprus in August of that year. It provided that the President of the republic would be a Greek Cypriot, and the Vice-President a Turkish Cypriot, both elected by their respective communities, and assisted by a cabinet in which there to be seven Greek ministers and three Turks. The President and Vice-President would have 'separately or jointly' the right of veto in matters affecting foreign affairs, defence and security. The legislature, of 50 members, would be divided between Greek and Turkish representatives in a 70–30 per cent ratio with simple majority voting, except that laws relating to municipalities or imposing taxes would require separate majorities of both the Greek and Turkish members. The civil service was to be divided in the same ratio, and there were to be separate Communal Chambers governing religious affairs, education, culture and personal status cases, as well as separate municipalities in Greek and Turkish areas. The constitution was accompanied by a Treaty of Establishment between Cyprus and Britain, providing for two base areas under British sovereignty in the south of the island, at Dhekelia and Akrotiri. A second treaty between Greece, Turkey and Cyprus provided for the stationing of 950 Greek and 650 Turkish troops on the island.

Under a Treaty of Guarantee, which was signed as part of the 1960 package between Cyprus, Britain, Greece and Turkey, the four states undertook to 'prohibit, so far as concerns them, any activity aimed at promoting, directly or indirectly, either union of Cyprus with any other State or partition of the Island' and guaranteed the independence of Cyprus and 'the state of affairs established by the Basic Articles of its constitution' (Article 2). Equally, under Article 1 of the treaty the Cyprus government promised 'not to participate, in whole or in part, in any political or economic union with any State whatsoever'. Finally, and most crucially, Article 4 of the treaty provided that if its provisions were violated, the three governments would consult with one another, but that: 'In so far as common or concerted action may not be possible each of the three guaranteeing Powers reserves the right to take action with the sole aim of re-establishing the state of affairs created by the present Treaty.'[76] For the Turkish side these provisions, while extremely complicated, seemed quite acceptable, since they gave it a guarantee against *enosis* and protection of the Turkish Cypriot community. On these grounds, Menderes' government could feel satisfied with the settlement even though it remained to be seen whether the Greek and Turkish Cypriots, or the two mainland governments, would be ready or able to make it work.

Turkey and the missile crisis, 1961–3

During 1960–1, the political attentions of most Turks and their western allies were almost entirely turned to domestic affairs, as the military first overthrew Adnan Menderes' government in May 1960, and then set about trying to reconstruct Turkish politics, at the cost of serious conflict within their ranks. Civilian government was eventually restored after general elections in October 1961, when an unstable coalition under İsmet İnönü was established.[77] Meanwhile, foreign policy failed to attract much more than passing attention. The Cyprus situation seemed to have stabilized, following the settlement of 1960. As already noted (p89), the military regime dropped Menderes' brief and inconclusive reconciliation with the USSR, turning down Soviet advances and confirming its loyalty to NATO and CENTO. Behind the scenes, however, decisions were being taken that were to project Turkey into a major international crisis in 1962.

In October 1959, the Menderes government had agreed with the Eisenhower administration that 15 Jupiter intermediate range missiles, armed with nuclear warheads, would be installed on Turkish territory. These were not the first nuclear weapons to appear in Turkey, since US aircraft armed with tactical nuclear weapons had been operating from Turkey for some time, but they significantly enhanced Turkey's potential role in a nuclear war. Although some members of the Turkish foreign ministry opposed the installation of the Jupiters on the grounds that they might provoke an attack by the USSR, they were overruled by the government and senior military commanders. The latter believed that the Jupiters would enhance Turkey's military strength, as a symbol of the alliance's readiness to use atomic weapons against any Soviet attack on Turkey. They were encouraged in this belief by the US military, since General Lauris Norstad, as SACEUR, stressed their military value in conversations with the Turks. The missiles were installed at a base near İzmir in the autumn of 1961, although they did not become operational until the spring of 1962. They were owned by Turkey, but the US retained custody of the warheads, and they could only be used with joint permission of the US and Turkish governments. Together with two similar squadrons of Jupiters deployed in Italy, they were targeted on 45 of the 129 Soviet medium and intermediate range missiles aimed at Europe.[78]

As early as 1959, the planned deployment of Jupiters in Turkey had been the subject of complaints by Khrushchev to Vice-President Richard Nixon. The Soviet leader repeated these protests publicly in May 1962. It is even suggested that he may have decided to install Soviet missiles in Cuba in retaliation for the Turkish Jupiters, or with a view to exchanging their removal for that of the Jupiters from Turkey, although this idea is disputed by several observers.[79] Meanwhile, both the Eisenhower and Kennedy administrations had realized that they would be outdated by the Polaris submarine-launched system, that they were inaccurate, and that they would be vulnerable to a Soviet first strike.[80] In April 1961, President John F. Kennedy asked for the deployment of the Turkish missiles to be reviewed. In the following month, Secretary of State Dean Rusk raised the issue with Selim Sarper, now the foreign minister in the military government. According to Rusk's later account, Sarper refused to withdraw the Jupiters since 'their parliament'[81] had only just approved the expenditures for installing them and that 'it would be very embarrassing to go right back to them and say that they would be taken out. And then he said it would be very bad for the morale of Turkey as a member of NATO if they were taken out before a Polaris submarine were in the Mediterranean to take their place' (which was then the case).[82] As Robert Komer, later the US ambassador to Turkey, wrote in a memo soon after the crisis: '[Robert] McNamara [Secretary of State for Defence] knows the JUPITERS are of no military value. But the Turks, Italians and others don't – and that's the whole point.'[83] George McGhee, who was then chairman of the Policy Planning Council, told the President in June 1961 that if the Jupiters were removed this would be seen as a sign of weakness, after Khrushchev's diplomatic offensive at the Vienna summit earlier that month, and pointed to General Norstad's recommendation of the missiles in earlier discussions with Sarper. During the spring and summer of 1962, Rusk twice raised the question again in talks with the Turks, without result, and Kennedy was told by the State Department that it would be unwise to go on pressing the point.[84]

It was after these fruitless discussions that the Cuban missile crisis erupted in October 1962, just as the Jupiters were being handed over to the Turkish authorities. The beginning of the end of the crisis came on the evening of 26 October, when Khrushchev wrote to Kennedy saying that he would withdraw the Soviet missiles from Cuba if the United States lifted its blockade on the island and agreed not to attack Cuba. However, in a second letter, delivered on the following morning, he made the withdrawal of the missiles from Cuba contingent on American withdrawal of the Jupiters from Turkey (the 'Turkey-for-Cuba trade').[85] The idea of such an exchange was discussed in Washington, but rejected, it is claimed, since it could have provoked further demands from Khrushchev, and because the Turks would much resent the implication that 'their interests were being traded off in order to appease an enemy', as the US ambassador in Ankara Raymond Hare explained.[86] Turgut Menemencioğlu, the Turkish ambassador in Washington, had already made it clear on 25 October that Turkey strongly resented being equated, in his words, 'with a country in the Caribbean, run by a bearded pirate, who had turned his island into a base for aggression against the free world'.[87] Kennedy's tactic was to reply only to Khrushchev's first letter, accepting the withdrawal of the Soviet missiles without a trade, and ignoring the second letter. On the following day (28 October) Khrushchev agreed to this, and the crisis was settled.[88]

On this basis, it appeared that the Soviet missiles were withdrawn from Cuba without the United States having to make any concessions on the Turkish Jupiters. This was the line that was steadfastly held to by both the Kennedy administration and the İnönü government. The last of the Jupiters were removed from Turkey on 24 April 1963, following an announcement by the new Turkish foreign minister, Feridun Cemal Erkin, that they would be replaced by Polaris submarines.[89] However, in his memoirs, which were published after his death in 1968, the President's brother and Attorney-General Robert Kennedy revealed that, on the President's instructions, he had met Anatoli Dobrynin, the Soviet ambassador in Washington, on the evening of 27 October (that is, before Khrushchev's letter agreeing to the withdrawal of the Soviet missiles from Cuba had been received). He had told the ambassador that if this were done 'it was our judgement that, within a short time after the crisis was over, these [Jupiter] missiles would be gone'.[90] Later, it appeared that he had actually made a more specific commitment to Dobrynin and that the US government would have been prepared to make it public if Khrushchev had not backed down first.[91]

The immediate effect of the crisis on Turkish thinking is hard to assess. Apparently, Turkish government officials strongly suspected there had been a Turkey-for-Cuba deal,[92] but they evidently decided not to make their suspicions public. Since it was not generally known about until much later, the incident failed to provoke public criticism and was anyway overshadowed by a far more bitter and open dispute between Turkey and the US over Cyprus that erupted in 1964. Although Turkish policy-makers failed to realize this at the time, the Jupiters had been far more of a danger than an advantage to Turkey. At the height of the crisis, the Soviet ambassador in Ankara had warned members of the Turkish government that a nuclear war was on their doorstep. In the event of a nuclear exchange between east and west, the Jupiters would almost certainly have been a Soviet nuclear target, making İzmir the Hiroshima of a potential third world war.[93] Clearly, in its dealings with both the USA and USSR, Turkey needed to be more cautious than it had been in 1959–62.

More directly, the removal of the Jupiters also removed an obvious obstacle to the development of better Turkish–Soviet relations. After 1963, there were still some American-supplied nuclear weapons in Turkey (as there still are), but these were short-range weapons, as supplied to other NATO armies. They were again subject to a 'dual-key' control system, and could reasonably be seen by the Soviets as being defensive rather than aggressive.[94] In the late spring of 1963, after the withdrawal of the Jupiters, a high-ranking Turkish parliamentary delegation visited the USSR for the first time since 1932. There were increased economic contacts between Turkey and the Soviets, and in October the newspaper *Cumhuriyet* published an article by Khrushchev claiming that there were now 'no serious reasons that could prevent the establishment of good neighbour relations between our two countries'.[95] This did not mean that the USSR was satisfied by Turkey's position after 1963, since it was still pressing for Turkish non-alignment, but it was at least less perturbed than it had been while the Jupiters were still on Turkish soil. A third conclusion would be that, since Turkish officials privately suspected at the time that there had been a Turkey-for-Cuba trade, then they could have reasonably concluded that, in a time of crisis, the USA might be willing to sacrifice Turkish interests for American ones,[96] and that exclusive reliance on American support might be risky. As George E. Gruen concluded in 1980, 'the seeds were sown for a lingering suspicion in Ankara that Washington might be tempted by superpower considerations to bargain away Turkey's security interests'.[97] This was to reinforce trends towards the adoption of more flexible policies towards the superpowers, which became apparent in the second half of the 1960s.

Turkish foreign policy, 1945–63: A balance sheet

Turkey's decision to join the western camp in the Cold War was virtually inevitable. Neutrality was not seen as a viable option for Turkey in the circumstances of the time, and the only serious obstacles to be overcome were not misgivings on the Turkish side, but initial reluctance to accept Turkey as a full member of the alliance on the part of western governments. Since the United States took some time to assess the geographical scope and intensity of the Cold War, while the British sought to use Turkey as part of a fruitless effort to preserve some of their previous role in the Middle East, Turkey's admission to the alliance was slow in coming, but none the less full when it did. Initially, the focus of conflict was the old issue of the Turkish straits, but this contest was already beginning to change its shape. In 1945–6, the question of Soviet naval access to the Mediterranean, and western access to the Black Sea, was still strongly contested, but the most problematic part of the Soviet project was the demand for bases at the straits. This was a new item on the agenda, which was a more fundamental threat to Turkey's independence and integrity. During the 1950s and afterwards, rights of naval passage through the straits became less crucial as the development of air power, nuclear weapons and inter-continental missiles ended the supremacy of conventional naval forces as strategic or diplomatic weapons.[98] Nevertheless, the fear that the USSR might try to take over Turkey as a means of controlling the straits was still the most important single reason for Turkey's attachment to NATO. Although successive Turkish governments were fiercely anti-communist, Turkey's commitment to the west derived from traditional considerations of territorial control and international power, not ideology. The perceived threat from communism may have heightened its worries, but did not create them originally.

Engagement in the alliance posed three potential risks for Turkey: first, that the western powers, primarily the United States, might reduce Turkey to a satellite; second, that it might drag Turkey into a global and possibly nuclear war originating in a conflict in which Turkey's national interests were only peripherally involved; and third, that Turkey might in turn have national interests that conflicted with those of the alliance as a whole. On the first score, there is no convincing evidence that the US controlled Turkey's domestic political system or intervened effectively in domestic politics to protect its own interests – indeed it did not need to do so, since internal opposition to the alliance was extremely weak. The fact that NATO was a multilateral alliance, including all the main western European states, also helped to diffuse the American role within it. Even at the point of crisis in 1960, when Menderes was overthrown, foreign policy was not an issue in the internal upheaval, and it appears that the US government did not even predict the coup, far less arrange it.[99] Nor did it make any moves to restore Menderes after the event. On the second score, the Turks themselves were evidently prepared to take risks in this regard – as, for instance, they did it 1950, when Turkish troops were sent to Korea, or in 1959, when they accepted the installation of the Jupiter missiles. On the other hand, the risk of involvement in a global nuclear war was only narrowly avoided at the time of the Cuban missile crisis in 1962, whose origins had little to do with Turkey's immediate interests, so the implicit dangers of the alliance did become obvious, if fortunately unrealized. On the third score, the Cyprus conflict did pose the risk of a clash with NATO – or at least with Greece – over an issue with which Turkey was closely concerned. As yet, however, it had not involved the danger of a conflict with the western powers, since the British were generally fairly supportive of the Turkish position, and the United States was not yet involved.

Two main criticisms can be made of Turkish diplomacy at the time. The first is that Turkey was insufficiently sensitive to the shift in Soviet policy that followed the death of Stalin, and should have made more effort to defuse its confrontation with the USSR after Khrushchev came to power. However, it is uncertain how much Turkey could have gained from such a shift, and likely that it could have lost important advantages. Even if Turkey could have gained from closer economic relations with the USSR, it might have lost heavily if western aid had been reduced as a result. Even if the Soviet security threat were reduced, the balance of military power would have been so heavily in Russia's favour, if Turkey had been neutral, that the risk of political subordination if not outright invasion would still have been serious. A second and more convincing criticism is that Turkey's policy in the Middle East was misconceived, and counterproductive. Certainly, Menderes' promotion of the Baghdad pact was based on a fundamental misperception of the interests and policies of the main Arab states, since they had no desire to line up in a Cold War conflict in which they felt quite uninvolved, and repudiated an alliance with the USA that was seen as the main patron of Israel. Menderes' aggressive attitude to Syria in 1957 almost certainly promoted the Soviet cause rather than obstructing it, and his threatened intervention in Iraq in 1958 could have produced a serious crisis in relations with both the USSR and the Arab states. A change of policy towards the region was thus a predictable outcome for the succeeding period.

5   Turkey and the Cold War, 1964–90
Global shifts and regional conflicts

The apparent relaxation of relations between the superpowers after 1962 was bound to have significant effects on the position of a front line state such as Turkey. In this new environment, Turkey's perceptions of an imminent military threat from the USSR declined, perhaps belatedly, as the focus of east–west conflict shifted away from Europe towards Africa, east Asia and the Middle East – a process which had begun in the mid-1950s. After 1962, there was a gradually growing realization that, even if there were a war in Europe, Turkey was not likely to be a primary Soviet target, especially if there were no nuclear missiles sited on its territory.[1] In effect, Turkey now had more room for manoeuvre than it had done during the earlier phase of the Cold War. In particular, it could take the risk of improving its relations with the USSR and the non-aligned nations without endangering its national security.

Some differences also arose between Turkey and its allies over strategic planning during the 1960s, as NATO began to adopt the strategy of 'flexible response', as an alternative to massive nuclear retaliation to an attack by the Warsaw Pact. This contained worrying aspects for the Turks, since it suggested that NATO might be willing to sacrifice Turkish territory so as to gain time in a superpower conflict, and was only accepted by Turkey, along with other members of the alliance, in 1967. Similarly, Turkey declined to cooperate in the proposal for a 'Multilateral Force' (that is submarines equipped with Polaris missiles and crews of mixed nationalities).[2] These changed perceptions coincided with and were reinforced by the emergence of the Cyprus dispute as a major and at times dominant element in Turkey's foreign policy. This brought out serious conflicts of interest between Turkey and the United States: in fact, between 1964 and 1980, relations between the two countries were more tense than at any other time in the post-war period. Difficulties in the relationship with Washington naturally strengthened the trend towards a less monocentric foreign policy on the Turkish side.

Turkish diplomacy was also affected by changes in domestic politics between 1960 and 1980. Until 1960, Turkey had been governed successively by İsmet İnönü's Republican People's Party (CHP) and the Democrat Party of Adnan Menderes. There had been sharp conflicts between the two parties, almost entirely on domestic issues, but both had, in their time, enjoyed large and firm parliamentary majorities that provided a relatively stable background for policy-making. This situation had not substantially altered during the military regime of 1960–1. However, when it left office, the military endowed Turkey with a new and more liberal constitution, combined with a proportionately representative electoral system, which vastly increased the range of views represented in parliament. Ideological positions that had been previously been virtually absent from public political discourse, notably socialism and Islamism with their concomitant foreign policy commitments, now became openly aired, even if they were far from gaining majority support. Greater plurality in the party structure also had important effects on the stability and effectiveness of government. In September 1960, the Democrat Party was dissolved by the military regime. Just one year later, Menderes and two of his former ministers (including the foreign minister Fatın Rüştü Zorlu) were hanged. However, this did not prevent the formation of a virtual successor, in the shape of the Justice Party (AP). Neither the CHP nor the AP, as the two main parties, won an overall majority in general elections held in September 1961, forcing İnönü to soldier on at the head of three shaky coalitions until February 1965, when a temporary government took over in preparation for the October 1965 elections. These were convincingly won by the Justice Party, now led by Süleyman Demirel, which gave Turkey what proved to be a rare interval of stable single-party government lasting until March 1971. At that point, the army intervened again and oversaw a semi-military regime, nominally under civilian '*supra* party' government, until 1973.

With the return to elected civilian politics in October 1973, hopes that a stable and effective administration could be formed were dashed, as no party won an overall majority in either of the two general elections held in 1973 and 1977. As a result, Turkey had no less than seven successive governments in as many years – first an unlikely coalition between the Republican People's Party, now led by Bülent Ecevit, and the pro-Islamist National Salvation Party (MSP) between January and November 1974, then a short-lived non-party caretaker government, followed by a right-wing coalition under Demirel known as the 'Nationalist Front' between March 1975 and June 1977. A minority government under Ecevit then lasted for less than two weeks, before being succeeded by a second 'Nationalist Front' under Demirel, which stayed in office until January 1978. With the help of defectors from the Justice Party, Ecevit then returned to the premiership, but his third government collapsed in October 1979, giving way again to Demirel, who this time headed a minority Justice Party government. Meanwhile, between 1977 and 1980, Turkey seemed to be heading towards a total political and economic collapse, thanks to weak and unstable government and a rising tide of political terrorism from violent extremists of both right and left, combined with soaring inflation and huge deficits in the balance of payments. This led almost inevitably to a third military takeover that overthrew Demirel's government in September 1980. The main effects of these turmoils were domestic, but they also had important consequences for Turkey's foreign relations. After 1973, the overriding preoccupation of governments was to hold onto power, or prevent their rivals from gaining it. While they might try to promote changed external policies, they had little opportunity to develop new strategies effectively, or do more than react to immediate crises. Their hold on power was tenuous, and policies had to be bargained for with fractious and demanding coalition partners. As a result, Turkish foreign policy became a prisoner of chronic domestic instability and economic crisis, making effective planning very hard to achieve or implement.[3]

Partial disengagement: Turkey, the superpowers and Cyprus, 1964–80

While changes in the global environment, and the missile crisis of 1962, certainly had some effect in promoting changes in Turkish policy during the 1960s, Cyprus turned out to be the crucial determining issue, since it awakened popular emotions that few other questions could have done. In 1959, after the Zürich agreements had been signed, İsmet İnönü has prophetically remarked: 'As long as both communities are not convinced that *enosis* is not possible in the long run, we will have a difficult time to ensure that other articles of the constitution are implemented.'[4] Unfortunately, this expectation proved well-founded. The constitutional settlement achieved in 1960 proved impossible to operate, since the Greek Cypriots, most of whom had apparently not abandoned the dream of *enosis*,[5] were little inclined to respect the rights that the Turkish Cypriots had been given under the constitution. Equally, the Turkish Cypriots were determined to exercise them to the full, even to the point of constitutional breakdown. In effect, power-sharing demanded a degree of collaboration and consensus from both sides that was sorely lacking. In November 1963, President Makarios put forward 'thirteen points' of constitutional amendment that, if accepted, would have removed most of the special rights of the Turkish Cypriots. This caused the effective withdrawal of the Turkish Cypriots from the government, and serious inter-communal fighting in which the Turks were the main sufferers. In the course of these and subsequent clashes about one third of them were driven from their homes, and became refugees in their own country, pushed back into a series of enclaves.[6]

As the crisis deepened during 1964, İnönü apparently decided on a policy of brinkmanship designed to induce the United States to broker a peaceful settlement. On 31 January, the British proposed that a NATO force should be sent to the island on a three-months' peacekeeping mission, during which the Turks would promise not to intervene. Reversing their previous stand, the Americans agreed to contribute troops to this operation, but the idea was flatly rejected by Makarios. As an alternative, the UN Security Council resolved on 4 March to create a UN peacekeeping force, but this was not organized in time to prevent further clashes.[7] At the beginning of June 1964, İnönü's government was seriously considering landing forces on the island, exercising its rights under Article 4 of the 1960 Treaty of Guarantee: in fact, on 2 June, the government decided to launch a military intervention (quite how it planned to do this is not clear).[8] However, on 4 June, the Prime Minister received a blunt letter from President Lyndon Johnson warning him that the other members of NATO 'have not had a chance to consider whether they have an obligation to protect Turkey against the Soviet Union if Turkey takes a step which results in Soviet intervention', and that Turkey could not use US-supplied weapons for an invasion of Cyprus. Given that the Soviet government had been strongly supportive of Makarios, this was not an empty threat.[9] In a visit to Washington on 22–3 June, İnönü was apparently persuaded that the United States would now take matters more firmly into its own hands, and both he and the Greek premier Georgios Papandreou agreed to the appointment of the former Secretary of State Dean Acheson as President Johnson's mediator.[10] It is impossible to know whether Turkey would have invaded Cyprus in 1964 if Johnson had not taken this action, possibly it would not have, since İnönü's approach was essentially cautious. Apart from the possibility of a Soviet reaction, the Turkish army would have had difficulty in carrying out the operation, due its lack of landing-craft.[11] In August 1964, units of the Greek Cypriot National Guard, which had been illegally established two months earlier and was led by General Georgios Grivas, threatened to wipe out the Turkish Cypriot enclave near Kokkina. In response, the Turkish Cypriots organized their own militia, but Turkey limited itself to air strikes against Greek Cypriot positions. Subsequently, something like peace was re-established on the island, but it was one which left the Turks at a grave disadvantage.

The most important effects of the 'Johnson letter' were felt in Turkish–American relations. Most Turks felt, quite simply, that the American intervention had shown that the US favoured the Greeks, since it had prevented Turkey from exercising its assumed military superiority, its only way of overcoming the Turks' numerical inferiority on the island. Cyprus was not the only source of Turkish–American frictions, since these were exacerbated by other problems such as the legal immunity of US military personnel in Turkey,[12] but it was easily the most important one. Anti-American protests were voiced most vociferously by the Turkish Worker's Party (commonly known by its Turkish acronym, TİP) Turkey's first legal Marxist party, which openly called for withdrawal from NATO and the severance of all political links with the United States. TİP competed in the general elections of 1965 and 1969, when it never won more than a tiny fraction of the vote,[13] and never had any share of government. Nonetheless, the party's strident anti-Americanism awakened wide sympathies, mainly because it managed to canalize strong nationalist sentiments along with its Marxist rhetoric. The reaction forced Demirel to at least be seen as protecting Turkish against US interests. In July 1969, after years of negotiation, a Defence Cooperation Agreement was signed between the two countries, in which the Turkish side sought to ensure that all joint defence activities were conducted within the limits of NATO commitments, and that all joint defence installations were the property of the Turkish republic. On this basis, there were some retrenchments of American freedom of action and a cutback of US personnel in Turkey.[14]

Turkish disenchantment with the United States also led to a rapprochement with the USSR, which had been on offer from the Soviet side for some time but hitherto rejected by the Turks. The perceived reduction in the Soviet threat to Turkey, combined with the realization that Soviet support for the Greek Cypriots seriously weakened Turkey's position on the Cyprus question, reinforced this important change of policy. On 8 August 1964, following the Turkish air strikes in Cyprus, the Soviet news agency TASS had warned that if Cyprus were invaded 'the Soviet Union will help the Republic of Cyprus to defend her freedom and independence ... and is prepared to begin negotiations on this matter immediately'.[15] Turkey had an obvious interest in reducing this threat, as the possibility of a conflict with the USSR over Cyprus made it more vulnerable to American pressure. Since the Soviet government had long sought some sort of accommodation with Turkey, the Soviet–Turkish détente developed quickly. A delegation from the Supreme Soviet, headed by Politburo member Nikolai Podgorny, visited Turkey in January 1965, initiating a series of official visits by the leaders of the two countries. The most visible product of the new relationship was in the economic field. In March 1967, Turkey accepted a $200 million credit from the USSR for seven industrial projects. This was followed by two further credits of $288 million and $700 million, in 1972 and 1975 respectively. By the end of the 1970s, Turkey was reported to have received more Soviet economic assistance than any other Third World state.[16] In 1972, the two countries signed a Declaration on the Principles of Good Neighbourly Relations, although this did not amount to much in practical terms. More immediately important for Turkey was a significant shift in the Soviet position on Cyprus, as the Soviet government evidently decided that it would be more profitable to try to accommodate the Turks than give unconditional support to the Greeks. After 1964, and especially after the *coup d'état* in Athens of April 1967 that brought a fanatically right-wing military government to power in Greece, Turkey and the USSR were united in strong opposition to *enosis* and 'the observance of the legitimate rights and interests of both communities in Cyprus'.[17] In particular, the Soviet Union sought to prevent a Greek takeover of Cyprus, which would have opened the way for the establishment of US bases on the island. This did not mean that Turkish policy on Cyprus had full Soviet support, but at least the Turks had secured an end to active hostility from Moscow.

During 1966–8, these changes led, for the first time, to a serious and open debate in Turkey about whether the country should remain in NATO. On the left, Professor A. Halûk Ülman, later a foreign policy adviser to Bülent Ecevit, argued the case for neutrality by claiming that membership of NATO required Turkey to maintain an oversized army, thus diverting resources away from civilian development projects, which would be a better protector against communism. Were there to be a conventional war in another theatre, the alliance would drag Turkey into it, even if it arose for reasons remote to Turkey's national interests. Were the war to be nuclear, then Turkey would become the victim of instant devastation. If Turkey were neutral but was nonetheless attacked by the USSR, then the US would assist it anyway since it could not allow the Soviets to dominate the Middle East. The contrary argument was put by other commentators such as the retired Admiral Sezai Orkunt, and İhsan Sabri Çağlayangil, Demirel's foreign minister. Çağlayangil took the most strongly pro-NATO line, arguing that membership of the alliance did not place unacceptable burdens on Turkey and that if it were neutral it would have to divert more rather than less resources to defence. Orkunt supported this point, adding that if Turkey quit NATO it would face serious shortages of military spare parts, almost all of which were American-supplied. Moreover, withdrawal from the alliance would seriously weaken Turkey in its conflict with Greece over Cyprus, since the United States might well increase military aid to Greece at Turkey's expense.

At the same time, Turkey continued to be heavily reliant on western, and especially American, economic assistance to close the gap in its external accounts, meet interest payments on its growing foreign debt and finance needed investments. After 1964, these were channelled through an aid consortium of the OECD, in which the United States took the lead, followed by what was then West Germany. During 1960–4, such transfers were running at an average of around $243 million per year, rising to an average of $284 million per year during 1965–9, equivalent to more than half of Turkey's foreign exchange earnings from trade and other sources. In spite of the growth in aid from the USSR, Turkey's foreign policy options remained somewhat restricted by its reliance on borrowing from the west. The balance of the argument thus came down in favour of remaining in NATO, while avoiding commitments to support the United States in the Middle East and other theatres, which might push Turkey into the position of a US satellite.[18]

These conclusions were reinforced by Turkish reactions to Soviet policies in other regions during the late 1960s. While Soviet spokesmen might profess friendship for Turkey, actions such as the Soviet invasion of Czechoslovakia in 1968, and the contemporary Soviet naval build-up in the eastern Mediterranean, inevitably weakened the case for neutrality. As İsmet İnönü, then the leader of the opposition, publicly concluded: 'We have examined the NATO agreement and announced our stand. The recent Czech events have shown how correct this stand was.' Foreign minister Çağlayangil underlined this point, warning that global détente had been 'gravely impaired' by events in Czechoslovakia.[19] As a result, a strong balance of opinion supported the idea that Turkey should stay in NATO, but avoid becoming stridently pro-American, and protect its own national interests within the alliance.

Turkish–US relations were also affected – this time more favourably – by a renewed crisis over Cyprus in 1967. Although Demirel had criticized İnönü's alleged lack of assertiveness in 1964, he in fact continued a cautious policy by beginning direct negotiations with Greece. These continued after the Greek colonels' coup and resulted in meetings between the Greek and Turkish Prime Ministers at the border towns of Keşan and Alexandroupolis (Dedeağaç) on 9–10 September 1967. During the talks, Demirel was prepared to accept the union of Cyprus with Greece in return for the grant of a Turkish sovereign base area (similar to those enjoyed by the British) but this condition was turned down by the Greeks.[20] Just over two months later, on 15 November, Cyprus again exploded when the Greek Cypriot National Guard attacked the two Turkish Cypriot villages of Kophinou and Aghios Theodhoros. After threatened air strikes from Turkey, the Greek Cypriots withdrew from the two villages the following day. However, on 17 November, Demirel decided to stiffen his response by demanding from the Greek government that it withdraw the 12,000 troops it had infiltrated into the island, well above the limits allowed by the 1960 settlement (see p97), and disband the National Guard. On the same day, parliament gave the government authority to send Turkish troops abroad – implicitly, to Cyprus.[21] Preparations were meanwhile made for a sea-borne invasion of Cyprus, although whether Turkey could or would have successfully accomplished this is open to some doubt, thanks to equipment shortages on the Turkish side, and the presence of the US Sixth Fleet, which might have intercepted it.[22] Greece rejected the Turkish demands on 22 November, but on the following day the former Secretary for Defence Cyrus Vance flew into Ankara as a personal emissary of the US President. Lyndon Johnson had evidently decided not to repeat the mistake of issuing a blunt veto to the Turks, but to try mediation. After some stalling, on 30 November, the Greek mainland government changed its tune by agreeing to withdraw its troops from Cyprus, disband the National Guard and recall Grivas. This did not mark a complete victory for the Turks, since Makarios later refused to dismantle the National Guard. However, Vance had persuaded the Greek mainland government to accept the most important Turkish demands, and thus helped to restore America's standing in Turkish opinion. The change in the Soviet attitude was also notable, since the USSR strongly opposed the junta in Athens and refused to criticize the expected Turkish invasion.[23]

During the following years, the main focus of concern in Turkey switched back to domestic problems, as the Demirel government was forced to resign by a military *pronunciamento* on 12 March 1971. For the next 30 months, Turkey was governed by a series of weak but supposedly 'supra-party' governments that, in fact, followed the off-stage directions of the military chiefs. All the available evidence suggests that the military intervention was an entirely home-grown event and that neither the US government nor its agencies played any part in bringing it about, although the Nixon administration was certainly quite supportive of the semi-military regime once it was established.[24] During 1971–3, the main bone of contention in Turkey's foreign relations was a dispute with the United States over the cultivation of the opium poppy, which was an important source of income for some Turkish farmers, especially in the province of Afyonkarahısar (the name means 'opium-black-castle'). The crop had been grown quite legally in Turkey for many years, since it is an important ingredient in legal pain-killing drugs. However, the Nixon administration was extremely concerned by the growth of heroin addiction in the United States and sought to ban opium cultivation in Turkey, to prevent diversion into the illegal market. In June 1971, the semi-military government under Nihat Erim yielded to American pressure, by agreeing to implement a complete ban on production, to begin in the autumn of 1972. This move stirred up a wave of popular opposition, on the grounds that Turkey had sacrificed an important source of legitimate income, merely to please the United States. Eventually, in July 1974, the succeeding civilian government under Bülent Ecevit revoked the ban, but implemented measures to prevent diversion into the illegal market by enforcing what is known as the 'poppy straw process' of harvesting. These measures were accepted in Washington: in fact the Ford administration encouraged the government in taking these measures, and the dispute was thus laid to rest.[25] Unfortunately, the Turkish (and Kurdish) criminal underworld still plays a role in the international heroin trade, but mainly because Turkey is an important transit route for drug-trafficking, rather than an original source of production.

Turkey returned to elected civilian government in 1974 with two new actors on the political stage. In May 1972, Bülent Ecevit unexpectedly captured the leadership of the Republican People's Party from the veteran İsmet İnönü, and then attempted to turn the party into a social democrat party on the western European model, while retaining the commitment to Kemalist secularism and espousing the idea of a more independent foreign policy within NATO. Meanwhile, Turkey's first successful Islamist party emerged, in the shape of the National Salvation Party (MSP) led by Necmettin Erbakan. The MSP had stridently anti-western views on cultural questions, but little in the way of a developed foreign policy apart from a strongly nationalist outlook. A coalition government of these two unlikely bed-fellows was formed in January 1974. Five months later, it faced the most severe foreign policy test encountered by any Turkish government since the late 1940s, when the Greek military junta sought to oust Makarios and effectively establish the union of Greece with Cyprus. In 1968, inter-communal negotiations on a new constitution had begun between Glafcos Clerides, representing the Greek Cypriots, and Rauf Denktash on the Turkish Cypriot side, but these broke down in 1973 as Makarios would not accept a settlement definitely ruling out *enosis*.[26] In November 1973, Colonel Demetrios Ioannides, who was fanatically hostile to Makarios and committed to achieving *enosis,* replaced Colonel Georgios Papadopoulos as the strongman of the Athens junta. Three months later, following the death of Grivas, the reconstructed junta took over full control of the Greek Cypriot National Guard and EOKA-B, the extremist successor to the EOKA terrorist organization of the 1950s. This produced a sharp reaction from Makarios on 6 July 1974, when he made public a letter he had sent to the Greek president, General Gizikis, demanding the immediate withdrawal of the 650 mainland Greek officers in the National Guard.[27] The Athens junta responded on 15 July, when Makarios was deposed by the

National Guard and EOKA-B, to be replaced by Nikos Sampson. Sampson was the worst possible choice from every viewpoint, since he had virtually no support in Cyprus and was notorious for his killings in EOKA's campaign against the British in the 1950s, not to mention his hatred of the Turks.

As co-guarantors of Cyprus' independence, the British were against military action, since there were thousands of British tourists and residents on the island who would have been vulnerable to retaliation by the Greeks, and the maintenance of the British bases was heavily dependent on cooperation from the Greek Cypriots. The British did however act to save Makarios, who was transported to London via the British base at Akrotiri. In Washington, President Nixon was embroiled in the final stages of the Watergate scandal, while his Secretary of State Henry Kissinger was preoccupied with Middle East peacemaking, following the Arab–Israeli war of October 1973. Hence the United States failed to take sufficiently strong action to defuse the crisis until it was too late. This left Turkey as the sole regional power that was likely to take a strong stand.

The Cypriot coup of 15 July caught Ecevit's government by surprise. It had few well-developed plans for what it sought to achieve in Cyprus, although it was committed to some sort of federal solution,[28] and opposed the return of Makarios, given his attitude in the inter-communal negotiations. In the conditions of the time, geographical federation would have been difficult to apply in Cyprus, since the Turkish Cypriots did not inhabit a single stretch of territory but were scattered in pockets around the island, complicating the military problem of protecting them. On the other hand, Turkey now had sufficient landing-craft and other equipment to carry out a successful invasion of Cyprus, provided it was not physically opposed by Britain or the United States. The expectation that this would not happen was a crucial factor in convincing the Turks that they could go ahead with the invasion if it were necessary. The Ecevit government also realized that it might provoke a war with Greece, but calculated that it could take this risk.[29] Turkey would base its action on Article 4 of the 1960 Treaty of Guarantee, although this allowed it to intervene only after consulting with the other guarantor powers, and with the sole aim of re-establishing the state of affairs set up by the treaty – that is, the independence and territorial integrity of Cyprus.[30]

On 16 July, the day after the Sampson coup, Ecevit held a meeting with his military commanders in the National Security Council, at which it was decided to carry out preparations for a landing, to be launched on 20 July. According to the military planning, the operation would be completed in two stages. In the first stage, Turkish forces would secure a bridgehead in the northern part of the island, after which negotiations would begin for a new constitutional settlement. If the Greeks refused this, then a second advance would be ordered to gain sufficient territory where the Turkish Cypriots could be settled for their security. Prior to the launch of the first operation, Turkey must first consult with the British and try to secure a diplomatic solution, though Ecevit was not hopeful that this could be achieved. The idea of a military intervention was strongly supported by Erbakan, though the former Prime Minister Nihat Erim was cautious. In private, Demirel attacked the proposal, on the grounds that it could provoke a war with Greece. Presciently, Demirel argued that even if Turkey did occupy Cyprus or part of it, world opinion might restore Makarios to power and the Turks would be left no better off. However, his party's parliamentary group was later to give full support to military intervention.[31]

On 17 July, Ecevit flew to London for emergency meetings with the British government. However, as he had expected, he was unable to persuade them to take joint action by allowing Turkish forces to operate from the British bases. Meanwhile, Nixon's Undersecretary of State Joseph Sisco also arrived in London to attempt mediation, but had virtually no effective diplomatic ammunition to persuade the two sides. Accordingly neither Sisco, Kissinger or the British could persuade Ecevit to call off the invasion, which was launched in the early morning of 20 July. Britain and the United States did not act effectively to prevent it, and Soviet government made it clear that it was prepared to accept a limited Turkish intervention provided the independence of Cyprus were preserved. More broadly, the fact that the Greek junta had put itself clearly in the wrong increased general acceptance of the Turkish action. By the time a cease-fire was brought about on 22 July through Resolution 353 of the UN Security Council, Turkish forces held a small triangle of territory in the north of the island. This still left about 50,000–60,000 Turkish Cypriots, or about half the Turkish Cypriot population, outside Turkish protection. It evidently fell short of what the Turkish military had planned to achieve during the first two days, since Turkish troops continued local advances after the cease-fire had been declared. Turkish Cypriot areas outside the northern triangle were still surrounded by the National Guard and apparently in grave danger. Immediately after the Turkish landings on 20 July, the Greek government decided in principle to declare war on Turkey, and on the following day Ioannides, now a Brigadier-General, demanded that the army should attack the Turks directly across the river Maritsa in Thrace. The Greek armed forces were quite unprepared for such an operation and the military regime fell apart. On 23 July, Constantine Karamanlis was recalled from exile to head a civilian government in Athens. Simultaneously, Sampson fell from power in Cyprus, and Glafcos Clerides was made head of a provisional Greek Cypriot government on 24 July.[32]

Peace talks between Britain, Turkey and the new Greek government opened in Geneva on 25 July. By 29 July they had reached a deadlock, but at that point Kissinger persuaded Ecevit that acceptance of Resolution 353 did not mean that Turkey would have to withdraw its forces immediately, and the parties signed a joint declaration on the following day. This represented a considerable success for the Turks since, while it confirmed the joint acceptance of a military standstill and the establishment of buffer zones between the two sides, it linked the withdrawal of Turkish forces to the achievement of 'a just and lasting solution acceptable to all parties concerned' and noted 'the existence in practice ... of two autonomous administrations' in the island – an implicit recognition that the former unitary republic could not be restored.[33]

The British, Greek and Turkish delegations, which were later joined by Clerides and Denktash, reassembled in Geneva on 9 August, supposedly to work out the basis of a new constitutional settlement. The need to secure the end of the threat to the Turkish Cypriots outside the triangle was also an important objective for the Turks. However, by the time the second Geneva conference began, the two sides had dug themselves in to irreconcilable positions. On the Turkish side, Erbakan favoured the idea of outright partition of Cyprus and was persuaded by Ecevit to accept the principle of an independent Cypriot state only on the basis of a geographical federation of the two communities. On the Greek side, Makarios, who was still in exile, opposed any constitutional negotiations with Turkey, and Georgios Mavros, the Greek foreign minister and representative at Geneva, would only accept negotiations on the basis of the 1960 constitution.

On 10 August, the second Geneva conference got down to business when Denktash put forward proposals for a bizonal federation, with a Turkish state in the north of the island. Under American pressure the Ankara government agreed two days later to what was known as the 'cantonal' plan, under which the Turkish Cypriots would be given six separate cantons, around existing settlements, within a federal structure, as an alternative. Some sort of federal solution was evidently favoured by both Kissinger and James Callaghan, the British Foreign Secretary. When the Turkish foreign minister Turan Güneş put the bizonal and cantonal plans to him on 13 August, Clerides asked for a 48-hour recess to consider the proposals. This was refused by Güneş, and the next day Turkish forces began a second advance, which effectively sectioned off the northern part of the island, from Kokkina in the west to Famagusta in the east. Neither Britain or the United States took any effective action to halt the second Turkish advance. When Clerides asked the Soviet observer at Geneva, Viktor Menin, for a limited Russian military presence in Cyprus, he was asked whether this had been cleared with the Americans, suggesting that there may have been a US–Soviet understanding that neither superpower would intervene unilaterally.[34] Although Turkey and the Turkish Cypriots were still committed in principle to maintaining an independent federal Cypriot state, the island was in practice partitioned (as some Turks argued it had been since 1963–4) with the Turks controlling about 36 per cent of its territory. About 150,000 Greek Cypriots were forced to flee as refugees to the south, while the 120,000 Turkish Cypriots regrouped in the north, completing the physical division.

After the second Turkish advance, Ecevit apparently expected that the Greek side would soon come back to the negotiating table,[35] but the Greeks solidly refused to return to Geneva. Turkey had a clear military superiority in Cyprus, but could not convert this into political influence, so as to gain a Cyprus settlement in accordance with its own objectives. Ecevit had enjoyed broad international support at the time of the first landings, but sacrificed it by embarking on the second offensive so precipitately. He also had difficulties in converting Erbakan to the idea of negotiations and this was one of the main factors leading to his resignation on 7 November 1974. In February 1975, Rauf Denktash proclaimed the 'Turkish Federated State of Cyprus' in the north, presumably as a preliminary to the negotiation of a federal constitution, but this move was unrecognized by any state except Turkey. On 28 April 1975, inter-communal negotiations began in Vienna under UN auspices. These failed to make any real progress until 12 February 1977, when Makarios and Denktash, meeting in Nicosia, agreed to four important guidelines on which future negotiations would proceed. For Makarios, this included the important concession that: 'We are seeking an independent, non-aligned, bi-communal Federal Republic.' The two sides also agreed to discuss what were called the 'three freedoms' – that is freedom of movement between the two parts of the island, freedom of settlement and the right to own property in either part – 'taking into consideration the fundamental basis of a bi-communal federal system'.[36] However, this potentially important turning-point failed to produce any positive results. Makarios died on 3 August 1977, to be succeeded by Spyros Kyprianou as Greek Cypriot president, but the two sides could not agree on the respective powers of the central government and constituent states, or the geographical division between the two. Hence the inter-communal negotiations dragged on, seemingly endlessly and fruitlessly, as Cyprus was overtaken on the list of Turkey's concerns by far more pressing domestic problems.[37]

While the Cyprus dispute ground on during the 1970s, relations between Greece and Turkey became further embittered by a series of bilateral conflicts. Of these, the most acute related to offshore mineral rights in the Aegean. As a signatory to the Geneva Convention on the Continental Shelf of 1958, which grants coastal states rights to seabed resources at a depth of less than 200 metres contiguous to their coasts, Greece claimed exclusive offshore mineral rights to about two thirds of the Aegean, since Greek islands extend to within a few miles of the coast of Turkey. Exploration licences to search for oil were granted by Greece in 1970, and a small commercial find was made near the northern island of Thassos in 1974. The Greek claim was disputed by Turkey, which suggested the division of resources by a median line down the middle of the Aegean, or joint exploration and production by the two countries. Conflict erupted in May 1974, when the Turks sent a survey ship into areas claimed by Greece, but was then overtaken by events in Cyprus later that year. After a second incident in July–August 1976, Greece made unsuccessful appeals on this issue to the UN Security Council and the International Court of The Hague. The dispute then subsided, although it remained unsettled, as Greece argued that it should be submitted for adjudication by the International Court, while Turkey preferred bilateral negotiations, with possible submission of unresolved issues to the Court. On the Turkish side, the conflict assumed importance not for economic reasons (the oil resources of the Aegean are thought to be limited) but out of the fear that claims to seabed resources might some day be converted into claims to sovereignty over the adjacent sea and air space.[38]

Similar fears were critical in a simultaneous dispute in which Greece claimed the right to extend its territorial waters from the present six miles to the internationally recognized norm of 12 nautical miles. Given the large number of Greek islands, this would give Greece control of about 64 per cent of the Aegean, compared with about 10 per cent for Turkey. Under international law, Greece would be obliged to allow innocent passage to both merchant shipping and warships of any nation through its territorial waters. Nonetheless, the Turks still concluded that they would be vulnerable to total enclosure by Greece. In June 1995, the Turkish parliament announced that a declaration by Greece of a 12-mile limit would be treated as a *casus belli,* raising the horrifying possibility that two NATO allies might actually go to war over this issue. The Greeks also fortified their Aegean islands, in spite of the demilitar-ization required by the Lausanne Treaty, while in 1975 Turkey reconstructed its Fourth Army as an 'Army of the Aegean', which was pointedly excluded from Turkey's commitment to NATO. Other disputes centred on the rights of the Turkish-Muslim minority in Thrace and the greatly depleted Greek commu-nity in Istanbul, as well as flight control rights in the Aegean. None of these conflicts are or were insoluble (indeed, the flight control dispute was settled in 1980) but they further embittered historical rivalries between the two nations and added to the problems created by Cyprus.[39]

The Cyprus crisis of 1974 also had important effects on Turkey's relations with the United States. Until this time, ethnic politics in Washington had not played a decisive role in the relationship,[40] but in September 1975, a powerful pro-Greek lobby in Congress secured the passage of a resolution banning military sales and aid to Turkey until the President could show that substantial progress had been registered towards a settlement of the Cyprus problem. The fact that there were an estimated 1.25 million Greek-Americans at the time, compared with only 54,000 Turkish-Americans,[41] gave the Greeks a clear advantage on this issue. The ban was opposed by President Ford and Secretary of State Henry Kissinger, but it nonetheless came into effect on 5 February 1975. In response, Demirel's government suspended the Defence Cooperation agreement of 1969, and in July ended all operations at all US facilities in Turkey, other than those deemed to have a purely NATO function. This had a serious effect in curtailing America's ability to monitor Soviet troop move-ments, as well as missile and underground nuclear tests in the southern region of the USSR, which depended on the use of radar and other facilities on Turkish soil. In fact, the signs are that the embargo had at least as damaging an effect on American military capabilities as on those of Turkey. In October 1975, under strong pressure from the Ford administration, Congress agreed to a partial lifting of the embargo, by limiting it to supplies covered by grants and deferred credit sales. Turkey was in any case able to circumvent US restrictions by buying supplies from other NATO countries, such as Italy and Germany. Certainly, the Turkish armed forces were seriously short of modern equipment by the late 1970s, but this was probably as much an effect of the government's critical financial straits and a desperate shortage of foreign exchange as it was the direct result of the arms embargo. In the event, the embargo was completely lifted by Congress in August 1978, allowing re-opening of the major US facilities in the following October.[42]

In view of the sharp public reaction in Turkey to the 'Johnson letter' of 1964, it is perhaps surprising that the arms embargo of 1975–8 had comparatively little political effect. There were no massive demonstrations against the United States, such as might have been expected, and Turkish comment was relatively restrained. After he took over the premiership at the beginning of 1978, Bülent Ecevit began to suggest that Turkey might pull out of NATO if the embargo were not lifted, causing consternation in Washington.[43] However, in fact there were no moves to withdraw Turkey from NATO's military structures, as Greece and France had done. The fact that the catharsis in US–Turkish relations had already been passed in the 1960s may have played a part in this, but the knowledge that opinions in Washington were divided also moderated Turkish reactions. Not only did the Ford administration clearly oppose the embargo, but Jimmy Carter, the successful candidate in the 1976 presidential elections, also changed his position on this issue. During the election campaign, he had indulged in some pro-Greek rhetoric, but after his inauguration he rapidly reversed his stance, in line with military and diplomatic opinion, and supported the total and unconditional lifting of the embargo in 1978. Nor is there any evidence that the arms embargo had any effect in softening Turkish policies on Cyprus, though it may have moderated anti-American feelings in Greece.[44]

In the late 1970s, the difficulties in Turkey's relationship with the United States, together with the perceived decline in the Soviet threat and Turkey's economic problems, persuaded Bülent Ecevit to adopt what he called 'a new national security concept and new defence and foreign policies'. Ecevit argued that Turkey was shouldering an unfairly large burden within NATO and was over-dependent on the US. Accordingly, it should slim down its forces, develop its own defence industries and 'establish an atmosphere of mutual confidence in our relations with the neighbouring countries'.[45] Ecevit appeared to adopt a more 'Third Worldist' stance than his predecessors. In July 1978, his foreign minister attended the non-aligned ministers meeting in Belgrade, and it was suggested that he sought an independent role for Turkey in NATO similar to that of Romania in the Warsaw Pact at the time. In June 1978, his government signed what was called a Political Document on the Principles of Good Neighbourly and Friendly Cooperation with the USSR, but this went much less far than the fully-fledged non-aggression pact that the Soviet government had been working for. During his visit to Moscow for the conclusion of the agreement, Ecevit announced that his government would be reducing its cooperation with the US and NATO, on the grounds that the USSR no longer constituted a threat to Turkish security. However this fell well short of closing down the US bases on Soviet soil, or a withdrawal from NATO, as the

Soviets had hoped.[46] As Ecevit explained it, his 'new concept of national defence ... should be compatible with our continued membership of NATO ... In spite of everything we do not intend to leave NATO'.[47] In practice, it was hard to see what Ecevit's policies amounted to in practical terms, besides a less committedly pro-American attitude. The only tangible example of this was his extreme reluctance to allow the US to use Turkish bases for flights by U-2 reconnaissance aircraft to monitor the expected strategic arms limitation agreement (SALT II) between the superpowers.[48] Apart from the fact that Ecevit never stayed in office for long enough to put any effective new strategies into operation, and was too beset by domestic problems, the more conservative administrations led by Demirel had also backed the idea of a more 'diversified' foreign policy and had, for instance, reacted sharply to the arms embargo. Hence, it has to be concluded that Turkey's disengagement from the western alliance during the 1970s was, at best, very partial, hesitant and uncertain.

Re-engagement, and the deconstruction of the Cold War, 1980–9

During the first half of the 1980s, Turkish foreign policies – in particular, its relations with the superpowers – entered a phase of re-engagement in the western alliance, in the sense that the previous tension in Turkish–American relations abated markedly, talk of altering Turkey's position within NATO subsided, and some of the old suspicion and hostility returned to Turkish–Soviet relations. As in the case of the previous phase, this realignment had both international and domestic political causes. At the end of the 1970s, global developments heightened tensions between the superpowers and re-established the importance of Turkey's role in the western alliance, as well as the Turks' attachment to the west. The Iranian revolution of February 1979 meant that Turkey was now the west's only ally in the northern tier and its value as a listening-post and barrier to any potential Soviet advance into the Middle East was reinforced. American anxieties regarding the future security of the region were further enhanced by the Soviet invasion of Afghanistan in December 1979. For American policy-makers such as Zbigniew Brzezinski, Jimmy Carter's national security adviser, the area to the east of Turkey was seen as an 'arc of crisis', with the possibility of a Soviet invasion or internal takeover of Iran envisaged as a distinct possibility. In retrospect, such scenarios may seem exaggerated, but they were genuinely believed in at the time, and informed western policy accordingly. Although it is improbable that Turkey's leaders believed that the Soviet Union was now on the point of invading Turkey, the invasion of Afghanistan severely weakened the case for detachment from NATO in domestic political debates, by demonstrating what could happen to a relatively weak nation on the borders of the USSR that opted for neutrality.[49] Even when the assumed threat to the Middle East abated during the 1980s, the perception on both sides that the Soviet Union was still a threat continued with the inauguration of Ronald Reagan as US President in 1981, and apparent immobilism on the part of the ailing gerontocracy of Leonid Brezhnev and his successors who still ruled in the Kremlin.

Changes in Turkey's domestic politics occurred slightly later than those in the global environment, but were no less influential in the redirection of foreign policy. On 12 September 1980, the descent into political anarchy and economic collapse was abruptly halted by Turkey's third coup since 1960, when the four force commanders of the Turkish armed forces, headed by Chief of Staff General Kenan Evren, overthrew Demirel's government and rapidly suppressed the terrorist organizations of both the ultra-left and ultra-right that had almost brought the country to its knees during the previous two years. Islamist, extreme nationalist and leftist organizations were closed and all the pre-coup parties dissolved. Stability was generally welcomed but the widespread human rights abuses by the regime provoked loud international criticism. In November 1982, a new constitution, more restrictive than its predecessor, was introduced, and Evren was declared President for the next seven years. While the military regime also succeeded in putting the economy back on the rails, its attempt to construct a civilian political system according to its own blueprint was far less successful. In the elections held in November 1983, the party favoured by the military and led by a retired general, Turgut Sunalp, was roundly defeated by Turgut Özal's Motherland Party, as the standard-bearer of the centre-right. After their suppression by the military, leftist forces failed to revive in the 1980s, and were bitterly divided by personal and other rivalries.

Meanwhile Özal, who won a second electoral victory in 1987, continued as Prime Minister until taking over from Evren as President in 1989. He provided Turkey with a period of stable single-party government that it had lacked since the late 1960s, as well as the possibility of constructing and executing a consistent foreign policy and consistent leadership. Constitutionally, Bülent Ecevit and Süleyman Demirel were banned from politics by the military regime until 1992, but this did not prevent them from setting up their own parties under proxy leaders (in Ecevit's case, his wife Rahşan) known as the Democratic Left Party and True Path Party, respectively. The two former leaders successfully campaigned for a removal of the bans in 1987. However, neither they nor a new centre-left party, the Social Democrat People's Party,[50] led by İsmet İnönü's son Erdal İnönü, succeeded in breaking Özal's grip on power until 1991. Similarly, Necmettin Erbakan effectively re-founded his former National Salvation Party as the Welfare Party. Having been prevented by the generals from competing in the 1983 elections, his party failed to win any seats in 1987. At this stage, Erbakan seemed to have been left in the wilderness, with part of his electoral base captured by the Motherland Party, which made a distinct bid for the support of moderate Islamic voters.[51]

The most distinctive feature of Özal's programme was a commitment to economic liberalization, mirroring that of Ronald Reagan and Margaret Thatcher. This was notably successful in restoring economic growth and Turkey's external balances, and created important ideological bonds with the contemporary western leaders. Like them, Özal believed that 'the second half of the seventies witnessed the failure, not only of the communist system, but also ... of the post-war model of society based on Keynesian economics and the welfare state'. In visionary mood, he hoped to see Turkey as a member of the European Community, in which: 'Her ethnocentricity will have come to an end; her conception of history, her foreign policy and her outlook on life will effectively have become secular. She will enjoy a truly global and humanist perspective, in which the pejorative distinction between Christians and others will have disappeared.'[52] Although this vision was far from realized, it can be seen as part of a process by which some of the tensions and mutual suspicions between Turkey and the west which had emerged during the 1960s and 1970s were being broken down.

The clearest sign of the new relationship with the United States was the signature of a new Defence and Economic Cooperation agreement in March 1980, for which the lifting of the arms embargo had obviously cleared the way. Under the new DECA, the US retained the use of its 12 most vital bases in Turkey, including İncirlik and essential intelligence gathering stations, while 13 other facilities reverted to exclusive Turkish use. The Carter administration also promised increased military and economic aid to Turkey, although this fell short of the Turks' ambitious military shopping list.[53] In subsequent years, annual US military assistance to Turkey peaked at $715 million in 1984, falling to $526 million in 1988, as the Cold War gradually scaled down. Nonetheless, Turkey was still the third largest recipient of US military assistance, after Egypt and Israel. In 1986, the reduction of conventional forces in western Europe allowed the US and other NATO members to transfer surplus military material to Turkey, along with Greece and Portugal. The DECA of 1980 also provided for the expansion of Turkey's own defence industries through the transfer of technology and equipment. The most prominent part of this programme was the establishment of a factory to produce the F-16 fighter, in collaboration with General Dynamics of the USA, which produced its first aircraft in 1987, but there were many similar projects.[54]

For both Turkey and successive US administrations, the most serious hurdle to the expansion of this relationship was strong pressure in Congress, from both pro-Greek and pro-Armenian lobbies, to limit US aid to Turkey, and to maintain a 10:7 ratio in aid to Turkey and Greece (that is, to allow $10 in aid to Turkey for every $7 in aid to Greece). After the expiry of the 1980 DECA in 1985, Turkey pushed hard for stronger guarantees on aid deliveries, and signed a new DECA only after Secretary of State George Schultz agreed that the administration would vigorously press Congress on this issue. In 1987, Congress nevertheless cut the proposed aid package to Turkey for 1988 from $914 million to around $570 million. This was accompanied by a determined but unsuccessful campaign by a group of pro-Armenian congressmen to have 24 April declared an official day of mourning for the 1.5 million Armenians whom they claimed had been killed by the Turks in 1915. In response, President Evren called off a long-planned trip to Washington and the government began to restrict US use of the İncirlik base. Although a Side Letter to the DECA remained unratified by the Turkish parliament, both sides agreed to operate it. Eventually, the agreement was renewed for another four years in 1988 since, it spite of the decline in the Soviet threat, Turkey still needed military, and some economic assistance, from the United States.[55]

Not surprisingly, the strengthening of ties between Turkey and the United States in the early 1980s was accompanied by growing tension in relations between Ankara and Moscow. The Soviet military intervention in Afghanistan was strongly criticized by the Turks. Although Turkey did not directly assist the Afghan *mujahiddin,* several thousand Afghan refugees of 'Turkic' (in fact, Kirghiz) extraction were given shelter in Turkey. The signature of the DECA in 1980 was a further setback for Soviet policy, and led to sharp attacks on the Turkish government in the Soviet press.[56] On the Turkish side, suspicions were increased by a Soviet military build-up in the Caucasus in the early 1980s, and the Soviet re-arming of Syria after the war in Lebanon of 1982.[57] Soviet aid to Turkey virtually dried up at the same time. The frosty relationship with the USSR continued until 1985, when Mikhail Gorbachev succeeded Konstantin Chernenko as Secretary General of the Soviet communist party. Essentially Gorbachev's policies centred on economic reconstruction and greater openness in the internal organization of the USSR, combined with cooperation rather than conflict with the west, and led eventually to the end of the Cold War by 1989–90.

Soviet policies towards Turkey during the Brezhnev era had been based on the 'national capitalism' school of thought within Soviet strategy. This had assumed that the large number of developing countries that were not of socialist orientation could nonetheless be brought round to pro-Soviet positions through the exploitation of contradictions between them and the advanced capitalist states. Under Gorbachev, this policy was seen to have failed. In spite of the conflicts between Turkey and the United States, and the impressive volume of Soviet aid to Turkey, it had paid almost no political dividends. Turkey was still a firm member of NATO, and there were still numerous US bases on Turkish soil. Problems in the US–Turkish relationship were the result of pressure by ethnic lobbies in Congress, not Soviet policy. Hence, the argument for 'economic interdependence' advanced under Gorbachev proposed that all states were part of a single global economic system, in which it was in the interests of all to cooperate.[58] During the second half of the 1980s, Turkey was able to develop better relations with both the Soviet Union and the western powers simultaneously, for the first time since the 1930s. The main effects of this transformation were seen in the economic field. Between 1987 and 1990, the bilateral trade volume between Turkey and the USSR more than quadrupled, from $476 million to $1.8 billion. The most important element in this was the supply of Russian natural gas to Turkey, through a pipeline via Bulgaria constructed in 1987. This resulted from an agreement reached in September 1984, shortly before Gorbachev came to power. Turkish contractors also began to win important construction contracts in the USSR. Meanwhile, the dramatic improvement in Turkey's external accounts under Özal meant that

Turkey now became a provider of credits to the USSR, rather than the other way round. In 1989, the Turkish Eximbank extended two credit lines of $150 million each to the Soviet Union for the purchase of Turkish consumer goods, with further and larger credits granted in 1991.[59]

While these momentous changes in global politics had significant effects on Turkey's relations with the superpowers, its local difficulties with Greece over the Aegean and Cyprus continued virtually unchanged. In Cyprus, the inter-communal negotiations dragged on until 1983 without result. In November of that year – just before the end of the military regime in Turkey – the Turkish Cypriots laid claim to national sovereignty by proclaiming the Turkish Republic of Northern Cyprus, with Rauf Denktash as president, but their state was refused international recognition by any government except that of Turkey. Since the Greek Cypriots now refused face-to-face discussions, the UN Secretary General Pérez de Cuellar pressed ahead with 'proximity talks' between the two sides. These came close to producing a new agreement in 1984, when Denktash accepted a constitutional package establishing a federal republic with a Greek Cypriot President and Turkish Cypriot Vice-President. Pérez de Cuellar had expected that President Kyprianou would accept this package at a summit meeting in New York in January 1985, but in the event he turned it down. No effective progress was made later, despite the succession of Kyprianou by Georgios Vassiliou as Greek Cypriot president in 1988.[60]

In bilateral relations with Greece, a significant hurdle was overcome when the military regime agreed to Greece's readmission to the military structures of NATO in 1980. However, the bilateral Aegean disputes between Greece and Turkey continued unsettled. The simmering tension between the two countries came back onto the boil in March 1987, when the Canadian-controlled oil company that had made the Thassos find announced that it would drill in an area outside Greek territorial waters and thus claimed by Turkey. This prompted the Turks to send their own survey ship, *Sismik I*, into the Aegean. Greek warships were reportedly prepared for action in response. The crisis was then defused when Turgut Özal announced that the *Sismik* would not sail into disputed waters unless the Greeks moved in to drill new wells. Confidential talks then began between the two sides, leading to a direct meeting between Özal and the Greek premier Andreas Papandreou at an economic conference in the Swiss resort of Davos in January 1988. This resulted in an agreement to avoid mutual antagonisms, or a repetition of the 1987 crisis. Regular contacts between diplomats, the military, the press and businessmen would be encour-aged to this end. Unfortunately, the so-called 'spirit of Davos' did not last and failed to resolve any of the substantive questions at issue between the two countries. By the end of the 1980s, Greek–Turkish relations had returned to their depressingly familiar situation of mutually suspicious stand-off.[61]

Elsewhere in the Balkans, the closing years of the Cold War had one erratic – and for those involved, tragic – effect. In the late 1980s the regime of Todor Zhivkov, Bulgaria's last and longstanding communist ruler, apparently sought to prop up its faltering domestic popularity by launching a campaign against the country's Turkish community. In spite of emigrations to what became Turkey during the Balkan wars and afterwards, the Turkish minority in Bulgaria during the 1980s still numbered about 900,000, or about 10 per cent of the total population of the country.[62] Under a treaty signed between Turkey and Bulgaria in 1925, the minority's rights and status were protected. Turkish governments took the view that, as Bulgarian citizens, the Bulgarian Turks had the right to fair treatment, but Turkey should respect Bulgaria's territorial integrity. Politically, Turkey needed to maintain good relations with Bulgaria if it could. Nonetheless, about 150,000 Bulgarian Turks were expelled to Turkey during 1950–1, apparently in revenge for Turkey's participation in the Korean war on the UN side. During the 1970s, another 116,000 emigrated to Turkey, under an agreement allowing for the re-union of divided families. Beginning in 1984, the Bulgarian authorities launched a campaign of forced assimilation and oppression, in which the Bulgarian Turks were obliged to adopt Bulgarian names or prevented from performing religious ceremonies. Many thousands were arrested and imprisoned, or uprooted from their homes, being forced into internal exile. Turkey protested, and gained support from such bodies as the United Nations and the Organization of the Islamic Conference, but to no effect. In 1989, the Zhivkov regime apparently panicked at the rise of organized protests among the Turks, by deciding to expel them *en masse.* During June–August 1989, around 312,000 people fled to Turkey, carrying what possessions they could. Large protest meetings were held in Istanbul, at which Turgut Özal issued empty threats of marching on Sofia. However, the scale of the exodus was such that, on 21 August, the government decided to re-impose visa requirements, which it had lifted in June, effectively stopping the flow. Fortunately, the crisis was ended in November 1989, when Zhivkov was overthrown, and conditions for the Turkish minority were rapidly improved.[63]

Turkey and the Middle East, 1964–89

While Turkey's relations with the superpowers were profoundly affected by global changes between the 1960s and 1980s, its relationship with its Middle Eastern neighbours followed a largely independent although fluid course, and was relatively unaffected by domestic political pressures. The shift in Turkish foreign policies in the mid-1960s was marked by a determined attempt to rebuild bridges with the Arab world. The most immediate reason for this was the aim of winning the Arab states away from their previous support for Makarios and, more broadly, to try to convince them that Turkey had abandoned the obviously futile approaches of the Baghdad pact. The pact was now severely criticized in Turkey for its alienation of Arab nationalism, and for allegedly subordinating Turkey's national interests to those of the western alliance.[64] By the mid-1970s, an important economic incentive had been added to this agenda. The oil price rises of 1973–4, followed by the further rises of 1980–1, combined with Turkey's growing consumption of imported oil, vastly increased its dependence on the Middle Eastern oil-exporting countries. Turkish exports to the Middle East were slow to develop in response, but when they did so during the 1980s the effects were impressive. As a result, Turkey's imports from the region rose from a trifling $64 million in 1970 to $2.8 billion in 1985, and its exports from $54 million to around $3 billion during the same period. For Turkish construction companies, who had a cumulative total of $15.5 billion worth of contracts by 1985, the region also became an important market, which had attracted around 200,000 emigrant Turkish workers.[65] All these interests entailed constructing better links with all the main Middle Eastern countries. Essentially, Turkish policy towards the region tried to uncouple its regional policy from its alliance with the western powers as far as possible, and to build up bilateral rather than multilateral linkages with the main states in the region. Above all, Turkish policy sought to avoid taking sides in regional disputes, either between states or within them.

As part of this approach, Turkey began to be a good deal more cautious in supporting the United States in the Middle East than it had been during the 1950s. The guideline for Turkish policy-makers was that they could not commit themselves to anything that could not at least be presented as part of their functions within NATO, and thus as an unavoidable alliance commitment, or as having an entirely humanitarian purpose. In the 1967 Arab–Israeli war, Turkey remained strictly neutral, and refused the US the use of its bases for refuelling or supply. The Demirel government supported UN Resolution 242 calling for Israeli withdrawal to its pre-war frontiers, although it refused to join the Arab states in condemning Israel as the 'aggressor'. While Turkey allowed the US to use Turkish bases to evacuate civilians from Jordan in 1970 and from Iran in 1979, during the Yom Kippur war of October 1973, it specifically forbade the US Air Force to use the İncirlik base for anything other than routine NATO missions. Turkey also refused to cooperate with the abortive mission to rescue the US hostages from Tehran in 1980. During the early 1980s, it also appears that it fought shy of providing bases for the proposed US Rapid Deployment Force in the Middle East. The furthest it was willing to go in this direction occurred in 1982, when the military regime accepted what was called a 'co-locator operating bases agreement' providing for the modernization of ten existing airfields in eastern Turkey, and the construction of two new ones. However, it was stipulated that these were to be used strictly in accordance with NATO defence plans.[66]

Turkey's attempts to adopt an even-handed policy in the Middle East were most in evidence in its policies towards the Arab–Israeli struggle, and during the Iran–Iraq war of 1980–8. On the first score, during the 1970s it began to adopt a more pro-Palestinian tilt. Its recognition of the PLO in 1976 and the opening of a PLO office in Ankara in 1979 were the most overt signs of this. However, the shift was slow and hesitant, mainly because Turkey was suspicious of collaboration between the Palestinians and leftist-cum-Kurdish terrorist movements in Turkey. Hence, Turkey was careful to limit its support to the PLO, rather than to the more radical Palestinian factions such as those headed by George Habash and Naif Hawatmeh, which were apparently supported by

Greece and Syria.[67] Another problematic factor in Turkey's relationship with the Arab states was its standing in the Organization of the Islamic Conference (OIC). Here, the obstacle did not derive from Turkey's continuing recognition of Israel or its links with the United States, but from its own secularist constitution and the determination of most of the political elite to preserve it. In 1969, when Demirel's foreign minister İhsan Sabri Çağlayangil attended the first Islamic Conference at Rabat, the move triggered off sharp criticism from the pro-secularist establishment in Turkey. In response, the government followed a generally low key approach, arguing that the Conference was not 'religious', and emphasizing the importance of its economic links with the Arab countries. Although Turkey played a full part in the OIC, its parliament never ratified the charter of the organization.[68]

This limited re-orientation towards the Islamic world may have been seen as part of the rise of political Islam in Turkey. However, although Necmettin Erbakan took his place in governments headed by both Ecevit and Demirel, he does not seem to have had much influence on foreign policy and his call for a rupture of Turkey's links with NATO and other western organizations went unheeded. In the Middle East, Turkey refused to break off relations with Israel, even though these were kept at a low level, to avoid exciting Arab susceptibilities. Like many other countries, Turkey was strongly critical of the Israeli annexation of east Jerusalem in 1980, and there was some sympathy among liberal as well as Islamist opinion for the Palestinian *intifada* that began in December 1987. On the other hand, there was important if quiet cooperation between the Turkish and Israeli security forces, notably in 1982 during the Israeli invasion of Lebanon, when the Israeli forces captured a number of Turkish terrorists and handed both them and information on Turkish and Armenian terrorist groups to the Turkish authorities. After 1986, Turkish–Israeli relations started to improve markedly, as the Turks began to realize the importance of winning the support of the pro-Israeli lobby in Washington as a means of overcoming their problems with the US Congress. Apparently under pressure from Washington, Turkey upgraded its relations with Israel in 1986 by sending a senior diplomat, Ekrem Güvendiren, to head its legation in Tel Aviv.[69] This accommodation was facilitated by the beginnings of the Arab–Israeli peace process, marked by the PLO's acceptance of Israel's existence and the principle of a 'two state solution' in Palestine in 1988. Just as the contemporaneous deconstruction of the Cold War made it possible to develop good relations with both the west and the USSR, so the changes in Middle Eastern politics made it easier to maintain friendships with both the Arabs and the Israelis.[70]

Turkish policies towards Iran and Iraq, two of its immediate neighbours, depended on walking another tightrope, especially during the war between the two countries of 1980–8. With Iraq, the task was not too difficult, since Ankara and Baghdad had no serious mutual disputes. Their common interests were reinforced by the emergence of powerful Kurdish separatist movements in both countries during the 1980s. With the beginnings of the revolt within

Turkey by militants of the Kurdistan Workers' Party (*Partiya Karkeren Kurdistan,* or PKK) in 1984, Özal's government was worried by the contemporary power vacuum in Iraqi Kurdistan. In October 1984, it concluded an agreement with Baghdad under which the Turkish forces could carry out 'hot pursuits' into Iraqi territory against the PKK, obviating the need to secure separate permission from Iraq on each occasion.[71] Potentially, relations with Iran could have been far more difficult to handle. So long as the Shah ruled, Turkish–Iranian relations were reasonably cooperative, and institutionalized through the Central Treaty Organization and its sister organization for 'Regional Cooperation and Development', or RCD (see pp93–4). Nonetheless, in the mid-1970s the Turks were somewhat perturbed by the Shah's exaggerated ambitions of turning Iran into the dominant power in the Middle East. In 1979, much more dramatically, the Iranian revolution turned Iran into a militantly Islamist and anti-western state, in direct opposition to Turkey's alignments, both domestic and international. Recognizing realities, Turkey was careful not to take an openly anti-Iranian attitude after the revolution, since it was anxious not to isolate Iran and thus possibly push it into the Soviet sphere of influence. Thus, when the United States imposed a trade embargo on Iran in November 1980, following the imprisonment of the US embassy hostages in Tehran, Turkey refused to follow suit. Hence, Turkey and Iran continued a correct if often frosty relationship.[72] The RCD organization was dissolved along with CENTO in 1979, but it was revived in 1985 as the Economic Cooperation Organization (ECO), with the initial membership of Iran, Turkey and Pakistan, and its headquarters in Tehran.

By the end of 1980, the outbreak of the Iran–Iraq war had turned Iranian attentions elsewhere, and made both Iran and Iraq heavily dependent on Turkey economically, both as a source of supply of non-military imports and as a transit route to the outside world. For Turkey, the main cost of the war was that it gave the Iraqi Kurds a chance to re-launch their campaign for an independent Kurdish state, with Iranian help, and provided the PKK with bases in Iraq for attacks on Turkish territory. However, this was outweighed by economic and broad strategic gains. In particular, their dependence on Turkey as a transit route and a source of imports gave the Iranians a solid reason for not alienating the Turks.[73] For Iraq, the oil export pipeline from Kirkuk to the Turkish port of Dörtyol, near İskenderun, originally built in 1977, was a vital lifeline, and it was expanded to a total capacity of 1.5 million barrels per day by 1987. Hence, Turkey reaped economic benefits from the war, as its exports to the two countries grew from $220 million in 1981 to just over $2 billion in 1985, at which point they accounted for more than a quarter of Turkey's total exports. In this case, fence-sitting turned out to be profitable, as well as the most politically prudent policy, although exports to the two countries decreased during 1986–8, as they apparently began to run short of funds.[74] Turkey was also lucky in that neither Iran or Iraq was able to win a clear-cut victory. For instance, when Iran captured the Iraqi Kurdish town of Halabjah in March 1988, there were fears in Ankara that it might move on to seize Kirkuk, allowing the Kurds to establish an autonomous state in Iraq, and cutting off the Kirkuk–Dörtyol pipeline. In the event, Iraqi forces recaptured Halabjah in June 1988, having earlier subjected the town to a barbaric poison-gas attack in which around 5,000 civilians died. As a result of the Iraqi counter-offensive, around 60,000 Kurdish refugees entered Turkey. After initial reluctance, they were settled in four separate camps in south-eastern Anatolia. Hence, when Iran accepted a UN-brokered ceasefire in July 1988, the end of the conflict caused relief in Ankara.[75]

This is not to suggest that Turkey's relations with all the Arab states developed positively during the 1980s. As usual, the relationship with Syria proved to be the most difficult to handle, as new disputes were added to Syria's longstanding grievance over the Turkish annexation of Alexandretta in 1939. While the Iraqi regime cooperated with Turkey against the Kurdish resistance, Syria actively supported it, by giving shelter to Abdullah Öcalan, the leader of the PKK, as well as logistical and training support to his organization in Syrian-occupied Lebanon. The conflict intensified, as Turkey launched its ambitious Southeast Anatolia Project to use the waters of the Euphrates and Tigris for electricity generation and irrigation, threatening the supply of water to Syria and Iraq, for whom this was a vital resource. In 1987, as Turkey was beginning construction of the giant Atatürk Dam on the Euphrates, Özal visited Damascus and secured an agreement with President Hafiz al-Assad under which Turkey would continue to supply a minimum average flow into Syria of 500 cusecs (cubic metres per second) in return for a Syrian commitment that neither country would support violent resistance groups operating in the territory of the other. On paper, this was a highly satisfactory conclusion for Turkey, but Syria later insisted that the 500 cusecs figure was acceptable only while the dam was being filled, and that an average flow of 600–700 cusecs would be demanded once it was completed. Nor did Syria halt its support for the PKK, in spite of constant denials. Meanwhile, Özal promoted an ambitious plan, christened the 'peace pipeline', to supply water from the Ceyhan and Seyhan rivers in Turkey (which are hydrologically separate from the Euphrates) to Syria, Jordan and western Saudi Arabia, and via a second 'Gulf Pipeline' to eastern Saudi Arabia and the smaller Arab Gulf states. This project never got off the drawing board, since the political problems of supply across so many states and the huge cost apparently make it impractical, although it showed the strength and direction of Özal's ambitions to make Turkey a major economic and political player in the region.[76]

Turkey and Europe, 1959–90

One of the effects of Turkey's membership of the western alliance was that its bilateral relations with the western European states became far less critical than they had been previously. Britain has a special role as a co-guarantor of the Cyprus settlement of 1960, while West Germany re-emerged as its biggest trading partner, enjoying a high prestige with the Turkish public at the time, as well as being a source of financial and military assistance.[77] However, political relations with the western European nations were important to Turkey mainly because they were partners of the United States, rather than as independent political actors in their own right, as they had been before 1945. The relationship began to change shape with the launch of the European Economic Community (EEC), originally consisting of Germany, France, Italy and the three Benelux countries, in 1957. In June 1959, Greece submitted an application for membership of the EEC, followed by Turkey the following month. The result was that Greece became an associate member of the Community in July 1961, to be followed again by Turkey, which signed an Associa-tion Agreement with Brussels on 12 September 1963. On the Turkish side, the reasons for the application were political rather than economic. International recognition as a member of the western community of nations had been an objective of Turkish leaders since the days of the *Tanzimat,* and was seen as a logical extension of Turkey's membership of NATO and other western institutions. The need to avoid being outflanked by Greece was also an important motive and almost certainly hastened the Turkish decision. The economic objective of gaining easier market access to the EEC, which already accounted for about 35 per cent of Turkey's exports, added to the incentive. On the Community side, there were some doubts, mainly in France, as to whether Turkey could be counted as a 'European' nation, but these were overcome by the recognition of Turkey's strategic role in the Cold War, the desire to be even-handed between Greece and Turkey, and the general desire to emphasize that the EEC was an expanding association, open to new members and cultures.[78]

While the main motivations for signing the Association Agreement of 1963 were political, its content was almost entirely economic. It outlined a process by which Turkey was to achieve a customs union with the Community, to be followed by possible full membership, to take place in three stages. During a preliminary stage, which was to last from 1964 to 1973, the EEC would extend preferential trading conditions to Turkey, plus some direct financial aid. This would be followed by a transition stage, during which both sides would eliminate tariff and other barriers to trade, so as to establish a customs union. Once the application of the Agreement had advanced far enough for Turkey to carry out the obligations of Community membership then, under Article 28, the parties would 'examine the possibility of the accession of Turkey to the Community'.[79] In this way, the existing member states did not commit themselves to accepting Turkey as a full member of the Community, as some Turkish commentators tried to argue, but they did at least agree to consider the question at some future date, provided Turkey could meet the conditions of membership.[80] Politically, the most important gain for Turkey was the symbolic recognition by Walter Hallstein, the president of the European Commission at the time, that 'Turkey is part of Europe'.[81]

The Association Agreement was accepted by Turkey in 1963 with little internal debate or dissent. However, this situation did not repeat itself in November 1970, when the two sides signed an Additional Protocol. This was to lay down the rules for application of the transition stage, scheduled to last from 1973 until 1980 at the earliest, or 1995 at the latest. Initially, the Community regarded Turkey's desire to proceed rapidly to the second stage as rather premature, since little preparation had been accomplished, but it was again persuaded by the political arguments in favour of developing the relationship. In Ankara, the Demirel government was firmly committed to the ultimate goal of full membership and unrealistically hoped that Turkey could precede Britain, Ireland, Denmark and Norway in this. However, new forces in Turkish politics, notably the Islamists led by Necmettin Erbakan, were firmly against the move on both ideological and protectionist grounds. Scepticism about the desirability of reducing tariff and other trade barriers was later to be shared by the Republican People's Party under Bülent Ecevit, and the more *étatist* school of thought within the state bureaucracy, notably in the State Planning Organization. Nonetheless, following the military intervention of March 1971, the Protocol was ratified by the Turkish parliament in July of that year.[82]

By the late 1970s, opposition to the arrangement became more vociferous, as the gradual removal of trade barriers became impeded. The Demirel administration complained that Turkey was not being given sufficient access to the Community's agricultural market and at the beginning of 1978, the Community began to impose restrictions on the import of cotton yarns and textiles, Turkey's main industrial exports.[83] Meanwhile, following the restoration of democratic government in Greece in 1974, the Karamanlis administration applied for full membership of the Community and eventually achieved this in 1981. Later, it was argued that by not submitting an application at the same time as Greece, Turkey missed the boat with the Community, which might have accepted both proposals together (or possibly have turned down both).[84] The position of Turkish migrant workers in the Community also became a critical issue, since by 1976 their number had reached around 600,000, plus about 1 million dependants, and their annual remittances to Turkey were running at about $1 billion per year. Under Article 36 of the Additional Protocol, the two sides were due to begin the process of allowing free movement of workers between Turkey and the Community in 1976. When the target date arrived, the EEC merely agreed to improve the freedom of movement of Turkish workers already in the Community, and to give the Turks priority if its manpower needs could not be met by other Community members, effectively making this commitment a dead letter.[85] In October 1978, beset by mounting political as well as economic problems, Ecevit's government froze Turkey's obligations under the Protocol. Progress was not resumed until after Demirel returned to power in October 1979, but was then halted once more by the military takeover of September 1980.

The earlier military interventions of 1960 and 1971 had provoked little or no reaction from the main European states, but that of 1980 was different. The European public was now more conscious of a need to protect democratic norms in allied states. The European Parliament, which was more concerned with issues of ideological principle than were the national governments or bureaucrats, now exercised more authority within the Community structures.

The European reaction also left Turkey's military rulers in a dilemma. On the one hand, they were firmly committed to a modernist, western identity for Turkey, and were thus concerned to defend and promote links with the western powers. On the other hand, their authoritarian streak was at odds with western Europe's commitment to democratic standards and its desire to see that Turkey adhered to them. In this way, Turkey's domestic regime, rather than just its foreign policies, became of prime importance in its relations with western Europe. On the surface, the United States was less vociferous than western Europe on the need to respect human rights and secure a rapid return to democratic government, but nevertheless it kept up some behind-the-scenes diplomatic pressure on Ankara in this direction. In effect both sides had to walk a tightrope. On their side, the western powers needed to keep the issue of democratization on the agenda, without pushing the Turkish government so far on this issue that it became totally alienated and unco-operative. On the other side, the generals needed to show sufficient concern for western susceptibilities without openly admitting that their policies were being partly dictated by their western allies (which would have under-mined their domestic standing) or restricting their freedom of manoeuvre domestically to an unacceptable degree. Fortunately both sides managed to walk the tightrope with a fair degree of success.[86]

The first reaction to the 1980 coup came from the Council of Europe, a separate body that Turkey had joined in 1949. Membership of the Council had mainly symbolic significance, since it lacked any economic or military clout, but the symbolism was nevertheless important to the Turkish elite as a mark of Turkey's European credentials. The Turkish delegation was with-drawn from the Council's Parliamentary Assembly shortly after the coup and not restored until some months after civilian rule had been re-established, although Turkey's membership of the Council was not formally suspended. More materially, in May 1981, the Turkey–EC Association Council agreed on a draft package of economic aid to Turkey, known as the Fourth Financial Protocol. In the following month the value of this was increased to 600 million ECU but, under pressure from the European Parliament, the release of this was made conditional on effective moves to restore democracy. In November 1981, following the generals' closure of all the previous political parties, the EC Commission hardened its position by deciding that, in these conditions, it would not resume any discussions on the release of the funds. Whether the withdrawal of aid by itself made a substantial difference to the military government's policies is hard to say with certainty – the previous case of the US arms embargo would suggest that it did not. However, its symbolical significance was considerable and probably played an unacknowledged role in encouraging the generals to return to democracy under acceptable conditions. At the same time, the western powers were able to promote their objectives without provoking an acrimonious or open break with Turkey.[87]

Although many western European observers had initial doubts about the democratic credentials of the restored civilian regime, Turgut Özal's accession to power in 1983 changed the picture dramatically, since he was committed in principle to liberalizing Turkey's international trade, regardless of the effects on relations with the Community. In fact, Özal told the Turkish parliament in 1987 that 'the aim of the economic liberalization programme and our reforms was to facilitate our integration into the European Community as a full member'.[88] This may have been something of a misrepresentation, since Özal would almost certainly have sought to liberalize the Turkish economy anyway, but his reforms certainly assisted the process of economic integration with the Community. In spite of Özal's personal attachment to Islam and occasional appeals to the moderate Islamist vote in domestic politics, he was convinced that this should not be a barrier to Turkey's eventual accession.[89] Accordingly, the removal of trade barriers was resumed after 1983, and in April 1987, Özal's government submitted a formal application for full membership. Although this turned out to be premature, what was now the European Community was bound to consider it, and the Commission prepared its official Opinion on the application. After a long delay, this was issued in December 1989 and formally accepted by the Community's Council of Ministers in February 1990. In essence, the Commission's Opinion was a polite rebuff of the Turkish application. In the economic sphere, it referred to the 'substantial development gap between the Community and Turkey', which meant that Turkey would have great difficulty in shouldering its obligations under the Community's economic and social policies. In the political context, it cited Turkey's disputes with Greece, the Cyprus problem and the fact that its human rights regime and 'respect for the identity of minorities' had 'not yet reached the level requited in a democracy'. On these grounds, it recommended that no accession negotiations should begin until after 1993 at the earliest, with no subsequent date set. In the meantime, the two sides should concentrate on the completion of the customs union, as planned in the Additional Protocol.[90] At the time the Opinion was issued, Commissioner Abel Matutes confirmed that Turkey was still eligible to become a full member of the Community in principle.[91] Nonetheless, it was clear that, not without reason, Turkey's western European partners were anxious to delay the process as long as possible.

Turkish diplomacy, 1964–79: Some critical assessments

Changes in global politics between the mid-1960s and late 1980s clearly gave Turkish diplomacy some new opportunities, but these were offset by new problems. As global conflicts softened, regional ones asserted themselves and were to prove just as hard to handle. In its relations with the superpowers, Turkey exploited the possibilities of a better relationship with the USSR successfully, although perhaps belatedly, by expanding economic opportunities and converting Moscow from a hostile to a neutral force on the Cyprus question. In effect, it exploited its ability to gain strategic rent, both economic and political, from both sides in the Cold War. However, there were fairly tight limits to détente between Turkey and its northern neighbour. Faced with the classic choice between alliance and neutrality, Turkey remained committed to the western alliance. In the last analysis, those who favoured neutrality lost the argument, because they could not show that the potential gains outweighed the likely losses and dangers. Admittedly, perceptions of the Soviet threat had substantially altered by the 1960s. The security of the straits – the centre of attention for both the Turks and the western powers for almost two centuries – became a less crucial question, thanks to the development of nuclear weapons and inter-continental missiles.[92] On the other hand, Turkey could not afford to break away from the western alliance, as an ultimate protection against the Warsaw Pact, as well as a source of military and economic aid which would probably not have been available otherwise. Turkish neutrality would probably have redounded to Greece's advantage, and Soviet policies in the Middle East and eastern Europe did not inspire the Turks with confidence. Ecevit's claim to have adopted new policies did not amount to much, beyond a change of tone, and was quite rapidly abandoned in the 1980s. Hence, Turkey's membership of NATO survived both the 'Johnson letter' of 1964 and the Congressional arms embargo of 1975–8. During the 1980s, most of the heat went out of the argument, as there were few objections to the strengthening of Turkey's links with the US in the first half of the decade, while in the second half, Özal was in the happy position of being able to continue Turkey's commitment to the alliance and improve its relationship with the USSR simultaneously

The two factors that made a successful foreign policy more difficult to execute between the mid-1960s and the 1980s were, first, the resurgence of local contests and interests which conflicted with those of the Cold War and, second, the irruption of domestic political factors and instabilities into foreign policy-making, both in Turkey and on the western side. Until 1964, foreign policy did not figure prominently in the contest between Turkey's two main parties, since there was a broad consensus on the need for the NATO alliance, and public opinion was not much exercised by foreign policy issues. Equally, western governments were mainly satisfied with Turkey's foreign policies, and relatively little concerned with its internal political practices. The Cyprus conflict changed this picture dramatically, since it brought out a clear clash between Turkey and the United States and excited such nationalist fervour in both Greece and Turkey that few other issues could have done. In Turkey, this effect was probably enhanced by long-run social and cultural changes, as an increasing number of ordinary citizens gained access to information about the outside world through newspapers and broadcasting, and became less inclined to leave foreign policy-making to the traditional elite of diplomats, generals and senior politicians. Balancing internal pressures with external realities became a difficult task, which was exacerbated by serious instability in internal politics, especially during the 1970s. For a time, leftist ideas had some influence on external relations, though the resurgence of politicized Islam seems to have had little direct effect on foreign policy, apart from destabilizing the domestic political system. During the 1970s, internal pressures also began to affect

American policies towards Turkey, mainly in the form of ethnic lobbies, of which Turkish diplomacy had little experience and was not skilled in countering. Similarly, the weaknesses of Turkish democracy, notably in the field of human rights, began to affect western European policies, which had hitherto paid little attention to Turkish domestic politics, being primarily motivated by Turkey's international strategic importance.

In dealing with that part of its foreign policy agenda that was not directly part of the Cold War contest, Turkish policy had mixed success. In handling the Cyprus problem in 1964 and 1967, İnönü and Demirel were both cautious. The 1967 experience was more successful from the Turkish viewpoint than that of 1964, but it still left the Turkish Cypriots in a hazardous and exposed position, with the essential problem of how to reconstruct the Cypriot state no nearer solution. The shocked public reaction in Turkey to the 'Johnson letter' of 1964 was evidently based on the misapprehension that since Turkey was strategically more important to NATO than Greece, and was a faithful member of the western alliance, the US would support Turkey against the Greeks. The opposite expectation, that the United States could not afford to be anything other than neutral in a dispute between two NATO allies, should have been apparent from the start but it was hard for the Turks to swallow. The crisis of 1974 was different, in that Turkey appeared to have a clearer mandate for intervention, under the 1960 Treaty of Guarantee. If Turkey had not invaded, then Cyprus would probably have been united with Greece, the Turkish Cypriots massacred or expelled, and the colonels' regime consolidated in Greece. Most of the blame for the crisis could clearly be laid at the door of the Greek junta, though both Makarios and the British and US governments failed to acquit themselves well – the last two through their failure to take sufficiently strong action against the junta at an early stage. On the Turkish side, Ecevit took a gamble that Greece would not attack Turkey in response (or that, if it did, Turkey could repel it), which turned out to be justified. On the other hand, by launching the second stage of the invasion so precipitately, without allowing Clerides the 48-hour recess he had asked for, Ecevit lost the moral advantage he had held at the time of the original Turkish landings. In the end he was no nearer to getting the Greeks to accept a workable federal settlement, since his expectation that the shock of the second invasion would force them to come back to the conference table in chastened mood proved misplaced. Its policy during the Cyprus crisis of 1974 was probably the furthest Turkey ever went to striking out on its own, independently of NATO, but the outcome suggested that it had little ability to dictate its own political terms in the ensuing situation. The struggle then proliferated into a series of bilateral Greek–Turkish disputes, for which Greece shared as much of the blame as Turkey. Ecevit and his successors could not resolve them, even though Özal's peace talks with Andreas Papandreou of 1988 prevented a head-on military collision.

The development of Turkey's relationship with western Europe followed a separate course, which was at least to some degree independent of the Cold

War. In launching the initiative, the Turks almost certainly underestimated the difficulties involved, but felt that they had little alternative. Membership of the new Europe was seen as a logical part of the Kemalist heritage, and abandoning the effort would have given Greece an easy advantage. On the other hand, Turkey's economic problems, and Ecevit's neutralist and *étatist* leanings, created difficulties that almost led to breakdown in the late 1970s. Whether Turkey actually missed an important opportunity in 1974–5, when it failed to follow Greece in applying for full membership of the Community, can be endlessly debated, but the argument is ultimately unprovable. In eventually submitting Turkey's application in 1987, Özal may also have overestimated his chances of securing a successful outcome, but by the time it came the Community's reply was widely expected, and Turkey received the best response it could reasonably have expected.

The Middle East was probably the most successful theatre for Turkish foreign policy at the time – the precise opposite of the experiences of the 1950s. Turkey's Middle Eastern relations were usually easier to handle, since they aroused fewer domestic political passions than conflicts with Greece or relations with the US. Even though they showed formal respect for the institutions of Islam, at the time most Turkish Muslims had little sense of identity with the Arab world and were disinclined to support its causes. So far as one can judge, this sentiment was reciprocated. Hence, the Turkish government's hopes that a more friendly approach towards the Arabs would induce them to swap sides, by abandoning their support for the Greek Cypriots in the United Nations and other bodies, was misplaced. On the other hand, the Turks were able to overcome some of the old suspicions that they were no more than America's gendarme in the Middle East, and to develop profitable commercial relations accordingly. During the Iran–Iraq war, they were able to turn an external conflict to their advantage by making both sides dependant on Turkish good will. Through careful diplomacy, relations with Israel were continued, even if this aroused Arab suspicions. The relationship with Syria was more problematic, and became complicated by Kurdish separatism in Turkey, and Syria's role in it, as well as the conflict over the Euphrates. As in the case of Cyprus, this created problems which were to last long after the end of the Cold War.

6 Turkish foreign policy after the Cold War

Strategic options and the domestic and economic environments

The end of the Cold War, the collapse of communist rule in eastern Europe and the dissolution of the USSR during 1989–91 altered Turkey's international environment as profoundly as either of the two previous transformations, of 1918–23 and 1945. The security threat from the Soviet Union, which had originally been the main cause of Turkey's attachment to the western alliance, had effectively ended. On the face of it, this restored the situation of the 1920s but in a more extreme degree, since the Soviet state had constitutionally dissolved, Russia had contracted territorially and a series of small successor states had emerged in the Black Sea region, central Asia and Transcaucasia. Having been previously surrounded on three sides by what was, in effect, a single state far more powerful than itself, Turkey was now surrounded by smaller neighbours that were weaker than itself both militarily and economically.[1] If policies had been determined purely by considerations of military security, and the western alliance had had no other functions, this should have allowed Turkey to revert to neutrality. That this did not happen was mainly due to the fact that the world of the 1990s was very different from that of the 1920s. The western military alliance acquired new missions to replace those of meeting the Soviet challenge, in which Turkey could play a role. Moreover, NATO was only one of a number of institutional and ideological bridges between Turkey and the west. Other non-military links, such as that with the European Union,[2] and Turkey's continued commitment to political and economic liberalism, meant that, for several years after the Cold War ended, there was a fairly high degree of continuity from the previous period.

Global changes: Foreign policy options and debates

Both in Turkey and abroad, the post-Cold War situation sparked off a quite unprecedented debate regarding where Turkey's international future lay, in which a wide variety of views were expressed. During 1989–90, some commentators suggested that the end of the Soviet threat had reduced Turkey's international influence, since it had now lost its role as the cornerstone of western security in the eastern Mediterranean. More broadly, it was argued that NATO would lose its importance, to be replaced by alternative security structures.[3] In this situation, Turkey might be seen as a strategic and political liability rather than an asset to the west – strategically because it had a host of complex regional security concerns (which, it was apparently assumed, were not shared by the western powers) and politically because of its non-membership of the European Community, its internal Kurdish problem, poor human rights record and conflicts with Greece. Turkey's leaders liked to present themselves to the western powers as a bridge between Europe and the Middle East and central Asia, but there was a risk that western Europe might prefer to see it as a barrier against a hostile 'other', left outside European structures. In the absence of closer ties with western Europe, this line of argument suggested that Turks would look elsewhere for new areas of opportunity, such as those in post-communist Russia or the newly independent states of central Asia and the Black Sea.[4] *In extremis*, it was occasionally argued, Turkey might abandon its alignment with the west, in favour of a 'Eurasian' alliance with countries to its east. This view was not unknown in the Turkish army: as an example, in March 2002 General Tuncer Kılınç, then the Secretary of the National Security Council, appeared to suggest that Turkey should leave NATO and form an alliance with Russia or even Iran. However, he was promptly slapped down by the Chief of the General Staff, General Hüseyin Kıvrıkoğlu, as well as the then Prime Minister Bülent Ecevit and President Ahmet Necdet Sezer.[5]

On the other side of the argument, less radical assessments proposed that Turkey's links to the west had not lost their importance to either side. The end of the Cold War had not been all bad news for Turkey, and it was suggested that its new opportunities were complementary rather than contradictory to its links with the western powers.[6] The idea that Turkey would be drawn away from the west by new opportunities in central Asia and elsewhere – that it might seek an 'Middle Eastern' or 'Turkic' identity rather than a 'western' one – was disputed by experienced observers such as Paul Henze, who pointed out that the supposed new choices were 'not contradictory or competitive, they are complimentary'. It was in the interests of western Europe and the United States to regard Turkey as an 'integral component' that could also 'maximise its relations with the Middle East and Central Asia', he claimed.[7] It could also be argued that an active policy outside Europe was important for Turkey partly because it increased the value of Turkish friendship for western policy-makers in the post-Cold War environment. Hence, as Ziya Öniş suggested, Turkey 'should look simultaneously to both the East and the West' and accept the fact that 'Islam constitutes an important part of its cultural heritage'.[8]

After 2002, when domestic politics altered course with the election victory of the Justice and Development Party (AKP), not all of Turkey's foreign policy was contested. Except on the radical-Islamist right and the ultra-left, as well as among occasional ultra-nationalists such as General Kılınç, it was generally accepted that Turkey needed to maintain its links with NATO and its bid to join the European Union. In relations with Turkey's 'near abroad', however, two contrasting visions had emerged. The first adopted a highly securitized approach, which accepted that the threat from Russia had ended but argued that Turkey was still surrounded by enemies and needed to continue with an intensely suspicious attitude to all its neighbours, having national security as the overriding concern. Thus, in an article published in 1996, Şükrü Elekdağ, formerly Under-Secretary at the Turkish foreign ministry and ambassador to Washington, argued that Turkey still faced the danger of a 'two and a half front war', the two main fronts being against Greece and Syria, who might act together, and the 'half' front being the internal struggle against the PKK.[9] Elsewhere, Elekdağ described Turkey as being 'besieged by a veritable ring of evil'.[10] This assumption was born out by Turkish defence spending during the 1990s, which, like that of Greece, continued to account for a larger share of its GDP than in the case of other NATO countries.[11] Critics could argue that this high rate of military expenditure derived partly from the influential role played by the military in internal politics, or the need to fight the PKK and confront Greece over Cyprus, both of which might have been avoided by more flexible policies.

Against this was the alternative doctrine, presented quintessentially by Professor Ahmet Davutoğlu, foreign policy advisor to the new Prime Minister Tayyip Erdoğan between 2002 and 2009, when he became foreign minister. One critic saw Davutoğlu as 'always the hero of his own narratives', but if nothing else he acquired a higher profile on the international stage than any of his recent predecessors, with his neat moustache normally framing a bemused smile, and a seemingly indefatigable diplomatic activism that earned his the soubriquet of 'Energizer Bunny' from State Department officials.[12] Although the AKP had distinctly Islamist origins, Davutoğlu rejected the classic Islamist worldview of inevitable and perpetual warfare between Muslims and 'infidels'. Instead, he argued that the Muslim world did not have the resources to develop a global strategy as an anti-systemic force. He went on to maintain that 'the history of civilisations is not composed only of clashes' and that 'a comprehensive civilisational dialogue ... is needed for a globally legitimate international order'.[13] In a book published in 2000, he developed his thesis by arguing that Turkey, thanks to its geographical position, possessed a 'strategic depth' that it had hitherto failed to exploit: it should move away from its previous 'threat assessment approach' to develop an active engagement in regional political systems in the Middle East, Asia, the Balkans and Transcaucasia.[14]

After the AKP had come to power, Davutoğlu gave further clues to his thinking, by suggesting that rather than acting as a mere 'bridge' between the west and the Muslim world, a previously repeated mantra of Turkish foreign policy spokesmen, Turkey should act as a 'central country', breaking away from a 'static and single-parameter policy' and becoming a 'problem solver' contributing to 'global and regional peace'.[15] He has expanded this by emphasizing: '[W]e don't want to be on the agenda of [the] international community as one item of crisis. We want to be in the international community to solve the crisis.'[16] Rather than concentrating purely on defence, Davutoğlu stressed that Turkey should work for 'zero problems' with all its neighbours. In accordance with these principles, and where possible, the AKP government tried to make greater use of 'soft power' – economic, political and cultural – in place of the alternative heavily securitized doctrine, especially in relations with its Middle Eastern neighbours.[17] In general, and although Davutoğlu certainly helped to give Turkish foreign policy a much higher international profile, it can be argued that, in practice, the two approaches – securitized nationalism and de-securitized liberalism – continued in uneasy tandem, and that the AKP leadership did not always stick strictly to its own declared principles. Unexpected events, like the so-called 'Arab Spring' of actual and attempted political liberalization in the Middle East in 2011, faced it with questions that Davutoğlu's grand vision had not always foreseen. This reflected both the internal balance of power between the AKP government and the state establishment, and hard external realities.

Some broader cultural changes also suggested that the context of policy-making was gradually changing. When the writer first visited Turkey in 1960–1, it still seemed quite isolated from the rest of the world – intensely patriotic but locked into an inward-looking ethnic nationalism, apparently stemming from a sense of insecurity, which sought to deny the Ottoman heritage as well as global currents. Problematic issues such as the Kurdish question or the fate of the Ottoman Armenians were simply excluded from the public discourse. Fifty years later, global as well as internal changes had worked an impressive transformation, at least in urban and middle class society. Globalized con-sumerism was the most obvious aspect of this, but change went deeper, as previously taboo subjects – such as the role of the non-Muslim minorities in late Ottoman Istanbul, Kurdish ethnicity or the relations between Sunni and Alevi Muslims – were openly discussed and even positively celebrated with exhibitions, concerts and the like. Multiculturalism was now seen as a source of strength rather than weakness. From being considered 'oriental', Istanbul had become 'cool', host to vibrant new artistic and intellectual currents. Istanbul was not the whole of Turkey of course. The new class of confident, outward-looking liberal intellectuals co-existed uneasily with a predominantly conservative society in most of Anatolia. Nonetheless, its emergence sug-gested that the Turkish worldview was gradually undergoing some profound transformations, with important implications for the future.

The domestic environment, 1990–2011

Whether Turkish governments could exploit the new opportunities apparently presented by the end of the Cold War, and how they would do so, also depended on whether they could depend on a stable domestic power base. During the 1990s, this was the Achilles' heel of Turkish foreign policy, since external problems were seriously exacerbated by internal weaknesses and conflicts. In the search for effective democratic government, the record of the 1990s was a generally dismal one. No single party won an overall majority in parliament in any of the three general elections – held in 1991, 1995 and 1999 – and Turkey slipped back into the position of chronic governmental instability that it had experienced during the 1970s, although the story of the slide into near-anarchy and eventual military takeover of 1978–80 was fortunately not repeated. It was not until 2002 that a stable government with a reliable majority was established under the AKP. This gave Tayyip Erdoğan's government a huge advantage over its predecessors, in which it had the chance to implement a much more concerted foreign policy.

Between 1987 and 1991, Turgut Özal's apparently solid hold on domestic political support was badly eroded by his government's economic failures, in particular, its failure to control inflation, which ran at an average annual level of 66 per cent between 1988 and 1991.[18] When he had succeeded Kenan Evren as President in 1989, Özal had been constitutionally obliged to sever all official links with the Motherland Party. However, in practice, he continued to control both the party and the government from behind the scenes. In this situation, his Prime Minister, Yıldırım Akbulut, failed to impress either the party or the public as an effective leader. In a party convention held in June 1991, he was successfully challenged by his former foreign minister, Mesut Yılmaz, who now took over as party chairman and Prime Minister. Unwisely, Yılmaz decided to call an early general election in October 1991, in which the Motherland Party came in a poor second, with 112 seats, well behind Süleyman Demirel's True Path Party (DYP), which won 179 seats. Erdal İnönü's Social Democrat Populist Party (SHP) won 91 seats. Although there was relatively little difference in terms of policies between the Motherland and True Path parties, the fierce rivalry between Demirel and Özal prevented any collaboration between the two, and Demirel formed an unwieldy coalition with the social democrats. His government lasted until 17 April 1993, when President Özal died suddenly of a heart attack. Since Demirel decided to take over the presidency, to which he was elected by parliament on 16 May, a new Prime Minister and leader of the True Path Party had to be found. Unexpectedly, a special party convention elected Mrs Tansu Çiller, who took over the premiership on 25 June 1993.

Tansu Çiller's installation aroused high hopes, since she was thought of as a liberal, and the appointment of a woman Prime Minister in a Muslim country was regarded as an important milestone. Her defects were her lack of political experience and her weak grip over the levers of power within her own party. Her government was also badly shaken by one of Turkey's periodic economic crises, in the spring of 1994, causing a rapid devaluation of the currency and a slump in economic growth. Loss of confidence in the government was compounded by unproven allegations of corruption against the Prime Minister and her husband, but was also affected by turmoils on the centre-left of the political spectrum that were beyond her control. In 1992 a group of MPs led by Deniz Baykal had left the SHP to re-establish the Republican People's

Party (CHP). This reunited with the SHP in February 1995, under Baykal's leadership and the CHP's title. In the following September, Baykal pulled his party out of the coalition. After an unsuccessful attempt by Mrs Çiller to form a minority government, a new DYP–CHP coalition was stitched together in November, but only on the condition, demanded by Baykal, that new elections be held on 24 December.

The serious governmental instability that had developed after 1993 was exacerbated by the results of the December 1995 elections, in which Necmettin Erbakan's pro-Islamist Welfare Party became the biggest single party in the assembly, with 158 of the 550 seats. The remainder of parliament was evenly split between the True Path and Motherland parties, with 135 and 132 seats respectively, to be followed by Bülent Ecevit's Democratic Left Party (DSP), which had 76 seats, and a much reduced CHP (49 seats). After months of fruitless bargaining, Mesut Yılmaz formed a coalition with Mrs Çiller on 12 March 1996, but this fell apart just one month later. Reversing her previous stand of fierce opposition to political Islamism, Tansu Çiller then formed an alliance with Necmettin Erbakan, resulting in a coalition between their two parties which took office on 26 June, with Erbakan as Premier. From the start, the coalition was wracked by dissent between its two constituents and was further weakened by the revelation of damaging links between parts of the government and the police service with organized crime, which was revealed by an automobile crash at Susurluk, in western Anatolia, on 3 November 1996.[19] Meanwhile, Erbakan's moves towards creeping Islamization (especially in education) aroused the ire of the staunchly secularist generals, as well as much of an emerging civil society. On 18 June 1997, in the face of repeated warnings from the military-dominated National Security Council, as well as mounting public protests, Erbakan resigned, hoping to reconstruct the government under Mrs Çiller's premiership. However, backbench defections from the DYP to a short-lived Democratic Turkey Party (DTP) robbed the coalition of its majority. Accordingly, President Demirel passed on the baton to Mesut Yılmaz, who formed a minority government, in coalition with Ecevit's DSP and the DTP, on 30 June 1997. Subsequently, in February 1998, the Welfare Party was closed down by order of the Constitutional Court for breaking articles of the constitution protecting secularism, and Necmettin Erbakan was banned from running for public office for the following five years. Nonetheless, a successor party was rapidly formed, in the shape of the Virtue Party, nominally under the leadership of Recai Kutan.

Yılmaz's third government (and Turkey's ninth since 1991) managed to hold on to power for 15 months, but was weakened from the start by its dependence on uncertain outside support by the CHP. On 25 November 1998, in the wake of unproven corruption allegations against the government, Baykal withdrew this lifeline and the government was defeated in a vote of confidence. On 30 July 1998, parliament had voted to hold early general elections in April 1999, To fill the gap, Ecevit formed a minority caretaker administration. The results of the poll, held on 18 April 1999, were a serious setback for Tansu Çiller, Mesut Yilmaz and Recai Kutan, whose tallies were reduced to 85, 86 and 111 seats respectively. They were also a disaster for the CHP, which failed to surmount the 10 per cent threshold, below which parties cannot win any seats in parliament. With 136 seats, Ecevit's DSP was now the biggest party in the assembly, but the surprise winner was the Nationalist Action Party (MHP), formerly the vehicle for Alparslan Türkeş and his brand of ultra-nationalism. Following Türkeş' death in 1997, the party leadership had been captured by the sober and distinctly uncharismatic Devlet Bahçeli, who succeeded both in converting the party to a more moderate but uncertain position and in making it the second biggest party in parliament by winning 129 seats in the elections. Although many DSP members had serious suspicions about the MHP,[20] Bahçeli took his place as deputy premier in a tripartite coalition with the DSP and the Motherland Party, under Ecevit's premiership, which took office on 28 May 1999.

On 17 August 1999, the Ecevit government's standing was shattered by a massive earthquake in the Gulf of İzmit, near Istanbul, in which more than 17,000 people lost their lives. State agencies – notably the army and the quasi-governmental Red Crescent organization – were quite unprepared for the disaster. Although the government made progress in its relations with the European Union, its chronic failures in handling the economy destroyed its popularity. An open row between Ecevit and Ahmet Necdet Sezer, who had succeeded Demirel as President in May 2001, produced a catastrophic economic crash. By the spring and summer of 2002, the Ecevit government was clearly falling apart. The Prime Minister's health (he was by now 77 years old) had been failing for some time. In May 2002 he was hospitalized twice with a variety of maladies and was unable to carry out his normal duties for around two months. In July 2002, his successful foreign minister, İsmail Cem, resigned to form his own New Turkey Party (YTP) where he was joined by 58 ex-DSP backbenchers, robbing the government of its majority. On 31 July 2002, parliament voted to hold general elections on 3 November.

The election campaign in the autumn of 2002 saw the emergence of a new actor on the national political scene. As a member of Necmettin Erbakan's Welfare Party, Recep Tayyip Erdoğan had been a successful mayor of Istanbul between 1994 and 1998, when he was convicted of 'stirring up hatred and enmity with regard to … religion' and sentenced to ten months in prison as well as a lifetime ban from participation in politics. Following the closure of the Welfare Party in 1998, Erdoğan emerged as the leader of a group within its successor, the Virtue Party, known as the 'renewalists'. This opposed Erbakan and sought to convert the party to a pro-western, liberal-conservative stance, with tinges of Islamism. After an unsuccessful attempt by the 'renewalists' to take over the leadership of the Virtue Party at its first national convention in May 2000, Erdoğan and his supporters set up the Justice and Development Party (AKP) on 14 August 2001. The new party abandoned Erbakan's former call for an Islamic order, and strongly backed the improvement of human rights and Turkey's bid to join the EU.

As the election results came in, it was clear that the AKP had won by a landslide. None of the previous ruling parties passed the 10 per cent threshold that they would have needed to win any seats in parliament. With around 46 per cent of the vote going to parties scoring less than 10 per cent (and thus effectively discounted) the AKP won 363 of the 550 seats on 34.3 per cent of the poll. As the only other party to pass the 10 per cent threshold, the CHP came in a poor second, with 19.4 per cent of the poll and 178 seats. Remarkably, the AKP repeated this performance in the following general elections, held in July 2007, increasing its score to 46.6 per cent, with the CHP getting 20.9 per cent and the MHP breaking through the threshold with 14.3 per cent of the votes. Thanks to the presence of the third party, the AKP's parliamentary representation was reduced slightly in 2007, to 341 seats, but this still left it with a massive majority of 132 seats over the combined opposition.[21]

In spite of its electoral successes, the AKP government faced a number of serious domestic challenges, mainly because it aimed to limit the power of the authoritarian secularist state elite, represented by the military, the judiciary and parts of the civil service, as well as the CHP. Initially, Erdoğan was constitutionally prevented from running for parliament, and thus becoming Prime Minister, thanks to his conviction of 1998. It was not until March 2003 that he overcame this obstacle, having used the AKP's parliamentary majority to amend the constitution. In the meantime his deputy, Abdullah Gül, served as Premier. In April 2007, Gül was elected to the presidency, following the retirement of the militantly secularist President Ahmet Necdet Sezer. However, this result was overruled by the Constitutional Court on highly dubious grounds. In response, the government decided to opt for general elections in July, which it won by a landslide. In the new assembly, Gül was duly elected President on 28 August. Parliament also passed a constitutional amendment, providing for the direct election of future Presidents by the voters for a maximum of two four-year terms. This was carried by a majority of just under 70 per cent in a national referendum held in October 2007.

The challenge to the government from the judicial authorities was not over, however. In February 2008, the MHP joined the AKP in passing a further amendment to the constitution, which would have allowed female university students to wear the traditional Muslim headscarf to class. This change was hotly opposed by the hard-line secularists as an allegedly unacceptable infringement of Kemalism and was annulled by the Constitutional Court on grounds that appeared to give it the quite unconstitutional right to overrule any amendment to the constitution. Worse was to come in March 2008, when the Chief Public Prosecutor of the Court of Cassation applied to the Constitutional Court for the closure of the AKP, on the grounds that it had become the 'focus of activities' aimed at destroying the secular character of the republic. The charge was rejected by a margin of just one vote in the panel of 11 judges.[22] Further challenges came from the military, which in April 2007 had issued a thinly-veiled threat of a *coup d'état* if Abdullah Gül were elected president – a threat from which it later backed off in the face of a harsh public reaction.

Later, the higher ranks of the army were battered by a series of allegations of attempted plots to overthrow the government, known as the 'Ergenekon', 'Cage Action' and 'Sledgehammer' plots, which erupted during 2008–10.[23] These resulted in the quite unprecedented arrest and trials of a number of senior retired and serving officers, which were still dragging on in 2012. Although it was far from certain that all those arrested were guilty as charged, the military suffered a severe loss of public prestige, which significantly weakened its hand as an independent political actor. The contest came to a head in July 2011 as the government refused to allow the promotion of 17 generals and admirals who had been accused of involvement in the 'Sledgehammer' conspiracy. In response, the Chief of the General Staff, General Işık Koşaner, resigned on 29 July, along with the commanders of the army, navy and air force, with General Koşaner claiming: 'I am unable to fulfil my responsibility to protect the rights of my personnel as the Chief of General Staff.' President Abdullah Gül reacted swiftly by appointing General Necdet Özel, the Commander of Gendarmerie and the only one of the four force commanders who had not resigned, as Commander of Land Forces. This paved the way for his appointment as Chief of the General Staff at the meeting of the High Military Council (YAŞ) held on 4 August 2011, at which new appointments to the command of the army, air force, navy and gendarmerie were also made.[24] In effect, the government had outmanoeuvred the soldiers and seriously reduced their ability to play an independent political role, in foreign relations as well as other public policy areas.

Meanwhile, the general elections held on 12 June 2011 came as further proof of the AKP's dominance over the political system. By increasing its share of the vote to just under 50 per cent, and winning 326 of the 550 seats in parliament, the AKP had now won three general elections in succession – the first time any party had achieved this since the days of Adnan Menderes' Democrat Party in the 1950s. Even more surprisingly, it had increased its share of the poll on each occasion. Although the CHP increased its vote share slightly, to just under 26 per cent, it was still failing to make much impression on the electorate, in spite of a change of leadership from Deniz Baykal to Kemal Kılıçdaroğlu in May 2010.[25] As a result, the main concern of those who had previously worried about instability and lack of direction in Turkish politics began to be replaced by the anxiety that the government had now become too powerful rather than too weak.

Turkey's Kurdish question

With the end of the Cold War, the Kurdish problem – in particular, the campaign of violence by the PKK – became Turkey's most important and immediate security issue, gathering pace during the early 1990s.[26] Until 1998, the PKK leader Abdullah Öcalan was an unacknowledged guest of the Syrian government and benefited from Syrian logistic support as well as the use of training camps in the Syrian-occupied Bekaa Valley in the Lebanon. The Kurdish cause also won more international publicity after Saddam Hussein's brutal repression of the Kurdish rebellion in Iraq, just after the Gulf war of 1991. On 5 April 1991, following the flight of around 500,000 mainly Kurdish refugees to the Iraqi–Turkish border and even larger numbers to that with Iran, the United Nations Security Council passed Resolution 688. Under the Resolution, an international force, initially numbering around 20,000 troops from 11 countries, established a 'safe haven' in northern Iraq, to which all the refugees had been able to return by the end of May.[27]

'Operation Provide Comfort', as it was initially known, solved the immediate problem of the refugees but exacerbated Turkey's internal Kurdish problem, since it attracted international attention to the Kurdish cause and provided a base (or at least a power vacuum) in northern Iraq from which PKK insurgents could attack targets in Turkey. Exploiting this position, and benefiting from continued support by Syria, the PKK was able to intensify its campaign. By 1993, it almost seemed on the verge of leading a mass popular uprising on the lines of the Palestinian *intifada* – running its own 'liberated zones', extorting taxes, suppressing activities by the other political parties and ruthlessly punishing alleged 'collaborators'.[28] In March 1993, and perhaps encouraged by rather vague and indirect contacts with President Özal via the Iraqi Kurdish leader Jelal Talabani,[29] Öcalan declared a unilateral ceasefire. However, this failed to provoke any effective political response by the Turkish government.[30] As a result, the war against the PKK was resumed at full scale.

After 1993, the PKK's chances of achieving long-run military success gradually receded. By 1994–5, the Turkish army and gendarmerie were starting to regain the upper hand in south-eastern Anatolia, where the fighting was concentrated, and by 1998 they had re-established control over most of the region. Turkey also became engaged in the struggle for power in northern Iraq, firstly by an incursion into Iraqi territory against the PKK in 1992, and then a far larger attack in 1995. These were followed by further operations in 1996 and afterwards, in which the Turkish forces collaborated with the *peshmerga* militia attached to the Kurdistan Democratic Party, led by Massoud Barzani.[31]

Meanwhile, successive Turkish governments took an uncertain but generally hawkish line against non-violent activities by Kurdish political groups in Turkey. After their establishment of a coalition government in November 1991, Süleyman Demirel and Erdal İnönü made a well-publicized visit to the south east, in which Demirel proclaimed that 'Turkey must recognize the Kurdish reality'.[32] The October 1991 elections also brought to parliament a group of 22 Kurdish MPs, elected on the SHP ticket, who then joined the People's Labour Party (HEP), Turkey's first distinctly pro-Kurdish party.[33] This was closed down by order of the Constitutional Court in June 1993, but its members officially left the party shortly before this took effect and were able to set up a successor party, known as the Democracy Party (DEP). In March 1994, Tansu Çiller's government engineered the arrest of 13 of DEP's

MPs by lifting their parliamentary immunities. The party was closed down and they were charged with treason. Six of them managed to flee abroad, but the remainder were imprisoned and one was murdered. A third pro-Kurdish party was then set up, as the People's Democracy Party (HADEP) under Murat Bozlak. This was allowed to compete in the 1995 and 1999 general elections, as well as the local elections of 1999. It emerged as the leading party in a number of south-eastern provinces on both occasions, and in 1999 succeeded in winning the mayoralties in Diyarbakır and a number of other south-eastern towns and cities. However, it won less than 5 per cent of the national vote on both occasions and thus failed to capture any seats in parliament. Officially, HADEP disavowed terrorism, but many of its grassroots supporters were also supporters of the PKK, and the party found it hard to distance itself from it.[34]

A turning point in the PKK's career came during the winter of 1998–9. After a fierce Turkish diplomatic offensive against Syria, backed up with the threat of military action, Hafiz al-Assad's government expelled Öcalan on 7 October 1998, and he left for Moscow (see pp233–4). On 12 November, he made a dramatic appearance in Rome airport, where he was arrested for carrying a false passport, and then tried to gain political asylum in Italy. The Italian authorities expelled their unwelcome guest on 16 January 1999, when he set off on another odyssey to Belarus, Russia and Greece. Öcalan eventually arrived at the Greek ambassador's residence in Nairobi, Kenya, on 2 February, carrying a Greek Cypriot diplomatic passport. On 16 February, he was captured by a Turkish security team while on his way to Nairobi airport and brought back to Turkey, where he was placed on trial before a State Security Court on 30 May.[35] On 29 June, the court sentenced him to death under Article 125 of the Turkish Penal Code, which makes it an offence to attempt to remove any part of Turkish territory from the control of the state, and he was found guilty of causing the deaths of thousands of innocent people. Under the constitution, if Öcalan were to be executed, parliament would have had to pass a positive vote to that effect. However, it failed to do so. Eventually, under strong pressure from the Council of Europe and the European Union, it abolished capital punishment altogether in 2002, and Öcalan's sentence was changed to life imprisonment. Meanwhile, the PKK declared a unilateral ceasefire in August 1999.[36]

Unfortunately, hopes of an end to the armed struggle against the PKK proved short-lived. Following the US-led invasion of Iraq in March 2003 and the establishment of a virtually independent Kurdish administration in northern Iraq under American protection, the PKK won a new lease of life, inducing it to end its ceasefire the following September. From bases in northern Iraq, the PKK's new campaign cost nearly 150 lives, including those of 37 civilians between 2003 and 2005.[37] After a short lull, the PKK launched a new series of assaults in the autumn of 2007, culminating in an attack on 21 October in which 12 Turkish soldiers were killed and another eight abducted.[38] These attacks naturally provoked a sharp dispute between the

Turkish government and the US authorities in Iraq, who proved to be unable, or unwilling, to take effective action against the PKK bases in Iraqi territory. It was only in November 2007, and under threat that Turkey might launch another unilateral cross-border military operation, that President George W. Bush agreed that the US would give the Turks 'real time' intelligence on the Iraqi-based PKK – in effect, giving the Turkish forces a green light for limited operations in northern Iraq (see p169).[39] Allegedly, the resulting attacks severely damaged the PKK's military strength, although it did not eliminate it.

As the conflict dragged on, it became gradually accepted in Turkey that it could not be ended by purely military means but had to be addressed at the political level also. In the 2007 elections, the Democratic Society Party (DTP), which had succeeded DEHAP in 2005 as the main pro-Kurdish party in Turkey and had unofficial links with the PKK, succeeded in evading the 10 per cent election barrage by running its candidates as nominal independents. This secured the election of 19 deputies who re-joined the DTP after taking their seats, with two others joining the party later. In this way, Kurdish nationalism gained a recognized voice in parliament. By the end of 2005, Tayyip Erdoğan was changing the official discourse, by accepting the existence of multiple ethnic identities within a common Turkish citizenship. In effect, the national identity was being redefined as civic rather than ethnic: Turkish Kurds often referred to themselves as *Türkiyeli* ('from Turkey') rather than *Türk*. As Erdoğan told a Kurdish audience in the remote south-eastern town of Şemdinli in November 2005: 'We will respect secondary identities – that is, a Turk will say "I am a Turk", a Kurd will say "I am a Kurd", a Laz will say "I am a Laz" – everyone will be obliged to respect this. But we all have a primary identity, as a citizen of the Turkish republic.'[40] The government was not prepared to accept Kurdish demands for political autonomy within Turkey, but ready to promote Kurdish cultural rights, on which it was under strong pressure from the European Union. As part of a package of constitutional amendments passed in August 2002, the Ecevit government had allowed radio and television broadcasting in Kurdish by the state broadcasting corporation (TRT) as well as Kurdish language education in private institutions: in July 2003, private radio and TV stations were also allowed to broadcast in Turkish. By 2010, there was a full-time Kurdish language channel on state television ('TRT 6') and a private Kurdish TV channel broadcasting from Gaziantep.[41] Some universities were setting up Kurdish language departments, although there were no Kurdish classes in state schools.

In the autumn of 2009, the AKP government appeared to be going further than this, when it launched what was called the 'Kurdish opening'. As originally planned, this would have included reform, if not abolition of the much criticized 'village guards' system, in which pro-government Kurds were armed and trained by the army to act as a sort of official militia, the establishment of elective Kurdish courses in state schools, and increased investment in development schemes in the south east.[42] Using the new links that the government was establishing with the Kurdish administration in Iraq, it was hoped to bring the majority of PKK fighters 'down from the mountains', by being resettled in Turkey. The 300-odd militants who were counted as leaders of the organization would not receive an amnesty but might be resettled in countries other than Turkey.[43]

The 'Kurdish opening' was certainly welcome, but most of it was left unimplemented, mainly because the government had underestimated the problems it faced. As a first step, 34 PKK members and their relatives (including four children) presented themselves at the Turkish–Iraqi border crossing post of Habur on 19 October 2009. After questioning by the Turkish judicial authorities, they travelled on to Diyarbakır, where they received a rapturous reception clearly orchestrated by the DTP. The government quickly realized that the PKK was turning the 'opening' into a propaganda coup for itself so on 24 October Tayyip Erdoğan announced 'a break' in the process.[44] Worse was to come on 11 December, when the Constitutional Court ordered the dissolution of the DTP on the grounds of 'its links with a terrorist organization and being the focal point of activities contrary to the indivisible integrity of the state'. While the Prime Minister stated that he opposed the closure of political parties, he had done nothing to prevent it in this case. In response, the DTP simply regrouped as the Peace and Democracy Party (BDP).[45] Although the BDP leadership was trying to promote a more moderate line, the 'Kurdish initiative' appeared to have dropped off the government's agenda: instead, it launched a 'democratic opening' of constitutional reforms, most of which did not address the Kurdish question directly (see pp191–2).

Moves towards a peace process in Turkey's Kurdish problem were not resumed until the autumn of 2010. By this stage, Turkey was getting extensive cooperation against the PKK from the Syrian government, as well as that of Iran, which was facing attacks by the 'Party for a Free Life in Kurdistan' (PJAK), an Iranian-Kurdish organization closely allied to the PKK. As a result, a number of PKK members were killed in operations in Iran and Syria, and around 200 were extradited to Turkey. There were also intense discussions with US intelligence officials and Massoud Barzani, the head of the Iraqi-Kurdish administration.[46] In the run-up to the constitutional referendum of 12 September (p192), the PKK declared another ceasefire, extending it in stages up to the end of February 2011.[47] Although the government denied that a deal had been struck with Abdullah Öcalan, state officials and intelligence officers were apparently in touch with him on his island prison of İmralı, and there were reports that, after the elections to be held in June 2011, parts of the 'Kurdish opening' might be revived.[48] Politically, there was no certainty that a settlement could be reached or that the PKK would finally lay down its arms, but at leat the government had accepted the need for a wide-ranging approach. If successful, this could have a significant effect on Turkey's external position, as well as its domestic politics, since the Kurdish problem had been a serious liability in its relations with the western powers (especially the European Union) as well as with its Middle Eastern neighbours.

Foreign policy-making: Actors, parties and public opinion

As previous chapters have explained, the circle of foreign policy actors had only begun to broaden in Turkey during the 1960s, as new political currents and a loosening of the consensus on foreign policy had started to develop.[49] The process of foreign policy-making is one of the least well-studied aspects of Turkish foreign policy and suggestions can often only be speculative or illustrated by occasional examples. Nonetheless, what could be described as the group of 'state actors' apparently continued to be the dominant decision-makers during the 1990s. These included, principally, the President, Prime Minister and foreign minister, plus the commanders of the armed forces (combined, since 1961, in the National Security Council) and the professional diplomats in the foreign ministry. Thanks to the weakness of successive governments, the military regained some of its role as an independent policy-maker.[50] There were also differences of approach between individuals within the state elite. In particular, during his period as President between 1989 and 1993, Turgut Özal was more visionary and more prepared to take risks and new policy directions than either his predecessors or his successor. More broadly, he tried to convert the presidency into an independent source of policy and power. After his death, Süleyman Demirel, who had taken relatively little interest in foreign policy during his previous stints as Premier, oversaw a return to a more conservative, traditionalist and institutionalized style in foreign policy.[51]

While the lack of detailed research makes it hard to be categorical, there were some fairly clear signs of a shift of the balance of power between foreign policy actors after the AKP came to power in 2002. In particular, the elected government increased its authority at the expense of non-elected officials, the army in particular. Although it is hard to be exact about this, populist currents, and public opinion generally, also appeared to become more influential. As examples, in 2004, in giving full support to the Annan peace plan for Cyprus, the government successfully overrode open objections by the military chiefs, although the plan was later rejected by the Greek Cypriots (pp199–200). Similarly, in 2007 it overcame attempts by the military to boycott the Kurdish Regional Government in northern Iraq, and to launch unilateral cross border operations into Iraqi Kurdistan (p237). The causes of this shift of power were almost entirely domestic – in particular, the army's loss of public standing due to the 'Ergenekon' and 'Sledgehammer' cases – and the outcome of the military appointments crisis of July–August 2011 (p143). Nonetheless it had important foreign policy implications, since the unelected state elite, especially the military, had lost its dominance in the direction of policy.

In Turkey, as in other countries, the available evidence indicates that most ordinary citizens attach far less importance to foreign policy than to domestic issues. Thus, a survey conducted by the Strateji-Mori polling organization in Istanbul in 1997 found that 57 per cent of the respondents described themselves as 'not-interested' in foreign policy, with only 23 per cent 'interested': not surprisingly, those with higher education were more likely to be interested than those without.[52] During election campaigns, opinion polls nearly always suggest that most voters attach primary importance to the state of the economy, with foreign policy well down in the list of priorities – if indeed it figures at all.[53] Similarly, the programmes and election manifestos of the political parties devote little space to foreign policy. As an example, the current programme of the AKP devotes almost all its attention to 'Basic Rights and Political Principles', the economy, public administration and social policies, with foreign policy only figuring as a short section at the end of the document, almost as an afterthought.[54]

Public opinion polls in Turkey on foreign policy questions should be treated very cautiously, since people may well give arbitrary or poorly-informed answers, so as not to appear ignorant. Thus, in a poll conducted in December 2010, an astonishing 42.6 per cent of respondents rated the United States as 'the biggest foreign threat directed against Turkey', although there was not the slightest sign that the USA was likely to attack the country: probably, people were simply using the opportunity to express their opposition to American policy in the Middle East.[55] More broadly, assessing the effects of shifts in opinion on foreign policy is extremely hard, due to the risk of confusing cause and effect. As an example, the decline of public support for Turkey's eventual membership of the European Union after 2004 (p192) appears to have been the result, rather than the cause, of growing political problems in the Turkey–EU relationship; in this case, public opinion was a dependent, not determinant variable. Nevertheless, the available evidence suggested that, with the passage of time, it was becoming more influential and more vocal in foreign policy-making, especially on issues that raised serious questions affecting national security, and on which there was extensive media coverage and general support. A prime example was the overwhelming public opposition to cooperation with the United States in the invasion of Iraq, in spite of reluctant support for the idea by the government; this resulted in the unexpected parliamentary vote of 1 March 2003 that refused to allow US troops to enter northern Iraq from Turkish territory (p167). The knowledge that public opinion supported a strongly critical attitude towards Israel, especially after the deadly Israeli bombardment of the Gaza strip during December 2008–January 2009, and the attack on the Turkish aid ship *Mavi Marmara* in May 2010, was almost certainly instrumental in determining Tayyip Erdoğan's increasingly anti-Israeli rhetoric: for once, he had a foreign policy issue on which he knew he had the bulk of public opinion behind him, and on which he knew people felt strongly – even those who did not support the AKP (pp230–1).[56] This made it virtually impossible to re-establish the previous entente with Israel, even if he had wanted to do so.

Party loyalties were generally reflected in the media, in which the main national dailies and commercial TV companies (that are in many cases owned by the same groups) supported a pro-western secularist position, while the minority of pro-Islamist newspapers and broadcasters adopted the opposite stance. The influential Feza Group, owning the newspaper *Zaman* and the TV channel Samanyolu, combined broad support for the AKP with a liberal rather than distinctly Islamist position. After 2002, the press was broadly divided into two camps, pro- and anti-AKP, with the former predictably supportive of the government's foreign policy, while the latter opposed it. The media as a whole could take stridently nationalist stands towards particular incidents – as for instance, in the crisis with Greece over the islet of Kardak (Imia) in 1996 – which made crisis management far more difficult (see p196). Similarly, extensive media coverage of both the bombardment of Gaza and the *Mavi Marmara* affair played a major role in stirring up the public reaction, deepening the Turkish–Israeli rift.

During the 1990s, there was much discussion of whether Turkey was developing a 'civil society' similar to those of western democracies, in which non-governmental organizations, such as business groups, trades unions and voluntary bodies, were coming to play a bigger role in the country's politics.[57] Of these, probably the most influential were business associations, notably the Turkish Industrialists' and Businessmen's Association (TÜSİAD) and the Union of Chambers (TTOBB). Both these groups, like the two main labour confederations, Türk-İş and DİSK, supported pro-western and anti-Islamist policies,[58] although the Islamist-nationalists had their own business association, MÜSİAD, and labour confederation (Hak-İş). Within Turkey, there were also emergent lobbies formed by people of particular ethnic origins. Besides the obvious case of the Kurds, these included citizens of Bulgarian, Bosnian, Chechen and Abkhazian origin, although just how influential they were at points of crisis can be disputed, particularly in Turkey's relationships with Russia, and its policies in the Balkans (see pp210, 202). Among other ethnic organizations, that of the Uighur refugees from China's Xinjiang province, had only a periodic impact (pp246–7). Other emerging non-governmental organizations that had some role in foreign policy included environmentalist groups such as the Turkish branch of Greenpeace, protesting against the passage of huge oil tankers through the Bosporus.[59]

Under the AKP, two NGOs with clearly Islamist sympathies began to have a significant impact on Turkey's international relations. The first was the educational and cultural movement established by the influential Nakshibendi religious leader Fethullah Gülen. In the current context, the most important of the Gülen movement's activities was the foundation of a chain of privately financed schools in an impressive range of countries, ranging from south-east Europe to central Asia, Africa and even the United States (pp224, 247). These projected conservative (though not specifically Islamic) values and had generally high academic standards. During the 1990s, the movement had been regarded with grave suspicion by the Turkish military and staunchly secularist politicians and bureaucrats, but under the AKP it achived a far wider degree of acceptance, and even moral support, as a unique attempt to promote Turkey's image on a global scale.[60]

Meanwhile, the most striking instance of NGO activism, which had highly controversial effects on foreign relations, was the crisis caused by the attempt by an aid convoy headed by the Turkish ship *Mavi Marmara* to break the Israeli blockade of Gaza in May 2010 (pp230–1). The lead organizer of the convoy, the Turkish-based 'Foundation for Human Rights and Freedoms and Humanitarian Relief' (İHH), was not entirely apolitical, since its main attachment was apparently to the radical-Islamist Felicity Party (*Saadet Partisi*, or SP). Nevertheless, in the country as a whole, most AKP supporters were almost certainly sympathetic to the aims of the blockade-runners, as were many supporters of other parties. Hence, the government was pushed into an international crisis by a non-governmental organization that it was hard to stop, for political if not for legal reasons.

The growing economic agenda

As in earlier decades, Turkish governments realized that their success or failure in delivering economic benefits, in the form of higher incomes and employment, and better social services, was the main criterion by which they would be judged by the electorate. A successful economic programme primarily required effective domestic policies. However, economic needs also became an important factor in foreign policy. In particular, Turkish governments had to try to prevent political conflicts with important trading partners, and avoid isolationist policies that could have cut them off from international financial markets or potential investors. An important effect of the end of the Cold War was that export markets in the former Soviet Union, which had previously been restricted by the state-controlled economic system, were now relatively open to Turkish, as to other exporters. At the same time, governments sought to use the country's growing economic power, relative to that of most of its immediate members, as an instrument in foreign policy. Increasing regional economic links and dependencies would, they believed, help to secure greater regional political stability. This approach was advocated, in particular, by Turgut Özal, during his term as President between 1989 and 1993, when he adopted the classic liberal concept that growing economic interdependencies between states would generate better political relations.[61] The same approach was energetically pursued by the AKP government after 2002, as part of the increased emphasis on 'soft power' as an instrument in foreign policy.

Economic trends after 1990 mirrored those that had begun during the 1980s. Gross National Product (GNP) continued to grow, from around $151 billion in 1990 to an estimated $1,029 billion by 2010, at exchange rate parities, or an average annual growth rate of around 3.6 per cent per year at constant prices. Meanwhile, exports rose from $13.0 billion in 1990 to $120.9 billion in 2010, and imports from $22.6 billion to $177.3 billion over the same period. As a result, total foreign merchandise trade, as a proportion of GNP, rose from 23.5 per cent to an estimated 40.6 per cent.[62] In effect, economic growth meant that external dependencies were also growing, as Turkey was increasingly integrated into the global economy.

Turkey's external accounts almost always showed a heavy deficit in merchandise trade, but part of this gap was covered by invisible items. Thus, in 2010, there was a visible trade deficit of $56.3 billion, but net income from services of around $14.2 billion. At $22.5 billion, tourism was easily the biggest item on the credit side. Allowing for net overseas interest payments of just under $8 billion, and income from migrants' remittances of around $1.4 billion, this left Turkey with an overall deficit on current account of $48.6 billion, which had to be filled by capital inflows.[63] The economy also moved higher up the technological ladder. By 2010, manufacturing industry accounted for just under 20 per cent of GNP, compared with just under 8 per cent for agriculture and 72.6 per cent for services.[64] Manufactured products now accounted for 92.6 per cent of total exports, and agricultural products for only 4.5 per cent. Heading the list of export items were textiles and clothing, at $21.6 billion, base metals at $14.5 billion and motor vehicles, consisting almost entirely of the well-known European, American, and Japanese brands, at $14.8 billion.[65]

While the Turkish economy was growing, until 2001 it was also plagued by very poor management by successive governments. Thanks to a massive public sector deficit, consumer price inflation ran at an average rate of around 75 per cent per annum between 1990 and 2000, and the exchange rate of the Turkish Lira fell from TL 2,609 to the US dollar in 1990 to TL 625,218 to the dollar in 2000. Meanwhile, the total outstanding external debt rose from $49.2 billion at the end of 1990, to $118.3 billion at the end of 2000, and the external debt service ratio (that is, interest payments as a proportion of GNP) to 35.4 per cent in 1998.[66] In effect, Turkey had a growing economy and foreign trade, but chronically high inflation, a very weak currency, and daunting external debts. Worse was to come in February 2001, when Prime Minister Ecevit had an open and bitter argument with President Sezer, in which the President accused Ecevit of failing to investigate reports of widespread malpractice at three state banks and failing to sack his Minister of Energy, who was accused of corrupt practices. This triggered off a panic in the already jittery markets, causing a stock market crash, with the collapse of two state banks and the inter-bank payments system. In the chaos, the currency devalued by almost 50 per cent in two months. According to different calculations, Gross Domestic Product (GDP) dropped by between 5.7 per cent and 7.5 per cent in 2001.[67] In the aftermath of the crisis, Kemal Derviş, a former Vice-President of the World Bank, was hastily appointed to the government, as minister of the economy, to draw up a stabilization plan under the auspices of the International Monetary Fund (IMF). In this, Turkey's relationship with the US government, which was strong at the time, was almost certainly a crucial factor: without the support of the Bush administration, it could be doubted that Turkey would have received such favourable treatment.[68] In May 2001, the government received a new credit line of $8 billion, in addition to $6 billion still available under a previous programme. In February 2002, this was succeeded by a new three-year stand-by agreement, in which the IMF granted another $17 billion in emergency credits.[69] In return, the government had to accept strict conditions, including tight fiscal targets so as to reduce the rampant public sector deficit, and establish the independence of the Central Bank, which was now free to fix interest rates. The recapitalization of the private banks and the restructuring of the state banking sector, rationalizing public employment, reforming the tax system and privatizing the large and cumbersome state sector of the economy were also important parts of the programme.[70]

With no alternative available, the Ecevit government began the implementation of this programme during 2001–2. This was continued by the succeeding AKP administration. In a dramatic turnaround of Turkey's previous economic performance, it came to be regarded as a prime example of a successful IMF restructuring exercise. As a report by the IMF of November 2007 concluded: 'Turkey has enjoyed a remarkable economic track record since the 2001 crisis.'[71] From more than 70 per cent at the beginning of 2002, the annual inflation rate, as measured by the consumer price index, fell to 9.3 per cent in 2004, and with one exception remained at less than 10 per cent thereafter.[72] As from 1 January 2005, the currency was redenominated by deleting the last six digits, so that everyday purchases no longer cost millions of Liras (at the time of writing in September 2011, the exchange rate stood at around TL 1.76 to the dollar). This corresponded to a decline in the consolidated central government deficit (hence, deficit financing by the government) to 3.6 per cent of estimated GDP in 2010.[73] Net foreign direct investment rose from a low point of $1 billion in 2002 to a high point of $19.9 billion in 2007, before falling back to $6.8 billion in 2008, in the wake of the global financial crisis.[74] Most crucially, economic growth was restored, with the average annual growth rate of GDP running at 6.9 per cent between 2002 and 2007.[75]

Thanks to its closer integration in to the global economy, Turkey could not escape the effects of the world financial crash of September–October 2008. Besides the fall in foreign direct investment, exports fell back from $132 billion in 2008 to $102 billion in 2009, thanks to the sharp fall in overseas demand, especially in the European Union.[76] In parallel, the annual growth rate of GDP fell from 4.7 per cent in 2007 to 0.7 per cent in 2008, to be followed by a drop of –4.7 per cent in 2009 (the first negative number recorded since 2001).[77] Two features distinguished this from previous economic crises, however. First, it was entirely exogenously generated, so that the government could not reasonably be blamed for the setback, limiting the political fallout. Second, Turkey had already undergone its banking crisis in 2001, and had taken the necessary measures. Hence, its financial system remained largely unaffected. The economy recovered remarkably quickly, with one estimate putting the GDP growth rate for 2010 at 8.1 per cent, or higher than any of the world's main economies but for China and India.[78]

The direction of Turkey's foreign trade had important implications for its foreign policies. In 1990, the then European Community accounted for just under 46 per cent of Turkey's total foreign merchandise trade (that is, exports plus imports) and trade with other OECD countries, primarily the USA and

Japan, for another 19 per cent. The Middle East accounted for 13 per cent of total trade, the USSR for 5 per cent and all other countries for the remaining 17 per cent.[79] By 1998, the most significant change had been the increased role of the countries of the former Soviet Union (officially grouped together as the Commonwealth of Independent States, or CIS) in Turkey's foreign trade, strengthening a trend which had begun in the 1980s. By 1996, the CIS accounted for about 12.7 per cent of Turkey's total foreign trade – a far higher proportion than during the Cold War – with the share of the EU increasing slightly to 49 per cent. Meanwhile, the share of the Middle East in total trade had shrunk to 5.9 per cent.[80] By 2010, there were further shifts in these patterns. The most striking trend was a decline in the EU's share of the total (in spite of the substantial geographical expansion of the EU since 1990) to just under 42 per cent, with a corresponding increase in that of the Middle East to 13.2 per cent, and of the CIS (mainly Russia) to 13.7 per cent.

Part of this shift was accounted for by rising oil and natural gas prices, and Turkey's growing consumption of both: in fact, securing reliable energy supplies at reasonable prices became a major task in Turkey's external relations. Since the economy was still at the stage of building up basic industries, economic growth meant a steady increase in the demand for energy. Thus, total primary energy consumption rose from 76.7 million tons oil equivalent (mtoe) in 2000 to almost 111 mtoe in 2010 – an increase of 45 per cent in ten years. Since Turkey's domestic energy resources are limited to lignite, some hard coal and hydro-power, virtually all crude oil and natural gas must be imported, and together account for around 58 per cent of total consumption. The rise in the consumption of natural gas has been particularly spectacular, from 14.6 billion cubic metres (bcm) in 2000 to 39 bcm in 2010.[81] Accordingly, building pipelines to bring gas from neighbouring countries – notably Russia, Azerbaijan and Iran, with Iraq a potential supplier – has become a crucial item in the foreign policy agenda, which is returned to later (pp208–9, 237, 241).

Turkey's need to secure reliable energy supplies to meet its own consumption is only part of the picture, however, since it is suggested that it could also serve as a 'energy bridge' between producers – especially of natural gas – in the Caspian basin and the Middle East, and customers in Europe. The Turkish route would be important for European consumers, partly because of the projected steady increase in Europe's demand for imported gas, with the expected decline of North Sea reserves, and partly because disputes between Russia and the Ukraine, through which Russian exports to Europe pass, have periodically threatened to interrupt supplies. For many European countries (Germany, France and Italy being the main exceptions) over-reliance on Russian gas was seen as a serious disability, especially in eastern Europe. Of the several international gas pipeline projects in which Turkey is involved, the only one which has actually so far got off the drawing board is a small-scale connector between the Turkish and Greek pipeline networks, taking gas imported by Turkey from Azerbaijan to its western neighbour, which was inaugurated in 2007 and supplies around 700 million cubic metres per year. If extended to Italy, as is planned, it could acquire some significance. However, it was overshadowed by the far bigger Nabucco project, which would aims to carry 31 billion cubic metres (bcm) of gas per year via a 3,300-kilometre pipeline across Turkey, and then through Bulgaria, Romania and Hungary to a distribution point in Baumgarten in Austria. A consortium of energy companies in each of the countries along the route would, plus Germany, construct and operate the pipeline.[82]

After years of preliminary planning, in 2009 the EU allocated €200 million from its European economic recovery package towards the project. This would be only a fraction of the total estimated cost of €8 billion, but was important as a symbol of the EU's commitment to Nabucco. In March 2010, Turkey became the last of the transit countries to ratify the Intergovernmental Agreement providing the legal framework for the project. A further financing package of up to €4 billion was agreed to in September 2010 by the European Bank for Reconstruction and Development, the European Investment Bank and the International Finance Corporation (part of the World Bank) and the consortium. Although the consortium originally planned to start construction in 2012, with the first gas flowing through the pipeline three years later, this planned completion date had been put back to 2017 by October 2011.[83] The main unanswered question hanging over the project was where the substantial gas supplies that were required would come from. Azerbaijan was identified as the first likely source, but even after expansion of its existing Shah Deniz gas field, in the Caspian, it was not expected to supply more than 10 bcm per year,[84] or only about a quarter of Nabucco's planned capacity (pp214–5). The next likely supplier was expected to be Turkmenistan, which has huge reserves of gas. Connecting its gas fields to Nabucco would raise serious political and technical problems, although the European Union announced in September 2011 that it would negotiate with Azerbaijan and Turkmenistan to bring Turkmen gas across the Caspian via an undersea pipeline. In the longer term, supplies from Iran and Iraq were also envisaged, although both these alternatives faced formidable political obstacles.[85] To sum up, if Nabucco were eventually to be built, it would potentially give Turkey enhanced international importance, although the outcome was still in doubt.

Besides Turkey's potential role in the international energy game, general commerce with countries outside Europe was also of growing importance, reflecting the shift in global economic power away from Europe and north America. Trade with Iraq, normally Turkey's biggest commercial partner in the Middle East, was restored by the lifting of UN sanctions against Iraq after Saddam Hussein's overthrow in 2003, and the gradual restoration of order in the country after 2005. Elsewhere, the east Asian countries were acquiring a growing role in Turkey's foreign trade: thus, China came from virtual insignificance to account for 6.5 per cent of Turkey's foreign trade by 2010. Data on Turkey's services income, broken down by country groups, are not available, except in the case of tourist entries: on this score, the western European countries were well in the lead, accounting for just over 49 per cent of the total in 2009, to be followed by the CIS, with 20 per cent, and visitors from the Middle East with 11 per cent. Meanwhile, a striking feature of Turkey's external commercial relations was that the United States, its main strategic ally, played a relatively insignificant role – accounting, for instance, for only 5.4 per cent of Turkey's total foreign trade in 2010.[86]

In terms of financial flows, Turkey's dependencies were still largely with the advanced industrial nations, although investors in the capital-rich oil exporting countries of the Middle East were acquiring an increasing role after 2005. In spite of the essential part the IMF had played in the restructuring programme after the 2001 crisis, by the end of 2008, of Turkey's total external liabilities of $183.4 billion, only about 18 per cent was accounted for by loans to the government, with around 22 per cent due to loans to the banking sector, and the remaining 60 per cent by loans to other sectors. The majority of these loans were provided by commercial banks, mainly in western Europe, the USA and Japan. In the growing inflow of investment capital, Middle Eastern investors were emerging as more important players, thus of the total inflow in 2007, around 80 per cent came from European countries, 8.4 per cent from the United States, and 6.8 per cent from the Middle East.[87]

Summarizing the effects of these trends on foreign policy is far from easy, but the first and most striking part of the emerging pattern was that, by 2011, Turkey was in a far stronger position economically than at any time in its recent past, enabling it to project a more powerful and effective international image and act as a pole of attraction to its smaller neighbours. It came to be identified as one of the world's most important emerging markets, and even likened to the 'BRIC' group of nations (Brazil, Russia, India and China) that were expected to oust western Europe, the USA and Japan from their former dominance of the global economy.[88] It also became a member of the G-20 group of the world's leading advanced and newly industrialized countries, increasing its engagement with global politics and providing a new forum for contacts between Turkish and world leaders.

This effect should not be overestimated, however. Turkey could be more confident internationally, but this did not mean that it could go it alone in world politics. By 2011, it had the world's seventeenth biggest economy, but it was still far smaller than those of the BRIC countries. Moreover, it was still seriously vulnerable at several points. The continuing deficit in the current account balance of payments – put in February 2011 at 6.4 per cent of GDP, or proportionately higher than that of any other European country[89] – meant that it was heavily dependent on capital inflows from abroad, some of which could go into reverse. Hence, it had to maintain a stable relationship with the capital-exporting countries, especially in Europe and the USA. Nor could it afford disputes with its Middle Eastern neighbours, given the importance of its cross-border trade. Maintaining tourism income, notoriously sensitive to political upsets, also required careful management of its foreign relations. The share of the EU in its foreign trade might be declining, but was still crucially important. Hence, there was still a huge economic incentive for continuing the quest for full EU membership, whatever the political problems. In short, Turkey now had a stronger and more confident international profile, but it still needed to be cautious, and mindful of the potential economic risks of over-ambitious policies.

7 Turkey and the west after the Cold War I

Turkey and the United States

During the 1970s and 1980s, it became possible to distinguish Turkey's relations with the United States from those with the other western powers. This trend continued after the end of the Cold War, but with important turning points and frequently contradictory trends in Turkey's relations with the European Union, on the one hand, and the United States on the other. Hence, what follows concentrates on the Ankara–Washington relationship, leaving the story of Turkey's bid to join the European Union to the following chapter.

In summary, relations between Ankara and Washington strengthened at the beginning of the 1990s, before fluctuating during the following years and then suffering a severe shock in 2003, with the American-led invasion of Iraq. The inauguration of the Obama administration at the beginning of 2009 appeared at first to herald a new start for Turkey's transatlantic links, but before long problems re-emerged. In the relationship with Washington, Turkey's relations with third parties – in particular, Israel, Iran and Iraq, including the Iraqi Kurds – were instrumental. These experiences had led to open questions about the basic orientation of Turkish foreign policy. The link with Washington still seemed to be of crucial importance, but more dependent on the convergence – or maybe divergence – of national interests than on broad perceptions of identity, and balanced by growing self-confidence and independence on the part of Turkish policy-makers. It was not until 2011 that US–Turkish relations seemed to have become re-established on a firmer basis, with broad agreement on most, but not all, the strategic issues facing the two governments.

Turkey and the United States after the Cold War: The first Gulf War and its aftermath, 1990–1

In 1992, when the Defence and Economic Cooperation Agreement (DECA) with the United States came up for renewal, it was extended for only one year. Turkey then asked for a renegotiation of its terms, but in practice the agreement was renewed automatically on an annual basis. Meanwhile, the American military presence in Turkey, with which the DECA was mainly concerned, was drastically reduced. This was part of America's global policy of reducing its military commitments worldwide, now that the Cold War was over. By the middle of 1994, eight of the 12 US military bases previously established in Turkey had been closed or handed over to the Turkish forces, although the vital NATO air base at İncirlik, near Adana, continued in operation. US military aid to Turkey was also scaled down substantially – partly because of congressional opposition over human rights and other issues, but partly also because there seemed to be less need for it, and it was discontinued altogether in 1999.[1]

In the early 1990s, the alliance between Turkey and the United States seemed firm because in many policy areas the two countries had common interests and common approaches. Both supported the admission of new eastern European members to NATO, achieved in the cases of Poland, Hungary and the Czech Republic in 1999,[2] and that of the states of the former Soviet Union to the Organization for Security and Cooperation in Europe (OSCE), NATO's Partnership for Peace programme, and the North Atlantic Cooperation Council. Although there were some differences between Turkey and the United States in their approaches to Russia, the US government strongly supported the plan to build an 'East–West energy corridor', linking the states of the Caspian basin to world markets via Turkey, and avoiding Russian territory (see pp213–5).[3] Turkey also played an active role in supporting actions by the United Nations, and then by the US and the rest of NATO, in Bosnia-Herzegovina, beginning in 1993–4. It appears that initially the Turkish foreign ministry may have been unenthusiastic about plans for a bombing campaign against the Serbs, following the eruption of the Kosovo crisis in 1998–9, but once the campaign began, Turkey gave it its full and active support – a policy in which the Turkish government was strongly supported by public opinion at home (see pp204–5).

For both sides, the Gulf crisis of 1990–1 was a critical turning point, since it gave Turkey an important role in US policy in the Middle East, which had been in abeyance since the collapse of the Baghdad Pact. Hence, it seems worthwhile to give a summary of this part of the story at this point.[4] Immediately after the Iraqi invasion of Kuwait on 2 August 1990, Turkey's reaction was uncertain, but Saddam Hussein's refusal to evacuate Kuwait and the imposition of an economic embargo on Iraq by the United Nations under Security Council Resolution 661 of 6 August, meant that the government was rapidly obliged to change course. Accordingly, on 8 August, it was announced that Turkey would suspend all commercial dealings with Iraq and close the oil pipeline from Kirkuk to Yumurtalık, which carried about half of Iraq's oil exports. After this, and as a war in the Gulf seemed ever more likely, the government was faced with three crucial questions: first, whether it would send troops to join the coalition forces in the Gulf; second, whether it would open a second front against Iraq along the Iraqi–Turkish border if war broke out; and third, whether it would allow the coalition powers (principally the United States) to use İncirlik for air attacks on targets in northern Iraq, given that this was not strictly within the base's NATO functions.

It appears that, left to himself, Turgut Özal would have given a positive reply to all three questions.[5] Constitutionally, the President's policy-making powers were limited, but Özal enjoyed the potential advantage that the Motherland Party had a large majority in parliament, and that the Prime Minister, Yıldırım Akbulut, was seen as a weak figurehead. With his regular contacts with world leaders, Özal apparently tried to act single-handedly in directing Turkish policy during the crisis. However, he had to face the fact that Turkish public opinion was distinctly unenthusiastic about the prospect of direct Turkish involvement in a war in the Gulf, in which no clear national interests seemed to be at stake.[6] This was reflected in parliament, where the opposition – consisting of Süleyman Demirel's True Path Party and the Social Democrat Populist Party led by Erdal İnönü – stood against Özal's activist policy. More crucially, an important segment of the Motherland Party, led by Akbulut's former foreign minister Mesut Yılmaz, effectively supported the opposition line.[7]

The strength of the opposition was important to Özal since, under Article 92 of the constitution, parliament would have to pass a special resolution authorizing the declaration of a state of war, the despatch of Turkish troops abroad, or the reception of foreign troops on Turkish soil.[8] Eventually, on 5 September, parliament passed the necessary resolution, but by this stage the opposition to direct involvement by Turkish forces in the looming Gulf War was clear enough. It was underlined by the successive resignations of first, the foreign minister, Ali Bozer, on 12 October, then of defence minister Safa Giray on 18 October, and finally of the Chief of the General Staff, General Necip Torumtay, on 3 December 1990.[9] It was only at the last minute, on 17 January 1991, as the air war in the Gulf was beginning, that parliament renewed its war powers vote to the government, and made it clear that this would include permission for the coalition air forces to use İncirlik and other air bases in Turkey for attacks on Iraq.[10]

As the war against Iraq raged during January–February 1991, coalition aircraft made regular sorties from İncirlik and were of substantial value to the allies in attacking Iraqi targets in the north of the country. Prior to the outbreak of the fighting, Turkish forces along the border with Iraq had also been built up to around 120,000 men, with air support and armour, to oppose an Iraqi ground attack, although the Turkish General Staff apparently judged that this was unlikely.[11] These reinforcements pinned down about eight Iraqi divisions in the north of the country, which could otherwise have been used against the coalition forces in the south. Although Turgut Özal had apparently urged that if Iraq broke up then Turkish forces should intervene in northern Iraq so as to seize the province of Mosul with the Kirkuk oilfield, this idea was dropped, as it was opposed by General Torumtay and the Turkish General Staff, on political as well as military grounds.[12] Turkey thus came through the conflict without having fired a shot in anger, and having rendered positive assistance to the allied cause.

Naturally enough, Turgut Özal was not inclined to underrate this contribution, and claimed in a television broadcast on 2 March 1991 that 'our country has passed a test with flying colours and has proved to the world at large that it a country that can be trusted'.[13] Soon afterwards, however, events took a grave turn for the worse as Saddam Hussein brutally suppressed the rebellion by the Kurds of north-eastern Iraq and around 500,000 destitute refugees fled to the border with Turkey, with even larger numbers fleeing across the Iraqi–Iranian frontier. Their presence faced the Turks with an unexpected dilemma. On the one hand, they could hardly deny any assistance to the refugees in their desperate plight, which was shown nightly on the world's television screens. On the other hand, they were most reluctant to allow them to settle in Turkish territory. On 7 April, Özal proposed a way out by suggesting that the UN should take control of territory in northern Iraq, so that the refugees could return to a 'safe haven'. This idea was then adopted by the British and US governments. Under UN Security Council Resolution 688 of 5 April 1991 an international force of around 20,000 troops was stationed at Silopi, near the border with Iraq, to support the operation. Virtually all the refugees had returned to Iraq by the end of May, as part of what was called 'Operation Provide Comfort'. The Silopi ground force was withdrawn in September 1991, but thereafter Saddam's forces were kept out of the safe haven by a special detachment of US, British and French aircraft based at İncirlik, which enforced a no-fly zone in Iraq north of the 36th parallel.[14] This left western policy quite heavily dependent on Turkish cooperation and consent, since the mandate for 'Provide Comfort' (in particular, permission to use the İncirlik base for a non-NATO operation) had to be regularly renewed by the Turkish parliament, normally at six-month intervals.

For Turgut Özal, the primary reason for supporting the coalition in the Gulf War was that it would re-establish Turkey's strategic importance in the eyes of the western powers, especially the US. Its effects on Turkey's relations with the Middle East was secondary to this. Hence, he seized the opportunity to demonstrate to the western governments that the alliance with Turkey would still be essential, even though the threat from Russia had ended. In effect, he wished to reinvent Turkey's value to the west. So far as the United States was concerned, he was largely successful, since 'Provide Comfort' depended on Turkish support. However, Özal had also hoped that the war would result in the fall of Saddam and his replacement with a democratic regime in Iraq that could work out a settlement with the Kurds, restore Baghdad's control in the north of the country, and thus prevent the PKK from using it as a base for its attacks in Turkey.[15] His hopes proved unfounded. In spite of economic sanctions, which were themselves costly for Turkey, Saddam retained his grip over most of the country. There was no internal settlement with the Kurds, and western policy effectively left a power vacuum in north-eastern Iraq that strengthened rather than weakened the PKK.

The alliance under stress, 1991–7

Quite frequently, it is argued that Özal's policy during the Kuwait crisis marked an important turning point, in which Turkey abandoned its non-interventionist policies in the Middle East, in favour of acting as a regional power for the first time since the demise of the Baghdad Pact.[16] Against this, it is suggested that, in practice, Turkish policies during the crisis did not really deviate from previous approaches, which essentially rested on preserving friendly relations with the Middle Eastern states while still paying due attention to Turkey's membership of the western alliance. Nor is the idea that Turkish policy was a 'one-man show' by Özal borne out by the record, since two important parts of his agenda – Turkish participation in the land force in the Gulf, and a 'second front' against Iraq – remained unrealized.[17] In fact, Turkish policy was a compromise between Özal's ambitions, and stiff domestic opposition from the public, parliament and the army. Probably, the most important shift in policy was the promotion of the safe havens plan in Iraq, since this involved Turkish engagement with the Iraqi Kurds, which Ankara had previously avoided, and implied that there might be an unofficial partition of Iraq. However, it has to be seen as an *ad hoc* arrangement to deal with an unexpected emergency, rather than part of a pre-planned strategy.

The economic cost to Turkey of maintaining trade sanctions against Iraq was also a serious one for the Turks since Iraq had previously been one of Turkey's most important trading partners, and its lost trade and other earnings probably cost its economy around \$2 billion per year.[18] In 1991, this was compensated for by special payments of around \$2.2 billion, mainly from Kuwait and Saudi Arabia. This fell back to around \$900 million in 1992, and then tailed off altogether.[19] Not surprisingly, Turkey pressed for the lifting of the sanctions, provided that Saddam Hussein adhered to the UN's conditions.

More critically, the question of continuing the mandate for 'Provide Comfort' turned out to be very contentious in Turkey, especially after Süleyman Demirel returned to power in November 1991. Opposition to the operation rested on the fear that the special force might be used by the US for other operations in the Middle East, over which Turkey had no control, or that it was part of a western project to promote the establishment on an independent Kurdish state, with serious implications for the future of Turkey's own Kurdish problem. At worst, this developed into what has been called the 'Sèvres syndrome' – that is, the suspicion that the western powers were bent on dismantling Turkey territorially, just as they had tried to do in the abortive Treaty of Sèvres of 1920 (see p32). After he assumed the presidency following Özal's death in April 1993, Demirel himself referred to the Sèvres Treaty, arguing that Turkey could never win the support of the west, however hard it tried to democratize its internal political system.[20] This complaint may have been voiced partly as an excuse not to implement the needed improvements in Turkey's human rights regime, but it also struck a sympathetic chord with nationalist opinion at home.

On the other side of the argument, the reasons for continuing 'Provide Comfort' were clear enough. These rested on the fact that Turkey could not afford to provoke an open conflict with the United States over an important part of American policy in the Middle East, and that so long as the 'Provide Comfort' force was based in Turkey, then the Turks retained at least some leverage over how it was used. On these and similar grounds, the Turkish military chiefs, who continued to maintain close relations with their American counterparts, were strongly in favour of continuing 'Provide Comfort'. While in opposition, both Süleyman Demirel and Erdal İnönü had opposed the operation, but once in power after 1991 they accepted it, as did both Tansu Çiller and Bülent Ecevit, during their respective premierships.[21] This was continued even during the turbulent period of the Erbakan–Çiller government of 1996–7, although the government managed to extract some cosmetic changes and the name of the operation was changed to 'Northern Watch' as from the beginning of 1997.[22]

Renewed entente, 1997–2002

After the Erbakan-led administration was ousted from power in June 1997, Turkish–US relations returned to a more normal state but essential problems still remained. Of these, the position and status of what was in effect a separate Kurdish political entity in Iraq was probably the most important. For Turkey, an immediate source of concern was that the PKK seized the opportunity to re-establish itself with bases in northern Iraq in territory nominally controlled by the Iraqi Kurds. In 1992, after the failure of negotiations between Saddam Hussein's government and the two main Kurdish groups in Iraq – that is, the Kurdistan Democratic Party (KDP) led by Massoud Barzani, and Jelal Talabani's Patriotic Union of Kurdistan (PUK) – elections were held for a regional parliament and the two leaders agreed to share power in a 'federated state'. This prospect was strongly opposed by Turkey, which was anxious to prevent the foundation of anything which might be presented as the nucleus of an independent Kurdistan. However, in 1994–6, as the entente between Barzani and Talabani broke down into civil war, international support for Kurdish independence waned, leaving the Turks with a less difficult task.[23] At the same time, the US turned a blind eye towards repeated military incursions by Turkey into northern Iraq against the PKK, which in several cases were carried out in collaboration with the KDP.[24] By 1998 Turkey and the US thus seemed to have reached an accommodation on this issue, in which Washington recognized Turkey's interests, while the Turks understood that, through their role in maintaining 'Northern Watch' they could exercise some influence over US policy.

This sense of Turkish–US accord on the Kurdish issue was further enhanced by the important help which the CIA and State Department apparently gave to Turkey in the capture of Abdullah Öcalan in February 1999 (see p145).[25] A few months later, in August 1999, the prompt and generous assistance given by both the US government and public to aid the victims of the İzmit earthquake disaster was widely appreciated.[26] When President Clinton visited Turkey in November 1999 for the Istanbul summit of the Organization for Security and Cooperation in Europe, he arrived three days early, so as to allow for talks with Prime Minister Ecevit and human rights and other non-governmental organizations, as well as addressing the Turkish parliament. With his wife and daughter, he visited the earthquake survivors in their tents, showing striking informality and sympathy, which was starkly contrasted with the usually dour and aloof demeanour of most of Turkey's own politicians.[27] A photograph of the President holding a baby who had survived the devastation was fondly remembered for many years afterwards.

Thus, by the end of the decade, the Turkish–American relationship seemed to have returned to a degree of warmth and popular support it had not known since the 1950s. The relationship was now referred to as a 'strategic partnership', although it was not clear exactly what this meant. Naturally, this strengthening of Turkish–US ties did not mean that Turkey was regarded as above criticism in the United States. Pressure from the US Congress over continuing restrictions on human rights in Turkey, and the Cyprus question, meant that arms deliveries and military aid were held up or curtailed.[28] At the beginning of 1990, Senator Robert Dole proposed a motion seeking to designate 24 April as 'a national day of remembrance of the Armenian genocide of 1915–23'[29] but this was defeated in the Senate. In November 2000, President Clinton successfully urged the Speaker of the House of Representatives to block a second resolution and it again fell by the wayside.[30]

Following Bill Clinton's departure from the White House in January 2001, some differences between Ankara and the new US administration under George W. Bush emerged, but these worries were sidelined by the horrific terrorist attacks in New York and Washington on 11 September 2001. In the view of a previous US ambassador in Ankara: 'Turkey's response to 11 September [was] everything one would expect of a "strategic partner".'[31] Most Turkish opinion had long had contempt for the Taliban regime in Afghanistan, which had been regarded as the epitome of reactionary fanaticism even by Turkey's own Islamists. A cabinet decree issued on 25 September 2001 allowed US forces to use Turkish air bases and air space in support of these operations. On 10 October, parliament endorsed a government proposal to send Turkish troops abroad (in effect, to Afghanistan) and receive foreign troops on Turkish soil, so as to meet the requirements of Article 92 of the constitution.[32] After the overthrow of the Taliban regime, attention was focused on the International Security Assistance Force (ISAF), which was set up in support of the new Afghan government under Hamid Karzai. On 15 February 2002, an advance party of 260 Turkish troops arrived in Kabul to join ISAF, with Turkey taking over the command of the force in June 2002 with a contingent of 1,400 soldiers.[33] The Turkish contingent has remained in Kabul ever since, assuming the command periodically in rotation. Although the Turkish public is not enthusiastic about this, its presence is generally appreciated by both the US (which needs to show that a Muslim country is participating) and Afghan government, while it avoids direct conflict with the Taliban.

The second Gulf War: Collision and tension, 2002–8

While the campaign in Afghanistan drew Turkey and the United States together, US policy towards Iraq continued to divide them, as it had on previous occasions. Even before 11 September, conservatives in Congress, together with the new Secretary for Defence, Donald Rumsfeld, endorsed a more aggressive policy towards Iraq, including arming the Iraqi opposition in the hope of toppling Saddam Hussein.[34] This was a key part of the 'neo-conservative' doctrine that the US needed to re-assert itself around the world, after the alleged timidity of the Clinton years. The horrific events of 9/11 strengthened this policy, brought forward most notably in President Bush's 'State of the Union' address to Congress in January 2002, in which the President linked Iraq, Iran and North Korea as an 'axis of evil'.

From the start, it was evident that Turkey would be very reluctant to give active support to US military action against Iraq, primarily because it feared that the result might be the territorial break-up of the country, with the emergence of an independent Kurdish state in the north. Like millions of other people around the globe, most Turks viewed the prospective invasion of Iraq as unnecessary and illegitimate, since it did not have clear United Nations backing. Given the deep divisions within the Iraqi opposition, it was likely that Saddam's overthrow, if it could be achieved, would produce chaos in Iraq, rather than an orderly transition.[35] There were also fears that another war in the Gulf would have damaging economic results for Turkey, as that of 1991 had done. Diplomatically, the Ecevit government's main initiative was to try to persuade the Iraqi president to accept UN resolutions for restarting the weapons inspection process, so as to forestall American military action, but repeated attempts to do this fell on deaf ears in Baghdad.[36] Ecevit took up his concerns during a visit to Washington on 15–19 January 2002.[37] By March, his stance against an attack on Iraq appeared to be hardening, as he told a meeting of EU leaders in Barcelona on 14 March, 'it is not necessary to undertake a military operation' since he claimed that 'Iraq has been under strict control and is not in a position to inflict harm on its neighbours'.[38]

By the time the AKP government was established in November 2002, it seemed ever more likely that the United States, with the support of at least some of its allies, would invade Iraq, but it was quite unclear what attitude Turkey would take. In spite of the sense of looming crisis, the question of Iraq barely figured in the 2002 election campaign and the AKP had no clear and declared policy positions on the issue. Essentially, it encountered the same problem that Turgut Özal had faced in 1990, in which the need to maintain the 'strategic partnership' with the USA conflicted with strong public opposition to any involvement in Iraq – even stronger, in fact, than on the earlier occasion.[39] In other respects, the problem was more acute than in 1990. First, there was no general international support for action against Iraq, as there had been over Kuwait, and no clear mandate for military action from the United Nations. UN Security Council Resolution 1441, of 8 November 2002, threatened Saddam Hussein with 'serious consequences' if he failed to comply with his disarmament obligations, but did not specifically authorize the use of force against him.[40] Second, the US government was asking Turkey to do far more than it had in 1990–1, when it confined itself to implementing the UN economic embargo and allowing the coalition air forces to use the İncirlik base. Instead, as Deputy Defence Secretary Paul Wolfowitz explained in a visit to Ankara on 3 December 2002, Washington now wanted Turkey to allow US forces to use Turkish territory to open a 'northern front' against Iraq – a similar plan to that which Turgut Özal had considered in 1990, but that he had been forced to drop by the Turkish General Staff. In preparation for this there would be a first stage, in which the US military would inspect bases and communications in Turkey, to be followed by a second, or 'site preparation stage'. The third stage would be the landing of US forces, prior to the invasion of Iraq. Although Wolfowitz claimed afterwards that Turkish support was assured, it appears that Abdullah Gül, as Prime Minister, only agreed to implement the first stage: the second two would depend on parliamentary permission, as required by Article 92 of the constitution.[41] Later, on 10 December, Tayyip Erdoğan, as the prospective Prime Minister, visited Washington for talks with President Bush. From this, his hosts gained the impression that he favoured the American plan, although he later said that he had not given any firm commitments, reflecting the strong opposition to the idea from within the cabinet and the AKP in parliament.[42]

During January and early February 2002, Abdullah Gül was heavily engaged in intense diplomacy, working with other Middle Eastern governments, to try to persuade Saddam Hussein to comply fully with the UN disarmament resolutions, or even step down from power, in which case Turkey would guarantee his personal security. These attempts proved fruitless and the Premier was accused of wasting time when he should have been preparing for the expected war, although he needed to show his own party that he had done his utmost to avoid one.[43] However, the decision as to whether to accept the US plan could not be put off indefinitely. As in the case of the previous Gulf crisis, it was clear that the attitude of the General Staff would be crucial. Essentially, the generals advised that an attack on Iraq would be most unwelcome, but since the US seemed determined to go ahead with it anyway, Turkey would be better off inside the American tent than outside. So as to exercise some leverage over the Iraqi Kurds – and maybe the US forces as well – they proposed that a Turkish force should occupy a 'buffer zone' 30–40 kilometres inside Iraq, if the invasion went ahead.[44] In this respect, they were reversing the position taken by General Necip Torumtay in 1990. The government broadly accepted this, although there were deep divisions within the cabinet on this issue.

On this basis, on 6 February 2003, parliament passed a resolution allowing US forces to implement the second, or 'site preparation' stage of the plan, and this was begun on 12 February.[45] Although it was under strong pressure from Washington to take a final decision as soon as possible, the government postponed a vote on implementing the third stage until 1 March. This would follow a meeting of the National Security Council (NSC), bringing together the President, government ministers and the armed forces commanders, which was scheduled for 28 February. Apparently, the government hoped that if the generals gave a green light to the plan, this would shift responsibility for what would almost certainly be an unpopular decision onto their shoulders. In the meantime, Turkish–US relations were further embittered by unseemly wrangling over the scale of financial compensation that Turkey was demanding from Washington, and clear signs that the Iraqi Kurds would strongly oppose any Turkish presence in the invasion force.[46] When the crucial NSC meeting was held, however, the military chiefs failed to give clear support for the invasion plan, saying merely that it had been 'evaluated', and effectively transferring the responsibility back to the government.[47] On 1 March, when the crucial ballot was held on the floor of the house, around 100 AKP deputies, along with the opposition parties, failed to support the resolution, so that it was defeated by the hairsbreadth margin of just three out of a total of 546 votes.[48]

Needless to say, parliament's decision of 1 March 2003 came as a severe shock to the Bush administration, which had not anticipated it (Paul Wolfowitz described it as a 'big, big mistake')[49] and triggered off the most serious crisis in Turkish–American relations since the 'Johnson letter' of 1964. For neoconservative critics, it was seen as part of an 'Islamist agenda' by the AKP, which aimed to 'undercut the West's war on terrorism'.[50] While this view was seriously exaggerated, and ignored the fact that the government had itself urged acceptance of the resolution, the 1 March vote certainly left Turkish policy in disarray, with no alternative plan prepared. In effect, Turkey was forced to watch developments in Iraq from the outside, with little influence over either the US or Iraqi actors, notably the Kurds. On 20 March, the day the invasion began, parliament passed a second resolution allowing coalition aircraft the use of Turkish air space. On 24 June, the US forces were allowed to use the İncirlik base and the port of Mersin, with a land bridge to the Iraqi frontier, for logistical support for their troops in Iraq.[51] In October 2003, the Turkish parliament passed a third resolution to allow Turkish troops, expected to number around 10,000–12,000, to participate in the international 'stabilization force' in Iraq. Although this idea had originally been supported, if not initiated, by the Pentagon, it was vetoed by the Iraqi Governing Council (the temporary government appointed by the Americans) and by Paul Bremer, Administrator of the Coalition Provisional Authority in Iraq.[52] The 'strategic partnership' thus seemed to have been abandoned by both sides, with the Iraqi Kurds – the one group in Iraq which was stridently anti-Turkish – now treated as America's best allies in the region.[53]

Tensions between Turkey and the US touched a high point on 4 July 2003, when 11 soldiers of the Turkish Special Forces in Iraq (a detachment of around 1,000 troops that had originally been stationed in northern Iraq as part of 'Northern Watch')[54] were arrested by US forces for what the State Department described as 'disturbing activities' and taken off for questioning with sacks over their heads. Although Donald Rumsfeld later apologized for the affair, it provoked a storm of protest in the Turkish media, with General Hilmi Özkök, the Chief of the General Staff, describing it as 'the biggest crisis of confidence' between Turkey and the US.[55] The later revelations of the torture of suspects in Abu Ghraib prison in April–May 2004, and the destructive US attack on Fallujah in the following November, caused further sharp criticisms of the Americans in the Turkish media.[56] In June 2004, President Bush visited Istanbul and attempted to shift the focus of his Iraq strategy by using Turkey as the launching pad for his 'Broader Middle East Initiative', intended to promote democratization throughout the region.[57] Since this project clearly had a 'Made in America' label, it failed to win more than marginal support in Turkey or elsewhere, or to overcome Turkish–American tensions. These were aggravated by a best-selling Turkish novel, *Metal Storm*, depicting a war between Turkey and the United States, and the Turkish film *Valley of the Wolves – Iraq,* in which the Americans were depicted as ruthless aggressors.[58] In response, an article in the *Wall Street Journal* in February 2005 headlined 'The Sick Man of Europe – Again' concluded that Turkey could become 'another second rate country: small minded, paranoid, marginal'.[59]

Subsequently, the politicians on both sides took steps to cool the atmosphere down but they could not disguise some serious and real causes of tension. In northern Iraq, the city of Kirkuk, the site of one of the country's richest oil fields, had traditionally been inhabited by a mixture of Kurds, Arabs and the Turcoman minority, regarded by many people in Turkey as their ethnic kin. Although it had been excluded from the area controlled by the Kurdistan Regional Government, the Kurdish leadership now claimed it as their prospective regional capital and there were fears in Turkey that the US authorities would not prevent this.[60] A more immediate threat came from the PKK, which exploited the power vacuum in northern Iraq to build up its presence in the territory and, in September 2003, ended the ceasefire it had declared in 1999. Although the resulting series of attacks was less serious than it had been when the PKK's campaign had been at its height during the 1990s, it was still bad enough. It was more difficult to suppress because the US occupation of Iraq made it impossible for the Turkish armed forces to conduct cross-border operations as they had earlier. The only forces that could have taken action against the PKK were those of the Iraqi Kurds, which were reluctant to act, and the United States, which did not want to stir up trouble for itself in Iraqi Kurdistan, the one part of Iraq which was both pro-American and relatively peaceful.[61]

Frustrated by the failure of attempts to set up a bilateral mechanism with the US military to address this issue,[62] Turkish forces along the border with Iraq were strongly reinforced during the spring of 2007, with suggestions from the military commanders that Turkey might take unilateral action against the PKK in Iraq, although the idea was strongly opposed by Tayyip

Erdoğan and the US government.[63] Given the inaction on the American side, the PKK launched a new series of assaults in Turkey the autumn of 2007, killing seven pro-government Kurdish militiamen and another five civilians on 29 September, and 13 soldiers on 8 October. In response, the government raised the stakes on 17 October by passing a motion in parliament allowing the despatch of Turkish troops to Iraq, irrespective of the US presence. This did not prevent another attack by the PKK on 21 October, in which another 12 soldiers were killed and eight abducted, but it turned out to be a successful use of coercive diplomacy.[64] When Tayyip Erdoğan visited Washington on 5 November 2007 for talks with George W. Bush, the US President evidently realized that he had to go some way to meet Turkish demands, since if he failed to do so there was the possibility that Turkey might act unilaterally in Iraq. Accordingly, declaring that the PKK was an enemy of the United States and Iraq as well as Turkey, he announced the establishment of a tripartite (that is, US–Turkish–Iraqi) coordination mechanism. More materially, he agreed that the US forces in Iraq would supply the Turkish military with 'real time' intelligence on the PKK bases and activities in Iraq – in effect, giving the Turkish forces a green light for cross-border operations, provided they did not attack non-combatants.[65]

The 5 November agreement changed the situation, both militarily and diplomatically, even if this was not generally recognized in Turkey. On the first score, after a series of targeted bombing raids by the Turkish air force on 16 and 22–3 December 2007, and 16 January 2008, a major land and air operation was carried out on 21–9 February 2008, in which it was claimed that 250 PKK militants had been killed, with 27 casualties on the Turkish side.[66] Admittedly, the PKK presence in Iraq was far from eliminated, but the Turkish armed forces now had a relatively free hand in dealing with it. Diplomatically, it removed the main bone of contention between Turkey and the United States. When President Abdullah Gül visited Washington in January 2008, he admitted that there had been 'some turmoil in relations in past years' but claimed that now 'a climate of confidence has emerged'.[67]

The Mercurial Alliance, 2009–11

A further improvement in relationship with Washington was expected following Barack Obama's convincing win in the US presidential elections of November 2008. After all, the new president had himself opposed the invasion of Iraq in 2003, so could hardly blame the Turks for not having supported it. A few months before he became foreign minister on 1 May 2009, Ahmet Davutoğlu visited Washington and was said to have been 'dazzled' by the Obama team, predicting that there would be 'a golden age in Turkish–American relations'.[68] For his part, President Obama clearly recognized Turkey's importance as a democratic Muslim country, which could help to heal the breach opened up between the USA and the Muslim world by the Iraqi operation. As the Turkish press reported appreciatively, his visit to Turkey on 6–7 April was his first to a Muslim nation since becoming President. His public statements clearly indicated his wish to mend fences with Turkey, overcoming complaints that he had previously supported Armenian calls for a genocide resolution in Congress. The new president referred to the relationship with Turkey as a 'model partnership' ('strategic' had evidently been dropped from the official vocabulary). More broadly, he used the Turkish parliament, which he addressed on 6 April, as a platform from which to reach out to the world's Muslims, declaring that 'the United States is not, and never will be, at war with Islam'.[69] This was a message which he repeated in a landmark visit to Cairo in June 2009.[70]

In 2009 and after, the American and Turkish governments cooperated in a number of important fields – notably through Turkey's continued contribution to the International Security Assistance Force in Afghanistan, as well as in the reconstruction of Iraq, politically as well as physically. The opening of direct relations between Ankara and the Kurdistan Regional Government in Iraq also removed a serious bone of contention between Ankara and Washington (pp237–8). However, the 'golden age' which Ahmet Davutoğlu had reportedly predicted failed to materialize. Barack Obama's election as President helped to mitigate anti-American sentiment in Turkey, but only slightly: a survey conducted in 2009 still found that only 14 per cent of the Turkish respondents took a favourable view of the United States, the worst rating for the US among all the surveyed countries.[71] This may be attributed to the gradual (if rather belated) reconfiguration of the strategic relationship between Washington and Ankara after the end of the Cold War, a more populist element in Turkish foreign policy-making with the relative decline of the old elite, notably the military, but above all to the American invasion and occupation of Iraq, which still left a bitter taste in Turkish mouths.[72] More specifically, new sources of tension arose, mainly due to Turkey's relations with two third parties, Iran and Israel. While the details of these relations are explored in a later chapter (pp230–1, 241–2) they also need to be brought into the story at this point, since they had crucial effects on the Turkish–US relationship.

On the first score, Turkey's relations with Iran had been a source of unease in Washington for several years before the beginning of the Obama presidency. The problem stemmed essentially from the fact that while the United States had had tense if not actively hostile relations with Iran ever since the overthrow of the Shah in 1979, Turkey could not afford, either politically or economically, to have a serious collision with its large and powerful neighbour. While economic sanctions against Iran are relatively cost-free for the United States, they would create serious costs for Turkey, which depends on Iran for a substantial proportion of its natural gas supplies as well as an important export market (p241). The most serious stumbling block, however, was the widespread suspicion that Iran was trying to develop its own nuclear weapons. Given the viscerally hostile attitude of President Mahmoud Ahmadinejad to both Israel and the United States, this became a major source of concern for US policy-makers in both the Bush and Obama presidencies. This contrasted with the Turkish attitude, which tended to downplay the idea that Iran had a nuclear weapons programme,[73] or argued that even if it did, Turkey would not be a potential target.[74]

The main cause of concern was Iran's programme to produce enriched uranium, which it claimed it would need as fuel for a research reactor, but could be used for the production of nuclear weapons. On 17 May 2010, after intense negotiations, Turkish and Brazilian representatives announced an agreement with Iran under which Iran would send 1,200 kilograms of low enriched uranium for deposit in Turkey, in return for which an unspecified country would deliver 120 kilograms of 20 per cent enriched uranium for use in the Iranian reactor. Ahmet Davutoğlu and his Brazilian counterpart, Celso Amorim, hailed this as an important breakthrough. However, it was regarded with serious scepticism by the US and other western governments, on the grounds that Iran simultaneously announced that it would continue its own 20 per cent enrichment programme, in defiance of UN Security Council resolutions. The deal was also criticized as an attempt to undercut a new package of sanctions against Iran, which were then under preparation in the Security Council.[75] Worse was to come on 9 June 2010, when the representatives of Turkey and Brazil, both non-permanent members of the Security Council, voted against the sanctions resolution, causing official 'disappointment' in Washington.[76] Professor Davutoğlu later explained that President Ahmadinejad had told him that Iran would consider the 17 May agreement terminated unless Turkey and Brazil voted against the resolution, but had to face a storm of complaints in the US media.[77]

While Turkish governments publicly downplayed the possible nuclear threat from Iran, they were not unaware of the fact that they needed to protect their country against it, even if the danger was not immediate. In September 2009, there was discussion of Turkey acquiring its own anti-missile defence capacity, probably the US Patriot missile system. However, the cost of this, at around $7.8 billion dollars, made this a less likely option.[78] As an alternative, in November 2010, Turkey joined other NATO members in supporting plans to construct a system protecting all NATO members, in which the US would clearly play the key role. The Turkish government's main concern was not to provoke Iran by naming it as a potential threat to the alliance, and this was eventually agreed. Accordingly, in September 2011, Turkish and US officials signed a memorandum providing for the construction of a radar station on a military base at Kürecik, near Malatya, in south-east Anatolia, which would act as the ears of the system. The missiles themselves would be carried by US warships in the eastern Mediterranean and later stationed at bases in Romania.[79] After the conflict over Iran, Turkey's participation in this project significantly reduced tensions between Ankara and Washington, since it demonstrated that Turkish sympathies were still on the western side, and that it could still play an essential role in NATO's defence plans.

Turkey's relations with Israel also deteriorated sharply in 2010, particularly after the end of May when Israeli forces attacked an aid convoy attempting to break the blockade of the Gaza strip, killing eight Turks and one US citizen aboard the Turkish ship *Mavi Marmara,* which was leading the flotilla (see pp230–1). The effect on Turkey's relations with the US was serious because, by this stage, it appeared that Barack Obama had quietly abandoned his initial attempts to build bridges with the Arab states, failing to sustain his attempts to push for a peace agreement between Israel and the Palestinians, and allowing American policy to slip back into default mode by giving almost unconditional support to Israel. In the aftermath of the *Mavi Marmara* attack, Israel suffered worldwide condemnation, with the United States left as virtually its only supporter.[80] As usual, this reflected the strongly pro-Israeli instincts of the US Congress, which gave unquestioning support to the Israeli actions.[81] In January 2011, a committee of enquiry appointed by the Israeli government declared that the attack on the *Mavi Marmara* was entirely in accordance with international law, eliciting bitter criticism from Abdullah Gül and Tayyip Erdoğan. By contrast, a US State Department spokesman described it as 'an independent report, credible and impartial and transparent'.[82] Further evidence of the gap between Ankara and Washington came in February 2011, when the United States vetoed a resolution supported by every other member of the Security Council (including staunch pro-American allies such as Britain), which would have condemned Israeli settlements in the occupied Palestinian territories as an obstacle to peace, provoking predictable criticisms from Ahmet Davutoğlu.[83] Turkey's conflict with the US on this issue was tempered by the fact that it was one on which the US government was itself out of tune with the rest of world opinion.

Effects and predictions

The main effects of these disagreements were to be seen in domestic opinion and the media rather than in government-to-government relations, but were none the less serious for that. According to one American observer, writing in January 2011, before the radar agreement was concluded, 'in the court of public opinion ... Turkey looks like the enemy of the United States' best friend in the Middle East [Israel] as well as the friend of its worst enemy [Iran]'.[84] At its extreme, anti-Turkish opinion in America maintained that Erdoğan's government was 'in tune with the fanatically anti-western principles of Saudi Wahhabi Islam' (in the words of a former member of George W. Bush's Department of Defence).[85] Another American commentator even drew a parallel between Erdoğan and Osama bın Laden, on the grounds that 'both seek to create a thoroughly anti-democratic, if not totalitarian, order'.[86] Even if such views were rejected, there were quite widespread assumptions that Turkey had somehow been 'lost', and that its basic orientations were now with 'Eurasia', or the Middle East, not the west. On the Turkish side, Turkish politicians certainly could have done more to remind their own constituents that, despite the evident problems, relations with the United States were still of vital importance to Turkey. Admittedly, the Turkish economy had recovered strongly from the crises of 2001 and 2008, but the continuing and apparently growing deficit in the balance of payments meant that Turkey was still heavily dependent on international financial institutions, in which the United States still played a dominating role, and in which political considerations were not ignored, as the experience of 2001 had shown (p152). In countering the PKK presence in Iraq, cooperation with the US authorities was still vital, as was the need to ensure a smooth US withdrawal from Iraq. On the other side, it was still essential for the United States to maintain collaboration with Turkey in Iraq's reconstruction after US forces left, and in the establishment of the NATO missile defence system. Given Turkey's growing popularity in the Arab world, friendship with Turkey would help US policy-makers in the rest of the Middle East, while Turkish participation in security and peacekeeping operations in Afghanistan and the former Yugoslavia helped to show the US had the support of a powerful and democratic Muslim country.

All the signs were that, by the autumn of 2011, these points were fully appreciated by President Obama and Secretary of State Clinton. This understanding could be seen as part of a swing back to a close partnership, even if this was not appreciated by public opinion in the two countries. At the same time, it was essential for both sides not to endow the relationship with too much emotional capital. As the experienced American observer Ian O. Lesser suggested in June 2010: 'The new Turkish–Western [read Turkish–US] relationship will be *à la carte* and driven by convergent national interests rather than amorphous notions of geopolitics and identity. It could still be a rough ride.'[87]

8   Turkey and the west after the Cold War II

Turkey and the European Union

Of all the candidates for accession to the European Union, Turkey has had the longest and most contested journey, lasting more than 50 years, and with no certain outcome yet in view. The journey was affected by the end of the Cold War, but not so dramatically as other aspects of Turkey's foreign relations. Having opened up to eastern Europe after the fall of communism, and thus accepted a massive geographical enlargement as an aim, the countries that formed the European Union (formerly the European Community) in 1993 were bound to face the question 'why not Turkey?' On the other hand, the political economic and cultural obstacles to Turkish accession, especially on the EU side, did not go away. Periodically, also, Turkish enthusiasm for the project has flagged in response. As Luigi Narbone and Nathalie Tocci point out, there has been a cyclical relationship between Turkey and the EU, with marked ebbs and flows in the integration process, and crucial interactions with Turkey's domestic politics.[1] During the 1990s, there was progress in the economic dimension with the institution of a customs union between the EU and Turkey in 1996, but the process then stalled and for a time it looked as though Brussels might abandon it altogether. This was succeeded by a dramatic turnaround in 1999, which ended with the landmark decision by the European Council in December of that year to accept Turkey as a candidate for full membership on the same terms as the other candidate countries – that is, that it should meet the 'Copenhagen criteria' of economic and political standards to allow accession negotiations to begin. After a delayed start, and in the face of domestic political conflicts, the Ecevit government began the process of 'harmonization', as it was referred to, in 2001, and this was continued by the AKP administration that took office in November 2002. The government received its reward in October 2005, when the accession negotiations were officially inaugurated.

After 2005, however, the process went into the doldrums. On the EU side, new leaders came to power in France and Germany who openly rejected the idea of eventual Turkish accession. Although the AKP government and the Turkish Cypriots had made determined moves to solve it, the continued dispute over Cyprus re-emerged as a crucial obstacle. Later, the global financial crisis of 2008–9, and the urgent need to prevent a collapse of their common currency in 2011, preoccupied most of the EU countries, apparently consigning their 'Turkish question' to the sidelines. On the Turkish side, the 'harmonization' process stalled, as the government was distracted by internal conflicts. By 2011–12, major political reforms were back on the government's planned agenda, but whether this would have significant effects on its quest for eventual accession was still far from certain.

At the outset, it should also be said that the story of Turkey's relations with the European Union has become easily the most thoroughly explored aspect of Turkish foreign policy, generating far more academic literature and think-tank reports than any other topic. At points it is also highly complex and technical. The result is that, for reasons of space, and to avoid deviations that will probably be of interest mainly to specialists, some significant aspects have been left out of this account. They include the economic dimension of the relationship, which is dealt with only briefly, and the Turkish role in planning a post-Cold War European security architecture. To be discussed properly, both these would require a separate chapter in themselves. Similarly, the position of Turkish migrants in western Europe and their impact on Turkish policy towards the EU has had to be left out for reasons of space. For the time being, all that can be done is to point readers interested in these issues towards some of the relevant literature.[2]

Economic advance and political stalemate, 1990–8

After its measured rebuff to Turkey's application for full membership in December 1989 (see p131) the European Commission attempted to sugar the pill in June 1990 by issuing what was unofficially known as the 'Turkey package' – alternatively as the 'Matutes package' – of policy initiatives.[3] This proposed that there should be a renewed effort to achieve a customs union between Turkey and the then European Community, (EC) as foreseen in the original Association Agreement of 1963, together with enhanced cooperation in the industrial and other fields, and release of the funds provided for in the Fourth Financial Protocol of 1981 (p130). The last step remained unachieved, since Greece continued its veto on activating the Protocol, but other parts of this project were taken up. At their meeting in Lisbon in June 1992, the EC heads of state and government agreed that 'the Turkish role in the present European political situation is of the greatest importance', and called for the further development of relations with Turkey in line with the plan envisaged in the Association Agreement (p128).[4] In November of the same year, the Association Council agreed to restart the process for implementing the customs union and a working programme for the achievement of this was agreed to at another meeting of the Council one year later. Meanwhile, at a meeting held in Copenhagen in June 1993, the European heads of government, meeting as the European Council of what was now the European Union, confirmed the decisions of the Lisbon summit and agreed on a series of conditions, known as the 'Copenhagen criteria', which new member states would have to meet. These included: first, the existence of stable democratic institutions providing for the rule of law, the respect of human rights and protection of minorities; second, the existence of a functioning market economy; and third, the ability to adhere to the principles of political, economic and monetary union.[5] There was not much doubt that Turkey could meet the second of these criteria, while the last seemed too vague to act as an exact yardstick, but the first condition was clearly very problematic in the Turkish case.

So far as the free movement of goods was concerned, the construction of the customs union proved easier to achieve than would have been the case earlier, since Turkey had in any case been moving fairly steadily towards a liberalized import regime since the early 1980s. Groups within the business community who had previously been worried about their ability to compete in an open market with western European industry had also been brought round to the opposite point of view.[6] Hence, the customs union agreement was eventually signed in Brussels at a meeting of the Association Council on 6 March 1995. It was expected to go into effect at the beginning of 1996, after further legal and tariff changes had been implemented by Turkey. Two important political conditions were attached to the agreement, however. The first was that, to overcome Greek objections, the EU agreed to start accession negotiations with the Greek Cypriot government of the Republic of Cyprus within six months after the end of the Intergovernmental Conference which was to consider revisions to the Maastricht Treaty (in effect, in 1998). This raised complex problems in Turkey's relations with Greece and with Cyprus which are returned to later, and which were likely to continue for some time (p180).

The second hurdle was that, to go into effect, the customs union agreement would have to be ratified by the European Parliament in Strasbourg. This was a more immediate problem, since successive resolutions of the parliament suggested that, even though the customs union was officially restricted to the economic field and would not oblige the EU to start accession negotiations with Turkey, Turkey's poor human rights regime and the government's handling of the Kurdish problem would have an important impact on the Parliament's decision. In 1994, it had strongly criticized the lifting of the parliamentary immunity of the MPs of the pro-Kurdish Democracy Party (DEP) and the closure of the party (pp144–5). More immediately, as soon as the customs union agreement was signed in March 1995, the Parliament passed a resolution condemning the Association Council for accepting it, on the grounds that it was inconsistent with Turkey's shortcomings in human rights, its policies on the Kurdish problem and the continuing dispute over Cyprus.[7]

In the European Parliament, opposition to the customs union continued during 1995, and was if anything intensified by the Çiller government's handling of the DEP case and the confirmation of long prison sentences on the party's former MPs in October. A package of minor constitutional changes pushed through by the government in July was judged quite insufficient.[8] None-theless, as the time drew near for a vote in the Parliament to ratify the agreement, the MEPs came under strong pressure to change their position from the EU member state governments, who were understandably reluctant to abandon an agreement they had already signed. Pressure in favour of the customs union also came from the United States, as well as from Tansu Çiller, who suggested that its implementation would act as a barrier to the further rise of Islamic radicalism in Turkey, an idea that was echoed by the French President Jacques Chirac. Hence, on 13 December 1995, the MEPs ratified the agreement (in some cases, with heavy hearts) by a majority of 343 to 149. However, in their resolution of 13 December, they also asked the EU Commission to monitor the human rights situation in Turkey closely and to report to the Parliament annually on this.[9]

In the economic sphere, the implementation of the customs union marked the most important milestone in the development of Turkey's relations with the EU and its predecessors since the signature of the Additional Protocol in 1970. As from the beginning of 1996, Turkey was obliged to abolish all import duties 'and charges having equivalent effect' on all merchandise imports from the EU, in return for a similar undertaking by Brussels, and to apply the EU's relatively low common external tariff in its trade with third countries. Although agricultural products were excluded from this provision, the two sides committed themselves to achieving free movement in this sector eventually. Turkey was also required to pass effective laws for the protection of patents and other intellectual property and to eliminate barriers to competition within the country.[10]

On balance, Turkey made more economic concessions under the customs union than did the EU, since it had previously had a protective trade regime, whereas the only important remaining barriers to trade that had to be lifted by the EU were quotas on the imports of textiles and garments (the removal of which was admittedly an important gain for Turkish exporters). Prior to the signature of the agreement, pessimists had predicted that the ending of trade barriers would be harmful to Turkey, since it would suck in a flood of imports, without giving Turkish industry equivalent gains in exports.[11] In practice, these fears were not borne out, as Turkish industry proved a good deal more resilient than expected. There was no evidence that free trade with the EU was driving Turkish industry to the wall – instead, the Turkish economy was gaining from easier access to western Europe, and more competition in the domestic market. Today, the application of the customs union does not seem to be a problematic aspect of the Turkey–EU relationship. At the time, also, Tansu Çiller could not have refused to go ahead with it, since to do so would have been tantamount to signalling to Brussels that Turkey had abandoned its ambitions of eventual accession to the EU. On the contrary, in December 1995, she publicly announced that 'the customs union is not enough for us, our basic goal is full membership of the European Union'.[12] Admittedly, Turkey still suffered from some economic disadvantages from the customs union arrangements, such as lack of access to the European agricultural market and free movement of labour with the EU. Nor was Turkey given any role in deciding EU policies that fundamentally affected it, such as determining the common external tariff. Nonetheless, the main Turkish complaint against the customs union was political, rather than economic – that is, that without full membership, Turkey was being consigned to second-class status in the European family of nations, or even being excluded from it altogether.

By implementing the customs union, the two sides had chalked up an important success. However, they had only been tackling the economic part of their agenda, which was easier to address. The political obstacles, which were harder to resolve, remained as real as ever. For the EU governments, the question of whether they should start accession negotiations with Turkey, or at least commit themselves to doing so at some point in the future, was now hard to avoid. In 1989–90, when they had been responding to the Turkish application of 1987, they had been able to shelve the question, but the hard decision could not be put off indefinitely. During 1996–7, the outlook was also badly affected by Turkey's highly unstable domestic politics. The installation of the coalition government led by Necmettin Erbakan in June 1996 had a damaging effect on Turkey's relations with the EU, as it did on relations with the US, and for much the same reasons. In the December 1995 election campaign, Erbakan's Welfare Party had strongly opposed the project to gain full membership of the EU, which it characterized as a 'Christian Union', and instead called for a 'Union of Muslim Countries', although it did accept the need to remove barriers to trade with Europe.[13] Erbakan had also suggested that Turkey might leave the customs union, or at least revise it (quite how was unclear).[14] Once in office, however, he came under strong pressure from his coalition partner, Tansu Çiller, to leave the customs union untouched, much as he had done in the case of the 'Provide Comfort' operation in Iraq. On the other hand, Turkey made no moves towards advancing the case for accession and Welfare Party spokesmen make it clear that they were opposed to the idea in principle on 'cultural' (read religious) grounds.[15] Tansu Çiller, as the foreign minister and the main architect of the customs union on the Turkish side, seemed to be caught between two fires.

The sense of alienation was heightened by similar moves on the European side. In March 1997, as Erbakan's attempts to stay in power were gradually failing, the leaders of the European Christian Democrat parties, including the German Chancellor Helmut Kohl and the former Belgian Premier Wilfred Martens, issued a joint declaration after a meeting in Brussels, claiming that 'the European Union is a civilisation project and within this civilisation project Turkey has no place'.[16] Apart from the arrogant and prejudiced implication that Turkey was not a 'civilized' country, this declaration was bound to have the worst possible effects in Turkey, since it implied that Turkey could never become a member of the EU, however much progress it made in political reform or economic modernization. In effect, Erbakan's argument that the EU was a 'Christian club' seemed to be confirmed. The impact of the Brussels declaration was strengthened in July 1997 by the launch by the Commission President Jacques Santer of his 'Agenda 2000' programme. This proposed that in 1998 accession negotiations should begin with eastern European countries in what became known as the 'fast track' – that is, Poland, Hungary, the Czech Republic, Slovenia and Estonia, with Turkey conspicuous by its absence.

Worse was to come on 12–13 December 1997, at Luxembourg meeting of the European Council, when Cyprus was added to the 'fast track' list, and a 'slower track' list was announced, including Bulgaria, Latvia, Lithuania, Romania and Slovakia, with which the EU would begin accession negotiations at some time in the future. The summit adopted a 'European Strategy for Turkey', which was invited to be included in the new European Conference bringing together all the applicant states and the existing EU members, but its omission from either list served as a deadening blow to Turkey's ambitions.[17] The European Council could also be accused of applying double standards, since it had not excluded Slovakia from the list of candidates, although the Commission had reported in July 1997 that it had not reached the required human rights criteria. In a statement issued immediately after the Luxembourg summit, the Turkish government argued that the Luxembourg decision was based on 'partial, prejudiced and exaggerated assessments'. It stated that the government would maintain its existing links with the EU, but that 'development of these relations is dependent on the EU's fulfilment of its obligations' – in effect, that Turkey would freeze its relations with Brussels until it was clearly put on the list of enlargement candidates.[18]

During 1998, the Yılmaz government adhered to this policy of disengagement. In November 1998, the Commission prepared a report that raised some hopes that Turkey might be put on the candidates list, but these were dashed when the EU leaders turned down the report at a summit in Vienna in the following month. During the latter part of 1998, the Yılmaz administration was in any case preoccupied by trying to preserve its own survival, while the caretaker government under Bülent Ecevit, which held the fort between January and April 1999, was too weak to take any new initiatives in either domestic or foreign policies. After the capture of the PKK leader Abdullah Öcalan in Nairobi in February 1999 (see p145) the failure of the EU to issue any sort of condemnation of Greece for its role in the affair (presumably because to do so would have raised uncomfortable questions about the actions of Italy and Germany)[19] did nothing to improve the atmosphere in relations between Ankara and Brussels.

The transformation: 1999–2005

Following the elections of April 1999, and the establishment of a new coalition under Bülent Ecevit, prospects began to improve. Ecevit supported a strongly nationalist line on the Cyprus question, but was committed to the widening of human rights in Turkey for domestic reasons, quite irrespective of its effects on Turkey's foreign relations. His coalition partners in the Nationalist Action Party led by Devlet Bahçeli, have been classified as 'defensive nationalists' in the sense that, nominally, they did not oppose the idea of EU accession, but were ill-prepared to accept the political adjustments – especially on the Kurdish question – that would make it possible. The Motherland Party, as the third coalition partner supported both EU accession and political and economic liberalization.[20] Among the EU states, also, the defeat of the German Christian Democrats in the 1998 elections and their replacement by a Social Democrat (SPD)–Green coalition under Gerhard Schröder, substantially improved the chances of a successful dialogue between Turkey and the EU, since the new German government seemed anxious to turn over a new leaf in Germany's relations with Turkey. When the European heads of government assembled in Helsinki on 9 December 1999, the uncertainties were overcome and the main EU governments, which by this stage clearly favoured Turkey's candidature, carried the day. Turkey was thus placed as a candidate for accession, along with the eastern European applicants, plus Cyprus and Malta, and on the basis of the same criteria as those applied to other candidate states. Important conditions were laid down to allow accession talks to begin. The EU would begin an 'enhanced dialogue' with Turkey on human rights, and Turkey would need to produce 'a pre-accession strategy to stimulate and support its reforms' so as to meet the Copenhagen criteria.[21] Like other candidate countries, Turkey was urged to settle all its border disputes with other countries (in this case, with Greece) failing which they should be brought to the International Court in The Hague.[22]

Among the Helsinki decisions, two crucial extra conditions affected the Cyprus dispute. In the first place, Turkey was required to support the efforts of the UN Secretary-General to reach a settlement, although no such obligation was placed on the Cypriot side.[23] Second, the Council conceded that if no inter-communal settlement had been reached by the time accession negotiations had been concluded, then 'the Council's decision on accession will be made without the above being a precondition. In this the Council will take account of all relevant factors' (what these might be was left entirely vague).[24] This turned out to be a fatal mistake by the EU leaders since, by assuring the Greek Cypriots they could be admitted to the Union anyway, they provided them with no incentive to reach a settlement with the Turks. How a country could be admitted if about 20 per cent of its population were left outside the EU was unexplained. As a later EU Commissioner for external relations, Chris Patten, confided to a US diplomat in 2004, 'Cyprus ... probably should not have been admitted ... but the Greeks insisted on Cypriot admission as the price of agreeing to some of the northern European candidates' (presumably, the Baltic republics).[25]

The conditions regarding Cyprus and relations with Greece evidently caused some misgivings on the Turkish side, and the EU had to send its representative for foreign affairs, Javier Solana, on a last-minute trip to Ankara to explain the details and overcome objections. However, Bülent Ecevit and his colleagues would have found it hard to give the EU an outright refusal, and the Prime Minister confirmed that Turkey had accepted the invitation late on 10 December. The following morning, Ecevit flew to Helsinki to join the assembled EU leaders and formally accept the offer. In Helsinki, he conceded that Turkey still had much ground to cover in improving its human rights regime, but said that these problems could be overcome, 'given the dynamism of the Turkish people and their attachment to democracy'.[26]

In line with the Helsinki decisions, in November 2000 the EU Commission issued its 'Accession Partnership Document', laying down in more detail the political reforms – in particular, the widening of civil liberties – that Turkey would have to implement before accession negotiations could start. Since Turkey could meet most of the economic requirements of the Copenhagen criteria relatively easily, this political reform programme became the most problematic part of the Turkey–EU agenda over the following decade, making Turkey's internal politics (notably, its constitutional and legal structures) a crucial factor in its external relations. It thus became hard to draw a clear dividing line between internal and external policies.

The 'Accession Partnership Document' was accepted by EU leaders at the meeting of the European Council in Nice in December 2000.[27] In the short term (that is, before the end of 2001), the Commission stipulated that the government should 'strengthen legal and constitutional guarantees for the right to freedom of expression' as well as freedom of association and peaceful assembly. In the medium term (of an unstated duration) it would need to 'guarantee the enjoyment by all individuals, without any discrimination ... of all human rights and fundamental freedoms'. On the critical issue of minority rights, in the short term Turkey was required to 'remove any legal provisions forbidding the use by Turkish citizens of their mother tongue in TV/radio broadcasting' (in effect, to allow broadcasting in Kurdish) and later to 'ensure cultural diversity and guarantee cultural rights for all citizens irrespective of their origin. Any legal provisions preventing the enjoyment of those rights should be abolished, including in the field of education'. The 'State of Emergency' regime in the south-eastern provinces, which severely restricted human rights in the affected areas, should also be withdrawn. As a short-term measure, the government should 'undertake all necessary measures to reinforce the fight against torture', which was regularly resorted to by the police as a means of extracting confessions from suspects, and to maintain the existing *de facto* moratorium on capital punishment, which had been in effect since 1984.[28] In the longer term, Turkey was required to abolish the death penalty entirely, and sign and ratify Protocol 6 of the European Convention on Human Rights (this allows signatory states to retain the death penalty only 'in respect of acts committed in time of war or of imminent threat of war').[29] Finally, the government would need to enact constitutional and legal changes to reduce the independent political role of the military – in particular by bringing the powers and functions of the military-dominated National Security Council into line with the practice of EU member states. For the Ecevit government, these goals were not easy to achieve. Within the ruling coalition, Devlet Bahçeli's Nationalist Action Party (MHP) strongly opposed anything seen as a concession to Kurdish nationalism, which its members tended to interpret as surrender to terrorism by the PKK. This affected the party's attitude to such questions as freedom of expression, as well as abolition of the death penalty or the granting of cultural rights to the Kurds. Hard-line conservative attitudes, which had to be overcome, were also common in parts of the state bureaucracy, the police and the military.

The government's first reaction to the Accession Partnership Document came in March 2001, when it issued its 'National Programme for the Implementation of the *Aquis*'. On paper, this appeared to meet most of the EU's requirements, but was notably vague on such crucial questions as the full abolition of the death penalty and whether permission would be given for broadcasting or education in Kurdish.[30] An important step towards implementing these reforms was taken some seven months later, on 4 October 2001, when parliament passed a package of 34 amendments to the constitution.[31] Under Article 76 of the constitution, constitutional amendments can only be passed by a two-thirds majority in parliament (that is, 367 votes) or a three-fifths majority (330 votes) plus approval in a national referendum. At the time, the government parties had around 340 seats, so they needed the support of the opposition parties to secure these changes without resorting to the cumbersome and possibly risky process of a referendum. Fortunately, this was secured, with relatively few backbench defections, since the opposition parties – including the pro-Islamist Felicity Party (*Saadet Partisi,* or SP) and the newly-formed Justice and Development Party (AKP) – did not wish to be presented as opponents of democratization. As part of this, the AKP took a clear step to abandon Muslim exceptionalism in favour of western-style liberalism, as the best way of protecting itself against the authoritarian secularist state establishment. In this way, a cross-bench alliance of pro-reform parties was put together.[32]

On the question of general restrictions of expression and association, the constitutional amendments of October 2001 were encouraging.[33] In particular, the new versions of Articles 13 and 14 of the constitution provided that basic rights and freedoms could only be limited for reasons stated in the constitution, and in accordance with 'the requirements of a democratic social order', but could not be used to justify actions 'with the aim of destroying the indivisible integrity of the state with its territory and nation, or abolishing the democratic and secular Republic depending on human rights'. This replaced the far wider (and at points dangerously vague) restrictions contained in the previous versions of these Articles, and brought the Turkish constitution into reasonably close correspondence with Article 10 of the European Convention on Human Rights.[34] The previous provision that 'No language prohibited by law shall be used in the expression and dissemination of thought' was removed from Article 26 of the constitution, with the similar restriction affecting the media being deleted from Article 28. However, this did not by itself allow Kurdish language broadcasting, which was separately forbidden under the broadcasting law.[35] Under an amendment to Article 38, the death penalty was abolished except in cases of 'war, the imminent danger of war, or terrorist crimes'. This brought the constitution into line with Protocol 6 of the European Convention, with the significant addition of 'terrorist crimes' – reflecting the refusal of the MHP to prevent parliament ordering the execution of the PKK leader Abdullah Öcalan, who was still in prison under sentence of death (p145). Finally, in an amendment to Article 118, civilians were given a majority of the seats in the National Security Council. Under the new wording, the Council was to submit its 'advisory decisions' to the government, which would then 'evaluate' them. This was far more restrictive than the previous wording, under which the government had been obliged to 'give priority consideration to the decisions' of the Council, although whether the military would instantly adopt a purely advisory role and purely on questions of national defence, as in western European democracies, remained questionable.

These changes brought about a qualified approval from the EU, although doubts were expressed as to whether the government would give effect to them, by altering the existing legal statutes affecting human rights. At the European Council meeting held in Laeken, Belgium, on 14–15 December 2001, the European heads of government welcomed the amendments, adding that the beginning of accession negotiations with Turkey had 'drawn nearer'.[36] More specifically, the annual 'Regular Report on Turkey's Progress Towards Accession', which was issued by the EU Commission on 13 November 2001, described the constitutional amendments as a 'significant step towards strengthening guarantees in the field of human rights and fundamental freedoms'. Nevertheless, Turkey still failed to meet the Copenhagen criteria, in the Commission's judgement.[37] In response, at the end of January 2002 Ecevit's government began the task of altering the laws affecting freedom of expression, by tabling amendments to Articles 312 and 159 of the Penal Code, as well as Article 8 of the 'Law for the Struggle against Terrorism' of 1991. After fierce disagreements between the MHP and the other parties in the coalition, according to the new version of Article 312, supposedly 'separatist' or anti-secularist statements would only be punishable if they were also issued 'in a manner which could be dangerous for public order'. However, Article 159, which critics argued could be used to punish anyone making critical statements about the armed forces or the government, remained virtually unchanged, but for a reduction in the maximum sentences allowed. Similarly the punishments specified under Article 8 of the 'Law for the Struggle against Terrorism' were reduced (these affected 'propaganda' deemed to be directed 'with the objective of destroying the indivisible integrity' of Turkey).[38] Later, on 26 March 2002, a second package of legal changes brought some liberalization of the laws affecting the press, the activities of associations and the closure of political parties, as well as the penalization of police officers found guilty of torture.[39] Nonetheless at a meeting of the Turkish–EU Association Council in April 2002, the EU side emphasized that Turkey still had to allow Kurdish broadcasting and other cultural rights, to abolish the death penalty in law and to withdraw the emergency regime in the south-eastern provinces, besides other changes, all of which had been clearly specified in the Accession Partnership Document some 17 months previously.[40]

In line with its commitment to liberalize the political system and push forward with Turkey's drive for EU membership, the AKP government that took office in November 2002 was able to continue the reform process without the burden of a reluctant coalition partner that had dogged Ecevit's efforts. Unlike its Islamist predecessors, it has been classified as 'conservative globalist' – that is, conservative on social and cultural issues, but globalist in its acceptance of Turkey's integration into the international economic and political system.[41] The first hurdle it faced was the European Council meeting held in Copenhagen in December 2002, at which it had hoped that the EU leaders might give a firm date for the start of the accession negotiations. Instead, the furthest the Council was prepared to go was to pledge that if it decided at its expected meeting in December 2004 that Turkey fulfilled the Copenhagen criteria, then accession negotiations would be opened 'without delay'. More ominously, it confirmed that although it confirmed a 'strong preference' for the reunion of Cyprus, it would not insist on this as a condition of Cypriot accession.[42]

While its early hopes remained unfulfilled, the AKP government put a brave face on the situation, and returned to the task of political reform. In June–July 2003, parliament passed what were known as the sixth and seventh 'harmonization packages' ('harmonization' that is, with the Copenhagen criteria). Two amendments that affected the rights of the Kurdish minority were: first, the complete withdrawal of Article 8 of the 'Law for the Struggle against Terrorism' of 1991; and second, permission for private radio and TV stations to broadcast in 'languages and dialects traditionally used by Turkish citizens in their daily lives' (even now Turkish officialdom still could not bring itself to speak openly of 'Kurdish').[43] Further amendments to Penal Code Article 159 provided that those who 'express ideas purely for the purpose of criticism, without indulging in insult, derision or vituperation' would not be punished. Changes to the law governing the powers and functions of the National Security Council and its Secretariat also restricted the decisions that the Council could take to those affecting the 'national security policy of the state', adding that these could only be 'advisory' for the government and providing that the Secretary-General of the Council could be a civilian, rather than a military officer, as had previously been required to be.[44] In response, the European Commission, in its progress report issued in November 2003, congratulated the government for having shown 'great determination in accelerating the pace of reforms', although it complained that implementation on the ground was uneven and called for the 'further alignment of civil military relations with European practice' and the exercise of full cultural rights (by implication, for the Kurds).[45]

Although not all these reforms were stipulated by the European Union, other important legal changes widened the scope of human rights in Turkey. Under a new Civil Code, originally enacted in December 2001, of which an updated version took effect in August 2003, husbands and wives were given equal rights in marriage, including parental rights over children and assets acquired during the marriage. Under a new Criminal Code passed in September 2004, which went into effect in April 2005, crimes against humanity and human trafficking were made criminal offenses, the punishments for 'honour killings' (that is, of female family members for alleged adultery) and torture were increased, violations of the right to privacy were criminalized, and incitements to hatred on the basis of social, racial, religious, sectarian or regional identities could only be punished if they represented a 'clear and present danger' to public security.[46] This left certain features of the Penal Code seriously restrictive of freedom of speech, but in general could be counted an important advance.

By 2004, the Cyprus problem had moved to the top of the Turkey–EU agenda, given that the Republic of Cyprus was expected to join the Union as a full member on 1 May 2004, along with nine other candidate countries, mainly from eastern Europe. While the details of negotiations over the future of the island are returned to later (p199) those aspects which vitally affected Turkey's relations with the EU need to be summarized at this stage. Despite strong opposition from its own military, as well as hard-line nationalist opinion, in January 2004, Tayyip Erdoğan's government took the bold step of backing the plan to reunite the island that had been promoted by the United Nations Secretary-General Kofi Annan. At a meeting with the Secretary-General in Davos, Switzerland, on 24 January, the Prime Minister agreed that if Greek and Turkish Cypriot negotiators could not reach full agreement, then the Turkish government would allow him to 'fill in the gaps' between the two sides, and then submit the plan to simultaneous referendums in the two parts of the island.[47] Since the Greek Cypriot President, Tassos Papadopoulos, objected to the Annan plan on several important points, the Secretary-General was left to fill in the outstanding points, and arrangements were made to hold the twin referendums on 24 April 2004.[48] According to the EU Commissioner for Enlargement, Günther Verheugen, the Greek Cypriot leadership had promised at the Helsinki summit of December 1999 not to obstruct a settlement,[49] while Kofi Annan later related that Papadopoulos had told him he would 'want to support' the peace plan.[50] Nonetheless, in the run-up to the referendum, the Greek Cypriot President came out strongly in favour of a 'no' vote, against majority support for the plan on the Turkish Cypriot side. Hence, while just under 65 per cent of the Turkish Cypriot voters approved the plan, the 'no' votes accounted for 76 per cent of the votes on the Greek Cypriot side, and the plan collapsed.

With the Greek Cypriots' rejection of the Annan plan, the EU was obliged to accept the Republic of Cyprus as a full member, even though it excluded the Turks: effectively, it had been trapped by its commitment at Helsinki in December 1999. In an attempt to soften the blow, Commissioner Verheugen announced that the EU would 'seriously consider' ways of ending the economic isolation of the Turkish Cypriots that had been imposed by the

European Court of Justice in 1994.[51] However, attempts to put this into effect were blocked by the Greek Cypriot government, which skilfully exploited the fact that it was now inside the EU, while the Turks were still outside, and could create numerous legal obstacles.

While the failure of the Annan plan was a serious setback, its effects on Turkey's drive for EU membership were initially limited by the fact that the Greek mainland government adhered to the policy it had effectively adopted in 1999, to the effect that Greece would be safer if Turkey were included in the Union rather than left out. Tassos Papadopoulos did not take the same view, since he frequently threatened to block Turkey's accession process as a means of leverage over Turkey to make further concessions over Cyprus.[52] Prior to the scheduled European Council meeting to be held in Brussels on 16–17 December 2004, he threatened to veto any decision to start accession negotiations with Turkey unless Ankara recognized his government as the sole sovereign power in the island,[53] but was persuaded to back down by the Athens government. In France, the ruling UMP party (*Union pour un mouvement populaire*) opposed the idea of Turkish accession in principle, whereas President Jacques Chirac was a lukewarm supporter (he defined his position by saying that 'Turkish integration into the EU would be desirable when it is possible').[54] Hence, the Brussels meeting held to its previous commitment, by declaring that accession negotiations with Turkey could start on 3 October 2005, provided Turkey signed an additional protocol to the customs union agreement of 1995, extending the customs union to the ten new member states, including Cyprus. In Ankara, the government was reluctant to do this, on the grounds that this would be tantamount to recognizing the Greek Cypriot government, but eventually did so in July 2005, with the proviso that this would 'not amount to any form of recognition of the Republic of Cyprus'.[55]

The other important conditions imposed by the EU at the Brussels summit were contained in a 'Negotiating Framework for Turkey' prepared by the Commission. These stipulated that the negotiations could be broken off if there were a 'serious and persistent breach in Turkey of the principles of liberty, democracy, respect for human rights and fundamental freedoms and the rule of law'. Bowing to pressure coming especially from Germany, where it was feared that full membership for Turkey would mean opening the floodgates to a torrent of Turkish migrant workers, the Negotiating Framework allowed for the possibility of permanent limitations on freedom of movement, besides limiting the access of new members to EU structural and agricultural funds. Finally, while it was accepted that the shared goal of the negotiations was Turkish accession, this would be an 'open-ended process' whose outcome could not be guaranteed', and that it would take into account 'the absorption capacity of the union'.[56] In fact, the 'absorption capacity' criterion had been referred to in the original list of criteria agreed to in Copenhagen in 1993, but had not been mentioned in any of the Commission's previous documents on Turkey.[57] Since 'absorption capacity' was quite undefined, this appeared to create the possibility that the EU might decide to deny accession to Turkey even if it met all the other Copenhagen criteria, provoking some serious private doubts in Ankara about just how fully the EU was committed to the project.

As 3 October 2005, the planned date for the official start of the accession negotiations to be held in Luxembourg, drew nearer, Turkey was aided by the fact that the British government, which strongly favoured Turkish accession, took over the rotating EU Presidency in the second half of the year. This helped to overcome objections by the Greek Cypriot government and last-minute obstructionism by the Austrian foreign minister, Ursula Plassnik, who was eventually bought off by a promise to start accession negotiations with Croatia, after prolonging the discussions into the early hours of 4 October.[58] To complete the accession process, Turkey was required to implement the 35 sections, or Chapters, of the EU's *acquis communautaire*, the body of EU legislation with which all member states are obliged to apply ('negotiations' seems something of a misnomer, since a candidate state could only 'negotiate' for postponements at agreed points).[59] Accordingly, discussions on six Chapters were officially opened, of which one Chapter, on science and research, was completed (or 'closed' in the official jargon) in June 2006.

In the doldrums: 2006–11

The official start of the accession negotiations in October 2005 was naturally hailed as a great achievement. Unfortunately, it ushered in a period in which progress in Turkey's accession process slowed to a crawl, at best, and increasing doubts about the project began to be expressed on both sides. These were also painful years for the European project as a whole, following the massive enlargement of 2004. 'Enlargement fatigue' was now used an explanation for reluctance to admit more new members to the EU: this mainly affected the Turkish case, although it was not confined to it. Attempts to reform the internal structures of the Union received a severe setback in 2005, when the proposed Constitutional Treaty was rejected in referendums in France and the Netherlands. For the next two years, the EU leaders were preoccupied by the task of preparing an alternative. This took the form of the Lisbon Treaty of 2007, which was eventually ratified in 2009. As soon as this was achieved, the aftermath of the global financial crash of 2008 hit Europe, producing the severe fiscal and sovereign debt crisis of 2010–11 in Greece, Ireland and Portugal, and turning European attentions inward once more. Given these serious internal problems, further enlargement – to Turkey in particular – naturally tended to slip down the priorities list of European policy-makers.

Against this discouraging background, three special factors were also instrumental in severely slowing down the Turkish accession process. First, changes in political leadership in Europe, in France and Germany in particular, meant that three European governments were now headed by parties opposed in principle to Turkish membership of the Union.[60] Austria had for some time been a known quantity, since there was general opposition in the country to the idea of Turkish entry. However, in April 2011, the Austrian President Heinz Fischer stated that his country favoured the continuation of accession negotiations, while repeating the formula that they would be 'open-ended'.[61] More ominously, in Germany the coalition of the Social Democrat party (SPD) and Greens lost power to the Christian Democrat party (CDU–CSU) in the general elections of September 2005. Like her party, the CDU leader Angela Merkel was opposed to the principle of Turkish accession, favouring an ill-defined offer of 'privileged partnership' – in effect, a polite way of saying 'no'. The Turkish government firmly rejected this, since it would apparently offer it no advantages other than those it already enjoyed under the customs union, condemning Turkey to second-class status.[62] On the other hand, the new German chancellor was constrained on two fronts. First, the elections had been held only weeks before the Luxembourg meeting and she did not form her government until the following month (November 2005). She correctly concluded that she had to abide by agreements reached by her predecessors and could not stop the beginning of the accession negotiations. Second, with no overall majority in the Bundestag, she was obliged to form a 'grand coalition' government with the SPD, which still supported the principle of Turkish accession. The new SPD leader, Frank-Walter Steinmeier, served as foreign minister. As a result, Angela Merkel could not stop Turkey's accession process while maintaining the coalition. This situation continued after the following general elections of September 2009, after which she formed a second coalition with the Free Democrat Party (FDP): this, like the SPD, did not oppose Turkish accession. As a result, the agreement between the two new coalition partners, like its predecessor, repeated that while the aim of the Turkey–EU negotiations was accession, the process was an open-ended one. The agreement made no mention of 'privileged partnership', saying merely that if the accession negotiations failed, then there should be an attempt to bind Turkey 'as closely as possible to European structures'. In practice, the German government took neither a positive nor negative line at European summits, but simply followed that of the other 26 member states.[63] The main effect of these changes was psychological, since they strengthened the impression in Turkey that the EU was unreliable and might eventually default on the commitments it had entered into in 1999 and 2005, reducing the incentive to meet the EU's conditions.

As already noticed, the French position was originally ambiguous, since the ruling UMP party opposed the Turkish accession process, whereas President Chirac conformed to the majority European view by accepting it. This ambiguity was ended in May 2007 when Nicolas Sarkozy, who joined Angela Merkel in arguing for 'privileged partnership' rather than full membership for Turkey, was elected to the Elysée Palace. His reasoning was geographical, being based on the fact that only about 3 per cent of Turkey's territory is in Europe, with the remainder in Asia Minor. How Cyprus could be considered part of the European continent if Turkey were not was left unexplained.

Equally, the fact that Turkey has been a member of the Council of Europe and NATO for more than half a century was quietly ignored. In 2007, the French government unilaterally blocked discussion of five Chapters of the *acquis*, arguing that agreement on these Chapters would only be necessary if Turkey were to become a full member of the EU, rather than downgraded to 'privileged partnership'.[64] Two months later, President Sarkozy proposed that a panel of 'wise men' should be appointed, to decide the future boundaries of the EU (presumably these would not include Turkey). However, in December 2007, the European Council scotched this idea by setting up a 'reflection group': what this was supposed to reflect on was not clear but it was stated that this was not to include the question of the EU's future borders.[65] President Sarkozy did not give up his anti-Turkish campaign, however. In 2008, he promoted a bill in the French National Assembly that would have made a referendum in France compulsory before any country with a population more than 5 per cent of that of France could be admitted to the Union (thus potentially excluding Turkey while admitting Croatia). The French Senate amended this, to affect any enlargements, but allowing the President to decide whether to call a referendum or leave the decision to the legislature.[66] In effect, if the UMP or something like it were in power at the time Turkey's accession negotiations were completed, then there would be a serious risk of a unilateral veto by France. Unfortunately, Nicolas Sarkozy's personal behaviour only worsened the tensions between Turkey and France. Following his election, he failed to visit Turkey until February 2011, when he was obliged to do so because France had taken over the presidency of the G-20 group of advanced and emerging economies. Even then, he confined his visit to a few hours, creating an impression of outright rudeness towards his hosts.[67]

The continuing Cyprus problem was the second major cause of the marked slow-down in Turkey's accession process. Following the government's signature of the additional protocol extending the customs union to the new member states, Tayyip Erdoğan and his colleagues refused to submit it for ratification by parliament. This was partly due to the belief that this might be interpreted as recognition of the Greek Cypriot government as the sole legitimate authority in the island, and partly due to the hope that Turkey might be able to use this issue as a means of pressuring the EU leaders to lift the trade embargo on Turkish Cyprus, as Günther Verheugen had suggested in 2004 (p185). According to the rules of the customs union, Turkey would be obliged to open its harbours and airports to Greek Cypriot ships and aircraft, which it refused to do. In January 2006, the Turkish government proposed that it would allow this, if the trade embargo on northern Cyprus were ended – an idea that was welcomed by Olli Rehn, Verheugen's successor as Commissioner for Enlargement, as well as the British and Italian governments, but predictably rejected by Tassos Papadopoulos.[68] At the meeting of the European Council held in Brussels in December 2006, the demand by Papadopoulos that the accession negotiations should be broken off altogether was rejected. However, the Council agreed that negotiation of eight Chapters, which were affected by the customs union, would be blocked until the Turkish parliament ratified the additional protocol and no Chapters could be 'closed', on the same condition. During 2009, progress on other Chapters was blocked by Cyprus. The result, when combined with the French vetoes, was that by 2010, of the 33 negotiable Chapters, 16 were either suspended or held up, while 13 had been opened and only one closed. Inter-communal negotiations on Cyprus continued, of which the details are narrated later (pp200–1): in the context of Turkish–EU relations, it suffices to say for now that they failed to make any headway and that the Cyprus problem continued to be a major obstacle to progress.

The third factor which helped to account for the growing impasse was the loss of momentum of the AKP government's political reform programme – although this may have been as much the result as the cause of growing opposition in Europe, since the two trends were mutually reinforcing (the Cyprus problem had a life of its own). As the perceptive German observer Heinz Kramer claimed in 2009, 'the very moment the Turkish political leadership lost trust in the readiness of the EU to stand by its commitments, it started to change its policy'.[69] A crucial development was the change in the attitude of the opposition parties, notably the Republican People's Party (CHP). Following the 2007 general elections, the AKP had 341 seats, so it still needed the support of the CHP to change the constitution without resort to a referendum (p182). Earlier, the CHP had been prepared to do this, but subsequently the party leader Deniz Baykal changed his tactics, making constitutional amendments harder to achieve. Hence, as Ziya Öniş argues, after 2005, as the AKP moved from a position of strong to 'qualified' support for accession, the CHP moved from qualified support to Euro-scepticism.[70] There were also internal upsets that distracted attention. In the spring and summer of 2007, the crisis over the election of a new President and the resultant general election and referendum preoccupied the government. This was succeeded by the crisis caused by the government's attempt to lift the ban on female students wearing Islamic headscarves to class, the resultant clash with the Constitutional Court and the attempt by the Chief Prosecutor of the Court of Cassation to have the Constitutional Court close down the AKP (p142). Thanks to this domestic turmoil during 2007–8, the government made little headway in meeting the EU's demands for further political reforms.

This is not to suggest that no progress was made at all during this period. As an example, in February 2008, parliament enacted a new and more liberal law on charitable and religious foundations. This significantly improved the property rights of the small non-Muslim minorities in Turkey – a topic on which the EU had been pressing the government.[71] Another repeated cause of complaint by the EU Commission as well as liberal domestic opinion was Article 301 of the new Criminal Code enacted in 2004 (p185), which virtually repeated the wording of the previous Article 159 (p184). This made insulting the 'Turkish identity' (*Türklük*) or state institutions a criminal offense, and thus acted as a severe restriction of freedom of speech. Under this Article, Turkey's

Nobel Prize-winning novelist, Orhan Pamuk, was prosecuted over remarks on the Armenian massacres of the First World War,[72] as was the prominent Turkish-Armenian journalist Hrant Dink, who was tragically murdered by nationalist fanatics in January 2007.[73] It was amended in April 2008, mainly by stipulating that the Minister of Justice would need to authorize any future prosecutions. This was far from an ideal solution, and also left several other clauses restricting freedom of speech on the statute book, but it did at least result in a sharp reduction in the number of prosecutions – a development welcomed by the Commission.[74]

These limited improvements nevertheless left the European Commission with a long list of reforms that the government had failed to achieve, starting with legislation to set up an Ombudsman's office to investigate citizens' complaints against state authorities (a bill to this effect had actually been passed in 2006, but later vetoed by the Constitutional Court on the grounds that it was not specifically allowed for in the constitution. It had not subsequently been resuscitated).[75] The Commission also stressed the need to improve the rights of the Kurdish minority as well as freedoms of speech and communication. It complained about the continuation of compulsory classes on religious culture in schools, and restrictions on the Greek Orthodox Ecumenical Patriarchate, established in Istanbul since the fall of the Byzantine Empire. On other issues – such as women's rights, 'honour killings' and forced marriages – its complaint was that the authorities were failing to enforce the law properly, although the improved legal framework was now in place.[76] In spite of urgings by the Commission, the government also failed to alter Articles 68 and 69 of the constitution, and Articles 78–83 of the Political Parties Law, under which it had itself narrowly escaped closure by the Constitutional Court in 2008 (p142), its explanation being that it had been unable to win the support of the opposition, so as to achieve the necessary two-thirds majority.[77]

By 2009, the fact that the political reform programme seemed to have lost its impetus was prompting the suggestion that the whole mechanism of 'conditionality compliance' on which the accession process depended had broken down.[78] It was against this background that the AKP government launched a new campaign to tackle the Kurdish problem in the autumn of 2009 known as the 'Kurdish opening' (pp146–7). Before long, this was effectively abandoned, but in April 2010 it was succeeded by what was known as a 'democratization package', consisting of a raft of constitutional reforms. These included important changes to the judicial system, notably the composition and structure of the Constitutional Court and the High Council of Judges and Prosecutors, and amendments authorizing civilian courts to try military personnel for 'crimes against the security of the State, constitutional order and its functioning', while preventing civilians being tried by military courts except in time of war. There were also significant amendments improving individual rights, including positive discrimination in favour of women, children, the elderly and disabled, and the protection of children. Through an alteration of Article 74 of the constitution, the long-planned Ombudsman's office could be established, and under a new version of Article 148, individuals could apply to the Constitutional Court on the grounds that one of their fundamental rights under the European Convention of Human Rights had been violated by public authorities.[79]

With the exception of a proposed change to Article 69, affecting the closure of political parties, all these amendments were passed by a three-fifths majority in parliament.[80] They were submitted to a national referendum, in which the 'yes' votes carried the day with the convincing majority of 58 to 42 per cent, on 12 September 2010. Not surprisingly, this result was welcomed by the EU.[81] In urging support for the amendments, both Prime Minister Erdoğan and foreign minister Davutoğlu pointed out that they would strengthen Turkey's case in negotiations with Brussels,[82] but this was not the main burden of the government's message. Significantly, the phrase 'harmonization package' was dropped from the official discourse: instead, it was argued that Turkey needed more democracy for its own sake and not because this would aid its progress towards EU accession.[83] Turkish politicians now talked of the 'Ankara criteria', implying that the reform process was now home-grown, not imposed by Brussels.[84] The EU's reaction was also muted, since it did not produce any significant advance in the accession negotiations. In the run-up to the general elections of June 2011, both the AKP and CHP urged that Turkey needed a new and more democratic constitution, but again the effects of this on the accession process (if there were any) were barely noticed.[85] In effect, political liberalization had acquired its own momentum in Turkey, detached from Turkey's relations with Europe, and the main obstacles to eventual accession were now on the European rather than on the Turkish side.

Explanations and expectations

At the end of 2011, there seemed to be a bigger question mark over Turkey's quest to join the European Union than at any time since the late 1990s. Public opinion polls in Turkey are not entirely reliable, and findings by different organizations are often inconsistent, but the signs were that, with the flagging of the accession process after 2005, public support for the project in Turkey had fallen from around 70 per cent in 2004 to around 40–50 per cent by 2010. However, even then around 15–30 per cent of respondents failed to express a definite opinion, so that the potential 'yes' votes still appeared to outnumber the 'no' votes by a fairly substantial margin.[86] By December 2011 Croatia, which had started accession negotiations on exactly the same time as Turkey, had already signed an accession agreement, whereas in the Turkish case, no new chapters in the negotiations had been opened for the previous 18 months. As a result, Turkey's relations with the EU were said to have frozen in a 'European winter' (in contrast to the 'Arab Spring'). The biggest immediate cause of the blockage was obstructionism by the Greek Cypriot government, but this was only part of the story. Immersed as it was in its own fiscal and economic problems, deriving from serious internal political divisions, the EU seemed to have shunted the Turkey negotiations into a siding. Nor was the

Cyprus problem the sole cause of the impasse: as Joseph Daul, the leader of the European People's Party, the biggest grouping in the European Parliament, emphasized, there was no guarantee that even if the Cyrpus problem were resolved, Turkey would eventually gain accession. He and his fellow Christian Democrats still opposed Turkish membership in principle, strengthening the suspicion that they were merely hiding behind Greek Cypriot vetoes. In response, an angry President Gül referred to the EU as a 'miserable Union'.[87] Earlier, the Minister of State, Ali İhsan Bağış, Turkey's chief negotiator with Brussels, had claimed that the EU needed Turkey more than Turkey needed the EU, while the economy minister and deputy premier Ali Babacan speculated that eventually Turkey might remain detached from the EU, like Norway. Nevertheless, as he admitted, Turkey should not abandon the target of accession (now posited as 2023, the centenary of the proclamation of the republic) since it still needed to catch up with European democratic standards.[88]

Although such statements confirmed a distinct slackening of enthusiasm for the European project, there was no official suggestion of abandoning it. From the start of his appointment as foreign minister, Ahmet Davutoğlu had emphasized that EU accession ought to be Turkey's top priority.[89] The AKP's manifesto for the 2011 elections put relations with the EU at the head of its list of foreign policy goals: while the party complained about the 'unfair and baseless opposition of some European countries', it claimed that the steps the government had taken had 'initiated a new phase in Turkey's EU membership process'.[90] Looking further abroad, for all the talk about the 'Eurasian' connection and the attempt to construct a free trade zone with Middle Eastern neighbours (p235), there were no alternative regional institutions with anything like the extent or durability of the European Union. Equally, going it alone, Norwegian-style, would leave Turkey weaker rather stronger *vis-à-vis* both Europe and the rest of the world. The opposition to Turkish accession in Europe stemmed essentially from the ruling parties in France and Germany but, as of 2011, both Angela Merkel and Nicolas Sarkozy faced re-election battles within the next two years and neither looked likely to win. With alternative governments in Paris and Berlin, the far more favourable European line-up of 1999–2005 would be restored. Turkey would need to seize this opportunity to unfreeze the relationship – in particular, by pressing ahead with further political liberalization, and by ratifying the additional protocol on the customs union, which could be done without prejudicing its position on recognition of the Greek Cypriot government pending a final settlement.[91] To overcome opposition in the existing member states, it also needed to win over more of public opinion to the idea of Turkish membership, rather than just concentrate on the political elite.[92] With the likelihood that the Turkish economy would be growing faster than that of the EU over the next decade, those in Europe who favoured Turkish accession – and they still constituted the vast majority of member state governments – needed to stress the substantial economic as well as political advantages which Turkish membership could bring.[93]

9 Turkey and regional politics after the Cold War I

Greece, Cyprus and the Balkans

Turkey, Greece and Cyprus

In a rapidly changing world, Turkey's relations with its Greek neighbours seem to have been the theatre of foreign policy which was least affected by the end of the Cold War. In both countries, the ideological and historical heritage was still powerful. The nationalist narratives of each nation emphasized their differences, but were painfully aware of their similarities, operating in unacknowledged symbiosis, with Greeks identifying Turks as 'the other', and vice versa.[1] The tensions and conflicts that had built up since the late 1950s continued unresolved as the 1990s turned out to be a decade of false starts and little progress that failed to unblock what appeared to be a condition of permanent stalemate. It was not until 1999, with a fundamental change in Greek policy, that day-to-day relations with Turkey's Aegean neighbour changed dramatically, although basic problems remained unresolved. As in previous years, the clash of interests and emotions over Cyprus lay at the heart of Greek–Turkish conflicts. Nonetheless, in 2004, Turkey made historic moves to solve the Cyprus dispute. Sadly, the olive branch was rejected by the Greek Cypriots and by 2011, the problem had returned to stalemate.

Following his election as President of Cyprus in February 1988, George Vassiliou restarted negotiations with Rauf Denktash, the Turkish Cypriot leader, in 1990. These failed to get off the ground since Denktash insisted that as a precondition both sides should be recognized as having 'sovereign status'. Expanding this argument, Denktash began to speak of the existence of two 'peoples', rather than 'communities', in Cyprus, implying that the Turkish Cypriots had the right of self-determination.[2] With the two sides unable to agree even on basic principles, the 1990 talks got nowhere. However, soon after the Gulf War of 1991, Turgut Özal tried a new tack when he proposed to President George Bush that quadripartite talks should be started between the two mainland governments, plus the Greek and Turkish Cypriot leaders. Comparing such a summit to the election of a Pope, Özal argued that an overall settlement could be hammered out in a 'marathon session'.

This idea was rejected by the Greeks, but it encouraged the UN Secretary-General, Boutros Boutros-Ghali to believe that a more flexible stance on the

Turkish side could lead to successful inter-communal negotiations. After unsuccessful talks in 1991, the Secretary-General produced in 1992 what was referred to as a 'Set of Ideas', designed to overcome existing differences, which were endorsed by a Security Council Resolution (No. 750) of 10 April 1992. On this basis, Denktash and Vasilliou arrived in New York in June 1992 for 'proximity talks', in which they sat in separate rooms with the Secretary-General shuttling between the two. These lasted until 14 August. In spite of long discussions, the talks became deadlocked over the territorial division between Greeks and Turks in a future federation, and the right of the Greek Cypriot refugees to return to their former homes in the north. Renewed direct talks between Denktash and Vassiliou were held under Boutros-Ghali's chairmanship between 28 September and 11 October 1992, but they failed to resolve either these or other differences over the powers of each community in a federal constitution.[3]

After the failure of the talks in 1992, prospects became further clouded by the election of Glafcos Clerides as President of Cyprus in February 1993. During his election campaign, Clerides had attacked the 'set of ideas', although it later became apparent that he would accept them with significant revision. Rather than making another direct attempt to produce an overall settlement, Boutros-Ghali then adopted a gradualist approach by proposing a series of 'confidence-building measures', designed to produce some areas of agreement that might later develop into a general reconciliation. These included, in particular, the re-opening of Nicosia airport, closed since 1974, to both the Greek and Turkish Cypriots, and the return to the Greeks of Varosha, the southern suburb of Famagusta, which had been occupied by the Turkish army in 1974 but never settled by the Turkish Cypriots. These proposals were accepted in principle by both sides, but a protracted series of talks, which lasted from May 1993 until May 1994 under UN and then US auspices, broke down over the details.[4]

Prospects for a constitutional settlement dimmed further in July 1994, when the European Court of Justice effectively banned Turkish Cypriot exports to the EU. This prompted the National Assembly of the Turkish Republic of Northern Cyprus (TRNC) to delete the reference to the possibility of a future confederation with the Greeks from the TRNC constitution and reject the idea of further talks on the confidence-building measures while the judgment was in force.[5] By 1995, Greek Cypriot attentions were concentrated on the prospect of joining the EU. As a condition for accepting the customs union agreement between Turkey and the EU, the Greek government insisted that accession negotiations with Cyprus would begin six months after the conclusion of the inter-governmental conference which was to review the Maastricht Treaty (p176). These negotiations duly began in January 1998, with George Vassiliou, as the Greek Cypriots' chief negotiator, nominally accepted as the representative of both sides of the island.[6]

During 1996–8, the seemingly intractable Cyprus dispute became further complicated by a re-eruption of direct conflict between Greece and Turkey and Turkey's worsening relations with the EU. In January 1996, a bizarre 'battle of the flags' broke out between Greece and Turkey following a maritime accident on the uninhabited rocky outcrop of Kardak (Imia in Greek), which lies just under four nautical miles off Turkey's Aegean coast, and 5.5 miles from the Greek island of Kalymnos. The mayor of Kalymnos first planted a Greek flag on the islet, but this was then removed by a group of journalists from the Turkish daily *Hürriyet* before a landing party from the Greek navy arrived to replace the Turkish flag with a Greek one. This incident – absurd as it seemed to outsiders – stoked up fierce nationalist passions on both sides. These were inflated by the press, since for the Turks it appeared to raise the possibility that Greece might try to claim sovereign rights over the whole Aegean. Fortunately, the risk of a direct armed clash between Greece and Turkey was avoided by rapid intervention by the American mediator Richard Holbrooke. However, attempts to widen this into a broader agreement over territorial rights in the Aegean failed to make progress.[7] A year later, in January 1997, tensions rose once more when the Clerides government announced that it had ordered a total of 48 S-300 air defence missiles from Russia, which would be able to hit targets on the Turkish mainland as well as in Cypriot airspace. This was treated as a provocative challenge by Tansu Çiller, then the foreign minister, who threatened that the Turkish air force would destroy the missiles if they were installed. Fortunately, in December 1998, Clerides was persuaded to back down under intense pressure from Washington.[8]

In June 1997, the installation of the coalition led by Mesut Yılmaz (p140) meant that there was now a government in Ankara prepared to mend its fences with the western powers and hence with Greece. At a NATO meeting in Madrid in July 1997, the Greek and Turkish governments expressed a commitment to peaceful relations, respect for each other's sovereignty and existing international treaties. This was accompanied by renewed talks between Denktash and Clerides under UN auspices, first in Troutbeck, New York, in July 1997, and then in Glion, Switzerland, in August. Neither of these encounters resulted in any progress, mainly because Denktash objected to the expected opening of accession negotiations between Cyprus and the EU without any Turkish Cypriot representation. Any short-run chances of a meaningful dialogue with Greece, or progress on the Cyprus issue, were further reduced by the decision of the EU's Luxembourg summit in December 1997, which confirmed Turkey's apparent exclusion from the enlargement process (p179).[9] As Christopher de Bellaigue suggests: 'At one ill-considered stroke, the EU had destroyed what leverage it possessed over the Turks.'[10]

It was not until 1999 that more hopeful prospects began to emerge. The Greek government's murky role in the Öcalan affair, made clear after his capture by the Turks in Nairobi in February 1999 (p145) produced a change of heart by Greece in its attitude to Turkey, illustrated by the dismissal of the hard-line and unpredictable foreign minister Theodore Pangalos, as well as the Ministers of the Interior and Public Order, immediately afterwards. The Greek Prime Minister, Costas Simitis, seemed anxious to turn over a new leaf in relations with Turkey. In May 1999, the new Greek foreign minister George Papandreou took up an offer made by his Turkish opposite number, İsmail Cem, for a dialogue on bilateral issues between the two countries. This developed with a series of meetings during the summer and autumn. The agenda was mainly limited to uncontroversial questions – such as trade, tourism and environmental protection – but included 'cooperation against terrorism' (a reference to the Turkish demand for a definite end to Greek support for the PKK). Controversial issues, such as seabed rights and territorial waters in the Aegean, were postponed until a later date.[11] External and unexpected events also gave a boost to the détente. The Turkish earthquake of 17 August 1999 (p141), to which the Greek people and government responded rapidly and generously, and the despatch of a Turkish aid team to help with rescue operations after an earthquake in Athens on 7 September, led to a dramatic reversal of hostile attitudes in the press, even if public opinion seemed to be slow to catch up with this.[12]

Of the various substantive obstacles to be overcome, Cyprus was still the most intractable. In November 1999, Rauf Denktash, who was evidently under strong pressure from the US and the UN on this point, agreed to join Clerides in proximity talks in New York under UN auspices. These failed to produce effective results, since Denktash pressed for a 'confederation', or a looser form of reunion than the 'federation' demanded by the Greeks, who feared that the 'confederal' formula might give the Turkish Cypriots the right to opt out of a future Cypriot state.[13] It was at this point that the broader context was transformed by the decision of the European Council, meeting in Helsinki in December 1999, that Turkey could be included as a candidate for eventual EU membership on the same basis as the other candidate countries. For the Turks and the Turkish Cypriots, the sting in the tail was that the Council was also pressured by Greece into agreeing that the Republic of Cyprus could be admitted to the EU even if there was no internal settlement (p180). While Turkey did not reject the principle of Cypriot accession, it had insisted that this could not precede an internal settlement and should be simultaneous with the accession of Turkey. On balance, however, Ecevit's government could not afford to turn down the possibility of eventual accession and had to accept the Helsinki terms. In view of the Helsinki decision, it was clear that the need to resolve the Cyprus problem was a pressing one for Turkey, since this was the main point at which its policies clearly conflicted with those of its broader foreign policy interests to develop and maintain its links with the western powers, and avoid involvement in regional conflicts. It was the only important foreign policy issue in which it had virtually no external support.

On the positive side, the Helsinki decisions gave a positive boost to the developing rapprochement between the mainland governments of Greece and Turkey. In January 2000, George Papandreou visited Ankara to sign agreements to encourage mutual investments and prevent double taxation, besides cooperation in fighting organized crime, preventing illegal immigration, promoting tourism and protecting the environment. If nothing else, the visit was significant in that it was the first trip to the Turkish capital by a Greek foreign minister for 36 years. It was reciprocated by İsmail Cem, who visited Athens on 3 February 2000. This produced five further agreements on non-contentious issues, such as cultural and economic cooperation.[14] However, it also left the most thorny questions in Greek–Turkish relations, in particular the long-standing disputes over offshore mineral rights and territorial waters in the Aegean, still unsettled (pp115–6). As the decisions of the Helsinki summit had made clear, Turkey would not be able to conclude accession negotiations with the EU, unless they were solved.[15] Further discussions between Cem and Papandreou continued over the next two years, and by April 2002, the harmony between them was so far advanced that they even agreed to carry out a joint mission to Ariel Sharon and Yasser Arafat in the hope of helping to defuse the Israeli–Palestinian crisis.[16]

This left the Cyprus problem as the most contentious and complex point of conflict between the two countries. In January, President Clerides and Rauf Denktash restarted direct talks on a future constitution brokered by Alvaro de Soto, the Special Adviser on Cyprus to UN Secretary-General Kofi Annan.[17] In accepting the idea of face-to-face discussions, Denktash had evidently decided on a change of tack, to the extent that he was evidently backing off his previous claim that the sovereignty of his self-proclaimed Turkish Republic of Northern Cyprus should be recognized before inter-communal talks could be restarted. Like their predecessors, however, the discussions ended nowhere, having signally failed to meet the original target of reaching an agreement by June 2002. Nevertheless, it led to a renewed attempt by Kofi Annan, who put forward the first version of a new settlement plan in November 2002, referred to as 'the most comprehensive and detailed plan for a solution to the Cyprus issue'.[18] To summarize, it envisaged the establishment of a bi-zonal federation, to be known as the United Cyprus Republic, with weak federal powers, and a single shared sovereignty prohibiting both partition and union with any other country. The Treaty of Guarantee provided by the 1960 agreements would remain in force (pp97–8). There would be a bi-cameral federal legislature including of a Chamber of Deputies of 48 members with representation of each community in accordance with its share of the population and a minimum of 12 Turkish Cypriot deputies. In the upper house, or Senate, there would again be 48 members, but with equal numbers of Greek and Turkish Cypriot representatives. The federal government, referred to as the Presidential Council, would have six voting and three non-voting members, with members drawn proportionately from each community. This would elect a President and Vice-President, one from each community, who would rotate in office every 20 months. In a territorial adjustment, the Turkish Cypriot territory would be reduced to 28 per cent of the island and there would be a timetable for the withdrawal of foreign troops, to leave 950 Greek and 750 Turkish soldiers. Freedom of settlement and freedom of property ownership between the two constituent states would be restricted for a defined period, or until Turkey became a full member of the EU.[19]

When it took office in November 2002, the AKP government gave full support to the Annan plan and it was hoped that agreement to proceed on this basis could be reached in time for the Copenhagen meeting of the European Council in December. However, Rauf Denktash blocked this effort. The Turkish military, in the person of the Commander of Land Forces, General Aytaç Yalman, gave him public support. This turned out to be a fatal mistake, since President Clerides would probably have accepted the plan whereas his successor, Tassos Papadopoulos, who was elected to the Greek Cypriot presidency in February 2003, opposed it. In this way, the brief window of opportunity to settle the problem was missed.[20] The need to reach an agreement was underlined by the decision of the European Council meeting in Copenhagen, confirming the previous Helsinki decision, to the effect that the Republic of Cyprus could be admitted to the EU on 1 May 2004 even if there were no previous internal settlement.

In December 2003, events appeared to take a more hopeful turn when Rauf Denktash's party lost control of the TRNC parliament. The following month, Mehmet Ali Talat, leader of the opposition Republican Turkish Party, which favoured a settlement, took office as Prime Minister with Rauf Denktash's son Serdar, who had broken with his father, as deputy premier and foreign minister. The new Turkish Cypriot government committed itself to reaching an agreement with the Greek Cypriots by 1 May 2004, in cooperation with Turkey.[21] Soon afterwards, on 23 January 2004, at a meeting of the National Security Council in Ankara, objections from the Chief of the General Staff, General Hilmi Özkök, as well as from President Ahmet Necdet Sezer were overruled, and it was agreed that the Annan plan should be supported.[22] On the following day, Tayyip Erdoğan met Kofi Annan on the sidelines of the World Economic Forum meeting in Davos, Switzerland, in which he agreed that if the Greek and Turkish Cypriot negotiators could not reach an accord, and provided the Greeks agreed, then the Secretary-General would 'fill in the gaps' between the two positions. The final version of the plan could then be put to separate referendums on the two sides of the island, prior to the planned date for Cypriot accession to the EU.[23] Accordingly, in March 2004 negotiations were held in Bürgenstock, Switzerland, attended by Kofi Annan, and President Papadopoulos for the Greek Cypriots, with Mehmet Ali Talat and Serdar Denktash for the Turkish Cypriots, as well as the foreign ministers of Greece and Turkey. In practice, Papadopoulos played only a marginal role in the negotiations, since he only made himself available for two of the six critical days of negotiation, leaving a number of non-agreed points that Kofi Annan was left to 'fill in'. It was on this basis that a final version of the plan was submitted to twin referendums on the island on 24 April 2004.[24]

In the run-up to the referendums, it became clear that the majority of Turkish Cypriots favoured the Annan plan, since if it were implemented then they would join the European Union as equal partners of the Greek Cypriots and their international isolation would be ended. Hence, it was no surprise that just under 65 per cent of Turkish Cypriot voters approved of the plan, with a turnout rate of 87 per cent. The same reasoning did not apply on the Greek Cypriot side, since the Republic of Cyprus would be admitted to the EU on 1 May anyway, without having to make any constitutional concessions. Moreover, although the Greeks had in theory accepted a federal solution since 1977, they had never properly thought through what this would mean, and how much it would differ from 'three decades of maximalist rhetoric and treasured myths', as the International Crisis Group, a Brussels-based think-tank, puts it.[25] Features of the plan that were highly controversial on the Greek side included Turkey's continued right to intervene under the Treaty of Guarantee, the fact that the withdrawal of Turkish troops and the return of territory would only be gradual, and the continuation of all treaties between Turkey and the TRNC.[26] In an emotional television address on 7 April, in which at one point he broke down in tears, President Papadopoulos urged his audience to give 'a resounding NO' in the referendum.[27] The Greek Cypriots responded by rejecting the plan by 76 to 24 per cent, in an 89 per cent turnout. Hence, the Annan plan was killed, and the Republic of Cyprus entered the European Union on 1 May 2004 as a purely Greek state, creating serious problems for the EU as well as Turkey and the Turkish Cypriots.

With the defeat of the settlement plan in April 2004, the Cyprus problem entered an awkward limbo.[28] Immediately after the referendums, the European Council issued a statement declaring that 'the Council is determined to put an end to the isolation of the Turkish Cypriot community and to facilitate the reunification of Cyprus',[29] but did virtually nothing to put these words into effect. Later, the Turkish government became embroiled in a complex dispute with Brussels over the extension of the Turkey–EU customs union agreement to the new member states, including Cyprus, which has been outlined earlier (pp186, 189). In spite of the bleak prospects, neither Turkey or the Turkish Cypriots could afford to refuse appeals from the UN to participate in more negotiations with the Greek Cypriot government, for fear that they would then be accused of blocking a possible solution. Accordingly, between 2006 and early 2008, Mehmet Ali Talat and Tassos Papadopoulos had more than 50 meetings, although these proved quite fruitless. In February 2008, events took a turn for the better when Papadopoulos was unexpectedly defeated in the Greek Cypriot presidential elections, to be succeeded by Demetris Christofias, leader of the nominally communist 'Progressive Party of the Working People' (AKEL). Hopes were raised by the fact that since both he and Talat enjoyed a long-established dialogue, as leaders of left-wing parties that opposed ethnic nationalism, they might be able to overcome the differences between the two sides.[30] However, after early successes, the talks became bogged down over some basic principles. With the failure of a more flexible approach to win tangible gains, Turkish Cypriot support for the peace process declined, so that when Talat ran for re-election as TRNC president in April 2010 he was defeated by Derviş Eroğlu, leader of the National Unity Party (UBP), and a known sceptic of federal reunification.[31] Thereafter, although both sides continued to go through the motions of continuing the talks, no progess was registered, and relations reverted to their normal state of deadlock. As this book was being completed at the end of 2011, it was expected that multilateral talks would be held in New York in 2012. In these, the two Cypriot sides would be joined by representatives of Greece, Turkey and the UN, plus possibly other UN members. However, it was still doubtful that a settlement could be reached, given the continuing differences between the Greek and Turkish Cypriot leaders.[32]

On the face of it, the story of links between the two mainland governments after 2002 was less depressing. The fact that Greece now supported the principle of Turkish accession to the EU, rather than opposing it as it had formerly, had obviously positive effects on Turkish attitudes. Rapprochement with Greece fitted well into Ahmet Davutoğlu's policy of 'zero problems with neighbours' (even if this had signally failed in the Cypriot case). Contacts between the two countries continued to develop, most notably with the visit of Costas Karamanlis to Ankara in January 2008 – the first visit by a Greek Premier to Turkey for 49 years. In a return trip to Athens in May 2010, Tayyip Erdoğan initiated a High Level Cooperation Council aiming to bring ministers from the two countries into regular consultations, so as to institutionalize their cooperation – a strategy that was extended to other countries (p235). In the economic sphere, there was a huge increase in bilateral trade, which rose in value from $903 million in 2002 to just under $3 billion in 2010, and the opening of a pipeline to supply natural gas from Turkey to Greece in November 2007.[33] There were also signs that the relationship was developing into a people-to-people rapprochement, rather than a purely governmental one, with proliferating cultural exchanges, business group contacts and youth exchanges, in which the EU was active in funding activities by civil society groups.[34] This constituted a rare and apparently successful use of 'second track diplomacy' in Turkish foreign policy. A crucial role was also played by the Ecumenical Patriarch Bartholomew I in his outspoken advocacy of Greek–Turkish reconciliation, in opposition to the outrightly racialist views of Archbishop Christodoulos, formerly head of the Church of Greece.[35] In diplomatic relations, a significant sign of the improvement was seen in April 2005, when a second clash over the Imia/Kardak islet arose between the two countries' coastguards but was rapidly defused by both governments.[36]

This is not to suggest that all was now sweetness and light in trans-Aegean relations. The long-running dispute over territorial waters had not gone away – in fact in 2005, the Turkish military actually reasserted the *casus belli* resolution passed by the Turkish parliament ten years earlier (p116).[37] Mutual complaints regarding the treatment of minority populations (Greek in Turkey, Turkish in Greece) continued. On its side, the Turkish government failed to take conciliatory and relatively cost-free steps that had long been advocated, such as the reopening of the Greek Orthodox seminary on the Marmara island of Heybeli (Halki), a partial withdrawal of its large contingent of troops from Cyprus, and recognition of the 'Ecumenical' title of Patriarch Bartholomew.[38] By 2011, although exploratory talks on the territorial waters and continental shelf disputes had begun after the EU Helsinki summit of December 1999, no progress had been reported, and the recourse to the International Court envisaged at Helsinki remained unimplemented (p180). In effect, since 2004, a plateau had been reached. The resultant 'cold peace'[39] was at least better than the previous confrontation. Nonetheless, the continuing Aegean disagreement, and even more the Cyprus dispute, still had to be counted as the least successful theatre of Turkey's post-Cold War foreign policy.

Turkey and the Balkans

While Turkey's policies towards Cyprus and Greece clearly conflicted with the interests of its NATO allies, the developing ethnic conflicts in the Balkans during the 1990s – especially in former Yugoslavia – had the opposite effect. The Turks were closely concerned with the developing western military role, first in Bosnia-Herzegovina, beginning in 1993, and then in Kosovo in 1999. Far from opposing it in principle, their main complaint, especially before 1995, was that it was not speedy or effective enough. Once NATO had become heavily involved in these and the neighbouring republics, Turkey was usually enthusiastic and active in its support.

This is not to suggest that formulating policies towards the Balkans was all plain sailing for Turkish policy-makers, since they faced a classic dilemma of reconciling internal political pressures with external realities. On the one hand, domestic public opinion strongly favoured the Muslim side in the bloody conflict in Bosnia, and later in Kosovo. Although the Bosnian Muslims are not ethnically Turkish, Turks saw Muslim Bosnia as the last remnant of a once powerful Muslim presence in south-east Europe. Turkish government spokesmen frequently emphasized that they regarded the Bosnian conflict as an humanitarian issue, not a battle between two religions. However, historical memories had not been eradicated. In Turkey, the public impression – which was hard to deny – was that the international community was standing idly by in the face of massacres and expulsion of an important Muslim community, much as they had done in the nineteenth century. Islamist and ultra-nationalist parties did their best to stoke up such feelings, which were reinforced by the fact that a claimed total of 4 million Turkish citizens were said to be of Bosnian origin, the descendant of refugees of the nineteenth and early twentieth centuries.[40] On the other hand, successive Turkish governments recognized that they could not intervene unilaterally or independently in Bosnia, partly because of its distance from Turkish territory and partly because Turkey could not afford to step too far out of line with the policies of its western allies, primarily the United States.[41] Hence, Turkish governments concentrated their efforts on drawing international attention to the plight of the Bosnian Muslims and pressing their allies to intervene on their behalf.

The Bosnian problem became a 'top foreign policy issue' for Turkey between 1992 and 1995, as the western powers failed to take effective measures to protect the Bosnian Muslims against the Serbs following the dissolution of

Yugoslavia.[42] In 1992, Turkey strongly supported the NATO decision to deploy a naval task force in the Adriatic to monitor the application of economic sanctions against Serbia, and the force was at one point commanded by a Turkish officer. Later, in April 1993, it sent a detachment of F-15 jets to join the NATO force based in Italy, which was to enforce the no-fly-zone over Bosnia. Turkish diplomats and politicians were meanwhile making it clear that, in their view, these efforts did not go far enough. At the Helsinki summit of the Conference on Security and Cooperation in Europe (CSCE)[43] in July 1992, Prime Minister Demirel tried to mobilize a pressure group including the central Asian republics and Azerbaijan in support of the Bosnian government, and urged President Bush to launch a major military intervention, similar to that against Iraq in 1991. In August 1992, the government also attempted to persuade the permanent members of the UN Security Council to adopt an 'Action Plan' calling for limited air strikes against the Serbs, although with no involvement of ground forces. Rebuffed by the western powers, Turkey turned to fellow Muslim countries, a campaign in which President Özal played a prominent role. In December 1992, Turkey joined other members of the Organization of the Islamic Conference in threatening to send arms to the Bosnian Muslims after 15 January 1993 if the UN had not taken adequate measures to protect them by then, although when the time came this threat remained unimplemented.[44]

Although these attempts to mobilize the Muslim countries proved quite unavailing, events during 1994–5 suggested that Turkey was beginning to succeed in its bid to play a more active role in the crisis. In the face of appalling tragedies and atrocities, the western powers were slowly coming round to a more robust view of their responsibilities in Bosnia. Once the UN had set up a special protection force for Bosnia (UNPROFOR) then Turkey pressed to be included in it. After some prevarication, in March 1994, the UN Secretary-General announced that a Turkish detachment would be accepted. Consisting of about 1,500 troops, it arrived in Bosnia in July 1994, and was stationed at the town of Zeneca, in the western part of the country, where its main task was to monitor the ceasefire between the local Croat and Bosnian-Muslim forces. Its presence was strongly attacked by Greece, but welcomed by both the Croat and Bosnian Muslims, besides helping to reassure Turkish opinion that Turkey was playing a direct and positive role in Bosnia.[45] Diplomatically, Turkey also enhanced its image as a helpful ally to the west by brokering an entente between the Croats and Bosnian Muslims, resulting in the establishment of a Muslim-Croat Federation under the Washington Agreement of March 1994. Turkey and Croatia developed close relations, mainly due to their common hostility to Serbia, but the entente also underlined the Turkish argument that the conflict in Bosnia-Herzegovina was not a straightforward war between Christians and Muslims. Meanwhile, it was reported that Turkey was covertly supplying arms to the Bosnian Muslims (presumably with American compliance) via Croatia, although these accounts could not officially be confirmed.[46]

The most critical turning point in the Bosnian story came in 1995, following the capture by the Serbs of Srebrenica and Zepa, two of the supposedly 'safe areas' in eastern Bosnia, in July and the massacre and flight of their inhabitants. On 30 August, NATO air forces at last launched all-out air attacks on Serbian ground positions in an operation known as 'Deliberate Force', which lasted until 14 September. Following these attacks, Croat forces recaptured large areas of Croatia previously taken by the Serbs, and the Belgrade government was forced to the conference table. Under the agreements signed at Dayton, Ohio on 21 November 1995, Bosnia-Herzegovina was reconstituted, nominally as a single state, consisting of the Muslim-Croat federation and the Bosnian Serb republic, or 'Republika Serbska'. These events effectively removed the Bosnian problem as a source of potential conflict between Turkey and the western powers, since NATO had now intervened effectively to protect the Bosnian Muslims. The Turkish peacekeeping force stayed on in Bosnia-Herzegovina as a useful part of the international implementation force (IFOR: reconstituted as the 'stabilization force', or SFOR, in 1996). During 1996, Turkey also joined the United States in playing a significant part in the US-led programme to train and equip the army of the Muslim-Croat federation, besides joining the Italian-led peacekeeping intervention in Albania in 1997 known as 'Operation Alba', and sending a military contingent to help rebuild the Albanian forces.[47]

Following the Dayton agreement, conflicts in the Balkans seemed to have become stabilized, up to the time of the eruption of the crisis in Kosovo in 1998–9. Although the UN Security Council had not specifically authorized the use of force in Kosovo, NATO began a campaign of intensive air strikes against Serbian targets in Kosovo and in Serbia itself on 23 March 1999, triggering off the expulsion of almost a million Kosovar Albanians into the neighbouring republics of Macedonia, Albania and Montenegro. The campaign lasted until 10 June, when Serbian forces were withdrawn from Kosovo, and an international peacekeeping force, known as KFOR, was installed in the province.[48] At the outset, it appears that the Turkish foreign ministry was not enthusiastic about the prospect of a NATO intervention in Kosovo. In the Balkan context, the official detachment of Kosovo from Yugoslavia – either as an independent state or as part of Albania – could have acted as a precedent for the territorial break-up of Macedonia, with its large Albanian minority, which Turkey strongly opposed. At worst, it could even have threatened to provoke a much wider Balkan war, in which Greece and Turkey could have been dragged in on opposite sides.[49] However, the sheer scale and brutality of the Serbian action against the Kosovar Albanians meant that Turkey, as a fellow-Muslim nation, could hardly stand aside. As President Demirel claimed, 'the people who have been subjected to cruelty in Kosovo are our brethren', and the crisis presented Turkey with the opportunity to demonstrate that it was a 'first class' member of NATO.[50] On these grounds, Turkey strongly supported the NATO action in Kosovo, providing a detachment of F-16 fighters, based in Italy that, according to the Turkish press, played an active role in the operation.

Around 8,000 refugees from Kosovo were accommodated in Turkey and substantial aid was sent to those taking temporary refuge in Albania.[51] Following the Serbian withdrawal from Kosovo, Turkey sent a detachment of around 1,000 troops to join KFOR, who arrived in July 1999. They were stationed in the town of Prizren, which is largely inhabited by Kosovo's minority of ethnic Turks.[52]

With the end of the fighting in Kosovo, the situation in the western Balkans stabilized. Following the ouster of Slobodan Milosevic as President of Serbia in 2000, and his succession by Vojislav Kostinica, Turkey re-established diplomatic links with Belgrade, and was able to rebuild its bridges with Serbia as well as develop its links with the other ex-Yugoslav republics. In this way, it came to acquire a valuable mediator role between Bosnia-Herzegovina, Serbia and Croatia. The process was not a smooth one, since Turkey was one of the first states to recognize Montenegro's declaration of independence in 2006. Its recognition of Kosovo as an independent state in 2008 (reversing its initial attitude) caused a serious clash with Belgrade, in which Serbia temporarily withdrew its ambassador from Ankara, and the Turkish embassy in Belgrade was attacked by a furious mob.[53] Nonetheless, links were fully restored by October 2009, when Abdullah Gül became the first Turkish President to visit Serbia for 23 years and declared that relations between the two countries had never been better. Following the visit, Ahmet Davutoğlu was engaged in intense shuttle diplomacy between Sarajevo and Belgrade that resulted in the adoption by the Serbian parliament of a 'Declaration of Srebrenica' in March 2010, officially apologizing for the massacre of 1995. Besides this, Turkey's most significant diplomatic achievement was brokering an agreement between Serbia, Bosnia-Herzegovina and Croatia, known as the 'Istanbul Declaration on Peace and Stability in the Balkans', signed in April 2010, in which the three governments pledged to improve cooperation and work towards integration with the European Union. With Turkey supporting the three states' bids for membership of NATO as well as eventual accession to the EU, there was strong concordance between Turkish and both EU and US policies.[54]

Elsewhere in the Balkans, the end of communism had its most dramatic effects for Turkey in the fall of the Zhivkov regime in Bulgaria in November 1989, which ended the Bulgarian campaign against the Turkish minority (p123). Subsequent Bulgarian governments recognized the cultural rights of the Turks, and allowed them to play a full part in Bulgaria's new democratic system. As a result, at least half of the 312,000 Turkish refugees from Bulgaria returned to their homes in 1990 and afterwards. Although anti-Turkish and anti-Roma racialism has re-emerged in Bulgaria, the 'Movement for Rights and Freedoms' (in effect, the Turkish ethnic party of Bulgaria) supported successive Bulgarian governments that followed the fall of communism. As a sign of the dramatic improvement in attitudes and policies, Turkey and Bulgaria signed a Treaty of Friendship, Neighbourly Relations and Security in 1992. While Bulgaria's small size and the poor state of its economy obviously restricted this, economic collaboration was also developed. By 1999,

Turkey was lobbying in Washington for Bulgaria's admission to NATO, achieved in March 2004, as well as its membership of the EU, which it joined in January 2007.[55]

This is not to suggest that Turkish diplomacy in the Balkans was above criticism. During one of his trips to Bosnia in 2009, Ahmet Davutoğlu had a rare lapse into 'neo-Ottomanism' (see pp254–5) when he remarked that 'the Ottoman centuries of the Balkans were a success story. Now we have to reinvent this'.[56] Such remarks might go down well with a Muslim audience in the Balkans, but were likely to have the opposite effect for the non-Muslim majority. More broadly, it is argued that Turkey's ambitions outran its resources, in a region where the EU and the United States wielded far more power, both hard and soft.[57] In other respects, Turkey's generally cautious approach in the Balkans during the 1990s appeared to have paid good dividends, since it had helped to prevent Bulgaria as well as Macedonia from slipping into an anti-Muslim or anti-Turkish Slavic bloc led by Greece. Equally, a 'Muslim belt' failed to emerge, as Turkish policy carefully avoided creating one.[58] At the beginning of the decade, there had been fears that rivalry between Greece and Turkey might become part of the Balkan problem, but this was avoided. Thanks to its earlier hostility towards Macedonia and its friendship with Serbia, Greece had been on the losing side in Balkan conflicts and the odd man out in NATO – in contrast to Turkey. These points seem to have been recognized by the Simitis government, which revised Greek policies in the Balkans, as well as softening Greek attitudes towards the Turks. In fact, as part of the dramatic thaw in relations between Ankara and Athens, the two governments even agreed to discuss joint projects on rebuilding Kosovo, and a common approach to Balkan security problems.[59] More broadly, while Turkey was far from being a dominant player in Balkan politics, its foreign policy-makers were entitled to conclude that, besides strengthening their links with NATO as a useful ally, they had played a positive role by helping to stabilize and pacify the region after the initial tragic period of conflict.

10 Turkey and regional politics after the Cold War II

Russia, the Black Sea, Transcaucasia and central Asia

For Turkey, as for the other NATO countries, the end of the Cold War had been a gradual process. As we have seen, Mikhail Gorbachev's accession to power in the USSR in 1985 had brought about a notable decline in Soviet–Turkish tensions and impressive progress in economic cooperation between the two countries (see pp121–2). This process was sealed in March 1991, when Presidents Gorbachev and Özal finally signed a Treaty of Friendship and Good Neighbourliness. Had conditions remained unchanged, Turkey might have continued this as a long-term entente with its northern neighbour, as it had in the 1920s and 1930s. Although Turkish policies towards Russia were far more cooperative than they had been during the Cold War, a full entente failed to emerge, mainly because the disintegration of the USSR in 1991 opened up a Pandora's box of regional conflicts – notably in the new Trans-caucasian republics of Georgia, Armenia and Azerbaijan, in which Turkey and Russia were on opposite sides politically. At the same time, Turkey had important reasons, both strategic and economic, for seeking to avoid a head-on collision with Moscow. As a result, it had to walk a delicate tightrope in its relations with Russia, balancing its sympathies for the Muslim and pre-dominantly Turkic nations of the Caucasus and central Asia, and its desire to prevent Moscow from regaining a monopoly of power in Russia's 'near abroad', with its need to promote its economic interests in Russia and avoid a direct clash with Russian military power.

Turkey and Russia after the Cold War

With the opening up of the Russian economy after the fall of communism, economic relations and dependencies became a critical part of the relationship. In 2008, trade between the two countries reached a total of just under $38 billion, or 11.3 per cent of Turkey's total foreign trade, compared with a total of $3.7 billion in 1996, making Russia Turkey's biggest single trading partner for the first time. Thanks to the global economic downturn, this figure dropped to $26.2 billion in 2010, but Russia was still Turkey's second biggest trading partner after Germany. The relationship was not symmetrical, how-ever, since Russia's exports to Turkey were far larger than Turkey's exports to

Russia ($21.6 billion in 2010, compared with $4.6 billion).[1] This was largely the result of the massive increase in Turkey's energy imports from its northern neighbour, particularly of natural gas, which was part of the switch to gas as a vital part of the country's total energy supplies (see pp154–5). Exact calculations are difficult, since by 2010, Turkey had contracted to import much more natural gas than it actually consumed (51.8 billion cubic metres [bcm] per year, compared with an actual consumption of 39 bcm), reflecting consistent over-contracting.[2] In 2011, Russia was reported to be responsible for just over two-thirds of Turkey's natural gas consumption, in addition to 20 per cent of its oil imports.[3] Gas was supplied from Russia via two pipelines, one entering Turkey from the west, via Bulgaria, opened in 1987, and the other, known as 'Blue Stream' running under the Black Sea to Samsun, which started operation in 2003.

Since it is currently cheaper to transport natural gas by pipeline rather than in liquid form by tanker (LNG), consumers are effectively tied to given producers by the infrastructure network and vice versa. While Turkey is thus dependent on Russia for an essential commodity, the reverse is not true: Russia's imports from Turkey – consisting mainly of food products, textile products and chemicals – could be replaced by other suppliers. To add to these dependencies, in 2010, Turkey signed a contract with the Russian company Rusatom to construct its first nuclear power plant at Akkuyu, on the Mediterranean coast.[4] On the positive side, by 2010, Turkish contractors had acquired construction contracts in Russia to the value of $32 billion. Following the abolition of visa requirements, there was also an annual flow of around 3 million tourists from Russia to Turkey.[5] Nonetheless, the fact was that in the economic sphere Turkey was far more dependent on Russia than Russia on Turkey. Inevitably, this led to tensions in the relationship – in particular, attempts by the Turkish side to reduce the price of the gas imported from Russia, or to ease the conditions under which Turkey was obliged to pay for a given amount of gas per year whether or not it actually used it (known as the 'take or pay' clauses).[6] Hence, Turkey had a strong incentive to diversify its sources of supply.

Paradoxically, there were suggestions that Russia might also play a role in Turkey's bid to become an international energy hub, as a meeting point for oil and gas pipelines from producing countries in the Middle East, Transcaucasia, central Asia and Russia, running west to consumers in Europe. Whether this could be achieved would be dependent largely on the realization of the Nabucco project (see p155) and whether energy pipelines could be built from Iran and Iraq as well as the Caspian (pp237, 241). A coincidental concern was that the rapid growth of crude oil exports in tankers sailing from Russia across the Black Sea and through the Turkish straits to the Mediterranean, posed the real risk of disastrous accidents in the Bosporus, where navigation is difficult anyway.[7] An explosion or oil spill in the middle of Istanbul, through which the Bosporus passes, could cause catastrophic environmental damage, to say nothing of potential loss of life. Under the Montreux

Convention of 1936 (p48), Turkey must allow free passage through the straits to all merchant ships in peacetime, but the government and (it can be argued) the global oil firms have a strong incentive to construct a bypass route if possible. In August 2009, Russian President Vladimir Putin and the Italian Prime Minister Silvio Berlusconi reached an agreement with Prime Minister Erdoğan to build a pipeline from the Turkish Black Sea port of Samsun to the Mediterranean coast at Ceyhan. This would allow oil from Russia and Kazakhstan to reach world markets without passing through the Bosporus, having a capacity of 50 million metric tons per year (approximately 1 million barrels per day). As an incentive to Russia, Turkey agreed to lift its objections to the construction of 'South Stream' – a planned pipeline to carry gas under the Black Sea from Russia to eastern Europe, bypassing the Ukraine, which would pass through Turkey's exclusive offshore economic zone.[8] By 2011, however, it appeared that both projects had fallen by the wayside. Although the Turkish side still seemed to be fully supportive of the Samsun–Ceyhan project, the Russian oil transport firm Transneft announced in September 2011 that it would be frozen as 'it cannot be implemented in the economic sense'.[9] On the one hand, 'South Stream' also appeared to be technically and financially unviable, and it was reported that the Russian authorities were planning to export gas in liquefied form (LNG) as an alternative.[10] If this were shipped out through the Bosporus, however, the accident risk would be even greater, creating further conflicts.

Turkey, the Black Sea and Transcaucasia

As President during the early 1990s, Turgut Özal attempted to exploit and expand economic links to other ex-communist countries by launching a regional organization, in the shape of the Black Sea Economic Cooperation project. This took official status at a meeting held in Istanbul in June 1992, which was attended by the heads of state or government of Turkey, Bulgaria, Romania, Moldova, Ukraine, Russia, Georgia, Armenia, Azerbaijan, Greece and Albania (although the last four are not strictly speaking Black Sea states, it was evidently thought politically inexpedient to exclude them). At the Istanbul summit, the 11 countries committed themselves to 'reduce or progressively eliminate obstacles [to trade] of all kinds', and to develop joint projects in the fields of transport, energy, mining, tourism and environmental protection.[11]

Institutionally, the BSEC project has a permanent secretariat in Istanbul with a rotating chair, and an annual meeting of the foreign ministers of the member states. At a meeting in Sofia in December 1993, it was decided to set up a Black Sea Foreign Trade and Development Bank, based in Salonica. After long delays, this was eventually inaugurated in June 1999.[12] In the economic sphere, it is hard to estimate whether the project had had any significant or independent effect. Turkey's total trade with all the BSEC states, taken together, rose from $6.8 billion in 1996 to $48.1 billion in 2010, but of the latter figure, $26.2 billion, or 54 per cent, was accounted for by Russia alone, signalling that in economic terms the other member states were still dwarfed by Russia.[13] Moreover, three of the BSEC members – Bulgaria, Romania and Greece – were now members of the European Union, a far more powerful economic alliance. To criticize the project on these grounds was, however, to ignore the argument that it had political rather than purely economic aims, being based on the idea that if the regional countries developed their economic interdependencies, they would become politically more cooperative. This ambition now seems too optimistic, since the complex contests between almost all the members – between Greece and Turkey, between Russia and Ukraine and Georgia, and between Azerbaijan and Armenia – proved too obdurate for any real sense of community to emerge. In principle the strategy was admirable, but was hard to achieve in practice.

A second important aspect of Turkey's policy in the Black Sea region was the aim of preventing it becoming a zone of direct conflict between Russia and the western powers – an aim which brought it into a degree of alignment with Russia. Thus, both countries participated in a multilateral naval force, known as BLACKSEAFOR, set up in 2001, which also included elements of the navies of Bulgaria, Romania, Ukraine and Georgia. Its stated operational purpose was to carry out search and rescue operations, humanitarian assistance and environmental protection, but it could also carry out operations mandated by the United Nations or the Organization for Security and Cooperation in Europe (OSCE). In line with this approach, Turkey was reluctant to support the idea of NATO membership for Ukraine and Georgia, to which Russia was adamantly opposed.[14]

Politically, the most serious points of tension between Turkey and Russia arose from Russian involvement in ethnic conflicts in the Caucasus and Transcaucasia, in which Turkey was not likely to take a pro-Russian position. The first of these was the Chechen rebellion against Russian rule during 1994–6 and 1999. In this conflict, Turkish popular sympathies were generally with the Chechens, as fellow-Muslims (although ethnically they are quite separate). It is estimated that there are around 25,000 Turkish citizens of Chechen descent, and a claimed total of around 5 million inhabitants of Turkey whose families originate from the north Caucasus and Transcaucasian regions as a whole (that is, Chechens, Circassians, Abkhazians, Azeris and others). These groups supported a number of solidarity and cultural organizations in Turkey, with links to ultra-nationalist and Islamist parties, and are reported to have collected money and sent unofficial volunteers to fight in Chechnya. However, successive Turkish governments were careful not to give substantial or open support to any of these groups, mainly for fear that this might tempt Russia into giving full financial or logistical backing to the PKK.[15] As a statement of intent, in February 1995, the two countries signed a security protocol providing for cooperation against terrorism and organized crime, with the implication that they would abstain reciprocally from involvement in either the Kurdish or Chechen conflicts.[16] This commitment was one that went right back to the original Turkish–Soviet treaty of 1921, albeit in somewhat changed circumstances (p36). The issue came to a head in November 1999, when Prime Minister Bülent Ecevit paid an official visit to Moscow just as the Russians were intensifying their attacks during their second campaign in Chechnya. Although Ecevit admitted that the war was causing 'serious humanitarian worries', he stuck to the line that the war was 'Russia's internal problem'.[17] Thereafter, the Chechen question effectively dropped off the Turkish–Russian diplomatic agenda.

Of the various disputes between the regional states, that between Armenia and Azerbaijan was the most critical for Turkey. Since Azerbaijan has rich deposits of oil and natural gas, both onshore and under the Caspian Sea, the contest had vital economic and strategic dimensions for both Turkey and the western energy-importing countries. As in the case of the conflict in Bosnia-Herzegovina, it created the difficult task of reconciling domestic political pressures with external realities. While Turkish public opinion strongly favoured the Azeris, as fellow-Muslims of Turkic ethnicity, the government could not afford to give much more than moral or economic support to Azerbaijan, for fear of provoking a direct military conflict with Armenia, which might broaden into a Russian–Turkish war. Meeting in Tashkent in May 1992, Russia, Tajikistan, Uzbekistan, Kirghizstan, Kazakhstan and Armenia signed a treaty setting up the Collective Security Treaty Organization (CSTO), under which they promised to support one another if they were attacked by any country that was not a member of the Commonwealth of Independent States, or CIS (that is, the former Soviet republics, less the Baltic states). This allowed Russia to station troops in Armenia, so that if Turkey had been involved in direct hostilities with Armenia it would also have found itself fighting Russia.[18] Military cooperation between Turkey and Azerbaijan included the training of Azeri officers in Turkey and Azerbaijan, but did not definitely go further than this.[19]

The violent conflict between Azerbaijan and Armenia began in January 1990, before the dissolution of the Soviet Union, when Soviet troops killed several hundred Azeris while occupying Baku, the capital of Azerbaijan, following attacks on the local Armenian minority. At this stage, Turkey still hoped and expected that the USSR would survive as a territorial unit. It supported Gorbachev's reform programme, and adhered to the view that the conflict was an internal Soviet problem.[20] However, events soon made this policy obsolete. On 30 August 1991, Azerbaijan declared its independence, followed by Armenia on 21 September. Meanwhile, on 2 September, Nagorno-Karabakh, the predominantly Armenian enclave within Azerbaijan, proclaimed itself a separate republic. On 26 November, the Azeri parliament withdrew the autonomous status that Nagorno-Karabakh had previously enjoyed under the Soviet constitution. In the euphoria of independence, the Azeris and Armenians had set themselves on a collision course. In Ankara, the outgoing Motherland Party administration of Mesut Yılmaz recognized Azerbaijan as an independent state on 9 November, and the succeeding government under

Süleyman Demirel extended this recognition to all the previous Soviet republics on 19 December 1991.

In the long run, Turkey needed peace and stability in Transcaucasia, and the chance to develop economic opportunities in all the countries of the region. In an ideal world, it would also have liked to act as a regional power-broker and arbiter. This ambition proved impossible to achieve, since it went well beyond its political, economic and military resources. Inter-state disputes made the task still harder. Had the three Transcaucasian republics formed some sort of federation, or at least cooperated with one another, they might have been able to resist Russia's drive to re-assert its power, to Turkey's advantage. Instead, they followed the dismal example of the Balkan states during the 1930s by picking quarrels with their neighbours (p46), allowing Russia an easy re-entry into the region.

Initially, attempts were made by Turkey to open up contacts with Armenia, and to persuade the Azeris to restore the autonomy of Nagorno-Karabakh,[21] but by February 1992, full scale fighting in and around the enclave had erupted. On 26 February, Armenian forces in Stepanakert, the capital of Nagorno-Karabakh, captured the Azeri-inhabited suburb of Khojali, massacring some 500 civilians and causing widespread public protests in Turkey. President Özal apparently supported a hawkish line, suggesting that 'we should frighten [the Armenians] a little', but he was not supported by Prime Minister Demirel, who still stressed the need to find a peaceful settlement between the Azeris and Armenians.[22] These hopes proved unavailing. On 28 February 1992, at Turkish prompting, the Council for Security and Cooperation in Europe (predecessor of the OSCE) condemned the alteration of frontiers by force and confirmed that Nagorno-Karabakh is part of Azerbaijan. This did not deter the Armenians, who by 11 May had captured the whole of Nagorno-Karabakh and opened up a corridor between the enclave and Armenia proper, through Lachin, besides shelling the western end of Nakhichevan, the geographically detached province of Azerbaijan that abuts onto Turkish territory.

The Armenian attack on Nakhichevan raised critical questions for Turkey, since the fighting had now moved close to its borders. An Armenian invasion of Nakhichevan would have been a clear infraction of the Turkish–Soviet Treaty of Friendship of 1921, declaring that Nakhichevan was part of Azerbaijan and could not be handed over to any other state (see p36). Whether Turkey could have claimed treaty rights to intervene militarily in Nakhichevan to protect the status quo was an open question,[23] but the Commander of Land Forces, General Mühittin Fisunoğlu, announced that 'all necessary preparations' had been made for possible military action.[24] In Moscow, the commander of the armed forces of the CIS, General Yevgeny Shaposhnikov, warned that any intervention by a third country (read Turkey) could lead to a major war, and a similar warning was issued by the Russian ambassador in Ankara, Albert Chernishev. Apparently, this was the closest Turkey and Russia came to a direct armed collision.[25] Fortunately, the cautious Demirel decided to attempt a diplomatic solution, by making a direct approach to Moscow. This proved successful. After emergency talks between Demirel and President Boris Yeltsin on 25–6 May 1992, the two leaders issued a declaration condemning the occupation of Lachin and the fighting on the border between Armenia and Nakhichevan, inducing the Armenians to break off their attacks two days later.[26]

This outcome reduced the tension between the two sides. Shortly afterwards, Turkey was able to increase its influence in Baku in June 1992, when Abulfez Elchibey, who was strongly favoured in Ankara, was elected President of Azerbaijan. In March 1993, an outline agreement was signed between Turkey and Azerbaijan to construct an oil pipeline from Baku via Georgia to the Turkish Mediterranean port of Ceyhan, near İskenderun (generally known as the Baku–Tiflis–Ceyhan, or BTC project). This was to become a centrepiece of Turkish policy in Transcaucasia since it would give Turkey an important role in the Caspian oil game and significantly reduce Russia's leverage over the Caspian states by avoiding Azerbaijan's existing export pipeline running through Russian territory.

In a peace-seeking move, Turkey sent a diplomatic mission to Armenia in August 1992, pointing out the economic advantages that Armenia could enjoy by establishing normal relations with Turkey, but these approaches fell flat as the war between the Azeris and the Armenians dragged on during 1992–3, with the Armenians clearly gaining the upper hand. Following a UN Security Council resolution of 6 April 1993 calling for the withdrawal of Armenian forces, Turkey joined Azerbaijan in declaring an economic blockade of Armenia, with both countries closing their borders with Armenia. On the Turkish side, the blockade was not complete, since an air corridor between Istanbul and the Armenian capital of Yerevan was opened in 2005, and there were commercial contacts between the two countries via Georgia. Armenian citizens could also visit Turkey freely and it was later estimated that up to 40,000 of them were actually working in Turkey without permits.[27] As it was, the economic blockade had virtually no effect on the ground, since by September 1993, Armenian forces had captured virtually all the territory between Nagorno-Karabakh and Armenia proper, as well as the land south of the enclave as far as the Azeri–Iranian border, forcing around 100,000 Azeris to become refugees in their own country, and occupying about 20 per cent of the total land area of Azerbaijan.[28] In June 1993, Turkey joined ten other nations – including the US, Germany, Russia, Armenia and Azerbaijan – in the so-called 'Minsk Group', set up by the CSCE as an attempt to resolve the conflict. In spite of seemingly endless meetings, this has failed to register any real progress. Meanwhile, a new and tougher Russian policy was demonstrated by a violent change of regime in Baku. On 4 June 1993, one of Abulfez Elchibey's rivals, ex-Colonel Suret Husseinov, who was evidently acting with covert Russian support, took over large quantities or arms and ammunition from departing Soviet forces. He seized the town of Ganja, in northern Azerbaijan, from where he marched to Baku, and overthrew Elchibey's

government. He failed to gain personal political power in Azerbaijan, however, which was taken over by Haydar Aliev, a former member of the Politburo of the USSR and President of Nakhichevan since 1991.[29]

In spite of its support for Elchibey, and initial opposition in Turkey to
Aliev's takeover, there was nothing effective the Turkish government could do
to reverse it.[30] Hence, by the end of August, Turkey and the western powers
were obliged to accept the *fait accompli*. This change of direction was made
easier by the fact that, once he had been established in power, Haydar Aliev's
actions suggested that he would not be a Russian puppet. Initially – apparently
under Russian pressure – he opposed the BTC pipeline project, but he then
changed his tune by confirming his approval of the Turkish route.[31] In effect,
he had met most of Turkey's main objectives, short of a settlement with the
Armenians, in that he had prevented Azerbaijan from becoming a Russian
satellite, and was prepared to allow Turkey an important indirect role in the
development of Caspian oil. From Turkey's viewpoint, Aliev's presidency also
had an important advantage over that of Elchibey, in that Aliev was more
circumspect in his diplomacy. In particular, he was less likely to be provoca-
tively hostile to Russia, or to Iran, with which Turkey could not afford a
serious conflict.[32] In October 2003, ill-health forced him to step down from
the presidency in favour of his son Ilham, who generally followed his father's
conservative foreign policies, with an authoritarian (and apparently highly
corrupt) domestic regime in which the Aliyev clan and its close associates
monopolized power.

In the continuing struggle over Nagorno-Karabakh, by late 1993, both the
Azeris and Armenians seem to have realized that they had fought one another to
a standstill. Hence, in May 1994, Russia was able to induce the defence ministers
of Azerbaijan, Armenia and Nagorno-Karabakh to sign a ceasefire, which
was also signed by the Russian minister of defence, Pavel Grachev.[33] Russia
had thus emerged as the effective peace-broker in the region. The ceasefire at
least stabilized the situation, although it left the Armenians in a dominant
position on the ground. Since then, the main developments in Turkey's relations with the Transcaucasian states have been: first, the development of
closer economic links with Azerbaijan, especially in energy supplies, but with
distinct ups and downs in the political relationship; second, a volatile but generally tense relationship with Armenia, with important implications for Turkish–
American relations; and third, concerns over the future of Georgia, occasioned
by the brief Russian–Georgian war of 2008. Each of these can be summarized.

On the first score, the main achievement for both sides was the completion
of the Baku–Tiflis–Ceyhan pipeline in 2005, after many years of delay caused
by Russian opposition, financing problems and disputes over transit fees. Owned
by a consortium led by the British company BP with a 30 per cent share,
and the Azeri state oil company SOCAR (25 per cent) plus a number of other
oil companies including the Turkish TPAO, the line is 1,768 kilometres long:
when working at full capacity it could transport 1 million barrels per day. To
achieve this volume, connection would probably have to be made with the

huge oilfields of Kazakhstan, on the north-eastern side of the Caspian. Nonetheless even without this, the BTC pipeline is still rated as an important asset for Azerbaijan, Georgia and Turkey, and helps to establish Turkey as an important transit route for Caspian oil.[34] In 2006, it was joined by the Baku–Tiflis–Erzurum (BTE) gas pipeline. This parallels the BTC line into eastern Turkey, feeding Caspian natural gas from Azerbaijan's offshore Shah Deniz gas-field into the Turkish domestic distribution network. It has an annual capacity of 8.8 billion cubic metres (bcm) although Turkey's take-up has been around six bcm per year.[35] Currently (2011) overland traffic between Turkey and Azerbaijan is by road through Georgia, since the only existing rail link, running through Armenia, has been closed since 1993. In 1998, Turkey and Georgia agreed to build a bypass line connecting the two countries' rail systems and thus linking Turkey and Azerbaijan by rail. After long delays, in September 2011, this was reported to be 60 per cent complete.[36]

These economic links strengthened the Turkey–Azerbaijan relationship, but were not problem-free and were affected by political disputes. Despite the oft-repeated mantra that Turkey and Azerbaijan were 'one nation with two states', serious tensions periodically broke the surface. These derived from each country's relations with third parties, as well as straightforward commercial disagreements. On the latter score, a two-year argument over the price of Turkey's gas imports from Azerbaijan was only eventually settled in October 2011, when Prime Minister Erdoğan and President Aliev signed a new gas supply agreement, which also provided for future gas imports from the second stage of development of the Shah Deniz field ('Shah Deniz II'). This was expected to supply 16 bcm annually, from 2016, of which six bcm would be used in Turkey and the remaining 10 bcm would be fed into the Nabucco pipeline to central Europe, assuming that project were completed (see p155). The economic benefits that Turkey derived from friendship with Azerbaijan were further underlined on 25 October 2011, when Prime Minister Erdoğan and President Aliiev jointly initiated the construction of a $5 billion oil refinery at Aliağa, near İzmir, which was said to be the largest single private investment yet realized in Turkey.[37] Meanwhile, however, Azerbaijan had been hedging its bets by bargaining with Nabucco's Russian rivals: the Azeri state company SOCAR was reported to be negotiating with Russia's Gazprom to feed two bcm per year into the Russian pipeline network, from which it could presumably be exported to western markets, if the Nabucco project or something like it failed to materialize.[38]

Predictably, these economic disputes were heavily influenced by political relations. These came under severe strain during Turkey's attempted diplomatic opening with Armenia in 2009 (see below), causing bitter resentment in Baku at Turkey's supposed 'betrayal'. According to diplomatic cables released by 'Wikileaks' in December 2010, US diplomats in Baku had reported the previous February that President Aliev had reacted strongly, and that 'he made clear his distaste for the Erdoğan government in Turkey, underscoring the "naivete" of their foreign policy and the failure of their initiatives'.[39] The tension was only overcome after Tayyip Erdoğan had made it clear that the Turkish parliament would not be called on to ratify the US-sponsored protocols with Armenia unless the Nagorno-Karabakh dispute was settled, thus meeting the main Azeri demand. Once this had been achieved, the pendulum swung to the opposite extreme in August 2010, when Presidents Aliev and Gül endorsed a 'Agreement on Strategic Partnership and Mutual Assistance' as well as the establishment of a 'Council of High Level Strategic Cooperation' between the two countries: these were duly ratified by the Azeri and Turkish parliaments, in December 2010 and March 2011 respectively.[40]

The agreements of 2010 were a clear sign of the re-establishment of the Turkish–Azeri entente, but they also had very disturbing implications, in that the 'Strategic Partnership' pact provided that, in the event of military aggression by a third party, each side would support the other 'using all possibilities'. This undertaking followed a worrying build-up of armaments on both sides and a continuing deadlock in the Nagorno-Karabakh peace talks. It also coincided with a Russian–Armenian agreement under which Russia prolonged its lease of a military and air base in Armenia for the following 34 years, allowing the forces based there to be used outside former Soviet territory.[41] These two commitments appeared to raise the threat that Turkey and Russia might be involved in a head-on military collision arising from a Caucasian conflict over which they lacked direct control – the one danger both sides had sought to avoid in 1992. Surprisingly, this risk received virtually no attention in the Turkish media. The main hope was that, in practice, if there were a renewed war between Armenia and Azerbaijan, both Russia and Turkey would stop short of carrying out their declared commitments in full. It was pointed out that Russia's commitment under the collective security treaty of 1991 did not extend to the territory of Nagorno-Karabakh: there was ambiguity in the agreements that might be used as leverage to deter aggressive strategies. On the Turkish side, officials argued that there were no firm commitments, and claimed that the Azeris concurred that the new agreements did not amount to a mutual defence pact. They emphasized that they were trying to persuade Baku that a new war would be a 'nightmare scenario'. If Azerbaijan were attacked, they suggested, public opinion in Turkey would force it to send arms to Azerbaijan but 'we are not talking about sending troops fighting side by side. We can't do that without NATO'.[42] These provisos were reassuring, but raised the question why Turkey had signed such apparently serious agreements if in practice they were so vague. If nothing else, the exercise served as a good example of the difficulty of balancing domestic expectations with external realities.

Following the ceasefire in Nagorno-Karabakh in 1994, Turkey's relations with Armenia – such as they were – continued to be affected by its relations with the United States, as well as the Armenian–Azeri confrontation. Thanks to a continuing campaign on this issue by Armenia, by 2010 more than 20 countries, including Argentina, Belgium, Canada, France, Italy and Russia, had recognized the Armenian massacres of the First World War as genocide.

However, with the exception of France and Russia, none of these was in a position to exercise much leverage over Turkey. Under President Sarkozy, France opposed Turkey's accession to the European Union anyway, regardless of the Armenian issue, while Russia was clearly Armenia's main supporter, for reasons that had little to do with the genocide question. Hence, given the strength of the pro-Armenian lobby in Congress, the campaign for genocide recognition had its most significant impact on Turkey's relations with Washington, and did not go away with the defeat of the proposed Congressional genocide resolution of November 2000 (p164). In January–February 2007, the issue again came to the top of the agenda, when a similar resolution was tabled in the House of Representatives. Later, however, it suffered from a loss of support in Congress and was abandoned by Nancy Pelosi, the House Speaker, in October 2007.[43] In the US presidential election campaign of 2008 both Barack Obama, the future Vice-President Joe Biden, and the then Senator Hillary Clinton, all stated that if they won office they would use the word genocide to describe the events of 1915.[44] In fact, once established in the White House, Barack Obama resisted pressure for a new genocide recognition resolution in Congress, but the issue was unlikely to go away indefinitely.

In line with the general liberalization in Turkish politics, there was some relaxation of the previous taboo on the subject, with the convening of an academic conference in Istanbul in 2005, and an apology campaign launched by some 200 Turkish intellectuals in December 2008, which was signed by around 30,000 people online. After the murder of the Turkish-Armenian journalist Hrant Dink in January 2007, more than 100,000 Istanbulis marched behind his coffin, with many carrying placards declaring 'We are all Armenian'.[45] Nonetheless, the government and most of the political establishment continued to deny that there had been a genocide. In April 2005, Tayyip Erdoğan attempted to address the question directly when he proposed that the Armenian and Turkish governments should set up an historical commission to examine the archives. This idea was supported by President George W. Bush but rejected by Robert Kocharian, Armenia's then President.[46] Nonetheless, behind the scenes talks between the two sides began in Switzerland in 2007. An unexpected breakthrough occurred in September 2008, when President Gül became the first Turkish head of state to set foot in Armenia, by visiting Yerevan for a World Cup qualifier football match between the two national teams. Subsequently, the Turkish government was evidently under pressure to reach a détente with Armenia, to head off another genocide recognition resolution, tabled in Congress in March 2009. The Armenian government also had a strong economic incentive to open up normal trading relations with Turkey if it could.[47]

After a false start in April 2009, the Swiss-mediated talks achieved what looked like dramatic success at the end of August as the two sides announced that they had initialled two protocols. Under the first of these, they would establish diplomatic relations, confirming the recognition of the existing frontier between the two countries (something that ultra-nationalist groups on the Armenian side had rejected) and opening the border. The second protocol would, among other things, establish an historical sub-commission to examine the First World War massacres – a reversal of the previous Armenian position.[48] The two protocols were formally signed by the foreign ministers of the two countries in Zurich on 10 October, with a beaming Hillary Clinton in attendance, provoking predictable complaints from Azerbaijan.[49] On 22 October, the Turkish government sent the two protocols to parliament for ratification, but without any timetable for achieving this. It soon became clear that Tayyip Erdoğan would not propose this without clear progress in settling the Nagorno-Karabakh dispute, which was lacking. There was a further hostile reaction in Turkey to a critical decision by the Armenian Constitutional Court in January 2010, on the grounds that this was 'against the essence of the normalization process'.[50] Worse was to follow in March 2010, when the House of Representatives Foreign Affairs Committee passed another resolution calling for the administration to recognize the Armenian massacres of 1915 as genocide. Although Secretary of State Clinton opposed the resolution, and it was anyway doubtful that it had sufficient congressional support to pass, this effectively marked the end of official attempts to achieve ratification of the two protocols, which had in any case not been carried through by Armenia.[51] The protocols remained moribund, if not quite dead. In April 2010, the Armenian government formally suspended the normalization process, and abandoned it in February 2011.[52]

Nonetheless, the likelihood that genocide recognition resolutions might again come before Congress as an almost annual event was a powerful reason for Ankara to pursue the path of reconciliation with Armenia if it could. Speaking at a conference in Harvard University in September 2010, Ahmet Davutoğlu admitted that he had been unable to apply his principle of 'zero problems with neighbours' to Armenia, but claimed that 'one way or another, today or tomorrow, we will achieve this too. This is our political commitment'.[53] Clearly, a key to this achievement would be tangible progress in the Azeri–Armenian peace process, but by 2011, the Minsk Group discussions had still registered virtually no advance, in spite of 18 years of talks. Nor were they likely to, it could be argued, without a distinct change of course by Russia. This seemed unlikely, since Armenia was the only country in the region still allied with Moscow, and hosted an important Russian military base. If the Nagorno-Karabakh dispute were resolved, Armenia could settle its differences with Turkey and Russia would be the loser. Hence, Moscow had every interest in holding up the Minsk process for as long as possible – maybe indefinitely.

The critical role of Russia as the dominant actor in Transcaucasia came to the fore also in the brief war between Russia and Georgia of August 2008. This came as a serious shock to the western powers, demonstrating Russia's readiness to resort to force, and forcing Turkey back to a precarious balancing act between Russia, Georgia, and the United States.[54] On 7–8 August, Georgia launched a military offensive against Russian forces in South Ossetia, legally a Georgian province but under Russian occupation since 1992. Russian ground and air forces responded strongly, while Russian naval forces blockaded part of Georgia's coast. By 14 August, the Georgians were in full retreat, with the Russians in occupation of the port of Poti and the central city of Gori, from where they advanced to within 55 kilometres of Tiflis. With mediation by France, which then occupied the rotating presidency of the European Union, a ceasefire agreement was signed on 15–16 August. Russian forces were withdrawn from most of Georgia in subsequent weeks, although parts of Abkhazia and South Ossetia previously held by the Georgians remained under Russian occupation.

In all this, Turkey could not do much more than act as a worried bystander, although it had an important interest in the outcome since the middle leg of the BTC pipeline passed through Georgia. In previous years, it had developed friendly relations with Georgia, having helped to build up Georgia's national army by cooperating in military education in Georgia, under NATO's Partnership for Peace plan. It had extended limited military aid, and consistently supported Georgia's territorial integrity (read, opposing the Russian occupation of South Ossetia and Abkhazia).[55] Economically, it had become Georgia's biggest trade partner. On the other hand, in 2008, the Georgian President Mikheil Saakashvili was strongly criticized for his foolhardiness in starting a war he could not win,[56] and Turkey was above all anxious to avoid a military collision with Russia. Its main diplomatic contribution was unveiled on 11 August by Tayyip Erdoğan, who put forward proposals for a Caucasus Cooperation and Stability Pact, to include Georgia, Russia, Azerbaijan, Armenia and Turkey. He first took this to Moscow, then to Tiflis (where, understandably, President Saakashvili was less than enthusiastic) and then Baku on 20 August. President Gül conveyed the plan to Armenian President Serge Sarkisian during his groundbreaking visit to Yerevan for the football match of 6 September.[57]

In a visit to Ankara on 2 September, the Russian foreign minister Sergei Lavrov expressed appreciation for Turkey's diplomatic efforts, but it led to some serious tensions in Ankara's relations with Washington. Public opinion in Turkey was still hostile to the US, thanks to the war in Iraq, but there was also concern that if the Bush administration took too hawkish a line towards the Russian action, this could have serious consequences for Turkey, as the NATO member closest to the scene of the fighting. The immediate point of conflict with Washington was the planned despatch of US navy vessels to Georgia, nominally to deliver aid but also important as symbolic support for Georgia against Russia. On 14 August, the Chairman of the US Joint Chiefs of Staff, General James Cartwright, announced that two hospital ships, the *Comfort* and *Mercy*, would be detailed for this purpose. At the cost of provoking resentment in Washington, the Turkish government refused to allow their passage through the straits into the Black Sea, on the grounds that their tonnage exceeded the limits allowed to non-Black Sea states under the Montreux Convention of 1936 (p48). Days afterwards, permission was given for the passage of three smaller ships that were within the Montreux limits.[58]

When the Turkish foreign minister Ali Babacan visited New York on 20 September 2008, Secretary of State Condoleezza Rice was quoted as saying that Turkey was 'a terrific ally, including in this most recent crisis' and that it was a 'very important power force in the Caucasus'.[59] Nonetheless, it appears that, at the time, the 'strategic partnership' had been far from perfect and that, at the very least, Condoleezza Rice's assessment of Turkey's role had an element of exaggeration. As it was, the outcome was far better than it might have been for Turkey. If the BTC pipeline had been permanently closed or – worse still – Russia had been allowed to continue in occupation of most of Georgia, then Turkey would have suffered severely and maybe even been projected back into the front line of a new Cold War. As it was, the pipeline was temporarily closed, but this was due to a fire in Turkish territory (apparently caused by the PKK) and not the Russian invasion of Georgia.[60] After the ceasefire, Russia returned to near to its pre-war occupation zone. Virtually no other states, apart from Venezuela and Nicaragua, have recognized the supposed independence of South Ossetia and Abkhazia. On the other hand, the limitation of Russia's gains was primarily due to the application of political pressure by the US and the European Union, and the likely appreciation on the Russian side that Russia was now integrated into the global economy and could not afford to go back to a Cold War-style confrontation with the west. Equally, it left Turkey with the realization that, despite the dissolution of the USSR, Moscow was still the most powerful individual actor in Transcaucasia, and that its own ability to determine outcomes in the region was both limited and dependent on cooperation with the western powers.

Turkey and central Asia

Among the many effects of the disintegration of the USSR on Turkey's international situation, the ending of Soviet rule in central Asia was one that attracted most attention at the time, since it suggested that Turkey might become an important regional player in a part of the world that had virtually been lifted out of international politics since the late nineteenth century. Five independent republics had now been established in the region – Kazakhstan, Uzbekistan, Kirghizstan, Turkmenistan and Tajikistan – but they all appeared to be weak and isolated. Turkey, it was hoped, would be the model for the evolution of the five new republics as democratic states with free market economies. Turkish governments at the time did nothing to discourage these ideas, but within a few years more realistic policies and expectations began to prevail. As a result, Turkey was left with a cultural and economic role in central Asia, but without much real political power.

Turkish policies in the five ex-Soviet republics to the east of the Caspian were formed by cultural and historical legacies as well as modern political and economic realities. Some Turkish politicians, such as Süleyman Demirel, speaking in February 1992, referred to a 'Turkish world', supposedly stretching from the Adriatic to the great wall of China.[61] If this implied a strong degree of cultural homogeneity over such a vast area, it was a serious exaggeration. In practice, a distinction had to be made between 'Turkish', meaning the inhabitants of Turkey and their language, and 'Turkic' – that is, speakers of languages related to Turkish, but far from identical to it. When people from different central Asian nations speak to one another or to outsiders, they will normally do so in Russian, since there is no 'standard' Turkic language, similar to Mandarin Chinese or modern literary Arabic.

This linguistic complexity is reinforced by ethnic and historical ones. Within central Asia, there is one important indigenous non-Turkic nation, the Tajiks, speaking a dialect of Persian, plus numerous smaller ones. More importantly, the period of tsarist and then Soviet rule saw a substantial immigration of Russians and the other Slavic peoples of Russia, besides Koreans and other ethnic groups. According to Soviet data of 1990–1, ethnic Russians accounted for around 38 per cent of the population of Kazakhstan and 22 per cent of that of Kirghizstan, with smaller proportions in the other three republics.[62] Historically, the connections between the Turkic peoples of central Asia and those of modern Turkey has been slight. There has been no single state including all the Turkic peoples since the days of Timur Lang, in the late fourteenth and early fifteenth centuries.[63] The historical break has been reinforced by geographical ones, since Turkey only has direct territorial contact with one Turkic state, the Azeri enclave of Nakhichevan, which is in turn separated from the rest of Azerbaijan by Armenian territory. The main roads and railways run from central Asia to Russia, not the west, and the overland journey from, say, Istanbul to Tashkent is long and arduous, in spite of much talk of reconstructing the ancient 'Silk Road' through central Asia to China. Thanks to these geographical factors, central Asia never came to have the critical position in Turkish foreign policy occupied by Transcaucasia, where Turkish interests were far more direct, and there was a more real risk of a head-on collision with Russia.

In the early twentieth century, Turkish ethnic nationalism developed a distinctly pan-Turkish bias, calling for the union of all the Turkic peoples, but the failure of Enver Pasha's ill-advised advance into the Caucasus of 1918 and the establishment of Soviet rule throughout the region during 1920–2 made the pan-Turkist project completely unrealistic (see pp28, 35–6). Atatürk's government needed the cooperation of Moscow in opposing the entente powers, and pan-Turkism continued only as the attachment of ultra-nationalists on the political fringes.[64] It may have enjoyed a brief and tentative revival in some official circles during 1941–2, with the German invasion of the USSR, but it was apparently never supported by İsmet İnönü, and was rapidly dropped after the Soviet victory at Stalingrad (p66). After 1991, it seemed for some to have come back onto the political agenda, as the veteran ultra-nationalist Alparslan Türkeş, the most prominent pan-Turkist in Turkish politics, was brought in from the cold, by accompanying high-level delegations to central Asia, but the renewed vision soon proved to be illusory.[65]

The main effect of the changes of 1991 was probably in Turkish self-confidence. After years of cold-shouldering by the western Europeans, and uneasy relations with their Middle Eastern neighbours, Turks suddenly realized that in central Asia there were hitherto little-known nations with whom they could claim kinship, and who seemed to be looking for friendship with Turkey. However, it was far from clear what this would mean in political terms. As Philip Robins remarked, by 1993, 'hard decisions based on interests rather than fanciful notions of ethnic solidarity are informing decisions on both sides'.[66] In all this, it was noticeable that while there are also substantial Turkic minorities in Iran and Afghanistan, Turkey veered away from any support for them, effectively limiting its official contacts with the 'Turkic world' to the former territories of the USSR (the case of the Turkic Uighur minority in the Chinese province of Xinjiang was more problematic, (see p246). For broad political reasons, it was important for Ankara to maintain correct relations with both Iran and China, while Afghanistan was simply too remote and chaotic to be a major focus for Turkish policy, even though Turkish troops played an important part in the International Security Assistance Force in Kabul (p164).[67]

Prior to the disintegration of the USSR, Turkish policy did nothing to encourage it, and much of the Turkish political elite appeared to accept the Soviet view that the indigenous peoples of central Asia were good Soviet citizens who would probably be Russianized gradually.[68] In March 1991, as Mikhail Gorbachev was trying to restructure the Soviet Union, Turgut Özal paid an official visit to the USSR, with trips to the Ukraine, Azerbaijan and Kazakhstan, in which agreements on technical and economic cooperation were signed, but Turkey still found itself ill-prepared to deal with the end of Soviet rule in central Asia. In September 1991, President Nursultan Nazarbayev of Kazakhstan became the first central Asian head of state to visit Turkey, but two Turkish fact-finding missions sent to the region at about this time did not recommend that Turkey should recognize the self-declared independence of the central Asian republics. It was not until 16 December 1991, following Turkey's recognition of Azerbaijan, that the government decided to grant recognition to all of them in principle, and only some time after that that it opened embassies in the region. This recognition was hastened by a round of visits to Ankara by Saparmurat Niyazov, Islam Karimov and Askar Akayev, the presidents of Turkmenistan, Uzbekistan and Kirghizstan, in December 1991.[69]

After this hesitant start, Turkish policy then seemed to jump to the opposite extreme of expectations. During 1992, this was encouraged by western policy, particularly that of the United States, which at this stage appears to have seen a power-vacuum left by the end of Soviet rule in central Asia that might be filled by radical Islamism, promoted by Iran, and looked to Turkey to prevent this. When Süleyman Demirel, as Prime Minister, visited Washington in February 1992, President Bush told him: 'Turkey is a model for the countries in the region, and especially to those newly independent republics of central Asia.'[70] Meanwhile, during a trip to several capitals in the region, Secretary of State James Baker urged the new republics to adopt the 'Turkish model' of economic and political development.[71] Initially, this rhetoric was warmly received by the central Asian leaders: for instance, in his visit to Turkey in December 1991, President Karimov declared that he looked up to Turkey as an 'elder brother', while President Akayev compared Turkey to the 'morning star' guiding the Turkic republics.[72] Demirel's visit to all the central Asian states except Tajikistan in April–May 1992, in which he claimed, among other things, that Turkey and the Turkic republics 'share the same blood, religion and language', is seen as marking the high point of this period of euphoria. Spurred on by exaggerated expectations, and without adequate prior consultation with the central Asian governments, the Turks prepared an ambitious agenda for the first 'Turkic summit' of the heads of government of all the Turkic states, to be held in Ankara in October 1992. During his central Asian tour, Demirel had referred to the idea of a sort of 'Turkic common-wealth' or 'association of independent Turkic states', although this would not be 'dominated' by Turkey. Other models suggested were that of the Nordic Union of Scandinavian countries. The summit was expected to produce a 'Ankara Political Declaration' and an Economic Declaration. On the latter score, President Özal hoped to work for a 'Turkic Common Market', with the gradual removal of all barriers to free trade and the development of new transport systems.[73]

In the event, the outcome of the first Turkic summit poured cold water on many of these ambitions, since by the autumn of 1992, the central Asian leaders had evidently come round to a more realistic assessment of their connection with Turkey, and the realization that adoption of anything like a pan-Turkist programme could create serious problems for them in their relations with Russia. Once the leaders of the new republics had assembled in Ankara, President Nazarbayev made it clear that he was against any grouping based on religious or ethnic criteria, and that Kazakhstan could only participate in regional cooperation schemes on the condition that they did not harm its commitments to other members of the Commonwealth of Independent States – a fairly clear sign that Russia should not be shut out. Russia's continued economic domination in most of the regional states was clearly influential here. For Uzbekistan, Islam Karimov broadly supported Nazarbayev's position, since he had an interest in supporting Russian policy in neighbouring Tajikistan, which was aimed at preventing the victory of Islamist and other opposition forces in the Tajik civil war. The other regional republics, such as Turkmenistan, were also suspicious of any 'Turkic Commonwealth' project for fear that this would lead to domination by Uzbekistan, rather than Turkey, given that Uzbekistan was the biggest state in central Asia in terms of population. Nor did any of the central Asian delegations support the Azeri cause over Nagorno-Karabakh, as Turkey had hoped. The result was that the two 'Ankara Declarations' had to be abandoned, and the summit merely produced a bland communiqué on political relations and another on economic cooperation. All this committed the participants to very little, beyond an agreement to hold regular future summits.[74]

Although several later 'Turkic summits', including Azerbaijan as well as the trans-Caspian 'Turkic' nations, have been held since then, the attempt to achieve economic or political union petered out after 1992, as Turkish leaders and spokesmen emphasized that Turkey simply sought to promote the development of the republics as independent, democratic and secular states, with liberal market economies.[75] Once the idea of a more ambitious union had been abandoned, the Turks concentrated their efforts on developing cultural and educational links with the region, as well as trade and investment. On the first score, 10,000 scholarships were given each year to enable central Asian students to attend Turkish high schools and universities. Technical assistance, training and cultural cooperation, and the development of small industries in the region were conducted under the aegis of the Turkish International Cooperation Agency (TICA), which was affiliated to the foreign ministry and established in 1992.[76] The ministry of education also opened schools in central Asia, teaching in Turkish and English besides the national languages, although these were outnumbered by privately owned Turkish schools, notably those run by the religious brotherhood led by Fethullah Gülen (p150), which by 1998 was reported to have 74 schools in all the central Asian republics except Tajikistan.[77] While the Turkish state tried to present itself as strictly secularist, it was apparent that part of the attempted Islamic revival in central Asia was being sponsored from Turkey by private initiatives. This caused some embarrassment to Turkey's official representatives, who initially opposed the Gülen movement's schools, notably in Uzbekistan, although this opposition apparently subsided later.[78]

In developing its economic relations with central Asia, the Turkish government started off by claiming that it would launch an aid programme worth $3 billion to the Turkic states, but it soon became apparent that this vastly outran Turkey's resources. Nonetheless, by 2011, Turkey had provided around $1.2 billion in credits to the new republics, while around 1,000 private Turkish firms were reported to have invested $3.7 billion in the region since 1992. Turkish construction companies had important contracts for building hotels, airports and industrial projects worth $15.5 billion. Trade turnover also increased exponentially, from a meagre total of $108 million in 1992 to just under $5.7 billion in 2010.[79]

Turkey's more modest programme in central Asia, although relatively successful, was not without its political problems. These mainly derived from the fact that most of the republics were run by highly autocratic regimes, normally dominated by middle-ranking members of the former communist *nomenklatura*, who strongly resisted anything that they saw as external interference in their internal affairs. On this issue, Turkish governments had to walk another tightrope. On the one hand, they did not want to provoke disputes with the central Asian autocrats that might damage Turkey's economic or other interests. On the other hand, as a working democracy, Turkey could not entirely ignore democratic standards in its foreign policy. Hence, the careful statement issued by the foreign ministry under the AKP government maintained that the 'specific conditions' in the regional states should be 'taken into consideration' when criticizing them on grounds of 'human rights and democracy'. On the other hand, it claimed that Turkey was urging them to advance human rights practices, since this would enhance 'internal peace', and accelerate their integration in to the international community.[80] Clashes over issues of this kind were most prominent in the case of Uzbekistan. After a series of earlier complaints by President Islam Karimov that Turkey had been harbouring movements opposing his regime, tensions between the two countries came to a head in 1999, following an unsuccessful attempt to murder the President. Two Uzbeks who were suspected of the crime fled to Turkey and were only extradited back to Uzbekistan after some delay.[81] Following a break, commercial and diplomatic relations between the two countries were eventually re-established, but the political stand-off continued: it was noticeable, for instance, that Uzbekistan failed to attend the 'Turkic summit' held in Istanbul in September 2010, continuing a boycott it had applied since 1998.[82]

After the beginning of the new century, international and domestic politics generally had a weakening effect on Turkey's links with central Asia. Under Vladimir Putin, Russian power and interests revived, just as US attentions switched to Iraq and Afghanistan, while China was also beginning to emerge as an important player in the region. In short, central Asia was no longer the focus of international attention in the way it seemed it might be in the early 1990s. In Turkey, Alparslan Türkeş, the latter-day leader of pan-Turkism, died in 1997. Under his successor Devlet Bahçeli, his Nationalist Action Party continued to put more emphasis on 'Turkic unity' than the other parties, but after 2002 it was confined to the fringes of Turkish politics. By contrast, the ruling AKP was associated with the Muslim, or 'Ottoman', rather than ethnic nationalist identity. Officially, there were still references to 'one nation and six states'[83] – an extension of the slogan normally applied to Azerbaijan (p215) – but this did not amount to much more than rhetoric. Admittedly, Turkey's cultural and economic links with the region were still impressive, and Turks still tended to regard the 'Turkic' republics as closer to them than any other group of nations, in spite of the geographical separation.[84] Without this emotional and cultural dimension, it seems most unlikely that they would have shown anything like the degree of interest and activity in central Asia, especially in the economic sphere, that they actually displayed. On the other hand, by 2011, the region did not seem central to Turkey's main foreign policy concerns and was not perceived as an alternative to its traditional alignment with the western powers or its growing role in the Middle East.

11 Turkey and regional politics after the Cold War III

The Middle East and the wider world

By the first decade of the twenty-first century, Turkey's role in the Middle East became a major focus of attention for both Turkish and foreign observers. The reasons were not hard to identify. While the risk of armed conflict in Europe had virtually disappeared, the Middle East remained one of the most insecure regions of the world, with no dominant regional power, and inter-state wars and violent internal upheavals a constant threat. Its crucial position in the world oil industry made it the focus for great power rivalries as well as conflicts between producers and consumers. Narrating Turkey's part in this story is not easy, however, since conflicts both between and within most states in the region, and unpredictable changes, made it hard to construct overall regional strategies. Hence, actions and reactions in relations with the five regional actors at the top of Turkey's agenda – Israel, the Palestinians, Syria, Iraq and Iran – are discussed one by one. This survey closes with two developments with important implications for the shape of Turkey's future diplomacy: first, the internal convulsions of the 'Arab Spring' of which the outcome was still uncertain as this book was being written, and second, Turkey's attempt to project itself onto the wider global stage, which appeared to be opening yet another chapter in the country's foreign policy.

Critics of the ruling AKP's policies frequently argued that Turkey's new activism in the Middle East was part and parcel of its supposedly Islamist commitments. An alleged illustration of this was that after 2002, Turkey began to play a more active part in the Organization of the Islamic Conference (p125) – in particular by successful lobbying for the election of Professor Ekmeleddin İhsanoğlu, born in Egypt of a Turkish family and formerly Professor of the History of Science at Ankara University, as its Secretary-General in 2005. Too much should not be read into this, however, since Professor İhsanoğlu, like the AKP government, was prominent in urging cooperation and dialogue, raher than confrontation between the Muslim world and the west. Moreover, the OIC was only one of many international organizations to which Turkey was attached, and far less instrumental in its foreign policy than, for instance, NATO, the European Union or the United Nations.

Turkey, Israel and the Palestinians

During the 1990s, it appeared to many observers that Turkey was abandoning its traditional policy of strict neutrality in the Arab–Israeli dispute, by developing an entente with Israel. Regional and global changes helped to explain this change of heart. On the one hand, the removal of the USSR as an important player in Middle Eastern politics left the radical Arab states, especially Syria, in a more exposed and isolated position, and meant that tensions with the Arab countries would not impact on Turkey's relations with Moscow, as they had done during the Cold War. There was widespread disillusionment in Turkey with the Arab countries, which had failed to support the Turkish cause over Cyprus and, in the case of Syria, gave active support to the PKK. Conflicts over the waters of the Tigris and Euphrates added to these tensions. More positively, the beginning of the Arab–Israeli peace process in 1991, followed by the signing of the Declaration of Principles by Yitzhak Rabin and Yasser Arafat in September 1993, made it possible for Turkey to develop much closer relations with Israel without provoking a rupture in its relations with the PLO and the main Arab states. Strategically, the prospective gains for Turkey from closer links with the Israelis derived mainly from the fact both countries had a common interest in opposing Syria, although the Turkish Foreign Ministry steadfastly denied that Turkey's agreements with Israel were directed against any other state. The expectation that they would increase Turkish influence in Washington, by securing the support of the powerful pro-Israel lobby in the US Congress, and that both countries could gain from technical military and economic cooperation, were additional incentives for the construction of a Turkish–Israeli entente.[1]

The new trend in Turkish policy began in December 1991, when the Demirel government upgraded its relations with both Israel and the PLO to ambassadorial level. Following the signature of the Declaration of Principles, Hikmet Çetin, Demirel's foreign minister, visited Israel in November 1993, to be followed by Tansu Çiller, now the Prime Minister, one year later, then by Demirel, as President, in March 1996. Significantly, both Tansu Çiller and Demirel took in visits to Gaza and the Palestinian authorities in east Jerusalem as part of their trips. These visits were reciprocated by those of the Israeli President, Prime Minister and foreign minister to Turkey.[2] The most significant result of these contacts was the Turkish–Israeli agreement on 'Military Training and Cooperation', which was signed in February 1996. Valid for five years, with subsequent renewal at annual intervals, it provided for mutual military visits and the acquisition of military know-how, besides joint exercises in which Israeli and Turkish pilots would train in one another's countries. There would be Turkish–Israeli cooperation in the manufacture of surface-to-air missiles and other advanced weapons systems, and the exchange of intelligence. An Israeli firm also contracted to modernize Turkey's 102 ageing F-4 and F-5 fighter planes.[3] In the civilian sphere, it was accompanied by a free trade agreement between the two countries, which was originally signed in March 1996 and eventually ratified by the Turkish parliament in April 1997.

The Turkish–Israeli military agreement was evidently reached primarily on the initiative of the Turkish armed forces chiefs, and was signed at a time when there was effectively no government in Turkey (officially, the country was under a caretaker government headed by Tansu Çiller). However, shortly afterwards, in June 1996, Turkish policy towards the Middle East became a domestic political football, as the coalition government headed by Necmettin Erbakan took over, with Mrs Çiller playing an awkward role as foreign minister. In opposition, Erbakan and his party had strongly denounced Israel, and Turkey's links with it. Once installed in office, he bowed to military pressure by reluctantly accepting the military cooperation and free trade agreements, much as he had done in the case of 'Operation Provide Comfort' (see p163). However, he also tried to steer an independent course, by keeping Israel at arm's length and supporting militant Palestinians who opposed the peace process.

In pursuit of his programme to develop an 'Islamic' foreign policy, Erbakan made a well-publicized trip to Iran, Pakistan, Singapore, Malaysia and Indonesia in August 1996, followed by a swing through Africa, taking in Egypt, Libya and (partly Muslim) Nigeria, in the following October. His visit to Libya was a political fiasco, as Muammar Gaddafi treated him to a public dressing-down over Turkey's developing links with Israel and openly called for the establishment on an independent Kurdish state. Having pushed forward his project at the level of bilateral contacts, he was then quick to develop it in the multilateral dimension, by setting up what was known as the D-8 ('developing-8') group of mainly Muslim nations, as an Islamic response to the G-7 and other western economic groupings.[4] This bizarre and embarrassing episode was ended in June 1997 by the resignation of the Erbakan government, under strong pressure from the military and parts of civil society (see p140).

Over the following five years, despite some differences between Turkish and Israeli approaches, the entente with Israel continued to be an important part of Turkish foreign policy. In particular, the Turkish military gained from access to Israel's advanced weaponry and intelligence, which could have been blocked in western Europe or the United States because of the Kurdish issue. Whether the existence of the Turkish–Israeli link was influential in inducing the Syrian President Hafiz al-Assad to expel Abdullah Öcalan from Syria in October 1998 must remain an open question, since the Israeli government stated at the time that it was neutral on this question, but the possibility is still there (see p145). In the economic sphere, both countries almost certainly gained from the free trade agreement, as the annual volume of trade between them grew from $407 million in 1995 to $1.4 billion in 2002. However the latter figure only represented around 1.6 per cent of Turkey's total foreign trade. Economically, Turkey was still far more dependent on trade with the Arab countries, mainly because of its imports of oil and natural gas: it also had important markets for foodstuffs and light industrial products in the Arab states.[5]

The main weakness of the Turkish–Israeli link was that Turkey could not ignore its relations with the main Arab countries and the Palestinians, and that the entente with Israel was thus quite heavily dependent on the progress of peace talks between Israel and the PLO. If the two sides pulled apart, then Turkey would be under pressure to opt for one side or the other, with no certainty that this would be Israel. Hence, the collapse of the 'Camp David II' negotiations in 2000 and the subsequent start of the 'second *intifada*' in the occupied territories had serious effects on the entente. Although it is impossible to substantiate this, it is also likely that the end of Turkey's confrontation with Syria in 1998 (p145) removed an important incentive for the alignment with Israel. In these circumstances, Turkish–Israeli relations had a roller coaster ride over the next eight years. By the spring of 2002, Turkish opposition to Israel's violent tactics against the PLO was causing sharp reactions from both secularist and 'Muslim democrat' politicians. As Prime Minister in April 2002, Bülent Ecevıt described Israeli attacks on the PLO in the West Bank as 'genocide against the Palestinian people', causing protests from the US Congress.[6] Later, in March 2004, the murder from an Israeli helicopter of Sheikh Ahmad Yasin, the spiritual leader of the militant Palestinian organization Hamas, was sharply criticized by his successor Tayyip Erdoğan as 'a kind of terrorism': Erdoğan used similar language ('terrorism by the state') to describe Israel's military drive into the Rafah strip in May 2004.[7]

The break was not permanent, however, since events moved in the opposite direction after the death of Yasser Arafat in November 2004 and the return to tentative peace negotiations. As a sign of the reconciliation, Abdullah Gül, as foreign minister, visited both Israel and the West Bank on 3–5 January 2005, laying a wreath at the holocaust memorial at Yad Vashem, prompting the Israeli newspaper *Haaretz* to speak of the 'deep affection that each country's people feel for the other'.[8] In spite of this, the relationship lurched back into confrontation one year later, in February 2006, when Khaled Mashal, the exiled leader of the radical Islamist Hamas, which had just won the Palestinian parliamentary elections but had previously carried out terrorist attacks in Israel, flew into Ankara for what was described as an unofficial visit. This caused highly hostile reactions in Israel, since it undermined Turkey's claim that it would have no truck with terrorists, notably those of the PKK.[9] The incident caused some bitter feelings at the time, but these had apparently been laid aside by November 2007, when the Israeli and Palestinian Presidents Shimon Peres and Mahmoud Abbas paid an unprecedented joint visit to Ankara, addressing the Turkish parliament and expressing a common hope for peace. Subsequently, President Peres successfully pressed for Turkish participation in the Annapolis peace conference, held on 27 November, while Turkey also lobbied successfully for Syrian participation.[10] Although the conference failed to yield tangible progress, it set the scene for Turkey's active involvement as a mediator between Syria and Israel in discussions over the return to Syria of the Golan Heights, occupied by Israel since the six-day war of 1967. Preparations for this took place between March 2007 and May 2008.

Over the following eight months (May–December 2008) four rounds of indirect talks between Syrian and Israeli officials were held in Istanbul, with Turkish officials shuttling between them, and important progress being registered. The process reached a high point on 23 December 2008, at a dinner between Tayyip Erdoğan and his Israeli counterpart Ehud Olmert, with the expectation that direct talks between Israel and Syria were in the offing.[11]

It was at this point, when success seemed so near, that disaster struck. On 28 December 2008, Israel launched its devastating 'Cast Lead' assault on the Gaza strip that lasted until 18 January 2009, causing thousands of Palestinian deaths. From this point on, the Syrian–Israeli peace process collapsed, leaving Tayyip Erdoğan convinced that he had been deliberately deceived by the Israelis, who were secretly preparing the assault just when their Prime Minister was supposedly talking peace in Ankara.[12] Admittedly, Israeli settlements had been subjected to fatal rocket attacks from Gaza, but to Turkish public opinion, as to that of most of the rest of the world, the Israeli response seemed grossly disproportionate. The diplomatic clash with Israel exploded dramatically on 29 January 2009, at a meeting on the fringes of the Davos Economic Forum in Switzerland with the unfortunate title 'Gaza, a Model for the Middle East'. After a heated exchange with Shimon Peres, in which he told the Israeli President 'you know very well how to kill', Tayyip Erdoğan turned to the session chairman saying 'one minute', then stalked out of the hall after the chairman refused to allow him a chance to respond to Peres.[13] The atmosphere was further soured just one year later, when the Israeli deputy foreign minister Danny Ayalon, a member of the rabidly anti-Arab *Israel Beitanu* party, publicly humiliated the Turkish ambassador Oğuz Çelikkol by seating him in a lower chair than himself for a televised interview and planting only an Israeli flag on the table, pointing this out to the assembled press in Hebrew (which the ambassador does not speak). The Israeli government later apologized, but by this stage the damage had been done. Turkish public opinion – like that of most countries – can accept setbacks, but not open insults.[14]

The collision between Israel and Turkey reached a climax in May 2010, in a way that neither side could have anticipated. The pro-Islamist Humanitarian Relief Foundation, mainly known by its Turkish acronym İHH,[15] had been set up in 1995 in response to the Bosnian crisis. Apparently, its informal political links were with the pro-Islamist Felicity Party (*Saadet Partisi*), led before his death in February 2011 by Necmettin Erbakan, rather than with the AKP, although Prime Minister Erdoğan clearly shared the primary aim of the İHH to end the Israeli blockade of Gaza. In late May 2011 the cruise liner *Mavi Marmara* ('Blue Marmara'), which the İHH had acquired, led a flotilla of five smaller cargo ships loaded with 10,000 tons of supplies and around 700 passengers from many countries, aiming to break the blockade. Prior to their departure, Ahmet Davutoğlu urged the leader of the İHH, Bülent Yıldırım, not to sail to Gaza, and the organization apparently promised that if it were challenged by the Israelis it would re-route to the Egyptian port of al-Arish. In the early hours of 31 May, in international waters 130 kilometres from the Israeli coast, the Israeli navy demanded that the flotilla change course for the Israeli port of Ashdod, but this was refused. The flotilla was surrounded by Israeli fast boats and helicopters, which quickly seized the five smaller ships and then boarded the *Mavi Marmara*. In the ensuing struggle, Israeli fire killed nine people at close range (eight Turkish citizens and one with US nationality) and wounded around 50 others. The surviving passengers were taken to Ashdod, where they were detained until 2 June, suffering serious mistreatment by the Israeli authorities.[16]

Predictably, the attacks sparked off a storm of protests in Turkey, on the grounds that nine innocent people had been killed and others mistreated after their detention, that the attack took place in international waters and that the Turkish government could not have legally prevented its citizens leaving the country. The governmment recalled its ambassador from Tel Aviv for consultations, cancelled joint military exercises with Israel and barred Israeli military flights over its airspace. Its demands were that the Israeli government should pay compensation to the victims or their families and should issue an apology. Israel experienced an unprecedented wave of criticism from European parliaments and civil society organizations, while the UN Human Rights Council appointed a three-man fact-finding panel. Both the Israeli and Turkish governments established separate enquiry commissions. Finally, on 2 August, UN Secretary-General Ban Ki-moon appointed a four-man enquiry panel headed by the former New Zealand Prime Minister Geoffrey Palmer and including Turkish and Israeli representatives.[17]

Unfortunately, this plethora of enquiries failed to resolve the bitter dispute between Ankara and Tel Aviv. Reporting in September 2010, the UN Human Rights Council report found that the Israeli forces had violated international law, listing a series of alleged crimes committed by them and claiming that there was 'clear evidence to support prosecutions'. The Israeli government rejected the report as 'biased, politicized and extremist'.[18] While the internal Turkish report took a similar line to the UN report, the Israeli internal enquiry found that both the raid on the flotilla and the blockade of Gaza were legal under international law – a conclusion rejected by Ankara. Meanwhile, Israel's hard-line foreign minister Avigdor Lieberman claimed that it was Turkey, not Israel, that should pay compensation.[19] Nonetheless, during the spring of 2011, the Turkish government acted cautiously, since it evidently hoped that some reconciliation with Israel might be arranged. Hence, in mid-May, it apparently persuaded the İHH not to join the planned repeat of the flotilla exercise in May 2011.[20] According to the Israeli newspaper *Haaretz*, the Israeli defence ministry was prepared to issue an apology to Turkey for the attack on the *Mavi Marmara*, and it appeared that Israel might offer compensation to the victims' families. However, Lieberman refused to issue an apology, claiming that this would 'harm Israel's national dignity'.[21] Later, this was confirmed by the Israeli defence minister Ehud Barak, who stated that Prime Minister Benjamin Netanyahu was 'on his way to reach a compromise, but was thwarted by Lieberman', provoking a near breakdown of the Israeli government.[22]

A turning-point came at the beginning of September, when the long-awaited UN Palmer committee report found that the Israel's attack on the *Mavi Marmara* had been 'excessive and unreasonable' but that its naval blockade of the Gaza strip was legitimate under international law.[23] The report was rejected by the Turkish government, which continued to demand an apology. On 2 September, it effectively expelled the Israeli ambassador in Ankara by reducing mutual diplomatic representation to Second Secretary level and ending its defence cooperation agreement with Israel (although in practice this had been moribund for some time).[24] Ahmet Davutoğlu also rejected the Palmer committee's finding that the Israeli blockade was legal, pointing out that it had not been endorsed by the United Nations and announcing that Turkey would apply to the International Court at The Hague for an advisory opinion on the legitimacy of the blockade.[25] Although both Israel and Turkey were under strong pressure from Washington to heal their rift, it was hard to see how this could be achieved without a change of government in Israel. Even if this happened, it seemed unlikely that the Turkey–Israel relationship would resume its former warmth unless serious progress were made in Arab–Israeli peace talks.

Turkey and Syria, 1987–2010

In the overall pattern of Turkey's relationships with its Arab neighbours in the 1990s, its relations with Syria were the most critical, since they posed the greatest risk of armed confrontation with another state. The collapse of the USSR and Turkey's entente with Israel tilted the balance of power in Turkey's favour, but these changes did not by themselves solve the conflicts between the two countries, or ensure that Ankara would have it all its own way in its confrontation with Damascus. Mutual tensions derived mainly from Syrian support for the PKK and, on the other side, Syria's determination to prevent unlimited Turkish use of the waters of the Euphrates, which threatened to deprive Syria of a vital resource. Syrian calls for the return of the province of Alexandretta, or Hatay, annexed by Turkey in 1939 (see pp50–1) could still produce ruptures between the two countries, but by the 1990s, it appeared that the Syrian government was placing this issue lower down on its list of priorities, apparently recognizing that the return of Alexandretta was probably an unachievable aim for Syria.

In theory, the agreement reached between Turgut Özal and President Hafiz al-Assad in 1987 should have provided the basis for the settlement of both the Euphrates waters dispute and Syrian support for the PKK (see p127). In fact, Syria failed to honour its undertaking to 'prevent the activities of organisations ... threatening or undermining the security and stability of the other party'.[26] When pressed by the Turks on this issue, the Syrian government flatly but unconvincingly denied that it gave support to the PKK, and even that Abdullah Öcalan was on its territory.[27]

Although a full discussion of this issue lies outside the scope of this book, it can be said in summary that the Euphrates problem – which affects Turkey's relations with Iraq as well as with Syria – derives essentially from the fact that water resources in the Middle East are becoming increasingly scarce, thanks to a fixed and relatively limited supply, combined with rising populations and living standards, and hence escalating demand for water both for agriculture and non-agricultural uses. Turkey's increased use of the Euphrates waters, especially after the completion of the Atatürk Dam in 1990 is only one aspect of this complicated problem, which centres around the fact that if all the three countries through which the river flows drew off all the water they claim they need, then their total demands would exceed the total supply of water in the river by a margin of about 60 per cent.[28] In talks during the 1990s, both Syria and Iraq claimed that the Syrian acceptance of the 500 cusecs figure in 1987 (p127) was valid only while the Atatürk Dam was being completed, and that subsequently Turkey should supply at least 700 cusecs.[29] Tension over the Euphrates question reached a critical point in January 1990, when the Turkish authorities interrupted the flow of the river to fill the storage reservoir behind the Atatürk dam. When Prime Minister Yıldırım Akbulut visited Baghdad in May 1990, the Iraqi government refused to renew the cross-border security agreement of 1984, allowing Turkey to enter Iraqi territory in pursuit of the PKK, which had lapsed in 1988 (p126). Subsequently, the Gulf crisis of 1990–1, and the resultant international embargo on Iraq, virtually lifted the Iraqis out as effective players in the dispute. Meanwhile, sporadic talks between Turkey and Syria over the following six years failed to produce any progress.[30]

Like the Euphrates dispute (and partly because of it), arguments between Turkey and Syria over the latter's role in supporting the PKK dragged on fruitlessly after 1990. It was not until the autumn of 1998 that any advance became visible. During September 1998, Turkey mounted a strong campaign against Syria, backed up by military force, in a bid to force Hafiz al-Assad to carry out his commitments under the 1987 and 1992 agreements. As Turkish troops and armour were moved towards the border, the Commander of Land Forces, General Atilla Ateş, visited Reyhanlı, just north of the Syrian frontier, and announced: 'If Turkey's expectations are not met we will earn the right to take any sort of precaution. Our patience has run out.'[31] Prime Minister Mesut Yılmaz added his voice to the campaign, saying that Syria had to end its support for the PKK, now that the latter had been defeated in Turkey. There was speculation that even if Turkey did not attack Syria by land, it might launch punishing air strikes against Syrian missile batteries or assumed PKK bases in Syria and the Lebanon, and the Syrian military were evidently aware that Syria would be the loser if there were a war with Turkey.[32]

This stung other Middle Eastern states – especially Egypt and Iran – into intense diplomatic activity. Egypt's President Hosni Mubarak had a clear interest in preventing a military collision between Turkey and Syria, given that Syria was a fellow Arab state, while Turkey was an ally of the United States, with which Egypt also had close relations. His mediation was evidently supported by Washington, which wished to draw Syria towards accepting a peace agreement with Israel. Iran, meanwhile, was Syria's closest friend in the Middle East, but could not afford to get dragged into an armed confrontation with Turkey (or vice versa). Fortunately, the Turks and Syrians were apparently ready to accept mediation by Egypt and Iran. Both Mubarak and the Iranian foreign minister Kemal Kharrazi paid emergency visits to Ankara and Damascus, which succeeded in defusing the crisis. On 7 October, Abdullah Öcalan was reported to have left Syria for Russia. Later, on 19–20 October, Uğur Ziyal, the deputy under-secretary at the Turkish Foreign Ministry, held talks in Adana with the Syrian General Adnan Badr al-Hassan. The two negotiators signed an agreement on 20 October 1998. This confirmed: 'Öcalan is no longer in Syria and permission will definitely not be given for him to re-enter the country.' Syria declared that it had closed down all PKK camps in its territory and that the PKK would not be allowed to re-establish itself in Syria. A direct hot-line to prevent future clashes would be established between Ankara and Damascus, and there would be joint inspection of security measures on both sides of the frontier.[33] Apparently, Turkey had come out of the crisis with its main objectives realized (except that Öcalan had not actually been returned to Turkey) and without having had to make good its military threats.

With this obstacle out of the way, Turkey was able to cultivate a remarkable and unexpected entente with Syria. For a time, this became the centre-piece of a broad and much more active Turkish role in the Middle East in general, in which Turkey seemed to be filling a regional power vacuum, now that the leading Arab states – notably Iraq and Egypt – had lost their former influence.[34] The fact that the Turkish parliament refused to back the US-led invasion of Iraq in 2003, and that it later took a strongly critical line against Israel, won the AKP government mass support in the Arab world, for which there was no historical precedent.[35] The first clear sign of this turnabout came in June 2000, following the death of Hafiz al-Assad, when President Ahmet Necdet Sezer visited Damascus for the funeral, becoming the first Turkish President to set foot in the Syrian capital since the foundation of the state in 1946. After some delays, Bashar al-Assad, who had succeeded his father as President of Syria, paid a return visit to Ankara in January 2004 – again, a diplomatic first.[36] The rapprochement continued until 2011, when the 'Arab Spring', and the Syrian regime's violent suppression of the burgeoning oppositional movement, threw Turkish–Syrian relations back into the melting pot.

Apart from the improvement in the psychological atmosphere, the most striking achievements of this new entente were the signing of a free trade agreement in December 2004, and the opening of the border between the two countries to visa-free travel in October 2009. On the first score, mutual trade increased dramatically, from $643 million in 2004 to just under $2.3 billion in 2010.[37] In October 2009, Ahmet Davutoğlu and the Syrian foreign minister Walid al-Moallem, meeting in Aleppo and the Turkish city of Gaziantep, signed an agreement lifting mutual visa requirements, then symbolically crossed over the border, raising the road barrier over their heads as they did so. Just over two months later, on 24 December 2009, Prime Minister Erdoğan visited Damscus for wide-ranging talks with President Assad, billed as the first top-level meeting of a 'High Level Strategic Cooperation Council' between the two countries.[38] In April 2009, the two states had even held joint military manoeuvres along the border, although these were apparently of limited scope.[39] By 2010, Davutoğlu was suggesting that the Turkish–Syrian entente could be broadened into a Middle Eastern free trade and free travel zone, embracing Turkey, Syria, Lebanon and Jordan, with ambitious suggestions that this could become 'the Middle East's version of the European Union'.[40]

Even at the height of the entente, these ambitions had nevertheless to be tempered by unresolved problems. Apart from hostile reactions from Israel, Turkey's friendship with Syria provoked sharp criticisms from Washington, especially under the George W. Bush administration, which regarded Syria with grave suspicion. These came to a head in April 2005, when President Sezer paid a second visit to Damascus at just the time that Washington was putting severe pressure on Syria following the murder of the former Lebanese premier Rafiq Hariri, allegedly at the hands of Syrian agents.[41] On a more positive note, as early as 2001, there were signs that the two sides might be moving towards a settlement of the Euphrates waters question,[42] while in December 2004, at the time of the signature of the free trade agreement, Turkish diplomats stated that they had 'reached an accord' with Syria over the Alexandretta dispute.[43] Nonetheless, it later became apparent that these old arguments were still sticking points between the two governments. According to reports at the time of Tayyip Erdoğan's visit to Damascus in December 2009, an agreement on the water issue could have been signed if Turkey had not demanded a formal withdrawal of the Syrian claim to Alexandretta/Hatay, which the Syrians refused.[44] At best, these two issues had been shelved, but they could be raised again if, for instance, a more democratic regime were established in Syria.

Turkey, Iraq and the Iraqi Kurds

Between the eruption of the Kuwait crisis in 1990 and the US-led invasion of Iraq in 2003, Turkey's policies towards Iraq and the Iraqi Kurds were effectively part of its internal Kurdish problem and its often problematic relationship with the United States, which have been related earlier (pp162–3). It was not until around 2005, when Iraq was beginning to establish new political institutions for the post-Saddam era, that Turkish–Iraqi relations began to resume a degree of autonomy. In this context, the future position of the Iraqi Kurds, and the status of the city of Kirkuk – contested by Kurds, Arabs and the local Turcomans – was nearly always the most contentious issue for Turkey (p168).[45] Fortunately, the signs were not always negative. Following elections to the Transitional National Council of Iraq in January 2005, Jalal Talabani, leader of the Patriotic Union of Kurdistan, was elected President of

Iraq in April. This was of fundamental importance to Turkey, since it meant that once one of the two main Kurdish leaders in Iraq occupied a position of power in Baghdad, then the Kurds had less interest in breaking away from the Iraqi state: Talabani himself later admitted that an independent Kurdish republic was 'only a dream'.[46] Turkish fears about the future of Iraq were further allayed in May 2005 when Ibrahim al-Ja'fari visited Ankara for his first trip abroad since taking office as Prime Minister of Iraq in the previous month, assuring his hosts that his government would not allow 'any group in Iraq [read, the PKK] to damage the security of neighbouring countries'.[47] Given the weakness of his government, it was doubtful that al-Ja'fari could himself ensure this, but it was clear that he was at least well aware of the danger.

When the new constitution of Iraq was put to a referendum in September 2005, it was strongly supported on behalf of Turkey by Abdullah Gül, as foreign minister.[48] The constitution provided that Iraq would be a federal republic. The Turkish government was obliged to accept this, since it realized that it could not tell the Iraqis what kind of constitution they could have. More significantly, the document contained two provisions, essential from the Turkish viewpoint: first, none of the new 'regions' of Iraq (of which the Kurdish region, now under the Kurdistan Regional Government, or KRG, was obviously the most crucial) could secede from the federation; second, a decision on the future status of Kirkuk would be postponed until a proper census could be held, by the end of 2007 at the latest.[49] With these points assured, in December 2005, in the run-up to Iraq's second round of parliamentary elections, Abdullah Gül played a positive role in persuading the leaders of the main Sunni Arab parties not to boycott the polls, as they had earlier threatened to do.[50]

Once these basic guidelines had been accepted, Turkey's relations with the government in Baghdad developed apace – the main problem being not that the Arab majority in Iraq was hostile to Turkey, but that it was itself riven by internal sectarian and tribal divisions, finding it hard to establish a stable and effective national government in the face of continuing terrorist attacks from extremists of both the Sunni and Shi'ite sects. Although an unstated Turkish aim was to prevent Iranian domination of Iraq, Turkey was careful not to take sides in the sectarian strife, trying to maintain balanced relations with both the Shi'ite and Sunni parties. On the other hand, it had little leverage over Iraq's turbulent domestic politics, which carried the constant risk of systemic breakdown or even civil war.

The development of economic links with Iraq was also vital for Turkey, given that, prior to the imposition of the UN sanctions regime in 1990, Iraq had been one of Turkey's major trading partners. With the gradual, if some-what halting recovery of the Iraqi economy, mutual trade more than trebled between 2004 and 2010, from just under $2 billion to just under $6.2 billion, consisting almost entirely of Turkish exports to Iraq, rather than the reverse.[51] There were two politically significant aspects of this revival: first, that they boosted economic activity in the Kurdish-inhabited south-east, thus potentially reducing the economic basis of the PKK's grassroots support; and second, that a substantial proportion of Turkey's exports went to the Kurdish region of Iraq, which thus acquired a significant economic dependence on Turkey.[52] In June 2010, the energy minister for the KRG claimed that the Kurdish region could supply 14–15 billion cubic metres of gas per year into the planned Nabucco pipeline, thus making the project viable (p155), although whether this could be achieved in the absence of an oil and gas law agreed with the Baghdad government, which was still in the balance, seemed very doubtful.[53] In the longer term, if the needed laws were passed, and once Iraq's substantial internal demand for gas had been met, it seemed perfectly possible that Iraq would become a vital part of the Nabucco project, strengthening the Turkish–Iraqi relationship as well as Turkey's role in Europe's energy supplies.

To achieve these economic advances, serious political obstacles had to be overcome, of which the Turkish–Kurdish relationship was easily the most problematic. Following an intensification of the PKK campaign in Turkey, Turkish forces along the border with Iraq were strongly reinforced in the spring of 2007. The Commander of Land Forces, General İrfan Başbuğ, proclaimed that the Turkish army could and should cross the border to take action against the PKK bases in northern Iraq, although he must have known that this would be opposed both by Tayyip Erdoğan and the US government, to say nothing of the Kurds in Iraq.[54] A potential clash with both the US and the Iraqi Kurds was fortunately defused by the Prime Minister's visit to Washington on 5 November, and President Bush's undertaking to give the Turkish forces 'real time' intelligence on PKK movements in Iraq – in effect, giving a green light to limited Turkish military action in Iraqi Kurdistan (p169). This easing of the situation eventually led to an important turnaround in Turkey's relations with the KRG. In February–March 2007, the Turkish military came out strongly against the establishment of any direct relations with the Iraqi Kurds, presumably with the idea that this would represent support for Kurdish separatism.[55] Nevertheless, within a few months, Turkish officials entered into a direct dialogue with the Iraqi Kurdish leadership, reflecting the general decline in the army's independent political power after the start of the 'Ergenekon' investigations (p143).[56]

Later, at the end of October 2009, Ahmet Davutoğlu became the first Turkish foreign minister to pay an official visit to Massoud Barzani, chairman of the KRG, in his regional capital of Arbil. In the resulting discussion, Barzani gave full support to the government's 'Kurdish opening' (pp146–7), although this later fell flat.[57] Barzani paid a return visit to Ankara in June 2010, with Tayyip Erdoğan making his first trip to Arbil in the following March.[58] During September–October 2011, the south-east was struck by a new wave of PKK attacks, in which several civilians were killed, culminating in the deaths of 24 soldiers on 18 October. This provoked another cross-border operation by the Turkish army against PKK camps in northern Iraq. In response, Barzani sent his nephew Nechirvan Barzani on an urgent visit to Ankara, and visited the Turkish capital himself on 4 November. In Ankara, he claimed that 'our security is linked' and that 'we will take every measure to strengthen our security'.[59] What this meant was unclear, since he also told journalists that he opposed military action against the PKK and that 'we have to pursue peaceful means'.[60] This fell far short of the Turkish agenda, which wanted military cooperation against the PKK. On the other hand, the psychological atmosphere between Ankara and Arbil had undoubtedly improved dramatically since 2007. In this respect, the 'zero problems with neighbours' policy had scored a limited success.

This partial rapprochement with the KRG was accompanied by growing cooperation with the Baghdad government, although this had always been less problematic. In 2009, the two governments set up a 'Strategic Cooperation Council', of which the first meeting was held in September 2009, between their respective foreign ministers. In the following month, Prime Minister Erdoğan and his Iraqi counterpart Nouri al-Maliki met in Baghdad for the first full meeting of the Council, at which they signed no less than 48 agreements. The list included an accord on security cooperation, in which the Iraqi side (unlike Barzani) apparently recognized Turkey's right to intervene in northern Iraq against the PKK. Other deals covered the operation of the Kirkuk–Yumurtalık pipeline, power supply and improved communications.[61] The mutual visits continued during 2011. By the close of the year, the most pressing issue for the two governments was the impending US military withdrawal from Iraq. According to the original planning, some US troops were to stay on in the country after December 2011 to train the Iraqi army. However, the Iraqi government rejected the US demand that they be granted legal immunity while in Iraq. Accordingly, Tayyip Erdoğan reportedly suggested that the Turkish army should take over the job.[62] If this happened, then Turkey would continue to play an important role in Iraq after the US departure, emphasizing the increased interdependence of the two states.

Turkey and Iran

During the 1990s, conducting relations with Iran continued to be a difficult test for Turkish diplomacy. Essentially, problems in the relationship were the product of the Iranian revolution of 1979, uncertainties in the direction of Iran's politics, and Turkey's continuing Kurdish problem, rather than the end of the Cold War. As in the 1980s, Turkey's commitment to state secularism, and its links with the west, could have put it on a collision course with the Islamic Republic. Nonetheless, Turkey needed to create a reasonably cooperative relationship with Iran if it could, for pragmatic political and economic reasons. Outright hostility could have induced the Iranians to give all-out support to the PKK. Had this happened, it could have had the most serious effects for Turkey, given the length of the Turkish–Iranian border in a remote and mountainous area. Economically, also, there was a substantial degree of actual or potential economic interdependence between the two countries.

While there were evident advantages for Turkey from a cooperative relationship with Iran, the obstacles to achieving it were also clear. In broad political terms, the rulers in Tehran were bound to regard Turkey with grave suspicion, as America's main ally in the Middle East alongside Israel. While the Iranian government might periodically sign mutual security agreements with Turkey, during the 1990s there were reciprocal suspicions on the Turkish side that militant sections of the Iranian regime were aiding ultra-Islamist terrorists active in Turkey, and that the PKK was able to use some bases in Iran, even though this support was not so important or consistent as that given by Syria. After 2000, the main cause of conflict was Iran's assumed aim of building its own nuclear arsenal that, as related earlier, put serious strain on Turkish–US relations (pp170–1).

Turkish suspicions that Iran was involved in sponsoring ultra-Islamist terrorism in Turkey came to the surface in 1993, following the murder of the widely respected and strongly pro-secularist journalist Uğur Mumcu, on 24 January. Four days later, an unsuccessful attempt was made on the life of Jak Kamhi, one of Turkey's leading businessmen, and a prominent member of Istanbul's Jewish community. Investigations were also launched into the murders two other pro-secularist journalists, Çetin Emeç and Turan Dursun, who had both been killed in 1990. The minister of interior, İsmet Sezgin, told a press conference on 4 February that 19 people had been arrested for these crimes, of whom the majority had confessed that they had been trained for terrorism in Iran.[63]

In the aftermath, the Turks decided to reach an agreement with Tehran designed to prevent the PKK using bases in Iran, or Iranian sponsorship of Islamist terrorism. In return, Turkey would promise not to allow attacks on Iran by the Mujahadeen-e Khalq, the Iranian organization of anti-regime Iranian militants, some of whose members had taken refuge in Turkey. Accordingly, in November 1993 the two governments signed a security protocol stipulating that neither would allow any terrorist organization hostile to the other to operate from its territory. In May 1994, this agreement appeared to be working, as Iran turned over several members of the PKK, plus the corpses of others, to the Turkish authorities. As part of the rapprochement, Süleyman Demirel paid an official visit to Tehran in July 1994 – the first Turkish President to do so since before the Iranian revolution.[64] Nonetheless, it appeared that by the spring of 1995, relations had again deteriorated: in fact, it seems that in May 1995, Tansu Çiller, as Prime Minister, proposed launching air attacks on assumed PKK bases in Iran, but was overruled on this by Demirel.[65]

During 1996–7, Turkey's relations with Iran became an important item in Necmettin Erbakan's attempt to re-orient Turkey's foreign relations towards the Muslim countries, and secularist resistance to it. The high point of Erbakan's project came with his visit to Tehran in August 1996, in the course of which he signed an agreement with the Iranians for the construction of a natural gas pipeline from Tabriz, in north-western Iran, to the eastern Turkish city of Erzurum, with a future extension westwards to Sivas and Ankara. There were actually strong economic reasons for pushing ahead with the project from the Turkish viewpoint: in fact, an outline agreement on the proposal had been signed the previous year, by Tansu Çiller's government. Nonetheless, Erbakan was happy to stress the 'Islamic' aspect of his policies, in the knowledge that it would cause severe misgivings in Washington.[66] Within Turkey, the conflict over relations with Iran became still more acute in December 1996, when the then Iranian President Hashemi Rafsanjani visited Ankara and Erbakan apparently tried to negotiate a defence cooperation agreement with Iran. This idea was hotly opposed by the Turkish military, which saw Iran as far more of an enemy than an ally, and was vetoed by the General Staff, indicating the severe ruptures over foreign policy at the time.[67]

As in other policy theatres, the Yılmaz administration was left with the job of re-adjusting Turkey's relations with Iran, after the fall of the Erbakan–Çiller coalition in June 1997. Turkey's links with Israel, as well as conflicts over policy towards the Iraqi Kurds, were still a serious point of friction, and caused Demirel to walk out of a meeting of the Organization of the Islamic Conference held in Tehran in December 1997.[68] After further clashes over alleged PKK bases in Iran in 1999, the two countries signed another security agreement on 13 August, under which they would carry out 'simultaneous operations' against insurgent bases on both sides of the border.[69] Fortunately, these agreements improved the atmosphere and set up a period of far more cooperative relations on both sides, even if these were still tempered by mutual suspicions and tensions.

Although the process is not quite clear, it appears that there were also other reasons for this improvement. Critics of the AKP would argue that it reflected a pro-Islamic bias on the part of the party's leadership. Admittedly, religious sympathies may have played a role in the margins of government thinking, but all the evidence is that material considerations were far more influential. First, the Turkish parliament's refusal to support the US-led invasion of Iraq in 2003 almost certainly affected Iranian perspectives on Turkey: in opposing the war, the two countries' foreign policies ran in parallel for the first time since the Iranian revolution. With the impending American withdrawal from Iraq at the end of 2011, Iran was left as the most powerful external actor, thanks to the large Shi'ite presence in the country. Turkey would almost certainly oppose Iranian domination of post-occupation Iraq (as would the US and the Arab Gulf countries) but handled the situation carefully, keeping its bridges open with both the religious sects in Iraq. Second, and more immediately, the development of an Iranian–Kurdish branch of the PKK created a strong common interest between the two countries: whereas the PKK had previously looked to Iran for support, it was now fighting against it. Third, the two countries developed a strong economic interdependence, which mitigated mutual suspicions. This left concern over Iran's apparent nuclear ambitions as the only serious bone of contention between them.

As in the case of the other Middle Eastern countries, Turkey's trade with Iran grew exponentially after the mid-1990s, from a total of just over

$1.1 billion in 1996 to almost $10.7 billion in 2010. Within this total, however, there was a huge imbalance in Iran's favour, with exports to Turkey reaching more than $7.6 billion in 2010, against imports of just over $3 billion.[70] Within this, oil and natural gas accounted for the vast majority of Turkey's imports from Iran: by 2010, the Tabriz–Erzurum pipeline, officially opened in 2001, provided around 19 per cent of Turkey's natural gas supplies.[71] This supply was not always a secure or easy one, due to periodic technical breakdowns and price disputes, but it made Iran Turkey's second most important source of gas, after Russia. Without this, Russia would have had a near-monopoly of the Turkish market. The potential for developing this trade should have been enormous, given that Iran's gas reserves are again second only to those of Russia: in suitable political conditions Iran could become a major source of gas for Europe, via the Nabucco project. With this in mind, in July 2007, Turkish and Iranian ministers signed a memorandum of understanding under which a second pipeline would be built, to carry 30 billion cubic metres (bcm) of gas per year from Iran to Turkey and Europe. Most of the gas would originate from Iran, but some would come by another existing pipeline to Iran from Turkmenistan. To help achieve this, the Turkish state petroleum corporation TPAO would develop Iran's South Pars gas field, planned to produce 20 bcm per year.[72] Politically, however, the project faced insuperable political obstacles from the United States, where government spokesmen strongly criticized the project.[73] Under the Iran–Libya Sanctions Act passed by the US Congress in 1996 (from which Libya was dropped in 2006) sanctions can be placed in the US on any company investing more than $20 million per year in Iran's energy sector. In effect, this deprived the project of international financing, so that it has remained moribund. While potentially important, it is unlikely to be achieved unless there is a dramatic change in Iran's political direction, and hence in its relations with the West.

While the activities of the PKK drove Turkey and Iran apart during the 1990s, after 2004, they brought them together, as an Iranian–Kurdish branch of the PKK, known as the Free Life Party of Kurdistan, or PJAK, began attacks into Iranian territory. The Iranian government alleges that PJAK is supported by the US, and a representative of the organization, Rahman Haj-Ahmadi, visited Washington in August 2007 in a bid for weapons and ammunition. His visit appears to have been in vain however, as he failed to get an interview with administration officials.[74] More concretely, in April 2008, a meeting of the Turkey–Iran High Security Commission signed a memorandum of understanding to increase cooperation and exchange intelligence on PKK/PJAK, while two months later General İrfan Başbuğ, then the Turkish Commander of Land Forces, confirmed that the two countries were coordinating military operations against it.[75] In October 2011, after further attacks by the PKK in Turkey, the visiting Iranian foreign minister Ali Akbar Salehi agreed to step up this collaboration, although details were unclear.[76] This virtual alliance against PKK/PJAK was accompanied by a fairly high degree of convergence in policies towards Iraq. While Turkey would oppose any attempt by Iran to take over Iraq after US forces were withdrawn, both countries were opposed to any partition of the country that would result in an independent Kurdistan, and both seemed to want to avoid a confrontation over Iraq's political future.

On the whole, Turkish governments seemed to have been successful in handling their prickly eastern neighbour, but their policies were not above criticism. On occasion, they seemed to be over-stepping the mark in their desire to placate the Iranian regime – as, for instance, in June 2009, when Tayyip Erdoğan and Abdullah Gül were among the first to congratulate Mahmoud Ahmadinejad after his highly contested re-election as Iran's President.[77] It could also be argued that while the AKP government had worked hard to smooth Iran's relations with the west – in particular, through its attempts to bring about a negotiated settlement of the nuclear dispute (pp170–1) – it had received remarkably little in return. As an example, the Iranian government continued to maintain good relations with Armenia, and did nothing to support Turkey and Azerbaijan in their conforntation with Yerevan. In a little-reported incident, in May 2011, three Turkish academics attending a conference in Tehran were arbitrarily arrested and held for almost two weeks with no explanation, and only released after intervention by foreign minister Davutoğlu.[78] Predictably, the Turkish participation in the NATO missile defence shield provoked harsh criticisms from Ahmadinejad and other Iranian officials, who argued that its sole purpose was to defend Israel. In spite of Turkey's confrontation with Tel Aviv, the Turks were accused of giving 'all-out support for the Israeli regime'.[79] As in many other cases, Turkey's relations with Iran were vitally affected by its relations with third parties, especially the US. In what appeared to be a zero-sum game, reconciliation with the US promoted conflict with Iran, and vice versa.

Turkey and the 'Arab Spring'

As in the case of their counter-parts in other countries, Turkey's diplomats were caught off-balance by the unexpected wave of revolts and revolutions that convulsed much of the Arab world in 2011. President George W. Bush's 'Broader Middle East Initiative' of 2004 had been a dismal failure (see p168), and it was widely assumed that the Muslim Middle East had been exempted from the 'Third Wave' of democratizations that followed the end of the Cold War.[80] Hence, like those of most other governments, Turkey's strategy towards the Arab world before 2011 was morally neutral, ignoring the fact that most Arab states were ruled by autocratic and sometimes brutal regimes, and adhering to the rubric of non-interference in the internal politics of other countries. As a crucial test case, it was very rare to find any criticism in Turkey of policy towards Syria, although this could be attacked as cosying up to a ruthless and corrupt dictatorship.[81] Hence, the rapid spread and important successes of the Arab uprisings provoked some rapid rethinking, in Ankara as in other capitals. Turkish foreign policy-makers also had to accept that, in spite of Turkey's activist policies in the region, it had little influence over events on the ground and had to adapt itself to changing circumstances.

Although the 'Arab Spring' also affected countries as diverse as Bahrain, Yemen and Algeria, the cases of Tunisia, Libya, Egypt and Syria were the most significant for Turkey, since these were countries in which the uprisings had the most profound effects and that were also of political and economic importance to Ankara. To summarize the story, the uprisings began in Tunisia in December 2010, leading to the ouster of President Zine el-Abidine Ben Ali on 14 January 2011. After an interim government including members of Ben Ali's party, a new administration under Beji Caid el-Sebsi was appointed, paving the way for elections to a Constituent Assembly in October 2011. Protests in Egypt started on 25 January 2011, continuing until 10 February, when President Hosni Mubarak ceded his powers to Vice-President Omar Suleiman. The Vice-President then announced that Mubarak had resigned and transferred power to the Egyptian armed forces. Egypt then moved towards elections and, hopefully, a new constitution. In Libya, widespread protests began in mid-February 2011, with the opposition, organized by a National Transitional Council (NTC) established in the eastern city of Benghazi. As forces loyal to Colonel Muammar Gaddafi threatened to overwhelm the rebels, the United Nations Security Council adopted its Resolution 1973 on 17 March 2011, under which NATO air forces (primarily those of France and Britain, with some US support) beginning a bombing campaign officially designed to protect civilians, but in effect giving vital assistance to the rebels. After what originally looked like a deadlocked civil war, the rebels captured Tripoli in late August, followed by Gaddafi's stronghold of Sirte on 20 October, killing the former dictator in the process. Abdurrahim el-Keib, who had no connection with the Gaddafi regime, was appointed Prime Minister by the NTC on 31 October.

The revolt in Syria was far more problematic and bitterly contested, mainly because the Ba'thist regime was relatively well-organized, traditionally enjoying support among the heterodox Alawi and other non-Sunni communities, and retaining control over the strongest units of the armed forces. Mass demonstrations against the regime did not develop until mid-March 2011, and then largely in Sunni areas, but they then did so in a rising crescendo, resulting in some defections from the army and a death toll put by the United Nations at 5,000 by the end of 2011. In response, the US and the European Union imposed sanctions such as travel bans and freezing of assets of prominent regime members, and – more importantly – a ban on oil imports from Syria. Unexpectedly, on 12 November, the Arab League, in which Turkey has observer status, voted to suspend Syria's membership, asking member states to withdraw their ambassadors from Damascus.[82]

In the case of Tunisia, a country in which Turkey did not have substantial economic or strategic interests, the overthrow of the Ben Ali regime happened quickly: hence, Ankara was left with the easy job of recognizing the *fait accompli*. In the Egyptian case, as early as 2 February 2011 – some time before the outcome was certain – Tayyip Erdoğan called on President Hosni Mubarak to heed the calls of the demonstrators in Cairo's Tahrir Square to step down.[83] His instinct paid off, as Turkey was clearly seen later as having supported the winning side. The case of Libya was more problematic, however, since there were around 30,000 Turkish workers in the country, mainly working for Turkish construction firms with valuable contracts in Libya. At the beginning of March, Erdoğan had strongly attacked the idea of NATO intervention in Libya. Instead, Turkey concentrated on organizing a mass evacuation of its own and other foreign nationals. It also engaged in fruitless talks with Colonel Gaddafi in the hope of persuading him to enact political reforms. However, on 24 March, foreign minister Davutoğlu announced an abrupt change of course, as Turkey moved round to support of the NATO air operation, supplying five surface ships and a submarine to help enforce the arms embargo against Libya.[84] By May the government was openly calling on Colonel Gaddafi to leave Libya, and on 3 July recognized the opposition administration, the Transitional National Council, as 'the true representative of Libya's people'.[85] Subsequently, Turkey acted as co-chair of the Libya Contact Group (LCG) of 28 countries which developed relations with the Council, hosting a meeting of the LCG in Istanbul on 25 August, and extending economic and humanitarian aid to Libya.[86]

For the Turks, the uprising in Syria against the Ba'athist regime that began in March 2011 raised the most serious problems. The previous entente with Damascus had been the centrepiece of Turkey's Middle Eastern policy, and the government had put a great deal of effort into developing economic and political relations with its southern neighbour. Initially, during April–May 2011, Tayyip Erdoğan tried to persuade President Bashar al-Assad to enact social and economic reforms but, as in the Libyan case, these attempts proved quite unavailing. The Syrian President made frequent promises of reform, but failed to carry them through, while his regime continued violent suppression of the protests. As late as mid-May, Erdoğan was still claiming that it was 'too early' to call on President al-Assad to leave office, but by mid-June he had clearly changed his tune, describing the regime's crackdown on the opposition as 'savagery'.[87] The possibility of a wave of refugees seeking sanctuary in Turkey was a major worry for Ankara, which appeared to be borne out in late June with the Ba'thist regime's onslaught against the opposition in northern Syria. At its high point, the influx brought more than 18,000 refugees into Turkey, where they were accommodated by the Turkish Red Crescent in tented encampments near the border. Fortunately, by late September the number had been reduced to around 7,500 as most of the refugees returned to Syria to look after their farms and businesses.[88] Besides accommodating the refugees, for which it won international respect, Turkey also hosted the sharply divided Syrian opposition movement, representatives of which launched the Syrian National Council (SNC) in Istanbul at the beginning of October.[89] Relations with Syria hit a new low on 12 November, when pro-regime demonstrators attacked the Turkish embassy in Damascus, along with that of Saudi Arabia, provoking sharp protests from Ankara and the evacuation of embassy officials' families.[90]

At this stage, however, it was not clear what else the government could do in response, besides show support for the SNC. Tayyip Erdoğan was said to have been in full accord on the need for sanctions against Syria when he met President Obama on 20 September,[91] and Turkey terminated joint economic projects with its southern neighbour. However, a full economic embargo seemed unlikely, since it could hurt Turkey, and the people of Syria, as much if not more than the regime. In October 2011, a senior defector from the Syrian army, Colonel Riad al-As'aad, who had established himself in Turkey, claimed to command a 'Free Syrian Army' of 15,000 deserters, but there was no clear indication that he was receiving official or logistical support in Turkey (he firmly denied that he had been getting any help from the Turks).[92] Instead, the SNC continued to insist on a campaign of peaceful resistance. Foreign minister Davutoğlu emphasized that Turkey could only become militarily involved in Syria 'if the situation becomes a security threat for us'[93] (presumably, if the regime took the suicidal step of allowing the PKK or some other group to attack Turkey from Syria).

A striking difference between Turkey's confrontation with Syria during 2011, and that of the earlier phase before 1998, was that its stand had significant support from the rest of the Middle East, with the single exception of Iran. On the last score, Turkish diplomacy was not inactive, with Prime Minister Erdoğan relating that he had warned President Ahmadinejad not to extend unstinting support to the Syrian regime.[94] In the broader arena, the extent of support for Erdoğan's policies in the rest of the Middle East was borne out by a startlingly successful tour that he made to Egypt, Libya and Tunisia on 12–16 September 2011. He received a particularly rapturous welcome in Cairo, where as many as 20,000 people were reported to have turned up at the airport to greet him at around 2am. He had a warm reception also in Tunis and Tripoli, among other cities, winning plaudits as 'the most popular public figure across the Arab world'.[95] It is likely that this mainly reflected his tough stance against Israel, as well as his support for the 'Arab Spring', plus the remarkable lack of alternative political leadership in the Middle East at the time. He was also quick to refute the idea that he had any sort of Islamist mission: instead, he urged his Arab audiences to follow the Turkish model of a secular state which 'has an equal distance to all religious groups', provoking criticisms from outright Islamists such as those of the Egyptian Muslim Brotherhood.[96] In this, he had the full support of the US government, demonstrating that, except on the Israeli issue, there was now a close convergence between Turkish and American strategies in the region.

Turkey and the wider world

Turkey's foreign policy during the twenty-first century has mainly concentrated on the well-established areas of concern, which have a direct bearing on its strategic and economic priorities and are outlined earlier in this book. Significantly, however, policy also started to reach out to more distant regions, where the Turks did not have immediate interests or ethnic, historical or cultural connections, such as East and South Asia, Latin America and sub-Saharan Africa. There seem to have been two main motives for this: first, economic, as the country's growing economy boosted contacts with new trading partners, especially the new economic power-houses like Brazil, India and China; second, the desire for greater activism in global politics, consistent with Turkey's strengthened economy and higher international profile. This was accompanied by an attempt to play a role on the broader international stage, where Turkey could project itself as a nation with a Muslim culture, but a modern and relatively democratic political system, which could act as a mediator or bridge between the Muslim world and the west.

Among the emerging global powers, China was easily the most important for Turkey, but this was not a problem-free relationship. Its most significant aspect was economic, corresponding to China's emergence as a major industrial power. As a result, Turkey's trade with China grew exponentially, from a mere $621 million in 1996 to almost $19.5 billion in 2010. As in the case of Turkey's trade with Japan and other East Asian countries, however, there was a huge imbalance in China's favour, with Turkey's imports from China reaching $17.2 billion in 2011, against $2.3 billion in exports.[97] Hence, Turkey had a major interest in expanding its exports to China, as well as encouraging inward investment by Chinese undertakings, or developing joint ventures in third countries. On the other side, China reportedly looked to cooperation with Turkey as a way of consolidating its power in the Muslim world, and as a gateway to expanded Chinese business in third markets, especially in the Middle East.[98]

During the early stages of the Cold War, Turkey's only encounter with communist China was as an enemy in the Korean War, and it was not until 1971 that it recognized the People's Republic. However, the main cause of conflict continued to be the fate of the Uighurs, a Turkic-Muslim minority living in China's south-western province of Xinjiang. Numbering around 9 million, the Uighurs resisted communist rule after 1949, as well as assimilation into the Han majority: several thousand took refuge in Turkey, setting up a series of communal associations calling for the 'liberation of eastern Turkistan'.[99] Turkish policy was caught between sympathy for a fellow-Turkic nation, and the realist need to cultivate its relations with Beijing. A striking illustration of this started in June 2009, when President Gül paid a six-day visit to China, calling for greater cooperation between the two countries, and winding up his visit in Xinjiang, where he inauspiciously described the Uighurs as the 'friendship bridge' between Turkey and China.[100] Less than a week later, riots broke out in Urumqi, the provincial capital, between Uighurs and Han Chinese immigrants. The disturbances were violently suppressed by the Chinese authorities, resulting in more than 150 deaths, with 800 people injured. In response, Tayyip Erdoğan described the Chinese action as an 'atrocity' and 'genocide': Abdullah Gül called for a transparent investigation of the massacre, while a demonstration of around 10,000 people in Istanbul demanded Turkish intervention and a boycott of Chinese goods.[101] Subsequently, however, the Chinese government appeared anxious to have the incident forgotten, with a senior official of the Chinese foreign ministry claiming that China wanted to improve relations with Turkey,[102] and an apparent change of course by the authorities in Xinjiang, who adopted softer tactics and poured extra funds into the development of the province.[103] By October 2010, when Chinese Premier Wen Jiabao paid a return visit to Turkey, all appeared to be sweetness and light (at least on the surface) as both sides called for increased economic collaboration and even 'strategic cooperation' – of an unspecified character – between the two countries.[104]

For students of Turkish foreign policy, a more surprising development under the AKP government was increased Turkish interest in sub-Saharan Africa, with whom the Turks had few historical connections, and where the economic advantages were less obvious or immediate than in the case of China. This gathered pace in 2008, mainly as a part of Turkey's successful campaign to be elected as a non-permanent member of the United Nations Security Council for the term 2009–10 – itself an indication of its drive to establish a higher international profile. To promote its cause, it hosted a 'Turkey–African Cooperation Summit' with the heads of state and other senior representatives from 50 African states in Istanbul in August 2008.[105] Apart from a new interest in African markets by Turkish businessmen, an important role in raising Turkey's image in Africa – lauded by visiting Turkish politicians – was played by the educational activities of the Gülen movement (p150), which established 15 schools with 4,000 students in Nigeria, plus a university college,[106] with another chain of schools in Kenya, Uganda and other African states. Humanitarian concerns were also at the forefront of Turkish interests in Africa, notably in Somalia, where the Turkish Red Crescent and private foundations launched an impressive campaign of famine relief and medical assistance in the late summer of 2011. In an article in the US journal *Foreign Policy* in October 2011, Tayyip Erdoğan drew attention to his country's aid to Somalia, which he had himself visited two months earlier, accusing the rest of the international community of neglecting its plight.[107] This may be seen as part of his drive to project himself as a world statesman – virtually unprecedented in post-war Turkish politics – but it reflected genuine humanitarian concerns.

Another important aspect of this new activism on the international stage was the AKP government's determination to counter the idea that the Muslim world and the west were locked into inevitable hostility – the 'Clash of Civilizations' thesis advanced by the American scholar Samuel P. Huntington.[108] This was one of the AKP's basic ideological commitments, reflecting Ahmet Davutoğlu's call for 'a comprehensive civilizational dialogue' between Islam and the west (p137). It also appealed to those in the European Union, such as the British Premier Tony Blair, who supported the idea of a multicultural Europe, and Turkish membership of it as a way to strengthen links with the

Muslim world.[109] Predictably, the idea of Turkey promoting the 'meeting of civilizations' was used by Tayyip Erdoğan as an additional argument in favour of Turkish accession.[110] The ideal opportunity to take this up occurred in March 2004, following the Madrid train bombings by al-Qaeda-inspired terrorists that killed 191 people. In response, the Spanish Premier José Luis Rodríguez Zapatero proposed an 'Alliance of Civilizations between the Western and the Arab and Muslim world'. This project was taken up by the UN Secretary-General Kofi Annan, with Erdoğan invited to co-sponsor it with Zapatero in June 2005. A 'High Level Group for the Alliance of Civilizations' was then set up, which prepared an 'Implementation Plan' presented to Annan's successor, Ban Ki-moon, in 2007.[111] Cynics may argue that all this amounted to no more than pious hopes – that, for instance, it did not stem rising Islamophobia among the ultra-right in Europe and elsewhere, and that other Muslim countries showed no real enthusiasm for it. Nevertheless, in the context of the evolution of Turkish foreign policy it marked another significant shift: for the first time, Turkey was projecting itself as a spokesman of the Muslim world, with Tayyip Erdoğan taking on a role that none of his predecessors would probably have wanted or have been able to assume.

12 Conclusions and prospects

In an attempt to draw conclusions from a long and tangled story, this chapter is divided into three sections. The first tries to assess the effects of historical changes on the foreign policy options of the late Ottoman Empire and the Turkish republic, and to identify the continuities as well as reorientations of its policies in successive periods up to the end of the Cold War. The second assesses the evolution of foreign policy during the 1990s, while the third assesses the changes and effects of the most recent decade. It tries to offer a critical analysis of the successes and failures of recent strategies, and to address some of the crucial questions facing Turkish policy-makers, as well as foreign practitioners and observers.

Historical changes and policy options

An underlying assumption of this book is that there have been some important elements of continuity, as well as change, in Turkish foreign policy since the days of the late Ottoman Empire. For most of the period surveyed (that is, from the late eighteenth century until 1914, and from 1939 until the 1980s), Turkey was a state under threat from other powers, normally Russia, and from internal ethnic rebellions during the nineteenth century. Between 1914 and 1918 it was unnecessarily embroiled in the First World War, and between 1919 and 1922 it was locked in a basic struggle for survival. During these periods, the dominant question for foreign policy-makers was whether they should seek an alliance with a major power, and if so, with whom. During the remaining periods, between 1923 and 1939, and again after 1990, the external threat was reduced. Nonetheless, the policy options adopted during the two periods were quite different.

Looking back at the nineteenth century, Ottoman foreign policy was essentially defensive. Its main purpose was to protect the territory, primarily in Europe, which the Empire retained, and to secure a period of peace in which the state could reconstruct its institutions and strengthen its resources. The main threat the Empire faced was the challenge posed by the rise in power of Russia and the emergence of nationalist movements among the Christian societies of the Balkans. There were also threats from other directions, notably from the Sultan's nominal vassal Mehmet Ali Pasha between 1831 and

1841. Given that they could not rely on their own resources to defeat these enemies, the Ottoman rulers had either to form an alliance with one or more of the European powers, or remain outside alliances and hope that the rivalries between the powers would deter any of them from destroying the Empire. During the confused period of the Napoleonic wars, the Empire switched sides no less than four times, forming periodic alliances with both Britain, France and Russia. Faced with the challenge from Mehmet Ali, it constructed a brief entente with Russia in 1833 and then a successful alliance with Britain, Austria, Prussia and Russia in 1840. Its participation in great power politics reached its peak with the alliance with Britain and France signed in 1854, which led to the Crimean War. The alignment with Britain nonetheless withered away after the Treaty of Berlin of 1878, under which the Empire lost most, but not all, of its territories in the Balkans. Under Abdul Hamid, the Ottomans first sought an alliance with Germany but, when this attempt failed, moved back to the second policy of uneasy neutrality. Although the Young Turk regime of 1908 investigated the possibility of alliances with all the main European powers except Russia, the formation of the two great alliances of the First World War made it more difficult to maintain the balancing act between them, and the Empire had no formal alliances until it fatefully joined Germany in 1914.

The period between 1918 and 1923 marked the nadir of Turkish power, in which the survival of a Turkish state was most in doubt. That Turkey managed to survive it was mainly due to the stubborn determination of its people and leaders to resist occupation and partition. However, the war-weariness of the entente powers and the divisions between them also played an important part. By reaching separate settlements with France and Italy, and an entente with the new Soviet state, the founders of the republic showed themselves adept at exploiting the remnants of the old balance of power system. Through it, they were effectively able to isolate the Greeks, and belatedly convince the British that supporting Greek ambitions was a losing game. After the signature of the Treaty of Lausanne in 1923, they reverted to a policy of neutrality between all the main European powers. This was partly because an alliance was unnecessary. The events of 1918–23 had ended the mismatch between the state's resources and its territorial commitments. Turkey had no important *terra irridenta* to recover, and Russia's power had temporarily been reduced by internal turmoil, so that it was not a serious threat to Turkey for the first time in more than a century. Apart from this, alliances were simply unavailable at the time. In the world of the 1920s, the expectation was that collective security agreements under the League of Nations would suffice to keep the peace. By the mid-1930s, however, this hope was evaporating as Turkey began to see a new security threat, first from Italy and then from Germany. After a rare and unsuccessful attempt to forge an alliance with the minor powers of the Balkans in 1934, the Turks began to look for agreements with the USSR, and with Britain and France, as a means of obtaining security in the Mediterranean and the Balkans, respectively. The first quest proved unavailing, and was abruptly blocked by the signature of the Nazi–Soviet pact in August 1939, but the second was eventually achieved in October 1939, as the tripartite treaty between Britain, France and Turkey.

At the beginning of the Second World War, it appears that İsmet İnönü's government was fully prepared to undertake its commitments to the British and French – in effect, to join them in operations against Italy if Mussolini joined the war. However, the unexpectedly rapid collapse of France in the early summer of 1940 changed the external parameters drastically. Henceforth, the Turks were determined to stay out of the war, and successfully resisted pressure from both sides to break their *de facto* neutrality – first by Germany, during 1940–1, and then by the British and Americans, during 1942–4. That İnönü's tactic succeeded was partly due to adroit diplomacy and foot-dragging by Turkey, and partly to sheer good luck – in particular, Hitler's decision to invade the USSR rather than the Middle East in 1941, and subsequent disagreements between the British and Americans about the wisdom of trying to bring Turkey into the war. Nonetheless, by 1945, Turkey was still in a position of great international danger, as the victorious Stalin demanded concessions from Ankara that, if realized, would probably have converted Turkey into a Soviet satellite. It was as yet unclear whether the western powers would resist him.

In the post-war world, and faced with the classic choice between alliance and non-alignment, Turkey was almost bound to take the first option. Unaided, it could not expect to hold off a direct attack by the Warsaw Pact for more than a limited time, especially if, as expected, this was launched against the straits. As a result, the principle obstacle to forging the alliance was not reluctance on the Turkish side, but misgivings on the part of the United States, which was initially anxious not to disperse its resources over too many potential fronts. The Korean War changed western perceptions, and resulted in the admission of Greece and Turkey into NATO in 1952. Thereafter, Turkey's alliance with the west was fairly unproblematic, until the Cyprus crisis brought about a serious clash of perceived interests between Turkey and the USA in 1964. In the succeeding phase, there were some calls in Turkey for a reconsideration of the alliance, and the government led by Bülent Ecevit in 1978–9 tried to follow a more independent line. However, the arguments in favour of remaining in NATO proved conclusive, and were strengthened during the period of the 'second Cold War' of the early 1980s. At the same time, Turkey avoided becoming a mere satellite of the United States and was, for instance, able to follow a quite independent policy towards Cyprus and the Middle East. The formation of the European Economic Community, and Turkey's associate membership of it beginning in 1963, added a new dimension to its relationships with the western powers, besides a new set of actual or potential dependencies.

After the Cold War: The shifting agenda of the 1990s

At first glance, the end of the Cold War might seem to have given Turkey the option of abandoning its alliance with the west, since the main cause of its original formation – the direct threat from the USSR – had now been removed. That this did not happen was partly the result of the redefinition of the alliance, which was now seen as having a general mission to protect peace and democratic values throughout Europe, and partly because the alliance had acquired value for its members quite outside the limited field of national defence. In effect, the original military alliance had been extended into a host of diverse theatres and was underpinned by Turkey's integration into the global economy. In effect, the previous determinants of middle power strategies, which had been based almost entirely on crude considerations of power and security, had arguably been overtaken by a much wider range of concerns.

During the 1990s, a striking feature of Turkish diplomacy was the growing differentiation of policy into five main theatres, affecting relations with the United States, the European Union, the Balkans and the countries of the former USSR, and the Middle East. The biggest handicap with which it had to cope was domestic political instability and periodic economic breakdown, which made it hard to construct or apply effective strategies. Hence, policies tended to be reactive rather than proactive. In the central theatre of relations with the United States, and with the NATO alliance as a whole, the administrations of George Bush senior and Bill Clinton put a high premium of preserving their links with Turkey. For their part, the Turks he normally took care to cultivate the relationship, although it passed through a severe test during the period of the Erbakan-led government in Turkey of 1996–7. In operations in which NATO was actively involved, notably in the former Yugoslavia, Turkey was a cooperative and useful member of the alliance, although certainly not a major player. For the United States, Turkey's main strategic importance derived from its important role in western policies in the Middle East, beginning with the Gulf crisis of 1990–1, and especially in Iraq. This was also the most problematic feature of the Turkish–American relationship, however, since policy towards Iraq (and sometimes towards Iran) was the only important point at which Turkish and US attitudes seemed to be in conflict.

In Turkey's relationship with western Europe, the record was far more mixed. The faults lay partly on the European side, since until the end of 1999, the EU nations never really decided what their approach to Turkey should be – in particular, whether they should treat it as a candidate for full membership. Hence, they hoped to postpone a decision for as long as possible. On their side, the Turks initially underestimated the obstacles to accession, and tended to resent European criticisms over human rights and the treatment of the Kurds as unwarranted intrusions into their internal affairs. Conflicts with Greece and the Cyprus question exacerbated the tensions. It was not until the end of the 1990s that a resolution seemed possible, as Greeks and Turks began to see the advantages of renouncing hostility and the European Union at last officially ranked Turkey as a candidate for possible accession. Nonetheless, at the turn of the century, Turkey still had to take the first serious steps to make this possible.

Although the dissolution of the USSR and the Warsaw Pact removed the main threat to Turkey's security, handling its relations with Russia was difficult for

Turkey. While Russian policies in the Balkans and Transcaucasia brought Ankara into conflict with Moscow, Turkey needed to preserve a workable relationship, since the two countries had important mutual economic interests, and Turkey could not afford to run the risk of a head-on military clash with Russia. The fear that, if provoked, Russia might give all-out support to the PKK was another reason for caution. In Transcaucasia, Turkish governments had to perform a similar balancing act between Azerbaijan and Armenia, with Turkish public sympathies clearly on the Azeri side. At the same time, Turkey was too weak to play the role of arbiter in the region and had very little leverage over Armenia. In central Asia, also, expectations that Turkey would emerge as a regional power also failed to materialize, but this was probably because Turkish policy-makers had set themselves too ambitious an agenda in the first place.

In the Middle East, the most striking change in Turkish policy was the emergence of the entente with Israel. On the positive side, this strengthened Turkey's influence in Washington, and helped to tip the balance of power in favour of Turkey in its confrontation with Syria. Turkey's position in the Middle East would almost certainly have been far weaker if the Arab states had united, or had been uniformly anti-western. A significant demonstration of this was Hafiz al-Assad's climb-down in his confrontation with Turkey in the autumn of 1998 over Abdullah Öcalan, which showed both an impressive degree of Turkish regional power and the anxiety of Egypt to play the role of mediator, rather than give full support to Syria. In Iraq, also, Turkish policy benefited from serious splits within the Kurdish leadership, apart from the fact that the US effectively turned a blind eye to its military incursions into Iraqi Kurdistan. In spite of periodic clashes, Turkey managed to preserve a working relationship with Iran which was of value both politically and (potentially) economically.

Since 2002: Towards a new foreign policy?

After its ascent to power in 2002, the Justice and Development Party (AKP) depicted the previous ten years as the 'lost decade', claiming that in foreign relations, as in other areas of public policy, it would break new ground. If nothing else, the main architect of its strategy, Ahmet Davutoğlu, changed the language of foreign policy debates: his concepts of 'strategic depth', and of Turkey as a 'central country' were attempts to fit policy into a holistic conceptual framework it had previously lacked (p137). The aim of 'zero problems with neighbours' was a clear reaction to the highly securitized – even xenophobic – nationalism that had previously been advanced. Overall, it was presented as an alternative to previous policies which had been 'dominated ... by caution, passivity, and adherence to the status quo'.[1] But just how new, and how successful, was the AKP's much-publicized strategy?

On the first score, it could be argued that the principles of the new policy were less new than the conditions in which it operated. The continuity provided by ten years of single party government – the first such period since the 1950s – made it possible for the AKP to carry out a degree of long-range planning, without the need to bargain with jealous coalition partners, which its predecessors had significantly lacked. The IMF-inspired reform programme that followed the economic crash of 2001 (first adopted, be it noted, by the previous Ecevit government) set Turkey on a course of balanced and relatively stable economic growth that enabled it to shake off the effects of the global crisis of 2008, making it a point of attraction rather than an assumed liability for its allies and significantly increasing its soft power. On the other hand, the claim to novelty ignored the important changes, such as more active regional policies and an emphasis on economic cooperation as a means of international problem-solving, which had been developed by Turgut Özal more than a decade earlier. The improvement in relations with neighbouring states, albeit without the 'zero problems' label, had begun with the reconciliation with Greece in 1999, and initiated in the case of Syria by the Yılmaz government's successful tactics in 1998. In this way, the AKP administration successfully exploited pre-existing opportunities, rather than creating new ones. Nor was Davutoğlu the sole author or practitioner of the new strategies: as President, Abdullah Gül played an active diplomatic role, while Tayyip Erdoğan could apparently strike out on his own – for example, in relations with Israel – reflecting his close contact with grassroots public opinion.[2]

More controversially, it was argued that the AKP's policies, far from being new, were 'neo-Ottoman', implying a reversion to pre-republican practices. The argument was complicated by the fact that 'neo-Ottomanism' was often advanced as a domestic policy principle of multiculturalism, resting on the idealized vision of an Ottoman Empire in which people with diverse religious and ethnic identities supposedly lived in harmony. This principle had been adopted by Turgut Özal and promoted by the journalist Cengiz Çandar, aiming to reinstate Ottoman history and culture as part of Turkish collective memory.[3] The principle of cultural pluralism was used to address the Kurdish question, and could be adopted as the basis of more liberal, less ardently nationalist, foreign policies. However, 'neo-Ottomanism' was usually interpreted differently in the foreign policy context, where it could also be used to refer to the idea that Turkey should be more active in the former Ottoman space, stretching from the Balkans to the Middle East and North Africa.[4] This was seen as corresponding to Ahmet Davutoğlu's emphasis on Turkey's role in its geographical neighbourhood, most of which had once been part of the Ottoman Empire, and was used by the AKP's radical critics in the USA and elsewhere as the basis of a highly exaggerated argument to the effect that the AKP was turning Turkey away from the west towards a 'neo-Ottomanism' inspired by Muslim radicalism.[5] It was even argued that 'neo-Ottomanism' was a 'misnomer', since AKP policy allegedly 'ignores Israel, the Balkans and the Caucasus'.[6] Interpreted as a concrete project to re-build the Ottoman state territorially, it could have had exactly the opposite effects to those intended, since it was likely to provoke hostile reactions in the Arab world and among Balkan Christians, for whom collective memories were those of Ottoman autocracy, rather than benign multiculturalism.[7] Admittedly, in 1997, Necmettin Erbakan had referred to his goal of 'the creation of a greater Turkey just as the Ottomans did',[8] but apart from one stray remark in Bosnia in 2009 (p206), Ahmet Davutoğlu avoided repeating this line. While pursuing what he called a 'multi-dimensional and dynamic ... foreign policy',[9] he vigorously denied that he had ever used the term 'neo-Ottoman', stressing that Turkey respected the independence and equal status of all regional states.[10] There are no firm grounds to dispute this claim.

At the same time, there were strong arguments to the effect that Davutoğlu's policies were over-ambitious and less successful than he claimed. As part of his conception of Turkey as a 'central country', with interests and engagement in both the Balkans, Transcaucasia and the Black Sea, central Asia and the Middle East, it had to be accepted that Turkey was not the most influential external actor in any of them. In south-east Europe this role was clearly played by the European Union, while in the Black Sea, Transcaucasia and central Asia, Russia was still the dominant power, despite the demise of the Soviet Union. In the Middle East there was no dominant power, but instead a group of roughly equal powers – consisting of Turkey, Egypt, Saudi Arabia, Iran, Israel and (in normal times) Iraq, plus a number of smaller and weaker states – all jostling for dominance in an unstable pattern of enmities and alliances reminiscent of nineteenth-century Europe. Turkey's ability to project its power into any of these regions could be limited. Thus, being a 'central country' meant negotiation and compromise, with no certainty of being able to achieve ideal results for Turkey – relations with Russia, Iran, Armenia, Cyprus and Iraqi Kurdistan being apt examples. This probably accounted for Davutoğlu's emphasis on soft power, and 'a balance between security and democracy', rather than old-fashioned military force, but still pointed up some of the limitations of his strategy.[11]

Critics were also likely to argue that, by late 2011, the 'zero problems with neighbours' policy was in tatters, with tense if not outrightly hostile relations with Armenia, Syria, Israel and the Republic of Cyprus, and far from problem-free links with Iran and the Iraqi Kurds. The difficulty, it could be argued, was that if the neighbour refused to accept what the Turks regarded as reasonable conditions, and had the support of other powerful states, then problems would go unsolved – examples being Armenia, Israel and Cyprus.[12] Equally, hostilities between pairs of neighbouring states made it impossible to achieve 'zero problems' with both of them, as was illustrated by the cases of Armenia/Azerbaijan and Israel/Syria (in fact, in the last case, Turkey managed to have bad relations with both, but could hardly have done otherwise, given Israel's refusal to reach a reasonable accommodation over the *Mavi Marmara* affair, and the Syrian regime's brutal suppression of the opposition movement in 2011). On the other hand, arguing that the 'zero problems' policy had failed to achieve ideal results did not destroy the proposal that, as a general principle, it had been worth attempting, and that it had at least been better than the alternatives. As Hugh Pope suggests, the AKP's zero-problems policy had been 'largely beneficial ... It marks Turkey's move away from a reflexive defensive foreign policy, a decades-old holdover from the aftermath of the Ottoman collapse, and toward outreach and faith in win-win outcomes'.[13]

A more general criticism of the AKP's foreign policy strategies was that they lacked focus, and required Turkey to punch well above its weight. Rather than spread developing relationships to Africa and east and south-east Asia, it could be argued, Turkey should have concentrated on trying to resolve long-running problems nearer home. The Cyprus issue and relations with Greece were crucial examples, since they had wide repercussions, especially in Turkey's relations with the European Union. Offshore territorial disputes with Greece were far from insoluble, and a more resolute effort to solve them could have been made – including a resort to the World Court in The Hague, if that were needed. By opening its airports and harbours to Greek Cypriot planes and shipping, while stating clearly that this did not imply recognition of the Greek Cypriot government as the sole legitimate authority in the island, Turkey could have broken through the legal logjam caused by the additional protocol to the customs union agreement (pp189–90) and thus revitalized its accession negotiations. The claim that the EU should first adhere to its earlier undertaking to lift its trade embargo on the Turkish Cypriot state ignored the argument that, by insisting on a *quid pro quo* for anything seen as a concession, Turkish diplomacy locked itself into a series of impasses. Other moves that could have been made at little cost would have been the reduction of the large Turkish military detachment in Cyprus, and the re-opening of the Greek Orthodox seminary on the Marmara island of Heybeli (Halki), which would have greatly improved the psychological climate between Turkey and the Greek Cypriots, and mainland Greece, respectively.

In relations with Africa and the Middle East, Turkish policy could be accused or adopting double standards. Turkey strongly attacked Israel and the Syrian regime for flagrant human rights abuses in the occupied territories and the suppression of the Syrian opposition, even though its own human rights regime still fell short of international norms. Equally, it ignored the obvious shortcomings of despotic regimes like those of Iran and, more conspicuously, Sudan. On the latter score, in 2008, there was sharp criticism of the government, both in Turkey and abroad, when the Sudanese president, Omar Hassan al-Bashir was twice invited to Turkey, although the United Nations estimated that his regime had killed around 300,000 people in its suppression of the Darfur rebellion. Tayyip Erdoğan even claimed that the Sudanese regime had not committed genocide in Darfur, arguing that 'it is not possible for those who belong to the Muslim faith to commit genocide'.[14] In November 2009, the government compounded its mistake by inviting al-Bashir to Istanbul for a meeting of the Organization of the Islamic Conference, although by this stage the International Criminal Court had issued a warrant for his arrest. On this occasion, the visit was cancelled, although whether this was due to Turkish insistence was unclear.[15] By December 2011, when Tayyip

Erdoğan was vociferously supporting the 'Arab Spring', declaring that there would be no peace in the Middle East 'as long as there are dictators who open fire and massacre their own people',[16] there was clearly a need to be far more sensitive to democratic values in foreign policy than previously in order to avoid glaring inconsistencies.

For Turkey's allies, the biggest question was whether its disputes with the USA, dating from the invasion of Iraq and the collapse of the Turkish–Israeli entente, meant that Turkey was now 'turning away from the west'. In the Turkey–EU context, something of the same question could be asked, given the fall in public support in Turkey for the European project. Both these questions required nuanced answers, since there were contradictory trends within both theatres.

In the Turkey–EU context, answering the question was easier, in the sense that since 2005 it had been the EU (or at least an important part of it) that had turned away from Turkey, rather than the other way round. Given that the proclaimed European common security and defence policy had barely got off the ground, the relationship turned almost entirely on progress, or lack of it, in the accession negotiations, and European attitudes towards the prospect of eventual Turkish accession, which were mixed. This did not mean that Turkey had abandoned its European vocation, however, as government statements frequently emphasized. Even if they had doubts about the sincerity of the EU's commitments, Turkish leaders would have gained nothing by officially abandoning the aim of accession, so long as there was a long-run chance of achieving it. Given that most EU governments were not hostile to the idea of Turkish accession in principle, it would have been foolish for Turkey to abandon its quest, given the political as well as economic advantages of EU membership. There was also the distinct possibility of changes of government in France and Germany, which would radically improve the climate, provided progress could be made in resolving the Cyprus problem.

The Turkey–US relationship was simpler in the sense that this was a straightforward engagement between two sovereign states, but more complicated in that it embraced a host of third-party problems. After the crisis caused by parliament's refusal to support the US-led invasion of Iraq in 2003, plus the breakdown of the entente with Israel in 2009–10, it was clear that the relationship was under severe strain. For neo-conservative commentators such as Michael Rubin and Daniel Pipes, questions about Turkey's direction were clear: under the AKP, Turkey had fallen into the grip of Islamist extremists, who were dragging it away from the west.[17] Other observers felt little difficulty in refuting these views, arguing that Turkey wanted to reach out to the Middle East to complement its relations with the west, not to replace them.[18] The AKP's re-engagement with the Middle East was a practical response to strategic realities, not a blind application of Islamist ideology, it was maintained.[19] In practice, the Turkish–US alliance was quite mercurial, and contingent on the ebb and flow of diplomatic convergences. By 2011, it appeared to be back on as firm a footing as ever. Differences over Iran and Israel were more than outweighed by the need of both Turkey and the US to secure stability in Iraq, Turkish participation in Afghan peacekeeping, Turkey's expected role in the anti-missile defence shield, and common support for the 'Arab Spring'. In response, Washington pledged support for Turkey in its struggle against the PKK.[20]

Admittedly, Congress was far less positive in its attitude towards Turkey than the White House, thanks to the power of the pro-Israel lobby. There were also worries that, if they abided by their rhetoric in the pre-primary campaigns and later won the 2012 presidential elections, then any of the Republican candidates could be far more hostile, even outrightly anti-Muslim.[21] Against this, it was a mark of Turkey's enhanced international importance, as well as the closeness of its ties with the west, that in September 2011, Barack Obama was reported to have placed more telephone calls in that year to Tayyip Erdoğan than to any other world leader except the British Premier David Cameron,[22] while Britain's foreign secretary William Hague revealed that he made as many calls to Ahmet Davutoğlu as to Hillary Clinton.[23] Occasionally, Turkish critics argued for an alternative 'Eurasian' alliance (whether this was to be with Russia, central Asia, China, or even Iran was never made clear) but this was at best a highly nebulous concept, without any historical, cultural or ideological underpinnings. In spite of the tensions, and in an un-ideal world, Turkey had was still likely to opt for its western engagement as the best alternative, reflecting a skilful diplomatic tradition stretching back for almost 250 years.

Notes

Introduction

1 Of the alternative conceptual frameworks, the most prominent are those developed by Turkey's current (2011) foreign minister Ahmet Davutoğlu which are outlined on pp137–8. These offer useful clues to Davutoğlu's thinking, but seem less satisfactory as an explanation of actual behaviour, especially in the historical past. Other literature treats Turkey as a 'pivotal state' in the international system. This takes off from the proposal by Robert S. Chase, Emily B. Hill and Paul Kennedy, that such a state is one 'whose fate is uncertain, and whose future will profoundly affect ... [its] surrounding regions' – a 'hot spot that could not only determine the fate of its region, but also affect international stability': (Robert S. Chase, Emily B. Hill and Paul Kennedy, 'Pivotal States and US Strategy', *Foreign Affairs*, 75:1 [1996] p33). Among other points, they identify the Ottoman Empire as 'a classical example of a pivotal state throughout the nineteenth century' (ibid, p34). In a recent overall study of Turkey's international policies, Graham E. Fuller refers to the 'pivotal state' label in his title, but does not develop it in his text: (*The New Turkish Republic: Turkey as a Pivotal State in the Muslim World* [Washington, DC: United States Institute of Peace Press, 2008]). The only thorough exploration of the idea in the Turkish context which the writer knows of is that of Alan O. Makovsky, in a paper published in 1999: ('Turkey', in Robert S. Chase, Emily B. Hill and Paul Kennedy (eds), *The Pivotal States: A New Framework for US Policy in the Developing World* [New York, NY, and London: W.W.Norton, 1999] pp88–119). Although the challenges to Turkey's stability that he identifies (notably from Islamist radicalism and the military-civilian political contest) now seem less acute than they were at the time he was writing, Makovsky provides an important analysis of Turkish–US relations. However, like that of his editors, his main focus is on US policy, and how it should be developed, rather than that of the 'pivotal state' itself, which is the main concern of this book.

2 These suggestions are based on the proposals of David Vital, *The Inequality of States: A Study of the Small Power in International Relations* (Oxford: Clarendon Press, 1967); Carsten Holbraad, *Middle Powers in International Politics* (London: Macmillan, 1984); and Robert L. Rothstein, *Alliances and Small Powers* (New York and London: Columbia University Press, 1968).

3 See Morton A. Kaplan, *System and Process in International Politics* (New York: Wiley, 1957) Preface and pp22–28, and A.J.P. Taylor, *The Struggle for Mastery in Europe, 1848–1918* (Oxford: Oxford University Press, 1954) ppxix–xxiv.

4 Annette Baker Fox, *The Power of Small States: Diplomacy in World War II* (Chicago: University of Chicago Press, 1959) pp1–4, 8–9.

5 Fred Halliday prefers a more complicated periodisation, seeing the period 1946–53 as 'Cold War I', that of 1953–69 as one of 'Oscillatory Antagonism', and starting the period of détente in 1969, running through to 1979: Fred Halliday, *The Making of the Second Cold War* (2nd edn, London: Verso, 1986) pp3, 10–11.
6 Data from William Hale, The *Political and Economic Development of Modern Turkey* (London: Croom Helm, 1981) pp18–19, 67, and *Statistical Yearbook of Turkey 2010* (Ankara: Turkish Statistical Institute, 2011) pp43, 45, 56. The population projection is from data issued by the Turkish Industrialists and Businessmen's Association (TÜSİAD) quoted in *Hürriyet* newspaper, 14 January 1999.
7 *Statistical Yearbook of Turkey 1998*, p654: 2011 data from website of Turkish Statistical Institute (www.tuik.gov.tr) national income statistics
8 Data from website of World Bank (www.worldbank.org).
9 Data from website of Turkish Statistical Institute (www.tuik.gov.tr) national income and foreign trade statistics.
10 See *The Economist*, 10–16 December 2011, p76.

1 Foreign relations of the late Ottoman Empire, 1774–1918

1 Quoted, F.R. Bridge, 'The Habsburg Monarchy and the Ottoman Empire, 1900–1918', in Marian Kent (ed.), *The Great Powers and the End of the Ottoman Empire* (London: Cass, 2nd edn, 1996) p42. Officially, Austria became 'Austria-Hungary' with the establishment of the Dual Monarchy in 1867. In this chapter it is referred to throughout simply as 'Austria'.
2 Feroz Ahmad, 'The Late Ottoman Empire', in ibid, p6.
3 See Roderic H. Davison, *Reform in the Ottoman Empire, 1856–1876* (Princeton: Princeton University Press, 1963) pp136–71. For shorter accounts, see, e.g., Bernard Lewis, *The Emergence of Modern Turkey* (London: Oxford University Press, 1961) pp381–4, and Stanford J. Shaw and Ezel Kural Shaw, *History of the Ottoman Empire and Modern Turkey* (Cambridge: Cambridge University Press, 1977) vol 2, pp83–91.
4 Shaw and Shaw, *History*, vol 2, p242.
5 This calculation excludes Serbia, the Danubian principalities, Egypt, and the rest of north Africa, which were only nominally under Ottoman rule at the time. Data from Nuri Akbayar, 'Tanzimat'tan Sonra Osmanlı Devleti Nüfusu', *Tanzimat'tan Cumhuriyet'e Türkiye Ansiklopedisi* (Istanbul: İletişim Yayınları, 1985) vol 5, pp1239–40.
6 Stanford J. Shaw, 'The Ottoman Census System and Population, 1831–1914', *International Journal of Middle East Studies* vol 9 (1978) pp325–38; Meir Zamir, 'Population Statistics of the Ottoman Empire in 1914 and 1918', *Middle Eastern Studies* vol 17 (1981) p100.
7 Erik J. Zürcher, *Turkey: A Modern History* (London: I.B. Tauris, 1993) pp12–13, disputes the idea that the *milletbaşıs* actually commanded their religious communities: instead, power was dispersed, with local communities enjoying some autonomy *vis-à-vis* local representatives of the Ottoman government. For an account of the *millet* system, and its reform in the nineteenth century, see Davison, *Reform*, Ch4.
8 For an excellent summary, see Hugh Poulton, *Top Hat, Grey Wolf and Crescent: Turkish Nationalism and the Turkish Republic* (London: Hurst, 1997) Ch2.
9 Akbayar, 'Tanzimat'tan Sonra', pp1242–3; Justin McCarthy, *Death and Exile: The Ethnic Cleansing of Ottoman Muslims, 1821–1922* (Princeton: Darwin Press, 1995) esp. pp1–5, 333–40.
10 F.A.K. Yasamee, *Ottoman Diplomacy: Abdülhamid II and the Great Powers, 1878–1888* (Istanbul: Isis, 1996) pp2–4, 45–6, and 'Abdülhamid II and the Ottoman Defence Problem', *Diplomacy and Statecraft* vol 4 (1993) pp22–3. For a summary

of Ottoman military reforms in the nineteenth century, see William Hale, *Turkish Politics and the Military* (London: Routledge, 1994) pp15–24, 28–9.

11 Notably, from Yasamee, *Ottoman Diplomacy.*

12 Ibid, pp30–9; Kemal Girgin, *Osmanlı ve Cumhuriyet Dönemleri Hariciye Tarihimiz (Teşkilat ve Protokol)* (Ankara: Türk Tarih Kurumu, 1992) pp15–18, 40–8: J.C. Hurewitz, 'Ottoman Diplomacy and the European State System', *Middle East Journal* vol 15 (1961) pp141–52; Lewis, *Emergence,* pp60–1: Shaw and Shaw, *History,* vol 2, pp62, 72–3: İlber Ortaylı, 'Osmanlı Dipolmasisi ve Dışişleri Örgütü', *Tanzimat'tan Cumhuryet'e Türkiye Ansiklopedisi* (see note 4) vol 1, pp278–81.

13 Quoted, Yasamee, *Ottoman Diplomacy,* p43.

14 This generalization needs some qualification, since it applied particularly to the latter half of the nineteenth century rather than the first. Until the 1860s, Britain's relatively small but professional army was roughly comparable in effectiveness to those of the main continental powers: after then, it fell well behind them, as first Prussia and then the other powers built up mass armies based on universal conscription. Britain failed to follow suit, preferring to concentrate expenditure on its navy. See A.J.P. Taylor, *The Struggle for Mastery in Europe, 1848–1918* (Oxford: Oxford University Press, 1954) ppxix–xxiv.

15 Yasamee, *Ottoman Diplomacy,* pp43–5, 107–9, 184–5 and 'Abdülhamid', pp20–1, 26–9; Selim Deringil, 'Aspects of Continuity in Turkish Foreign Policy: Abdülhamid II and İsmet İnönü', *International Journal of Turkish Studies* vol 4 (1987) pp39–43.

16 See, in particular, M.S. Anderson, *The Eastern Question, 1774–1923: A Study in International Relations* (London: Macmillan, 1966), and J.A.R. Marriott, *The Eastern Question: An Historical Study in European Diplomacy* (Oxford: Clarendon Press, 4th edn, 1940). More Turkish-centred studies are those of Yasamee, *Ottoman Diplomacy*; Shaw and Shaw, *History,* vol 2, Chs1–4, and Zürcher, *Turkey,* Chs1–8.

17 Anderson, *Eastern Question,* ppxi–xii, 1–9, 13–20; Marriott, *Eastern Question,* pp151–4, 158, 163–4.

18 Anderson, *Eastern Question,* pp26–47; Marriott, *Eastern Question,* pp167–73.

19 Anderson, *Eastern Question,* pp48–50, 53–7, 67–8, 73–6; J.C.B. Richmond, *Egypt, 1798–1952* (London: Methuen, 1977) pp36–8, 47–9, 62–9.

20 Anderson, *Eastern Question,* pp65–73, 77–87, 95–107; Marriott, *Eastern Question,* pp183, 221–45; Richmond, *Egypt,* pp50–62. On Russia's rights at the straits under the 1833 and previous treaties, see J.C. Hurewitz, 'Russia and the Turkish Straits: a Revaluation of the Origins of the Problem', *World Politics* vol 14 (1961–2) pp607–32.

21 Quoted, Frank Edgar Bailey, *British Policy and the Turkish Reform Movement: A Study in Anglo-Turkish Relations, 1826–1853* (Cambridge, MA: Harvard University Press, 1942) p209.

22 Ibid, p228. Bailey's argument is confirmed by the work of other scholars, working from Ottoman sources – notably, Lewis, *Emergence*; Shaw and Shaw, *History*; and Davison, *Reform.*

23 Anderson, *Eastern Question,* pp116–43; Marriott, *Eastern Question,* pp256–78; Shaw and Shaw, *History,* vol 2, pp140–1. On the last point, see Hurewitz, 'Ottoman Diplomacy', pp151–2. For the texts of the *Hatt-i Şerif* and the *Hatt-i Hümayun,* see Bailey, *British Policy,* pp277–9, 287–91.

24 In 1866, Ottoman suzerainty in Moldavia and Wallachia became a pure formality, following internal upheavals. Serbia also became virtually independent, although under strong Austrian influence, following the withdrawal of the last Ottoman garrisons in 1867. Conflict between the Druzes and Maronites in the Lebanon had meanwhile led to French intervention and the establishment of the autonomous district (*sancak*) of Mount Lebanon in 1861. See Anderson, *Eastern Question,* pp152–8, 164–6; Shaw and Shaw, *History,* vol 2, pp141–4, 147–9.

25 For details, see Robert Devereux, *The First Ottoman Constitutional Period* (Baltimore: Johns Hopkins Press, 1963). Following his deposition, Abdul Aziz committed suicide in June 1876.

26 Strictly speaking, this was not part of the treaty of Berlin but agreed to by a separate convention between the British and Ottoman governments signed in June 1878. In return, Britain was supposed to aid the Ottoman Empire if Russia attacked it in the east. The British did not officially annex Cyprus until 1914.

27 Anderson, *Eastern Question*, pp169–73, 178–217, 226; Shaw and Shaw, *History*, vol 2, pp158–67, 172–4, 182–4, 186–91.

28 Yasamee, *Ottoman Diplomacy*, pp24–30, 89–90.

29 Ibid, pp51, 80–1, 84, 184–6, 189–91, 255–9.

30 E.M. Earle, *Turkey, the Great Powers and the Baghdad Railway* (New York: Macmillan, 1923) pp40, 43, 53, 68–70, 104–6; Charles Issawi, *An Economic History of the Middle East and North Africa* (London: Methuen, 1982) p69; H.C. Meyer, 'German Economic Relations with South-Eastern Europe, 1870–1914', *American Historical Review* vol 62 (1951–2) p85; Anderson, *Eastern Question*, pp263–7.

31 Feroz Ahmad, *The Young Turks: The Committee of Union and Progress in Turkish Politics, 1908–1914* (Oxford: Oxford University Press, 1969) pp1–13; Shaw and Shaw, *History*, vol 2, pp206–11, 266–7, 273–9; Anderson, *Eastern Question*, pp262–3, 268–78.

32 Although the annexation of Bosnia-Herzegovina provoked the most serious concerns among the European powers, the clash with Bulgaria was a more immediate worry for the Ottoman government, since Bulgaria was well-armed and could have launched an assault on Ottoman territory before the Turks could have mobilized in response. In the event, war was avoided, and the Ottoman parliament recognized Bulgaria's independence in April–May 1909. For details, see Hasan Ünal, 'Ottoman Policy during the Bulgarian Independence Crisis, 1908–9: Ottoman Empire and Bulgaria at the Outset of the Young Turk Revolution', *Middle Eastern Studies* vol 34 (1998) pp140, 147, 165–6.

33 Under the treaty of Ouchy of 15 October 1912: Italy also gained 'temporary' possession of the Dodecanese islands, in the southern Aegean.

34 Shaw and Shaw, *History*, vol 2, pp279–87, 290–2, 298–305.

35 Hasan Ünal, 'Young Turks Assessments of International Politics, 1906–9', *Middle Eastern Studies* Vol.32 (1996) pp30–44, reprinted in Sylvia Kedourie (ed.), *Turkey; Identity, Democracy, Politics* (London and Portland, OR: Cass, 1996) and 'Ottoman Policy', pp135, 137–9, 167.

36 Joseph Heller, *British Policy towards the Ottoman Empire, 1908–1914* (London: Frank Cass, 1983) pp13, 23–6, 29–31, 78, 98–100; Feroz Ahmad, 'Great Britain's Relations with the Young Turks, 1908–14', *Middle Eastern Studies* vol 2 (1965–6) pp309–15; Elie Kedourie, 'Young Turks, Freemasons and Jews', *Middle Eastern Studies* vol 7 (1971) pp89–104.

37 Heller, *British Policy*, pp11, 16, 35, 53, 63–4, 74–5, 80; Ahmad, 'Great Britain's Relations', pp309, 319–21.

38 Heller, *British Policy*, pp78–80; Shaw and Shaw, *History*, vol 2, pp292–8; Mustafa Aksakal, *The Ottoman Road to War in 1914: The Ottoman Empire and the First World War* (Cambridge: Cambridge University Press, 2008) p77.

39 Aksakal, *Ottoman Road to War*, pp15, 34.

40 Heller, *British Policy*, p134.

41 Aksakal, *Ottoman Road to War*, pp69, 96–8.

42 Quoted, Heller, *British Policy*, pp136–7.

43 Ahmad, 'Great Britain's Relations', p325.

44 Ibid, pp324–5; Anderson, *Eastern Question*, pp311–14; Shaw and Shaw, *History*, vol 2, pp310–12; Ulrich Trumpener, 'Turkey's Entry into World War I: An Assessment

of Responsibilities', *Journal of Modern History* vol 34 (1962) pp369–80, and, 'Germany and the End of the Ottoman Empire', in Kent (ed.), *Great Powers,* p124.

45 Shaw and Shaw, *History,* vol 2, pp315–17, adhere to the Turkish account, whereas Zürcher, *Turkey,* p121, believes that there was a centrally controlled policy of extermination, ordered by Talat and an inner circle within the Young Turk regime. For a review of the dispute, see Gwynne Dyer, 'Turkish "Falsifiers" and Armenian "Deceivers": Historiography and the Armenian Massacres', *Middle Eastern Studies* vol 12 (1976) pp99–107.

46 See Frank Weber, *Eagles on the Crescent: Germany, Austria and the Diplomacy of the Turkish Alliance, 1914–1918* (Ithaca and London: Cornell University Press, 1970) pp135–6, 153–4.

47 Gwynne Dyer, 'The Turkish Armistice of 1918: 1 – The Turkish Decision for a Separate Peace, Autumn 1918', *Middle Eastern Studies* vol 8 (1972) pp143–6, 150–1, 158–69.

48 Full text in Gwynne Dyer, 'The Turkish Armistice of 1918: 2 – A Lost Opportunity: The Armistice Negotiations of Moudros', *Middle Eastern Studies* vol 8 (1972) pp340–1.

49 The only such case which springs to mind is that of the Turkish Cypriots.

50 See Poulton, *Top Hat,* pp265–9. This process was not completed until some time after the First World War, under the population exchanges provided for by the treaty of Lausanne: see p40.

2 Resistance, reconstruction and diplomacy, 1918–39

1 Strictly speaking, Mustafa Kemal did not become 'Kemal Atatürk' until 1934, when the adoption of surnames became compulsory in Turkey. When referring to events before 1934, other personalities are referred to by their first names, with their later surnames in brackets.

2 For the text of the Treaty of Sèvres and the attached agreement between Britain, France and Italy, see J.C. Hurewitz (ed.), *Diplomacy in the Near and Middle East: A Documentary Record, 1914–1956* (Princeton: Van Nostrand, 1956) vol 2, pp81–9. For a full description, with maps, see Baskın Oran, 'Sèvres Barış Antlaşması', in Baskın Oran (ed.), *Türk Dış Politikası,* (Istanbul: İletişim Yayınları, 2001) vol 1, pp124–38.

3 That is, the secret Treaty of London of April 1915 and the St. Jean de Maurienne agreement of April 1917: for texts, see Hurewitz, *Diplomacy,* vol 2, pp11–12, 23–5. For details of the negotiations between the entente powers over the future of Turkey between 1918 and 1920, see Harry N. Howard, *The Partition of Turkey: A Diplomatic History, 1913–1923* (New York: Fertig, 1966) pp217–41.

4 Quotation from Atatürk's 'Great Speech' (effectively, his memoirs): *Speech Delivered by Ghazi Mustapha Kemal, President of the Turkish Republic, October 1927* (Leipzig: K.F. Koehler, 1929) p58.

5 Roderic H. Davison, 'Turkish Diplomacy from Mudros to Lausanne', in Gordon A. Craig and Felix Gilbert (eds), *The Diplomats, 1919–1939* (New York: Atheneum, 1974) vol 1, p179.

6 From Article 1 of the National Pact. Turkish text in A. Suat Bilge, et al., *Olaylarla Türk Dış Politikası* (Ankara University, Political Science Faculty, 1969) pp13–14: English translation in Hurewitz, *Diplomacy,* vol 2, pp74–5.

7 Bülent Gökay, *A Clash of Empires: Turkey Between Russian Bolshevism and British Imperialism, 1918–1923* (London: I.B. Tauris, 1997) pp77–8.

8 Kemal Girgin, *Osmanlı ve Cumhuriyet Dönemleri Hariciye Tarihimiz (Teşkilat ve Protokol)* (Ankara: Türk Tarih Kurumu, 1992) pp118–23.

9 M.S. Anderson, *The Eastern Question, 1774–1923: A Study in International Relations* (London: Macmillan, 1966) p368.

10 Marian Kent, 'British Policy, International Diplomacy and the Turkish Revolution', *Internatonal Journal of Turkish Studies* vol 3 (1985–6) pp33–8.

11 Gökay, *Clash of Empires*, pp52–60.

12 Quoted, Jacob M. Landau, *Pan-Turkism: From Irredentism to Cooperation* (London: Hurst, 1995) p74.

13 This territory had been ceded by the Ottoman Empire to Russia under the Treaty of Berlin of 1878, but evacuated by Russia under the Brest–Litovsk Treaty between the Bolsheviks and the central powers of March 1918. The Turks, in turn, had evacuated it eight months later under the terms of the Mudros armistice, and it had hence been occupied by Armenia.

14 Salahi Ransdan Sonyel, *Turkish Diplomacy, 1913–1923: Mustafa Kemal and the Turkish National Movement* (London and Beverly Hills: Sage, 1975) pp48–65; Gökay, *Clash of Empires*, pp85–112; Bülent Gökay, 'Turkish Settlement and the Caucasus, 1918–20', in Sylvia Kedourie (ed.), *Turkey; Identity, Democracy, Politics* (London and Portland, OR: Cass, 1996) pp45–76, reprinted from *Middle Eastern Studies* vol 32 (1996) pp45–76; Bülent Gökay, *Soviet Eastern Policy and Turkey, 1920–1991: Soviet Foreign Policy, Turkey and Communism* (London and New York: Routledge, 2006) pp20–4. For the text of the Turco-Soviet treaty of 1921, see Hurewitz, *Diplomacy*, vol 2, pp95–7. Among other things, under Article 3, the treaty provided that the enclave of Nakhichevan 'shall form an autonomous territory under the protection of Azerbaijan, on condition that the latter cannot transfer this protectorate to any third state' (read, Armenia). For further information on early communist movements in Turkey, see George S. Harris, *The Origins of Communism in Turkey* (Stanford: Hoover Institution, 1967), and for a detailed study of Turco-Soviet relations between 1919 and 1921, see A. Suat Bilge, *Güç Komşuluk: Türkiye-Sovyetler Birliği İlişkileri, 1920–1964* (Ankara: Türkiye İş Bankası Kültür Yayınları, 1992) pp26–78.

15 See Gökay, *A Clash of Empires*, pp109–11 and *Soviet Eastern Policy*, pp28–9. For details of the war materiel sent by the Bolsheviks to the nationalists, see Stefanos Yerasimos, *Türk-Sovyet İlişkileri, Ekim Devrimden 'Milli Mücadele'ye* (Istanbul: Gözlem Yayınları, 1979) pp631–6.

16 Gökay, *A Clash of Empires*, p86.

17 Ibid, pp123–7; Sonyel, *Turkish Diplomacy*, pp96–107, 135–9; Davison, 'Turkish Diplomacy', pp188–90, 192–3. For the full text of the 'Franklin–Bouillon Pact', see Hurewitz, *Diplomacy*, vol 2, pp98–100.

18 Sonyel, *Turkish Diplomacy*, pp161–73; Davison, 'Turkish Diplomacy', pp196–7; Osman Okyar, 'Turco-British Relations in the Inter-War Period: Fethi Okyar's Missions to London', in William Hale and Ali İkhsan Bağış (eds), *Four Centuries of Turco-British Relations* (Walkington: Eothen Press, 1984) pp71–4.

19 Sonyel, *Turkish Diplomacy*, pp173–82; Davison, 'Turkish Diplomacy', pp198–9; Gökay, *A Clash of Empires*, pp136–46.

20 Quoted, A.L. Macfie, *The Straits Question, 1908–36* (Thessaloniki: Institute for Balkan Studies, 1993) p181.

21 For the details, see Howard, *Partition*, pp281–5, and Baskın Oran, 'Lausanne Barış Antlaşması' in Oran (ed.), *Türk Dış Politikası*, vol 1, pp223–32. Italy had originally been granted 'temporary' possession of the Dodecanese after the Turco-Italian war of 1912: see above p262, footnote 33. For the full text of the treaty of Lausanne, see *Treaty of Peace with Turkey and other Instruments signed at Lausanne on July 24, 1923* (London: HMSO, 1923: Cmd 1929).

22 The new rules were laid down in a 'Convention on the Regime of the Straits', attached to the treaty of Lausanne. For details, see Hurewitz, *Diplomacy*, vol 2, pp124–7; Oran 'Lausanne', pp232–5: Harry N. Howard, *Turkey, the Straits and*

US Policy (Baltimore and London: Johns Hopkins University Press, 1974) pp113–26, 303–13; A.L. Macfie, 'The Straits Question: The Conference of Lausanne (November 1922–July 1923)', *Middle Eastern Studies* vol 15 (1979) pp211–38, and Macfie, *Straits Question*, pp181–211.

23 Quoted, David McDowall, *A Modern History of the Kurds* (London: I.B. Tauris, 1996) p190.

24 The British-controlled Turkish Petroleum Company (TPC) had obtained a concession covering the Mosul province from the Ottoman government just before the outbreak of the First World War. On the other side, the Ankara government granted a concession for, among other things, the oil rights in Mosul to an American consortium headed by Admiral Colby M. Chester, Commander Arthur Chester and Colonel Clayton Kennedy (the 'Chester concession') in April 1923. See Peter J.Beck, '"A Tedious and Perilous Controversy": Britain and the Settlement of the Mosul Dispute, 1918–26', *Middle Eastern Studies* vol 17 (1981) p258. On the Chester concession, see Selim İlkin, 'The Chester Railway Project', in Türkiye İş Bankası, *International Symposium on Atatürk (17 22 May 1981): Papers and Discussions* (Ankara: Türkiye İş Bankası Kültür Yayınları, 1984) pp769–817, and Bilmez Bülent Can, *Demiryolundan Petrole Chester Projesi (1908–1923)* (Istanbul: Tarih Vakfı Yurt Yayınları, 2000).

25 See Doğu Perinçek (ed.), *Mustafa Kemal Eskişehir-İzmit Konuşmaları* (Istanbul: Kaynak Yayınları, 1993) pp94–7.

26 Beck, 'Mosul Dispute', pp256–61; Howard, *Partition*, pp297–301; Sonyel, *Turkish Diplomacy*, pp195–6, 223–5.

27 See p9.

28 *Treaty of Peace ... Protocol relating to Certain Concessions Granted in the Ottoman Empire*, p203; *Commercial Convention*, p157. On the economic effects of the tariff limitation, see William Hale, 'The Traditional and Modern in the Economy of Kemalist Turkey', in J.M. Landau (ed.), *Atatürk and the Modernization of Turkey* (Boulder, CO: Westview Press, 1984) pp153–70.

29 Z.Y. Hershlag, *Turkey, an Economy in Transition* (The Hague: van Keulen, 1958) p21.

30 The population figures cited here are taken from Erik Zürcher, *Turkey: A Modern History* (London: I.B. Tauris, 1993) pp171–2. Other sources cite far higher figures for the total of Greek refugees and deportees.

31 Mehmet Gönlübol and Cem Sar, *Atatürk ve Türkiye'nin Dış Politikası 1919–1939* (Ankara: Milli Eğitim Basımevi, 1963) p90, footnote 86; quoted, Malik Mufti, 'Daring and Caution in Turkish Foreign Policy', *Middle East Journal* vol 52, no 1 (1998) p33.

32 These events are well-described and analysed in a large body of literature: see, in particular, Erik J. Zürcher, *The Unionist Factor: The Role of the Committee of Union and Progress in the Turkish National Movement* (Leiden: Brill, 1984) and *Political Opposition in the Early Turkish Republic: The Progressive Republican Party 1924– 1925* (Leiden: Brill, 1991). On the Sheikh Saiyid rebellion, see McDowall, *Modern History*, pp194–8. On the 1930 experiment, see Walter F. Weiker, *Political Tutelage and Democracy in Turkey: The Free Party and its Aftermath* (Leiden: Brill, 1973).

33 From Grew's memoirs: quoted in Feroz Ahmad, 'The Historical Background of Turkey's Foreign Policy', in Lenore G. Martin and Dimitris Keridis (eds), *The Future of Turkish Foreign Policy* (London and Cambridge, MA: MIT Press, 2004) p18.

34 This was subsequently commuted as a single cash payment of £500,000 sterling.

35 Stephen F. Evans, *The Slow Rapprochement: Britain and Turkey in the Age of Kemal Atatürk, 1919–38* (Walkington: Eothen Press, 1982) pp80–97; Beck, 'Mosul Dispute', pp261–73; McDowall, *Modern History*, pp143–6; Bilge, et al., *Olaylarla*, pp75–82: Aptülahat Akşin, *Atatürk'ün Dış Politika İlkeleri ve Diplomasisi* (Ankara: Türk Tarih Kurumu, 1991) pp126–31.

36 Bilge, et al., *Olaylarla*, pp67–75.
37 Dilek Barlas and Serhat Güvenç, 'Turkey and the Idea of a European Union during the Inter-war Years, 1923–39', *Middle Eastern Studies* vol 35, no 3 (2009) pp432–7.
38 Bilge, *Güç Komşuluk*, p112
39 Quoted, Brock Milman, 'Turkish Foreign and Strategic Policy, 1934–42', *Middle Eastern Studies* vol 31 (1995) p491.
40 Milman, 'Turkish Policy', p487; Bilge, et al., *Olaylarla*, p156
41 Cem Emrence, 'Rearticulating the Local, Regional and Global: The Greek–Turkish Rapprochement of 1930', *Turkish Studies* vol 4, no 3 (2003) pp31–2.
42 Bilge, et al., *Olaylarla*, pp87–90, 119; Melek Fırat, 'Yunanistan'la İlişkiler', in Oran (ed.), *Türk Dış Politikası*, vol 1, pp344–5.
43 Quoted, Dilek Barlas, *Etatism and Diplomacy in Turkey: Economic and Foreign Policy Strategies in an Uncertain World, 1929–1939* (Leiden, New York and Cologne: Brill, 1998) p156; see also Yücel Güçlü, 'Turco-British Relations on the Eve of the Second World War', *Middle Eastern Studies* vol 39, no 4 (2003) pp165–6.
44 Quoted, Milman, 'Turkish Policy', p489. See also Mustafa Türkeş, 'The Balkan Pact and its Immediate Implications for the Balkan States, 1930–34', *Middle Eastern Studies* vol 30 (1994) pp122–30.
45 Türkeş, 'Balkan Pact', pp131–41; Barlas, *Etatism and Diplomacy*, pp142–5; Bilge, et al, *Olaylarla*, pp106–14; Milman, 'Turkish Policy', p491.
46 Bilge et al., *Olaylarla*, p120: Milman, 'Turkish Policy', pp485–86.
47 Barlas, *Etatism and Diplomacy*, pp130–1.
48 During the Kurdish rebellion centred on Mount Ararat in 1929–30, rebel forces had moved into Turkey from Iranian territory, but conflict with Iran on this point had been removed by the subsequent Turco-Iranian frontier agreement: see McDowall, *Modern History*, pp204–6.
49 Bilge, et al., *Olaylarla*, pp114–17; Akşin, *Atatürk'ün*, pp198–9; Atay Akdevelioğlu and Ömer Kürkçüoğlu, 'Orta Doğu'yla İlişkiler' in Oran (ed.), *Türk Dış Politikası*, vol 1, pp365–9.
50 The story first appeared 19 years later in an unsigned article in the magazine *Caucasus*, entitled 'Atatürk–MacArthur Astounding Political Prophets' (no 1, 1951, pp1–4); it is repeated in, for example, Milman, 'Turkish Policy', p505 footnote 27, Akşin, *Atatürk'ün*, pp163–5, and (unattributed) in Altemur Kılıç, *Turkey and the World*, (Washington: Public Affairs Press, 1959) p59. However, if it took place in the form described then one would expect to find some record of it in contemporary or near-contemporary accounts and no such record can be found. The writer is very grateful to Dr Andrew Mango for advice and information on this point.
51 Conversation between Atatürk and Loraine of May 1936: quoted, Milman, 'Turkish Policy', p488.
52 Quoted, ibid, p490, from British Foreign Office records.
53 Montreux Convention, Articles 10, 11, 14 and Annex II B. For the full text of the Convention, with Annexes, see Turkish Straits Voluntary Watch Group, *Turkish Straits: New Problems, New Solutions* (Istanbul: Isis, for Foundation for Middle East and Balkan Studies, 1995) pp10–24. For details on the Montreux negotiations, see Howard, *Straits*, pp130–60; Macfie, *Straits Question*, pp213–27; Evans, *Slow Rapprochement*, pp100–1; Kudret Özersay, 'Montreux Boğazlar Sözleşmesi', in Oran (ed.), *Türk Dış Politikası*, vol 1, pp370–84.
54 Montreux Convention, Articles 18–21, 24.
55 Milman, 'Turkish Policy', p492.
56 Selim Deringil, *Turkish Foreign Policy during the Second World War: An 'Active' Neutrality* (Cambridge: Cambridge University Press, 1989) pp12–27, 31–40. See also Hershlag, *Turkey*, pp113–14, and William Hale, *The Political and Economic Development of Modern Turkey* (London: Croom Helm, 1981) pp55–59.

57 The latter loan was agreed as part of the alliance between the three countries of October 1939.
58 Milman, 'Turkish Policy', pp493–7; Deringil, *Foreign Policy*, pp35–8; Türkayya Ataöv, *Turkish Foreign Policy, 1939–1945* (Ankara University, Political Science Faculty, 1965) p9.
59 In, for instance, opposing Atatürk's policy at the Nyon conference as being too pro-British and confrontational. He was also more cautious in his approach to the Alexandretta dispute in 1936–8: Barlas, *Etatism and Diplomacy*, p113.
60 Bilge, *Güç Komşuluk*, pp120–8.
61 Gordon Waterfield, *Professional Diplomat: Sir Percy Loraine of Kirkharle Bt., 1880–1961* (London: Murray, 1973) p221.
62 In accordance with the arrangements agreed to at the conference of Nyon, September 1937, see Yücel Güçlü, 'The Nyon Arrangement of 1937 and Turkey', *Middle Eastern Studies* vol 38, no 1 (2002) pp61–3. On İnönü's attitude, see ibid, p64.
63 Güçlü, 'Turco-British Relations', p172.
64 Ibid, pp179, 181–7; Frank Marzari, 'Western–Soviet Rivalry in Turkey, 1939', Part I, *Middle Eastern Studies* vol 7 (1971) pp67–9, 72: quotations from ibid, p72.
65 Figures from Robert B. Satloff, 'Prelude to Conflict: Communal Interdependence in the Sanjak of Alexandretta 1920–36', *Middle Eastern Studies* vol 22 (1986) p154, and Avedis K. Sanjian, 'The Sanjak of Alexandretta (Hatay): Its Impact on Turkish–Syrian Relations (1939–56)', *Middle East Journal* vol 10 (1956) p380.
66 See Yücel Güçlü, 'The Controversy over the Delimitation of the Turco-Syrian Frontier in the Period between the Two World Wars', *Middle Eastern Studies* vol 42, no 4 (2006) pp641–57.
67 In fact, it remained a dead letter, since it was not ratified by the French National Assembly.
68 Satloff, 'Prelude', pp173–6; Sanjian, 'Sanjak', pp380–1; Marzari, 'Western–Soviet Rivalry', Part I, pp71–2. For a Turkish account, see Bilge, et al., *Olaylarla*, pp137–44.
69 Frank G.Weber, *The Evasive Neutral: Germany, Britain and the Quest for a Turkish Alliance in the Second World War* (Columbia and London: University of Missouri Press, 1979) pp40–4.
70 Yücel Güçlü, 'Turkish–German Relations from Montreux to the Second World War', *Turkish Yearbook of International Relations* vol 29 (1999) p70, and 'Turkish German Relations on the Eve of World War Two', *Turkish Studies* vol 1, no 2 (2000) p87.
71 Weber, *Evasive Neutral*, pp29–33, 36, 45; Franz von Papen, *Memoirs*, tr. Brian Connell, (London: Andre Deutsch, 1952) pp446–9; Sir Hughe Knatchbull-Hugessen, *Diplomat in Peace and War* (London: John Murray, 1949) p149: Ataöv, *Foreign Policy*, p65.
72 Marzari, 'Western–Soviet Rivalry', Part I, pp69–70, 73–7, and Part II, pp201–8; Deringil, *Foreign Policy*, pp75–84; Weber, *Evasive Neutral*, p39.
73 Marzari, 'Western–Soviet Rivalry', Part II, pp209–15; Deringil, *Foreign Policy*, pp85–8; Ataöv, *Foreign Policy*, pp54–8; see also Bilge, *Güç Komşuluk*, pp134–48.
74 Hurewitz, *Diplomacy*, vol 2, pp227–8; Marzari, 'Western–Soviet Rivalry', Part II, p215; Milman, 'Turkish Policy', pp496–7; Deringil, *Foreign Policy*, pp88–91, 189–92.
75 Güçlü, 'Turkish–German Relations on the Eve', p76.
76 See Milman, 'Turkish Policy', pp486–8. Milman's account of Atatürk's attitude towards Hitler is based on that of Lord Kinross, *Atatürk, the Rebirth of a Nation* (London: Weidenfeld and Nicolson, 1964) p322, but unfortunately Kinross does not give a source for his information. Atatürk's contempt for Mussolini, however, is well attested.
77 Deringil, *Foreign Policy*, pp59–64.

3 Turkey and the Second World War, 1939–45

1 Annette Baker Fox, *The Power of Small States: Diplomacy in World War II* (Chicago: University of Chicago Press, 1959) pvii.

2 For a summary of these arguments, see Brock Milman, 'Turkish Foreign and Strategic Policy 1934–42', *Middle Eastern Studies* vol 31 (1995) pp483–4, and *The Ill-Made Alliance: Anglo-Turkish Relations 1939–1940* (Montreal and Kingston: McGill-Queens University Press, 1998) pp374–8.

3 Edward Weisband, *Turkish Foreign Policy, 1943–1945: Small State Diplomacy and Great Power Politics* (Princeton: Princeton University Press, 1973) p249.

4 Ibid, pp33–71; Selim Deringil, *Turkish Foreign Policy during the Second World War: an 'Active' Neutrality* (Cambridge: Cambridge University Press, 1989) pp41–57.

5 Milman, *Ill-Made Alliance*, pp296–303, 330–3, quotations from pp299, 332; Milman, 'Turkish Policy', pp498–501; Selim Deringil, 'The Preservation of Turkey's Neutrality During the Second World War: 1940', *Middle Eastern Studies* vol 18 (1982) p34; Deringil, *Foreign Policy*, p97; Sir Hughe Knatchbull-Hugessen, *Diplomat in Peace and War* (London: Murray, 1949) p148.

6 Milman, *Ill-Made Alliance*, pp328, 343–57; Deringil, *Foreign Policy*, pp39, 93–5, and 'Preservation', pp31–2; Türkkaya Ataöv, *Turkish Foreign Policy, 1939–1945*, (Ankara University, Political Science Faculty, 1965) pp76–8.

7 Quoted, Milman, *Ill-Made Alliance*, p370.

8 Deringil, *Foreign Policy*, pp97–102, and 'Preservation', pp34–8.

9 Frank G.Weber, *The Evasive Neutral: Germany, Britain and the Quest for a Turkish Alliance in the Second World War* (Columbia and London: University of Missouri Press, 1979) pp49–51; Deringil, *Foreign Policy*, pp104–5.

10 Deringil, *Foreign Policy*, p40.

11 Fox, *Small States*, pp11–12.

12 A.L. Macfie, 'The Turkish Straits in the Second World War, 1939–45', *Middle Eastern Studies* vol 25 (1989) pp240–1; Ataöv, *Foreign Policy*, pp78–9.

13 See William Hale, 'Anglo-Turkish Trade since 1923: Experiences and Problems', in William Hale and Ali İhsan Bağış (eds), *Four Centuries of Turco-British Relations* (Walkington: Eothen Press, 1984) pp112–13. Data are taken from the Turkish official Statistical Yearbooks (*İstatistik Yıllığı*) for the years in question.

14 Ibid, p113; Ataöv, *Foreign Policy*, p71.

15 Quoted, Knatchbull-Hugessen, *Diplomat*, p167.

16 Deringil, *Foreign Policy*, p108.

17 Quoted, Ataöv, *Foreign Policy*, p87.

18 Deringil, *Foreign Policy*, pp102–15, and 'Preservation', pp38–48; Knatchbull-Hugessen, *Diplomat*, pp161–2, 166–7.

19 Necmeddin Sadak, 'Turkey Faces the Soviets', *Foreign Affairs* vol 27 (1949) p453.

20 Texts in J.C. Hurewitz (ed.), *Diplomacy in the Near and Middle East: A Documentary Record: 1914–1956* (Princeton: Van Nostrand, 1956) vol 2, pp226–30.

21 Macfie, 'Turkish Straits', pp241–2; Bruce R. Kuniholm, *The Origins of the Cold War in the Near East* (Princeton: Princeton University Press, 2nd edn, 1994) p25. See also Franz von Papen, *Memoirs*, tr. Brian Connell (London: Andre Deutsch, 1952) pp465–8.

22 Y. Olmert, 'Britain, Turkey and the Levant Question during the Second World War', *Middle Eastern Studies* vol 23 (1987) pp438–43. Quotation from ibid, p443.

23 Weber's account, drawing on British records, suggests that the British could have prevented hostile action by Rashid Ali if they had chosen to do so, and that the British Ambassador in Iraq, Sir Kinahan Cornwallis, supported by Churchill, provoked the conflict with him in order to topple him (Weber, *Evasive Neutral*, pp86–9).

24 In April 1942, a year after the crisis, Hugessen wrote a private letter to Sir Orme Sargent, the deputy under-secretary of state in the Foreign Office, stating (in Weber's words) that 'the Turks would have much preferred to participate in the violent repression of Rashid Ali's regime and then to have remained on patrol in Iraq, as either Britain or Germany's ally, to keep the situation there quiet' (ibid, pp89–90). Hugessen does not mention any of this in his memoirs.

25 Lukasz Hirszowicz, *The Third Reich and the Arab East* (London: Routledge & Kegan Paul, 1966) pp159–64. According to British reports, Saracoğlu refused permission for the transit of arms from Syria to Iraq (Deringil, *Foreign Policy*, p124) but the German reports, cited by Hirszowicz, contradict this. Deringil also admits that 'the Turks ended up allowing some war material to reach Iraq from the Axis in mid-May', though they stalled with the Germans for long enough to allow the British to regain control (ibid, p125).

26 Hirszowicz, *Third Reich*, pp170, 181–4; Olmert, 'Levant Question', pp444–7. On 3 June, Saracoğlu told von Papen that Turkey was considering occupying the Baghdad railway up to Aleppo for strategic reasons (Deringil, *Foreign Policy*, p125) but the Turks evidently then abandoned the proposal.

27 A. Suat Bilge, et al., *Olaylarla Türk Dış Politikası* (Ankara University, Political Science Faculty, 1969) p166.

28 Quoted, Ataöv, *Foreign Policy*, pp102–3.

29 Weber, *Evasive Neutral*, pp93–5.

30 Deringil, *Foreign Policy*, p121 (quotations from German documents). In his memoirs, von Papen refers to these negotiations only vaguely, saying that he had been trying to 'convert Turco-German relations from their attitude of non-belligerence into a condition of true neutrality and friendship' (von Papen, *Memoirs*, p478).

31 Deringil, *Foreign Policy*, pp121–2; Bilge, et al., *Olaylarla*, pp168–70; Ataöv, *Foreign Policy*, pp92–4. For the text of the treaty, see Hurewitz, *Diplomacy*, vol 2, p231, from where the quotations are taken.

32 Knatchbull-Hugessen, *Diplomat*, pp169–70; Weber, *Evasive Neutral*, p102. Von Papen confirms that the Turks kept the British informed about their negotiations with Germany (von Papen, *Memoirs*, p478) although whether these included the discussion of a full alliance is unclear.

33 Quoted, Deringil, *Foreign Policy*, p135.

34 Hirszowicz, *Third Reich*, pp197–201; Robin Denniston, *Churchill's Secret War: Diplomatic Decrypts, the Foreign Office and Turkey, 1942–44* (Stroud: Sutton Publishing and New York: St Martin's Press, 1997) p59.

35 Quoted, Deringil, *Foreign Policy*, p124.

36 Denniston, *Secret War*, pp53, 66.

37 Deringil, *Foreign Policy*, pp130–2; Ataöv, *Foreign Policy*, pp96–7; Weber, *Evasive Neutral*, pp111–17, 123–6; Charles Warren Hostler, *Turkism and the Soviets* (London: Allen & Unwin, 1957) p175. For further background on pan-Turkism in Turkey at this time, see Jacob M. Landau, *Pan-Turkism: From Irredentism to Cooperation* (London: Hurst, 1995) pp90–7, 110–35.

38 Weisband, *Foreign Policy*, pp101–15; Deringil, *Foreign Policy*, pp129, 135–6; Gül İnanç, 'The Politics of "Active Neutrality" of the Eve of a New World Order: The Case of Turkish Chrome Sales during the Second World War', *Middle Eastern Studies* vol 42, no 6 (2006) pp909–11; Fox, *Small States*, pp20, 29. Figures for Turkey's foreign trade are calculated from the Turkish Statistical Yearbook for 1942, see Hale, 'Anglo-Turkish Trade', p113. In fact, the British purchased 151,000 tons of chromite in 1941, or three times as much as they had contracted for, under a pre-emptive purchasing programme. On the other hand, Turkish deliveries of chromite to Germany in 1943 were only about half the amount provided for in the Clodius agreement (Weisband, *Foreign Policy*, pp105–7).

39 It was however publicized in a series of articles by C.L. Sulzberger in *The New York Times* in September 1943: David Brown, 'Foreword', in Faik Ökte, *The Tragedy of the Capital Tax*, tr. Geoffrey Cox (London: Croom Helm, 1987) pxiii.

40 See Stanford J. Shaw, *Turkey and the Holocaust* (New York: New York University Press, 1993).

41 For further details see Ökte, *Capital Tax*, also Edward C. Clark, 'The Turkish Varlık Vergisi Reconsidered', *Middle Eastern Studies* vol 8 (1972) pp205–16, and Weisband, *Foreign Policy*, pp231–6. The percentages cited here are drawn from Clark, 'Varlık Vergisi', p209.

42 Denniston, *Secret War*, p48. Quotations from Ataöv, *Foreign Policy*, p98, quoting British and Turkish sources. See also Sadak, 'Turkey', p458.

43 Deringil, *Foreign Policy*, pp127–8.

44 Quoted, Knatchbull-Hugessen, *Diplomat*, p181.

45 Deringil, *Foreign Policy*, pp131–2; Harry N. Howard, *Turkey, the Straits and US Policy* (Baltimore and London: Johns Hopkins University Press, 1974) p169.

46 Howard, *Straits*, p165.

47 Knatchbull-Hugessen, *Diplomat*, p180; Denniston, *Secret War*, p76.

48 Howard, *Straits*, pp170–1; Deringil, *Foreign Policy*, p142–3. On disputes between Churchill and Eden over this, see also Denniston, *Secret War*, pp7, 10, 76–7.

49 Weisband, *Foreign Policy*, pp119–32.

50 Ibid, pp133–9; Ataöv, *Foreign Policy*, pp106–9.

51 Deringil, *Foreign Policy*, pp150–1; Weisband, *Foreign Policy*, pp163–6; Denniston, *Secret War*, pp111–23. Weber relates that Turkey refused to join in the operation with its own forces because the British refused to transfer sovereignty over the islands to Turkey, but this in not confirmed by the other sources cited: Weber, *Evasive Neutral*, pp181–3.

52 Quoted, Weisband, *Foreign Policy*, p179.

53 Ibid, pp176–85; Howard, *Straits*, pp178–82; Kuniholm, *Origins*, pp34–9.

54 Howard, *Straits*, pp182–8; Kuniholm, *Origins*, pp39–40.

55 Knatchbull-Hugessen, *Diplomat*, p197.

56 Quotations from Weisband, *Foreign Policy*, p208, Howard, *Straits*, p188, Weisband, *Foreign Policy*, p214.

57 Weisband, *Foreign Policy*, pp201–15; Howard, *Straits*, pp188–94; Deringil, *Foreign Policy*, pp159–63; Kuniholm, *Origins*, pp44–9.

58 Deringil, *Foreign Policy*, pp163–4. The Cicero affair is almost certainly the best-known incident in Knatchbull-Hugessen's career, and von Papen relates that he valued the information produced by Cicero highly (von Papen, *Memoirs*, pp507–18), although it does not seem to have had much significant effect on Turkish foreign policy at the time. For more information, see Denniston, *Secret War*, pp128–40, which also provides a guide to the voluminous literature on Cicero.

59 Howard, *Straits*, pp199, 204; Weisband, *Foreign Policy*, pp271–2; Kuniholm, *Origins*, p41; Macfie, 'Turkish Straits', p245.

60 Howard, *Straits*, p205; Weisband, *Foreign Policy*, pp290–2; Deringil, *Foreign Policy*, p176. For further information on the October 1944 agreement, see Kuniholm, *Origins*, pp109–16.

61 Weisband, *Foreign Policy*, pp236–7, 249–50. On the last point, see also Landau, *Pan-Turkism*, pp117–18.

62 Weisband, *Foreign Policy*, pp228–9; Howard, *Straits*, p199;: Kuniholm, *Origins*, pp52–3.

63 Deringil, *Foreign Policy*, pp55–7, 170–2; Weisband, *Foreign Policy*, pp261–8; Süleyman Seydi and Steven Morewood, 'Turkey's Application of the Montreux Convention in the Second World War', *Middle Eastern Studies* vol 41, no 1 (2005) pp92–4.

64 Howard, *Straits*, pp197–8; Weisband, *Foreign Policy*, pp257–9, 268–73; Gül İnanç, 'The Politics of "Active Neutrality" of the Eve of a New World Order: the

Case of Turkish Chrome Sales During the Second World War', *Middle Eastern Studies* vol 42, no 6 (2006), p913. Turkey broke diplomatic relations with Japan in November 1944.

65 Weber, *Evasive Neutral*, p202; Howard, *Straits*, p203; Weisband, *Foreign Policy*, pp277–84; Kuniholm, *Origins*, pp62–4, 217–18.
66 Quoted, Macfie, 'Turkish Straits', p245.
67 Deringil, *Foreign Policy*, p176; Ataöv, *Foreign Policy*, p124; Kuniholm, *Origins*, pp111–12.
68 Howard, *Straits*, pp212–17; Kuniholm, *Origins*, pp219–20; A.L. Macfie, 'The Straits Question at the Potsdam Conference: The British Position', *Middle Eastern Studies* vol 23 (1987) pp75–6.
69 Milman, *Ill-Made Alliance*, pp371, 378.
70 This argument is strongly advanced by Sadak, 'Turkey', p459.
71 See, for example, Knatchbull-Hugessen, *Diplomat*, pp203–4; Ataöv, *Foreign Policy*, pp130–4.
72 See, for example, Fox, *Small States*, pp41–2; Deringil, *Foreign Policy*, pp184–5; Kuniholm, *Origins*, pp68–9.
73 The writer has dealt with this topic more fully elsewhere, see William Hale, *The Political and Economic Development of Modern Turkey* (London: Croom Helm, 1981) pp70–1, 74–8.
74 See Weisband, *Foreign Policy*, p325.
75 Deringil, *Foreign Policy*, p166.

4 Turkey and the Cold War, 1945–63: the engagement phase

1 Quoted, Bruce R. Kuniholm, *The Origins of the Cold War in the Near East* (Princeton: Princeton University Press, 2nd edn, 1994) p255.
2 For instance, the survey of the British and American diplomatic archives for the post-war period by Ekavi Athanassopoulou does not reveal any such suggestion, although she refers to the possible link; Athanassopoulou, *Turkey – Anglo-American Security Interests* (London: Cass, 1999) p73. It is noticeable, however, that in an article written in 1954 addressing an American audience, George McGhee, the US ambassador in Turkey between 1951 and 1953, emphasized that Turkey had now become 'a democracy in practice as well as form', and that under Menderes it was committed to 'giving maximum encouragement to free enterprise and foreign investment'; McGhee, 'Turkey Joins the West', *Foreign Affairs* vol 32 (1954) pp626–9.
3 See Dankwart A. Rustow, 'Transitions to Democracy: Turkey's Experience in Historical and Comparative Perspective', in Metin Heper and Ahmet Evin (eds), *State, Democracy and the Military: Turkey in the 1980s* (Berlin: de Gruyter, 1988) p245 note 10 and George S. Harris, *Troubled Alliance: Turkish-American Problems in Historical Perspective, 1945–1971* (Washington, DC: American Enterprise Institute for Public Policy Research and Hoover Institution, 1972) p39.
4 For fuller accounts of Turkey's domestic politics during this period, see in particular Kemal H. Karpat, *Turkey's Politics: The Transition to a Multi-Party System* (Princeton: Princeton University Press, 1959); Feroz Ahmad, *The Turkish Experiment in Democracy, 1950–1975* (London: Hurst, for Royal Institute of International Affairs, 1977) pp11–17; and Erik J. Zürcher, *Turkey: A Modern History* (London and New York: I.B. Tauris, 1993) pp215–52.
5 Officially, the Soviet fiction was that the territories were being demanded by the Soviet Republics of Armenia and Georgia, rather than the USSR as such. See Bruce R. Kuniholm, 'Turkey and the West Since World War II', in Vojtech Mastny and R. Craig Nation (eds), *Turkey Between East and West: New Challenges for a Rising Regional Power* (Boulder, CO: Westview, 1996) p45.

6 Athanassopoulou, *Turkey – Anglo-American*, pp44–5.
7 Kuniholm, *Origins*, pp255–9; Harry N. Howard, *Turkey, the Straits and US Policy* (Baltimore and London: Johns Hopkins University Press, 1974) pp216–19.
8 Athanassopoulou, *Turkey – Anglo-American*, p43.
9 A.L. Macfie, 'The Straits Question at the Potsdam Conference: The British Position', *Middle Eastern Studies* vol 23 (1987) pp77–9.
10 Necmeddin Sadak, 'Turkey Faces the Soviets', *Foreign Affairs* vol 27 (1949) p460.
11 Athanassopoulou, *Turkey – Anglo-American*, pp46, 53.
12 For text, see Howard, *Straits*, pp326–7. Under Article 29 of the convention, proposals for amendment could be submitted at the end of each five-year period following its entry into force: 9 November 1946 would have been one such date.
13 Quoted, Kuniholm, *Origins*, p297, and Howard, *Straits*, p239. For a broader debate about the issues involved, see Melvyn Leffler, 'The American Conception of National Security and the Beginnings of the Cold War', *American Historical Review* vol 89 (1984) pp346–81, and Bruce Kuniholm's 'Reply' in the same volume, pp385–90.
14 Kuniholm, *Origins*, pp317–19, 335–7, 356–7.
15 Quoted, Howard, *Straits*, pp243, 246.
16 Kuniholm, *Origins*, pp372–3.
17 Ibid, pp410–17. For the text of the 'Truman Doctrine', see ibid, pp458–63.
18 Sadak, 'Turkey', p461.
19 Figures from William Hale, *The Political and Economic Development of Modern Turkey* (London: Croom Helm, 1981) pp74–5. See also Athanassopoulou, *Turkey – Anglo-American*, pp70–5.
20 Athanassopoulou, *Turkey – Anglo-American*, pp105, 109–14, 116, 130; Ekavi Athanassopoulou, 'Western Defence Developments and Turkey's Search for Security in 1948', in Sylvia Kedourie (ed.), *Turkey: Identity, Democracy, Politics* (London: Cass, 1996) pp78–9, 86, 89–93, 99–102, reprinted from *Middle Eastern Studies* vol 32 (1996) pp77–108.
21 Quoted, Athanassopoulou, *Turkey – Anglo-American*, p130.
22 A. Suat Bilge, et al., *Olaylarla Türk Dış Politikası* (Ankara University, Political Science Faculty, 1969) pp242–3.
23 Quoted, George C. McGhee, *The US–Turkish–NATO Middle East Connection* (London: Macmillan, 1990) p60.
24 Quoted, Füsun Türkmen, 'Turkey and the Korean War', *Turkish Studies* vol 3, no 2 (2002) p169.
25 Ibid, pp172–6; Cameron S. Brown, 'The One Coalition they Craved to Join: Turkey in the Korean War', *Review of International Studies* vol 34, no 1 (2008) pp94–7; John M. Vander Lippe, 'Forgotten Brigade of the Forgotten War: Turkey's Participation in the Korean War', *Middle Eastern Studies* vol 36, no 1 (2000) pp96–8; Athanassopoulou, *Turkey – Anglo-American*, pp163–5.
26 McGhee, *US–Turkish*, pp72–4: Bilge, et al., *Olaylarla*, pp244–5.
27 Kuniholm, 'Turkey and the West', pp48–9.
28 McGhee, *US–Turkish*, pp78–85; Athanassopoulou, *Turkey – Anglo-American*, pp196–7, 200–1.
29 The 'Middle East Command' proposal was followed by another unrealized British plan for a 'Middle East Defence Organization' (MEDO), see Behçet K. Yeşilbursa, 'Turkey's Participation in the Middle East Command and its admission to NATO, 1950–52', *Middle Eastern Studies* vol 35, no 4 (1999) pp71–4, 81–96, and 'The American Concept of the "Northern Tier" Defence Project and the Signing of the Turco-Pakistani Agreement, 1953–54', ibid, vol 37, no 3 (2001) pp59–65; John C. Campbell, *Defense of the Middle East: Problems of American Policy* (New York: Praeger, 1960) pp40–8; Michael M. Bishku, 'Turkey and its Middle Eastern

Neighbours since 1945', *Journal of South Asian and Middle Eastern Studies* vol 15 (1992) p57.

30 Athanassopoulou, *Turkey – Anglo-American*, p220

31 Ibid, pp218–20, 227–8; McGhee, *US–Turkish*, pp87–8; Bilge, et al., *Olaylarla*, pp247–52.

32 Quoted, Kuniholm, 'Turkey and the West', p45.

33 Harris, *Troubled Alliance*, p56.

34 Quoted, Athanassopoulou, 'Turkey's Search', p85.

35 Philip A. Petersen, 'Turkey in Soviet Military Strategy', *Foreign Policy* (Ankara: Foreign Policy Institute) vol 13 (1986) p75.

36 See Aclan Sayılgan, *Solun 94 Yılı, 1871–1965* (Ankara: Mars Matbaası, 1968) p260.

37 Türkmen, 'Turkey and the Korean War', p170; Ahmad, *Experiment*, p391; Hüseyin Bağcı, *Demokrat Parti Dönemi Dış Politikası* (Ankara: İmge Kitabevi, 1990) pp24–8. On other issues, İnönü's Republican People's Party fully supported Turkey's accession to NATO in 1952, and (less enthusiastically) the Baghdad Pact of 1954. (McGhee, *US–Turkish*, p92 and 'Turkey', p617; Bilge, et al., *Olaylarla*, p279). Later, however, the party criticized Turkey's attachment to the Eisenhower Doctrine of 1957, its support of American intervention in the Lebanon in 1958 and the coopera-tion agreement with the United States of March 1959 (Harris, *Troubled Alliance*, pp66–9; Bağcı, *Demokrat Parti*, p97). İnönü also criticized the Zürich and London agreements on Cyprus of 1959, see Suha Bölükbaşı, *Turkish–American Relations and Cyprus* (Lanham, MD: University Press of America, for White Burkett Miller Center of Public Affairs, University of Virginia, 1988) pp35–6. However, this had virtually no effect on government policy at the time.

38 Bağcı, *Demokrat Parti*, p77.

39 Quoted, Ferenc A. Vali, *Bridge across the Bosporus: The Foreign Policy of Turkey* (Baltimore and London: Johns Hopkins Press, 1971) pp174–5. See also Alvin Z. Rubinstein, *Soviet Policy Toward Turkey, Iran and Afghanistan: The Dynamics of Influence* (New York: Praeger, 1982) pp14–15. Officially, the claim to Kars and Ardahan was supposed to have been dropped by the Soviet Republics of Georgia and Armenia, see note 5.

40 Hale, *Political and Economic*, pp106–7.

41 Duygu Bazoğlu Sezer, 'Turkey's Security Policies', in Jonathan Alford (ed.), *Greece and Turkey: Adversity in Alliance* (London: Gower, for International Institute of Strategic Studies, 1984) pp56–7; Kemal H. Karpat, 'Turkish–Soviet Relations', in Kemal H. Karpat, et al., *Turkey's Foreign Policy in Transition* (Leiden: Brill, 1975) pp86–7; Rubinstein, *Soviet Policy*, p17.

42 Bölükbaşı, *Turkish-American Relations*, pp48–9; A.H. Ulman and R.H.Dekmejian, 'Changing Patterns in Turkish Foreign Policy', *Orbis* vol 11 (1967) pp774–5.

43 Sezer, 'Turkey's Security', pp64–5; Kuniholm, 'Turkey and the West', pp50–1; Hale, *Political and Economic*, pp104–5, 108–10, 230. See also Baran Tuncer, 'External Financing of the Turkish Economy and its Foreign Policy Implications', in Kemal H. Karpat (ed.), *Turkey's Foreign Policy in Transition* (Leiden: Brill, 1975) pp218–21. Figures for total US aid cited here exclude PL480 wheat deliveries. The annual average growth of GNP at constant prices ran at 6.4 per cent between 1950 and 1960, although there was a marked slowdown in the late 1950s

44 See Ulman and Dekmejian, 'Changing Patterns', p773, and William Hale, *Turkish Politics and the Military*, (London: Routledge, 1994) p120.

45 Bruce R. Kuniholm, 'Turkey and NATO: Past, Present and Future', *Orbis* vol 27 (1983) p424.

46 Vali, *Bridge*, p227; Andrew Wilson, *The Aegean Dispute* (London: International Institute for Strategic Studies, Adelphi Papers No 155, 1980) p3.

47 Bilge, et al., *Olaylarla*, pp255–68 ; Vali, *Bridge*, pp199–201. In fact, Yugoslavia was not represented at Bandung, although Tito certainly became one of the prime

supporters of non-alignment: as Fred Halliday points out, the Bandung conference was one of Afro-Asian rather than non-aligned states, and the non-aligned
movement as such was not established until the Brioni conference of 1961 (Fred
Halliday, 'The Middle East, the Great Powers and the Cold War', in Yezid Sayigh
and Avi Shlaim (eds), *The Cold War and the Middle East* (Oxford: Clarendon
Press, 1997) p18). As an indicator of this, Turkey's then foreign minister Fatin
Rüştü Zorlu attended the Bandung conference but used it as a platform to attack
the idea of neutrality in the Cold War. Later, Zorlu told the Turkish parliament
that he had attended on western insistence, presumably so that the pro-western
viewpoint would at least be represented (Bilge, et al., *Olaylarla*, pp291–4). Zorlu
also boasted that he had 'knocked Nehru down' at Bandung, in his attacks on the
Indian premier's advocacy of non-alignment (quoted, Bishku, 'Turkey', p63).

48 Bağcı, *Demokrat Parti*, pp43–4.
49 Şule Toktaş, 'Turkey's Jews and their Immigration to Israel', *Middle Eastern Studies*
vol 42, no 3 (2006) pp506, 511, 513.
50 Amikam Nachmani, *Israel, Turkey and Greece: Uneasy Relations in the Eastern
Mediterranean* (London: Cass, 1987) pp5–12, 44–5, 61–3; McGhee, *US–Turkish*,
pp124–60, 186–207; Baruch Gilead, 'Turkish–Egyptian Relations 1952–57',
Middle Eastern Affairs vol 10 (1959) p357; Ara Sanjian, 'The Formulation of the
Baghdad Pact', *Middle Eastern Studies* vol 33 (1997) pp229–31.
51 See G.E.K., 'The Turco-Egyptian Flirtation of Autumn 1954', *The World Today*
vol 12 (1956) pp450–3, and Gilead, 'Turkish–Egyptian', pp359–60.
52 İsmail Soysal, 'The Baghdad Pact', in İsmail Soysal, *Between East and West: Studies
on Turkish Foreign Relations* (Istanbul: Isis, 2001) pp206–9, 219–22; Ayşegül
Sever, 'The Compliant Ally? Turkey and the West in the Middle East, 1954–58',
Middle Eastern Studies vol 34 (1998) p75; Sanjian, 'Formulation', pp242–5. For
the text of the Baghdad pact, see *Middle East Journal* vol 5 (1955) pp177–8; for
earlier drafts, see Sanjian, 'Formulation', pp248–57.
53 Soysal, 'Baghdad Pact', pp223–5; Campbell, *Defense*, pp49–54, 57–62; Bilge, et al.,
Olaylarla, pp273–88.
54 Ayşegül Sever, 'A Reluctant Partner of the US over Suez? Turkey and the Suez
Crisis', in Simon C. Smith (ed.), *Reassessing Suez 1956: New Perspectives on the
Crisis and its Aftermath* (Aldershot and Burlington, VT: Ashgate, 2008) pp124–7,
131; Campbell, *Defense*, pp49–54, 57–62; Bilge, et al., *Olaylarla*, pp273–88, 303;
Bağcı, *Demokrat Parti*, pp80–1. After the Suez crisis, Turkey also withdrew its
ambassador from Tel Aviv, although not severing diplomatic relations, 'until the
Palestinian question is resolved' – in fact, until 1991 (quoted, Bishku, 'Turkey and
its Middle Eastern Neighbours since 1945', *Journal of South Asian and Middle
Eastern Studies* (1992) vol 15, p61).
55 Quoted, Vali, *Bridge*, p285.
56 Perhaps unexpectedly, Turco-Iraqi relations were restored quite quickly after this
and a Turkish delegation attended celebrations in Baghdad marking the first
anniversary of the coup in July 1959. Probably, the main reason for this was that
Iraq's new ruler Abdul Karim Qassem refused to join the then United Arab
Republic of Egypt and Syria, and expressed sympathy towards Turkey. By this
stage, the Turks had evidently decided that the Baghdad pact was truly dead and
that they would have to make the best of a bad job. Iraq's rivalry with Syria, and
Turkish hostility towards Damascus, probably played an additional part in the
reconciliation. See ibid, p301.
57 Campbell, *Defense*, pp191–2, 242–3; William Hale and Julian Bharier, 'CENTO,
RCD and the Northern Tier: A Political and Economic Appraisal', *Middle Eastern
Studies* vol 8 (1972) p218.
58 McGhee, *US–Turkish*, pp149–56, quotation p156; Yeşilbursa, 'American Concept',
p66; Sanjian, 'Formulation', pp229–31.

59 Soysal, 'Baghdad Pact', pp226–30; Bishku, 'Turkey', p58; Sever, 'Compliant Ally?' pp76–80.
60 See, for example, Campbell, *Defense*, pp121–4, 127–31, 140–5, quotation p122. See also Bağcı, *Demokrat Parti*, pp83–5.
61 Quoted, Philip Robins, *Turkey and the Middle East* (London: Frances Pinter, for Royal Institute of International Affairs, 1991) p26.
62 George E. Gruen, 'Ambivalence in the Alliance: U.S. Interests in the Middle East and the Evolution of Turkish Foreign Policy', *Orbis* vol 24 (1980) p372; Sever, 'Compliant Ally?', pp81–3. As Sever suggests (p86), Menderes may have blown up the contest with Syria to distract the Turkish public from economic complaints, in view of the upcoming general elections held on 27 October 1957, but there is no documentary evidence of this. Bağcı, however, repeats this suggestion, arguing that once Menderes had won the elections, he rapidly wound the crisis down (Bağcı, *Demokrat Parti*, p9).
63 Quoted, Sever, 'Compliant Ally?', p83.
64 See ibid, pp83–4; Bağcı, *Demokrat Parti*, p97; and Robins, *Turkey and the Middle East*, p27. On the last point, George S. Harris supports the first argument, and Richard D. Robinson the second: see Harris, *Troubled Alliance*, pp65–6, and Richard D. Robinson, *The First Turkish Republic* (Cambridge, MA: Harvard University Press, 1963) p187. Following the revolution in Iraq, American and British military planners had themselves prepared contingency measures for a joint military intervention in Iraq. This project was supported by Duncan Sandys, Britain's hawkish minister of defence, but was turned down by the Amrericans and the British Foreign Office, on the grounds that it was not feasible militarily, plus the expectation that the new Iraqi ruler, Abdul Karim Qasim, would act as a counterpoint to Nasser in the Middle East. See Stephen Blackwell, 'A Desert Squall: Anglo-American Planning for Military Intervention in Iraq, July 1958–August 1959', *Middle Eastern Studies* vol 35 (1999) pp3–4.
65 According to Nachmani, 'Israel would enjoy the support of the Turkish "giant" and of its army', in return for 'scientific cooperation in highly sensitive spheres', Israeli technical and economic assistance and the export of Israeli military equipment to Turkey (Nachmani, *Israel, Greece and Turkey*, p75). See also Robins, *Turkey and the Middle East*, p77.
66 Bağcı, *Demokrat Parti*, p97.
67 Suha Bölükbaşı, 'The Johnson Letter Revisited', *Middle Eastern Studies* vol 29 (1993) pp507–8. This situation can perhaps be seen as similar to that in Alexandretta between 1921 and 1936, see p50.
68 Sanjian, 'Formulation', p243.
69 Tozun Bahceli, *Greek–Turkish Relations since 1955* (Boulder, CO: Westview, 1990) pp36–40.
70 Quoted, Robert Stephens, *Cyprus, a Place of Arms: Power Politics and Ethnic Conflict in the Eastern Mediterranean* (London: Pall Mall, 1966) p138, from Eden's memoirs, *Full Circle* (London: Cassell, 1960) p414.
71 Menderes unconvincingly claimed that the riots were the work of 'communist' provocateurs, and some restitutions were made. The government's responsibility was however made clear when Menderes and his colleagues were placed on trial following the coup of 27 May 1960: see Walter F.Weiker, *The Turkish Revolution, 1960–1961* (Washington, Brookings Institution, 1963) pp33–35.
72 For instance, in its submission to the United Nations of 1954 the Greek government did not even mention the existence of a Turkish community on the island (Vali, *Bridge*, p237).
73 Ibid, pp236–45; Stephens, *Cyprus*, pp139–50; Stanley Kyriakides, *Cyprus: Constitutionalism and Crisis Government* (Philadelphia, PA: University of Philadelphia Press, 1968) pp37–42; Suat Bilge, 'The Cyprus Conflict and Turkey', in Karpat, et al., *Turkey's Foreign Policy*, pp137–43.

74 Stephens, *Cyprus*, pp157–60, 163–7; Kyriakides, *Cyprus*, pp48–52; Bahceli, *Greek–Turkish*, pp44–6.
75 Quoted, Bölükbaşı, *Turkish–American Relations*, p36.
76 For the text of the constitution, and the accompanying Treaty of Establishment and the Treaty of Guarantee, see *Cyprus* (London: HMSO, Cmnd. 1093, 1960), from where these quotations are taken (pp86–7). For a more detailed discussion of the constitution, see Kyriakides, *Cyprus*, pp55–71.
77 For details, see Weiker, *Turkish Revolution*; Ahmad, *Experiment*, pp147–76; and Hale, *Turkish Politics*, pp119–49.
78 Kuniholm, 'Turkey and the West', pp51–2, and information from Mr İsmail Soysal.
79 Süleyman Seydi, 'Turkish–American Relations and the Cuban Missile Crisis', *Middle Eastern Studies* vol 46, no 3 (2010) p440; Donald L. Hafner, 'Bureaucratic Politics and "Those Frigging Missiles": JFK, Cuba, and US Missiles in Turkey', *Orbis* vol 21 (1977) p330. Hafner argues that the eventual offer by Khrushchev for such an exchange was merely 'a hasty, uncoordinated gesture designed to salvage some gain from a bad situation'.
80 Kuniholm, 'Turkey and the West', pp51–2; Barton J. Bernstein, 'The Cuban Missile Crisis: Trading the Jupiters in Turkey?', *Political Science Quarterly* vol 95 (1980) pp99–100 and 'Reconsidering the Missile Crisis: Dealing with the Problem of the American Jupiters in Turkey', in James A. Nathan (ed.), *The Cuban Missile Crisis Revisited* (New York: St Martin's Press, 1992) pp58–9, 65–6.
81 Presumably a reference to the unelected Constituent Assembly, which had been set up by the military regime in January 1961.
82 Dean Rusk, interviewed in James G. Blight and David A. Welch, *On the Brink: Americans and Soviets Reexamine the Cuban Missile Crisis* (New York: Noonday Press, 1989) p173.
83 Quoted, Kuniholm, 'Turkey and the West', p53.
84 Ibid, p52; Robert F. Kennedy, *Thirteen Days: A Memoir of the Cuban Missile Crisis* (New York: Norton, 1961) pp72–3; Bernstein, 'Reconsidering', pp62–3; see also McGhee, *US–Turkish*, p166, and Hafner, 'Bureaucratic Politics', pp309–11.
85 Kennedy, *Thirteen Days*, pp64–8, 71–2, 160–4.
86 Quoted, Bernstein, 'Reconsidering', p76.
87 Quoted, Seydi, 'Turkish–American', p443.
88 Kennedy, *Thirteen Days*, pp80–2.
89 Bernstein, 'Reconsidering', pp98–9; James A. Nathan, 'The Heyday of the New Strategy', in Nathan (ed.), *Cuban Missile Crisis,* p23; Bilge, et al., *Olaylarla*, p352.
90 Kennedy, *Thirteen Days*, pp86–7.
91 Bernstein, 'Reconsidering', p96; Blight and Welch, *On the Brink*, pp83–4.
92 The writer is very grateful to Dr Süleyman Seydi for advice on this point.
93 Vali, *Bridge*, p129; Nazih Uslu, *Turkey's Relationship with the United States, 1960–1975* (Ph.D. thesis, University of Durham, 1994) pp184–5.
94 Press conference given by Süleyman Demirel in February 1970, reprinted in Harris, *Troubled Alliance*, p236.
95 Quoted, Rubinstein, *Soviet Policy*, p19.
96 In 1970, İsmet İnönü complained openly that this had been done in 1962, in spite of his earlier denials, see ibid, p93, n10, and Seydi, 'Turkish–American', p451.
97 Gruen, 'Ambivalence', p369. Interestingly, Gruen reaches this conclusion without reference to Robert Kennedy's secret offer to Dobrynin.
98 An apt illustration of this was the lack of Turkish or western opposition to the passage of the Soviet aircraft carrier *Kiev* through the straits in 1976, see p282, n92.
99 Weiker, *Turkish Revolution*, pp13 n17, 160.

5 Turkey and the Cold War, 1964–90: global shifts and regional conflicts

1 This is suggested by Alvin J. Rubinstein, *Soviet Policy Toward Turkey, Iran and Afghanistan: The Dynamics of Influence* (New York: Praeger, 1982) p25.

2 Ferenc A. Vali, *Bridge across the Bosporus: The Foreign Policy of Turkey* (Baltimore and London: Johns Hopkins Press, 1971) pp120–1; Mehmet Gönlübol, 'NATO, USA and Turkey', in Kemal H. Karpat (ed.), *Turkey's Foreign Policy in Transition* (Leiden: Brill, 1975) pp43–5; Faruk Sönmezoğlu, *ABD'nin Türkiye Politikası (1964–1980)* (Istanbul: Der Yayınevi, 1995) p37.

3 For fuller accounts of Turkey's domestic politics between 1961 and 1980, see Feroz Ahmad, *The Turkish Experiment in Democracy, 1950–1975* (London: Hurst, for Royal Institute of International Affairs, 1977) pp177–388, Erik J. Zürcher, *Turkey: A Modern History* (London and New York: I.B. Tauris, 1993) pp253–91, and C.H. Dodd, *The Crisis of Turkish Democracy* (2nd edn, Wistow: Eothen Press, 1990) Chs1–2.

4 Quoted, Suha Bölükbaşı, 'The Johnson Letter Revisited', *Middle Eastern Studies* vol 29 (1993) p510.

5 As a sign of this, in 1960 Makarios himself alluded to the idea that 'the realisation of our hopes and dreams is not complete under the Zurich and London Agreements': quoted, Zenon Stavrinides, *The Cyprus Conflict: National Identity and Statehood* (Wakefield: Loris Stavrinides, 1976) p40. As late as June 1967 – after the Colonels' takeover in Athens – the Greek Cypriot House of Representatives passed a resolution calling for 'uniting the whole and undivided Cyprus with the Motherland, without any intervening stages', while the following October Makarios told a Greek Cypriot newspaper that 'the real victory will be achieved when Cyprus will be annexed to Greece without any concessions whatever' (quoted, ibid, p64).

6 For details, see Robert Stephens, *Cyprus, a Place of Arms: Power Politics and Ethnic Conflict in the Eastern Mediterranean* (London: Pall Mall, 1966) pp168–94, and Stanley Kyriakides, *Cyprus: Constitutionalism and Crisis Government* (Philadelphia, PA: University of Philadelphia Press, 1968) pp72–157.

7 Bölükbaşı, 'Johnson Letter', pp506, 513–15.

8 Sönmezoğlu, *ABD'nin Türkiye Politikası*, p14.

9 For the full text of the 'Johnson letter' and İnönü's reply, see *Middle East Journal* vol 20 (1966) pp386–93. The letter was supposed to be secret, but in fact tendentious versions of it reached the Turkish press at the time, suggesting even that the United States would have been prepared to use force to prevent Turkey from invading Cyprus. In 1965, the two governments belatedly agreed to make the full text public, but by this time most of the damage to US–Turkish relations had been done: see Parker T. Hart, *Two NATO Allies at the Threshold of War: Cyprus: a Firsthand Account of Crisis Management, 1965–1968* (Durham, NC, and London: Duke University Press, 1990) p15.

10 Bölükbaşı, 'Johnson Letter', p517.

11 Ibid, p521; Suha Bölükbaşı, *Turkish–American Relations and Cyprus* (Lanham, MD: University Press of America for White Burkett Miller Center of Public Affairs, University of Virginia, 1988) pp66–8. Turkey had no landing-craft at the time, and would have had to transport troops to Cyprus in ordinary cargo vessels and small boats, running the risk of heavy casualties and unacceptable delays. There is also some mystery about the timing of the planned operation, if there was one. Interviewed on 12 June 1963, İnönü stated that an invasion had been planned for 4 June, but that 'one day before I was warned by Washington not to use American arms for purposes not approved by America. Mr Johnson said that if the Russians took action, our NATO guarantees might not hold' (quoted, Jacob

M. Landau, *Johnson's 1964 Letter to İnönü and Greek Lobbying of the White House* (Jerusalem: Hebrew University of Jerusalem, Jerusalem Papers on Peace Problems 28, 1979) pp6–7). However, the 'Johnson letter' was not delivered until 5 June. Assuming that İnönü was not mis-quoted, or had not become badly confused over dates only one week after the event, this suggests either that he had received another warning from Johnson prior to the 'Johnson letter', or possibly that he had decided to abandon the planned invasion the day before the letter was delivered.

12 These disputes had in fact begun during the 1950s, see George S. Harris, *Troubled Alliance: Turkish–American Problems in Historical Perspective, 1945–1971* (Washington, DC: American Enterprise Institute for Public Policy Research and Hoover Institution, 1972) pp56–61. See also Sönmezoğlu, *ABD'nin Türkiye Politikası*, pp44, 50–1.

13 To be exact, 3 per cent in 1965 and 2.8 per cent in 1969.

14 See Harris, *Troubled Alliance*, pp128–47, 160–9; Ferenc A. Vali, *Bridge Across the Bosporus: The Foreign Policy of Turkey* (Baltimore and London: Johns Hopkins Press, 1971) pp137–46.

15 Quoted, Rubinstein, *Soviet Policy*, p30.

16 Bruce R. Kuniholm, 'Turkey and NATO: Past, Present and Future', *Orbis* vol 27 (1983) p427.

17 Quoted, Rubinstein, *Soviet Policy*, p32. On Soviet–Turkish relations during the 1960s and early 1970s, see ibid, pp26–32, and A.H. Ulman and R.H. Dekmejian, 'Changing Patterns in Turkish Foreign Policy, 1959–67', *Orbis* vol 11 (1967) pp779–80.

18 Vali, *Bridge*, pp158–63; Baran Tuncer, 'External Financing of the Turkish Economy and its Foreign Policy Implications', in Karpat (ed.), *Turkey's Foreign Policy*, pp218–24. Tuncer appears to exaggerate the last point, but his data only run up to 1969, before the level of Soviet aid reached substantial proportions.

19 Quoted, Vali, *Bridge*, pp83, 209. The impact of the Soviet occupation of Czechoslovakia in Turkey was accentuated by the fact that, following his removal from Prague, Alexander Dubcek was briefly stationed in Ankara as Czech ambassador.

20 Bölükbaşı, *Turkish–American*, pp132–3; for a slightly different account, see Cihat Göktepe, 'The Cyprus Crisis of 1967 and its Effects on Turkey's Foreign Relations', *Middle Eastern Studies* vol 41, no 3, (2005) p435.

21 Sönmezoğlu, *ABD'nin Türkiye Politikası*, p23; Göktepe, 'Cyprus Crisis', p439.

22 By 1967, Turkey still only had two landing-craft, six helicopters and 150 parachutes: troops would have had to be landed from conventional vessels and their position would have been precarious: Bölükbaşı, *Turkish–American*, p135.

23 Ibid, pp133–46; Harris, *Troubled Alliance*, pp122–4; Clement H. Dodd, *The Cyprus Imbroglio* (Hemingford Grey: Eothen Press, 1998) p27; Göktepe, 'Cyprus Crisis', pp440–1.

24 For further details on the events of March 1971, see Ahmad, *Experiment*, pp288–91 and William Hale, *Turkish Politics and the Military* (London: Routledge, 1994) pp184–93.

25 See James W. Spain, 'The United States, Turkey and the Poppy', *Middle East Journal* vol 29 (1975) pp295–309.

26 For details, see Polyvios G. Polyviou, *Cyprus: Conflict and Negotiation, 1960–1980* (London: Duckworth, 1980) pp62–126 and Dodd, *Cyprus Imbroglio*, pp27–9.

27 For the full text of Makarios's letter, which was written on 2 July, see Necati Ertekün, *The Cyprus Dispute and the Birth of the Turkish Republic of Northern Cyprus* (Nicosia: Rustem, 2nd edn, 1984) pp236–9.

28 The coalition protocol issued by the Ecevit government in January 1974 called for a federal settlement, and foreign minister Turan Güneş confirmed the government's opposition to a 'unitary state', but it appears that it was willing to reduce

this to a 'functional federation' – in other words, a power-sharing agreement broadly similar to the 1960 constitution, but recognizing the Turkish Cypriots as a separate community. On the other hand, the Turkish Cypriot leaders, notably Rauf Denktash, preferred the idea of a geographically-based federation. See Bölükbaşı, *Turkish–American*, pp178–9. After the Sampson coup, the Ecevit government also adopted this position.

29 Information from a senior member of the foreign ministry at the time. The Turkish forces now had 100 landing-craft, 15,000 parachutes and 100 helicopters. At the time of the initial landings on 20 July, 70 per cent of the landing craft were held back from the operation and kept in readiness for an invasion of the Greek Aegean islands, suggesting that if Greece had counterattacked, Turkey would have occupied the islands as a later bargaining chip (Bölükbaşı, *Turkish–American*, pp189, 195).

30 See pp97–8.

31 Bölükbaşı, *Turkish–American*, pp185–90; Mehmet Ali Birand, *30 Hot Days*, (London, Nicosia and Istanbul: Rustem, 1985) pp1–11, originally published in Turkish as *30 Sıcak Gün* (Istanbul: Milliyet Yayınları, 1975).

32 Birand, *Hot Days*, pp6–9, 11–14, 17–25, 36–7, 41–2, 47–8; Bölükbaşı, *Turkish–American*, pp191–7; Theodore A. Couloumbis, *The United States, Greece and Turkey: The Troubled Triangle* (New York: Praeger, 1983) pp90–6.

33 For the full text of the declaration, see Ertekün, *Cyprus Dispute*, pp248–9. For other accounts of the first Geneva conference, see Birand, *Hot Days*, pp61–76 and Bölükbaşı, *Turkish–American*, pp200–2.

34 The incident is related by Polyviou (*Cyprus*, p177) who attended the conference as a Greek Cypriot delegate, and Bölükbaşı, *Turkish–American*, p211. Birand, who also attended as a journalist, relates that he told Güneş that 'the Soviet Union had pledged support for Greece', but does not suggest that this included military support (Birand, *Hot Days*, pp81–2). For detailed accounts of the second Geneva conference, from different viewpoints, see ibid, pp81–113; Bölükbaşı, *Turkish–American*, pp202–11; Polyviou, *Cyprus*, pp162–85.

35 Bölükbaşı, *Turkish–American*, p211.

36 For full text, see Ertekün, *Cyprus Dispute*, p278, and Polyviou, *Cyprus*, pp205–6.

37 For details of the intercommunal negotiations between 1974 and 1980, see Ertekün, *Cyprus Dispute*, pp37–103; Polyviou, *Cyprus*, pp203–17; A.J.R. Groom, 'The Process of Negotiation, 1974–93' in C.H. Dodd (ed.), *The Political, Social and Economic Development of Northern Cyprus* (Hemingford Grey: Eothen, 1993) pp16–45.

38 Andrew Wilson, *The Aegean Dispute* (London: International Institute for Strategic Studies, Adelphi Paper No 155, 1980) pp4–10, 13–14, 22–3, 30; Suha Bölükbaşı, 'The Turco-Greek Dispute: Issues, Policies and Prospects', in C.H. Dodd (ed.), *Turkish Foreign Policy: New Prospects* (Wistow: Eothen, 1992) pp33–8.

39 Wilson, *Aegean Dispute*, pp3, 6–7, 11–12, 16–18, 23–4; Couloumbis, *The United States, Greece and Turkey: The Troubled Triangle* (New York: Praeger, 1983) pp117–30; Bölükbaşı, 'Turco-Greek Dispute', pp38–49.

40 The 'Johnson letter' of 1964 may have been partly the result of Greek–American lobbying (see Landau, *Johnson's 1964 Letter*) but there were almost certainly strong strategic reasons for Johnson's policy at the time – notably the fear of a strong Soviet reaction.

41 Couloumbis, *Troubled Triangle*, p108.

42 Ibid, pp103–6; Richard C. Campany Jr, *Turkey and the United States: The Arms Embargo Period* (New York: Praeger, 1986) pp55–6, 63–4; Duygu Bazoğlu Sezer, 'Turkey's Security Policies', in Jonathan Alford (ed.), *Greece and Turkey: Adversity in Alliance* (London: Gower, for International Institute for Strategic Studies, 1984) pp64–5; Rubinstein, *Soviet Policy*, p47.

43 Sönmezoğlu, *ABD'nin Türkiye Politikası*, p112.

44 Couloumbis, *Troubled Triangle*, pp106–7; Campany, *Turkey*, p63; Sezer, 'Security Policies', p67.
45 Bülent Ecevit, 'Turkey's Security Policies', in Alford (ed.), *Greece and Turkey*, p138. This is the text of an address delivered to the International Institute of Strategic Studies in London while he was Prime Minister in May 1978.
46 Rubinstein, *Soviet Policy*, pp40–1; Gareth Winrow, 'Gorbachev's New Political Thinking and Turkey', paper delivered to conference of British International Studies Association, University of Warwick, December 1991, p7.
47 Statement in Bonn, 12 May 1978, quoted, Wilson, *Aegean*, p25.
48 George E. Gruen, 'Ambivalence in the Alliance: US Interests in the Middle East and the Evolution of Turkish Foreign Policy', *Orbis* vol 24 (1980) p376.
49 For an overall assessment of these changes, see Duygu Bazoğlu Sezer, 'Turkey and the Western Alliance in the 1980s', in Atila Eralp, Muharrem Tünay and Birol Yeşilada (eds), *The Political and Socioeconomic Transformation of Turkey* (Westport, CT: Praeger, 1993) pp218–20.
50 The party was formed in 1985, following a merger between the Social Democracy Party, led by İnönü, and the previous People's Party.
51 For fuller accounts of Turkish politics during the 1980s, see Dodd, *Crisis*, Ch3–5; Nicole and Hugh Pope, *Turkey Unveiled: Atatürk and After* (London: Murray, 1997) Ch10–13; Hale, *Turkish Politics*, pp246–300; Kemal H. Karpat, 'Turkish Democracy at Impasse: Party Politics and the Third Military Intervention', *International Journal of Turkish Studies* vol 2 (1981). For a detailed narrative of the coup of 1980 and the events leading up to it, see Mehmet Ali Birand, *The Generals' Coup in Turkey: An Inside Story of 12 September 1980*, tr. M.A. Dikerdem (London: Brassey's Defence Publishers, 1987).
52 Turgut Özal, *Turkey in Europe and Europe in Turkey* (Nicosia: Rustem, 1991) pp300, 304.
53 Gruen, 'Ambivalence', pp365–6; Rubinstein, *Soviet Policy*, p51.
54 George E. Gruen, 'Turkey Between the Middle East and the West', in Robert O. Freedman (ed.), *The Middle East from the Iran Contra Affair to the Intifada* (New York: Syracuse University Press, 1991) p404; Ömer Karasapan, 'Turkey's Armaments Industries', *Middle East Report* January–February 1987, pp27–31.
55 Gruen, 'Turkey', pp405–6; Mahmut Bali Aykan, 'Turkish Perspectives on Turkish–US Relations Concerning Persian Gulf Security in the Post-Cold War Era: 1989–95', *Middle East Journal* vol 50 (1996) p345. See also the writer's contribution to Itamar Rabinovich, Haim Shaked and Ami Ayalon (eds), *Middle East Contemporary Survey* vol 11, 1987 (Boulder, CO: Westview Press, 1989) p673.
56 Rubinstein, *Soviet Policy*, pp42–3, 48–50.
57 Ali L. Karaosmanoğlu, 'Turkey's Security and the Middle East', *Foreign Affairs* vol 62 (1983) pp159, 173.
58 Winrow, 'Gorbachev's New Political Thinking', pp2–4, 8–9. Winrow's analysis follows that of David E. Albright, 'The USSR and the Third World in the 1980s', *Problems of Communism* vol 38 (1989) pp50–70.
59 Winrow, 'Gorbachev's New Political Thinking', pp10–11.
60 Dodd, *Cyprus Imbroglio*, pp37–42.
61 For details, see the writer's contribution to the 1987 edition of *Middle East Contemporary Survey* (vol 11) p672 (see note 55) and the 1988 edition (vol 12) p765.
62 This figure apparently excluded the Pomaks – that is, Bulgarian-speaking Muslims.
63 Kemal Kirişci, 'Post Second World War Immigration from the Balkan Countries to Turkey', *Turkish Review of Balkan Studies* (Istanbul, annual) vol 2 (1994/5) pp176–8; *Turkey Almanac 1989* (Ankara: Turkish Daily News, 1989) pp406–9; Hugh Poulton, *Top Hat, Grey Wolf and Crescent: Turkish Nationalism and the Turkish Republic* (London: Hurst, 1997) pp299–302.

64 Mahmut Bali Aykan, 'The Palestinian Question in Turkish Foreign Policy from the 1950s to the 1990s', *International Journal of Middle East Studies* vol 25 (1993) p94; Kemal H. Karpat, 'Turkish and Arab–Israeli Relations', in Karpat, et al., *Turkey's Foreign Policy in Transition*, pp122–5.

65 Philip Robins, *Turkey and the Middle East* (London: Pinter, for Royal Institute of International Affairs, 1991) pp100–7.

66 Kuniholm, 'Turkey and NATO', pp426, 438–9; Aykan, 'Palestinian Question', pp95, 97; Gruen, 'Ambivalence', pp372–3, 377; Karaosmanoğlu, 'Turkey's Security', pp160, 163, 168–70.

67 M. Hakan Yavuz and Mujeeb R. Khan, 'Turkish Foreign Policy Toward the Arab–Israeli Conflict: Duality and the [*sic*] Development', *Arab Studies Quarterly* vol 14 (1992) pp80–1; Aykan, 'Palestinian Question', p98: Bülent Aras, 'The Impact of the Palestinian–Israeli Peace Process in Turkish Foreign Policy', *Journal of South Asian and Middle Eastern Studies* vol 20 (1997) pp57–9.

68 Michael M. Bishku, 'Turkey and its Middle Eastern Neighbours since 1945', *Journal of South Asian and Middle Eastern Studies* vol 15 (1992), p65; Aykan, 'Palestinian Question', p99; Karaosmanoğlu, 'Turkey's Security', p167.

69 Yavuz and Khan, 'Turkish Foreign Policy', p81.

70 Aras, 'Impact', pp60–2; Aykan, 'Palestinian Question', pp104–5; Gruen, 'Turkey between Middle East and West' pp413–15; Robins, *Turkey and the Middle East*, pp79–86.

71 In fact, the first Turkish incursion into northern Iraq occurred in May 1983, see Suha Bölükbaşı, 'Turkey Copes with Revolutionary Iran', *Journal of South Asian and Middle Eastern Studies* vol 13 (1989) p103.

72 Ibid, pp95–99: John Calabrese, 'Turkey and Iran: Limits of a Stable Relationship', *British Journal of Middle Eastern Studies,* Vol.25 (1998) pp77–78.

73 Bölükbaşı, 'Turkey Copes', pp99–101.

74 See Henri J. Barkey, 'The Silent Victor: Turkey's Role in the Gulf War', in Efraim Karsh (ed.), *The Iran–Iraq War: Impact and Implications* (London: Macmillan, in association with Jafee Center for Strategic Studies, Tel Aviv University, 1989) pp135–9. After 1985, Turkey's exports to the two countries fell back, in line with the decline in oil prices, and the Turks had difficulty in persuading the Iraqis to pay their existing commercial debts. In the case of trade with Iran, there were also complaints by the Iranians about the way it was conducted, see ibid, pp139–40, and Bölükbaşı, 'Turkey Copes', pp100–1. See also Robins, *Turkey and the Middle East*, pp53–4, 58–62, 103. On the rise of the PKK, and Kurdish politics during the 1980s, see David McDowall, *A Modern History of the Kurds* (London: I.B. Tauris, 1996) pp418–31; Michael M.Gunter, *The Kurds in Turkey* (Boulder, CO: Westview, 1990) pp57–91, and Kemal Kirişci and Gareth Winrow, *The Kurdish Question and Turkey: an Example of Trans-state Ethnic Conflict* (London: Cass, 1997) pp126–36.

75 Bölükbaşı, 'Turkey Copes', pp105–6; McDowall, *Modern History*, pp357–61.

76 Robins, *Turkey and the Middle East*, pp49–52, 87–99. On the Euphrates dispute, see also Suha Bölükbaşı, 'Turkey Challenges Iraq and Syria: the Euphrates Dispute', *Journal of South Asian and Middle Eastern Studies* vol 16 (1993) pp9–32, and Gün Kut, 'Burning Waters: The Hydropolitics of the Euphrates and Tigris', *New Perspectives on Turkey* Fall (1993), pp1–17. For the texts of the 1987 agreements between Turkey and Syria, see H. Fahir Alaçam, 'Turkish–Syrian Relations', *Turkish Review of Middle East Studies* (Istanbul) vol 8 (1994/5) pp12–14. Distribution of the waters of the Tigris and Euphrates also involves conflict between Turkey and Iraq, see p233.

77 See Vali, *Bridge*, pp107, 154–6.

78 Selim İlkin, 'A History of Turkey's Association with the European Community', in Ahmet Evin and Geoffrey Denton (eds), *Turkey and the European Community*

(Opladen: Leske and Budrich, 1990) pp35–6; Roswitha Bourguignon, 'The History of the Association Agreement between Turkey and the European Community', in ibid, p52; Mehmet Ali Birand, 'Turkey and the European Community', *World Today* vol 38 (1978) pp52–3; Heinz Kramer, 'Turkey and EC's Southern Enlargement', *Aussenpolitik* vol 35 (1984) pp101–4.

79 Association Agreement, Article 28. For the full text of the Agreement, and of the Additional Protocol of 1970, see *Official Journal of the European Communities: Information and Notices,* vol 16, no C 113.

80 For instance, Seyfi Taşhan suggests that Turkey became an associate member of the EEC 'with the understanding that it would eventually become a full member' (Taşhan, 'The Case for Turkish Membership', in Ahmet Evin and Geoffrey Denton (eds), *Turkey and the European Community* (Opladen: Leske and Budrich, 1990) pp71–2). However, Bourguignon is far more guarded, confirming that 'full membership was not automatically fixed by the agreement' (Bourguignon, 'Association Agreement', p53). See also John Redmond, *The Next Mediterranean Enlargement of the European Community: Turkey, Cyprus and Malta?* (Aldershot: Dartmouth Publishing Co., 1993) p26.

81 Quoted, Redmond, *Next Mediterranean Enlargement,* p23.

82 İlkin, 'Turkey's Association', pp40–4.

83 Bourguignon, 'Association Agreement', pp55–6; Kramer, 'Turkey and EC', pp105–7.

84 The first suggestion seems quite far-fetched, since the obstacles to Greek accession, both economic and political, were far less than in the case of Turkey. However, it might have been a useful diplomatic ploy for the Turks, and some western parliamentarians hinted to them at the time that they should submit an application, see David Barchard, *Turkey and the West* (London: Routledge and Kegan Paul for Royal Institute of International Affairs, 1985) pp64–5.

85 See Nusret Ekin, 'Turkish Labor in the EEC', in Werner Gumpel (ed.), *Die Türkei auf dem Weg in die EG* (Munich and Vienna: R. Oldenbourg, 1979) pp88–94, 96, and İsmet Ergün, 'The Problem of Freedom of Movement of Turkish Workers in the European Community', in Denton and Evin (eds), *Turkey,* pp185–6, 189–90.

86 See İhsan D. Dağı, 'Democratic Transition in Turkey, 1980–83: the Impact of European Diplomacy', *Middle Eastern Studies* vol 32 (1996), pp125–9, 138–9, reprinted in Sylvia Kedourie (ed.), *Turkey; Identity, Democracy, Politics* (London and Portland, OR: Cass, 1996).

87 Ibid, pp129–32, 137–9; Barchard, *Turkey and the West,* pp58–9; Bourguignon, 'Association Agreement', pp58–9.

88 Quoted, Meltem Müftüler, 'Turkish Economic Liberalization and European Integration', *Middle Eastern Studies* vol 31 (1995) p85.

89 See Özal, *Turkey in Europe,* pp281–304.

90 For the full text of the Opinion, see Commission des Communautés Européennes, Sec (89) 2290, 'Avis de la Commission sur la demande d'adhésion de la Turquie à la Communauté' (Brussels, December 1989).

91 'Press Conference by Mr Matutes on Membership of Turkey to the Community' (Brussels, Commission of the European Communities, December 1989: ref BIC/ 89/393).

92 The most striking illustration of this occurred in 1976 when the Soviet aircraft-carrying cruiser *Kiev* steamed through the straits to the Mediterranean. On most criteria, the *Kiev* and her sister ships could be defined as aircraft carriers, whose passage was forbidden under the Montreux Convention. However, the Soviet navy classified her as an 'anti-submarine cruiser', and both the Turkish and NATO authorities accepted her passage. This partly reflected Turkey's desire not to provoke the USSR where possible, and partly to the fact that the *Kiev's* presence did not produce a fundamental alteration of the balance of power in the Mediterranean. The development of ship-borne missiles also rendered many of the

Montreux rules quite obsolete, since they referred to tonnage and the size of ships' guns, which were virtually irrelevant in the nuclear age. See Barry Buzan, 'The Status and Future of the Montreux Convention', *Survival* vol 18 (1976) pp242–7.

6 Turkish foreign policy after the Cold War: strategic options and the domestic and economic environments

1 Obviously, this statement does not hold true if one counts Russia as a 'neighbour' of Turkey, however, the essential point about the transformation for the Turks was that it left Russia far weaker than previously.

2 Officially, the European Community became the European Union when the Treaty of Maastricht went into effect in November 1993.

3 See Sabri Sayarı, 'Turkey, the Changing European Security Environment and the Gulf Crisis', *Middle East Journal* vol 46 (1992) pp10–11.

4 Ian O. Lesser, 'Bridge or Barrier? Turkey and the West After the Cold War', in Graham E. Fuller, et al., *Turkey's New Geopolitics: From the Balkans to Western China* (Boulder, CO: Westview, 1993) pp102, 129. Lesser elaborates his argument in a later paper, 'Turkey's Strategic Options', *International Spectator* (Rome) vol 34, no 1 (1999) p82.

5 *Hürriyet*, 7 March 2002; website of NTV television, Istanbul (www.ntvmsnbc.com) 8 March 2002; *Radikal*, 12 March 2002.

6 See the comments by Bülent Ecevit in *Cumhuriyet*, 27 December 1989, and Gareth M. Winrow, 'NATO and the Out-of-Area Issue: the Positions of Turkey and Italy', *Il Politico* (Pavia) vol 58 (1993) p640. For a Turkish perspective, see also Gülnur Aybet, 'NATO's New Missions', *Perceptions* (Ankara) vol 4, no 1 (1999) pp65–78.

7 Paul B. Henze, 'Turkey: Toward the Twenty-First Century', in Fuller, et al., *Turkey's New Geopolitics*, p2.

8 Ziya Öniş, 'Turkey in the Post-Cold War Era: in Search of Identity', *Middle East Journal* vol 49 (1995) pp 48–9.

9 Şükrü Elekdağ, 'Two and a Half War Strategy', *Perceptions* (Ankara) vol 1, no 1 (1996) p57.

10 Quoted, Malik Mufti, 'Daring and Caution in Turkish Foreign Policy', *Middle East Journal* vol 52, no 1 (1998) p34 (from an article by Şükrü Elekdağ in *Milliyet*, 15 April 1996).

11 See *The Military Balance, 1998/99* (London: Oxford University Press for International Institute of Strategic Studies, 1998) pp55, 67.

12 James Traub, 'Turkey's Rules', *New York Times,* 20 January 2011.

13 Ahmet Davutoğlu, 'The Clash of Interests: An Explanation of the World (Dis) Order', *Perceptions* (Ankara) vol 2, no 4 (1997–8).

14 Ahmet Davutoğlu, *Stratejik Derinlik: Türkiye'nin Uluslararası Konumu* (Istanbul: Küre Yayınları, 2000) esp. pp183–208. See also Alexander Murinson, 'The Strategic Depth Doctrine of Turkish Foreign Policy', *Middle Eastern Studies* vol 42, no 6 (2006) pp945–55.

15 Ahmet Davutoğlu, 'Türkiye Merkez Ülke Olmalı', *Radikal,* (Istanbul, daily) 26 February 2002. See also his article 'Turkey's Foreign Policy Vision: An Assessment of 2007', *Insight Turkey* vol 10, no 1 (2008) pp78–9.

16 Quoted, Traub, 'Turkey's Rules'.

17 See Tarık Oğuzlu, 'Soft Power in Turkish Foreign Policy', *Australian Journal of International Affairs* vol 61, no 1 (2007) pp92–5.

18 Data from *Country Report, Turkey*, 1st Qtr 1993 (London: Economist Intelligence Unit) p3. Nicole and Hugh Pope add valuable information on the Özal period, in *Turkey Unveiled: Ataturk and After* (London: Murray, 1997) Ch11–13.

19 For further details see William Hale, 'Turkey's Political Landscape: A Glance at the Past and the Future', *International Spectator* (Rome) vol 34, no 1 (1999) p31, and Hugh Poulton, 'The Turkish State and Democracy', in ibid, pp60–1.

20 Notably Mrs Rahşan Ecevit, see the interview with her in *Milliyet*, 15 May 1999.

21 For these and other details of domestic politics at the time, see William Hale and Ergun Özbudun, *Islamism, Democracy and Liberalism in Turkey: The Case of the AKP* (London and New York: Routledge, 2010) Ch5–7.

22 See ibid, pp39–40, 63–4, 73–5, 115, 127–8, 156.

23 See ibid, pp91–2, 94–5. On the 'Cage Action Plan' and 'Sledgehammer', see *Today's Zaman* (Istanbul, daily) 17, 21, 23, 24 November 2009 and 22, 25 January 2010.

24 BBC news website (www.bbc.co.uk/news), 29 July 2011; *Milliyet*, 4 August 2011.

25 Election results from *Hürriyet*, 14 June 2010.

26 For fuller accounts of Turkey's Kurdish problem during the 1990s see David McDowall, *A Modern History of the Kurds* (London: I.B. Tauris, 1996) Ch20; Robert Olson (ed.), *The Kurdish Nationalist Movement in the 1990s: Its Impact on Turkey and the Middle East* (Lexington, KY: University of Kentucky, 1996); Michael M.Gunter, *The Kurds and the Future of Turkey* (New York: St Martin's Press, 1997) Ch3; Kemal Kirişci and Gareth Winrow, *The Kurdish Question and Turkey: An Example of Trans-state Ethnic Conflict* (London: Cass, 1997) Ch5–6; Henri J. Barkey and Graham E. Fuller, *Turkey's Kurdish Question* (Lanham, MD: Rowman and Littlefield, 1998) Ch3–6, and 'Turkey's Kurdish Question: Critical Turning Points and Missed Opportunities', *Middle East Journal* vol 51 (1997); Philip Robins, 'The Overlord State: Turkish Policy and the Kurdish Issue', *International Affairs* vol 69 (1993).

27 See p161. See also Kemal Kirişci, 'Turkey and the Kurdish Safe Haven in Northern Iraq', *Journal of South Asian and Middle Eastern Studies* vol 19 (1996) pp21–3, and Mahmut Balı Aykan, 'Turkey's Policy in Northern Iraq, 1991–95', *Middle Eastern Studies* vol 32 (1996) pp345–6.

28 Kemal Kirişci, 'The Kurdish Question and Turkish Foreign Policy', in Lenore G. Martin and Dimitris Keridis (eds), *The Future of Turkish Foreign Policy* (Cambridge, MA, and London: MIT Press, 2004) p283.

29 See Gunter, *The Kurds and the Future of Turkey*, pp75–7, and William Hale, 'Turkey', in Ami Ayalon (ed.), *Middle East Contemporary Survey 1993* vol 17 (Boulder, CO: Westview, 1995) pp678–79, p695 n22.

30 See Barkey and Fuller, *Turkey's Kurdish Question*, p70.

31 See William Hale, *Turkey, the US and Iraq* (London: Saqi Books, in association with London Middle East Institute, 2007) Ch3; Robert Olson, 'The Kurdish Question and Turkey's Foreign Policy, 1991–95: From the Gulf War to the Incursion Into Iraq', *Journal of South Asian and Middle Eastern Studies* vol 19 (1995) p20; Barkey and Fuller, *Turkey's Kurdish Question*, Chs2–5.

32 Quoted, *Milliyet*, 9 December 1991.

33 HEP had originally been formed by deputies elected on the SHP ticket in 1987 but had then been expelled from the party by Erdal İnönü in 1989. For the 1991 elections, they re-established a temporary alliance with the SHP.

34 Henri J. Barkey, 'The People's Democracy Party (HADEP): The Travails of a Legal Kurdish Party in Turkey', *Journal of Muslim Minority Affairs* vol 18 (1998) pp129–38; Barkey and Fuller, *Turkey's Kurdish Question*, pp84–9; Gunter, *The Kurds and the Future of Turkey*, p73.

35 Kirişci, 'Kurdish Question', p278. For further details on Öcalan's peregrinations between October 1998 and February 1999, see *Briefing* (Ankara, weekly) 22 February 1999, pp20–1.

36 *Milliyet*, 30 June 1999; Kirişci, 'Kurdish Question', pp278–9.

37 *The Economist* (London, weekly) 21 July 2005.

38 *Hürriyet*, 22 October 2007.
39 Website of CNNTurk television, Istanbul (www.cnnturk.com) 5 November 2007.
40 *Hürriyet*, 21 November 2005. The Laz are an ethnic minority living in the Black Sea region of Turkey. Şemdinli had attracted national attention earlier that month when a bomb explosion in a bookshop in the town killed one bystander and injured another 13 people. On strong evidence, this was the work of two plain-clothes non-commisioned officers in the paramilitary gendarmerie, aided by a former convicted PKK terrorist (ibid, 11 November 2005). In spite of promises by Tayyip Erdoğan that those responsible would be brought to book, none of the culprits were punished.
41 *Today's Zaman*, 8 August 2010.
42 *Radikal*, 16 September 2009; *Today's Zaman*, 18, 24 September 2009.
43 *Radikal*, 18 September 2009.
44 *Hürriyet Daily News* (Istanbul, daily) 25 October 2009.
45 Ibid, 15,18 December 2009; *Hürriyet*, 11 December 2009.
46 *Today's Zaman*, 16 July 2010; *Hürriyet Daily News*, 23 September 2010.
47 *Hürriyet Daily News*, 18 August, 30 September 2010; *Hürriyet*, 2 November 2010; CNNTurk website, 1 March 2011.
48 *Hürriyet Daily News*, 19 August 2010; *Today's Zaman*, 23, 24 September 2010; *Radikal*, 25 September 2010.
49 The following account draws partly on the writer's article, 'Foreign Policy and Turkey's Domestic Politics', in David Shankland (ed.), *The Turkish Republic at 75 Years* (Hemingford Grey: Eothen, 1999).
50 See Lesser, 'Turkey's Strategic Options', p81.
51 Sayarı, 'Turkey, Changing', pp18–20.
52 Selim Oktar, 'The Turkish Foreign Policy Environment: A Public Opinion Perspective', paper presented to the Conference 'The Domestic Context of Turkish Foreign Policy', The Washington Institute for Near East Policy, Washington, DC, July 1997.
53 For 2002, see the poll conducted by Yönelim Araştırma, reproduced in Ali Eşref Turan, *Türkiye'de Seçmen Davranışı: Öncedeki Kırılmalar ve 2002 Seçimi* (Istanbul: Bilgi Üniversitesi Yayınları, 2004) p273, Table 68, and that conducted by A & G Araştırma, reported in Tarhan Erdem, 'İkı parti seçmeni AKP'ye gitti', *Radikal*, 6 November 2002. For 2007, see the poll conducted by KONDA, reported in *Radikal*, 25 July 2007.
54 *Adalet ve Kalkınma Partisi Programı*, from the party website (www.akparti.org.tr).
55 Metropoll Stratejik ve Sosyal Araştırması, *Türkiye Siyasal Durum Araştırması, Aralık 2010* (from www.metropoll.com.tr).
56 See ibid, and Metropoll, *Davos Krizi, Ocak 2009* (from www.metropoll.com.tr).
57 See, for example, Binnaz Toprak, 'Civil Society in Turkey', in Augustus R. Norton (ed.), *Civil Society in the Middle East*, vol 2 (Leiden: Brill, 1995); Nilüfer Göle, 'Towards an Autonomization of Politics and Civil Society in Turkey', in Metin Heper and Ahmet Evin (eds), *Politics in the Third Turkish Republic* (Boulder, CO: Westview, 1994) and Jenny B.White, 'Civic Culture and Islam in Urban Turkey', in Chris Hann and Elizabeth Dunn (eds), *Civil Society: Challenging Western Models* (London: Routledge, 1996).
58 However, until the mid-1990s, there had been differences of views within the business community, particularly on the customs union with the EU: see Mükerrem Hiç, *Turkey's Customs Union with the European Union: Economic and Political Prospects* (Ebenhausen: Stiftung Wissenschaft und Politik, 1995) pp17,19.
59 See, for example, *Radikal*, 4 July 2002.
60 For further details, see M. Hakan Yavuz and John L. Esposito (eds), *Turkish Islam and the Secular State: The Gülen Movement* (Syracuse, NY: Syracuse University Press, 2003).

61 On Özal's policies, see Soli Özel, 'On Not Being a Lone Wolf: Geography, Domestic Plays, and Turkish Foreign Policy in the Middle East', in Geoffrey Kemp and Janice Gross Stein (eds), *Powder Keg in the Middle East: the Struggle for Gulf Security* (Lanham, MD: Rowman and Littlefield, 1995) pp167–70. For a fuller discussion of economic issues in Turkish foreign policy during the 1990s, see the writer's article 'Economic Issues in Turkish Foreign Policy', in Alan Makovsky and Sabri Sayarı (eds), *Turkey's New World: Changing Dynamics in Turkish Foreign Policy* (Washington, DC: Washington Institute for Near East Policy, 2000).

62 Data for 1990 from Economist Intelligence Unit, *Country Report, Turkey*, 4th Qtr 1993, p3. For 2010, foreign trade data from website of Central Bank of the Republic of Turkey (ww.tcmb.gov.tr); data from website of Turkish Statistical Institute [Türkstat] Ankara [www.tuik.gov.tr] vary slightly: national income data from State Planning Organization, Ankara, *Medium Term Program (2010–2012)* Annex, Table 1.

63 Balance of payments data from website of Central Bank of Turkey.

64 National income date from State Planning Organization, Ankara, *Medium Term Program (2011–2013) Main Macroeconomiuc and Fiscal Targets, 11 October 2010*, Table 1.

65 Foreign trade data from Türkstat website.

66 Economist Intelligence Unit, *Country Report, Turkey*, 4th Qtr 1994, p3, 2nd Qtr 1999, p5, January 2004, p5.

67 Ibid, October 2003, pp28–9. For further details on the 2001 crisis and its background, see Ziya Öniş, 'Domestic Politics versus Global Dynamics: Towards a Political Economy of the 2000 and 2001 Financial Crises in Turkey'; Hakan Tunç, 'The Lost Gamble: The 2000 and 2001 Turkish Financial Crises in Comparative Perspective'; and Fikret Şenses, 'Economic Crisis as an Instigator of Distributional Conflict: the Turkish Case in 2001', all in *Turkish Studies* vol 4, no 2 (2003).

68 Öniş, 'Domestic Politics versus Global Dynamics', p17; Bülent Aliriza, 'Turkey and the Global Storm', *Insight Turkey* (quarterly, Ankara) vol 3, no 4 (2001) p33.

69 Economist Intelligence Unit, *Turkey, Country Profile, 2005*, p38.

70 For the details, see the government's Letter of Intent to the IMF of 3 April 2002, from the IMF website (www.imf.org/external/np/loi/2002/tur/02/index.htm).

71 International Monetary Fund, *Turkey, Selected Issues*, IMF Country Report No 07/364, November 2007, p2.

72 Inflation data from website of Central Bank of Turkey.

73 Data for 2001 from Economist Intelligence Unit, *Turkey, Country Profile, 2005*, p70; for 2010, *The Economist* (London, weekly) 26 February 2011, p94.

74 Data from website of Central Bank of Turkey.

75 Data from Turkstat website.

76 Foreign trade data from ibid, these vary slightly from those issued by the Central Bank.

77 National income data from Turkstat, *Turkey's Statistical Yearbook 2009*, p356, Table 21.1.

78 *The Economist*, 26 February 2011, p93.

79 *Statistical Yearbook of Turkey 1990* (Ankara: State Institute of Statistics, 1991) pp492–3.

80 *Briefing*, 8 March 1999, p36, 22 March 1999, p32.

81 Energy consumption data from *BP Statistical Review of World Energy, June 2011* (London: British Petroleum, 2001) pp23, 40, 41.

82 Katinka Barysch, *Should the Nabucco Pipeline Project be Shelved?* (Washington, DC: Transatlantic Academy, Paper Series, May 2010) pp5–6, 14; other data from Nabucco Pipeline Project website, 2011 (www.nabucco-pipeline.com).

83 Barysch, *Nabucco*, p5; other data from Nabucco Pipeline Project website and website of the Austrian energy company OMV, a major shareholder in the project (www.omv.com).

84 That is, in addition to 6 bcm per year for domestic consumption in Turkey, see p154.
85 Barysch, *Nabucco*, pp11–14; *Today's Zaman*, 12 September 2011. See also Bill Park, *Modern Turkey: People, State and Foreign Policy in a Globalized World* (London and New York: Routledge, 2012) pp151–3.
86 Foreign trade and tourism statistics from Turkstat website.
87 Data from Central Bank of the Republic of Turkey, *International Investment Position Report, December 2008*, pp19–20, and Table X, pp45–6.
88 In the view of the Belgian newspaper *De Tijd*, Turkey had become 'the BRIC nation in the EU's backyard', reported in *Hürriyet Daily News*, 5 July 2010.
89 Estimate for 2010, *The Economist*, 26 February 2011, p94.

7 Turkey and the west after the Cold War I: Turkey and the United States

1 Mahmut Bali Aykan, 'Turkish Perspectives on Turkish–US Relations Concerning Persian Gulf Security in the Post-Cold War Era', *Middle East Journal* vol 50 (1996) pp345–6; Kemal Kirişci, 'Turkey and the United States: Ambivalent Allies', in Barry Rubin and Thomas Keaney (eds), *Friends of America: US Allies in a Changing World* (London and Portland, OR: Frank Cass, 2001) p127.
2 At one point, while she was Premier, Tansu Çiller threatened to veto NATO enlargement if Turkey were not included in that of the EU, but this turned out to be an empty threat.
3 Kirişci, 'Turkey and the United States', p121. See also Gülnur Aybet, 'NATO's New Missions', *Perceptions* (Ankara) vol 4, no 1 (1999) p73.
4 The following account is based on the writer's earlier book, *Turkey, the US and Iraq* (London: Saqi Books, in association with London Middle East Institute, 2007) pp37–64. For other accounts, see Philip Robins, *Turkey and the Middle East* (London: Pinter, for Royal Institute of International Affairs, 1991) pp69–70, and 'Turkish Policy in the Gulf Crisis: Adventurist or Dynamic?' in C.H. Dodd (ed.), *Turkish Foreign Policy: New Prospects* (Wistow: Eothen Press, for Modern Turkish Studies Programme, SOAS, 1992); Sabri Sayarı, 'Turkey: the Changing European Security Environment and the Gulf Crisis', *Middle East Journal* vol 46 (1992) pp13–14, 16–20; and William Hale, 'Turkey, the Middle East and the Gulf Crisis', *International Affairs* vol 68 (1992).
5 In a television interview in January 1991, Özal claimed that, after August 1990, he had wanted to send a Turkish detachment to join the coalition forces in the Gulf, see *Summary of World Broadcasts* (London, BBC) 22 January 1991. The idea was apparently turned down by General Necip Torumtay, the Chief of the General Staff, see his memoirs, Necip Torumtay, *Orgeneral Torumtay'ın Anıları* (Istanbul: Milliyet Yayınları, 1994) p112. On the question of opening a second front against Iraq, see below, notes 9 and 12.
6 According to a poll published by the Istanbul daily *Hürriyet* in September 1991, 61 per cent of respondents stated that they opposed Turkish involvement in the prospective Gulf War, cited by M. Hakan Yavuz and Mujeeb R.Khan, 'Turkish Foreign Policy toward the Arab–Israeli Conflict: Duality and the [*sic*] Development', *Arab Studies Quarterly* vol 14 (1992) pp84–5.
7 Yılmaz had resigned as foreign minister in February 1990, stating at the time that he had done so 'because there was no possibility left for my working comfortably' in the government: (quoted, *Milliyet*, 22 February 1990). However, there was speculation that he resented frequent interference in the work of his ministry by the President and other members of the cabinet.
8 Under Article 92, parliamentary permission would not be needed if such action were required by 'international treaties to which Turkey is a party [in effect, the

North Atlantic treaty] or by the rules of international courtesy', but neither of these conditions applied in this case.

9 In Bozer's case, there was widespread speculation at the time that this was the case, although the minister merely accused 'those playing a role behind the scenes' of causing his resignation: (*Milliyet*, 13 October 1990). Safa Giray's departure from the government apparently had little to do with the Gulf crisis, but mainly derived from a dispute with Akbulut over the composition of the Istanbul delegation to the Motherland Party's annual convention for 1991. In his memoirs and in later interviews, Torumtay made it clear that he and his fellow generals opposed proposals by Özal that Turkey should open a second front against Iraq if war broke out (Torumtay, *Anilar*, pp115–16, and in statements in Mehmet Ali Birand and Soner Yalçın (eds), *The Özal: Bir Davanın Öyküsü* (Istanbul: Doğan Kitapçılık, 2001) pp430–3, 440–2).

10 *Financial Times*, 18 January 1991.

11 However, the General Staff did consider it 'probable' that Saddam Hussein might launch air or missile attacks against Turkey, and prepared plans for counter-attacks by the Turkish air force against Iraq in response; Torumtay, *Anilar*, p113.

12 See above, note 9. In their account, Nicole and Hugh Pope confirm that Özal had wanted to open a second front in Iraq, basing this on information from Güneş Taner, a minister of state at the time. According to Taner's statement, the Americans supported the idea, but the Turkish government decided that the United Nations would force Turkey to leave Mosul if it occupied the province, there was no money to pay for the campaign, and the General Staff 'forecast that 40,000–50,000 Turkish lives would be lost in an offensive'. Nicole and Hugh Pope, *Turkey Unveiled: Atatürk and After* (London: Murray, 1997) p220. For other statements by Özal, to the effect that he wanted Turkey to occupy Mosul, see ibid, p226.

13 *Summary of World Broadcasts*, 4 March 1991.

14 Kemal Kirişci, 'Turkey and the Kurdish Safe Haven in Northern Iraq', *Journal of South Asian and Middle Eastern Studies* vol 19 (1996) pp21–3; Mahmut Balı Aykan, 'Turkey's Policy in Northern Iraq, 1991–95', *Middle Eastern Studies* vol 32 (1996) pp345–6.

15 Pope and Pope, *Turkey Unveiled*, p228: Aykan, 'Turkey's Policy', p345.

16 See, for example, Meltem Müftüler-Baç, 'Turkey's Predicament in the Post-Cold War Era', *Futures* vol 28 (1996) p259.

17 Aykan, 'Turkey's Policy', p344.

18 Writer's estimate at the time, for the Economist Intelligence Unit. Turkish estimates were a good deal higher than this: for instance, in 1993, the government estimated the total loss since the embargo began as $20 billion over a four-year period, or an average of $5 billion per year; see Aykan, 'Turkey's Policy', pp353–4.

19 See the writer's contributions to Ami Ayalon (ed), *Middle East Contemporary Survey* for 1991 (vol 15) p713, and 1992 (vol 16) p773 (Boulder, CO: Westview, 1993, 1995).

20 Aykan, 'Turkish Perspectives', p357 note 57; see also Kemal Kirişci, 'Turkey and the United States', pp126–8 and 'The Kurdish Question and Turkish Foreign Policy', in Lenore G. Martin and Dimitris Keridis (eds), *The Future of Turkish Foreign Policy* (Cambridge, MA, and London: MIT Press, 2004) pp291–2. On the 'Sèvres syndrome' in general, see Dietrich Jung, 'The Sèvres Syndrome: Turkish Foreign Policy and its Historical Legacies', *American Diplomacy* vol 8, no 2 (2003).

21 Aykan, 'Turkey's Policy', pp354–5; see also Michael M.Gunter, *The Kurds and the Future of Turkey* (New York: St Martin's Press, 1997), pp98–9.

22 Philip Robins, 'Turkish Foreign Policy under Erbakan', *Survival* vol 39, no 2 (1997) p85.

23 Robert Olson, 'The Kurdish Question and Turkey's Foreign Policy, 1991–95: From the Gulf War to the Incursion into Iraq', *Journal of South Asian and Middle Eastern Studies* vol 19 (1995) p2.

24 See Asa Lundgren, *The Unwelcome Neighbour: Turkey's Kurdish Policy* (London: I.B. Tauris, 2007) pp78–81.
25 Officially, the US denied any direct involvement in Öcalan's capture, though it referred vaguely to diplomatic and intelligence operations in the affair: see *Briefing* (Ankara, weekly) 1 March 1999, p25. See also *The New York Times*, 20 February 1999, and *Milliyet*, 21 February 1999.
26 A notable exception was that of the Minister of Health, Osman Durmuş, of the Nationalist Action Party, who claimed that the hospital ship sent by the US Navy was not needed. However, this and similar remarks by the minister provoked harsh criticism in the Turkish press: *Milliyet*, 23 August 1999, headlined the story 'An Amazing Mentality'.
27 *Briefing*, 22 November 1999, pp7, 28; 29 November 1999, p3; *International Herald Tribune*, 22 November 1999.
28 Aykan, 'Turkish Perspectives', p351.
29 *Briefing*, 5 March 1990, p3.
30 See Ekavi Athanassopoulou, 'American Turkish Relations since the End of the Cold War', *Middle East Policy* vol 8 no 3 (2001) p155.
31 Mark R. Parris, 'Turkey and the US: A Partnership Rediscovered', *Insight Turkey* (Istanbul, quarterly) vol 3, no 4 (2001) pp3–4.
32 Ibid, p5; *Radikal*, 25 September 2001; website of NTV television, Istanbul (www.ntvmsnbc.com) 10 October 2001
33 Murat Yetkin, *Tezkere: Irak Krizinin Gerçek Öyküsü* (Istanbul: Remzi, 2004) p39. For a more detailed account and analysis by the writer of events narrated in this section, see Hale, *Turkey, the US and Iraq*, Ch4–6.
34 Aylin Şeker Görener, 'US Policy towards Iraq: Moral Dilemmas of Sanctions and Regime Change', *Turkish Review of Middle East Studies* (Istanbul, annual) vol 12 (2001) p43.
35 Masaki Kakizaki, 'Anti-Iraq War Protests in Turkey: Global Networks, Coalitions and Context', *Middle Eastern Studies,* Vol.47, No.1 (2011) pp83–84: Fikret Bila, *Sivil Darbe Girişimi ve Ankara'da Irak Savaşları* (Ankara, Ümit Yayıncılık, 2003) p192.
36 See *Radikal*, 10 January 2002; *Briefing,* 4 February 2002, p8; NTV website, 9 February 2002.
37 *Briefing*, 21 January 2002, pp3–4; *Radikal*, 17 January 2002.
38 Quoted, Nicole Pope, 'Concerns over Iraq', *Middle East International* 22 March 2002, p19.
39 See the polling results cited by Nasuh Uslu, Metin Toprak, İbrahim Dalmış and Ertan Aydın, 'Turkish Opinion towards the United States in the Context of the Iraq Question', *MERIA Journal* vol 9, no 3 (2005) pp2–3 and Table 14.
40 Text from http://daccessdds.un.org/doc/UNDOC/GEN/N02/682/26.
41 Bill Park, 'Turkey, the United States, and Northern Iraq', in Paul Cornish (ed.), *The Conflict in Iraq, 2003* (Basingstoke and New York: Palgrave Macmillan, 2004) p81; Yetkin, *Tezkere*, pp99–101; James E.Kapsis, 'The Failure of the US–Turkish Pre-war Negotiations: an Overconfidant United States, Political Mismanagement and a Conflicted Military', *MERIA Journal* vol 9, no 3 (2005) p1.
42 Philip Robins, 'Confusion at Home, Confusion Abroad: Turkey between Copenhagen and Iraq', *International Affairs* vol 79, no 3 (2003) p561 and 'The Opium Crisis and the Iraq War: Historical Parallels in Turkey–US Relations', *Mediterranean Politics* vol 12, no 1 (2007) p20; Yetkin, *Tezkere*, pp99–101; Bila, *Sivil Darbe*, pp196–7.
43 Yetkin, *Tezkere*, pp131–2, 143–4; Bila, *Sivil Darbe*, p217 ; Robins, 'Confusion', pp63–4.
44 *Milliyet*, 29 December 2002.
45 *Radikal*, 7 February 2003; *Hürriyet*, 12 February 2003.
46 Kapsis, 'Failure', p3; *The Economist*, 27 February 2003; Bila, *Sivil Darbe*, p221.

47 *Hürriyet*, 28 February 2003.
48 In fact, the 'yes' votes outnumbered the 'no' votes (264 votes to 250) but the parliamentary rules required the resolution to be passed by an absolute majority of the whole house (i.e., 267 votes), thanks to abstentions, this was not achieved, by a margin of three votes.
49 Quoted, Daniel Pipes, 'Turkey's Radical Turn', *New York Post*, 5 August 2003.
50 Jonathan Eric Lewis, 'Replace Turkey as a Strategic Partner?', *Middle East Quarterly* vol 13, no 2 (2006) p46. This argument rested on the highly dubious claim, which was unsupported by any provable and material evidence, that the AKP had received 'billions of dollars from Persian Gulf and other Islamist sources' (ibid). For more in this exaggerated vein, see Michael Rubin, 'Green Money, Islamist Politics in Turkey', ibid, vol 12, no 1 (2005) pp13–23. For a more sober, but still pessimistic assessment, which fails to put any of the blame for the deterioration on the Bush administration, see Joshua W. Walker, 'Reexamining the US–Turkish Alliance', *The Washington Quarterly* vol 31, no 1 (2007–8).
51 *Briefing*, 12 May 2003; *Hürriyet*, 24 June 2003.
52 NTV website, 7 October, 24 October 2003; *The Economist*, 18 October 2003; *Financial Times* (London) 8 November 2003; Michael Rubin, 'A Comedy of Errors: American–Turkish Diplomacy and the Iraq War', *Turkish Policy Quarterly* vol 4, no 1 (2005) p5.
53 See for instance, the comments by Thomas Oliphant, 'A Lesson for Turkey from Kurdish Allies', *Boston Globe* 13 April 2003, quoted by Cengiz Çandar, 'Turkish Foreign Policy and the War on Iraq', in Martin and Keridis (eds), *Future of Turkish Foreign Policy*, p53.
54 The exact number is disputed, see Lundgren, *Unwelcome Neighbour*, p81.
55 Yetkin, *Tezkere*, pp220–2; *Hürriyet*, 5, 8 July 2003; NTV website, 7, 8, 15, 17 July 2003; Bill Park, 'Between Europe, the United States and the Middle East: Turkey and European Security in the Wake of the Iraq Crisis', *Perspectives on European Politics and Society* vol 5, no 3 (2004) p501.
56 On the latter, see *Hürrıyet*, 27 November 2004.
57 'President's Remarks at Galatsaray University', 29 June 2004, from the White House website (www.whitehouse.gov/news/releases/2004/06).
58 Ioannis N. Grigoriadis, 'Friends No More? The Rise of Anti-American Nationalism in Turkey', *Middle East Journal* vol 64, no 1 (2010) pp60–1; Aylin Güney, 'Anti-Americanism in Turkey, Past and Present', *Middle Eastern Studies* vol 44, no 3 (2008) pp482–3; John C.K. Daly, *US–Turkish Relations: A Strategic Relationship Under Stress* (Washington, DC: The Jamestown Foundation, 2008) p8; David Arnett, 'Problems of Perception and Vision: Turkey and the US', *Turkish Policy Quarterly* vol 7, no 1 (2008) p16.
59 Robert J. Pollock, 'The Sick Man of Europe – Again', *Wall Street Journal* 16 February 2005.
60 Bill Park, *Turkey's Policy Towards Northern Iraq: Problems and Perspectives*, London, International Institute of Strategic Studies, Adelphi Paper 374, 2005, pp22, 35, 49–53; Lundgren, *Unwelcome Neighbour*, pp112–16.
61 The US authorities also claimed that they lacked sufficient ground troops to take on the PKK in Iraq, but the Turkish side found this hard to believe, see Arnett, 'Problems of Perception', p21.
62 Notably the appointment of two 'special coordinators', retired Generals Joseph Ralston for the US and Edip Başer for Turkey, in 2006; both resigned in the following year. See *Today's Zaman*, 6 October 2007.
63 *Turkish Daily News*, 14 March, 13 April 2007; website of CNN Turk television, Istanbul (www.cnnturk.com) 12 June 2007.
64 Website of NTV television, Istanbul (www.ntvmsnbc.com) 1 October 2007; *Hürriyet*, 9, 21, 22 October 2007; Daly, *US-Turkish Relations*, pp19–20.

65 CNN Turk website, 5 November 2007.
66 *Hürriyet*, 16 December 2007, 22 February 2008; BBC News website (http://news vote.bbc.co.uk) 22, 25 December 2007, 29 February 2008; *Today's Zaman*, 16 January 2008.
67 *Today's Zaman*, 9 January 2008.
68 James Traub, 'Turkey's Rules'.
69 *Milliyet*, 6 April 2009; quotation from the *Guardian* (London daily) 6 April 2009.
70 See, for example, BBC News website, 4 June 2009.
71 Cited in Grigoriadis, 'Friends No More?', p59. Just how seriously such findings should be taken may be doubted, however: see above, p149.
72 Ibid, pp61–2.
73 Tayyip Erdoğan was widely criticized for having allegedly dismissed the idea as 'gossip' in an interview in the *Guardian* in October 2009 (see, for example, BBC News website, 26 October 2009). In fact, he did not use this phrase, although he did claim that Iran's nuclear programme had purely peaceful purposes (*Guardian*, 26 October 2009). On the other hand, President Gül has been quoted as saying that he did think Iran was aiming to produce nuclear weapons, see International Crisis Group, *Turkey's Crises over Israel and Iran* (Brussels: International Crisis Group, Europe Report No 208, 8 September 2010) p12 n111.
74 Ian O. Lesser, 'Turkey, Iran and Nuclear Risks', *Turkish Policy Quarterly* vol 3, no 2 (2004) pp84–5, 92–3, and 'Can Turkey Live with a Nuclear Iran?' research paper issued by German Marshall Fund, Washington, DC (www.gmfus.org) 2 March 2009.
75 BBC News website, 17 May 2010.
76 NTV website, 11 June 2010.
77 Traub, 'Turkey's Rules' (see note 67).
78 *Hürriyet*, 13 September 2009; *Hürriyet Daily News*, 17 September 2009.
79 *Today's Zaman*, 14 September 2011; *Hürriyet*, 4 October 2011.
80 International Crisis Group, *Turkey's Crises*, pp8–9.
81 Ibid, p17.
82 BBC News website, 23 January 2011; *Today's Zaman*, 25 January 2011. On the earlier United Nations report, see *Today's Zaman*, 23 September 2010.
83 Ibid, 1 March 2011.
84 Traub, 'Turkey's Rules' (see note 67).
85 David Schenker, 'A NATO without Turkey', *Wall Street Journal*, 5 November 2009, quoted, International Crisis Group, *Turkey's Crises*, p18.
86 Daniel Pipes, 'A Democratic Islam?' *Jerusalem Post*, 17 April 2008. This drew a sharp response from Namık Tan, the Turkish ambassador in Tel Aviv, rejecting the 'totally baseless and unacceptable comparison' with bin Laden, ibid, 24 April 2008.
87 Ian O. Lesser, 'Rethinking Turkish–Western Relations: A Journey Without Maps', research paper issued by German Marshall Fund, Washington, DC (www.gmfus. org) 30 June 2010.

8 Turkey and the west after the Cold War II: Turkey and the European Union

1 Luigi Narbone and Nathalie Tocci, 'Running Around in Circles? The Cyclical Relationship between Turkey and the European Union', in Susannah Verney and Kostas Ifantis (eds), *Turkey's Road to European Union Membership: National Identity and Political Change* (London and New York: Routledge, 2009) p21.
2 For recent studies of the economic aspects, see Tevfik F. Nas, 'Economic Dimension: the Turkish Economy from the 1960s to EU Accession', in Armağan Emre Çakır (ed.), *Fifty Years of EU–Turkey Relations a Sisyphean Story* (London and New

York: Routledge, 2011) pp46–66, and references in Ziya Öniş and Fikret Şenses (eds), *Turkey and the Global Economy: Neo-Liberal Restructuring and Integration in the Post-Crisis Era* (London and New York: Routledge, 2009). On the position and role of Turkish migrants in the EU, see, for exampe, Fulya Kip Barnard, 'The Role of Turkish Migration and Migrants in Turkey's Relations with the EU', in İdris Bal (ed.), *Turkish Foreign Policy in [the] Post Cold War Era* (Boca Raton, FL: Brown Walker, 2004) pp181–95. On Turkey and European security policy, see the previous edition of this book, William Hale, *Turkish Foreign Policy, 1774–2000* (London and Portland OR: Frank Cass, 2nd edn, 2002] pp229–32, 353–4; Şebnem Udum, 'Turkey and the Emerging European Security Framework', *Turkish Studies* vol 3, no 2 (2002); Mahmut Balı Aykan, 'Turkey and European Security and Defence Identity/Policy (ESDI/P): A Turkish View', *Journal of Conrtemporary European Studies* vol 13, no 3 (2005); Miguel Medina Abelan, *Turkey, the European Security and Defence Policy, and Accession Negotiations* (Ankara: Middle East Technical University, 2009, from http://sinan.ces.metu.edu.tr/dosya/miguelwp1.pdf); Pinar Bilgin, 'Security Dimension: A Clash of Security Cultures? Differences between Turkey and the European Union Revisited', in Çakır (ed.), *Fifty Years*, pp67–82.

3 In preparing this summary of Turkey–EU relations between 1990 and 1996, the writer has drawn on two earlier papers: see William Hale, 'Turkey: A Crucial but Problematic Applicant', in John Redmond (ed.), *Prospective Europeans: New Members for the European Union* (New York and London: Harvester Wheatsheaf, 1994), and William Hale, 'Turkey and the EU: The Customs Union and the Future', *Boğaziçi Journal* (Istanbul) vol 10, no 1 (1997). For fuller accounts of events during the 1990s, see also the chapter on Turkey in John Redmond, *The Next Mediterranean Enlargement of the European Community: Turkey, Cyprus and Malta* (Aldershot: Dartmouth, 1993); Meltem Müftüler-Baç, *Turkey's Relations with a Changing Europe* (Manchester and New York: Manchester University Press, 1997) especially Ch5–6; and Heinz Kramer, 'Turkey and the European Union: A Multi-Dimensional Relationship with Hazy Perspectives', in V. Mastny and R. Craig Nation (eds.), *Turkey Between East and West: New Challenges for a Rising Regional Power* (Boulder, CO: Westview, 1996).

4 Quoted, Müftüler-Baç, *Turkey's Relations*, p95.

5 Ibid, pp95–6; Ali Resul Usul, *Democracy in Turkey: The Impact of EU Political Conditionality* (London and New York: Routledge, 2011) pp50–1; Kramer, 'Turkey and the European Union', pp210–11; Meltem Müftüler-Baç, 'The Never-Ending Story: Turkey and the European Union', *Middle Eastern Studies* vol 34, no 4 (1998) p241.

6 Meltem Müftüler, 'Turkish Economic Liberalization and European Integration', *Middle Eastern Studies* vol 31, no 1 (1995) pp92–5. On the last point, see Mükerrem Hiç, *Turkey's Customs Union with the European Union: Economic and Political Prospects,* (Ebenhausen: Stiftung Wissenschaft und Politik, 1995) pp17–19.

7 Müftüler-Baç, *Turkey's Relations*, pp90–1; Heinz Kramer, 'The EU–Turkey Customs Union: Economic Integration Amidst Political Turmoil', *Mediterranean Politics* vol 1, no 1 (1996) pp60, 67.

8 Kramer, 'EU–Turkey Customs Union', pp68–9.

9 Ibid, pp70–1; Müftüler-Baç, *Turkey's Relations*, p94.

10 'Decision 1/95 of the EC–Turkey Association Council of 22 December 1995', *Official Journal of the European Communities* vol 39 L35 (13 February 1996) Articles 4–6, 13, 25, 31–2.

11 See, for example, Canan Balkır, 'Turkey and the European Community: Foreign Trade and Direct Foreign Investment in the 1980s', in Canan Balkır and Allan M. Williams (eds), *Turkey and Europe* (London and New York: Pinter, 1993) p129.

12 Quoted, *Milliyet*, 17 December 1995.

13 Welfare Party 1995 election manifesto, pp6–7, 29.
14 See *Milliyet*, 14 December, 17 December 1995.
15 Philip Robins, 'Turkish Foreign Policy under Erbakan', *Survival* vol 39, no 2 (1997) p86.
16 Quoted, Müftüler-Baç, 'Never-Ending Story', p240.
17 Gülnür Aybet, 'Turkey and European Institutions', *International Spectator* (Rome) vol 34, no 1, (1999) p107.
18 'Statement by the Turkish Government on 14 December 1997, Concerning the Presidency Conclusions of the European Council Held on 12–13 December 1997 in Luxembourg', reprinted in *Perceptions* (Ankara) vol 2, no 4 (1997–8) pp154–6.
19 This was suggested by Bülent Ecevit, in an interview for *Milliyet*, 20 February 1999.
20 Ziya Öniş, 'Conservative Globalists versus Defensive Nationalists: Political Parties and Paradoxes of Europeanisation in Turkey', in Verney and Ifantis (eds), *Turkey's Road*, pp39–40.
21 *Presidency Conclusions, Helsinki European Council, 10 and 11 September 1999*, para 12 (from www.consilium.europa.eu/uedocs).
22 Ibid, para 4.
23 Ibid, paras 12 and 9(a) (taken together).
24 Ibid, para 9(b).
25 '04BRUSSELS1868, DINING WITH CHRIS: RANDOM THOUGHTS FROM RELEX' dated 24 April 2004 (one of the 'Wikileaks' cables, from http://213.251.145.96/cable/2004/04/04BRUSSELS1868.html). On the second point, see also Ziya Öniş, 'Greek–Turkish Relations and the European Union: A Critical Perspective', *Mediterranean Politics* vol 6, no 3 (2001) p37.
26 Reuters, 11 December 1999.
27 English text of the Accession Partnership Document, *Briefing*, 13 November 2000, pp16–24. The following summary deals only with the most politically critical points.
28 The then existing text of the Penal Code specified the death penalty for a number of offences, including 'political' crimes. However, under Article 87 of the constitution, death sentences could only be carried out if they were confirmed by a majority vote of parliament. No such confirmations had been voted through since 1984, leaving a large number of prisoners (including the PKK leader Abdullah Öcalan) on a kind of 'death row'.
29 For the full text of the Convention and its Protocols see, for example, Ian Brownlie (ed.), *Basic Documents on Human Rights* (Oxford: Clarendon Press, 3rd edn, 1992) pp326–62.
30 English text, *National Programme, Introduction and Political Criteria (Unofficial Translation)* on website of Prime Ministry, General Secretariat of EU Affairs (www.abgs.gov.tr).
31 These came into effect on 27 October 2001, when all but one of them were endorsed by President Sezer. For the full text of the constitution in English, including these and later amendments, see the website of the Grand National Assembly of Turkey (www.tbmm.gov.tr/anayasa/constitution.htm). For a more detailed summary of the reform programme, see Ergun Özbudun and Serap Yazıcı, *Democratization Reforms in Turkey (1993–2004)* (Istanbul: TESEV, 2004); Ergun Özbudun and Ömer Faruk Gençkaya, *Democratization and the Politics of Constitution Making in Turkey* (Budapest and New York: Central European University Press, 2009) and William Hale and Ergun Özbudun, *Islamism, Liberalism and Democracy in Turkey: The Case of the AKP* (London and New York: Routledge, 2010) Ch5.
32 *Briefing*, 8 October 2001, pp3–5. For further details on the last point, see İhsan Dağı, 'Rethinking Human Rights, Democracy and the West: Post-Islamist Intellectuals in Turkey', *Critique: Critical Middle Eastern Studies* vol 13, no 2 (2004); İhsan Dağı, 'Transformation of Islamic Political Identity in Turkey: Rethinking

the West and Westernization', *Turkish Studies* vol 6, no 1 (2005); İhsan Dağı, 'The Justice and Development Party: Identity, Politics and Human Rights Discourse in the Search for Security and Legitimacy', in M. Hakan Yavuz (ed.), *The Emergence of a New Turkey: Democracy and the AK Parti* (Salt Lake City, UT: University of Utah Press, 2006); Ziya Öniş, 'Globalization and Party Transformation: Turkey's Justice and Development Party in Perspective', in Peter Burnell (ed.), *Globalising Democracy: Party Politics in Emerging Democracies* (London and New York: Routledge, 2006). On the attitudes of political parties more broadly, see Gamze Avcı, 'Turkish Political Parties and the EU Discourse in the Post-Helsinki Period', in Mehmet Uğur and Nefis Canefe (eds), *Turkey and European Integration: Accession Prospects and Issues* (London and New York: Routledge, 2004) and Meltem Müftüler-Baç, 'Turkey's Political Reforms and the Impact of the European Union', *South European Society and Politics* vol 10, no 1 (2005).

33 For a more detailed account, see William Hale, 'Human Rights, the European Union, and the Turkish Accession Process', in Ali Çarkoğlu and Barry Rubin (eds), *Turkey and the European Union: Domestic Politics, Economic Integration and International Dynamics* (London and Portland, OR: Frank Cass, 2003) pp107–21.

34 Article 10 provides that freedom of expression may be subjected to such restrictions 'as are necessary in a democratic society, in the interests of national security, territorial integrity or public safety, [or] for the prevention of disorder or crime', among other things.

35 That is, the 'Law for the Establishment of Radio and Television Enterprises and their Broadcasts' (Law No.3984) of 1994, Article 4, see Human Rights Watch, *Turkey: Human Rights and the European Union Accession Partnership*, section on 'Ensuring Language Rights', from website of Human Rights Watch (www.hrw.org/reports/2000/turkey2).

36 Website of NTV television, Istanbul (www.ntvmsnbc.com) 15 December 2001.

37 Commission of the European Communities, '2001 Regular Report on Turkey's Progress towards Accession' (Brussels, 13 November 2001: SEC [2001] 1756) sections 1 (Introduction) and 1.2.

38 *Radikal*, 31 January 2002: NTV website, 6 February, 7 February 2002; *Hürriyet*, 7 February 2002.

39 See NTV website, 27 March 2002, and *Milliyet*, 27 March 2002.

40 *Radikal*, 18 April 2002.

41 Öniş, 'Conservative Globalists', p40.

42 *Copenhagen European Council, 12 and 13 December 2002, Presidency Conclusions* (Brussels: Council of the European Union, 15917/02, 29 January 2003, from www.european-council.europa.eu/council-meetings/conclusions.aspx).

43 NTV website, 19 July 2003.

44 Ibid, 30 July 2003.

45 *2003 Regular Report on Turkey's Progress towards Accession* (Brussels: European Commission, 2003, from www.avrupa.info.tr/Files/File/Docs/2003pdf) pp23, 43–5.

46 For the English text of the Civil Code, see www.tesev.org.tr/userfiles/image/turkey. For a translation of the Penal Code, see http://legislationonline.org/documents, and for a summary see Hale and Özbudun, *Islamism, Democracy and Liberalism*, p62.

47 *Turkish Daily News* (Ankara, daily) 26 January 2004

48 Clement Dodd, 'Constitutional Features of the UN Plan for Cyprus and its Antecedents', *Turkish Studies* vol 6, no 1 (2005) pp39–40, 45.

49 International Crisis Group, *Cyprus: Reversing the Drift towards Partition* (Brussels: International Crisis Group, Europe Report no 190, 10 January 2008) p4.

50 Quoted, ibid, p4.

51 BBC News website (http://news.bbc.co.uk) 24 April 2004.

52 James Ker-Lindsay, 'The Policies of Greece and Cyprus towards Turkey's EU Accession', *Turkish Studies* vol 8, no 1 (2007) pp46–8.

53 NTV website, 3 November 2004.

54 Ibid, 20 July 2004.

55 *Hürriyet*, 30 July 2005.

56 Text of the Negotiating Framework from the Washington Institute for Near East Policy, Washington, DC (www.washingtoninstitute.org/documents).

57 European Commission, *European Council in Copenhagen 21–22 June 1993: Conclusions of the Presidency* (SN180/1/93 REV1) p13. See also Usul, *Democracy*, pp56–7.

58 *Hürriyet*, 4 October 2005.

59 Of the 35 Chapters, two are non-negotiable (that is, Chapter 34 'Institutions' and Chapter 35 'Other Issues').

60 For further exploration of European opinion on the question of Turkish accession – both for and against – see Nathalie Tocci, 'Elite Opinion Dimension: Behind the Scenes of Turkey's Protracted Accession Process: European Elite Debates', in Çakır (ed.), *Fifty Years*, pp83–103; and Hakan Yılmaz, 'Turkish Identity on the Road to the EU: Basic Elements of French and German Oppositional Discourse', in Verney and Ifantis (eds), *Turkey's Road*, pp79–91.

61 *Today's Zaman*, 1 May 2011.

62 Website of CNN Turk television, Istanbul (www.cnnturk.com) 29 November 2004; *Hürriyet*, 30 November 2004.

63 *Today's Zaman*, 15 November 2009. Quotation from Hugh Pope, 'EU and Turkey Edge Back from the Brink' (5 January, 2010), report for the International Crisis Group, Brussels (www.crisisgroup.org).

64 Semih İdiz, *Turkey's 'French Problem'* (Paris and Brussels: Institut Français des Relations Internationales, Note Franco-Turque No 3, 7 Mai 2010) p4

65 *The Economist* (London, weekly) 22 December 2007.

66 *The Turko File: France,* 16 June, 19 July 2008 (http://turkofile.wordpress.com/category/france).

67 *Today's Zaman*, 26 February 2011. By contrast, President Gül had earlier spent several days in Paris on an official visit

68 Ayşe Aslıhan Çelenk, 'The Restructuring of Turkey's Policy towards Cyprus: the Justice and Development Party's Struggle for Power', *Turkish Studies* vol 8, no 3 (2007) p360; NTV website, 25 January 2006; *Hürriyet*, 28 January 2006; CNN Turk website, 31 January 2006; *The Economist*, 28 January 2006.

69 Heinz Kramer, *Turkey's Accession Process to the EU: The Agenda behind the Agenda* (Berlin: Stiftung Wissenschaft und Politik, SWP Comments 25, October 2009) p3.

70 Ziya Öniş, 'Contesting for Turkey's Political "Centre": Domestic Politics, Identity Conflicts and the Controversy over EU Membership', *Journal of Contemporary European Studies* vol 18, no 3 (2010) p368.

71 *Turkey 2008 Progress Report* (Brussels: Commission of the European Communities, 5 November 2008, SEC [2008] 1334) pp17, 23.

72 *Hürriyet*, 16 December 2005. In the event, the prosecution was dropped over a technicality (*Turkish Daily News*, 24 January 2006).

73 *Radikal*, 3 May 2006, 20 January 2007.

74 *2008 Progress Report* (see note 71) pp15, 17, 23.

75 *Turkey 2009 Progress Report* (Brussels: Commission of the European Communities, 14 October 2009, SEC [2009] 1334) pp9, 15.

76 See the frequent references in ibid, pp6–29, and the *2008 Progress Report* (see note 71) pp6–26.

77 *Hürriyet Daily News*, 15 December 2009.

78 Kramer, *Turkey's Accession Process,* p1

79 See Ergun Özbudun, *The Constitutional System of Turkey, 1876 to the Present* (New York: Macmillan, 2011) Ch9. For the English text of the amendments, as originally proposed, see Prime Ministry [of Turkey], Secretariat General for European Affairs, *Constitutional Amendments Proposal* (5 April 2010) (from www.aqbgs.gov.tr/files/BasinMusavirlik/const_amndments.pdf).
80 *Hürriyet*, 4 May 2010; *Today's Zaman*, 8 May 2010.
81 *Today's Zaman*, 8 May 2010.
82 Ibid, 10 April 2010; *Zaman* (Istanbul, daily) 24 March 2010.
83 See, for instance, the comments by Tayyip Erdoğan, reported in *Today's Zaman*, 7 May 2010 and *Radikal*, 6 June 2010.
84 Öniş, 'Contesting for Turkey's Political "Centre"', p366.
85 As an example, the AKP's manifesto for the 2011 elections devoted eight pages to 'democratization', 'strong political institutions', 'a strong civil society' and 'a new constitution', but only two sentences to the effect that this would strengthen the bid for accession: Justice and Development Party, *Türkiye Hazır, Hedef 2023: 12 Haziran 2011 Genel Seçımleri Seçim Beyannamesi* (Ankara: AK Parti, 2011) pp9–16.
86 Data for 2004–8 from the EU source Eurobarometer, reproduced in Armağan Emre Çakır, 'Introduction', in Çakır (ed.), *Fifty Years*, p5, and for 2008–10 from Eurobarometer, 'Standard EB 74, Autumn 2010' (from http://ec.europa.eu/public_opinion/archives/eb/eb74_fact_tr_en_pdf). These figures suggest support for EU membership fell fairly consistently between 2004 and 2008, but then stabilized at around 40 per cent. On the other hand, according to the Turkish polling organization Metropoll Stratejik ve Sosyal Araştırmalar, support rose from 55.5 per cent in 2007 to 69.1 per cent in 2008, before falling back to 49.7 per cent in 2010 (from the website www.metropoll.com.tr). The writer's conclusion is that there has been a fall in public support in Turkey for the project over the last 5–6 years, but the data are erratic and inconsistent.
87 *Today's Zaman*, 11 December 2011.
88 Ibid, 22 April 2011; *Hürriyet Daily News*, 21 April 2011. Later, President Gül repeated the idea of the 'Norwegian option' as a possible outcome, *Today's Zaman*, 1 May 2011.
89 Öniş, 'Contesting for Turkey's Political "Centre"', pp370–71.
90 Justice and Development Party, *Türkiye Hazır*, p151.
91 International Crisis Group, *Cyprus: Reversing the Drift*, p10.
92 Öniş, 'Contesting for Turkey's Political "Centre"', p362.
93 Tocci, 'Elite Opinion', pp84–5.

9 Turkey and regional politics after the Cold War I: Greece, Cyprus and the Balkans

1 Umut Özkırımlı and Spyros A. Sofos, *Tormented by History: Nationalism in Greece and Turkey* (London: Hurst, 2008) p2.
2 Clement H. Dodd, *The Cyprus Imbroglio* (Hemingford Grey: Eothen, 1998) pp42–3, 46–7, quotation p43.
3 Ibid, pp44–51; Suha Bölükbaşı, 'Boutros Ghali's Cyprus Initiative in 1992: Why Did it Fail?', *Middle Eastern Studies* vol 31, no 3 (1995) pp469, 471–6; Keith Kyle, *Cyprus: In Search of Peace* (London: Minority Rights Group International, 1997) pp27–9. For the text of Boutros-Ghali's 'Set of Ideas' and his 'non-map', see Dodd, *Cyprus Imbroglio*, pp141–61.
4 Dodd, *Cyprus Imbroglio*, pp53–9; Bölükbaşı, 'Boutros Ghali's Cyprus Initiative', pp474–5; Kyle, *Cyprus*, p30; Suha Bölükbaşı, 'The Cyprus Dispute in the Post-Cold War Era', *Turkish Studies Association Bulletin* vol 18 (1994) p18.
5 Dodd, *Cyprus Imbroglio*, pp67–8 ; Kyle, *Cyprus*, p31.

6 Christopher de Bellaigue, 'Conciliation in Cyprus?' *Washington Quarterly* vol 22, no 2 (1999) pp189–90.
7 See Ekavi Athanassopoulou, 'Blessing in Disguise? The Imia Crisis and Turkish–Greek Relations', *Mediterranean Politics* vol 2, no 3 (1997) pp77, 85–7. For a statement by the Turkish Foreign Ministry on the Kardak/Imia dispute, see 'Turkish Documents Regarding Issues between Turkey and Greece', *Turkish Review of Balkan Studies* vol 3 (1996/7) pp143–7.
8 Theodora Kalaitzaki, 'US Mediation in Greek–Turkish Disputes since 1954', *Mediterranean Quarterly* vol 16, no 2 (2005) pp122–3.
9 Athanassopoulou, 'Blessing in Disguise?', p90 ; Dodd, *Cyprus Imbroglio*, pp101–7, 190–2.
10 De Bellaigue, 'Conciliation', p190.
11 *Milliyet*, 26, 29 June 1999; *Briefing* (Ankara, weekly) 2 August 1999, pp12–13; *Financial Times*, 10 September 1999. See also Ahmet Evin, 'Changing Greek Perspectives on Turkey: an Assessment of the Post-Earthquake Rapprochement', *Turkish Studies* vol 5, no 1 (2004) p8. On the last point, see the interview with Bülent Ecevit in *Newsweek*, 1 November 1999.
12 See Ali Çarkoğlu and Kemal Kirişci, 'The View from Turkey: Perceptions of Greeks and Greek–Turkish Rapprochement by the Turkish Public', *Turkish Studies* vol 5, no 1 (2004) esp. pp122, 126, 137ff.
13 Oliver P. Richmond, 'Ethno-Nationalism, Sovereignty and Negotiating Positions in the Cyprus Conflict: Obstacles to a Settlement', *Middle Eastern Studies* vol 35, no 3 (1999) p48.
14 *Briefing*, 24 January 2000, p14; Reuters, 5 February 2000.
15 *Presidency Conclusions, Helsinki European Council, 10 and 11 September 1999*, para 12 (from www.consilium.europa.eu/uedocs).
16 Website of NTV television, Istanbul (www.ntvmsnbc.com) 9 April 2002.
17 Clement Dodd, *Storm Clouds Over Cyprus: A Briefing* (Hemingford Grey: Eothen, 2nd edn, 2002) p62.
18 Ahmet Sözen and Kudret Özersay, 'The Annan Plan: State Succession or Continuity', *Middle Eastern Studies* vol 43, no 1 (2007) p138.
19 Ibid, p130; Clement Dodd, 'Constitutional Features of the UN Plan for Cyprus and its Antecedents', *Turkish Studies* vol 6, no 1 (2005) pp45–9; Kudret Özersay, 'Simultaneous Referenda in Cyprus: Was it a "Fact" or an "Illusion"?', ibid, vol 6, no 3 (2005) pp383–6; Ahmet Sözen, 'A Model of Power-Sharing in Cyprus: From the 1959 London-Zurich Agreements to the Annan Plan', ibid, vol 5, no 1 (2004) pp65–9.
20 See Ayşe Aslıhan Çelenk, 'The Restructuring of Turkey's Policy towards Cyprus: The Justice and Development Party's Struggle for Power', *Turkish Studies* vol 8, no 3 (2007) pp351–2, 356; Müge Kınacıoğlu and Emel Oktay, 'The Domestic Dynamics of Turkey's Cyprus Policy: Implications for Turkey's Accession to the European Union', ibid, vol 7, no 2 (2006) pp263–6; Ziya Öniş and Şuhnaz Yılmaz, 'Greek-Turkish Rapprochement: Rhetoric or Reality?', *Political Science Quarterly* vol 123, no 1 (2008) p139.
21 *Hürriyet*, 12 January 2004; NTV website 12 January, 20 January 2004.
22 Çelenk, 'Restructuring', p357.
23 *Turkish Daily News*, 24 January 2004.
24 International Crisis Group, *Cyprus: Reversing the Drift to Partition* (Brussels: International Crisis Group, Europe Report No 190, 10 January 2008) p4 n27.
25 Ibid, p4.
26 Ibid, p4 n23.
27 Text supplied to the writer by the Cyprus High Commission in London.
28 International Crisis Group, *Cyprus: Reunification or Partition?* (Brussels: International Crisis Group, Europe Report No 201, 30 September 2009) p1.

29 European Council statement of 26 April 2004, quotation p1 n5.

30 Ibid, p2

31 International Crisis Group, *Cyprus: Six Steps towards a Settlement* (Nicosia/Istanbul/Brussels: International Crisis Group, Europe Briefing No 61, 22 February 2011) p3.

32 *Today's Zaman*, 1, 2, 6 November 2011.

33 *Hürriyet*, 18 November 2007. Trade data from Turkish Statistical Institute (www.tuik.gov.tr).

34 Bahar Rumelili, 'Civil Society and the Europeanization of Greek–Turkish Cooperation', *South European Society and Politics* vol 10, no 1 (2005) p48ff.

35 Iaonnis N. Grigoriadis, 'The Orthodox Church and Greek–Turkish Relations: Religion as a Source of Rivalry or Reconciliation?' in Jeffrey Haynes (ed.), *Religion and Politics in Europe, the Middle East and North Africa* (London and New York: Routledge, 2010) pp60–6. Fortunately, after the death of Archbishop Christodoulos in January 2008, the Holy Synod of Greece elected a far more moderate successor (ibid, p67).

36 Bahar Rumelili, 'Transforming Conflicts on EU Borders: The Case of Greek–Turkish Relations', *Journal of Common Market Studies* vol 45, no 1 (2007) p107 n2.

37 Ibid, p120.

38 Öniş and Yılmaz, 'Greek–Turkish Rapprochement', pp146–7.

39 Heinz Kramer, *AKP's 'New' Foreign Policy between Vision and Pragmatism* (Berlin: Stifting Wissenschaft und Politik, Working Paper FG2, June 2010) p24.

40 Estimate by the director of the Society of Solidarity and Assistance to the Refugees from Yugoslavia [in Turkey], cited by Kemal Kirişci, 'New Patterns of Turkish Foreign Policy Behavior', in Çiğdem Balım (ed.), *Turkey: Political, Social and Economic Challenges in the 1990s* (Leiden: Brill, 1995) p7. Another estimate puts the figure at one fifth of the population, which if true would amount to more than 14 million people on present (2011) numbers; İlhan Uzgel, 'The Balkans: Turkey's Stabilizing Role', in Barry Rubin and Kemal Kirişci (eds), *Turkey in World Politics: an Emerging Multiregional Power* (London: Lynne Rienner, 2001), p49.

41 Philip Robins, 'Coping with Chaos: Turkey and the Bosnian Crisis', in Richard Gillespie (ed.), *Mediterranean Politics*, vol 1 (1994) (annual, London: Pinter) p112; Duygu Bazoğlu Sezer, 'Turkey in the New Security Environment in the Balkan and Black Sea Region', in Vojtech Mastny and R. Craig Nation (eds), *Turkey between East and West: New Challenges for a Rising Regional Power* (Boulder, CO: Westview Press, 1996) p82.

42 Şule Kut, 'Turkish Policy towards the Balkans', in Alan Makovsky and Sabri Sayarı (eds), *Turkey's New World: Changing Dynamics in Turkish Foreign Policy* (Washington, DC: Washington Institute for Near East Policy, 2000) p82.

43 Renamed the Organization for Security and Cooperation in Europe (OSCE) in 1994.

44 Robins, 'Coping with Chaos', pp122–4; Kirişci, 'New Patterns', pp7–10.

45 *Independent*, 2 July 1994; *The Times* (London) 9 July 1994.

46 Robins, 'Coping with Chaos', pp125–6; John Roper, 'The West and Turkey: Varying Roles, Common Interests', *International Spectator* (Rome) vol 24, no 1 (1999) p94; Miomir Zuzul, 'Croatia and Turkey: Toward a Durable Peace in Southeastern Europe', *Perceptions* (Ankara) vol 3 (1998) pp82–8. After his retirement in 1994, former Chief of the General Staff Doğan Güreş stated that Turkey had secretly supplied arms to the Bosnian Muslims; Uzgel, 'The Balkans', p66 n12.

47 Gülnür Aybet, *NATO's Developing Role in Collective Security* (Ankara: Ministry of Foreign Affairs, Center for Strategic Research, 1999) pp18–20; Roper, 'The West and Turkey', p95.

48 Aybet, *NATO's Developing Role*, pp32–4.

49 See the 'Statement on Kosovo' signed at the NATO summit in Washington in April 1999, paragraph 14; full text reprinted in Aybet, *NATO's Developing Role*, pp63–5.

50 Quoted, *Briefing*, 24 May 1999, p18.
51 Ibid, 29 March 1999, pp14–15; 12 April 1999, pp14–16
52 Ibid, 12 July 1999, pp14–15.
53 *Turkish Daily News*, 21 February 2008; *Radikal*, 22 February 2008
54 Loic Poulain and Akis Sakellariou, 'Western Balkans: Is Turkey Back?', paper issued by Center for Strategic and International Studies, Washington, DC (http://csis.org) 25 April 2011, p2; James Traub, 'Turkey's Rules', *New York Times*, 20 January 2011.
55 See Turkish and Bulgarian reports reproduced in *Summary of World Broadcasts* (London, BBC) 15–16 October 1999.
56 Quoted, Poulain and Sakellariou, 'Western Balkans', p1.
57 Ibid, p5.
58 Kut, 'Turkish Policy', pp80, 88.
59 *Financial Times*, 10 September 1999; Ekavi Athanassopoulou, 'Greece, Turkey, Europe: Constantinos Simitis in Premiership Waters', *Mediterranean Politics* vol 1, no 1 (1996) p116; Othon Anastasakis, 'Greece and Turkey in the Balkans: Cooperation or Rivalry?' *Turkish Studies* vol 5, no 1 (2004) pp46–7, 50–2, 58.

10 Turkey and regional politics after the Cold War II: Russia, the Black Sea, Transcaucasia and central Asia

1 Data from Turkish Statistical Institute website (www.tuik.gov.tr), foreign trade statistics.
2 Data for contracted total from the website of the Turkish state pipeline company, BOTAŞ (www.botas.gov.tr); for actual consumption from *BP Statistical Review of World Energy, June 2011* (London: British Petroleum, 2011) p23. On the latter point, see Gareth M. Winrow, 'Turkey and the East–West Gas Transportation Corridor', *Turkish Studies* vol 5, no 2 (2004) pp28–32.
3 Data from BOTAŞ website (see previous note). Other gas suppliers were Iran (19 per cent) and Azerbaijan (13 per cent). Gas was also contracted to be imported as liquid natural gas (LNG) from Algeria and Nigeria (10 per cent).
4 Şaban Kardaş, 'Turkey Strengthens Nuclear Cooperation with Russia', *Eurasia Daily Monitor* vol 7, no 213, November 2010 (from www.jamestown.org).
5 Data from website of Turkish Ministry of Foreign Affairs (www.mfa.gov.tr) and *Today's Zaman*, 3 October 2011.
6 As, for instance, on the occasion of a visit to Moscow by Prime Minister Erdoğan in March 2011; Şaban Kardaş, 'Erdogan's Moscow Visit Produces Mixed Results', *Eurasia Daily Monitor* vol 8, no 54, March 2010.
7 See the statement on the Turkish Foreign Ministry website (www.mfa.gov.tr) 'Türk Boğazları'. This reports the number of tankers transiting the Bosporus as 4,248, with a total tonnage of 'dangerous materials' (primarily crude oil) of 60.1 million metric tons in 1996, rising to 10,054 passages and 143.9 million metric tones in 2007.
8 Website of NTV television, Istanbul (www.ntvmsnbc.com), 7 August 2009; see also Bill Park, *Modern Turkey: People State and Foreign Policy in a Globalised World* (London and New York: Routledge, 2012) pp149–50.
9 *Hürriyet Daily News*, 8 September 2011.
10 Vladimir Socor, 'Putin Looks for LNG Exit from South Stream', *Eurasia Daily Monitor* vol 8, no 49 (11 March 2011).
11 'Summit Declaration of Black Sea Economic Cooperation', June 1992 (copy kindly supplied by Ministry of Foreign Affairs, Ankara).
12 *Briefing*, 28 June 1999, p26.
13 Data from Turkish Statistical Institute website (www.tuik.gov.tr), foreign trade statistics.

14 Hasan Ulusoy, 'A New Formation in the Black Sea: BLACKSEAFOR', *Perceptions* (Ankara) vol 6, no 4 (2001–2) pp51–2; Suat Kınıklıoğlu, *The Anatomy of Turkish–Russian Relations* (Washington, DC: Brookings Institution, 2006) pp2–3, 11–13; Graham E. Fuller, *The New Turkish Republic: Turkey as a Pivotal State in the Muslim World* (Washington, DC: US Institute for Peace Press, 2008) p132; Ian O. Lesser, 'Turkey's Regional Role: Harder Choices Ahead', *Turkish Policy Quarterly* vol 7, no 2 (2008) p35.

15 Gareth M. Winrow, 'Turkey and the Newly Independent States of Central Asia and Transcaucasus', *MERIA Journal* vol 2, no 2 (1997), and 'Turkey's Relations with the Transcaucasus and the Central Asian Republics', *Perceptions* (Ankara) vol 1, no 1 (1996) pp129–30. In fact, Russia did give some political support to the PKK but apparently did not go further than that; Robert Olson, 'Turkish and Russian Foreign Policies, 1991–97: The Kurdish and Chechnya Questions', *Journal of Muslim Minority Affairs* vol 18, no 2 (1998) pp212–15, 218–19.

16 Suha Bölükbaşı, 'Ankara's Baku-Centered Transcaucasia Policy: Has It Failed?' *Middle East Journal* vol 51 (1997) p90.

17 Interview on TRT television, Ankara, 4 November 1999; see *Summary of World Broadcasts*, 6 November 1999, and *International Herald Tribune*, 29 November 1999.

18 See Gareth M. Winrow, 'A Region at the Crossroads: Security Issues in Post-Soviet Asia', *Journal of South Asian and Middle Eastern Studies* vol 18 (1994) p14; and Robert V. Barylski, 'Russia, the West and the Caspian Energy Hub', *Middle East Journal* vol 49, no 2 (1995) pp220–1. Azerbaijan signed the pact in September 1993, following the takeover by Haydar Aliev. However, it has not allowed Russian troops to be stationed on its territory, except for one Russian radar base.

19 Alexander Murinson, *Turkey's Entente with Israel and Azerbaijan: State Identity and Security in the Middle East and Caucasus* (London and New York: Routledge, 2010) p58.

20 For further details on these and subsequent events up to 1994, see the writer's two earlier papers, 'Turkey, the Black Sea and Transcaucasia', in John F.R. Wright, Suzanne Goldenburg and Richard Schofield (eds), *Transcaucasian Boundaries* (London: UCL Press, 1996) pp54–68, and 'Turkey and Transcaucasia', in David Menashri (ed.), *Central Asia Meets the Middle East* (London: Frank Cass, 1998) pp150–67.

21 Graham E. Fuller, 'Turkey's New Eastern Orientation', in Graham E. Fuller and Ian O. Lesser (eds), *Turkey's New Geopolitics: From the Balkans to Western China* (Boulder, CO: Westview, 1993) p78.

22 *Milliyet*, 6 March, 14 March 1992.

23 Bülent Ecevit claimed that this was so (*Cumhuriyet*, 25 May 1992), although the 1921 treaty appears to give Turkey far fewer rights than it had, for instance, under the 1960 Cyprus Treaty of Guarantee.

24 Quoted, *Mideast Mirror* (London, daily) 19 May 1992.

25 Ibid, 21 May 1992; *Milliyet*, 21 May 1992.

26 *Milliyet*, 27 May 1992; *Independent*, 28 May 1992.

27 International Crisis Group, *Turkey and Armenia: Opening Minds, Opening Borders* (Brussels: International Crisis Group, Europe Report No 199, 2009) p2.

28 It is claimed that more than a million Azeris have been forced to leave their homes since the start of the conflict in 1988; Svante E. Cornell, 'Turkey and the Conflict in Nagorno Karabakh: A Delicate Balance', *Middle Eastern Studies* vol 34 (1998) p51. See also Svante E. Cornell, 'Undeclared War: The Nagorno Karabakh Conflict Reconsidered', *Journal of South Asian and Middle Eastern Studies* vol 20 (1997) p9.

29 *Briefing*, 14 June 1993, p14; 21 June 1993, pp10–11.

30 *Milliyet*, 23 June 1993. In April–May 1995, a group of Azeri opposition leaders led by former President Ayaz Mutalibov, in coalition with Turkish ultra-nationalists and possibly with elements of the Turkish intelligence services, attempted to launch a coup to oust Aliev. Although the details are obscure, this was apparently thwarted by Demirel, who had established a close rapport with the Azeri president; Murinson, *Turkey's Entente*, pp20, 60, 126.

31 *Milliyet*, 12 August 1993.

32 During his presidency, Elchibey had tactlessly stated that Iran was doomed, and that Iranian Azerbaijan would be united with his republic within five years; see Cornell, 'Undeclared War', p13. Statements of this kind evidently caused severe misgivings in Ankara, which fully supported Azerbaijan's independence within its existing frontiers, but did not want to stir up the cauldron by supporting vague Azeri claims to Iranian Azerbaijan.

33 Dimitry Furman and Carl Johan Asenius, 'The Case of Nagorno-Karabakh (Azerbaijan)', in Lena Jonson and Clive Archer (eds), *Peacekeeping and the Role of Russia in Eurasia* (Boulder, CO: Westview, 1996) pp147–9.

34 Jonathan Elkind, 'Economic Implications of the Baku–Tibilisi–Ceyhan Pipeline' in Central Asia-Caucasus Institute, *The Baku–Tibilisi–Ceyhan Pipeline: Oil Window to the West* (Washington, DC: Johns Hopkins University, 2005) p43; Gökhan Bacık, 'Turkey and Pipeline Politics', *Turkish Studies* vol 7, no 2 (2006) p301; Paul A. Williams and Ali Tekin, 'The Iraq War, Turkey, and Renewed Caspian Energy Prospects', *Middle East Journal* vol 62, no 3 (2008) pp388, 397; Carol R. Saivetz, 'Tangled Pipelines: Turkey's Role in Energy Export Plans', *Turkish Studies* vol 10, no 1 (2009) p97.

35 'Shah Deniz taps primed', *Upstream Online*, 14 September 2006 (www.upstreamonline.com).

36 Report on the website www.lojiport.com, 26 September 2011.

37 *Today's Zaman*, 25 October 2011.

38 *Hürriyet Daily News*, 25 October 2011; Şaban Kardaş, 'Turkish-Azeri Deal May Herald New Competition in Southern Corridor', *Eurasia Daily Monitor* vol 7, no 115, 15 June 2010; Vladimir Socar, 'Nabucco Pipeline, Azerbaijan's Shah Deniz Field Require Synchronised Development', ibid, vol 7, no 164, 14 September 2010.

39 Quoted, *Hürriyet Daily News*, 1 December 2010.

40 *Today's Zaman*, 18 August 2010. The details were not published in the Turkish press, but see the reports by Stratfor Global Intelligence (www.stratfor.com) 22 December 2010, and *Baku Today* (www.bakutoday.net) 11 March 2011.

41 International Crisis Group, *Armenia and Azerbaijan: Preventing War* (Brussels: International Crisis Group, Europe Briefing No 60, February 2011) pp5–8, 15. On the last point, see *Hürriyet Daily News*, 26 August 2010.

42 International Crisis Group, *Armenia and Azerbaijan*, pp14–15, quotation p15.

43 John C.K. Daly, *US–Turkish Relations: A Strategic Relationship Under Stress* (Washington, DC: Jamestown Foundation, 2008) pp9–13; *Radikal*, 25 October 2007.

44 International Crisis Group, *Turkey and Armenia: Opening Minds, Opening Borders* (Brussels: International Crisis Group, Europe Briefing No 199, 4 May 2009), p3.

45 Ibid, pp23–5.

46 Website of CNN Turk television, Istanbul (www.cnnturk.com) 14 April 2005.

47 International Crisis Group, *Turkey and Armenia*, pp2–3.

48 *Hürriyet*, 1 September 2009; *Today's Zaman*, 1, 2 September 2009; Hugh Pope, 'Turkey and Armenia vow to heal past wounds', *International Crisis Group* (www.crisisgroup.org) 1 September 2009. For the text of the two protocols, see *Hürriyet*, 1 September 2009.

49 *Today's Zaman*, 11 October 2009; BBC News website, 11 October 2009.

50 *Today's Zaman*, 11 December 2009; on the latter point see Şaban Kardaş, 'Turkey Reacts to Armenian Constitutional Court's Decision on Protocols', *Eurasia Daily Monitor* vol 7, no 17 (26 January 2010).

51 *Hürriyet Daily News*, 5 March 2010; *Today's Zaman*, 19, 30 March 2010

52 Vladimir Socor, 'Armenia Suspends US–backed Normalization of Relations with Turkey', *Eurasia Daily Monitor* vol 7, no 81 (27 April 2010); Emil Danielyan, 'Turkish–Armenian Accords Pronounced Dead by Yerevan', ibid, vol 8, no 31 (14 February 2011).

53 *Today's Zaman*, 30 September 2010.

54 Igor Torbakov, *The Georgia Crisis and Russia–Turkish Relations* (Washington, DC: Jamestown Foundation, 2008) pp6–7.

55 Ibid, p9; Mustafa Aydın, 'Foucault's Pendulum: Turkey in Central Asia and the Caucasus', *Turkish Studies* vol 5, no 2 (2004) p12.

56 See, for instance, the commentary article in *Today's Zaman*, 12 August 2008, headlined 'Strategic Blunder led Georgia into South Ossetia Folly'.

57 See Bülent Alireza, 'Turkey and the Crisis in the Caucasus', commentary article for Center for Strategic and International Studies, Turkey Project, Washington, DC, 9 September 2008.

58 Ibid. See also *Today's Zaman*, 18, 20, 21, 22 August 2008.

59 Quoted, *Turkish Daily News*, 24 September 2008.

60 *Today's Zaman*, 20 August 2008.

61 Gareth M. Winrow, *Turkey in Post-Soviet Central Asia* (London: Royal Institute of International Affairs, 1995) p17; İdris Bal, *Turkey's Relations with the West and the Turkic Republics: The Rise and Fall of the 'Turkish Model'* (Aldershot: Ashgate, 2000) p51.

62 Gareth M. Winrow, 'Regional Security and National Identity: The Role of Turkey in former Soviet Central Asia', in Çiğdem Balım (ed.), *Turkey: Political, Social and Economic Challenges in the 1990s* (Leiden: Brill, 1995) p31 (citing Soviet data of 1990–1).

63 Winrow, *Turkey in Post-Soviet Central Asia*, pp6–7.

64 See Jacob M. Landau, *Pan-Turkism: From Irredentism to Cooperation* (London: Hurst, 1995) Ch3.

65 On Türkeş' pan-Turkist ideas and their relationship to Islamism, see Hugh Poulton, *Top Hat, Grey Wolf and Crescent: Turkish Nationalism and the Turkish Republic* (London: Hurst, 1997) pp147–50, 155–8; and Bal, *Turkey's Relations*, pp64–5.

66 Philip Robins, 'Between Sentiment and Self-Interest: Turkey's Policy toward Azerbaijan and the Central Asian States', *Middle East Journal* vol 47 (1993) p592.

67 General Dostum, the then Uzbek warlord in northern Afghanistan, did, however, visit Turkey in 1996, and requested Turkish government aid for his forces, apparently unsuccessfully; Gareth M. Winrow, 'Turkey and the Newly Independent States'. With regard to Iran, the fact that Abulfaz Elchibey, the President of Azerbaijan during 1992–3, was prone to call for 'reunion' with the Azeris of northwestern Iran was also a cause of embarrassment for Turkey.

68 Paul B. Henze, *Turkey: Toward the Twenty-First Century* (Washington, DC: Rand Corporation, n.d.) p31.

69 Winrow, *Turkey in Post-Soviet Central Asia*, pp11–12; Philip Robins, 'Turkey's Ostpolitik: Relations with the Central Asian States' in David Menashri (ed.), *Central Asia Meets the Middle East* (London: Cass, 1998) pp131–3.

70 Quoted, Robins, 'Turkey's Ostpolitik', p135.

71 Ibid, p135; Heinz Kramer, 'Options for Turkish Foreign Policy: Central Asia and Transcaucasus', unpublished paper (1997) p3.

72 Winrow, *Turkey in Post-Soviet Central Asia*, p13.

73 Robins, 'Turkey's Ostpolitik', pp133, 136–7; Winrow, *Turkey in Post-Soviet Central Asia*, p19.

74 Winrow, *Turkey in Post-Soviet Central Asia*, pp33–8; Robins, 'Turkey's Ostpolitik', pp137–40; Winrow, 'A Region at the Crossroads', pp16–17.
75 Robins, 'Between Sentiment and Self-Interest', p600; Winrow, 'Regional Security', p34; Heinz Kramer, 'Will Central Asia Become Turkey's Sphere of Influence?', *Perceptions* (Ankara) vol 1, no 1 (1996) p116.
76 Kramer, 'Options', pp11–12.
77 Bayram Balcı, 'Fethullah Gülen's Missionary Schools in Central Asia and their Role in the Spreading of Turkism and Islam', *Religion, State and Society* vol 31, no 2 (2003) p157; see also Berna Turan, 'National Loyalties and International Undertakings: The Case of the Gülen Community in Kazakhstan', in M. Hakan Yavuz and John L. Esposito (eds), *Turkish Islam and the Secular State: The Gülen Movement,* (Syracuse, NY: Syracuse University Press, 2003) pp184–207.
78 Balcı, 'Fethullah Gülen', p165.
79 Trade data for 1992 from Bal, *Turkey's Relations*, p84, for 2011 from Turkish Statistical Institute website (www.tuik.gov.tr), foreign trade statistics (for Kazakhstan, Kirghizstan, Uzbekistan and Turkmenistan). Other date from website of Turkish Ministry of Foreign Affairs (www.mfa.gov.tr), 'Turkey's Relations with Central Asian Republics'.
80 From website of Turkish Ministry of Foreign Affairs website (www.mfa.gov.tr), 'Turkey's Relations with Central Asian Republics'.
81 *Briefing*, 21 June 1999, pp14–15; 12 July 1999, p15.
82 *Hürriyet*, 17 September 2010; *Today's Zaman*, 17 September 2010.
83 *Hürriyet*, 17 September 2010.
84 Thus, respondents to a public opinion poll conducted by the Ankara-based International Strategic Research Organization (USAK) in August 2009 ranked all four of the 'Turkic' central Asian republics, plus Azerbaijan, as among the 14 nations judged to be 'Turkey's friends' in the world, whereas only three NATO countries (USA, Italy and Germany) were included in the list: Uluslarası Stratejik Araştırmalar Kurumu, *USAK Dış Politika Algılama Anketi,Ağustos 2009,* p7 (from www.usak.org.tr)

11 Turkey and regional politics after the Cold War III: the Middle East and the wider world

1 Ayşegül Sever, 'The Arab–Israeli Peace Process and Turkey since the 1995 Interim Agreement', *Turkish Review of Middle East Studies* (Istanbul) vol 9 (1996/7) pp121, 125; M. Hakan Yavuz, 'Turkish–Israeli Relations through the Lens of the Turkish Identity Debate', *Journal of Palestine Studies* vol 27 (1997) pp26–7.
2 Mahmut Bali Aykan, 'The Palestinian Question in Turkish Foreign Policy from the 1950s to the 1990s', *International Journal of Middle East Studies* vol 25 (1993) p106; Bülent Aras, *Palestinian–Israeli Peace Process and Turkey* (Commack, NY: Nova Science Publishers, 1998) p134; Kemal Kirişci, 'Post Cold-War Turkish Security and the Middle East', *MERIA Journal* no 2 (1997); Mahmut Bali Aykan, 'The Turkey–US–Israel Triangle: Continuity, Change and Implications for Turkey's Post-Cold War Middle East Policy', *Journal of South Asian and Middle Eastern Studies* vol 22 (1999) pp6–7.
3 For further details, see Amikam Nachmani, 'The Remarkable Turkish–Israeli Tie', in Amikam Nachmani, *Turkey and the Middle East* (Tel Aviv: Begin-Sadat Center for Strategic Studies, Bar Ilan University, 1999, reprinted from *Middle East Quarterly* vol 5 [1998]) pp24–6.
4 Besides Turkey, the members of the 'D-8' were Bangladesh, Egypt, Indonesia, Iran, Malaysia, Nigeria and Pakistan. Notable absentees among the Arab countries were Saudi Arabia and the other Gulf states, Jordan, Syria and Iraq: apparently,

these governments refused to take Erbakan or his ideas seriously. The title was changed to 'D-8' from 'M-8' or 'Muslim', apparently because the latter sounded too provocative. See Philip Robins, 'Turkish Foreign Policy under Erbakan', *Survival* vol 39, no 2 (1997) pp93–4; and Sabri Sayarı, 'Turkey and the Middle East in the 1990s', *Journal of Palestine Studies* vol 26 (1997) p52

5 By comparison, Turkey's total trade with the Arab countries of the Middle East and North Africa in 2002 was around $8.7 billion, or more than six times the total for Israel. Data for 1992 from *Statistical Yearbook of Turkey 1998*, p525; for 2002, from Turkish Statistical Institute website (www.tuik.gov.tr), foreign trade statistics.

6 *Hürriyet*, 17 April 2002.

7 Ibid, 22, 25 March 2004; *Turkish Daily News*, 26 March, 21 May 2004.

8 Quoted, *Briefing*, 10 January 2005, p8.

9 *Hürriyet*, 17 February 2006; website of NTV television, Istanbul (www.ntvmsnbc.com) 17 Fenruary 2006.

10 *Today's Zaman*, 13, 14, 22 November 2007.

11 See Kemal Kirişci, Nathalie Tocci and Joshua Walker, *A Neighbourhood Rediscovered: Turkey's Transatlantic Value in the Middle East* (Washington, DC: German Marshall Fund of the United States, Brussels Forum Paper Series, 2010) p9.

12 International Crisis Group, *Turkey's Crises over Israel and Iran* (Brussels: International Crisis Group, Europe Report No 208, 2010) p3.

13 *Hürriyet*, 30 January 2009.

14 Ibid, 12, 13 January 2010.

15 Its full title in Turkish is *İnsan Hak ve Hürriyetleri İnsani Yardım Vakfı* ('Human Rights and Freedoms Humanitarian Relief Foundation') but it normally translates this simply as 'Humanitarian Relief Foundation': see the organization's website (www.ihh.org.tr).

16 International Crisis Group, *Turkey's Crises*, pp4–8; United Nations, *Report of the Secretary-General's Panel of Inquiry on the 31 May 2010 Flotilla Incident, July 2011* [the 'Palmer Committee Report'] (released by the *New York Times*, 2 September 2011) pp45, 50, 59, 61.

17 International Crisis Group, *Turkey's Crises*, pp8–9.

18 Quotations from *Today's Zaman*, 23 September 2010.

19 *Hürriyet*, 8 December 2010: BBC News website (www.bbc.co.uk/news) 23 January 2011.

20 *Today's Zaman*, 17 May, 17 June 2011.

21 Ibid, 7, 24 June, 17 July 2011.

22 Ibid, 19 September 2011; *Hürriyet*, 19 September 2011.

23 Palmer Committee Report (see note 16) pp45, 54.

24 BBC News website, 6 September 2011; *Hürriyet Daily News*, 2 September 2011

25 BBC News website, 3 September 2011.

26 In the words of Article 5 of the 1987 agreement: for the full text, see H. Fahir Alaçam, 'Turkish–Syrian Relations', *Turkish Review of Middle East Studies* (Istanbul) vol 8 (1994/5) pp12–14.

27 Suha Bölükbaşı, 'Turkey Challenges Iraq and Syria: The Euphrates Dispute', *Journal of South Asian and Middle Eastern Studies* vol 16 (1993) pp22–3; see also İlter Turan, 'Water and Turkish Foreign Policy', in Lenore G. Martin and Dimitris Keridis (eds), *The Furure of Turkish Foreign Policy* (Cambridge, MA, and London: MIT Press, 2004) pp193–208. On the last point, see Meliha Benli Altunışık and Özlem Tür, 'From Distant Neighbours to Partners? Changing Syrian-Turkish Relations', *Security Dialogue* vol 37, no 2 (2006) p237.

28 See Ayşegül Kibaroğlu, 'Prospects for Cooperation in the Euphrates–Tigris River Basin' *Turkish Review of Middle East Studies* (Istanbul) vol 8 (1994/5) p143; and Turkish Ministry of Foreign Affairs (MFA), 'Water Issues between Turkey, Syria and Iraq', *Perceptions* (Ankara) vol 1, no 2 (1996) p87.

29 See MFA, 'Water Issues', p102.
30 Bölükbaşı, 'Turkey Challenges', pp23–25; MFA, 'Water Issues', pp98–100.
31 Quoted, *Briefing*, 21 September 1998, p10.
32 Ibid, 12 October 1998, pp16–17; Ö. Zeynep Oktav Alantar, 'The October 1998 Crisis: A Change of Heart of Turkish Foreign Policy Towards Syria?', *Cahiers d'études sur la Méditerranée orientale et le monde turco-iranien* no 31 (2001) pp143–5.
33 *Briefing*, 12 October 1998, pp16–17; 19 October 1998, pp11–12; 26 October 1998, pp11–12; Alantar, 'October 1998 Crisis', pp145–6.
34 Suggested by *The Economist*, 29 October 2009,
35 See Mensur Akgün, Gökçe Perçinoğlu and Sabiha Senyücel Gündoğar, *The Perception of Turkey in the Middle East* (İstanbul: Turkish Economic and Social Studies Foundation [TESEV], 2009).
36 Altunışık and Tür, 'From Distant Neighbours', pp239, 241.
37 Data from Turkish Statistical Institute website (www.tuik.gov.tr), foreign trade statistics.
38 *Today's Zaman*, 14 October, 24 December 2009.
39 *Hürriyet*, 28 April 2009.
40 *Today's Zaman*, 27 September 2010.
41 Altunışık and Tür, 'From Distant Neighbours', pp242–3.
42 Ibid, p242; *Turkish Daily News*, 14 April 2005; *Radikal*, 15 April 2005.
43 Burak Akıncı, 'Newly Found Friendship Between Turkey and Syria', *Middle East Online* (www.middle-east-on-line.com) 23 December 2004.
44 *Today's Zaman*, 24 December 2009.
45 For further details on the Kirkuk question, and Turkey's policies towards it up to January 2005, see International Crisis Group, *Iraq: Allaying Turkish Fears over Kurdish Ambitions* (Brussels: International Crisis Group, Middle East Report No 35, 2005) pp2–8.
46 Quoted, *Hürriyet*, 9 November 2005.
47 Quoted, *Turkish Daily News*, 21 May 2005.
48 Website of NTV television, Istanbul (www.ntvmsnbc.com) 17 October 2005.
49 Text of the constitution from the website of the Iraqi Transitional Government (www.iraqigovernment.org).
50 *Hürriyet*, 5 December 2005.
51 Data from Turkish Statistical Institute website (www.tuik.gov.tr), foreign trade statistics.
52 Amberin Zaman, 'Turkey and the Iraqi Kurds: from Red Lines to Red Carpets', *Analysis* (Washington, DC: German Marshall Fund of the United States, 14 May 2010) p2.
53 *Hürriyet Daily News*, 7 June 2010.
54 *Turkish Daily News*, 14 March, 13 April 2007; CNN Turk website, 12 June 2007.
55 NTV website, 15 February 2007; *Turkish Daily News,* 17, 21 February 2007; Meliha Benli Altunışık, 'World Views and Turkish Foreign Policy in the Middle East', *New Perspectives on Turkey* no 40 (2009) pp179–80.
56 *Today's Zaman*, 14 May, 4 June 2007.
57 Ibid, 31 October 2009; *Radikal*, 1 November 2009.
58 *Hürriyet Daily News*, 5 June 2010; NTV website, 29 March 2011.
59 *Today's Zaman*, 20 October, 4 November 2011.
60 *Hürriyet Daily News*, 4 November 2011; *Radikal*, 5 November 2011.
61 *Radikal*, 19 September 2010; *Today's Zaman*, 16 August 2010.
62 *Today's Zaman*, 31 October 2010.
63 Ankara Radio, 4 February 1993, in *Summary of World Broadcasts*, 6 February 1993. See also *Milliyet*, 3 February 1993; and Hugh Pope, 'Pointing Fingers at Iran', *Middle East International*, 5 February 1993. For other connections between

ultra-Islamist political movements in Turkey and Iran, see John Calabrese, 'Turkey and Iran: Limits of a Stable Relationship', *British Journal of Middle Eastern Studies* vol 25, no 1 (1998) pp84–5.

64 Michael M. Gunter, *The Kurds and the Future of Turkey* (New York: St Martin's Press, 1997) p96; Robert Olson, 'The Kurdish Question and Turkey's Foreign Policy, 1991–95: From the Gulf War to the Incursion into Iraq', *Journal of South Asian and Middle Eastern Studies* vol 19 (1995) pp8–10; Michael M. Gunter, 'Turkey and Iran Face Off in Kurdistan', *Middle East Quarterly* vol 5, no 1 (1998) p35.

65 Gunter, *Kurds and the Future*, p96; Kemal Kirişci, 'The Kurdish Question and Turkish Foreign Policy', in Lenore G. Martin and Dimitris Keridis (eds), *The Future of Turkish Foreign Policy* (Cambridge, MA, and London: MIT Press, 2004) p294.

66 *Briefing*, 19 August 1996, pp4–5; Calabrese, 'Turkey and Iran', pp83–4; Robins, 'Turkish Foreign Policy under Erbakan', pp90–1.

67 Kirişci, 'Kurdish Question', p295.

68 See Gunter, 'Turkey and Iran', p40.

69 *Milliyet*, 27, 28 July 1999; *Briefing*, 9 August 1999, pp13–14, 16 August 1999, p9; Anatolia Agency, 17 October 1999 (in *Summary of World Broadcasts*, 19 October 1999).

70 Data from Turkish Statistical Institute website (www.tuik.gov.tr), foreign trade statistics.

71 Data from the Turkish state pipeline company BOTAŞ.

72 *Turkish Daily News*, 16 July 2007.

73 Ibid, 22 September 2007; *Today's Zaman*, 24 September 2007.

74 *Turkish Daily News*, 6, 11 August 2007; see also Daphne McCurdy, 'Turkish–Iranian Relations: When Opposites Attract', *Turkish Policy Quarterly* vol 7, no 2 (2008) p96.

75 McCurdy, 'Turkish–Iranian Relations', pp98–9.

76 *Today's Zaman*, 21 October 2011.

77 CNN International website (www.cnn.com) 16 June 2009.

78 *Today's Zaman*, 14 October 2011.

79 Ibid, 10 October 2011.

80 Samuel P. Huntington, 'Democracy's Third Wave', in Larry Diamond and L.F. Plattner (eds), *The Global Resurgence of Democracy* (Baltimore, MD, and London: Johns Hopkins University Press, 1993).

81 For a rare exception, see Farid Ghadry, 'Syrian–Turkish Relations', *Turkish Policy Quarterly* vol 4, no 2 (2005).

82 BBC News website, 12 November 2011.

83 Cengiz Çandar, 'Tebrikler, Mısır'ın halkına ve Türkiye'nin Başbakanı'na', *Radikal*, 2 February 2011.

84 BBC News website, 25 March 2011; *Radikal*, 24 March 2011.

85 *Hürriyet Daily News*, 3 May 2011; BBC News website, 3 July 2011.

86 'Conclusions of the Libya Contact Group Meeting, Istanbul, 25 August 2011', from website of Ministry of Foreign Affairs (www.mfa.gov.tr).

87 *Hürriyet Daily News*, 13 May 2011; *Today's Zaman*, 11 June 2011.

88 *Hürriyet Daily News*, 25 September 2011.

89 BBC News website, 2 October 2011.

90 *Hürriyet*, 13, 14 November 2011.

91 *Today's Zaman*, 21 September 2011.

92 BBC News website, 16 November 2011.

93 *Today's Zaman*, 7 October 2011.

94 Ibid, 15 September 2011; on the last point, see Rania Abouzeid, 'Unfriending Assad: Turkey, Iran and Even Hizbullah Begin to Rethink Syria', *Time*, 29 August 2011.

95 *Today's Zaman*, 12 September 2011.
96 Ibid, 14 September 2011; *Hürriyet Daily News*, 15 September 2011.
97 Data from Turkish Statistical Institute website (www.tuik.gov.tr), foreign trade statistics
98 Abdullah Bozkurt, 'Enlistment of Turkish Help from a Chinese Perspective', *Today's Zaman,* 15 November 2011.
99 For further information on the Uighurs of Xinjiang and their connections with Turkey, see Graham E. Fuller, 'Turkey's New Eastern Orientation', in Graham E. Fuller and Ian O. Lesser (eds), *Turkey's New Geopolitics: From the Balkans to Western China* (Boulder, CO: Westview, 1993) pp73–4; and Gareth M. Winrow, 'Turkey's Relations with the Transcaucasus and the Central Asian Republics', *Perceptions* (Ankara) vol 1, no 1 (1996) p138.
100 *Today's Zaman*, 25, 26, 28 June 2009, quotation from ibid, 30 June 2009.
101 Ibid, 11, 14 July 2009.
102 Ibid, 31 July 2009.
103 Ibid, 15 November 2011.
104 *Hürriyet Daily News*, 8 October 2010.
105 *Today's Zaman*, 19 August 2008.
106 Ibid, 15 December 2010.
107 Recep Tayyip Erdoğan, 'The Tears of Somalia', *Foreign Policy*, 10 October 2011.
108 Samuel P. Huntington, 'The Clash of Civilizations', *Foreign Affairs* vol 72, no 3 (1993).
109 See his remarks quoted in the *Guardian* (London, daily) 30 September 2005.
110 Ali Balcı and Nebi Miş, 'Turkey's Role in the Alliance of Civilizations: A New Perspective in Turkish Foreign Policy?', *Turkish Studies* vol 9, no 3 (2008) p393.
111 For further details see ibid, pp392–401.

12 Conclusions and prospects

1 Malik Mufti, 'Daring and Caution in Turkish Foreign Policy', *Middle East Journal* vol 52, no 1 (1998) p45.
2 Ziya Öniş, 'Multiple Faces of the "New" Turkish Foreign Policy: Underlying Dynamics and a Critique', *Insight Turkey* vol 13, no 1 (2011) pp49, 53.
3 Yılmaz Çolak, 'Ottomanism vs. Kemalism: Collective Memory and Cultural Pluralism in 1990s Turkey', *Middle Eastern Studies* vol 42, no 4 (2006) pp592–3. See also Ioannis N. Grigoriadis, '*Türk* or *Türkiyeli*? The Reform of Turkey's Minority Legislation and the Rediscovery of Ottomanism', ibid, vol 43, no 3 (2007) pp432–5.
4 Nora Fisher Onar, *Neo Ottomanism, Historical Legacies and Turkish Foreign Policy* (Istanbul: Center for Economic and Foreign Policy Research [EDAM] Discussion Paper Series 2009/03, from www.scribed.com) pp9–10.
5 Michael Rubin, 'Shifting Sides? The Problems of Neo-Ottomanism', *National Review Online*, 10 August 2004 (www.meforum.org).
6 Soner Çağaptay, *The AKP's Foreign Policy: The Misnomer of Neo-Ottomanism*, (Washington, DC: Washington Institute for Near East Policy, 2009, from www.washingtoninstitute.org).
7 Şuhnaz Yılmaz and İpek K. Yosmaoğlu, 'Fighting the Spectres of the Past: Dilemmas of Ottoman Legacy in the Balkans and Middle East', *Middle Eastern Studies* vol 44, no 5 (2008) pp679–80.
8 Quoted, M. Hakan Yavuz, 'Turkish Identity and Foreign Policy in Flux: The Rise of neo-Ottomanism', *Critique, Critical Middle Eastern Studies* vol 7, no 12, (1998) p23.
9 Ahmet Davutoğlu, 'Turkey's Zero-Problems Foreign Policy', *Foreign Policy*, 20 May 2010, p5.

10 See, for instance, his remarks reported in the website of CNN Turk television (www.cnnturk.com) and *Today's Zaman,* 25 November 2009. This was apparently in response to an article by Delphine Strauss, 'Turkey's Ottoman Mission', *Financial Times,* 23 November 2009.

11 Davutoğlu, 'Turkey's Zero-Problems', p4.

12 'Powerful states' here includes the European Union, in the case of Cyprus (Russia in the case of Armenia, and the USA in that of Israel).

13 Hugh Pope, 'Turkey, Pax Ottomana?', from website of the International Crisis Group (www.crisisgroup.org) (no pagination) originally published in *Foreign Affairs* vol 86, no 6 (2010).

14 Quoted, Carol Migdalowitz, 'AKP's Domestically Driven Foreign Policy', *Turkish Policy Quarterly* vol 9, no 4 (2010/11) p41.

15 *Hürriyet Daily News,* 6, 7 November 2009; website of CNN Turk television, 8 November 2009.

16 *Hürriyet Daily News,* 12 December 2011

17 See, for example, Rubin, 'Shifting Sides?' or Daniel Pipes, 'Is Turkey Going Rogue?' *National Review Online,* 27 September 2011 (www.meforum.org); see also Walid Zafar, 'Daniel Pipes Is Off Iran: The Real Bad Guy Is Turkey', *Political Correction,* 16 December 2010 (http://politicalcorrection.org/fpmatters).

18 Ömer Taşpinar, *Turkey's Middle East Policies: Between Neo-Ottomanism and Kemalism* (Washington, DC: Carnegie Endowment for International Peace, Carnegie Middle East Center, September 2008) pp14–15.

19 Nicholas Danforth, 'Ideology and Pragmatism in Turkish Foreign Policy: From Atatürk to the AKP', *Turkish Policy Quarterly* vol 7, no 3 (2008) pp90–4.

20 See the reports in *Hürriyet Daily News,* 1 December 2011, and *Today's Zaman,* 22, 25 September, 28 October, 1 November 2011.

21 *Today's Zaman,* 21 September, 2, 27 November 2011.

22 According to the *Los Angeles Times,* reported in *Today's Zaman,* 16 October 2011.

23 William Hague, interviewed by Andrew Rawnsley and Toby Helm, *Guardian,* 1 October 2011.

Bibliography

Official publications and documents

Britain

Treaty of Peace with Turkey and other Instruments signed at Lausanne on July 24, 1923 (London: HMSO, 1923, Cmd 1929)
Cyprus (London: HMSO, 1960, Cmd 1093)

EC/EU

Official Journal of the European Communities: Information and Notices, vol 16, no C 113 (texts of Association Agreement of 1963 and Additional Protocol of 1970)
Commission des Communautés Européennes, Sec (89) 2290, 'Avis de la Commission sur la demande d'adhésion de la Turquie à la Communauté' (Brussels, December 1989)
'Decision 1/95 of the EC–Turkey Association Council of 22 December 1995', *Official Journal of the European Communities* vol 39 L35 (13 February 1996)
'Press Conference by Mr Matutes on Membership of Turkey to the Community' (Brussels: Commission of the European Communities, December 1989, ref BIC/89/393)
'Accession Partnership Document' [for Turkey], November 2000, reprinted in *Briefing* (Ankara, weekly) 13 November 2000, pp16–24
'Presidency Conclusions, Helsinki European Council, 10 and 11 September 1999', from www.consilium.europa.eu/uedocs.

Turkey

'Constitution of the Republic of Turkey (as amended on October 17, 2001)', website of the Grand National Assembly of Turkey (www.tbmm.gov.tr/anayasa/constitution.htm)
'Statement by the Turkish Government on 14 December 1997, Concerning the Presidency Conclusions of the European Council Held on 12–13 December 1997 in Luxembourg', reprinted in *Perceptions* (Ankara) vol 2, no 4 (1997–8)
'Turkish Documents Regarding Issues between Turkey and Greece', *Turkish Review of Balkan Studies* vol 3 (1996/7)
Prime Ministry, General Secretariat of EU Affairs, 'National Programme, Introduction and Political Criteria (Unofficial Translation)', from www.abgs.gov.tr

Prime Ministry, Secretariat General for European Affairs, *Constitutional Amendments Proposal* (5 April 2010), from www.abgs.gov.tr/files/BasinMusavirlik/const_amnd ments.pdf

United Nations

Report of the Secretary-General's Panel of Inquiry on the 31 May 2010 Flotilla Incident, July 2011 [the 'Palmer Committee Report'] (released by the *New York Times*, 2 September 2011)

United States

US Energy Information Administration, 'Caspian Sea Region: Natural Gas Export Options', (February 2002),'Turkey', and 'Caspian Sea Region: Oil Export Options' (February 2002), website of the US Energy Information Administration (www.eia. doe.gov)

Serial publications

Country Report: Turkey (London: Economist Intelligence Unit, quarterly)
Middle East Contemporary Survey (Boulder, CO: Westview Press, annual)
Statistical Yearbook of Turkey/Türkiye İstatistik Yıllığı (Ankara: State Institute of Statistics, normally annual, in English and Turkish)
The Military Balance (London: Oxford University Press for International Institute of Strategic Studies, annual)
Turkey Almanac (Ankara: Turkish Daily News, annual: now discontinued)
BP Amoco Statistical Review of World Energy (London: BP Amoco [previously BP], annual)
Regular Report on Turkey's Progress towards Accession (Brussels: Commission of the European Communities, normally issued in November of each year)

Official websites

Central Bank of the Republic of Turkey www.tcmb.gov.tr
International Monetary Fund www.imf.org
Nabucco Pipeline Project www.nabucco-pipeline.com
Turkish Foreign Ministry www.mfa.gov.tr
Turkish State Pipeline Company (BOTAŞ) www.botas.gov.tr
Turkish Statistical Institute www.tuik.gov.tr
World Bank www.worldbank.org

Turkish newspapers, news magazines and TV websites

BBC news website www.bbc.co.uk/news
Briefing (Ankara, weekly)
Cumhuriyet (Istanbul, daily: www.cumhuriyet.com.tr)
Hürriyet (Istanbul, daily: www.hurriyet.com.tr)
Hürriyet Daily News (Istanbul, daily: www.hurriyetdailynews.com.tr, prior to December 2008 published as *Turkish Daily News*)

Milliyet (Istanbul, daily: www.milliyet.com.tr)
Radikal (Istanbul, daily: www.radikal.com.tr)
Todays Zaman (Istanbul, daily: www.todayszaman.com)
Website of CNNTurk television, Istanbul www.cnnturk.com
Website of NTV television, Istanbul www.ntvmsnbc.com
Zaman (Istanbul, daily: www.zaman.com.tr)

Books and articles

Abelan, Miguel Medina, *Turkey, the European Security and Defence Policy, and Accession Negotiations* (Ankara: Middle East Technical University, 2009)

Abouzeid, Rania, 'Unfriending Assad: Turkey, Iran and Even Hizbullah Begin to Rethink Syria', *Time*, 29 August 2011

Ahmad, Feroz, 'Great Britain's Relations with the Young Turks, 1908–14', *Middle Eastern Studies* vol 2 (1965–6)

——*The Young Turks: The Committee of Union and Progress in Turkish Politics, 1908–1914* (Oxford: Oxford University Press, 1969)

——*The Turkish Experiment in Democracy, 1950–1975* (London: Hurst, for Royal Institute of International Affairs, 1977)

——'The Late Ottoman Empire', in Marian Kent (ed.), *The Great Powers and the End of the Ottoman Empire* (London: Cass, 2nd edn, 1996)

——'The Historical Background of Turkey's Foreign Policy', in Lenore G. Martin and Dimitris Keridis (eds), *The Future of Turkish Foreign Policy* (London and Cambridge, MA: MIT Press, 2004)

Akbayar, Nuri, 'Tanzimat'tan Sonra Osmanlı Devleti Nüfusu', *Tanzimat'tan Cumhuriyet'e Türkiye Ansiklopedisi* (Istanbul: İletişim Yayınları, 1985) vol 5

Akdevelioğlu, Atay and Ömer Kürkçüoğlu, 'Orta Doğu'yla İlişkiler', in Baskın Oran (ed.), *Türk Dış Politikası,* (Istanbul: İletişim, 2001) vol 1

Akgün, Mensur, Gökçe Perçinoğlu and Sabiha Senyücel Gündoğar, *The Perception of Turkey in the Middle East* (Istanbul: Turkish Economic and Social Studies Foundation [TESEV], 2009)

Akıncı, Burak, 'Newly Found Friendship Between Turkey and Syria', *Middle East Online* (www.middle-east-on-line.com) 23 December 2004

Aksakal, Mustafa, *The Ottoman Road to War in 1914: The Ottoman Empire and the First World War* (Cambridge: Cambridge University Press, 2008)

Akşin, Aptülhat, *Atatürk'ün Dış Politika İlkeleri ve Diplomasisi* (Ankara: Türk Tarih Kurumu, 1991)

Alaçam, H. Fahir, 'Turkish–Syrian Relations', *Turkish Review of Middle East Studies* (Istanbul) vol 8 (1994/5)

Alantar, Ö. Zeynep Oktav, 'The October 1998 Crisis: A Change of Heart of Turkish Foreign Policy towards Syria?', *Cahiers d'études sur la Méditerranée orientale et le monde turco-iranien* no 31 (2001)

Albright, David E., 'The USSR and the Third World in the 1980s', *Problems of Communism* vol 38 (1989)

Alireza, Bülent, 'Turkey and the Crisis in the Caucasus', commentary article for Center for Strategic and International Studies, Turkey Project, Washington, DC, 9 September 2008

——, 'Turkey and the Global Storm', *Insight Turkey* vol 3, no 4 (2001)

Altunışık, Meliha Benli, 'World Views and Turkish Foreign Policy in the Middle East', *New Perspectives on Turkey* no 40 (2009)

Altunışık, Meliha Benli and Özlem Tür, 'From Distant Neighbours to Partners? Changing Syrian–Turkish Relations', *Security Dialogue* vol 37, no 2 (2006)

Anastasakis, Othon, 'Greece and Turkey in the Balkans: Cooperation or Rivalry?' *Turkish Studies* vol 5, no 1 (2004)

Anderson, M.S., *The Eastern Question, 1774–1923: A Study in International Relations* (London: Macmillan, 1966)

Aras, Bülent, 'The Impact of the Palestinian–Israeli Peace Process in Turkish Foreign Policy', *Journal of South Asian and Middle Eastern Studies* vol 20 (1997)

——*Palestinian–Israeli Peace Process and Turkey* (Commack, NY: Nova Science Publishers, 1998)

Arnett, David, 'Problems of Perception and Vision: Turkey and the US', *Turkish Policy Quarterly* vol 7, no 1 (2008)

Ataöv, Türkaya, *Turkish Foreign Policy, 1939–1945* (Ankara University, Political Science Faculty, 1965)

Atatürk, Kemal, *Speech Delivered by Ghazi Mustapha Kemal, President of the Turkish Republic, October 1927* (Leipzig: K.F. Koehler, 1929)

Athanassopoulou, Ekavi, 'Ankara's Foreign Policy Objectives after the End of the Cold War: Making Policy in a Changing Environment', *Orient* vol 36 (1995)

——'Greece, Turkey, Europe: Constantinos Simitis in Premiership Waters', *Mediterranean Politics* vol 1 (1996)

——'Western Defence Developments and Turkey's Search for Security in 1948', *Middle Eastern Studies* vol 32, no 2 (1996): reprinted in Sylvia Kedourie (ed.), *Turkey: Identity, Democracy, Politics* (London: Cass, 1996)

——'Blessing in Disguise? The Imia Crisis and Turkish–Greek Relations', *Mediterranean Politics* vol 2 (1997)

——*Turkey – Anglo-American Security Interests* (London: Cass, 1999)

——'American–Turkish Relations since the End of the Cold War', *Middle East Policy* vol 8 (2001)

Avcı, Gamze, 'Turkish Political Parties and the EU Discourse in the Post-Helsinki Period', in Mehmet Uğur and Nefis Canefe (eds), *Turkey and European Integration: Accession Prospects and Issues* (London and New York: Routledge, 2004)

Aybet, Gülnür, *NATO's Developing Role in Collective Security* (Ankara: Ministry of Foreign Affairs, Center for Strategic Research, 1999)

——'Turkey and European Institutions', *International Spectator* (Rome) vol 34 (1999)

——'NATO's New Missions', *Perceptions* (Ankara) vol 4, no 1 (1999)

Aydın, Mustafa, 'Foucault's Pendulum: Turkey in Central Asia and the Caucasus', *Turkish Studies* vol 5, no 2 (2004)

Aykan, Mahmut Bali, 'The Turkey–US–Israel Triangle: Continuity, Change and Implications for Turkey's Post-Cold War Middle East Policy', *Journal of South Asian and Middle Eastern Studies* vol 22 (1999)

——, 'Turkey and European Security and Defence Identity/Policy (ESDI/P): A Turkish View', *Journal of Contemporary European Studies* vol 13, no 3 (2005)

——, 'The Palestinian Question in Turkish Foreign Policy from the 1950s to the 1990s', *International Journal of Middle East Studies* vol 25 (1993)

——, 'Turkey's Policy in Northern Iraq, 1991–95', *Middle Eastern Studies* vol 32, no 4 (1996)

——, 'Turkish Perspectives on Turkish–US Relations Concerning Persian Gulf Security in the Post-Cold War Era: 1989–95', *Middle East Journal* vol 50, no 3 (1996)

Bacık, Gökhan, 'Turkey and Pipeline Politics', *Turkish Studies* vol 7, no 2 (2006)

Bağcı, Hüseyin, *Demokrat Parti Dönemi Dış Politikası* (Ankara: İmge Kitabevi, 1990)

Bahceli, Tozun, *Greek–Turkish Relations since 1955* (Boulder, CO: Westview, 1990)

Bailey, Frank Edgar, *British Policy and the Turkish Reform Movement: A Study in Anglo-Turkish Relations, 1826–1853* (Cambridge, MA: Harvard University Press, 1942)

Bal, İdris, *Turkey's Relations with the West and the Turkic Republics: The Rise and Fall of the 'Turkish Model'* (Aldershot: Ashgate, 2000)

Balcı, Ali and Nebi Miş, 'Turkey's Role in the Alliance of Civilizations: A New Perspective in Turkish Foreign Policy?' *Turkish Studies* vol 9, no 3 (2008)

Balcı, Bayram, 'Fethullah Gülen's Missionary Schools in Central Asia and their Role in the Spreading of Turkism and Islam', *Religion, State and Society* vol 31, no 2 (2003)

Balkır, Canan, 'Turkey and the European Community: Foreign Trade and Direct Foreign Investment in the 1980s', in Canan Balkır and Allan M.Williams (eds), *Turkey and Europe* (London and New York: Pinter, 1993)

Barchard, David, *Turkey and the West* (London: Routledge and Kegan Paul for Royal Institute of International Affairs, 1985)

Barkey, Henri J. and Graham E. Fuller, 'Turkey's Kurdish Question: Critical Turning Points and Missed Opportunities', *Middle East Journal* vol 51, no 1 (1997)

——*Turkey's Kurdish Question* (Lanham, MD: Rowman and Littlefield, 1998)

Barkey, Henri J., 'The Silent Victor: Turkey's Role in the Gulf War', in Efraim Karsh (ed.), *The Iran–Iraq War: Impact and Implications* (London: Macmillan, in association with Jafee Center for Strategic Studies, Tel Aviv University, 1989)

——'The People's Democracy Party (HADEP): The Travails of a Legal Kurdish Party in Turkey', *Journal of Muslim Minority Affairs* vol 18 (1998)

Barlas, Dilek, *Etatism and Diplomacy in Turkey: Economic and Foreign Policy Strategies in an Uncertain World, 1929–1939* (Leiden, New York and Cologne: Brill, 1998)

Barlas, Dilek and Serhat Güvenç, 'Turkey and the Idea of a European Union During the Inter-war Years, 1923–39', *Middle Eastern Studies* vol 35, no 3 (2009)

Barnard, Fulya Kip, 'The Role of Turkish Migration and Migrants in Turkey's Relations with the EU', in İdris Bal (ed.), *Turkish Foreign Policy in Post Cold War Era* (Boca Raton, FL: Brown Walker, 2004)

Barylski, Robert V., 'Russia, the West and the Caspian Energy Hub', *Middle East Journal* vol 49, no 2 (1995)

Barysch, Katinka, *Should the Nabucco Pipeline Project be Shelved?* (Washington, DC: Transatlantic Academy, Paper Series, May 2010)

Beck, Peter J., '"A Tedious and Perilous Controversy": Britain and the Settlement of the Mosul Dispute, 1918–26', *Middle Eastern Studies* vol 17, no 2 (1981)

Bellaigue, Christopher de, 'Conciliation in Cyprus?' *Washington Quarterly* vol 22 (1999)

Bernstein, Barton J., 'The Cuban Missile Crisis: Trading the Jupiters in Turkey?', *Political Science Quarterly* vol 95 (1980)

——'Reconsidering the Missile Crisis: Dealing with the Problem of the American Jupiters in Turkey', in James A. Nathan (ed.), *The Cuban Missile Crisis Revisited* (New York: St Martin's Press, 1992)

Bila, Fikret, *Sivil Darbe Girişimi ve Ankara'da Irak Savaşları* (Ankara: Ümit Yayıncılık, 2003)

Bilge, A. Suat, 'The Cyprus Conflict and Turkey', in Kemal H. Karpat, et al., *Turkey's Foreign Policy in Transition* (Leiden: Brill, 1975)

Bilge, A. Suat, *Güç Komşuluk: Türkiye-Sovyetler Birliği İlişkileri, 1920–1964* (Ankara: Türkiye İş Bankası Kültür Yayınları, 1992)

Bilge, A. Suat, et al., *Olaylarla Türk Dış Politikası* (Ankara University, Political Science Faculty, 1969)

Bilgin, Pinar, 'Security Dimension: A Clash of Security Cultures? Differences between Turkey and the European Union Revisited', in Emre Çakır (ed.), *Fifty Years of EU–Turkey Relations a Sisyphean Story* (London and New York: Routledge, 2011)

Birand, Mehmet Ali and Soner Yalçın (eds), *The Özal: Bir Davanın Öyküsü* (Istanbul: Doğan Kitapçılık, 2001)

Birand, Mehmet Ali, *30 Hot Days* (London, Nicosia and Istanbul: Rustem, 1985), originally published in Turkish as *30 Sıcak Gün* (Istanbul: Milliyet Yayınları, 1975)

——'Turkey and the European Community', *World Today* vol 38 (1978)

——*The Generals' Coup in Turkey: An Inside Story of 12 September 1980*, tr. M.A. Dikerdem, (London: Brassey's Defence Publishers, 1987)

Bishku, Michael M., 'Turkey and its Middle Eastern Neighbours since 1945', *Journal of South Asian and Middle Eastern Studies* vol 15 (1992)

Blackwell, Stephen, 'A Desert Squall: Anglo-American Planning for Military Intervention in Iraq, July 1958–August 1959', *Middle Eastern Studies* vol 35, no 3 (1999)

Blight, James G. and David A. Welch, *On the Brink: Americans and Soviets Reexamine the Cuban Missile Crisis* (New York: Noonday Press, 1989)

Bölükbaşı, Suha, *Turkish–American Relations and Cyprus* (Lanham, MD: University Press of America, for White Burkett Miller Center of Public Affairs, University of Virginia, 1988)

——'Turkey Copes with Revolutionary Iran', *Journal of South Asian and Middle Eastern Studies* vol 13 (1989)

——'The Turco-Greek Dispute: Issues, Policies and Prospects', in C.H. Dodd (ed.), *Turkish Foreign Policy: New Prospects* (Wistow: Eothen, for Modern Turkish Studies Programme, SOAS, 1992)

——'Turkey Challenges Iraq and Syria: the Euphrates Dispute', *Journal of South Asian and Middle Eastern Studies* vol 16 (1993)

——'The Johnson Letter Revisited', *Middle Eastern Studies* vol 29, no 3 (1993)

——'The Cyprus Dispute in the Post-Cold War Era', *Turkish Studies Association Bulletin* vol 18 (1994)

——'Boutros Ghali's Cyprus Initiative in 1992: Why Did it Fail?', *Middle Eastern Studies* vol 31, no 3 (1995)

——'Ankara's Baku-Centered Transcaucasia Policy: Has It Failed?', *Middle East Journal* vol 51, no 1 (1997)

Bourguignon, Roswitha, 'The History of the Association Agreement between Turkey and the European Community', in Ahmet Evin and Geoffrey Denton (eds), *Turkey and the European Community* (Opladen: Leske and Budrich, 1990)

Bozkurt, Abdullah, 'Enlistment of Turkish Help from a Chinese Perspective', *Today's Zaman*, 15 November 2011

Bridge, F.R., 'The Habsburg Monarchy and the Ottoman Empire, 1900–1918', in Marian Kent (ed.), *The Great Powers and the End of the Ottoman Empire* (London: Cass, 2nd edn, 1996)

Brown, Cameron S., 'The One Coalition they Craved to Join: Turkey in the Korean War', *Review of International Studies* vol 34, no 1 (2008)

Brown, David, 'Foreword', in Faik Ökte, *The Tragedy of the Capital Tax*, tr. Geoffrey Cox (London: Croom Helm, 1987)

Brownlie, Ian (ed.), *Basic Documents on Human Rights* (Oxford: Clarendon Press, 2nd edn, 1981)

Buzan, Barry, 'The Status and Future of the Montreux Convention', *Survival* vol 18 (1976)

Çağaptay, Soner, *The AKP's Foreign Policy: the Misnomer of Neo-Ottomanism*, (Washington, DC: Washington Institute for Near East Policy, 2009: from www.washingtoninstitute.org)

Çakır, Armağan Emre, 'Introduction', in Armağan Emre Çakır (ed.), *Fifty Years of EU–Turkey Relations a Sisyphean Story* (London and New York: Routledge, 2011)

Calabrese, John, 'Turkey and Iran: Limits of a Stable Relationship', *British Journal of Middle Eastern Studies* vol 25 (1998)

Campany, Richard C., Jr, *Turkey and the United States: The Arms Embargo Period* (New York: Praeger, 1986)

Campbell, John C., *Defense of the Middle East: Problems of American Policy* (New York: Praeger, 1960)

Can, Bilmez Bülent, *Demiryolundan Petrole Chester Projesi (1908–1923)* (Istanbul: Tarih Vakfı, Yurt Yayınları, 2000)

Çandar, Cengiz, 'Turkish Foreign Policy and the War on Iraq', in Lenore G. Martin and Dimitris Keridis (eds), *The Future of Turkish Foreign Policy* (Cambridge, MA, and London: MIT Press, 2004)

——'Tebrikler, Mısır'ın halkına ve Türkıye'nin Başbakanı'na', *Radikal*, 2 February 2011

Çarkoğlu, Ali, and Kemal Kirişci, 'The View from Turkey: Perceptions of Greeks and Greek–Turkish Rapprochement by the Turkish Public', *Turkish Studies* vol 5, no 1 (2004)

Çelenk, Ayşe Aslıhan, 'The Restructuring of Turkey's Policy towards Cyprus: The Justice and Development Party's Struggle for Power', *Turkish Studies* vol 8, no 3 (2007)

Chase, Robert S., Emily B. Hill and Paul Kennedy, 'Pivotal States and US Strategy', *Foreign Affairs* vol 75, no 1 (1996)

Clark, Edward C., 'The Turkish Varlık Vergisi Reconsidered', *Middle Eastern Studies* vol 8 (1972)

Çolak, Yılmaz, 'Ottomanism vs. Kemalism: Collective Memory and Cultural Pluralism in 1990s Turkey', *Middle Eastern Studies* vol 42, no 4 (2006)

Cornell, Svante E., 'Undeclared War: the Nagorno Karabakh Conflict Reconsidered', *Journal of South Asian and Middle Eastern Studies* vol 20 (1997)

——'Turkey and the Conflict in Nagorno Karabakh: A Delicate Balance', *Middle Eastern Studies* vol 34, no 1 (1998)

Couloumbis, Theodore A., *The United States, Greece and Turkey: The Troubled Triangle* (New York: Praeger, 1983)

Dağı, İhsan D., 'Democratic Transition in Turkey, 1980–83: The Impact of European Diplomacy', *Middle Eastern Studies* vol 32, no 2 (1996), reprinted in Sylvia Kedourie (ed.), *Turkey; Identity, Democracy, Politics* (London and Portland, OR: Cass, 1996)

——'Rethinking Human Rights, Democracy and the West: Post-Islamist Intellectuals in Turkey', *Critique: Critical Middle Eastern Studies* vol 13, no 2 (2004)

——'Transformation of Islamic Political Identity in Turkey: Rethinking the West and Westernization', *Turkish Studies* vol 6, no 1 (2005)

——'The Justice and Development Party: Identity, Politics and Human Rights Discourse in the Search for Security and Legitimacy', in M. Hakan Yavuz (ed.), *The*

Emergence of a New Turkey: Democracy and the AK Parti (Salt Lake City, UT: University of Utah Press, 2006)

Daly, John C.K., *US–Turkish Relations: a Strategic Relationship under Stress* (Washington, DC: Jamestown Foundation, 2008)

Danforth, Nicholas, 'Ideology and Pragmatism in Turkish Foreign Policy: From Atatürk to the AKP', *Turkish Policy Quarterly* vol 7, no 3 (2008)

Danielyan, Emil, 'Turkish–Armenian Accords Pronounced Dead by Yerevan', *Eurasia Daily Monitor* vol 8, no 31, 14 February 2011

Davison, Roderic H., *Reform in the Ottoman Empire, 1856–1876* (Princeton: Princeton University Press, 1963)

——'Turkish Diplomacy from Mudros to Lausanne', in Gordon A. Craig and Felix Gilbert (eds), *The Diplomats, 1919–1939* (New York: Atheneum, 1974) vol 1

Davutoğlu, Ahmet, 'The Clash of Interests: An Explanation of the World (Dis)Order', *Perceptions* (Ankara) vol 2, no 4 (1997–8)

——*Stratejik Derinlik: Türkiye'nin Uluslararası Konumu* (Istanbul: Küre Yayınları, 2000)

——'Türkiye Merkez Ülke Olmalı', *Radikal* (Istanbul, daily) 26 February (2002)

——'Turkey's Foreign Policy Vision: An Assessment of 2007', *Insight Turkey* vol 10, no 1 (2008)

——'Turkey's Zero-Problems Foreign Policy', *Foreign Policy* 20 May 2010

Denniston, Robin, *Churchill's Secret War: Diplomatic Decrypts, the Foreign Office and Turkey, 1942–44* (Stroud: Sutton Publishing, and New York: St Martin's Press, 1997)

Deringil, Selim, 'The Preservation of Turkey's Neutrality During the Second World War: 1940', *Middle Eastern Studies* vol 18, no 1 (1982)

——'Aspects of Continuity in Turkish Foreign Policy: Abdülhamid II and İsmet İnönü', *International Journal of Turkish Studies* vol 4 (1987)

——*Turkish Foreign Policy during the Second World War: An 'Active' Neutrality* (Cambridge: Cambridge University Press, 1989)

Devereux, Robert, *The First Ottoman Constitutional Period* (Baltimore: Johns Hopkins Press, 1963)

Dodd, C.H., *The Crisis of Turkish Democracy* (Wistow: Eothen Press, 2nd edn, 1990)

——*Storm Clouds Over Cyprus: A Briefing* (Hemingford Grey: Eothen, 2nd edn, 2002)

——*The Cyprus Imbroglio* (Hemingford Grey: Eothen, 1998)

Dodd, Clement, 'Constitutional Features of the UN Plan for Cyprus and its Antecedents', *Turkish Studies* vol 6, no 1 (2005)

Dyer, Gwynne, 'The Turkish Armistice of 1918: 1 – The Turkish Decision for a Separate Peace, Autumn 1918', *Middle Eastern Studies* vol 8, no 2 (1972)

——'The Turkish Armistice of 1918: 2 – A Lost Opportunity: The Armistice Negotiations of Moudros', *Middle Eastern Studies* vol 8, no 3 (1972)

——'Turkish "Falsifiers" and Armenian "Deceivers": Historiography and the Armenian Massacres', *Middle Eastern Studies* vol 12, no 1 (1976)

Earle, E.M., *Turkey, the Great Powers and the Baghdad Railway* (New York: Macmillan, 1923)

Ecevit, Bülent, 'Turkey's Security Policies', in Jonathan Alford (ed.), *Greece and Turkey: Adversity in Alliance* (London: Gower, for International Institute of Strategic Studies, 1984)

Eden, Sir Anthony, *Full Circle* (London: Cassell, 1960)

Ekin, Nusret, 'Turkish Labor in the EEC', in Werner Gumpel (ed.), *Die Türkei auf dem Weg in die EG* (Munich and Vienna: R. Oldenbourg, 1979)

Elekdağ, Şükrü, 'Two and a Half War Strategy', *Perceptions* (Ankara) vol 1, no 1 (1996)

Elkind, Jonathan, 'Economic Implications of the Baku–Tibilisi–Ceyhan Pipeline', in Central Asia-Caucasus Institute, *The Baku–Tibilisi–Ceyhan Pipeline: Oil Window to the West* (Washington, DC: Johns Hopkins University, 2005)

Emrence, Cem, 'Rearticulating the Local, Regional and Global: The Greek–Turkish Rapprochement of 1930', *Turkish Studies* vol 4, no 3 (2003)

Erdoğan, Recep Tayyip, 'The Tears of Somalia', *Foreign Policy* 10 October 2011

Ergün, İsmet, 'The Problem of Freedom of Movement of Turkish Workers in the European Community', in Ahmet Evin and Geoffrey Denton (eds), *Turkey and the European Community* (Opladen: Leske and Budrich, 1990)

Ertekün, Necati, *The Cyprus Dispute and the Birth of the Turkish Republic of Northern Cyprus* (Nicosia: Rustem, 2nd edn., 1984)

Evans, Stephen F., *The Slow Rapprochement: Britain and Turkey in the Age of Kemal Atatürk, 1919–38* (Walkington: Eothen Press, 1982)

Evin, Ahmet, 'Changing Greek Perspectives on Turkey: An Assessment of the Post-Earthquake Rapprochement', *Turkish Studies* vol 5, no 1 (2004)

Fırat, Melek, 'Yunanistan'la İlişkiler', in Baskın Oran (ed.), *Türk Dış Politikası,* (Istanbul: İletişim, 2001) vol 1.

Fox, Annette Baker, *The Power of Small States: Diplomacy in World War II* (Chicago: University of Chicago Press, 1959)

Fuller, Graham E., 'Turkey's New Eastern Orientation', in Graham E. Fuller and Ian O. Lesser (eds), *Turkey's New Geopolitics: From the Balkans to Western China* (Boulder, CO: Westview, 1993)

——*The New Turkish Republic: Turkey as a Pivotal State in the Muslim World* (Washington, DC: United States Institute of Peace Press, 2008)

Furman, Dimitry and Carl Johan Asenius, 'The Case of Nagorno-Karabakh (Azerbaijan)', in Lena Jonson and Clive Archer (eds), *Peacekeeping and the Role of Russia in Eurasia* (Boulder, CO: Westview, 1996)

G.E.K., 'The Turco-Egyptian Flirtation of Autumn 1954', *The World Today* vol 12 (1956)

Ghadry, Farid, 'Syrian–Turkish Relations', *Turkish Policy Quarterly* vol 4, no 2 (2005)

Gilead, Baruch, 'Turkish–Egyptian Relations 1952–57', *Middle Eastern Affairs* vol 10 (1959)

Girgin, Kemal, *Osmanlı ve Cumhuriyet Dönemleri Hariciye Tarihimiz (Teşkilat ve Protokol)* (Ankara: Türk Tarih Kurumu, 1992)

Gökay, Bülent, 'Turkish Settlement and the Caucasus, 1918–20', *Middle Eastern Studies* vol 32, no 2 (1996), reprinted in Sylvia Kedourie (ed.), *Turkey; Identity, Democracy, Politics* (London and Portland, OR: Cass, 1996)

——*A Clash of Empires: Turkey Between Russian Bolshevism and British Imperialism, 1918–1923* (London: I.B. Tauris, 1997)

——*Soviet Eastern Policy and Turkey, 1920–1991: Turkey and Communism* (London and New York: Routledge, 2006)

Göktepe, Cihat, 'The Cyprus Crisis of 1967 and its Effects on Turkey's Foreign Relations', *Middle Eastern Studies* vol 41, no 3, (2005)

Göle, Nilüfer, 'Towards an Autonomization of Politics and Civil Society in Turkey', in Metin Heper and Ahmet Evin (eds), *Politics in the Third Turkish Republic* (Boulder, CO: Westview, 1994)

Gönlübol, Mehmet and Cem Sar, *Atatürk ve Türkiye'nin Dış Politikası 1919–1939* (Ankara: Milli Eğitim Basımevi, 1963)

Gönlübol, Mehmet, 'NATO, USA and Turkey', in Kemal H. Karpat, et al., *Turkey's Foreign Policy in Transition* (Leiden: Brill, 1975)

Görener, Aylin Şeker, 'US Policy towards Iraq: Moral Dilemmas of Sanctions and Regime Change', *Turkish Review of Middle East Studies* (Istanbul: Annual) vol 12 (2001)

Grigoriadis, Ioannis N., '*Türk* or *Türkiyeli?* The Reform of Turkey's Minority Legislation and the Rediscovery of Ottomanism', *Middle Eastern Studies* vol 43, no 3 (2007)

——*Trials of Europeanization: Turkish Political Culture and the European Union* (New York: Palgrave Macmillan, 2009)

——'Friends No More? The Rise of Anti-American Nationalism in Turkey', *Middle East Journal* vol 64, no 1 (2010)

——'The Orthodox Church and Greek–Turkish Relations: Religion as a Source of Rivalry or Reconciliation?' in Jeffrey Haynes (ed.), *Religion and Politics in Europe, the Middle East and North Africa* (London and New York: Routledge, 2010)

Groom, A.J.R., 'The Process of Negotiation, 1974–93' in C.H. Dodd (ed.), *The Political, Social and Economic Development of Northern Cyprus* (Hemingford Grey: Eothen, 1993)

Gruen, George E., 'Ambivalence in the Alliance: US Interests in the Middle East and the Evolution of Turkish Foreign Policy', *Orbis* vol 24 (1980)

——'Turkey Between the Middle East and the West', in Robert O. Freedman (ed.), *The Middle East from the Iran Contra Affair to the Intifada* (New York: Syracuse University Press, 1991)

Güçlü, Yücel, 'Turkish–German Relations from Montreux to the Second World War', *Turkish Yearbook of International Relations* vol 29 (1999)

——'Turkish–German Relations on the Eve of World War Two', *Turkish Studies* vol 1, no 2 (2000)

——'The Nyon Arrangement of 1937 and Turkey', *Middle Eastern Studies* vol 38, no 1 (2002)

——'Turco-British Relations on the Eve of the Second World War', *Middle Eastern Studies* vol 39, no 4 (2003)

——'The Controversy over the Delimitation of the Turco-Syrian Frontier in the Period Between the Two World Wars', *Middle Eastern Studies* vol 42, no 4 (2006)

Güney, Aylin, 'Anti-Americanism in Turkey, Past and Present', *Middle Eastern Studies* vol 44, no 3 (2008)

Gunter, Michael M., *The Kurds in Turkey* (Boulder, CO: Westview, 1990)

——*The Kurds and the Future of Turkey* (New York: St Martin's Press, 1997)

——'Turkey and Iran Face Off in Kurdistan', *Middle East Quarterly* vol 5 (1998)

Hafner, Donald L., 'Bureaucratic Politics and "Those Frigging Missiles": JFK, Cuba, and US Missiles in Turkey', *Orbis* vol 21 (1977)

Hale, William, *The Political and Economic Development of Modern Turkey* (London: Croom Helm, 1981)

——'Anglo-Turkish Trade since 1923: Experiences and Problems', in William Hale and Ali İhsan Bağış (eds), *Four Centuries of Turco-British Relations* (Walkington: Eothen, 1984)

——'The Traditional and Modern in the Economy of Kemalist Turkey', in J.M. Landau (ed.), *Ataturk and the Modernization of Turkey* (Boulder, CO: Westview Press, 1984)

——'Turkey, the Middle East and the Gulf Crisis', *International Affairs* vol 68 (1992)

——'Turkey: A Crucial but Problematic Applicant', in John Redmond (ed.), *Prospective Europeans: New Members for the European Union* (New York and London: Harvester Wheatsheaf, 1994)

——*Turkish Politics and the Military* (London: Routledge, 1994)

——'Turkey', in Ami Ayalon (ed.), *Middle East Contemporary Survey 1993* vol 17 (Boulder, CO: Westview, 1995)

——'Turkey, the Black Sea and Transcaucasia', in John F.R. Wright, Suzanne Goldenburg and Richard Schofield (eds), *Transcaucasian Boundaries* (London: UCL Press, 1996)

——'Turkey and the EU: the Customs Union and the Future', *Boğaziçi Journal* (Istanbul) vol 10 (1997)

——'Turkey and Transcaucasia', in David Menashri (ed.), *Central Asia Meets the Middle East* (London: Cass, 1998)

——'Foreign Policy and Turkey's Domestic Politics', in David Shankland (ed.), *The Turkish Republic at 75 Years* (Hemingford Grey: Eothen, 1999).

——'Turkey's Political Landscape: a Glance at the Past and the Future' *International Observer* (Rome) vol 34 (1999)

——'Turkey: Economic Issues in Turkish Foreign Policy', in Alan Makovsky and Sabri Sayarı (eds), *Changing Dynamics of Turkish Foreign Policy* (Washington, DC: Washington Institute for Near East Policy, 2000)

——*Turkish Foreign Policy, 1774–2000* (London and Portland, OR: Frank Cass, 2nd edn, 2002)

——'Human Rights, the European Union, and the Turkish Accession Process', in Ali Çarkoğlu and Barry Rubin (eds), *Turkey and the European Union: Domestic Politics, Economic Integration and International Dynamics* (London and Portland, OR: Frank Cass, 2003)

——*Turkey, the US and Iraq* (London: Saqi Books, in association with London Middle East Institute, 2007)

Hale, William and Julian Bharier, 'CENTO, RCD and the Northern Tier: A Political and Economic Appraisal', *Middle Eastern Studies* vol 8 (1972)

Hale, William and Ergun Özbudun, *Islamism, Democracy and Liberalism in Turkey: The Case of the AKP* (London and New York: Routledge, 2010)

Halliday, Fred, *The Making of the Second Cold War* (London: Verso, 2nd edn, 1986)

——'The Middle East, the Great Powers and the Cold War', in Yezid Sayigh and Avi Shlaim (eds), *The Cold War and the Middle East* (Oxford: Clarendon Press, 1997)

Harris, George S., *The Origins of Communism in Turkey* (Stanford: Hoover Institution, 1967)

——*Troubled Alliance: Turkish–American Problems in Historical Perspective, 1945–1971* (Washington, DC: American Enterprise Institute for Public Policy Research and Hoover Institution, 1972)

Hart, Parker T., *Two NATO Allies at the Threshold of War: Cyprus: A Firsthand Account of Crisis Management, 1965–1968* (Durham, NC, and London: Duke University Press, 1990)

Heller, Joseph, *British Policy Towards the Ottoman Empire, 1908–1914* (London: Cass, 1983)

Henze, Paul B., *Turkey: Toward the Twenty-First Century* (Washington, DC: Rand Corporation, n.d.)

——'Turkey: Toward the Twenty-First Century', in Graham E. Fuller, et al., *Turkey's New Geopolitics: From the Balkans to Western China* (Boulder, CO: Westview, 1993)

Hershlag, Z.Y., *Turkey, an Economy in Transition* (The Hague: Van Keulen, 1958)

Hiç, Mükerrem, *Turkey's Customs Union with the European Union: Economic and Political Prospects* (Ebenhausen: Stiftung Wissenschaft und Politik, 1995)

Hirszowicz, Lukasz, *The Third Reich and the Arab East* (London: Routledge and Kegan Paul, 1966)

Holbraad, Carsten, *Middle Powers in International Politics* (London: Macmillan, 1984)

Hostler, Charles Warren, *Turkism and the Soviets* (London: Allen and Unwin, 1957)

Howard, Harry N., *The Partition of Turkey: A Diplomatic History, 1913–1923* (New York: Fertig, 1966)

——*Turkey, the Straits and US Policy* (Baltimore and London: Johns Hopkins University Press, 1974)

Human Rights Watch, *Turkey: Human Rights and the European Union Accession Partnership*, www.hrw.org/reports/2000/turkey2

Huntington, Samuel P., 'Democracy's Third Wave', in Larry Diamond and L.F. Plattner (eds), *The Global Resurgence of Democracy* (Baltimore, MD, and London: Johns Hopkins University Press, 1993)

——, 'The Clash of Civilizations?' *Foreign Affairs*, Vol.72 (1993)

Hurewitz, J.C. (ed.), *Diplomacy in the Near and Middle East: A Documentary Record, 1914–1956* (Princeton: Van Nostrand, 1956)

——'Ottoman Diplomacy and the European State System', *Middle East Journal* vol 15, no 2 (1961)

——'Russia and the Turkish Straits: A Revaluation of the Origins of the Problem', *World Politics* vol 14 (1961–2)

İdiz, Semih, *Turkey's 'French Problem'* (Paris and Brussels: Institut Français des Relations Internationales, Note Franco-Turque No 3, 7 Mai 2010)

İlkin, Selim, 'The Chester Railway Project', in Türkiye İş Bankası, *International Symposium on Atatürk (17–22 May 1981): Papers and Discussions* (Ankara: Türkiye İş Bankası Kültür Yayınları, 1984)

——'A History of Turkey's Association with the European Community', in Ahmet Evin and Geoffrey Denton (eds), *Turkey and the European Community* (Opladen: Leske and Budrich, 1990)

İnanç, Gül, 'The Politics of "Active Neutrality" of the Eve of a New World Order: The Case of Turkish Chrome Sales During the Second World War', *Middle Eastern Studies* vol 42, no 6 (2006)

International Crisis Group, *Iraq: Allaying Turkish Fears over Kurdish Ambitions* (Brussels: International Crisis Group, Middle East Report No 35, 2005)

——*Cyprus: Reversing the Drift to Partition* (Brussels: International Crisis Group, Europe Report No 190, 10 January 2008)

——*Cyprus: Reunification or Partition?* (Brussels: International Crisis Group, Europe Report No 201, 30 September 2009)

——*Turkey and Armenia: Opening Minds, Opening Borders* (Brussels: International Crisis Group, Europe Report No 199, 4 May 2009)

——*Turkey's Crises over Israel and Iran* (Brussels: International Crisis Group, Europe Report No 208, 2010)

——*Armenia and Azerbaijan: Preventing War* (Brussels: International Crisis Group, Europe Briefing No 60, February 2011)

——*Cyprus: Six Steps Towards a Settlement* (Nicosia, Istanbul and Brussels: International Crisis Group, Europe Briefing No 61, 22 February 2011)

Issawi, Charles, *An Economic History of the Middle East and North Africa* (London: Methuen, 1982)

Jung, Dietrich, 'The Sèvres Syndrome: Turkish Foreign Policy and its Historical Legacies', *American Diplomacy* vol 8, no 2 (2003)

Justice and Development Party, *Türkiye Hazır, Hedef 2023: 12 Haziran 2011 Genel Seçimleri Seçim Beyannamesi* (Ankara: AK Parti, 2011)

——*Adalet ve Kalkınma Partisi Programı*, from the party website www.akparti.org.tr (accessed 23 February 2012)

Kakizaki, Masaki, 'Anti-Iraq War Protests in Turkey: Global Networks, Coalitions and Context', *Middle Eastern Studies* vol 47, no 1 (2011)

Kalaitzaki, Theodora, 'US Mediation in Greek–Turkish Disputes since 1954', *Mediterranean Quarterly* vol 16, no 2 (2005)

Kaplan, Morton A., *System and Process in International Politics* (New York: Wiley, 1957)

Kapsis, James E., 'The Failure of the US–Turkish Pre-war Negotiations: An Over-confidant United States, Political Mismanagement and a Conflicted Military', *MERIA Journal* vol 9, no 3 (2005)

Karaosmanoğlu, Ali L., 'Turkey's Security and the Middle East', *Foreign Affairs* vol 62 (1983)

Karasapan, Ömer, 'Turkey's Armaments Industries', *Middle East Report* January–February 1987

Kardaş, Şaban, 'Turkey Reacts to Armenian Constitutional Court's Decision on Protocols', *Eurasia Daily Monitor* vol 7, no 17, 26 January 2010

——'Erdogan's Moscow Visit Produces Mixed Results', *Eurasia Daily Monitor* vol 8, no 54, March 2010

——'Turkish–Azeri Deal May Herald New Competition in Southern Corridor', *Eurasia Daily Monitor* vol 7, no 115, 15 June 2010

——'Turkey Strengthens Nuclear Cooperation with Russia', *Eurasia Daily Monitor* vol 7, no 213, November 2010

Karpat, Kemal H., *Turkey's Politics: The Transition to a Multi-Party System* (Princeton: Princeton University Press, 1959)

——'Turkish and Arab–Israeli Relations', in Kemal H. Karpat et al., *Turkey's Foreign Policy in Transition* (Leiden: Brill, 1975)

——'Turkish-Soviet Relations', in Kemal H. Karpat et al., *Turkey's Foreign Policy in Transition* (Leiden: Brill, 1975)

——'Turkish Democracy at Impasse: Party Politics and the Third Military Intervention', *International Journal of Turkish Studies* vol 2 (1981)

Kedourie, Elie, 'Young Turks, Freemasons and Jews', *Middle Eastern Studies* vol 7, no 1 (1971)

Kennedy, Robert F., *Thirteen Days: A Memoir of the Cuban Missile Crisis* (New York: Norton, 1961)

Kent, Marian, 'British Policy, International Diplomacy and the Turkish Revolution', *Internatonal Journal of Turkish Studies* vol 3 (1985–6)

Ker-Lindsay, James, 'The Policies of Greece and Cyprus towards Turkey's EU Accession', *Turkish Studies* vol 8, no 1 (2007)

Kibaroğlu, Ayşegül, 'Prospects for Cooperation in the Euphrates–Tigris River Basin' *Turkish Review of Middle East Studies* (Istanbul) vol 8 (1994/5)

Kılıç, Altemur, *Turkey and the World* (Washington, DC: Public Affairs Press, 1959)

Kınacıoğlu, Müge and Emel Oktay, 'The Domestic Dynamics of Turkey's Cyprus Policy: Implications for Turkey's Accession to the European Union', *Turkish Studies* vol 7, no 2 (2006)

Kınıklıoğlu, Suat, *The Anatomy of Turkish–Russian Relations* (Washington, DC: Brookings Institution, 2006)

Kinross, Lord, *Ataturk, the Rebirth of a Nation* (London: Weidenfeld & Nicolson, 1964)

Kirişci, Kemal, 'Post Second World War Immigration from the Balkan Countries to Turkey', *Turkish Review of Balkan Studies* (Istanbul, annual) vol 2 (1994/5)

——'New Patterns of Turkish Foreign Policy Behaviour', in Çiğdem Balım (ed.), *Turkey: Political, Social and Economic Challenges in the 1990s* (Leiden: Brill, 1995)

——'Turkey and the Kurdish Safe Haven in Northern Iraq', *Journal of South Asian and Middle Eastern Studies* vol 19 (1996)

——'Post Cold-War Turkish Security and the Middle East', *MERIA Journal* no 2 (1997)

——'Turkey and the United States: Ambivalent Allies', in Barry Rubin and Thomas Keaney (eds), *Friends of America: US Allies in a Changing World* (London: Cass, 2001)

——'The Kurdish Question and Turkish Foreign Policy', in Lenore G. Martin and Dimitris Keridis (eds), *The Future of Turkish Foreign Policy* (Cambridge, MA, and London: MIT Press, 2004)

Kirişci, Kemal and Gareth Winrow, *The Kurdish Question and Turkey: An Example of Trans-state Ethnic Conflict* (London: Cass, 1997)

Kirişci, Kemal, Nathalie Tocci and Joshua Walker, *A Neighbourhood Rediscovered: Turkey's Transatlantic Value in the Middle East* (Washington, DC: German Marshall Fund of the United States, Brussels Forum Paper Series, 2010)

Knatchbull-Hugessen, Sir Hughe, *Diplomat in Peace and War* (London: Murray, 1949)

Kramer, Heinz, 'Turkey and EC's Southern Enlargement', *Aussenpolitik* vol 35 (1984)

——'The EU–Turkey Customs Union: Economic Integration amidst Political Turmoil', *Mediterranean Politics* vol 1 (1996)

——'Turkey and the European Union: A Multi-Dimensional Relationship with Hazy Perspectives', in V. Mastny and R. Craig Nation (eds), *Turkey Between East and West: New Challenges for a Rising Regional Power* (Boulder, CO: Westview, 1996)

——'Will Central Asia Become Turkey's Sphere of Influence?', *Perceptions* (Ankara) vol 1, no 1 (1996)

——'Options for Turkish Foreign Policy: Central Asia and Transcaucasus', unpublished paper (1997)

——*Turkey's Accession Process to the EU: The Agenda Behind the Agenda* (Berlin: Stiftung Wissenschaft und Politik, SWP Comments 25, October 2009)

——*AKP's 'New' Foreign Policy between Vision and Pragmatism* (Berlin: Stifting Wissenschaft und Politik, Working Paper FG2, June 2010)

Kuniholm, Bruce R., 'Turkey and NATO: Past, Present and Future', *Orbis* vol 27 (1983)

——*The Origins of the Cold War in the Near East* (Princeton: Princeton University Press, 2nd edn, 1994)

——'Turkey and the West Since World War II', in Vojtech Mastny and R. Craig Nation (eds), *Turkey Between East and West: New Challenges for a Rising Regional Power* (Boulder, CO: Westview, 1996)

Kut, Gün, 'Burning Waters: The Hydropolitics of the Euphrates and Tigris', *New Perspectives on Turkey* Fall (1993)

Kut, Şule, 'Turkish Policy towards the Balkans', in Alan Makovsky and Sabri Sayarı (eds), *Turkey's New World: Changing Dynamics in Turkish Foreign Policy,* (Washington, DC: Washington Institute for Near East Policy, 2000)

Kyle, Keith, *Cyprus: In Search of Peace* (London: Minority Rights Group International, 1997)

Kyriakides, Stanley, *Cyprus: Constitutionalism and Crisis Government* (Philadelphia: University of Philadelphia Press, 1968)

Landau, Jacob M., *Johnson's 1964 Letter to İnönü and Greek Lobbying of the White House* (Jerusalem: Hebrew University of Jerusalem, Jerusalem Papers on Peace Problems 28, 1979)

——*Pan-Turkism: from Irredentism to Cooperation* (London: Hurst, 1995)

Leffler, Melvin, 'The American Conception of National Security and the Beginnings of the Cold War', *American Historical Review* vol 89 (1984)

Lesser, Ian O., 'Bridge or Barrier? Turkey and the West After the Cold War', in Graham E. Fuller et al., *Turkey's New Geopolitics: From the Balkans to Western China* (Boulder, CO: Westview, 1993)

——'Turkey's Strategic Options', *International Observer* (Rome) vol 34 (1999)

——'Turkey, Iran and Nuclear Risks', *Turkish Policy Quarterly* vol 3, no 2 (2004)

——'Turkey's Regional Role: Harder Choices Ahead', *Turkish Policy Quarterly* vol 7, no 2 (2008)

——'Can Turkey Live with a Nuclear Iran?', research paper issued by German Marshall Fund, Washington, DC, www.gmfus.org, 2 March 2009

——'Rethinking Turkish–Western Relations: A Journey Without Maps', research paper issued by German Marshall Fund, Washington, DC, www.gmfus.org, 30 June 2010

Lewis, Bernard, *The Emergence of Modern Turkey* (London: Oxford University Press, 1961)

Lewis, Jonathan Eric, 'Replace Turkey as a Strategic Partner?', *Middle East Quarterly* vol 13, no 2 (2006)

Lundgren, Asa, *The Unwelcome Neighbour: Turkey's Kurdish Policy* (London: I.B. Tauris, 2007)

Macfie, A.L., 'The Straits Question: The Conference of Lausanne (November 1922–July 1923)', *Middle Eastern Studies* vol 15, no 2 (1979)

——'The Straits Question at the Potsdam Conference: The British Position', *Middle Eastern Studies* vol 23, no 1 (1987)

——'The Turkish Straits in the Second World War, 1939–45', *Middle Eastern Studies* vol 25, no 2 (1989)

——*The Straits Question, 1908–36* (Thessaloniki: Institute for Balkan Studies, 1993)

Makovsky, Alan O., 'Turkey', in Robert S. Chase, Emily B. Hill and Paul Kennedy (eds), *The Pivotal States: A New Framework for US Policy in the Developing World* (New York and London: W.W. Norton, 1999)

Mango, Andrew, 'European Dimensions', *Middle Eastern Studies* vol 28 (1992)

——*Atatürk* (London: Murray, 1999)

Marriott, J.A.R., *The Eastern Question: An Historical Study in European Diplomacy* (Oxford: Clarendon Press, 4th edn, 1940)

Marzari, Frank, 'Western–Soviet Rivalry in Turkey, 1939' (in two parts) *Middle Eastern Studies* vol 7, nos 1–2 (1971)

McCarthy, Justin, *Death and Exile: The Ethnic Cleansing of Ottoman Muslims, 1821–1922* (Princeton: Darwin Press, 1995)

McCurdy, Daphne, 'Turkish–Iranian Relations: When Opposites Attract', *Turkish Policy Quarterly* vol 7, no 2 (2008).

McDowall, David, *A Modern History of the Kurds* (London: I.B. Tauris, 1996)

McGhee, George C., 'Turkey Joins the West', *Foreign Affairs* vol 32 (1954)

McGhee, George C., *The US–Turkish-NATO Middle East Connection* (London: Macmillan, 1990)

Metropoll Stratejik ve Sosyal Araştırması, *Davos Krizi, Ocak*, from www.metropoll.com.tr (2009)

——*Türkiye Siyasal Durum Araştırması, Aralık*, from www.metropoll.com.tr (2010)

Meyer, H.C., 'German Economic Relations with South-Eastern Europe, 1870–1914', *American Historical Review* vol 62 (1951–2)

Migdalowitz, Carol, 'AKP's Domestically Driven Foreign Policy', *Turkish Policy Quarterly* vol 9, no 4 (2010/11)

Milman, Brock, 'Turkish Foreign and Strategic Policy, 1934–42', *Middle Eastern Studies* vol 31, no 3 (1995)

——*The Ill-Made Alliance: Anglo-Turkish Relations 1939–1940* (Montreal and Kingston: McGill-Queens University Press, 1998)

Mufti, Malik, 'Daring and Caution in Turkish Foreign Policy', *Middle East Journal* vol 52, no 1 (1998)

Müftüler-Baç, Meltem, 'Turkey's Political Reforms and the Impact of the European Union', *South European Society and Politics* vol 10, no 1 (2005).

Müftüler, Meltem, 'Turkish Economic Liberalization and European Integration', *Middle Eastern Studies* vol 31, no 1 (1995)

Müftüler-Baç, Meltem, 'Turkey's Predicament in the Post-Cold War Era', *Futures* vol 28 (1996)

——*Turkey's Relations with a Changing Europe* (Manchester and New York: Manchester University Press, 1997)

——'The Never-Ending Story: Turkey and the European Union', *Middle Eastern Studies* vol 34, no 4 (1998)

Murinson, Alexander, 'The Strategic Depth Doctrine of Turkish Foreign Policy', *Middle Eastern Studies* vol 42, no 6 (2006)

——*Turkey's Entente with Israel and Azerbaijan: State Identity and Security in the Middle East and Caucasus* (London and New York: Routledge, 2010)

Nachmani, Amikam, *Israel, Turkey and Greece: Uneasy Relations in the Eastern Mediterranean* (London: Cass, 1987)

——'The Remarkable Turkish–Israeli Tie', in Amikam Nachmani, *Turkey and the Middle East* (Tel Aviv: Begin-Sadat Center for Strategic Studies, Bar Ilan University, 1999), reprinted from *Middle East Quarterly* vol 5 (1998)

Narbone, Luigi and Nathalie Tocci, 'Running Around in Circles? The Cyclical Relationship between Turkey and the European Union', in Susannah Verney and Kostas Ifantis (eds), *Turkey's Road to European Union Membership: National Identity and Political Change* (London and New York: Routledge, 2009)

Nas, Tevfik F., 'Economic Dimension: The Turkish Economy from the 1960s to EU Accession', in Armağan Emre Çakır (ed.), *Fifty Years of EU–Turkey Relations a Sisyphean Story* (London and New York: Routledge, 2011)

Nathan, James A., 'The Heyday of the New Strategy', in James A. Nathan (ed.), *The Cuban Missile Crisis Revisited* (New York: St Martin's Press, 1992)

Oğuzlu, Tarık, 'Soft Power in Turkish Foreign Policy', *Australian Journal of International Affairs* vol 61, no 1 (2007)

Oktar, Selim, 'The Turkish Foreign Policy Environment: A Public Opinion Perspective', paper presented to the Conference 'The Domestic Context of Turkish Foreign Policy', The Washington Institute for Near East Policy, Washington, DC, July 1997

Ökte, Faik, *The Tragedy of the Capital Tax*, tr. Geoffrey Cox (London: Croom Helm, 1987)

Okyar, Osman, 'Turco-British Relations in the Inter-War Period: Fethi Okyar's Missions to London', in William Hale and Ali İkhsan Bağış (eds), *Four Centuries of Turco-British Relations* (Walkington: Eothen, 1984)

Olmert, Y., 'Britain, Turkey and the Levant Question during the Second World War', *Middle Eastern Studies* vol 23, no 4 (1987)

Olson, Robert, 'The Kurdish Question and Turkey's Foreign Policy, 1991–95: From the Gulf War to the Incursion Into Iraq', *Journal of South Asian and Middle Eastern Studies* vol 19 (1995)

——*The Kurdish Nationalist Movement in the 1990s: Its Impact on Turkey and the Middle East* (Lexington, KY: University of Kentucky, 1996)

——'Turkish and Russian Foreign Policies, 1991–97: The Kurdish and Chechnya Questions', *Journal of Muslim Minority Affairs* vol 18, no 2 (1998)

Onar, Nora Fisher, *Neo Ottomanism, Historical Legacies and Turkish Foreign Policy* (Istanbul: Center for Economic and Foreign Policy Research [EDAM] Discussion Paper Series 2009/03, from www.scribed.com)

Öniş, Ziya, 'Turkey in the Post-Cold War Era: in Search of Identity', *Middle East Journal* vol 49, no 1 (1995)

——'Greek–Turkish Relations and the European Union: a Critical Perspective', *Mediterranean Politics* vol 6, no 3 (2001)

——'Domestic Politics versus Global Dynamics: Towards a Political Economy of the 2000 and 2001 Financial Crises in Turkey', *Turkish Studies* vol 4, no 2 (2003)

——'Globalization and Party Transformation: Turkey's Justice and Development Party in Perspective', in Peter Burnell (ed.), *Globalising Democracy: Party Politics in Emerging Democracies* (London and New York: Routledge, 2006)

——'Conservative Globalists versus Defensive Nationalists: Political Parties and Paradoxes of Europeanisation in Turkey', in Susannah Verney and Kostas Ifantis (eds), *Turkey's Road to European Union Membership: National Identity and Political Change* (London and New York: Routledge, 2009)

——'Contesting for Turkey's Political "Centre": Domestic Politics, Identity Conflicts and the Controversy over EU Membership', *Journal of Contemporary European Studies* vol 18, no 3 (2010)

——'Multiple Faces of the "New" Turkish Foreign Policy: Underlying Dynamics and a Critique', *Insight Turkey* vol 13, no 1 (2011)

Öniş, Ziya and Fikret Şenses (eds), *Turkey and the Global Economy: Neo-Liberal Restructuring and Integration in the Post-Crisis Era* (London and New York: Routledge, 2009)

Öniş, Ziya and Şuhnaz Yılmaz, 'Greek–Turkish Rapprochement: Rhetoric or Reality?', *Political Science Quarterly* vol 123, no 1 (2008)

Oran, Baskın, '"Sèvres Barış Antlaşması" and "Lausanne Barış Antlaşması"', in Baskın Oran (ed.), *Türk Dış Politikası* (Istanbul: İletişim, 2001) vol 1

Ortaylı, İlber, 'Osmanlı Dipolmasisi ve Dışişleri Örgütü', *Tanzimat'tan Cumhuriyet'e Türkiye Ansiklopedisi* (Istanbul: İletişim Yayınları, 1985) vol 1

Özal, Turgut, *Turkey in Europe and Europe in Turkey* (Nicosia: Rustem, 1991)

Özbudun, Ergun, *The Constitutional System of Turkey, 1876 to the Present* (New York: Macmillan, 2011)

Özbudun, Ergun and Ömer Faruk Gençkaya, *Democratization and the Politics of Constitution Making in Turkey* (Budapest and New York: Central European University Press, 2009)

Özbudun, Ergun and Serap Yazıcı, *Democratization Reforms in Turkey (1993–2004)* (Istanbul: TESEV, 2004)

Özel, Soli, 'On Not Being a Lone Wolf: Geography, Domestic Plays, and Turkish Foreign Policy in the Middle East', in Geoffrey Kemp and Janice Gross Stein (eds), *Powder Keg in the Middle East: The Struggle for Gulf Security* (Lanham, MD: Rowman and Littlefield, 1995)

Özersay, Kudret, 'Montreux Boğazlar Sözleşmesi', in Baskın Oran (ed.), *Türk Dış Politikası* (Istanbul: İletişim, 2001) vol 1.

——'Simultaneous Referenda in Cyprus: Was it a "Fact" or an "Illusion"?' *Turkish Studies* vol 6, no 3 (2005)

Özkırımlı, Umut and Spyros A. Sofos, *Tormented by History: Nationalism in Greece and Turkey* (London: Hurst, 2008)

Park, Bill, 'Between Europe, the United States and the Middle East: Turkey and European Security in the Wake of the Iraq Crisis', *Perspectives on European Politics and Society* vol 5, no 3 (2004)

——'Turkey, the United States, and Northern Iraq', in Paul Cornish (ed.), *The Conflict in Iraq, 2003* (Basingstoke and New York: Palgrave Macmillan, 2004)

——*Turkey's Policy Towards Northern Iraq: Problems and Perspectives*, London, International Institute of Strategic Studies, Adelphi Paper 374 (2005)

——*Modern Turkey: People, State and Foreign Policy in a Globalized World* (London and New York: Routledge, 2012)

Parris, Mark R., 'Turkey and the US: A Partnership Rediscovered', *Insight Turkey,* vol 3, no 4 (2001)

Perincek, Doğu (ed.), *Mustafa Kemal Eskişehir-İzmit Konuşmaları* (Istanbul: Kaynak Yayınları, 1993)

Petersen, Philip A., 'Turkey in Soviet Military Strategy', *Foreign Policy* (Ankara: Foreign Policy Institute) vol 13 (1986)

Pipes, Daniel, 'Is Turkey Going Rogue?' *National Review Online* 27 September 2011 (www.meforum.org)

Pollock, Robert J., 'The Sick Man of Europe – Again', *Wall Street Journal* 16 February (2005).

Polyviou, Polyvios G., *Cyprus: Conflict and Negotiation, 1960–1980* (London: Duckworth, 1980)

Pope, Hugh, 'Pointing Fingers at Iran', *Middle East International* 5 February 1993

——'Turkey and Armenia vow to heal past wounds', International Crisis Group, Brussels (www.crisisgroup.org) 1 September 2009

——'EU and Turkey Edge Back from the Brink', International Crisis Group, Brussels, www.crisisgroup.org, 5 January 2010

——'Turkey, Pax Ottomana?' *Foreign Affairs* vol 86, no 6 (2010)

Pope, Nicole, 'Concerns over Iraq', *Middle East International* 22 March 2002

Pope, Nicole and Hugh Pope, *Turkey Unveiled: Atatürk and After* (London: Murray, 1997)

Poulain, Loic and Akis Sakellariou, 'Western Balkans: Is Turkey Back?', paper issued by Center for Strategic and International Studies, Washington, DC (http://csis.org) 25 April 2011

Poulton, Hugh, *Top Hat, Grey Wolf and Crescent: Turkish Nationalism and the Turkish Republic* (London: Hurst, 1997)

——'The Turkish State and Democracy', *International Observer* (Rome) vol 34 (1999)

Redmond, John, *The Next Mediterranean Enlargement of the European Community: Turkey, Cyprus and Malta?* (Aldershot: Dartmouth Publishing Co., 1993)

Richmond, J.C.B., *Egypt, 1798–1952* (London: Methuen, 1977)

Richmond, Oliver P., 'Ethno-Nationalism, Sovereignty and Negotiating Positions in the Cyprus Conflict: Obstacles to a Settlement', *Middle Eastern Studies* vol 35, no 3 (1999)

Robins, Philip, *Turkey and the Middle East* (London: Pinter, for Royal Institute of International Affairs, 1991)

——'Turkish Policy in the Gulf Crisis: Adventurist or Dynamic?' in C.H. Dodd (ed.), *Turkish Foreign Policy: New Prospects* (Wistow: Eothen Press, for Modern Turkish Studies Programme, SOAS, 1992)

——'Between Sentiment and Self-Interest: Turkey's Policy toward Azerbaijan and the Central Asian States', *Middle East Journal* vol 47, no 4 (1993)

——'The Overlord State: Turkish Policy and the Kurdish Issue', *International Affairs* vol 69 (1993)

——'Coping with Chaos: Turkey and the Bosnian Crisis', in Richard Gillespie (ed.), *Mediterranean Politics*, vol 1 (1994) (annual, London: Pinter)

——'Turkish Foreign Policy under Erbakan', *Survival* vol 39, no 2 (1997)

——'Turkey's Ostpolitik: Relations with the Central Asian States' in David Menashri (ed.), *Central Asia Meets the Middle East* (London: Cass, 1998)

——'Confusion at Home, Confusion Abroad: Turkey between Copenhagen and Iraq', *International Affairs* vol 79, no 3 (2003)

——'The Opium Crisis and the Iraq War: Historical Parallels in Turkey–US Relations', *Mediterranean Politics* vol 12, no 1 (2007)

Robinson, Richard D., *The First Turkish Republic* (Cambridge, MA: Harvard University Press, 1963)

Roper, John, 'The West and Turkey: Varying Roles, Common Interests', *International Spectator* (Rome) vol 34 (1999)

Rothstein, Robert L., *Alliances and Small Powers* (New York and London: Columbia University Press, 1968)

Rubin, Michael, 'Shifting Sides? The Problems of Neo-Ottomanism', *National Review Online* 10 August 2004 (www.meforum.org)

——'A Comedy of Errors: American–Turkish Diplomacy and the Iraq War', *Turkish Policy Quarterly* vol 4, no 1 (2005)

——'Green Money, Islamist Politics in Turkey', *Middle East Quarterly* vol 12, no 1 (2005)

Rubinstein, Alvin Z., *Soviet Policy Toward Turkey, Iran and Afghanistan: The Dynamics of Influence* (New York: Praeger, 1982)

Rumelili, Bahar, 'Civil Society and the Europeanization of Greek–Turkish Cooperation', *South European Society and Politics* vol 10, no 1 (2005)

——'Transforming Conflicts on EU Borders: The Case of Greek–Turkish Relations', *Journal of Common Market Studies* vol 45, no 1 (2007)

Rustow, Dankwart A., 'Transitions to Democracy: Turkey's Experience in Historical and Comparative Perspective', in Metin Heper and Ahmet Evin (eds), *State, Democracy and the Military: Turkey in the 1980s* (Berlin: de Gruyter, 1988)

Sadak, Necmeddin, 'Turkey Faces the Soviets', *Foreign Affairs* vol 27 (1949)

Saivetz, Carol R. 'Tangled Pipelines: Turkey's Role in Energy Export Plans', *Turkish Studies* vol 10, no 1 (2009)

Sanjian, Ara, 'The Formulation of the Baghdad Pact', *Middle Eastern Studies* vol 33, no 2 (1997)

Sanjian, Avedis K., 'The Sanjak of Alexandretta (Hatay); its Impact on Turkish–Syrian Relations (1939–56)', *Middle East Journal* vol 10, no 4 (1956)

Satloff, Robert B., 'Prelude to Conflict: Communal Interdependence in the Sanjak of Alexandretta 1920–36', *Middle Eastern Studies* vol 22, no 2 (1986)

Sayarı, Sabri, 'Turkey, the Changing European Security Environment and the Gulf Crisis', *Middle East Journal* vol 46, no 1 (1992)

——'Turkey and the Middle East in the 1990s', *Journal of Palestine Studies* vol 26 (1997)

Sayılgan, Aclan, *Solun 94 Yılı, 1871–1965* (Ankara: Mars Matbaası, 1968)

Şenses, Fikret, 'Economic Crisis as an Instigator of Distributional Conflict: The Turkish Case in 2001', *Turkish Studies* vol 4, no 2 (2003)

Sever, Ayşegül, 'The Arab–Israeli Peace Process and Turkey since the 1995 Interim Agreement', *Turkish Review of Middle East Studies* (Istanbul) vol 9 (1996/7)

——'The Compliant Ally? Turkey and the West in the Middle East, 1954–58', *Middle Eastern Studies* vol 34, no 2 (1998)

——'A Reluctant Partner of the US over Suez? Turkey and the Suez Crisis', in Simon C. Smith (ed.), *Reassessing Suez 1956: New Perspectives on the Crisis and its Aftermath* (Aldershot and Burlington, VT: Ashgate, 2008)

Seydi, Süleyman, 'Turkish–American Relations and the Cuban Missile Crisis', *Middle Eastern Studies* vol 46, no 3 (2010)

Seydi, Süleyman and Steven Morewood, 'Turkey's Application of the Montreux Convention in the Second World War', *Middle Eastern Studies* vol 41, no 1 (2005)

Sezer, Duygu Bazoğlu, 'Turkey's Security Policies', in Jonathan Alford (ed.), *Greece and Turkey: Adversity in Alliance* (London: Gower, for International Institute of Strategic Studies, 1984)

——'Turkey and the Western Alliance in the 1980s', in Atila Eralp, Muharrem Tünay and Birol Yeşilada (eds), *The Political and Socioeconomic Transformation of Turkey* (Westport, CT: Praeger, 1993)

——*Turkey's Political and Security Interests and Policies in the New Geostrategic Environment of the Expanded Middle East* (Washington, DC, Henry L. Stimson Center, Occasional Paper No 19, 1994)

——'Turkey in the New Security Environment in the Balkan and Black Sea Region', in Vojtech Mastny and R. Craig Nation (eds), *Turkey Between East and West: New Challenges for a Rising Regional Power* (Boulder, CO: Westview, 1996)

Shaw, Stanford J. and Ezel Kural Shaw, *History of the Ottoman Empire and Modern Turkey* (Cambridge: Cambridge University Press, 1977)

Shaw, Stanford J., 'The Ottoman Census System and Population, 1831–1914', *International Journal of Middle East Studies* vol 9 (1978)

——*Turkey and the Holocaust* (New York: New York University Press, 1993)

Socar, Vladimir, 'Armenia Suspends US-Backed Normalization of Relations with Turkey', *Eurasia Daily Monitor* vol 7, no 81, 27 April 2010

——'Nabucco Pipeline, Azerbaijan's Shah Deniz Field Require Synchronised Development', *Eurasia Daily Monitor* vol 7, no 164, 14 September 2010

——'Putin Looks for LNG Exit from South Stream', *Eurasia Daily Monitor* vol 8, no 49, 11 March 2011

Sönmezoğlu, Faruk, *ABD'nin Türkiye Politikası (1964–1980)* (Istanbul: Der Yayınevi, 1995)

Sonyel, Salahi Ransdan, *Turkish Diplomacy, 1913–1923: Mustafa Kemal and the Turkish National Movement* (London and Beverly Hills: Sage, 1975)

Soysal, İsmail, 'The Baghdad Pact', in İsmail Soysal, *Between East and West; Studies on Turkish Foreign Relations* (Istanbul: Isis, 2001)

Sözen, Ahmet, 'A Model of Power-Sharing in Cyprus: From the 1959 London–Zurich Agreements to the Annan Plan', *Turkish Studies* vol 5, no 1 (2004)

Sözen, Ahmet and Kudret Özersay, 'The Annan Plan: State Succession or Continuity', *Middle Eastern Studies* vol 43, no 1 (2007)

Spain, James W., 'The United States, Turkey and the Poppy', *Middle East Journal* vol 29, no 3 (1975)

Stavrinides, Zenon, *The Cyprus Conflict: National Identity and Statehood* (Wakefield: Loris Stavrinides, 1976)

Stephens, Robert, *Cyprus, a Place of Arms: Power Politics and Ethnic Conflict in the Eastern Mediterranean* (London: Pall Mall, 1966)

Taşhan, Seyfi, 'The Case for Turkish Membership', in Ahmet Evin and Geoffrey Denton (eds), *Turkey and the European Community* (Opladen: Leske and Budrich, 1990)

Taşpinar, Ömer, *Turkey's Middle East Policies: Between Neo-Ottomanism and Kemalism* (Washington, DC: Carnegie Endowment for International Peace, Carnegie Middle East Center, September 2008)

Taylor, A.J.P., *The Struggle for Mastery in Europe, 1848–1918* (Oxford: Oxford University Press, 1954)

Tocci, Nathalie, 'Elite Opinion Dimension: Behind the Scenes of Turkey's Protracted Accession Process: European Elite Debates', in Armağan Emre Çakır (ed.), *Fifty Years of EU–Turkey Relations: a Sisyphean Story* (London and New York: Routledge, 2011)

Toktaş, Şule, 'Turkey's Jews and their Immigration to Israel', *Middle Eastern Studies* vol 42, no 3 (2006)

Toprak, Binnaz, 'Civil Society in Turkey', in Augustus R. Norton (ed.), *Civil Society in the Middle East* (Leiden: Brill, 1995) vol 2

Torbakov, Igor, *The Georgia Crisis and Russia–Turkish Relations* (Washington, DC: Jamestown Foundation, 2008)

Torumtay, Necip, *Orgeneral Torumtay'ın Anıları* (Istanbul: Milliyet Yayınları, 1994)

——'Turkey's Military Doctrine', *Foreign Policy* (Ankara: Foreign Policy Institute) vol 15, no 1–2 (1990)

Traub, James, 'Turkey's Rules', *New York Times* 20 January (2011)

Trumpener, Ulrich, 'Turkey's Entry into World War I: an Assessment of Responsibilities', *Journal of Modern History* vol 34 (1962)

——*Germany and the Ottoman Empire, 1914–1918* (Princeton: Princeton University Press, 1968)

——'Germany and the End of the Ottoman Empire', in Marian Kent (ed.), *The Great Powers and the End of the Ottoman Empire* (London: Cass, 2nd edn, 1996)

Tunç, Hakan, 'The Lost Gamble: the 2000 and 2001 Turkish Financial Crises in Comparative Perspective', *Turkish Studies* vol 4, no 2 (2003)

Tuncer, Baran, 'External Financing of the Turkish Economy and its Foreign Policy Implications', in Kemal H. Karpat (ed.), *Turkey's Foreign Policy in Transition* (Leiden: Brill, 1975)

Turan, Ali Eşref, *Türkiye'de Seçmen Davranışı: Öncedeki Kırılmalar ve 2002 Seçimi* (Istanbul: Bilgi Üniversitesi Yayınları, 2004)

Turan, Berna, 'National Loyalties and International Undertakings: The Case of the Gülen Community in Kazakhstan', in M. Hakan Yavuz and John L. Esposito (eds), *Turkish Islam and the Secular State: The Gülen Movement,* (Syracuse, NY: Syracuse University Press, 2003)

Turan, İlter, 'Water and Turkish Foreign Policy', in Lenore G. Martin and Dimitris Keridis (eds), *The Future of Turkish Foreign Policy* (Cambridge, MA, and London: MIT Press, 2004)

Türkeş, Mustafa, 'The Balkan Pact and its Immediate Implications for the Balkan States, 1930–34', *Middle Eastern Studies* vol 30, no 1 (1994)

Turkish Ministry of Foreign Affairs (MFA), 'Water Issues between Turkey, Syria and Iraq', *Perceptions* (Ankara) vol 1, no 2 (1996)

Turkish Straits Voluntary Watch Group, *Turkish Straits: New Problems, New Solutions* (Istanbul: Isis, for Foundation for Middle East and Balkan Studies, 1995)

Türkmen, Füsun, 'Turkey and the Korean War', *Turkish Studies* vol 3, no 2 (2002)

Udum, Şebnem, 'Turkey and the Emerging European Security Framework', *Turkish Studies* vol 3, no 2 (2002)

Ulman, A.H. and R.H. Dekmejian, 'Changing Patterns in Turkish Foreign Policy, 1959–67', *Orbis* vol 11 (1967)

Uluslarası Stratejik Araştırmalar Kurumu, Ankara, *USAK Dış Politika Algılama Anketi, Ağustos*, from www.usak.org.tr, (2009)

Ulusoy, Hasan, 'A New Formation in the Black Sea: BLACKSEAFOR', *Perceptions* (Ankara, quarterly) vol 6, no 4 (2001–2)

Ünal, Hasan, 'Young Turks Assessments of International Politics, 1906–9', *Middle Eastern Studies* vol 32, no 2 (1996)

——'Ottoman Policy During the Bulgarian Independence Crisis, 1908–9: Ottoman Empire and Bulgaria at the Outset of the Young Turk Revolution', *Middle Eastern Studies* vol 34, no 4 (1998), reprinted in Sylvia Kedourie (ed.), *Turkey Before and After Atatürk: Internal and External Affairs* (London and Portland, OR: Cass, 1999)

Uslu, Nazih, *Turkey's Relationship with the United States, 1960–1975* (Ph.D. thesis, University of Durham, 1994)

Uslu, Nasuh, Metin Toprak, İbrahim Dalmış and Ertan Aydın, 'Turkish Opinion towards the United States in the Context of the Iraq Question', *MERIA Journal* vol 9, no 3 (2005)

Usul, Ali Resul, *Democracy in Turkey: The Impact of EU Political Conditionality* (London and New York: Routledge, 2011)

Uzgel, İlhan, 'The Balkans: Turkey's Stabilizing Role', in Barry Rubin and Kemal Kirişci (eds), *Turkey in World Politics: An Emerging Multiregional Power* (London: Lynne Rienner, 2001)

Vali, Ferenc A., *Bridge Across the Bosporus: The Foreign Policy of Turkey* (Baltimore and London: Johns Hopkins Press, 1971)

Vander Lippe, John M., 'Forgotten Brigade of the Forgotten War: Turkey's Participation in the Korean War', *Middle Eastern Studies* vol 36, no 1 (2000)

Vital, David, *The Inequality of States: A Study of the Small Power in International Relations* (Oxford: Clarendon Press, 1967)

von Papen, Franz, *Memoirs*, tr. Brian Connell (London: Andre Deutsch, 1952)

Walker, Joshua W., 'Reexamining the US–Turkish Alliance', *Washington Quarterly* vol 31, no 1 (2007–8)

Waterfield, Gordon, *Professional Diplomat: Sir Percy Loraine of Kirkharle Bt., 1880–1961* (London: Murray, 1973)

Weber, Frank G., *Eagles on the Crescent: Germany, Austria and the Diplomacy of the Turkish Alliance, 1914–1918* (Ithaca and London: University Press, 1970)

——*The Evasive Neutral: Germany, Britain and the Quest for a Turkish Alliance in the Second World War* (Columbia and London: University of Missouri Press, 1979)

Weiker, Walter F., *The Turkish Revolution, 1960–1961* (Washington, DC: Brookings Institution, 1963)

——*Political Tutelage and Democracy in Turkey: The Free Party and its Aftermath* (Leiden: Brill, 1973)

Weisband, Edward, *Turkish Foreign Policy, 1943–1945: Small State Diplomacy and Great Power Politics* (Princeton: Princeton University Press, 1973)

White, Jenny B., 'Civic Culture and Islam in Urban Turkey', in Chris Hann and Elizabeth Dunn (eds), *Civil Society: Challenging Western Models* (London: Routledge, 1996)

Williams, Paul A. and Ali Tekin, 'The Iraq War, Turkey, and Renewed Caspian Energy Prospects', *Middle East Journal* vol 62, no 3 (2008)

Wilson, Andrew, *The Aegean Dispute* (London: International Institute for Strategic Studies, Adelphi Papers No 155, 1980)

Winrow, Gareth M., 'Gorbachev's New Political Thinking and Turkey', paper delivered to conference of British International Studies Association, University of Warwick, December 1991

——'NATO and the Out-of-Area Issue: The Positions of Turkey and Italy', *Il Politico* (Pavia) vol 58 (1993)

——'A Region at the Crossroads: Security Issues in Post-Soviet Asia', *Journal of South Asian and Middle Eastern Studies* vol 18 (1994)

——'Regional Security and National Identity: The Role of Turkey in former Soviet Central Asia', in Çiğdem Balım (ed.), *Turkey: Political, Social and Economic Challenges in the 1990s* (Leiden: Brill, 1995)

——*Turkey in Post-Soviet Central Asia* (London: Royal Institute of International Affairs, 1995)

——'Turkey's Relations with the Transcaucasus and the Central Asian Republics', *Perceptions* (Ankara) vol 1, no 1 (1996)

——'Turkey and the Newly Independent States of Central Asia and Transcaucasus', *MERIA Journal* no 2 (1997)

——'Turkey and the East–West Gas Transportation Corridor', *Turkish Studies* vol 5, no 2 (2004)

Yasamee, F.A.K., 'Abdülhamid II and the Ottoman Defence Problem', *Diplomacy and Statecraft* vol 4 (1993)

——*Ottoman Diplomacy: Abdülhamid II and the Great Powers, 1878–1888* (Istanbul: Isis, 1996)

Yavuz, M. Hakan and John L. Esposito (eds), *Turkish Islam and the Secular State: The Gülen Movement* (Syracuse, NY: Syracuse University Press, 2003)

Yavuz, M. Hakan, and Mujeeb R. Khan, 'Turkish Foreign Policy Toward the Arab–Israeli Conflict: Duality and the [sic] Development', *Arab Studies Quarterly* vol 14 (1992)

Yavuz, M. Hakan, 'Turkish–Israeli Relations Through the Lens of the Turkish Identity Debate', *Journal of Palestine Studies* vol 27 (1997)

——'Turkish Identity and Foreign Policy in Flux: The Rise of Neo-Ottomanism', *Critique, Critical Middle Eastern Studies* vol 7, no 12 (1998)

Yerasimos, Stefanos, *Türk-Sovyet İlişkileri, Ekim Devrimden Milli Mücadele'ye* (Istanbul: Gözlem Yayınları, 1979)

Yeşılbursa, Behçet K., 'Turkey's Participation in the Middle East Command and its Admission to NATO, 1950–52', *Middle Eastern Studies* vol 35, no 4 (1999)

——'The American Concept of the "Northern Tier" Defence Project and the Signing of the Turco-Pakistani Agreement, 1953–54', *Middle Eastern Studies* vol 37, no 3 (2001)

332 *Bibliography*

Yetkin, Murat, *Tezkere: Irak Krizinin Gerçek Öyküsü* (Istanbul: Remzi, 2004)

Yılmaz, Hakan, 'Turkish Identity on the Road to the EU: Basic Elements of French and German Oppositional Discourse', in Susannah Verney and Kostas Ifantis (eds), *Turkey's Road to European Union Membership: National Identity and Political Change* (London and New York: Routledge, 2009)

Yılmaz, Şuhnaz and İpek K. Yosmaoğlu, 'Fighting the Spectres of the Past: Dilemmas of Ottoman Legacy in the Balkans and Middle East', *Middle Eastern Studies* vol 44, no 5 (2008)

Zafar, Walid, 'Daniel Pipes Is Off Iran: The Real Bad Guy Is Turkey', *Political Correction,* 16 December 2010 (http://politicalcorrection.org/fpmatters).

Zaman, Amberin, 'Turkey and the Iraqi Kurds: From Red Lines to Red Carpets', *Analysis* (Washington, DC: German Marshall Fund of the United States, 14 May 2010)

Zamir, Meir, 'Population Statistics of the Ottoman Empire in 1914 and 1918', *Middle Eastern Studies* vol 17, no 1 (1981)

Zürcher, Erik J., *The Unionist Factor: The Role of the Committee of Union and Progress in the Turkish National Movement* (Leiden: Brill, 1984)

——*Political Opposition in the Early Turkish Republic: The Progressive Republican Party 1924–1925* (Leiden: Brill, 1991)

——*Turkey: A Modern History* (London: I. B. Tauris, 1993)

Zuzul, Miomir, 'Croatia and Turkey: Toward a Durable Peace in Southeastern Europe', *Perceptions* (Ankara) vol 3 (1998)

Index

Abbas, Mahmoud: 229
Abdul Aziz, Sultan: 20
Abdul Hamid II, Sultan: 13, 21, 23:
  foreign policy: 21–24
Abdul Mejid, Prince and Caliph: 38, 41
Abdul Mejid, Sultan: 18
Aberdeen, Lord, 19
Abkhazia: 219–20
ABM system, in Turkey: 171, 242
Abu Ghraib prison scandal, 2004: 168
Acheson, Dean: 84, 86, 107
Adana conference (1943): 70
Additional Protocol (Turkey-EEC, 1970):
  128–29
Adrianople: see Edirne
Afghanistan: 46, 118, 121, 164–65, 222
Africa: Turkey's policy towards: 247
Afyon (Afyonkarahisar): 37, 110
Aghios Theodhoros: 110
Ahmad, Feroz: 27
Ahmadinejad, Mahmoud: 170–71, 242,
  245
Ahmed Jemal Pasha: 24, 26, 28
AK Party: see Justice and Development
  Party
Akayev, Askar: 222–23
Akbulut, Yıldırım: 139, 160, 233
AKEL (Progressive Party of the Working
  People, Cyprus): 200
Akerman, Convention of (1825): 17
AKP: see Justice and Development Party
Akrotiri: 97, 112
Al-As'aad, Riad: 245
Al-Assad, Bashar: 234–35, 244–45
Al-Assad, Hafiz: 127, 145, 228, 233–34
  (see also Syria)
Albania: and Ottoman empire: 10, 22, 24:
  and Turkish republic: 51, 204–5
Al-Bashir, Omar Hassan: 256
Alexander I, Tsar: 16

Alexandretta (Hatay) dispute: 50–51, 127,
  232, 235: naval base: 89
Alexandropol (Leninakan, Gümrü),
  treaty of: 36
Alexandroupolis (Dedeağaç): 110
Al-Gaylani, Rashid Ali: see Rashid Ali
Al-Hassan, Adnan Badr: 234
Ali Pasha: 19
Ali Riza Pasha: 33
Aliağa, oil refinery: 215
Aliev, Haydar: 214
Aliev, Ilham: 214–16
Al-Ja'fari, Ibrahim: 236
Alliance of Civilizations: 248
Al-Maliki, Nouri: 238
Al-Moallem, Walid: 234
Al-Said, Nuri: 92–93, 95–96
Amasya protocol (1919): 33
Amorim, Celso: 171
Annan, Kofi: 198, 248: Annan Peace Plan
  (for Cyprus): 148, 185, 198–99
Annapolis peace conference (on Middle
  East, 2007): 229
Antalya: 37
Arab revolt (1916): 27
'Arab spring': 138, 242–45
Arafat, Yasser: 227, 229
Aras, Tevfik Rüştü: 42, 44, 46–47, 49–
  50
Arbil: 237
Ardahan: 29, 50, 74 n.14, 112, 114, 122
Armenia: and Ottoman empire: 17, 22:
  and Turkey, 1919–23: 32, 35–36: after
  Cold War: 211–18: and Nagorno-
  Karabakh conflict: 211–14, 216, 218
Armenian genocide resolutions: 164, 170,
  216–18
Armenian terrorists: 125
Armenian-American lobby: 120, 164,
  217